BIO CONTROL
IN PROTECTED CULTURE

KEVIN M. HEINZ, ROY G. VAN DRIESCHE,
AND MICHAEL P. PARRELLA, EDITORS

Ball Publishing | Batavia, Illinois

Ball Publishing
335 N. River St.
P.O. Box 9
Batavia, IL 60510
www.ballpublishing.com

Cover design by Lisa Weistroffer.
Interior design by Nancy DuPont, Bay Graphics, Inc.

Library of Congress Cataloging-in-Publication Data
  Biocontrol in protected culture / Kevin M. Heinz, Roy G. Van Driesche, and Michael P. Parrella, editors.
       p. cm.
     Includes index.
     ISBN 1-883052-39-4 (hardcover : alk. paper)
  1. Greenhouse plants—Diseases and pests—Biological control. 2. Insect pests—Biological control. I. Heinz, Kevin M. II. Van Driesche, Roy. III. Parrella, Michael P. (Michael Peter), 1951–
     SB936.B55 2005
     631.5'83—dc22   2004012378

Printed and bound in Singapore by Imago.
10 09 08 07 06 05 04   1 2 3 4 5 6 7 8 9

CONTENTS

CONTRIBUTORS

The editors would like to extend a special thanks to the many people who contributed their research and time to this book:

Albajes, Ramon; Centre UdL-IRTA; Universitat de Lleida., Avda Rovira Roure, 191, 25198—Lleida, Spain; +34 973 70 25 71; ramon.albajes@irta.es

Alomar, Oscar; Centre de Cabrils, IRTA; Ctra de Cabrils, s/n., 08348—Cabrils (Barcelona), Spain; +34 93 750 75 11; oscar.alomar@irta.es

Avilla, Jesús; Centre UdL-IRTA; Universitat de Lleida., Avda Rovira Roure, 191, 25198 – Lleida. Spain; +34 973 70 25 81; jesus.avilla@irta.es

Bennison, Jude; ADAS; ADAS Boxworth, Boxworth, Cambridge CB3 8NN, United Kingdom; +44 (0) 1954 268225; jude.bennison@adas.co.uk

Blümel, S.; Austrian Agency of Health and Food Safety, Institute of Plant Health, Spargelfeld-str. 191, A-1226 Wien, Austria; +43-1-73216-5154; Sbluemel@ages.at

Bolckmans, K.; Koppert Biological Systems, Veilingweg 17, P.O. Box 155, 2650 AD Berkel en Rodenrijs, the Netherlands; KBolckmans@koppert.nl

Braman, S. K.; Department of Entomology, University of Georgia; UGA/CAES/Griffin Campus, 1109 Experiment St., Griffin, GA 30224, USA; 1-770-228-7236; kbraman@griffin.uga.edu

Broadbent, A. B.; Agriculture and Agri-Food Canada, 1391 Sandford St., London, Ontario, N5V 4T3, Canada; 1-905-457-1470, ext. 251; broadbentb@agr.gc.ca

Brødsgaard, H. F.; Department of Crop Protection; Danish Institute of Agricultural Sciences, Research Centre Flakkebjerg, DK-4200 Slagelse, Denmark; +45 58 11 33 00; henrik.brodsgaard@agrsci.dk

Castañé, Cristina ; Centre de Cabrils; IRTA, Centra de Cabrils, s/n, 08348—Cabrils (Barcelona), Spain; +34 93 750 75 11; cristina.castane@irta.es

Chau, Amada; Department of Entomology; Texas A&M University, College Station, TX 77843-2473, USA; 1-979-862-3407; achau@tamu.edu

Chow, Andrew; Department of Entomology; Texas A&M University, College Station, TX 77843-2473, USA; 1-979-862-3407; achow@tamu.edu

Costello, R. A.; British Columbia Ministry of Agriculture, Food and Fisheries, Abbotsford Agriculture Centre, 1767 Angus Campbell Road, Abbotsford, British Columbia, V3G 2M3, Canada; 1-604-556-3031; bob.costello@gems4gov.bc.ca

Gabarra, Rosa; Centra de Cabrils; IRTA., Centra de Cabrils, s/n, 08348—Cabrils (Barcelona), Spain; +34 93 750 75 11; rosa.gabarra@irta.es

Gillespie, D.; Agriculture and Agri-Food Canada, Pacific Agri-Food Research Centre, POB 1000, 6947 #7 Highway Agassiz, British Columbia, V0M 1A0, Canada; 1-604-796-2221; GillespieD@agr.gc.ca

Gill, Stanton; University of Maryland and Montgomery College, CMREC, 11975 Homewood Road, Ellicott City, Maryland 21042, USA; 1-301-596-9413; sgill@umd.edu

Hassan, S.; Federal Research Centre, Institute for Biological Control, Heinrich Str. 243, D-64287 Darmstadt, Germany; s.hassan@bba.de

Heinz, Kevin; Department of Entomology, Texas A&M University, College Station, TX 77843-2473, USA; 1-979-845-2510; KMHeinz@tamu.edu

Hoddle, M.; Department of Entomology, University of California, Riverside, CA 92521, USA; 1-909-787-4714; mark.hoddle@ucr.edu

Jacobson, Rob; Stockbridge Technology Centre Ltd., Cawood, Selby, North Yorks, YO8 3TZ, United Kingdom; +44(0) 1757 268275; robjacobson@stcnyorks.co.uk

Keil, Cliff; Department of Entomology & Wildlife Ecology, University of Delaware, Newark, DE 19717, USA; 1-302-831-8882; Keil@udel.edu

Landa, Z.; Department of Plant Sciences, University of South Bohemia, Ceske Budejovice, Czech Republic; Zlanda@zf.jsu.cz

Leppla, N. C.; University of Florida, Department of Entomology & Nematology, Bldg. 970, P.O. Box 110620, Gainesville, FL 32611, USA; 1-352-392-1901, ext. 120; NCLeppla@mail.ifas.ufl.edu

Lindquist, Richard (retired); Department of Entomology, Ohio Agricultural Research and Development Center, Wooster, OH 44691, USA; rlindquist@olympichort.com

Martin, N. A.; New Zealand Institute for Crop & Food Research Ltd., Mount Albert Research Centre, Private Bag 92 169, Auckland, New Zealand; +64-9-815 4200; MartinN@crop.cri.nz

Murphy, G. D.; Ontario Ministry of Agriculture and Food, P.O. Box 7000, Vineland, Ontario L0R 2E0, Canada; 1-905-562 4141, ext. 106; graeme.murphy@omaf.gov.on.ca

Nicoli, G. (deceased); Istituto di Entomologia "G. Grandi", University of Bologna, via Filippo Re 6, 40126 Bologna, Italy

Oetting, R. D.; Department of Entomology, University of Georgia; UGA/CAES/Griffin Campus, 1109 Experiment St., Griffin, GA 30224, USA; 1-770-412-4714; roettin@griffin.uga.edu

Osborne, L. S.; University of Florida, Mid-Florida Research & Education Center, 2727 Binion Road, Apopka, FL 32703-8504, USA; 1-407-884-2034, ext. 163; lso@mail.ifas.ufl.edu

Parrella, Michael; Department of Entomology, University of California, One Shields Ave., Davis, CA 95616, USA; 1-530-752-1606; Mpparrella@ucdavis.edu

Peña, Jorge; University of Florida, Tropical Research & Education Center, 18905 SW 280th St., Homestead, FL 33031-3314, USA; 1-305-246-7001, ext. 223; jepe@ifas.ufl.edu

Ramakers, P. M. J.; Applied Plant Research, Division Glasshouse Horticulture, P.O.B. 8, 2670 AA Naaldwijk, the Netherlands; +31 174 636811, mobile: +31 317 478904; pierre.ramakers@wur.nl

Raupp, M. J.; University of Maryland, Department of Entomology, 4112 Plant Sciences Building, University of Maryland, College Park, MD 20742, USA; 1-301-405-8478; mraupp@umd.edu

Raworth, D. A.; Agriculture and Agri-Food Canada, Pacific Agri-Food Research Centre, POB 1000, 6947 #7 Highway, Agassiz, British Columbia, V0M 1A0, Canada; 1-604-796-2221; RaworthD@agr.gc.ca

Sanderson, John; Department of Entomology, Cornell University, Ithaca, NY 14853-2604, USA; 1-607-255-5419; jps3@cornell.edu

Shipp, J. L.; Agriculture and Agri-Food Canada, Greenhouse and Processing Crops Research Centre, Harrow, Ontario, N0R 1G0, Canada; 1-519-738-2251; shippl@agr.gc.ca

Short, Ted; Department of Food, Agriculture, and Environmental Science, Ohio Agricultural Research and Development Center, Wooster, OH, 44691, USA; 1-330-263-3855; Short.2@osu.edu

Shrewsbury, P. M.; University of Maryland, Department of Entomology, 4112 Plant Science Bldg., College Park, MD 20742, USA; 1-301-405-7664; pshrewsbury@umd.edu

Tanigoshi, L. K.; Department of Entomology, Washington State University, Vancouver Research & Extension Unit, 1919, NE 78th St., Vancouver, WA 98665-9752, USA; 1-360-576-6030; Tanigosh@wsu.edu

Valentin, Ronald; Foliera Incorporated, Foliera Incorporated, 4655 Bartlett Road, Beamsville, Ontario, L0R 1B1, Canada; 1-905-563-1066; RonaldValentin@Foliera.com

van der Linden, Anton; Applied Plant Research, Wageningen University and Research Centre, P.O. Box 118, 2770 AC Boskoop, the Netherlands; +31 (0) 172 236728; anton.vanderlinden@wur.nl

Van de Veire, M.; Laboratory of Agrozoology, Faculty of Agricultural and Applied Biological Sciences, Ghent University, Coupure Links 653 B 9000 Ghent, Belgium; +32 9 264 61 48; marc.vandeveire@Ugent.be

van Lenteren, Joop; Laboratory of Entomology, P.O. Box 8031, 6700 EH, Wageningen University, the Netherlands; + 31 317 482327; Joop.vanLenteren@wur.nl

Van Driesche, Roy; Department of Entomology, University of Massachusetts, Fernald Hall, Amherst, MA 01003, USA; 1-413-545-1061; vandries@nre.umass.edu

White, Phil; Plant Pathology & Microbiology Department, Horticulture Research International, Plant Pathology & Microbiology, Horticulture Research International, Wellesbourne, Warwick, CV35 9EF, United Kingdom; +44 01789 470382

Yano, E.; National Agricultural Research Center, 3-1-1, Kannondai, Tsukuba, Ibaraki, 305-8666, Japan; +81-29-838-8846; yano@affrc.go.jp

INTRODUCTION

There are over 140 species of insects and mites that are known to be pests in greenhouses, glasshouses, and various other protected agricultural production schemes. With introduction, augmentation, and preservation of natural enemies as a foundational principle, other compatible techniques may be integrated to develop economic, effective, and sustainable management strategies for these arthropod pests. This book is the most comprehensive overview to date of challenge encountered in developing practical biological control solutions to arthropod pest problems, but too provides an elaborate menu of biological control options for a diverse array of pest problems occurring on various crops grown in equally diverse environments.

The core audience for this book is agricultural professionals, yet the material is sufficiently thought-provoking that it is expected to find its way onto the bookshelves of biological control researchers and into college-level classrooms specializing in biological control or pest management. Each of the authors involved with the project is a researcher who works closely with commercial greenhouse growers. The book outlines the principles and applications of biological control for management of arthropod pests infesting protected cultures—greenhouses, glasshouses, and shaded structures.

After presenting the fundamental principles of biological control–based pest management within protected culture, several chapters address the prerequisites for a successful program in terms of greenhouse/glasshouse structure, working with providers of natural enemies, practical aspects of sampling, and management of insecticides. Several chapters address biological control of specific pests and identify those practices that work and those that do not in vegetable and ornamental crop production systems. Current implementation and the future of biological control–based pest management systems in the most important protected crops worldwide are presented in the concluding chapters.

Biological control within protected cultivation is practiced to varying degrees throughout the world under quite different social, economic, and technical conditions. Contributions to the book reflect such a diversity of situations: from the total reliance on biological control in the high-technology glasshouses of northern Europe and Canada to difficulties of its use in the open-air structures common to the Mediterranean region, temperate eastern Asia, and South America. Furthermore, the ensemble of authors represents a global view of the subject in terms of geographic location, expertise, and perspective (including research, extension, allied industries, and regulator). Yet the structure of the book permits easy comparison of viewpoints associated with the different pests and crop production systems. Probably no book published to date has offered such a complete treatment of biological control in protected culture.

1

AN OVERVIEW OF BIOLOGICAL
CONTROL IN PROTECTED CULTURE

R. G. Van Driesche
Department of Entomology
University of Massachusetts, Amherst, MA
and
K. M. Heinz
Department of Entomology
Texas A & M University, College Station, TX

Early naturalists, having observed predators and other natural enemies killing
pest species in nature, speculated that manipulation of predacious insects might control
pests infesting greenhouse crops. Erasmus
Darwin (1800) first suggested that aphids in
hothouses be controlled by the artificial use
of predacious syrphid fly larvae. Fifteen years
later, Kirby and Spence (1815) noted the
desirability of discovering methods for artificially increasing the population of lady
beetles for aphid control in greenhouses.
There is no documentation to indicate these
suggestions led directly to actual use of aphid
biological control; Hussey (1985) reported
that the first case of biological control within
greenhouses was the culturing and releasing
of the parasitoid *Encarsia inaron* (Walker) (=
E. partenopea Masi [Polaszek, Evans, and
Bennet 1992]) for biological control of greenhouse whitefly, *Trialeurodes vaporariorum*
(Westwood), in England. This first attempt
failed to produce desirable levels of control,
presumably because the parasitoid is ineffective during hot summer days.

The first successful biological pest
control of greenhouse crops occurred in 1926
when dark-colored (parasitized) whitefly
were discovered in the greenhouse of an
English tomato grower. The responsible parasitoid, *Encarsia formosa* Gahan, was subsequently found to provide control of the pest,
and commercial production was begun
(Speyer 1927, Hussey 1985). Production was
curtailed in 1949 and ceased in 1956, due to
competition from newly developed insecticides (Hussey 1985). Within a few years,
resistance to several insecticides was
observed in the spider mite *Tetranychus
urticae* Koch (Bravenboer 1960). Discovery
of *Phytoseiulus persimilis* Athias-Henriot, an
effective spider mite predator first encountered in German greenhouses containing
orchids imported from Chile, revived biological control in European greenhouses
(Bravenboer and Dosse 1962). Interest in
whitefly biological control resumed in the
early 1970s after severe whitefly outbreaks
took place. Rediscovery of *E. formosa* and
development of improved methods for

1

rearing and shipping of natural enemies led to an effective and widely accepted whitefly biological control program. Since this revival, the number of researchers studying biological pest control in protected culture, and the number of countries in which biological control methods are used, has increased steadily.

The total worldwide area covered by greenhouses is 370,500 acres (150,000 ha) (van Lenteren and Woets 1988). Small-scale application of biological control in greenhouses started in 1968 with the use of the predatory mite *P. persimilis;* only one commercial company produced this natural enemy at the time. *E. formosa* was added to the list of commercially reared species in 1970, and by 1997 forty-one parasitoids and predators of greenhouse pests were marketed by one or more of the 142 suppliers of beneficial organisms in North America (Hunter 1997). The total greenhouse area now under biological control is about 29,640 acres (12,000 ha) and represents 30% of the northern vegetable production greenhouse area in which the method is most easily applied (van Lenteren and Woets 1988). The method is applied mainly in vegetables, although recently the development of biological control for ornamental crops has been actively investigated.

In this chapter, we study the three approaches to conducting biological control in protected cultures. Associated with each approach is a set of prerequisites, practices, and expectations. These aspects are reviewed, and examples are provided to illustrate essential points. The constantly changing landscape of plant cultivation within protected cultures will continue to pose challenges to existing biological control practices, several of which we will discuss in this chapter. In the final section of the chapter, we will address the safety of biological control to humans, to other nontarget organisms, and to the environment.

Ways to Use Biological Control

Biological control is the use of living natural enemies to suppress pest populations. Natural enemies of insects and mites include parasitic wasps that use pests as hosts for their offspring, predators that consume their prey, and pathogens that cause disease (see chapter 6 for a review of key natural enemies used in greenhouses). Nonchemical pest control methods that do not use living natural enemies—such as pheromones, sticky traps, or plant breeding—are not considered biological control.

Biological control can be applied in three basic ways:

Importation

This method, also called the "classical" method, is commonly used when local natural enemies are likely to be insufficiently specialized to suppress a pest of foreign origin. A goal of this approach is to gain permanent suppression of the pest by creating a self-reproducing population of an effective species of natural enemy. Therefore, this method tends to be most successful in permanent, undisturbed habitats and is rarely used in greenhouse production. In the relatively permanent plant collections residing in conservatories and atria, importation biological control has been successful in providing long-term control of whitefly, scale, and mealybug populations. For example, in some situations, the brown soft scale (*Coccus hesperidum* L.) can be permanently controlled in indoor plantscapes after establishing a population of the encyrtid wasp *Metaphycus alberti* (Howard) (Stauffer and Rose 1997).

Augmentation

Prolonged establishment of a natural enemy is not always possible, as, for example, in short-cycle flower crops. In these situations, crop protection and pest suppression may be achieved through release of parasitoids or predators, or through application of pathogens as biopesticides to augment the number of natural enemies present. Releasing the parasitoid wasp *E. formosa* and the predacious mite *P. persimilis* for control of whiteflies and spider mites on vegetable crops are examples of augmentative biological control (Chant 1961, Hussey and Parr 1965, Markkula and Tittanen 1976, van Lenteren et al. 1977, Mori and Saito 1979, van Lenteren and Woets 1988). If releases occur only at the beginning of the crop, followed by natural reproduction of the agent used, the term *seasonal inoculative release* applies. If little or no reproduction of the released agent occurs and releases are made repeatedly, the method is described as *inundative release*. Application of formulated pathogens is a special case of inundative release, known as the *biopesticidal approach*.

Conservation

The living natural enemies used for biological control of pest populations require a set of indispensable conditions for their existence. Greenhouse conditions that may influence the ability of natural enemies to survive and reproduce include the physical and climatic environments, the crop plant, and other pest control practices. The temperature of a greenhouse, for example, may be too high or too low for some species of natural enemies, but not others. The use of fungicides to control foliage plant diseases may be in conflict with the use of biopesticides that contain entomopathogenic fungi or with the use of other kinds of natural enemies. In addition, plant traits, such as toxic compounds, nutrition, morphology, and phenology, that may confer resistance to plant pests may also adversely affect beneficial insects.

Factors Shaping Choice of Biological Control Methods and Agents

The nature of protected culture strongly influences the relative applicability of these various forms of biological control in individual greenhouses, conservatories, or interiorscapes. Of special importance are the rate of turnover in the crop or plant collection, the types and levels of plant damage acceptable to the end user, the needs for other pest control applications, the costs of the natural enemies, and their effectiveness. Thus, in general terms, we predict that biological control is likely to be easier

- in long-term rather than short-term crops,
- in vegetables rather than ornamentals,
- in crops having few pests other than the one targeted for biological control,
- in a crop in which the target pest does not attack the part of the plant that is sold,
- in a crop in which the targeted pest does not transmit diseases in the crop.

Turnover in the crop or planting

Importation biological control is likely to be most successful in the relatively permanent plant collections residing in conservatories and in the atria of public buildings. Within these sites, the habitat (i.e., vegetation) remains in place for long periods, and renewal of vegetation occurs piecemeal rather than en masse. This allows both pests and their natural enemies to survive by moving between plants. In addition, the permanence of the vegetation acts to reduce the fluctuations in temperature and availability of moisture, which further favors the long-term survival of natural-enemy populations.

In contrast, greenhouses containing crops with short production cycles are characterized by the emptying of entire ranges during harvest, followed soon after by the starting of new crop plants from different sources. This turnover in vegetation prevents the use of classical biological control. In such cases, inoculative releases must be used to reestablish the natural enemy with each new crop, as, for example, is done on tomatoes and cucumbers when the aphelinid wasp *E. formosa* is released for whitefly control in a series of new crops. However, even under these cropping patterns, some kinds of pest and natural-enemy species may carry over between crops. Some parasitoids, such as the *Synacra* sp. (Hellqvist 1994) that attacks larvae of fungus gnats (*Bradysia* sp.), may persist in greenhouses between crops. This parasitoid breeds in fungus gnat larvae that live in the soil on the greenhouse floor as well as in pots. In large greenhouses, where harvests are staggered, highly mobile natural enemies—such as *Diglyphus* sp. that attacks *Liriomyza* leafminers, or *E. formosa* that attacks whiteflies—may inoculate new crops adjacent to older plants within the same range.

Types and levels of plant damage acceptable to the end user

Degrees of pest suppression required for commercial success vary by crop and context. The level of pest suppression needed strongly affects the degree to which biological control is economically practical. Greater levels of whitefly suppression, for example, are needed to meet the needs of commercial flower production than are needed for the production of vegetable crops. In vegetable crops, only the fruit reaches the customer. Consequently whiteflies affect vegetable crop profitability only if whiteflies transmit crop diseases, if high densities reduce fruit number or size, or if honeydew or sooty mold soils fruits. Moderate levels of whiteflies on foliage often have little effect on vegetable crops and can be permitted. In contrast, on potted flower crops, the entire plant will reach the customer, and whitefly numbers on leaves that might be acceptable to a tomato grower may cause economic loss to a poinsettia grower. Cut flower crops may tolerate higher levels of some pests if they are confined to the parts of plants, such as lower leaves or to main stems that do not reach the consumer. Pests that transmit diseases or cause serious damage to the marketed portion of the crop must be controlled to a greater degree than indirect pests that do not.

Harmonization with control of other pests

Broad-spectrum insecticides frequently disrupt natural enemies by reducing their abilities to survive and reproduce and thus should be avoided when implementing biological control. For example, longtailed mealybugs (*Pseudococcus longispinus* [Targioni-Tozzetti]) infesting pothos ivy (*Epipremnum aureum* [Linden and Andréy] Bunt) planted in hotel atria can be permanently suppressed by establishment of the encyrtid wasp *Pseudaphycus angelicus* (Howard) (Goolsby 1994). Secondary outbreaks of spider mites also occur on pothos ivy. To preserve biological control of the longtailed mealybug, releases of mite predators such as *P. persimilis* are used, rather than widespread application of persistent-contact insecticides.

Similarly, if augmentative releases of natural enemies are to be effective, the pest management methods used for all other pests must be compatible with the natural enemies released. In roses, for example, extensive use of sulfur fumigation for control of powdery mildew is incompatible with releases of *P. persimilis* for control of spider mites (Simmonds1972). To resolve this conflict and still employ biological spider mite control, other methods of powdery mildew control must be used.

In short-term flower crops, silverleaf whitefly (*Bemisia argentifolii* Bellows and Perring = *Bemisia tabaci* [Gennadius] strain B) and greenhouse whitefly (*T. vaporariorum*) can be suppressed on poinsettia through the repeated release of aphelinid parasitoids. To be effective, other poinsettia pests must be controlled in compatible ways. Use of *Bacillus thuringiensis* Berliner var. *israelensis* (Gnatrol) or nematodes (Xgnat, ScanMask), for example, can suppress fungus gnats. In contrast, splashing the foliage of a soil-applied pesticide with a long residual such as chlorpyrifos (Duraguard) would conflict with the use of whitefly parasitoids and reduce their effectiveness.

Cost

The cost of biological control, relative to other pest control options, is an important consideration for most growers in choosing whether to use biological control. In assessing relative costs, it is useful to distinguish between *discovery costs* and *implementation costs*. Discovery costs are incurred while locating, testing, and developing mass-rearing methods for a new natural enemy of a target pest. Implementation costs are those costs that users must bear to employ a natural enemy once it has been discovered.

Discovery costs have been best documented for classical biological control projects in which continued rearing of the natural enemies is not required. The cost-to-benefit ratios associated with classical biological control, averaged over many projects, are 30:1. This rate of return is more cost-effective than the 5:1 cost-to-benefit ratio associated with the discovery of a new chemical control program (DeBach 1964, Huffaker and Messenger 1976, Tisdell 1990, DeBach and Rosen 1991). One factor contributing to the large difference between discovery costs for biological and for chemical control is the $2 million expended for finding a new natural enemy, compared to the $25 million invested for developing a new insecticide (van Lenteren 1990).

Figures are lacking on the discovery cost-to-benefit ratio of developing new augmentative biological control projects, which is the approach most commonly taken with biological control in greenhouses. The discrepancy in cost-to-benefit ratios between augmentation biological control and chemical control versus importation biological control and chemical control are likely to be less. The recurring costs associated with continuous mass production of the natural enemies necessary for augmentation biological control are unique to this approach. Further, parasitoids and predators are generally not subject to patent protection, and commercial insectaries find it more difficult to recover investment costs than is the case with investments in development of new chemicals.

Implementation costs of augmentative biological control, measured by the prices paid by growers for the purchase of biological control agents, may or may not be competitive in greenhouse crops with those of chemical controls, depending on the price of the agent, the price of competing chemical control and the effectiveness of the biological control agent at a given release rate. Implementation costs of biological control for many vegetable crops grown in European glasshouses have been lower than the costs of chemical pest control (in terms of cost of control agents versus chemicals and labor costs of each approach). In 1980, for example, chemical control of whitefly in European greenhouses was twice as expensive as biological control with *E. formosa* (Ramakers 1982). Similarly, chemical control of the spider mite *T. urticae* is almost twice as expensive as biological control with predatory mites (van Lenteren 1990). As a result, biological control in tomato, cucumber, and sweet pepper frequently provides total and cost competitive control of the arthropod pests associated with these important crops.

In flower crops, biological control has not been widely employed because in general the level of control is either inadequate or the approach is more costly than chemical control. An exception to this is whitefly control in poinsettia (*Euphorbia pulcherrima* Willd. ex Koltz). In this crop, the use of the parasitoid *Eretmocerus eremicus* Rose and Zolnerowich (Hymn.: Aphelinidae) (combined with use limited use of an insect growth regulator) at 0.5 females per plant per week is competitive in price with the use of pesticides for control of whitefly (U.S. $0.21 per plant per season for biological control and $0.14 for chemical control) (Van Driesche et al. 2002) and costs under commercial use of biological control can be as low as U.S. $0.10-0.14 per pot per season (Van Driesche and Lyon 2003).

Biological effectiveness

Grower use of biological control increases after field trials demonstrate the biological effectiveness of particular release rates of particular agents. Data from such practical tests identify the appropriate natural enemy species for release, minimum release rates, management errors that must be avoided, and other information needed for successful use. Unlike pesticides, for which chemical companies usually develop efficacy data, natural enemies are often marketed before scientific data on their effectiveness are available. In some instances, independent researchers conduct trials to investigate the efficacy of new biological control agents. Results from these trials are delivered to growers and advisors through personal contacts with cooperative extension, articles in research and trade journals and books, and oral presentations at meetings sponsored by scientific societies and various industry groups. We will discuss the value of science-based efficacy testing in more detail later in this chapter. But first we will review the general practice of importation, augmentation, and conservation biological control relative to crop production in protected culture.

Classical Biological Control

Classical biological control is the most widely used form of biological control in outdoor crops, but it is seldom practiced in protected culture. The focus in protected culture has been on augmentative releases of natural enemies due to the ephemeral nature of many of the crops grown in greenhouses and the frequent need to suppress pest outbreaks to virtually undetectable levels in very short periods of time. Under these conditions, classical biological control has limited application. Two avenues do, however, exist for increasing the application of classical biological control in protected culture: permanent plantings and carryover systems between plantings.

Development of biological control systems in permanent plantings

Some plant collections in conservatories and in atria of commercial buildings are virtually permanent, and if properly managed are suitable sites for long-term establishment of biological control agents. Examples include brown soft scale on ficus, longtailed mealybug on pothos ivy, and greenhouse and silverleaf whiteflies on a variety of plants. In practice, even these situations may require more than the single release of a natural enemy to achieve its permanent establishment or to maintain suitable levels of pest suppression; in some cases, the need for repeated releases may be very infrequent. Other pest control methods may also be needed so that an integrated pest management program may be used, rather than classical biological control alone.

Development of carryover techniques for use to link discrete crops

For some pests, it may be possible to develop ways to carry natural enemy populations over between crops. This is analogous to the same problem that exists for some outdoor crops in which natural enemies experience reduced effectiveness because their populations must periodically discover and colonize new crop patches (Van Driesche and Bellows 1996). This approach would blend both conservation and importation, depending on the origin of the natural enemy.

Linkages can sometimes be created between plantings by manipulating features such as planting date or the spatial arrangement of crop patches in the landscape (Vorley and Wratten 1987). While relatively little attention has been given to such interactions in the context of protected culture, some kinds of natural enemies persist in greenhouses, as, for example, the eucoilid parasitoid *Hexatoma* sp. that attacks shore flies (*Scatella stagnalis* Fallén) and the diapriid *Synacra* sp. that attacks fungus gnats (*Bradysia* spp.). Because these pests and parasitoids occur not only in potted soil but also in the soil or alga deposits on greenhouse floors, these agents may persist even after greenhouses have been emptied between crops. Manipulation of greenhouse management practices to favor the carryover of these parasitoids should be possible. Success would make greenhouses more stable with respect to populations of these pests. While some use of remedial biological control (such as the use of *B. thuringiensis* var. *israelensis* in pots) might still be needed, the frequency of need for such treatments may be reduced by natural enemy conservation, and the overall level of control may improve. Also, conservation of natural enemies may facilitate biological control of some pests that cannot easily be controlled by other forms of biological control.

Augmentative Biological Control

Seasonal inoculative releases

This approach to biological control relies on limited numbers of releases of natural enemies early in the crop. The method is based on the expectation that releases will lead to the establishment of a self-reproducing population of the parasitoid or predator and that the agent will increase its numbers sufficiently over several generations to control the pest. Seasonal inoculative releases of *E. formosa* are used regularly in northern Europe to provide good control of greenhouse whitefly on tomato and sweet pepper (Woets and van Lenteren 1976, van Lenteren et al. 1977).

Releases of whitefly natural enemies may use several different methods, including the early introduction of both the pest and the parasitoid ("pest in first" method, Gould et al. 1975), staggered releases of the parasitoid only ("dribble" method, Parr et al. 1976, Stenseth and Aase 1983), and use of in-greenhouse rearing systems based on innocuous alternative hosts reared on live plants placed in the greenhouse ("banker plant" method, Stacey 1997). Of these, the dribble method is most widely used. To achieve biological control of greenhouse whitefly, releases of the parasitoid *E. formosa* begin at planting in anticipation of natural development of a whitefly population and continue at a low rate of one parasitoid pupa per plant on a weekly basis until parasitized nymphs are found in the crop, at which time *E. formosa* release rates are modified according to the levels of parasitism observed within the crop. Using this method, *E. formosa* releases on vegetable crops now exceed 11,850 acres (4,800 ha) of production annually (van Lenteren and Woets 1988, van Lenteren 1995).

Seasonal inoculative releases of *P. persimilis* to suppress two-spotted spider mite (*T. urticae*) occurs on about 19,760 acres (8,000 ha) of greenhouse crops (van Lenteren, 1995). Releases of various parasitoids (*Diglyphus begini* [Ashmead], *Diglyphus isaea* [Walker], *Dacnusa sibirica* Telenga, and others) are made for control of *Liriomyza* spp. Open rearing units of the predatory mite *Neoseiulus* (= *Ambylseius*) *cucumeris* (Oudemans) (fig. 1.2) are used to inoculate vegetable crops with this mite for thrips control.

Leafminers in crops such as tomato and chrysanthemum have also been investigated as targets of biocontrol (Wardlow 1984; Heinz, Nunney, and Parrella 1993). The aphid *Myzus persicae* (Sulzer) can be suppressed during in long-season productions of chrysanthemum by inoculative release of the braconid parasitoid *Aphidius matricariae* Haliday (Scopes 1970).

Figure 1.1. Parasitoids used in whitefly biological control (here, *Encarsia formosa*) are released into crops by hanging cards with parasitized whitefly glued to them. The wasps emerge from the whitefly and distribute themselves throughout the production area as they search for whitefly nymphs. Rates of parasitization are increased by suspending cards under foliage infested with third-instar whitefly. *Photo: K. M. Heinz.*

Seasonal inoculative release of parasitoids or predators (as opposed to inundative releases) lowers the cost of control because fewer agents must be purchased and released. Much pest control is achieved by the offspring of released agents, which have reared themselves, at no cost, in the greenhouse during the course of the crop. This method, however, has three important limitations.

First, there must be enough seasonal time for the parasitoid or predator to develop—through two or more generations—and achieve sufficient numbers to suppress the pest. Potentially this problem might be overcome in short-season crops if there are many plantings grown in overlapping sequence within the same greenhouse ranges. In such cases, while any individual group of crop plants may be present for a relatively short time, the pest and parasitoid populations can come into balance over the longer time frame of multiple overlapping plantings. For example, in potted chrysanthemums in Texas, even though any one set of plants requires only six to nine weeks to reach maturity, sequential plantings of the crop are present for a nine-month period.

Second, crops on which seasonal inoculative releases are made will likely experience significant increases in pest density before the natural enemy population increases sufficiently to suppress the pest population to low levels. Seasonal inoculative releases of *E. formosa* in tomatoes, for example, were

Figure 1.2. Predatory mites used in biological control of thrips are frequently released into crops using these self-contained rearing units. The predatory mites feed on non-pestiferous mites housed within the paper sachets, and the predators disperse into the crop as their numbers increase. Use of these self-contained rearing units reduces the cost to the consumer and provides a prolonged period of predator releases over time. *Photo: K. M. Heinz.*

associated with about a thousandfold increase in whitefly density before control by the parasitoid occurred (Foster and Kelly 1978). Temporarily high populations may be of no consequence or may reduce the quality of the crop even after control is achieved, particularly for flower crops in which foliage with numerous cast exuviae of pests might be considered damaged because of the unattractiveness of the visible insect parts.

Third, the exact timing of population

interactions between host and parasitoid may bring varying results in actual pest control and not be predictable with sufficient accuracy for use on crops with tightly timed markets, such as flowers grown for specific holidays (e.g., poinsettias and Easter lilies). Such variability may place the entire crop at risk because the crop would have no value if it could not be sold precisely on time.

Inundative releases

Inundative augmentative releases of parasitoids and predators are expected to result in an immediate suppression of the pest due to action of the natural enemies released, and whether such releases lead to the establishment of a self-reproducing population of natural enemies is less important (fig. 1.3). Inundative releases are used when seasonal inoculative releases provide insufficient levels of control at the appropriate time within the crop cycle.

In short-term flower crops such as poinsettia, whitefly populations must be maintained at low levels throughout the crop cycle. Reliance on seasonal inoculative releases of *E. formosa* is less effective in this crop than it is for whitefly control of vegetables for several reasons. First, the number of whitefly on the plant that can be tolerated by the producer is much lower on potted flower crops than on vegetable crops because the entire plant is sold. In tomatoes, moderate levels of whitefly on leaves are acceptable, provided whitefly numbers do not lead to contamination of fruit with sooty mold. In contrast, detection of whitefly on poinsettia foliage by wholesalers, retailers, or customers may result in rejection of the plants at the

Figure 1.3. Inundative releases of predatory mites are often accomplished by releasing them directly onto plants infested with pestiferous mites. Because the predator mites are very small, they are often mixed with an inert carrier to facilitate there spread throughout the production range. *Photo: J. L. Shipp.*

point of sale. Second, flower crops such as poinsettia that must be sold at fixed dates (major holidays) must be free of whiteflies on schedule. The system does not allow for a week or two more for parasitoids to suppress whitefly numbers, should populations develop at rates different than expected.

Weekly releases of parasitoids such as *E. formosa* or the more recently commercialized species *Eretmocerus eremicus* (formerly known as *Eretmocerus californicus* Howard) can be used to suppress whitefly populations in poinsettia. Used at rates of between 0.5 and 3 females per plant per week, high levels of whitefly nymphal mortality (95 to 99%) result (Hoddle, Van Driesche, and Sanderson 1997a, b, c; Van Driesche et al. 2002). At these release rates, host feeding and superpara-

sitism reduce successful production of offspring by parasitoids to very low levels and the parasitoid functions more like a non-reproduction population of predators (via host feeding).

Problems associated with inundative releases of parasitoids and predators relate mostly to cost. Because more agents are being released over the course of the crop, the cost of biological control is higher. For example, *E. eremicus* can control whiteflies on poinsettia in the northeastern United States reliably if weekly releases of three female wasps are made. The cost associated with this release rate for a sixteen-week crop cycle is $1.18 per single-stemmed plant. Given that the wholesale value for a 6-in. (15-cm) pot poinsettia is about $5.00, this control cost is too high. To overcome this problem, integration of parasitoid releases with limited mid-season (weeks seven and eight) applications of a compatible selective pesticide, such as an insect growth regulator, is recommended. Integration reduces total control costs because a lower release rate (0.5 or 1.0 female wasps per plant per week instead of 3) may be used at a cost of U.S. $0.21–0.38 (Van Driesche et al. 2001, 2002). In practical use by growers, costs have been further reduced to the range of U.S. $0.10–0.14 (Van Driesche and Lyons, 2003).

Biopesticidal Applications of Insect Pathogens and Nematodes

Natural outbreaks of pathogens or nematodes seldom provide useful pest control in greenhouses. However, some pathogens are commercially reared and sold as formulated products that may be applied when and where pest control is needed; this pest control method is called the *biopesticidal approach.*

Biopesticides are applied with conventional pesticide application machinery. Storage requirements of biopesticides may be equivalent to those for pesticides (for *B. thuringiensis* products), or storage under cool (41 to 61°F [5 to 16°C]) conditions may be required. Some biopesticides may be sensitive to environmental conditions at the application site (fungal spores need minimum levels of humidity to germinate; nematodes are harmed by desiccation). Residual efficacy of biopesticides is often more limited than that of chemical pesticides, but biopesticides' short residuals and their greater selectivity make them easier to integrate with parasitoids

and predators. In addition, the risk of phytotoxicity is lower with biopesticides than with chemical pesticides. In general, biopesticides are compatible with most pesticides.

Bacterial biopesticides (*B. thuringiensis*–based products) may be used in greenhouses to control miscellaneous Lepidoptera such as beet armyworm (*Spodoptera exigua* Hübner) when these invade greenhouses. Because these compounds must be ingested by the lepidoptera larvae and because they are slow to kill their host, bacterial biopesticides are most effective and provide the highest level of crop protection when targeted at first or second instars of the pest. Also, dipteran-active strains (*B. thuringiensis* var. *israelensis*) may be used to suppress fungus gnats.

Several genera of entomopathogenic fungi have been considered for use as biopesticides. However, currently only one species of fungus, *Beauveria bassiana* (Balsamo) Vuillemin, is being marketed in North America (as BotaniGard or Naturalis) for insect control in crops. This fungus has potential application in greenhouse crops for control of aphids, whiteflies, and thrips. Efficacy of fungal bioinsecticides, however, is often variable, and this has inhibited widespread adoption of such products (Hall 1982; Schaaf, Van Der Malais, and Ravensberg 1990).

Nematodes in the families Steinernematidae and Heterorhabditidae are used in greenhouses for control of pests with soildwelling life stages. *Steinernema feltiae* (Filipjev) and *Steinernema carpocapsae* (Weiser) are marketed for control of fungus gnats in greenhouses and mushroom houses (Harris, Oetting, and Gardner 1995). Development of products employing new species or methods of application is being pursued and may lead to effective use of nematodes against additional pests. Integration of nematodes with parasitoids as a means of reducing the cost associated with inundative releases of *D. begini* for leafminer control on chrysanthemums was investigated by Sher, Parrella, and Kaya (2000), but integration was unsatisfactory because the nematode reduced survival of immature parasitoids.

Conservation of Natural Enemies

Conservation of natural enemies in greenhouses is an essential part of biological control programs based either on classical biological control or augmentative releases. In broad terms, conservation of natural enemies consists of creating as favorable an environment as possible for natural enemies. Factors that affect natural enemies can include

- the physical environment (temperature, daylength, ventilation, etc.),
- use of pesticides in the greenhouse,
- access to necessary foods,
- effects of plants,
- conflicts with other natural enemies used in the crop.

The physical environment

Temperature may strongly affect the relationship between a natural enemy and the target pest. *E. formosa*, for example, works best at temperatures around 73°F (23°C) (Helgesen and Tauber 1974). At low temperatures, population-growth rates of *E. formosa* are reduced, but so are those of the whitefly host, and population suppression of the pest by the

parasitoid is still possible (van Lenteren and Hulspas-Jordaan 1987). High greenhouse temperatures (over 95°F [35°C]) were found to be unfavorable for *E. tricolor* Foerster (Artigues et al. 1987), as are temperatures over 82°F (28°C) to the braconid *Aphidius colemani* Viereck (Goh, Kim, and Han 2001, Kim and Kim 2003), the aphid parasitoid in greatest use in greenhouse crops..

High relative humidities (95% or greater) are needed by spores of some entomopathogenic fungi to germinate (Connick, Lewis, and Quimby 1990) and thus to be effective at killing the target pest. Manipulation of greenhouse environments to provide short periods of high humidity is technically feasible. Complications may arise, depending on the exact levels of humidity needed and the crop species; the conditions necessary for germination of entomopathogenic fungal spores may also promote germination of spores of fungi that cause diseases in plants. Soil moisture and texture are important factors affecting nematode survival and movement, which is related to host finding and hence the level of control achieved (Kaya 1990).

Some kinds of natural enemies—such as some strains of the aphid predator *Aphidoletes aphidimyza* (Rondani), the predacious mite *Neoseiulus cucumeris* (Oudemans), and the predacious bugs *Orius* spp.—enter a reproductively inactive state called *diapause* when they mature under short daylength (less than twelve to fourteen hours of light per day) (Gilkeson and Hill 1986, Rodriguez-Reina et al. 1994, van den Meiracker 1994). During inoculative biological control programs, it may be important to use supplemental lighting to avoid diapause induction and to secure high levels of natural enemy reproduction within the greenhouse. Alternatively, special non-diapausing strains of the natural enemies may be employed (e.g., Gilkeson and Hill 1986).

Use of pesticides in the greenhouse

Conflicts between natural enemies and pesticides applied to the crop can prevent biological control agents from being effective. Conflicts with pesticides may arise directly from their toxicity to natural enemies, or they may arise indirectly by their depletion of the pest population to levels too low to sustain the natural enemy population. The likelihood of conflict varies by the group of natural enemy, the kind of pesticide, and the application method (Jebson 1989, Croft 1990). Nematodes and pathogens are generally compatible with most pesticides, including insecticides. Uses of insecticides and miticides should be expected to conflict with releases of parasitoids and predators; however, there are exceptions. Standardized methods for testing of insecticide compatibility with natural enemies have been developed by a work group within the International Organization for Biological Control (Hassan 1989). Testing guidelines and results from these tests are presented in chapter 7.

Access to necessary foods

Some parasitoids and predators may benefit from access to foods that either complement their diet of pests or replace it when pest populations are temporarily below levels necessary to sustain the natural enemy population. These foods may be materials like the sugary honeydew that is associated with the pest to be controlled, or they may be mate-rials that are artificially supplied (e.g., Mensah 1996). Several studies have demonstrated pollen applications to be a promising method to enhance populations of phytoseiid mites preying upon western flower thrips, *Frankliniella occidentalis* (Pergande) (Hessein and Parrella 1990, Ramakers 1995).

Effects of plants

Plant features can strongly affect natural enemies, changing both the efficiency of their foraging and the rate of their population growth. Both of these influences can directly affect the success of the natural enemy in controlling the pest population. Natural enemies, for example, may forage less efficiently on leaves with a high number of long trichomes ("hairs") (Hulspas-Jordaan and van Lenteren 1978) or of trichomes that exude sticky or toxic materials (De Ponti, Steenhuis, and Elzinga 1983). However, such host plant-related differences in foraging efficiency do not always translate into differences in biological pest control (Heinz and Zalom 1996). Thus, detailed information about the effects of plant features on natural enemy behavior and population dynamics is necessary if host-plant resistance and biological control are to be integrated successfully. When developing new varieties, natural enemies may be conserved by avoiding the development of plants with unfavorable features and, conversely, by actively endowing plants with features that are favorable to natural enemies, such as nectaries (for food) or domatia (which act as refuges for some predators, such as phytoseiids) (Boethel and Eikenbary 1986, Walter and O'Dowd 1992).

Conflicts with other natural enemies

In some cases, it may be necessary or desirable to use two or more natural enemies simultaneously in a crop (e.g., Hommes 1992). Some combinations of natural enemies have high compatibility, while other combinations may be in conflict. Applications of *B. thuringiensis*, for example, have no effect on the simultaneous use of parasitoids or predators for whitefly, leafminer, or mite control. Similarly, use of entomopathogenic fungi such as *Aschersonia aleyrodis* Webber is compatible with such aphelinid wasps as *E. formosa* (Ramakers and Samson 1984, Fransen and van Lenteren 1993, 1994). Some whitefly predators, such as the mirid bug *Macrolophus caliginosus* Wagner and the coccinellid beetle *Delphastus catalinae* (Horn), have also been found to be compatible with whitefly parasitoids (Heinz and Nelson 1995, Sampson and King 1996). Similarly, the predacious bug *Orius tristicolor* (White) and the predacious mite *N. cucumeris* may be used together for control of western flower thrips (Gillespie and Quiring 1992).

Major Issues Affecting Adoption of Biological Control

Issues strongly affecting growers' decisions about using biological control agents in protected culture include: Does it work? Does it work every time? Can I afford it? Are natural enemies easy to order, store, and apply? Is there a natural enemy for each kind of pest I have?

Efficacy

Efficacy data are available only for a limited number of natural enemies used in protected culture. Unlike pesticides, natural enemies (apart from bacteria and viruses used as biopesticides) are not subject to patent protection. Consequently, producers have immediate competition for production of new agents and in most cases cannot afford to invest in their development. Unlike pesticides, for which chemical companies pay to develop efficacy data, natural enemies are often marketed before scientific data on effectiveness are available. An exception to this occurs in Holland, where the government requires data on efficacy before a natural enemy may be marketed for pest control.

When efficacy data from producers are not available, university or government researchers may in some instances run trials to investigate the efficacy of new biological control agents (e.g., Hamlen 1978; Parrella, Jones, and Christies 1987; Chambers, Long, and Helyer 1993; Gabarra, Castañé, Albajes 1995; Grafton-Cardwell, Ouyang, and Striggow 1997; Hoddle, Van Driesche, and Sanderson 1997a, 1997b, 1997c). However, relatively few of the species marketed for use in protected culture have benefited from this type of assessment. Instead, more agents are sold based on a general knowledge of the agent's biology (i.e., that the agent eats or parasitizes the pest it is marketed to control) and on testimonials from other users. Testimonial evidence is a form of information commonly used by people in many areas of endeavor, including pest control. If one grower has used a biological control agent and escaped pest damage, he may induce others to use the agent by describing the favorable outcome he experienced.

Testimonial data, however, have several major drawbacks. First, such information almost always lacks the two essential features of an experiment: controls and replication. The lack of untreated plots (controls) means that growers have nothing in particular against which to compare how well use of the agent worked, except their memory of other crops in other years when they did not use the agent. Such comparisons are prone to error. Pest pressure varies widely, and lack of pest damage is interesting only if pests were actually present. Without controls, there is no way to know the degree of pest pressure that was "successfully" resisted by the use of a biological control agent. Replication is necessary for documenting the variability of the result observed, and lack of replication introduces great uncertainty about the reliability of the outcome. If the agent worked in this place this year, can we safely assume it will work in most years and most locations?

In picking agents to use in protected culture, only agents for which efficacy trials have been conducted should be used on a large scale. Efficacy trials are also needed to provide information on the minimum effective rate of release, the optimal release methods, and management errors that must be avoided if releases are to suppress the target pest. Replicated experimental efficacy trials conducted under realistic commercial conditions are the only sure means to obtain such information. However, in many cases, such information will be lacking and growers using untried agents must recognize the limitations of producers or researchers to advise them reliably. For biopesticides and nema-

todes, more information is likely to be available on efficacy of particular products.

Predictability

Growers want biological control agents to reliably control the pest every time. Predictability of natural enemies is influenced by the extent of our knowledge about particular natural enemies and their sensitivity to variation in the environment. The most reliable results are obtained from use of natural enemies that have been tested experimentally under commercial conditions at many locations. Protected culture conditions are quite variable. Agents that work under one grower's conditions may not work under another's.

Environmental variation also affects the efficacy of many kinds of natural enemies. Natural enemies, because they are living organisms, are much more sensitive to environmental factors than are chemical pesticides. Nematodes, for example, are influenced by the species of the pest, by the nature of the soil, and by the level of soil moisture. Viruses are influenced by ultraviolet light (the severity of this problem being determined by the physical structure protecting the crop). Fungi are perhaps the most variable in their performance, with the level of infectiveness fluctuating strongly in response to relative humidity during critical periods shortly after application. Effectiveness of parasitoid or predator releases varies if greenhouses are particularly hot or particularly cold, and it may differ by the size of the house or the degree or manner of ventilation.

Knowing the correct identification of the pest targeted for biological control and of the natural enemy species released is an essential but often overlooked element for successful biological control. For example, the braconid wasp *A. colemani* may be used successfully for control of some aphids (e.g., cotton aphid, *Aphis gossypii* Glover and green peach aphid, *Myzus persicae* [Sulzer]) (Messing and Rabasse 1995) but not others (foxglove aphid, *Aulacorthum solani* [Kaltenbach] and potato aphid, *Macrosiphum euphorbiae* [Thomas]) (van Steenis 1992). More than 30 species of aphids occur in protected culture, depending on geographic location and the crop, and commercially available aphid parasitoids will be effective for only some of these species. Growers attempting control with untested parasitoid/aphid combinations may be unsuccessful; such failures stem from failing to correctly define the pest problem relative to the extent of our knowledge.

Quality and cost of reared agents

To work effectively, natural enemies must be of adequate quality for the intended use and have such quality reliably. To help improve the quality of reared natural enemies, standardized tests to assess the quality of insects reared in insectaries have been developed (e.g., Bigler 1991; Nicoli, Benuzzi, and Leppla 1994; van Lenteren 2003; and see chapter 31 of this work). Important factors for measuring the quality of reared natural enemies include the number of natural enemies in a shipment (relative to the stated number), the sex ratio, the emergence rate (if sold as pupae), the percentage of malformed individuals (unable to walk or fly), the short-term survival (% for one or two days), and the ability of the agent to find and to feed on, or oviposit in, the target host. Schemes to periodically test the production of insectaries for these features have been

developed and are applied at the discretion of individual producers.

Blind trials assessing the quality of reared agents have been conducted by independent researchers in some cases (ordering agents from commercial sources and then subjecting them to various measures of quality). O'Neil et al. (1998), in one such study, found that most shipments arrived on time, but that the number of natural enemies received often differed significantly from the number ordered, from only half as many to several-fold more than the number ordered. The proportion of the natural enemies ordered that arrived alive also varied, with some shipments having as few as a quarter of the insects purchased still alive upon receipt by the grower. The severity of these problems varied by the species of natural enemy ordered and by the supplier. Growers need to check the quality of the products they purchase and to avoid use of species or suppliers that prove unsatisfactory.

Shipping, storage, and application methods

For most parasitoids and predators, effective shipping requires use of rapid delivery service (<5 days), together with suitable packing materials and coolants to stabilize and lower temperatures. Longer delivery times are usually unsatisfactory because emergence or death may occur en route. The need for fast delivery increases the shipping cost. Purchase of natural enemies produced in other countries may significantly increase shipping time, as delays may occur in customs or at the distributor.

Storage characteristics of pathogens used as biopesticides are generally good, and for many species they are equivalent to the storage requirements of chemical pesticides, although refrigeration may be required. Nematodes have a shelf life of up to eight weeks if stored at 61°F (16°C) or below. Refrigeration may be used but is not required. For parasitoids and predators, storage at 50 to 61°F (10 to 16°C), but not colder, allows agents to be held for a few days, but immediate application is recommended. Lack of the ability to be stored means that such agents must be purchased frequently, increasing shipping costs and exposing the user to interruptions in product availability.

Suppliers recommend application methods for most natural enemies. For biopesticides and nematodes, application methods are similar to those used for chemical pesticides. For predators and parasitoids, application is usually done by hand—shaking agents into foliage of crop—or by dispersing cards or bags containing the agent.

Range of available natural enemies

A dilemma facing growers wishing to use biological control arises in some cases if biological control agents are available for only some members of the crop's pest complex. This situation arises in part because effective biological control agents have not been found for some pests, such as western flower thrips. In addition, as pesticide use on crops decreases in favor of biological control (for the major pests), minor pests or new species not formerly encountered may occur as pests in the crop. For example, in the United Kingdom the glasshouse leafhopper, *Hauptidia maroccana* (Melichar), is

becoming an increasingly important pest of tomatoes, coincident with the reduction in pesticide usage (Jacobson and Chambers 1996). Solution of these problems will require continued investment in research to develop new species of biological control agents suitable for these additional pest species.

Safety of Biological Control in Protected Culture

Risks of biological control through the introduction of new species must be carefully considered before importation and the start of commercial distribution (van Lenteren et al. 2003). The safety of a new biological control agent's use in protected culture should be evaluated relative to the agent's potential to be a nuisance pest itself or have adverse effects on people or crops, or, if established outdoors, harm nontarget invertebrates.

Potential to cause nuisance problems

Released natural enemies should not bite, sting, or contaminate food. In general, these problems have not arisen, in part because species with obvious abilities to bite or sting (such as vespid wasps [yellow jackets] and ants) are not used as augmentative biological control agents in protected culture. However, the biology of each new species must be carefully considered. The coccinellid *Harmonia axyridis* (Pallas), an Asian species now used in greenhouses for aphid control, has become a domestic nuisance species in the United States and Europe because of it ability to establish outdoors and then enter homes in large numbers in the fall of the year when it aggregates to enter overwintering sites (Bathon 2003).

Effects on humans

Apart from allergies, there are no known risks to the health of greenhouse workers from the release of parasitoids or predators, and the use of these agents is a distinct improvement in worker safety over the use of many pesticides. However, body parts from many kinds of commercially released natural enemies (and the pests also) can break off, become airborne and be inhaled or contact the skin. This may lead to allergies in greenhouse workers. Such is the case, for example, with the predatory mite *A. cucumeris*, which is released in large quantities against thrips (Groenewould et al. 2002). Workers should avoid inhalation of dust from such products and protect skin of forearms from direct contact.

Nematodes used in protected culture (various species of *Steinernema* and *Heterorhabditis*) have been extensively tested and never observed to infect man or other mammals (e.g., Gaugler and Bousch 1979). Currently, the only bacterial species used in insect pest control in protected culture is *B. thuringiensis*. Strains of this species in commercial use do not infect man or domestic animals under normal circumstances. Currently no insect viruses are being used for pest control in protected culture, but the *Autographa californica* Speyer virus and the celery looper virus are baculoviruses with broad host ranges that might be used in the future. No cases of infection by baculoviruses are known in any vertebrates (Podgwaite

1986), and the host ranges of these viruses appear to be restricted to the arthropods. Most of the fungi used as commercial pest control agents do not infect man or other vertebrates (Podgwaite 1986, McCoy and Heimpel 1980). Health concerns have been recognized for some entomopathogenic fungi. Prolonged exposure to *B. bassiana*, for example, can cause allergies in humans (York 1958).

Effects on crop plants

Risk of damage to the crop plant from released parasitoids is nil. Risk from releasing predators is low and has not been a problem in the past. But some predacious Hemiptera, such as species of *Macrolophus* and *Dicyphus* (Lucas and Alomar 2002) and some mites, do feed on plants when prey are scarce. Whether this occurs frequently enough to be of any importance must be evaluated on a case-by-case basis.

To native nontarget species

Releases of some kinds of natural enemies may be incompatible with other operations such as farming of silk moths, birdwing butterflies, or other Lepidoptera. *Trichogramma* releases or applications of either *B. thuringiensis* or baculovirus products in the vicinity of such activities may cause damage to the farmed insect species. Conflict with these same types of agents might also arise if these biological control tools were used to suppress pest Lepidoptera in butterfly houses.

Species of natural enemies imported for use in augmentative biological control may establish permanently in the outdoor environment. This occurred, for example, with the

European mantid, *Mantis religiosa* L., following the international sale of its egg cases, and with the predacious mite *P. persimilis*, following its release among California strawberries (McMurtry et al. 1978). Although use in greenhouses separates released agents somewhat from the outdoor environment, during warm months opportunities exist for agents released in greenhouses to move outdoors and to perhaps establish.

Also, in many instances, the line between protected culture and outdoor farming is not strong, as, for example, in Floridian shade house production of palms and other nursery plants, or in strawberries grown outdoors in temporary early-season plastic tunnels. Consequently, requests to import nonnative species of arthropods for augmentative biological control should be reviewed with the potential establishment of the agents in mind.

Augmentative use of some nonindigenous species may conflict with the conservation of rare native species in the same feeding guilds, especially on islands. Native lacewings of islands such as Hawaii (Tauber, Johnson, and Tauber 1992), for example, might be reduced in density if highly competitive species of nonnative congeners became established through use in either classical biological control or in augmentative biological control outdoors or in protected culture. Frank and McCoy (1994) analyzed the range of biological control agents for sale in Florida relative to their potential for establishment and their effect on native species. Outdoor releases posed greater risks than releases in protected culture, but even such indoor releases may lead to escapes. Consequently, prudence dictates that the consequences of

establishment be considered before sale is permitted in a given country.

To other biological control agents or pollinators

In general, honeybees are not affected by *B. thuringiensis* (Vandenberg 1990). Baculoviruses should be safe for use in commercial greenhouses in which agents such as the wasp *E. formosa* and the predacious mite *P. persimilis* are used. Entomopathogenic fungi vary in the breadth of their host ranges and may kill some beneficial insect species that ingest or contact fungal spores. Larvae of the ladybird beetle *Cryptolaemus montrouzieri* Mulsant (the mealybug destroyer), for example, suffered 50% mortality when fed the spores of *B. bassiana*. Adult beetles were not affected (Flexner, Lighthart, and Croft1986). Honeybee workers suffered 29% mortality when fed spores of *Hirsutella thompsonii* Fisher (Cantwell and Lehnert 1979). These effects, however, are small in comparison with those caused by use of chemical pesticides under the same circumstances.

References Cited

Artigues, M., J. Avilla, M. J. Sarasua, and R. Albajes. 1987. *Encarsia tricolor* vs. *Encarsia formosa*: Their use in biological control of *Trialeurodes vaporariorum* in Spanish conditions. *IOBC/WPRS Bulletin* 10:18–22.

Bathon, H. 2003. Invasive natural enemy species, a problem for biological plant protection. *DgaaE Nachrichten* 17 (1): 8.

Bigler, F., ed. 1991. Fifth Workshop of the IOBC Global Working Group, Quality control of mass reared arthropods, Wageningen, the Netherlands, 25–28 March.

Boethel, D. J., and R. D. Eikenbary, eds. 1986. *Interactions of Plant Resistance and Parasitoids and Predators of Insects.* New York: John Wiley and Sons.

Bravenboer, L. 1960. De chemische en biologische bestrijding van de Spintmijt *Tetranychus urticae* Koch. *Publikatie Proefstn Groenten-en Fruiteelt onder Glas te Naaldwijk* no. 75:85.

Bravenboer, L., and G. Dosse. 1962. *Phytoseiulus riegeli* Dosse als predator einiger shcadmilben aus der *Tetranychus urticae* gruppe. *Entomologia Experimentalis et Applicata* 5:291–304.

Cantwell, G. E., and T. Lehnert. 1979. Lack of effect of certain microbial insecticides on the honeybee. *Journal of Invertebrate Pathology* 33:381–82.

Chambers, R. J., S. Long, and N. L. Helyer. 1993. Effectiveness of *Orius laevigatus* (Hem.: Anthorcoridae) for the control of *Frankliniella occidentalis* on cucumber and pepper in the U.K. *Biocontrol Science and Technology* 3:295–307.

Chant, D. A. 1961. An experiment in biological control of *Tetranychus telarius* (L.) (Acarina: Tetranychidae) in a greenhouse using the predacious mite *Phytoseiulus persimilis* Athias-Henriot (Phytoseiidae). *Canadian Entomologist* 93:437–43.

Connick, W. J., Jr., J. A. Lewis, and P. C. Quimby, Jr. 1990. Formulation of biocontrol agents for use in plant pathology. In *New Directions in Biological Control*, ed. R. R. Baker and P. E. Dunn, 345–372. New York: Alan R. Liss.

Croft, B. A. 1990. *Arthropod Biological Control Agents and Pesticides*. New York: John Wiley and Sons.

Darwin, E. 1800. *Phytologia; Or, The Philosophy of Agriculture and Gardening*. Dublin: P. Byrne.

Debach, P., ed. 1964. *Biological Control of Insect Pests and Weeds*. London: Chapman and Hall.

Debach, P., and D. Rosen. 1991. *Biological Control by Natural Enemies*. Cambridge: Cambridge University Press.

De Ponti, O. M. B., M. M. Steenhuis, and P. Elzinga. 1983. Partial resistance of tomato to the greenhouse whitefly (*Trialeurodes vaporariorum* Westw.) to promote biological control. *Mededlingen Faculteit Landbouwwetenschappen, Rijksuniversiteit Gent* 48:195–98.

Flexner, J. L., B. Lighthart, and B. A. Croft. 1986. The effects of microbial pesticides on non-target, beneficial arthropods. *Agriculture, Ecosystems and Environment* 16:203–54.

Foster, G.N., and A. Kelly. 1978. Initial density of glasshouse whitefly (*Trialeurodes vaporariorum* [Westwood], Hemiptera) in relation to the success of suppression by *Encarsia formosa* Gahan (Hymenoptera) on glasshouse tomatoes. *Horticultural Research* 8:55–62.

Frank, J. H., and E. D. McCoy. 1994. Commercial importation into Florida of invertebrate animals as biological control agents. *Florida Entomologist* 77:1–20.

Fransen, J. J., and J. C. van Lenteren. 1993. Host selection and survival of the parasitoid *Encarsia formosa* on greenhouse whitefly, *Trialeurodes vaporariorum*, in the presence of hosts infected with the fungus *Aschersonia aleyrodis*. *Entomologia Experimentalis et Applicata* 69:239–49.

———. 1994. Survival of the parasitoid *Encarsia formosa* after treatment of parasitized greenhouse whitefly larvae with fungal spores of *Aschersonia aleyrodis*. *Entomologia Experimentalis et Applicata* 71:235–43.

Gabarra, R., C. Castañé, and R. Albajes. 1995. The mirid bug *Dicyphus tamaninii* as a greenhouse whitefly and western flower thrips predator on cucumber. *Biocontrol Science and Technology* 5:475–88.

Gaugler, R., and G. M. Bousch. 1979. Nonsusceptibility of rats to the entomogenous nematode, *Neoaplectana carpocapsae*. *Environmental Entomology* 8:658–60.

Gilkeson, L. A., and S. B. Hill. 1986. Genetic selection for and evaluation of nondiapause lines of predatory midge, *Aphidoletes aphidimyza* (Rondani) (Diptera: Cecidomyiidae). *Canadian Entomologist* 118:869–79.

Gillespie, D. R., and D. J. M. Quiring. 1992. Competition between *Orius tristicolor* (White) (Hemiptera: Anthocoridae) and *Amblyseius cucumeris* (Oudemans) (Acari: Phytoseiidae) feeding on *Frankliniella occidentalis* (Pergande) (Thysanoptera: Thripidae). *Canadian Entomologist* 124:1123–28.

Goh, H., J. Kim, and M. Han. 2001. Application of *Aphidius colemani* Viereck for control of the aphid in the greenhouse. *Journal of Asia-Pacific Entomology* 4 (2):171-174.

Goolsby, J. A., III. 1994. Biological control of longtailed mealybug, *Pseudococcus longispinus* (Targioni-Tozzetti) (Homoptera: Pseudococcidae) in the interior plantscape. Ph.D. diss., Department of Entomology, Texas A&M University, College Station.

Gould, H. J., W. J. Parr, H. C. Woodville, and S. P. Simmonds. 1975. Biological control of glasshouse whitefly (*Trialeurodes vaporariorum*) on cucumbers. *Entomophaga* 20:285–92.

Grafton-Cardwell, E. E., Y. Ouyang, and R. A. Striggow. 1997. Predaceous mites (Acari: Phytoseiidae) for control of spider mites (Acari: Tetranychidae) in nursery crops. *Environmental Entomology* 26:121–30.

Groenewould, G. C. M., C. de G. in 't Veld, A. J. van Oorschot-van Nes, N. W. de Jong, A. M. Vermeulen, A. W. van Toorenenbergen, A. Burdorf, H. de Groot, and R. G. van Wijk. 2002. Prevalence of sensitization to the predatory mite *Amblyseius cucumeris* as a new occupational allergen in horticulture. *Allergy* 57: 614-619.

Hall, R. A. 1982. Control of whitefly, *Trialeurodes vaporariorum* and cotton aphid, *Aphis gossypii* in glasshouses by two isolates of the fungus *Verticillium lecanii*. *Annals of Applied Biology* 101:1–11.

Hamlen, R. A. 1978. Biological control of spider mites on greenhouse ornamentals using predaceous mites. *Proceedings of the Florida State Horticultural Society* 91:247–49.

Harris, M. A., R. D. Oetting, and W. A. Gardner. 1995. Use of entomopathogenic nematodes and a new monitoring technique for control of fungus gnats, *Bradysia coprophila* (Diptera: Sciaridae), in floriculture. *Biological Control* 5:412–18.

Hassan, S. A. 1989. Testing methodology and the concept of the IOBC/WPRS working group. In *Pesticides and Non-Target Invertebrates*, ed. P. C. Jebson, 1–18. Wimborne, U.K.: Intercept.

Heinz, K. M., and J. M. Nelson. 1995. Interspecific interactions among natural enemies of *Bemisia* in an inundative biological control program. *Biological Control* 6:384–93.

Heinz, K. M., and F. G. Zalom. 1996. Performance of the predator *Delphastus pusillus* on *Bemisia* resistant and susceptible tomato lines. *Entomologia Experimentalis et Applicata* 81:345–52.

Heinz, K. M., L. Nunney, and M. P. Parrella. 1993. Toward predictable biological control of *Liriomyza trifolii* (Diptera: Agromyzidae) infesting greenhouse cut chrysanthemums. *Environmental Entomology* 22:1217–33.

Helgesen, R. G., and M. J. Tauber. 1974. Biological control of greenhouse whitefly, *Trialeurodes vaporariorum* (Aleyrodidae: Homoptera) on short-term crops by manipulating biotic and abiotic factors. *Canadian Entomologist* 106:1175–88.

Hellqvist, S. 1994. Biology of *Synacra* sp. (Hym., Diapriidae), a parasitoid of *Bradysia paupera* (Dipt., Sciaridae) in Swedish greenhouses. *Journal of Applied Entomology* 117:491–97.

Hessein, N. A., and M. P. Parrella. 1990. Predatory mites help control thrips on floriculture crops. *California Agriculture* 44:19–21.

Hoddle, M. S., R. G. Van Driesche, and J. P. Sanderson. 1997a. Biological control of *Bemisia argentifolii* (Homoptera: Aleyrodidae) on poinsettia with inundative releases of *Encarsia formosa* "Beltsville strain" (Hymenoptera: Aphelinidae): Can parasitoid reproduction augment inundative releases? *Journal of Economic Entomology* 90:910–24.

———. 1997b. Biological control of *Bemisia argentifolii* (Homoptera: Aleyrodidae) on poinsettia with inundative releases of *Encarsia formosa* (Hymenoptera: Aphelinidae): Are higher release rates necessarily better? *Biological Control* 10:166–79.

———. 1997c. Biological control of *Bemisia argentifolii* (Homoptera: Aleyrodidae) on poinsettia with inundative releases of *Eretmocerus* sp. nr. *californicus* (strain AZ) (Hymenoptera: Aphelinidae): Do release rates and plant growth affect parasitism? *Bulletin of Entomological Research* 88:47–58.

Hommes, M. 1992. Biological control of aphids on capsicum. *Bulletin OEPP/EPPO* 22:421–427.

Huffaker, C. B., and P. S. Messenger, eds. 1976. *Theory and Practice of Biological Control.* New York: Academic Press.

Hulspas-Jordaan, P.M., and J. C. van Lenteren. 1978. The relationship between host-plant leaf structure and parasitization efficiency of the parasitic wasp *Encarsia formosa* Gahan (Hymenoptera: Aphelinidae). *Mededlingen Faculteit Landbouwwetenschappen, Rijksuniversiteit Gent* 43:431–40.

Hunter, C.D. 1997. *Suppliers of Beneficial Organisms in North America.* Sacramento, Calif.: California Environmental Protection Agency.

Hussey, N. W. 1985. History of biological control in protected culture. In *Biological Pest Control: The Glasshouse Experience*, ed. W. N. Hussey and N. Scopes, 11–22. Ithaca, N.Y.: Cornell University Press (Poole, U.K.: Blandford Press).

Hussey, N. W., and W. J. Parr. 1965. Observations on the control of *Tetranychus urticae* Koch on cucumbers by the predatory mite *Phytoseiulus riegeli* Dosse. *Entomologia Experimentalis et Applicata* 8:271–81.

Jacobson, R. J., and R. J. Chambers. 1996. Control of glasshouse leafhopper (*Hauptidia maroccana*: Homoptera, Cicadellidae) within an IPM programme in protected tomatoes. *IOBC/WPRS Bulletin* 19:67–70.

Jebson, P. C., ed. 1989. *Pesticides and Non-Target Invertebrates.* Wimborne, U.K.: Intercept.

Kaya, H. K. 1990. Soil ecology. In *Entomopathogenic Nematodes in Biological Control*, ed. R. Gaugler and H. K. Kaya, 93–155. Boca Raton, Fla.: CRC Press.

Kim, Y. and J. Kim. 2003. Biological control of aphids on cucumber in plastic greenhouses using banker plants. *Korean Journal of Applied Entomology* 42:81-84.

Kirby, W., and W. Spence. 1815. *An Introduction to Entomology.* London: Longman, Brown, Green and Longmans.

Lucas, É. and O. Alomar. 2002. Impact of *Macrolophus caliginosus* presence on damage production by *Dicyphus tamaninii* (Heteroptera: Miridae) on tomato fruits. *Journal of Economic Entomology* 95: 1123-1129.

Markkula, M., and K. Tittanen. 1976. "Pest in first" and "natural infestation" methods in the control of *Tetranychus urticae* Koch with *Phytoseiulus persimilis* Athias-Henriot on glasshouse cucumbers. *Annales Agriculturae Fenniae* 15:81–5.

McCoy, C. W., and A. M. Heimpel.1980. Safety of the potential mycoacaricide, *Hirsutella thompsonii,* to vertebrates. *Environmental Entomology* 9:47–9.

McMurtry, J. A., E. R. Oatman, P. H. Phillips, and G. W. Wood. 1978. Establishment of *Phytoseiulus persimilis* (Acari: Phytoseiidae) in southern California. *Entomophaga* 23:175–79.

Mensah, R. K. 1996. Suppression of *Helicoverpa* spp. (Lepidoptera: Noctuidae) oviposition by use of the natural enemy food supplement Envirofeast. *Australian Journal of Entomology* 35:323–29.

Messing, R. H. and J. M. Rabasse. 1995. Oviposition behaviour of the polyphagous aphid parasitoid *Aphidius colemani* Viereck (Hymenoptera: Aphidiidae). *Agriculture, Ecosystems and the Environment* 52:13-17.

Mori, H., and Y. Saito. 1979. Biological control of *Tetranychus urticae* Koch (Acarina: Tetranychidae) populations by three species of phytoseiid mites (Acarina: Phytoseiidae). *Journal of the Faculty of Agriculture of Hokkaido University* 59:303–11.

Nicoli, G., M. Benuzzi, and N. C. Leppla, eds. 1994. Proceedings of the Seventh Workshop of the IOBC Global Working Group, Quality control of mass reared arthropods. Rimini, Italy, September 13–16, 1993.

O'Neil, R. J., K. L. Giles, J. J. Obrycki, D. L. Mahr, J. C. Legaspi, and K. Katovich. 1998. Evaluation of the quality of four commercially available natural enemies. *Biological Control* 11:1–8.

Parr, W.J., H. J. Gould, N. H. Jessop, and F. A. B. Ludlam. 1976. Progress towards a biological control program for glasshouse whitefly (*Trialeurodes vaporariorum*) on tomatoes. *Annals of Applied Biology* 83:349–363.

Parrella, M. P., V. P. Jones, and G. D. Christie. 1987. Feasibility of parasites for biological control of *Liriomyza trifolii* (Diptera: Agromyzidae) on commercially grown chrysanthemum. *Environmental Entomology* 16:832–37.

Podgwaite, J. D. 1986. Effects of insect pathogens on the environment. In *Biological Plant and Health Protection: Biological Control of Plant Pests and of Vectors of Human and Animal Diseases*, ed. J. M. Franz, 279–87. International Symposium of the Akademie der Wissenschaften und der Literatur, November 15–17, 1984, at Mainz and Darmstadt. *Fortschritte der zoologie* 32: Gustav Fischer Verlag, Stuttgart, Germany.

Polaszek, A., G. A. Evans, and F. D. Bennett. 1992. *Encarsia* parasitoids of *Bemisia tabaci* (Hymenoptera: Aphelinidae, Homoptera: Aleyrodidae): A preliminary guide to identification. *Bulletin of Entomological Research* 82:375–92.

Ramakers, P. M. J. 1982. Biological control in Dutch glasshouses: Practical applications and progress in research. In *Integrated Crop Protection: Proceedings of a Symposium Held at Valence, France, 18–19, June 1980*, ed. P. Graffin, 265–70. Rotterdam, the Netherlands: Balkema.

Ramakers, P. M. J. 1995. Biological control using oligophagous predators. In *Thrips Biology and Management*, ed. B. L. Parker, M. Skinner, and T. Lewis, 225–29. NATO ASI Series A: Life Sciences, vol. 276.

Ramakers, P. M. J., and R. A. Samson. 1984. *Aschersonia aleyrodis*, a fungal pathogen of whitefly, II. Application as a biological insecticide in glasshouses. *Zeitschrift für Angewandte Entomologie* 97:1–8.

Rodriguez-Reina, J. M., F. Ferragut, A. Carnero, and M. A. Peña. 1994. Diapause in the predacious mites *Amblyseius cucumeris* (Oud.) and *Amblyseius barkeri* (Hug.): Consequences of use in integrated control programmes. *Journal of Applied Entomology* 118:44–50.

Sampson, A. C., and V. J. King. 1996. *Macrolophus caliginosus*, field establishment and pest control effect in protected tomatoes. *IOBC/WPRS Bulletin* 19:143–46.

Schaaf, D. A., M. Van Der Malais, and W. J. Ravensberg. 1990. The use of *Verticillium lecanii* against whitefly and thrips in glasshouse vegetables in the Netherlands, Proceedings and abstracts. Fifth International Colloquium on Invertebrate Pathology and Microbial Control, Adelaide, Australia.

Scopes, N. E. A. 1970. Control of *Myzus persicae* on year-round chrysanthemums by introducing aphids parasitized by *Aphidius matricariae* into boxes of rooted cuttings. *Annals of Applied Biology* 66:323–27.

Sher, R. B., M. P. Parrella, and K. K. Kaya. 2000. Biological control of the leafminer *Liriomyza trifolii* (Burgess): implications for intraguild predation between *Diglyphus begini* Ashmead and *Steinernema carpocapsae* (Weiser). *Biological Control* 17: 155-163.

Simmonds, S. P. 1972. Observations on the control of *Tetranychus urticae* on roses by *Phytoseiulus persimilis*. *Plant Pathology* 21:163–65.

Speyer, E. R. 1927. An important parasite of the greenhouse whitefly (*Trialeurodes vaporariorum*) Westwood. *Bulletin of Entomological Research* 17:301–8.

Stacey, D. L. 1997. "Banker" plant production of *Encarsia formosa* Gahan and its use in the control of glasshouse whitefly on tomatoes. *Plant Pathology* 26:63–6.

Stauffer, S., and M. Rose. 1997. Biological control of soft scale insects in interior plantscapes in the USA. In *Soft Scale Insects: Their Biology, Natural Enemies and Control*, vol. 7b, ed. Y. Ben-Dov and C. J. Hodgson, 183–205. Amsterdam: Elsevier.

Stenseth, C., and I. Aase. 1983. Use of the parasite *Encarsia formosa* (Hym.: Aphelinidae) as a part of pest management on cucumbers. *Entomophaga* 28:17–26.

Tauber, C. A., J. B. Johnson, and M. J. Tauber. 1992. Larval and developmental characteristics of the endemic Hawaiian lacewing, *Anomalochrysa frater* (Neuroptera: Chrysopidae). *Annals of the Entomological Society of America* 85:200–6.

Tisdell, C.A. 1990. Economic impact of biological control of weeds and insects. In *Critical Issues in Biological Control*, ed. M. Mackauer, L. E. Ehler, and J. Roland, 301–16. Wimborne, U.K.: Intercept.

Vandenberg, J. D. 1990. Safety of four entomopathogens for caged adult honeybees (Hymenoptera: Apidae). *Journal of Economic Entomology* 83:755–59.

van den Meiracker, R. A. F. 1994. Induction and termination of diapause in *Orius* predatory bugs. *Entomologia Experimentalis et Applicata* 73:127–37.

Van Driesche, R. G., and T. S. Bellows, Jr. 1996. *Biological Control*. New York: Chapman and Hall.

Van Driesche, R. G., M. S. Hoddle, S. Lyon, and J. P. Sanderson. 2001. Compatibility of insect growth regulators with *Eretmocerus eremicus* (Hymenoptera: Aphelinidae) for whitefly (Homoptera: Alyerodidae) control on poinsettia: II. *Biological Control* 20:132–146.

Van Driesche, R. G., S. Lyon, K. Jacques, T. Smith, and P. Lopes. 2002. Comparative cost of chemical and biological whitefly control in poinsettia: is there a gap? *Florida Entomologist* 85:488-493.

Van Driesche, R. G. and S. Lyon. 2003. Commercial adoption of biological control-based IPM for whiteflies in poinsettia. *Florida Entomologist* 86: 481-3.

van Lenteren, J. C. 1990. Integrated pest and disease management in protected crops: The inescapable future. *IOBC/WPRS Bulletin* 8 (5):91–9.

———. 1995. Integrated pest management in protected crops. In *Integrated Pest Management: Principles and Systems Development*, ed. D. R. Dent, 311–43. London: Chapman and Hall.

———(ed.). 2003. *Quality Control and Production of Biological Control Agents: Theory and Testing Procedures.* Wallingford, United Kingdom, CABI Publishing.

van Lenteren, J.C., and P. M. Hulspas-Jordaan. 1987. *Encarsia formosa* can control greenhouse whitefly at low temperature regimes. *IOBC/WPRS Bulletin* 10:87–91.

van Lenteren, J. C., and J. Woets. 1988. Biological and integrated control in greenhouses. *Annual Review of Entomology* 33:239–69.

van Lenteren, J. C., J. Woets, N. Van Der Poel, W. Van Boxtel, S. Van De Merendonk, R. Van der Kamp, H. Nell, and L. Sevenste-van der Lelie. 1977. Biological control of the greenhouse whitefly *Trialeurodes vaporariorum* (Westwood) (Homoptera: Aleyrodidae) by *Encarsia formosa* Gahan (Hymenoptera: Aphelinidae) in Holland, an example of successful applied ecological research. *Mededlingen Faculteit Landbouwwetenschappen, Rijksuniversiteit Gent* 42:1333–42.

Van Lenteren, J. C., D. Babendreier, F. Bigler, G. Burgio, H. M. T. Hokkanen, S. Kuske, A. J. M. Loomans, I. Menzler-Hokkanen, P.C. J. van Rijn, M. B. Thomas, M. G. Tommasini, and Q.-Q. Zeng. 2003. Environmental risk assessment of exotic natural enemies used in inundative biological control. *BioControl* 48: 3-38.

van Steenis, M. J. 1992. Suitability of *Aphis gossypii* Glov., *Macrosiphum euphorbiae* (Thom.), and *Myzus persicae* Sulz. (Hom.: Aphididae) as hosts for several aphid parasitoid species (Hym.: Braconidae). *Bulletin OILB/STROP* 16 (2):157-160.

Vorley, V. T. , and S. D. Wratten. 1987. Migration of parasitoids (Hymenoptera: Braconidae) of cereal aphids (Hemiptera: Aphididae) between grassland, early-sown cereals, and late-sown cereals in southern England. *Bulletin of Entomological Research* 77:555–68.

Walter, D. E., and D. J. O'Dowd. 1992. Leaf morphology and predators: Effect of leaf domatia on the abundance of predatory mites (Acari: Phytoseiidae). *Environmental Entomology* 21:478–84.

Wardlow, L. R. 1984. Monitoring the activity of tomato leafminer (*Liriomyza bryoniae* Kalt.) and its parasites in commercial glasshouses in southern England. *Mededlingen Faculteit Landbouwwetenschappen, Rijksuniversiteit Gent* 49:781–91.

Woets, J., and J. C. van Lenteren. 1976. The parasite-host relationship between *Encarsia formosa* (Hym., Aphelinidae) and *Trialeurodes vaporariorum* (Hom., Aleyrodidae). VI. Influence of the host plant on the greenhouse whitefly and its parasite *Encarsia formosa*. *IOBC/WPRS Bulletin* 4:151–64.

York, G. T. 1958. Field tests with the fungus *Beauveria* sp. for control of the European corn borer. *Iowa State College Journal of Science* 33:123–29.

2

Biological Control as a Component of IPM Systems

R. G. Van Driesche
Department of Entomology
University of Massachusetts, Amherst, MA
and
K. M. Heinz
Department of Entomology
Texas A & M University, College Station, TX

Introduction

Few greenhouse crops have only one pest. Poinsettia has only whiteflies (two species) as a major insect pest. Minor pests of this crop are fungus gnats, and an important disease is *Botrytis cinerea* Pers.: Fr. So, even in this relatively simple crop, growers using biological control for the major insect pest (whitefly) must also consider how they should manage other pests in a compatible way. For crops such as tomatoes or roses, the need to develop a network of compatible control strategies is even greater and more complicated, since these crops are hosts to numerous pests. Furthermore, pest complexes have a tendency to increase rather than decrease in size. New pests may invade, as *Bemisia argentifolii* Bellows and Perring (= "B" strain of *Bemisia tabaci* [Gennadius]) did in 1986 in the United States and as *Frankliniella occidentalis* (Pergande) did during the 1990s in many greenhouse production regions of Europe. Also, local native species formerly excluded from greenhouses by use of broad-spectrum pesticides may invade crops and become new pests.

How, then, should growers using biological control proceed to construct integrated pest management systems with biological control as the foundation? This is a complex question, and we have dealt with it in this book at several levels. In chapters 20 through 29, full crop-specific IPM programs are presented and analyzed for chrysanthemums, poinsettias, cut flowers, foliage plants, woody ornamentals, bedding plants, cucumbers, sweet pepper, tomatoes, and mushrooms. In these chapters, recommendations are made about the best approaches for integrating controls needed for specific groups of pests. A topic that routinely comes up in this regard is how to integrate biological control agents with chemical pesticides. Chapter 7 covers the principles of this topic in depth.

Here we will present the broad view of what it means to integrate biological control into an IPM system. We will parallel the general discussion on biological control-based integrated pest management systems developed by Van Driesche and Bellows (1996), and readers interested in additional material on biological control for outdoor crops should refer to that reference. Here, we discuss the following issues:

- *Control foundations*—What is the most important pest to be controlled, and how must that be achieved?
- *Stimuli for change*—What changes are forcing growers to move away from past practices? For example, have pests become resistant to formerly useful pesticides, or have important pesticides been banned from use? Have government regulations modified the availability of pest management strategies?
- *Control combinations and their issues*—What issues are involved when we try to integrate two or more different kinds of control?
- *Techniques*—What tools do we have at our disposal for such integration?

Control Foundations

Most crops have one or more key pests that must be successfully controlled to produce a marketable harvest. Controls employed for such key pests form the foundation for the crop's pest management system around which all other control decisions must be coordinated. Pest management systems may rest on foundations either of chemical control, cultural control, biological control, or control through plant resistance, depending on what is required for control of the key pests.

Chemical foundations

In the production of cut roses, powdery mildew and spider mites are often the key pests. Control of powdery mildew currently requires use of an effective fungicide because rose varieties in use lack resistance to the pest. Spider mites potentially could be controlled with either acaricides or predacious mites. A conflict exists, however, between sulfur vaporization (for control of mildew) and use of predacious mites. Since many growers prefer to rely on sulfur for disease control, mildew becomes the defining key pest whose control approach determines the kind of IPM foundation (chemical) used in the crop. Controls for other pests (such as spider mites) are then adjusted around the chemical control of this key pest. Much of the potential for biological control of such lesser pests is not realized because pesticides applied for control of key pests also harm natural enemies. We will address the solution to this rose pest management dilemma later in this chapter.

Biological control foundations

In crops in which natural enemies control the key pest, biological control forms the foundation for pest management. Biological control–based systems are most likely to develop if a significant key pest is the successful target of biological control early in the history of the production of the crop. In tomatoes and cucumbers, whitefly is a key pest, but one that can be controlled well with releases of the parasitoid *Encarsia formosa* Gahan. The requirement to conserve this key natural enemy acted subsequently to influence choices about methods that could be used to control other pests in the crop. Chemical controls could not be employed except in ways that were not disruptive to this key parasitoid. These crops were later invaded by western flower thrips. Because any widespread use of nonselective pesticides in the crops would both disrupt whitefly biological control and kill bumblebees used in the crop to enhance pollination, efforts to find controls for western flower thrips have focused on biological control methods rather than pesticides.

Mixed foundation systems

Not every crop has a clearly defined control strategy as a pest management foundation. Crops may lack well-defined key pests, or pests may be amenable to either chemical or biological control. In such systems, consequences of choices made about control are likely to accumulate, leading the system toward the development of a foundation based on the dominant control method, such as pesticide, biological control, host plant resistance, or cultural practices. Strawberries grown in plastic tunnels, for example, may be affected by spider mites, plant-feeding mirid bugs, and gray mold (*B. cinerea*). Mites can be suppressed by use of either acaricides or augmentative releases of predacious mites. Mirid bugs cannot be easily suppressed by biological control methods within single fields within a crop cycle, but they have the potential to be suppressed regionally in North America by introduced parasitoids from Europe (Day et al. 1998). Finally, even gray mold, traditionally suppressed with fungicides, has potential to be controlled by biological control methods, using antagonistic fungi distributed by pollinators (Peng, Sutton, and Kevan 1992). In such systems, development of the pest control foundation will depend on choices made by researchers, pest management consultants, and farmers.

Practices employed will channel decisions, affecting the development of controls for remaining pests. Use of biological controls for one pest may stimulate use of biological control for additional pests. Choosing chemical controls may make use of biological controls less likely. Chemical controls for *Lygus* bugs, for example, may make releases of predacious mites ineffective, resulting in the use of acaricides. Use of some fungicides may reduce the reproductive rates of predacious mites (Dong and Niu 1988), making biological mite control less effective.

Forces Driving Changes in IPM Methods

Many pest control systems are based primarily on the use of pesticides. Initial efforts at improving pest management in such cases is often largely pesticide management, in that the quantity of pesticide used is reduced by pest monitoring, use of damage thresholds, and calibration of machinery, but most pest control is still achieved by the use of pesticides. Changing such systems to ones based on biological control or controls other than the use of chemical pesticides is a subject of interest in many countries. In principle, several routes might lead to such transitions: incremental modifications, new crop production methods or control methods for key pests, development of pesticide resistance by key pests, legal restrictions on essential pesticides, or development of biological controls for key pests.

Incremental modifications

A commonly held belief is that chemical-based control systems can be modified gradually into ones in which few or no pesticides are used by a series of small changes, requiring only small adjustments by growers in any given year. In practice, this goal is often difficult to achieve because chemical practices are in many ways antagonistic to biological control. Opportunities to modify such practices through use of physiologically selective pesticides will be limited by the finite number of pesticides registered for use on the crop. Efforts to employ ecologically selective methods of pesticide application will be limited by constraints on retaining effectiveness of the pesticides against the target pests. Dosages reduced below certain levels may be ineffective. While incremental methods are most acceptable to growers, more far-reaching changes are often needed to achieve IPM systems based on biological control methods.

New crop production or pest control methods

One approach that is often involved in converting a pesticide-based IPM system to one based on biological control is the development of some alternative method to control a common pest in the crop. Use of *Bacillus thuringiensis* Berliner or nematodes instead of persistent broad-spectrum insecticides to control fungus gnats in potted flower crops, for example, allows for biological control of whiteflies to be implemented. The incompatibility of many insecticides with the wide use of bumblebees (*Bombus terrestris* L.) for pollination of tomato, eggplant, strawberry, and melon crops also promoted the use of biological pest control in vegetables. In general, any nondisruptive control method that replaces or hinders the regular use of a broad-spectrum pesticide will increase the opportunity to achieve biological control in the crop. Methods to replace chemical pesticides include nematodes, pathogens, traps, mating disruption with pheromones, and host-plant resistance. Elimination of formerly required pesticide applications is particularly valuable if these are early-season applications. This allows time for natural-enemy populations to colonize and reproduce in the crop without immediately being suppressed by pesticide treatments.

Development of pesticide resistance

When a key pest becomes highly resistant to most available pesticides, the ability of growers to effectively suppress the pest with chemically based pest management systems may be lost. At this point, the system is without definite shape and growers are amenable to changing the basis for pest control in the crop. The development of pesticide-resistant spider mites was a driving force in converting greenhouse vegetables from pesticide-based systems to ones based on biological control; predators offered the only means of suppressing these pesticide-resistant spider mite populations.

Loss of registered pesticides

The ability to continue to employ chemical pest control systems may also be lost if important pesticides are banned or if greenhouse crop registrations are given up by chemical companies as unprofitable in view of tighter regulatory standards. For example, termination in the United States of the registration of the aphicide pirimicarb reduced the opportunities to integrate chemical and biological control of aphids in some crops.

Passage of the U.S. Food Quality Protection Act in 1996 is significantly restricting the use of organophosphates, carbamates, and several dithiocarbamate fungicides on greenhouse crops. Governmental support for biological control research and implementation also complements tighter restrictions on the use of insecticides. For example, the Danish Environmental Protection Agency has recently promoted several initiatives to broaden the use of biological control (Enkegaard et al. 1999).

Development of biological controls for key pests

Biological control research may produce solutions to long-standing pest control problems. Once found, these solutions may be quickly adopted and become the industry standard practice. Efforts to develop effective biological control methods for *Bemisia* whiteflies (Hoddle, Van Driesche, and Sanderson 1997a, 1997b, 1997c; Van Driesche et al. 2001) and western flower thrips (see reviews by Parker, Skinner, and Lewis 1995; Lewis 1997; Van Driesche et al. 1988) on flower crops are examples of such research programs.

Control Combinations and Their Issues

In general, four combinations of biological control and other factors are possible in IPM systems: (1) biological and chemical control, (2) biological and cultural controls or practices, (3) biological control and pest-resistant plants, and (4) two or more different types of biological control. Each has its own approaches and concerns.

Biological and chemical control

To varying degrees, most insecticides and acaricides adversely affect natural enemies (Croft 1990), as do some fungicides and herbicides. The use of such materials may prevent the use of biological controls in the same crop. Indeed, residues present on cuttings or young plants purchased from other growers may affect a grower's ability to use biological control agents, in some cases for a month or more. The damage done to natural enemies by pesticides can be reduced by either lowering the amount applied, seeking selective pesticides that are safer to natural enemies (physiological selectivity), or altering the way in which pesticides are applied to reduce contact with natural enemies (ecological selectivity) (see chapter 7).

Physiological selectivity of pesticides may be employed by screening key natural enemies for susceptibility to pesticides registered for use on the crop to determine if any of the available pesticides are less damaging to important natural enemies or if adequate pest control might be achieved at lower doses. Substituting stomach poisons for contact pesticides may protect some types of natural enemies. Substituting inherently less toxic materials, such as insect growth regulators, pheromones, or microbial pesticides (like those based on toxins of *B. thuringiensis*), or using lower doses can also reduce conflicts between natural enemies and pesticides. For example, lowered doses of sulfur via vaporization (lower quantities, shorter periods of vaporization) can be used to promote the integration of sulfur for powdery mildew control and predatory mites for spider mite control in roses (Hanna et al. 1997).

Ecological selectivity of materials that are toxic to natural enemies can be achieved if the materials are applied in ways that minimize contact with natural enemies. Use of the granular form of imidacloprid for control of sucking insects such as aphids or whiteflies would, for example, have little effect on the use of biological control agents on the foliage for control of thrips or spider mites. Thripstick, a deltamethrin product once used in Europe, controlled onion thrips (*Thrips tabaci* Lindeman) in greenhouse cucumbers without disrupting whitefly biological control because the pesticide was applied only to the rock wool substrate in which the plants were rooted (where the thrips pupated) (Pickford 1984). This treated area was not visited by *E. formosa*; thus, whitefly biological control was not affected. Another approach to integration of natural enemies and pesticides is to employ pesticide-resistant natural enemies (Hoy 1982, Hoy et al. 1990). For example, a strain of *Neoseiulus californicus* (McGregor) resistant to bifenthrin (Talstar) is under study in Florida for use in controlling spider mites in crops in which other pests such as aphids, scales, or mealybugs are being suppressed with this pyrethroid (Osborne, Ehler, and Nechols 1985).

Biological and cultural controls or practices

In general, cultural practices and natural enemies are less likely to be in conflict than pesticides and natural enemies are. However, some conflicts can exist. Traps, for example, catch natural enemies as well as pests, and if deployed in too great a density may depress natural enemy numbers. In greenhouse tomatoes, picking off the old leaves at the bottom of the plant may selectively remove the leaves bearing the most whitefly parasitoid pupae.

Biological control and pest-resistant plants

The use of pest-resistant plants is usually considered compatible with the use of natural enemies. In some instances, however, characters conferring pest resistance on plants may reduce the effectiveness of biological control agents. Some suppressive traits of resistant plants may be internal to the plant (e.g., secondary plant compounds) and have little direct contact with natural enemies but may have secondary effects if compounds are exuded onto the surface of the plant or if such compounds change host chemistry or quality (see Kashyap, Kennedy, and Farrar 1991; Barbour, Farrar, and Kennedy 1993; Gillespie and Quiring 1994). Plant traits that have external manifestations may directly affect natural enemies. High trichome densities on stems of tomatoes (*Lycopersicon lycopersicum* [Linnaeus] Karsten ex Farwell) in greenhouses in the Netherlands acted as barriers to dispersal of the predacious mite *Phytoseiulus persimilis* Athias-Henriot, a predator commonly released on the crop for mite control (van Haren et al. 1987). In cucumber and tomato, the efficacy of searching by the parasitoid *E. formosa* for its host, the greenhouse whitefly, *Trialeurodes vaporariorum* (Westwood), is greatly reduced by the presence of stiff foliar trichomes that slow the parasitoid's walking and also force the parasitoid to expend more time grooming if the trichomes are coated with sticky honeydew (see Price et al. 1980, Li et al. 1987). The effect of such plant features on natural enemies varies, however, with the natural enemy species. For the whitefly predator *Delphastus pusillus* (LeConte) (Coleop.: Coccinellidae), Heinz and Zalom (1995, 1996) found no effect on predation rate from variation in density of nonglandular trichomes on tomato leaves.

Two or more different types of biological control

In pest management systems based primarily on biological control, several types of natural enemies may be required for control of various members of the pest complex. This is increasingly the case in greenhouse crops. Predatory mites, whitefly parasitoids, and predators for thrips may all be required, for example, in greenhouse pepper crops. In some crops, it may be necessary to combine the release of aphid parasitoids with microbial pesticides such as *B. thuringiensis* to suppress lepidopteran larvae. Potential conflicts that may arise in such complex systems include predators that eat one of the other natural enemies and pathogens that kill the hosts of one of the parasitoids. For example, Cloutier and Johnson (1993) found that the thrips predator *Orius tristicolor* (White) also fed on the predatory mite *P. persimilis* when both were used for control of greenhouse pests. In such cases, avoiding conflict is often a matter of timing releases so that one natural enemy does not encounter the other immediately upon release; or that the natural enemies released specialize in different developmental stages of a single target pest or they specialize in different target pests all together. Such conflicts among natural enemies have been termed *intraguild predation*.

For pathogens and parasitoids attacking the same species, conflicts caused by elimina-

tion of the host population for the parasitoids can be managed by adjusting the rate and degree of coverage of the microbial pesticide to lower the rate of kill, leaving some hosts to be parasitized. Trials may be needed to determine if the actions of two or more biological control agents are compatible. Application of the fungus *Aschersonia aleyrodis* Webber was found by Ramakers and Samson (1984) to be compatible with the use of *E. formosa* in greenhouse crops for control of the whitefly *T. vaporariorum*, because its use did not alter the ratio of parasitized and nonparasitized whiteflies.

Techniques to Integrate Methods

Several techniques are available to integrate natural enemies into pest management systems, with the goal that biological control will provide the foundation for control in the system. These include (1) natural enemy monitoring, (2) using natural enemy numbers in models to predict the outcomes of natural enemy–pest interactions at the population level, (3) assessment of compatibility of natural enemies with pesticides and new crop varieties, (4) assessment of effects of cultural practices on natural enemies, and (5) techniques for direct natural enemy management.

Natural enemy monitoring and thresholds

If control of pests is to be based on the action of natural enemies, methods must be available to measure the abundance of key species or groups of natural enemies at various times in order to determine if they are sufficiently abundant to maintain the pest under control.

Thresholds must be developed that define what levels of natural enemy abundance are reliably associated with effective pest control. These thresholds may take various forms, including predator-to-prey ratios or proportions of hosts parasitized (Martin and Dale 1989), and they vary among crops and within crop cycles. Threshold values are higher and much less variable in ornamentals than in vegetables. Further, threshold values tend to increase within a crop cycle during the approach and production of the harvestable fruit, foliage, or flowers. For control of whitefly infesting greenhouse tomatoes, *E. formosa* is often introduced immediately after planting. As long as no whiteflies are observed, release rates of approximately 1.5 *E. formosa* per m^2 per week continue. As soon as a whitefly infestation is detected, release rates are increased to 3 *E. formosa* per m^2 per week. When the level of parasitism in the plant is at least 85%, parasitoid release rates may be reduced or releases may cease provided additional outbreaks do not occur.

Using natural enemy numbers in pest models

Given monitoring methods for both pests and natural enemies, information on natural enemy abundance can be incorporated into models used to make management decisions about pest control. Decision charts developed by Martin and Dale (1989) related proportions of leaves in greenhouse crops infested with the greenhouse whitefly (*T. vaporariorum*) and levels of parasitism in ways that allowed determinations to be made as to whether or not chemical pest controls were needed. A simple computer model developed by Heinz, Nunney, and Parrella (1993) for

biological control of *Liriomyza trifolii* (Burgess) infesting greenhouse cut chrysanthemums generated population data for both the natural enemy and pest within the context of an augmentation biological control program. Growers monitoring population trends in their greenhouses using foliage (Jones and Parrella 1986) and sticky card (Parrella and Jones 1985; Heinz, Parrella, and Newman 1993) sampling methods (for a general overview, see chapter 5) could compare their actual pest and natural-enemy population levels to the levels predicted by the model and make changes to their pest management strategies as necessary.

Models in their most sophisticated form can also incorporate factors that affect crop profitability. This allows pest management decisions to be based on information that accurately reflects the likely economic benefit of specific pest control options. Such models should include information on the level of the pest (suggesting possible losses), the levels of key natural enemies (suggesting possibility for biological control to reduce these losses), costs of pest control options, current crop load of marketable produce, and current crop price. Collectively, these factors define the value of the harvested crop at risk, which determines the amount of pest control that is economical to implement.

Compatibility of natural enemies and pesticides

When chemical pesticides are required to supplement the control of one or more members of a pest complex, care must be taken not to employ pesticides that will destroy the biological control systems operating against other pests in the crop. To choose pesticides with appropriate properties, pesticides must be screened to determine their effects on the important natural enemies in the system. Methods for such screening are discussed in more detail in chapter 7. Hassan (1977, 1985) and Vogt (1994) provide standardized protocols for testing effects of pesticides on various specific types of natural enemies, especially species used in greenhouse crops, under laboratory, semifield, and field conditions. Growers can use the results of such investigations by referring to "side effects" guides published by various insectaries, such as Koppert Biological Systems (http://www.koppert.com and then look for Side Effects button).

Natural enemies, crop varieties and cultural practices

Crop breeders continue to introduce new cultivars, which perpetuates the need to screen cultivars for their compatibility with key natural enemies. Biological control considerations are likely to influence both the kinds of characters incorporated into new varieties and the optimal intensity of such characters (van Emden 1991). In addition to avoiding the addition of characters to plants that hurt natural enemies, opportunities exist in plant breeding to add positive features to plants (such as nectaries and hiding places used by predator mites, called *domatia*) that help natural enemies (Cortesero, Stapel, and Lewis 2000).

Just as crop variety and pesticide use affect the environment in which natural enemies must function, so do various cropping practices, such as soil and water management, weed control, planting and harvesting schedules, and crop residue handling practices. Bieri et al. (1989), for example, compared the effects of two different irrigation systems used in greenhouse cucumber (*Cucumis sativus* Linnaeus) production in Switzerland on biological control of mites and thrips. The role of such factors in shaping the degree to which natural enemies are effective against pests is large, and modifications to cultural practices should be actively explored in the process of developing pest management systems based on biological control.

Direct provisioning of resources to natural enemies

Efforts to develop pest management systems based on biological control agents can also include direct manipulation of resources important to natural enemies being used in the crop. In greenhouse cucumbers, open-rearing units (banker plants) have been used to aid establishment of aphid natural enemies for the control of *Aphis gossypii* Glover (Bennison and Corless 1993). Banker plants, comprised of wheat or barley seedlings infested with bird-cherry aphids, *Rhopalosiphum padi* (Linnaeus), enhanced early establishment of *Aphidius colemani* Viereck and *Aphidoletes aphidimyza* (Rondani), enabling rapid and prolonged control of *A. gossypii*. Additionally, viability of the parasitoids emanating from the banker plants was believed to be greater than that of wasps emerging from the standard method of spreading parasitoid pupae, mixed with vermiculite, throughout the greenhouse.

In greenhouse crops with western flower thrips, pollen resources are important to *Orius* bugs and some species of predatory mites. In crops or at time lacking pollen, artificial application of pollen may be a means to stimulate population increase in such predators, with the expectation that larger predator populations will result in more intense levels of predation on the thrips (van Rijn, van Houten, and Sabelis 1999).

Conclusion

As discussed in subsequent chapters, biological control–based IPM programs are prevalent in many protected cropping systems. This is especially true for vegetables relative to ornamentals. Prior to 1970, biological pest control was rare to nonexistent within protected culture (van Lenteren and Woets 1988). In Denmark, more than 98% of all vegetable acreage is under biological control (Enkegaard et al. 1999). Rapid rates of adoption have also been observed for vegetables grown in Austria (Pleininger and Blümel 1999), Canada (Murphy and Broadbent 1996), France (Courbet and Maisonneuve 1999), Japan (Ogata 1999), the Netherlands (Fransen 1996), New Zealand (Martin, Workman, and Marais 1996), and the United States (Casey et al. 1999; Heinz, Thompson, and Krauter 1999).

Until recently, implementation of biological control–based IPM programs within ornamentals has been infrequent. Changes in government policies, pest biologies, consumer demands, and biological control technologies have stimulated adoption of biological pest control in ornamental commodities. In Denmark, 30 to 35% of the ornamental acreage within protected culture is under biological control (Enkegaard et al. 1999). As discussed in later chapters, biological control–based IPM programs within ornamen-

tals have been most successful in controlling pests of propagation crops of ornamentals (Heinz and Parrella 1990) and cut flowers, and only recently have successes in potted and bedding plants been experienced. These programs are most common on nonexport flowers or crops in which only a select portion of the crop needs to be protected (e.g., vegetables). In conservatories and interior landscapes, where relatively high pest levels are frequently tolerated, programs are also becoming more common (van Lenteren and Woets 1988). Provided the conditions promoting the biological control–based IPM throughout the world remains intact, the acreage and crops protected by this strategy should continue to grow.

References Cited

Barbour, J. D., R. R. Farrar, and G. G. Kennedy. 1993. Interaction of *Manduca sexta* resistance in tomato with insect predators of *Helicoverpa zea*. *Entomologia Experimentalis et Applicata* 68 (2):143–55.

Bennison, J. A., and S. P. Corless. 1993. Biological control of aphids on cucumbers: Further development of open rearing units or "banker plants" to aid establishment of aphid natural enemies. *IOBC/WPRS Bulletin* 16 (2):5–8.

Bieri, M., F. Zwygart, G. Tognina, and G. Stadler. 1989. The importance of soil water content for the biological control of *Thrips tabaci* Lind. on cucumbers in the greenhouse. *Mitteilungen der Schweizerischen Entomologischen Gesellschaft* 62:28.

Casey, C., B. Murphy, M. Parrella, and J. MacDonald. 1999. Development of an integrated pest management program for fresh cut roses in U.S. greenhouses. *IOBC/WPRS Bulletin* 22 (1):29–32.

Cloutier, C., and S. G. Johnson. 1993. Predation by *Orius tristicolor* (Hemiptera: Anthocoridae) on *Phytoseiulus persimilis* (Acarina: Phytoseiidae): Testing for compatibility between biocontrol agents. *Environmental Entomology* 22 (2):477–82.

Cortesero, A. M., J. O. Stapel, and W. J. Lewis. 2000. Understanding and manipulating plant attributes to enhance biological control. *Biological Control* 17 (1):35–49.

Courbet, S., and J. C. Maisonneuve. 1999. Biological pest control in greenhouses in France during 1998. *IOBC/WPRS Bulletin* 22 (1):37–40.

Croft, B. A. 1990. *Arthropod Biological Control Agents and Pesticides*. New York: John Wiley and Sons.

Day, W. H., J. M. Tropp, A. T. Easton, R. F. Romig, R. G. Van Driesche, and R. J. Chianese. 1998. Geographic distributions of *Peristenus conradi* and *P. digoneutis* (Hymenoptera: Bracondiae), parasites of the alfalfa plant bug and the tarnished plant bug (Hemiptera: Miridae) in the northeastern United States. *Journal of the New York Entomological Society* 106:69–75.

Dong, H. F., and L. P. Niu. 1988. Effect of four fungicides on the establishment and reproduction of *Phytoseiulus persimilis* (Acari: Phytoseiidae). *Chinese Journal of Biological Control* 4:1–5.

Enkegaard, A. D., D. Funck Jensen, P. Folker-Hansen, and J. Eilenberg. 1999. Present use and future potential for biological control of pests and diseases in Danish greenhouses. *IOBC/WPRS Bulletin* 22 (1):65–8.

Fransen, J. J. 1996. Recent trends in integrated and biological pest and disease control in the Netherlands. *IOBC/WPRS Bulletin* 19 (1):43–6.

Gillespie, D. R., and D. J. M. Quiring. 1994. Reproduction and longevity of the predatory mite, *Phytoseiulus persimilis* (Acari: Phytoseiidae) and its prey, *Tetranychus urticae* (Acari: Tetranychidae) on different host plants. *Journal of the Entomological Society of British Columbia* 91:3–8.

Hanna, R., F. G. Zalom, L. T. Wilson, and G. M. Leavitt. 1997. Sulfur can suppress mite predators in vineyards. *California Agriculture* 51 (1):19–21.

Hassan, S. A. 1977. Standardized techniques for testing side-effects of pesticides on beneficial arthropods in the laboratory. *Zeitschrift für Pflanzenkrankheiten und Pflanzenschutz* 84:158–63.

———. 1985. Standard methods to test the side-effects of pesticides on natural enemies of insects and mites developed by the IOBC/WPRS Working Group "Pesticides and Beneficial Organisms." *Bulletin OEPP/EPPO* 15:214–55.

Heinz, K. M., L. Nunney, and M. P. Parrella. 1993. Toward predictable biological control of *Liriomyza trifolii* (Diptera: Agromyzidae) infesting greenhouse cut chrysanthemums. *Environmental Entomology* 22 (6):1217–33.

Heinz, K. M., and M. P. Parrella. 1990. Biological control of insect pests on greenhouse marigolds. *Environmental Entomology* 19 (4):825–35.

Heinz, K. M., M. P. Parrella, and J. P. Newman. 1993. Time efficient use of yellow sticky traps in monitoring insect populations. *Journal of Economic Entomology* 85:2263–9.

Heinz, K. M., S. P. Thompson, and P. C. Krauter. 1999. Development of biological control methods for use in southwestern U.S. greenhouses and nurseries. *IOBC/WPRS Bulletin* 22 (1):101–4.

Heinz, K. M., and F. G. Zalom. 1995. Variation in trichome-based resistance to *Bemisia argentifolii* (Homoptera: Aleyrodidae) oviposition on tomato. *Journal of Economic Entomology* 88:1494–1502.

———. 1996. Performance of the predator *Delphastus pusillus* on *Bemisia* resistant and susceptible tomato lines. *Entomologia Experimentalis et Applicata* 81:345–52.

Hoddle, M., R. G. Van Driesche, and J. Sanderson. 1997a. Biological control of *Bemisia argentifolii* (Homoptera: Aleyrodidae) on poinsettia with inundative releases of *Encarsia formosa* "Beltsville strain" (Hymenoptera: Aphelinidae): Can parasitoid reproduction augment inundative releases? *Journal of Economic Entomology* 90 (4):910–24.

———. 1997b. Biological control *of Bemisia argentifolii* (Homoptera: Aleyrodidae) on poinsettia with inundative releases of *Eretmocerus* sp. nr. *californicus* (strain AZ) (Hymenoptera: Aphelinidae): Do release rates and plant growth affect parasitism? *Bulletin of Entomological Research* 88:47–58.

———. 1997c. Biological control of *Bemisia argentifolii* (Homoptera: Aleyrodidae) on poinsettia with inundative releases of *Encarsia formosa* (Hymenoptera: Aphelinidae): Are higher release rates necessarily better? *Biological Control* 10:166–79.

Hoy, M. A. 1982. Aerial dispersal and field efficacy of a genetically improved strain of the spider mite predator *Metaseiulus occidentalis*. *Entomologia Experimentalis et Applicata* 32:205–12.

Hoy, M. A., F. E. Cave, R. H. Beede, J. Grant, W. H. Krueger, W. H. Olson, K. M. Spollen, W. W. Barnett, and L. C. Hendricks. 1990. Release, dispersal, and recovery of a laboratory-selected strain of the walnut aphid parasite *Trioxys pallidus* (Hymenoptera: Aphidiidae) resistant to azinphosmethyl. *Journal of Economic Entomology* 76:383–8.

Jones, V. P., and M. P. Parrella. 1986. The development of sampling strategies for larvae of *Liriomyza trifolii* in chrysanthemum. *Environmental Entomology* 15:268–273.

Kashyap, R. K., G. G. Kennedy, and R. R. Farrar. 1991. Mortality and inhibition of *Helicoverpa zea* egg parasitism rates by *Trichogramma* in relation to trichome/methyl ketone-mediated insect resistance of *Lycopersicon hirsutum* f. *glabratum*. *Journal of Chemical Ecology* 17 (12):2381–96.

Lewis, T., ed. 1997. *Thrips as Crop Pests*. Wallingford, U.K.: CAB International.

Li, Z. H., F. Lammes, J. C. van Lenteren, P. W. T. Huisman, A. van Vianen, and O. M. B. DePonti. 1987. The parasite-host relationship between *Encarsia formosa* (Hymenoptera: Aphelinidae) and *Trialeurodes vaporariorum* (Homoptera: Aleyrodidae). XXV. Influence of leaf structure on the searching activity of *Encarsia formosa*. *Journal of Applied Entomology* 104:297–304.

Martin, N. A., and J. R. Dale. 1989. Monitoring greenhouse whitefly puparia and parasitism: A decision approach. *New Zealand Journal of Crop and Horticultural Science* 7:115–23.

Martin, N. A., P. J. Workman, and T. Marais. 1996. IPM for greenhouse crops in New Zealand: Progress, problems and prospects. *IOBC/WPRS Bulletin* 19 (1):99–102.

Murphy, G. D., and A. B. Broadbent. 1996. Adoption of IPM by the greenhouse floriculture industry in Ontario, Canada. *IOBC/WPRS Bulletin* 19 (1):107–10.

Ogata, Y. 1999. Integration of biological and chemical control in case of Japan. *IOBC/WPRS Bulletin* 22 (1):189–91.

Osborne, L. S., L. E. Ehler, and J. R. Nechols. 1985. Biological control of the two-spotted spider mite in greenhouses. Bulletin, Agricultural Experiment Stations, University of Florida, 0096-607X, 853. Gainesville, Fla.: Agricultural Experiment Stations, Institute of Food and Agricultural Sciences, University of Florida.

Parker, B. L., M. Skinner, and T. Lewis, eds. 1995. *Thrips Biology and Management*. NATO ASI Series. Series A: Life Sciences vol. 276. New York: Plenum Press.

Parrella, M. P., and V. P. Jones. 1985. Yellow traps as monitoring tools for *Liriomyza trifolii* (Diptera: Agromyzidae) in chrysanthemum greenhouses. *Journal of Economic Entomology* 78:53–6.

Peng, G., J. C. Sutton, and P. G. Kevan. 1992. Effectiveness of honeybees for applying the biocontrol agent *Gliocladium roseum* to strawberry flowers to suppress *Botrytis cinerea*. *Canadian Journal of Plant Pathology and Reviews of Canadian Phytopathology*. 14 (2):117–29.

Pickford, R. J. J. 1984. Evaluation of soil treatment for control of *Thrips tabaci* on cucumbers [*Phytoseiulus persimilis*, *Encarsia formosa*]. *Annals of Applied Biology* 104 (suppl.):18–9.

Pleininger, S., and S. Blümel. 1999. Implementation and development of IPM in greenhouse crops in Austria. *IOBC/WPRS Bulletin* 22 (1):193–6.

Price, P. W., C. E. Bouton, P. Gross, B. A. McPheron, J. N. Thompson, and A. E. Weiss. 1980. Interactions among three trophic levels: Influence of plants on interactions between insect herbivores and natural enemies. *Annual Review of Ecology and Systematics* 11:41–65.

Ramakers, P. M. J., and R. A. Samson. 1984. *Aschersonia aleyrodis*, a fungal pathogen of whitefly. II. Application as a biological insecticide in glasshouses. *Zeitschrift für Angewandte Entomologie* 97:1–8.

Van Driesche, R. G., and T. S. Bellows. 1996. *Biological Control*. New York: Chapman and Hall.

Van Driesche, R. G., K. M. Heinz, J. C. van Lenteren, A. Loomans, R. Wick, T. Smith, P. Lopes, J. P. Sanderson, M. Daughtrey, and M. Brownbridge. 1988. *Western Flower Thrips in Greenhouses: A Review of Its Biological Control and Other Methods*. Amherst, Mass.: University of Massachusetts.

Van Driesche, R. G., M. Hoddle, S. Lyon, and J. Sanderson. 2001. Compatibility of insect growth regulators with *Eretmocerus eremicus* (Hymenoptera: Aphelinidae) for whitefly (Homoptera: Aleyrodidae) control on poinsettia II. *Biological Control* 20 (2):132–146.

van Emden, H. F. 1991. The role of host plant resistance in insect pest mis-management. *Bulletin of Entomological Research* 81:123–6.

van Haren, R. J. F., M. M. Steenhuis, M. W. Sabelis, and O. M. B. de Ponti. 1987. Tomato stem trichomes and dispersal success of *Phytoseiulus persimilis* relative to its prey *Tetranychus urticae*. *Experimental and Applied Acarology* 3:115–21.

van Lenteren, J. C., and J. Woets. 1988. Biological and integrated pest control in greenhouses. *Annual Review of Entomology* 33:239–69.

van Rijn, P. C. J., Y. M. van Houten, and M. W. Sabelis. 1999. Pollen improves thrips control with predatory mites. Integrated control in glasshouses. *IOBC/WPRS Bulletin* 22 (1):209–12.

Vogt, H., ed. 1994. Side-effects of pesticides on beneficial organisms: Comparison of laboratory, semi-field, and field results. *IOBC/WPRS Bulletin* 17 (10):1–178.

3

EFFECTS OF GREENHOUSE STRUCTURE AND FUNCTION ON BIOLOGICAL CONTROL

R. K. Lindquist
Department of Entomology
The Ohio State University/OARDC, Wooster, Ohio

and

T. L. Short
Food, Agricultural, & Biological Engineering Department
The Ohio State University, Wooster, Ohio

Van Lenteren (2000) estimated there were 741,290 acres (300,000 ha) of greenhouses worldwide, and biological control was used on about 37,065 acres (15,000 ha) to suppress insects or mites. Why is biological control successful on 5% of the area covered by greenhouse, and either not used or unsuccessful in the vast majority of greenhouses? A comparison of the systems using biological control with those relying on other pest management strategies may generate an answer to this question.

Biological control will be easiest to implement and most successful under the following circumstances: First, the crop is produced in a traditional greenhouse (i.e., a glass or double-layered polyethylene-covered structure) located in a temperate climate with a prolonged cold season during which no outdoor crops can grow and where there is no insect or mite pest activity outside of the greenhouse. Second, the greenhouse is properly designed for heating and ventilating, and

it contains a computer-controlled environmental monitoring and control system. Third, the greenhouse produces a long-term vegetable crop such as tomato, sweet pepper, or cucumber. Last, there is a crop-free period during which routine sanitation measures (e.g., weed control, algae removal, growing media disinfestation) can be carried out.

In contrast, biological control will be most difficult to implement and therefore least successful in the following circumstances: First, the crop is produced in a plastic-covered tunnel located in a tropical or subtropical area without a prolonged cold season and with cultivated and uncultivated vegetation growing near the structure all year. Second, the greenhouse has no heating or ventilation system or environmental monitoring and control system. Third, short-term, high-value ornamental crops are produced for export. And fourth, there is continuous crop production.

From the above, one can readily ascertain that many factors influence the success of biological pest control, including the crop, the pest's biology, the choice of natural enemies, and natural-enemy release rates. These factors and their successful integration are the subject of many of the chapters of this book. Here we will examine the effects of greenhouse structure, function, and location on biological control programs.

Greenhouse Structure

Greenhouse structures that are marginally or highly appropriate for growing plants in a given climatic area are usually also marginal or good for insect and mite management. In northern Europe and North America, greenhouse structures typically are covered with glass, a double layer of polyethylene, or a layer of polycarbonate (fig. 3.1). In contrast, in subtropical and Mediterranean areas, structures are usually covered with only a single layer of polyethylene and sometimes are open-sided, tunnel greenhouses (figs. 3.2 and 3.3). The tremendous variation in structural designs and environmental-control systems often makes it difficult to properly match design features with growing practices (see

Figure 3.2. Unheated greenhouse covered by a single layer of plastic in the Mediterranean region. *Photo: T. Short.*

Nelson 1991 for a review of structural types and environmental controls).

The structural design of greenhouses affects the success of biological control by allowing (or not allowing) easy manipulation of the internal greenhouse environment. Greenhouses in temperate areas must have sophisticated environmental controls—including heating, cooling, and ventilation systems—to help regulate conditions in the greenhouse for proper plant growth. If greenhouse temperature, humidity, and air movement can be controlled to some extent, there are several potential advantages beyond

Figure 3.1. Heated, glass-covered greenhouses in northern Europe. *Photo: R. Lindquist.*

Figure 3.3. A plastic-covered greenhouse with open sides in the Mediterranean region. *Photo: R. Lindquist.*

providing optimum conditions for crop production. Some of these advantages include fewer pest and disease outbreaks and a more hospitable environment for beneficial insects, mites, and biopesticides.

Benefits of environmental control in pest management

Shipp, Boland, and Shaw (1991) noted that manipulating the greenhouse environment, especially temperature and humidity, was probably the most underutilized tactic in insect and mite pest management. Plant pathologists have used greenhouse environmental manipulation for years to control some fungal and bacterial plant pathogens (Jarvis 1992), but very little research has been done to use this strategy against insect and mite pests. The key to using environmental controls in an insect and mite management program is to know how environmental conditions affect both the pest and the biological control agent. Environmental control systems can be used to collect information, which can then be used to estimate durations of pest- and natural enemy–development cycles (Mumford 1992). Of the important greenhouse pest–natural enemy interactions, most studies have focused on that between greenhouse whitefly (*Trialeurodes vaporariorum* [Westwood]) and its parasitoid (*Encarsia formosa* Gahan) on various crops (e.g., Burnett 1949, Helgesen and Tauber 1974, Stenseth 1976, Osborne 1982, van Roermund and van Lenteren 1992). These studies have shown that at temperatures above 68°F (20°C), the parasitoid *E. formosa* develops faster than its whitefly host, making it a good control agent. However, as Osborne (1982) noted, the thermal threshold (the minimum temperature needed for development) was lower (46.9°F [8.3°C]) for greenhouse whiteflies than for the parasitoid (54.9°F [12.7°C]), thus yielding a population-growth advantage to the pest at low temperatures. Temperature records from computerized greenhouses provide a further opportunity (as suggested by Mumford [1992] and Clarke et al. [1994]) to predict pest outbreaks and to track the population interplay between pest and natural enemy by computing the developmental times of both pest and parasitoid stages (measured in day degrees). Using these data, one can project the numbers of pests and natural enemies by their developmental stages. This information can be useful in timing initial releases of the parasitoid, making natural-enemy introductions more efficient.

In a similar way Osborne and Peña (1997) used temperature records and other environmental factors to track the interaction between the two-spotted spider mite, *Tetranychus urticae* Koch, and its predator, *Phytoseiulus persimilis* Athias-Henriot. They found that at temperatures between 59 and 86°F (15 and 30°C), *P. persimilis* develops more rapidly than *T. urticae* (table 3.1), but at temperatures above 86°F (30°C), conditions favor *T. urticae*. Results have not been consistent, however, possibly due to differences in experimental methods and variability in the strains of *P. persimilis* used. Use of such information is most feasible in greenhouses whose structures allow temperatures to be modified to favor biological control. If a greenhouse structure makes temperature change unfeasible, automated collection of temperature data should be implemented as a minimum standard. Automated systems can be installed and maintained relatively inex-pensively, and they permit effortless moni-toring of environmental variables that can then be used to forecast the likely success of biological control releases or the need for other control measures.

Table 3.1. Effect of Temperature on Development Times (Days*) of *Tetranychus urticae* Koch and *Phytoseiulus persimilis* Athias-Henriot on Greenhouse Roses.**

Mite species	59°F (15° C)	68°F (20° C)	86°F (30° C)
T. urticae	36.3	16.6	7.3
P. persimilis	25.2	9.1	5.0

*Days from first oviposition of the parental mites to first oviposition of their daughters
**Adapted from Sabelis (1981)

Humidity levels (and their interaction with temperature) also affect the efficacy of natural enemies (e.g., Shipp and Gillespie 1993; van Houten and van Lier 1995; Shipp and van Houten 1997; Shipp, Ward, and Gillespie 1996; Osborne and Peña 1997). For example, phytoseiid mite predators used for spider mite and thrips (e.g., western flower thrips, *Frankliniella occidentalis* [Pergande]) control are affected by both temperature and moisture. At temperatures between 50 and 86°F (10° and 30°C), mite predators generally do better under high relative humidity than low relative humidity. Because moisture tends to be higher in double-layered poly-covered greenhouses, the predatory mite *Neoseiulus cucumeris* Oudemans provides better western flower thrips control in plastic-rather than in glass-covered greenhouses (Murphy 1997). Knowledge of these relation-ships can help extension agents, growers, and scouts to estimate the likelihood of success in particular structures. Also, in structures that are somewhat unfavorable to mite predators (e.g., glasshouses with excessively low humidity), it may be possible to modify crop management (such as irrigation methods) to enhance relative humidity and to make the greenhouse a site for successful biolog-ical control.

Moisture levels also strongly affect the success of mycoinsecticides, more so than temperature (Osborne and Landa 1992, van Lenteren 1995). Murphy et al. (1998) applied the fungus *Beauveria bassiana* (Balsamo) Vuillemin for control of western flower thrips in laboratory and greenhouse experiments. In laboratory trials using two concentrations of *B. bassiana*, western flower thrips mortality increased as humidity increased (table 3.2). In commercial greenhouse tomato and cucumber operations, application of emulsifiable suspension formulation of *B. bassiana* resulted in infection levels of 41 to 89% for *F. occidentalis* and 49 to 91% for *T. vaporariorum* four to eleven days post applica-tion under standard production conditions (Shipp et al. 2003). Helyer et al. (1992) demonstrated that by raising the relative humidity in the greenhouse on programmed cycles (two nights of high humidity followed by two nights of ambient humidity), control of chrysanthemum pests by the fungus *Verticillium lecanii* (Zimmerman) Viegas was much improved.

Use of environmental controls to modify temperature or humidity levels in greenhouses in favor of better biological control can become complicated if several different natural enemies are then released against a variety of pests. For example, one could easily imagine a rose greenhouse receiving releases of *E. formosa* for biological whitefly control and releases of *P. persimilis* for biological control of spider mites. In this case, the grower would have to balance the optimal temperature for the natural enemies with the optimal temperature for crop growth. Similarly, humidity manipulations to enhance thrips predators or the efficacy of entomopathogenic fungi need to be done within limits acceptable for management of plant diseases.

Table 3.2. Effect of Relative Humidity at 79°F (26°C) on *Frankliniella occidentalis* (Pergande) Mortality Seven Days after Application of a Wettable Powder Formulation of *Beauveria bassiana* (Balsamo) at Two Concentrations.*

Concentration**	% Mortality at		
	60% rh	75% rh	90% rh
0.9 g	40.8	57.4	80.0
1.8 g	47.5	86.5	97.1

*Data modified from Murphy et al. (1998)
**4.4×10^{10} spores/g

Pest management problems in greenhouses without environmental controls

If greenhouses have no environmental control capabilities, significant problems with pest management and crop production will be commonplace. In subtropical and Mediterranean climates, snow and extremely cold temperatures are rare, and, consequently, greenhouses are frequently constructed with light framing and without environmental control equipment. For example, in the Middle East and southern Europe, greenhouses rarely have adequate ventilation or other controls to moderate temperatures (Alebeek and van Lenteren 1992; Garcia, Greatex, and Gomez 1997). The same is true of the very large greenhouses used to produce ornamental crops in Colombia (personal observation). Many of these single-layer, plastic-covered, naturally ventilated structures (fig. 3.4) span several hectares. With this configuration, daytime temperatures can become very warm in the interior of the greenhouse.

Inadequate temperature controls and ventilation cause two problems related to pest management. First, pests such as spider mites

Figure 3.4. A large greenhouse in Colombia covering several hectares.
Photo: R. Lindquist.

and western flower thrips can increase rapidly at high temperatures (Robb 1989), which favor pest development but are harmful to beneficial insects and mites (Osborne and Peña 1997). Second, the warm air in the greenhouse contains moisture that condenses on plants at sundown and leads to development of powdery mildew on susceptible plants. Fungicide applications (especially sulfur fumigation) are then likely to be essential for suppression of mildew and other plant pathogens, but these applications can be harmful to the predatory mites needed to control spider mites and thrips. Lack of proper environmental controls, thus, can hasten an increasing spiral of pest intensity.

Overcoming problems caused by greenhouse structure

There are two ways to overcome the environmental problems found in greenhouses located in warm areas. Either pest management can be adjusted to fit the greenhouse design, or producers can design and build better greenhouses. In some cases, harmful effects of temperature and humidity on natural enemies can be reduced by using local species of beneficial insects and mites that are better adapted to the local conditions (van Lenteren 1995). For example, Sekeroglu and Kazak (1993) found a strain of *P. persimilis* in Turkey that was better adapted to local conditions and provided better biological control of spider mites than did imported strains of this predator. However, some of the benefits reported from local natural enemies may have been due to better quality of local natural enemies, compared with the same species shipped long distances.

Changes in such features as the material used to cover the greenhouse may provide opportunities to make greenhouses more favorable to biological control. For example, greenhouse coverings that filter out certain parts of the light spectrum have been shown to reduce incidence of some plant pathogens. Elad and Shtienberg (1997) reported that a green-pigmented polyethylene cover, which filtered out parts of the far-red spectrum, reduced the incidence of diseases caused by *Botrytis cinerea* Persoon by 35 to 75%. Recovering existing greenhouses with such materials might lead to a general reduction in the number of fungicide applications needed on a crop. This, in turn, should make the crop more suitable for several kinds of predators and parasitoids. However, trials monitoring the activity of bumblebees (used for pollination in greenhouse tomatoes) in commercial double polyethylene greenhouses have found that bee activity is greater and bee loss through the gutter ventilation system is lowest when coverings transmit high levels of UV light (Moradin et al. 2001). Thus, more research on greenhouse coverings that have selective light-filtering characteristics is needed.

Despite the above-cited problems with crop production and pest management that are associated with naturally ventilated greenhouses, not all such structures are the same. There is increasing interest in designing naturally ventilated greenhouses for both low- and high- technology applications. Aerodynamic modeling, which is made possible by modern computers, has resulted in naturally ventilated commercial greenhouses with ventilation equal to, or better than, fan-ventilation systems (Short and

Duyne 1996; Short 1998; Kacira, Short, and Stowell 1998). These structures can be of any length, but must be no wider than thirty meters.

Care needs to be taken in choosing a ventilation design. For example, figure 3.5 shows temperature profiles for two naturally ventilated greenhouses with different designs. One (fig. 3.5 top) has top vents that open, but no side vents. The other (fig. 3.5 bottom) also has an open side vent. With no side vent,

temperatures are much higher along both sides and along the floor. These temperature extremes could result in poor crop growth, as well as more severe pest and disease problems in these areas. Temperature problems caused by such design features can also be harmful to beneficial insects and mites. Temperatures in the greenhouse with the open side vent are relatively even across the structure, rising only slightly on the side opposite the vent.

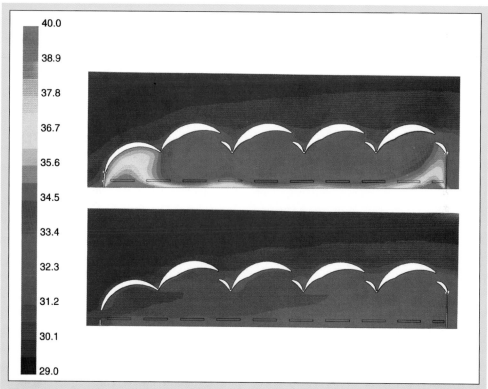

Figure 3.5. Computer-predicted temperature profiles in two naturally ventilated greenhouses on a summer day, with top vents fully open and the side vent facing the prevailing wind open or closed. The top profile predicts temperatures in the greenhouse with only top vents open, whereas the bottom profile predicts temperatures with the side vent open. Predictions made for a wind of 5.5 mph (2.5 m/sec). *Data from T. L. Short.*

Properly designed greenhouses with natural ventilation have a number of advantages, including: (1) low energy requirements; (2) lack of any restrictions on greenhouse length; (3) inside air temperatures that can be maintained very close to outside air temperatures; and (4) low temperature gradients across the greenhouse. Natural ventilation, combined with shading by thermal screens, can provide good climatic conditions, both for crop growth and for successful biological control. Improved ventilation will provide humidity control, which will reduce problems with plant pathogens. In addition, the installation of an internal fogging system can provide increased humidity when required. A simulation model with integrated global radiation input has been developed to predict leaf wetness duration during the day to optimize the impact of fogging on greenhouse temperature and humidity conditions, but at the same time minimize the impact of leaf wetness on disease outbreaks (Zhang and Shipp 2002). Such features will help with biological insect and mite management programs.

Pest movement into greenhouses

Insect and mite movement into greenhouses can occur almost anywhere during the warm season when growing vegetation, cultivated or uncultivated, surrounds the greenhouse. Greenhouses in warm climates are vulnerable to active outdoor pests throughout much of the year, in contrast with those in northern areas, where pest invasions occur only in fall and spring months. Warmer climates generally have more pest species, and those pests reproduce more rapidly than in temperate climates. The open-sided greenhouses found in many Mediterranean, tropical, and subtropical areas allow virtually unrestricted movement of pests into and out of the structures (see fig. 3.3). This is equally true for modern, naturally ventilated greenhouses, as described above. Even the open ventilators and mechanical evaporative-cooling systems used in many modern greenhouses allow pest movement into the greenhouse and disrupt biological controls. Heinz, Nunney, and Parrella (1993) cited this as a disrupting influence for biological control of the leafminer *Liriomyza trifolii* Burgess in California greenhouses. Pest movement into greenhouses is an especially serious problem when viruses and their vectors, such as western flower thrips and tospoviruses, are involved (Ramakers and Rabasse 1995; Garcia, Greatex, and Gomez 1997), and invasions of such pests can make their management very difficult.

Beneficial insects and mites, however, can also move into greenhouses from surrounding areas. If, as is often the case, these natural enemies are polyphagous (e.g., lacewings, pirate bugs, coccinellid beetles), they can have a stabilizing effect on growth of pest populations. This inward movement of natural enemies can contribute to more successful biological control in warmer areas (Ramakers and Rabasse 1995, Nicoli and Burgio 1997). Changing pesticide-use patterns from regular conventional organophosphate, carbamate, or pyrethroid insecticide applications to products that are less harmful to natural enemies will facilitate this movement of beneficial species into greenhouses. Growers need patience, as the movement of natural enemies into greenhouses typically follows only after the movement of pest species.

Restricting movement of pests into greenhouses

Another way in which the structure of a greenhouse can affect pest management and biological control is through the use of screening to isolate the crop from outside influences. Growers who have installed screens over greenhouse openings frequently report fewer insect pest problems (Berlinger et al. 1993, Robb 1995). In theory, any greenhouse, whether naturally or mechanically ventilated, can utilize screens. The most important part of installation is that the air-exchange surface area must be increased when screened to compensate for the reduced airflow. The amount of surface increase required will depend on the size of holes in the screen and can be easily calculated. The screen hole size required will depend on the species of pests to be excluded. Table 3.3 (adapted from Bethke and Paine 1991) shows the screen hole sizes that have been shown to exclude several major pests. Due to their narrow body shape, thrips are the most difficult insects to exclude. Greenhouses with mechanical ventilation systems can have screens installed over all openings. For naturally ventilated structures, installation of screening can be difficult, but still possible. In such cases, screening is often installed only on the sides facing the prevailing wind (Robb 1995) or only to exclude such large pests as moths and beetles (fig. 3.6). In warmer areas, screens are sometimes used when pest movements are most troublesome and when heat loads are not excessive (Nicoli and Burgio 1997).

Greenhouses may be constructed (and existing greenhouses retrofitted) with positive air-pressure systems, designed both to provide cooling and to keep air flowing out of all greenhouse openings. In greenhouses with positive air pressure, the fan inlet is screened and the airflow out of the greenhouse restricts inward movement of pests ("PPC has uses …" 1994, Dole and Wilkins 1999).

Greenhouse Function

Greenhouse function—that is, what is being produced in the greenhouse—has a significant effect on the ease or difficulty of

Table 3.3. Maximum Size of Holes in Screening for Excluding Some Major Insect Pests.

Pest	Hole Size	
	Microns	**Inches**
Aphid (*Aphis gossypii* Glover)*	340	0.013
Leafminer (*Liriomyza trifolii* Burgess)	640	0.025
Western flower thrips (*Frankliniella occidentalis* [Pergande])	192	0.0075
Whitefly (*Bemisia argentifolii* Bellows and Perring)	462	0.018

*Winged aphids are larger than whiteflies, but require a smaller hole size because of their wing placement or behavior. Table adapted from Bethke and Paine (1991).

Figure 3.6. Screening installed to exclude moths and beetles in a greenhouse in Colombia.
Photo: R. Lindquist.

achieving biological control of pests. This is true despite the fact that similar pest groups attack both ornamentals and vegetables. Most of the successful biological control programs within greenhouses have occurred in vegetable crops—mainly tomato, cucumber, and sweet pepper—and where the greenhouses are located in temperate climates. There are also some biological control programs on ornamental crops, and nearly all of these are located in temperate areas (Fransen 1992).

The history of biological control development and implementation is described elsewhere (see especially chapters 1 and 4) and in other publications (Hussey and Scopes 1985, van Lenteren and Woets 1988, van Lenteren 1995, Ramakers and Rabasse 1995, Albajes et al. 1999). Use of biological control in greenhouses began in northern Europe and

continues to be concentrated in that geographic region. The Netherlands and the United Kingdom had more than 50% of the greenhouse area in the world when biological control programs for key pests were first developed. Most of the greenhouses using biological controls were producing tomatoes (van Lenteren and Woets 1988). Other important factors that affected the development and implementation of biological control were that (1) pesticide resistance among key pests (especially spider mites) forced a search for alternative controls; (2) strong research and advisory services existed in both the Netherlands and the United Kingdom for developing and implementing the alternative controls; (3) a group of educated, experienced growers was willing to use the alternative controls; and (4) there were sources for the necessary beneficial insects and mites.

The development and implementation of biological control–based pest management programs is hindered when one or more of these four factors are missing (e.g., Alebeek and van Lenteren 1992; Greatrex 1997; Garcia, Greatex, and Gomez 1997). Other factors that can influence the feasibility of biological pest control in a particular crop or country include acceptable injury thresholds, details of the cropping system, pesticide availability, and economic factors.

Injury threshold levels

Economic-injury levels generally are higher on vegetable crops than on ornamentals, even though similar pests attack these crops. Some insect or mite injury to the leaves of a vegetable crop, in which the fruit is the marketed product, can be tolerated without any yield loss. Biological control of pests on ornamentals, however, is often more difficult simply because the value of these crops is based on their aesthetics rather than on their yield (Fransen 1992; Parrella, Murphy, and Fogg 1997). Many ornamental plants, such as potted plants, are sold with both leaves and flowers present, and on such plants any visible feeding injury may detract from the crop's appearance, making the crop difficult to sell, even if plant growth is not affected. Plants produced for export are usually expected to meet a requirement of zero tolerance for the presence of insects, mites, and feeding injury. More flexibility exists with cut flowers or potted and bedding plants produced for local markets. For cut flower crops such as rose, gerbera (*Gerbera jamesonii* Bol. ex Adlam), chrysanthemum, carnation (*Dianthus caryophyllus* L.), and gypsophila (*Gypsophila* spp.), damaged leaves can be removed after harvest and the undamaged flowers sold. In addition, some markets are willing to relax damage-tolerance levels in an effort to reduce pesticide use and increase the use of biological control agents. For example, a group of Dutch chrysanthemum producers may export to Sweden chrysanthemums containing some damage, provided the producers have followed specified plant-production procedures (van Oosten 1992).

Economic-injury thresholds have been developed more frequently for vegetable crops and have generally been ignored for ornamentals (Shipp et al. 1998, Dik and Albajes 1999, Hao et al. 2002). Although damage thresholds are being developed for pests such as whiteflies, leafminers, and thrips (Sanderson, Davis, and Ferrentino 1994, Parrella 1995), for some ornamental crops progress is slow, due to the ease of quantifying injury thresholds in terms of fruit yield and quality rather than in terms of the aesthetic qualities so important in flower crops.

Economic-injury thresholds for ornamentals are further complicated by their failure to address the issue of grower attitudes toward risk (Mumford 1992). There are three problems with economic thresholds on high-value greenhouse crops: First, there is a high investment in greenhouse crops so there is a greater need for risk avoidance. Second, the probability of total crop loss when control strategies fail is very high. Most growers feel that preventative pesticide applications will provide protection against this crop loss without the need to bother with economic thresholds. The cost of pest control for most crops is 1 to 5% (van Lenteren 1995)—or 7.5% of production costs (Murphy et al. 1998)—so growers feel they can afford chemical control costs without the perceived risk associated with biological controls. Third, the increase of pests in greenhouses may be too rapid to decide if a threshold has been reached, even if one is established. To address this third concern, some researchers and extension specialists advocate the use of preventative biological control, whereby natural enemies are released according to schedule, even when pest densities are below detectable levels.

The use of postharvest disinfestation methods (Hara 1994) on ornamental crops will improve chances that crops produced with biological (or reduced-chemical) control methods will pass quarantine inspection.

Crop production systems

Monocultures vs. mixed crops

Vegetables are usually produced in monocultures, and between harvest and planting there is a period without any crop plants in the greenhouse. This crop-free period can greatly enhance the opportunity for effective biological pest control. During the crop-free period, the greenhouses can be disinfected of pathogens, the weeds can be removed, and arthropod pests eliminated. The biological control program can be initiated soon after replanting, presumably when pest numbers are low. The crop-free period in vegetable production also provides multiple chances for biological control. Should a biological control program fail within a vegetable greenhouse, alternate rescue methods may be implemented for the duration of the crop cycle and a revamped biological control program used with the next crop.

The benefits associated with monocultures are often not present for many ornamental crop growers. Even though some long-lived ornamentals (e.g., roses and poinsettias) appear to be produced in monocultures, many plantings are diverse collections of many cultivars, which can differ in their susceptibility to pests. Flower growers in northern Europe, Colombia, Ecuador, and some other countries often produce only one or a few ornamental crops, but these crops commonly are grown in a continuous cycle. Consequently, the crop-free period, so helpful in vegetable production, may not exist. Many other growers produce a diverse array of ornamental crops, each with its own pest complex, as polycultures in single greenhouses. Managing multiple pests on multiple crops may become burdensome for an individual grower, and it may raise the cost of biological control to economically unacceptable levels.

Crop duration

Biological pest management tends to be most successful when applied to vegetable crops with relatively long (greater than six months) crop cycles. This allows time for beneficial insects and mites to be introduced, become established, and eventually control the pests. Many ornamental crops are produced in a matter of seven or eight weeks, which greatly reduces the time available for natural enemies to successfully control pest populations.

Crop spatial architecture

Plant spacing within a crop is very important for biological control, especially where predators are involved (Osborne et al. 1995). The efficiency of predatory mites increases significantly if plants are closely spaced. Most ornamentals are grown with definite spacing between plants for light and ventilation.

Changes in such production practices might improve chances for biological control. The bent-stem technique, now used in some greenhouse rose-production facilities, should help biological control of pests such as *T. urticae* and *F. occidentalis*. In this method, lateral stems are bent down to increase the photosynthetic base for flower production. Total flower production is not increased, but the flowers that are produced are of higher quality, commanding higher market prices. Instead of open aisles between rose beds, the aisles are filled with living rose stems, facilitating predator movement. Also, the denser mass of foliage at the bases of plants raises humidity, which increases predator survival (Pellett, Furguson, and Zary1998).

Choosing the correct time and context in which to begin a biological control program can also lead to greater success. Osborne et al. (1995) suggested that using *P. persimilis* on spider mite–susceptible stock or on mother plants would improve biological control of *T. urticae* on foliage plant crops. Stock plants are grown very closely together for a long time, and spider mites are the only major pests of many species of foliage plants, providing greater opportunity for biological control.

Pesticide availability

In many countries there are more pesticides registered for use on greenhouse-grown ornamental crops than on vegetable crops. This is largely due to differences in registration requirements for food and non-food crops. For a pesticide to be registered for use on edible crops, a safe residue level at harvest must be established. The cost of establishing these safe pesticide residue levels for greenhouse food crops may be too high an investment for the pesticide manufacturer to justify because the production acreage is so small compared with that for field-grown crops. Ornamental plants are exempt from the residue-tolerance requirements established for edible crops, so pesticide registration is faster and less expensive. Because of the greater availability of pesticides and the perceived risks of changing to biological control cited above, growers of ornamental plants have fewer incentives to move away from pesticides—as long as effective products are available.

Economics of biological control

Seasonal inoculative control

Approaches to biological control differ with cropping systems. Vegetable growers tend toward the use of seasonal inoculative releases of natural enemies, while growers of ornamental crops rely more on inundative releases. Seasonal (once to several times per year) inoculative biological control relies on releases of precise numbers of natural enemies and is more economical in terms of costs for natural enemies. Relatively few beneficial insects and mites are required to provide pest suppression because the biological control agents reproduce in the crop, leading to control throughout the entire season (Ramakers and Rabasse 1995). Because the natural enemies are expected to survive and reproduce at rates necessary to control the target pest, the development of inoculative-control programs requires detailed information on the specific crop pest–natural enemy relationships.

Recently, similar scientific approaches have been applied to several natural enemy–pest relationships associated with ornamental crops. For example, Heinz (1998) studied the patterns of green peach (*Myzus persicae* [Sulzer]) and melon aphid (*Aphis gossypii* Glover) infestations on greenhouse chrysanthemums in an effort to determine how two natural enemies, *Chrysoperla rufilabris* (Burmeister) and *Aphidius colemani* Viereck, respond to changing aphid infestations over time and space. The aphid parasitoid *A. colemani* was more effective at locating aphids than the lacewing predator *C. rufilabris*. For another pest–natural enemy system, Heinz, Nunney, and Parrella (1993) published a relatively simple mathematical model to predict the numbers of *Diglyphus begini* Ashmead to release for biological control of leafminers (*L. trifolii*) on chrysanthemums. Information gained from studies such as these can help to make the use of biological control agents more efficient.

Inundative releases

Another approach to biological control, used mostly on ornamentals, is to make regular (weekly or biweekly) inundative introductions of natural enemies for control of one or more pest species. Hoddle, Van Driesche, and Sanderson (1997a, 1997b) studied inundative introductions of *E. formosa* (Beltsville strain) and *Eretmocerus eremicus* Rose and Zolnerowich for control of the whitefly *Bemisia argentifolii* Bellows and Perring on poinsettia. Wardlow and O'Neal (1992) and Wardlow (1998) advocated using all possible pest- and disease-prevention methods to minimize problems (sanitation, screening, cultivar selection), along with regular introductions of beneficial insects and mites for control of expected pests. Introduction rates are based on research and grower experience. The objective

is to keep pest numbers as close to zero as possible to meet market standards. It is well established that regular inundative introductions of beneficial insects and mites can effectively control most pests of ornamental plants. However, this method will be economically feasible only in areas where prices for beneficial organisms are low, relative to the market value of the crop. Once pest numbers are lowered, fewer beneficial insects and mites will be needed, reducing control costs.

Challenges to Additional Implementation of Biological Control

The increase in greenhouse production in warmer areas, with lower construction, labor, and energy costs, is likely to continue, especially as transportation systems and postharvest handling methods improve. The low input costs in these areas mean that crops can be produced less expensively than those grown in areas with higher energy and labor costs, even if production per unit area is less (e.g., southern versus northern Europe, Colombia versus the United States). While current greenhouse design in these areas may make biological control difficult, new natural-ventilation designs may overcome that problem. Change is slow, however, due to a reluctance to change productions systems that work or that are perceived to work.

For the last thirty years, building a better greenhouse in many parts of the world has relied on the use of well-designed fan and evaporative pad ventilation systems (Short 1999). While those systems continue to be highly effective, there is a growing interest in designing and using naturally ventilated greenhouses for both highly sophisticated as well as completely unsophisticated growing operations. Modifications in greenhouse design features have typically been made with little engineering input. While grower testimonials abound, real data have been almost nonexistent until recently. Engineers, horticulturists, pathologists, and entomologists need to work together to better understand the interactions among greenhouse structure, the environment within the greenhouse, and their influences on plant and integrated pest management. Better ventilation can greatly improve disease control and minimize the use of chemicals. Better ventilation can eliminate temperature extremes and increase the probability of having consistent and reliable integrated pest control.

Most biological control programs have been developed for, and implemented in, vegetable glasshouses located in northern European countries. Currently, most of the world's greenhouse area is now located in subtropical or Mediterranean climate areas. Further, ornamentals are now produced in about 50% of the greenhouse area. Much of the production in these systems is for export, so crops must meet the quality standards of the importing, rather than the exporting, countries. As noted in the introductory paragraphs of this chapter, these expanding production areas possess many of the characteristics that typically hinder the implementation of biological control.

One rather large mistake made by many growers and advisors has been to use the successful biological control programs in northern Europe as exact models for other areas. Early attempts at biological control in southern European greenhouses using the system of precise natural-enemy introductions based on the northern European model generally were not successful and were called an "unmitigated disaster" by Greatrex (1997). The emphasis is now on developing workable biological control systems for local areas that follow only partially the original models developed in northern Europe.

The worldwide movement of plant material (mostly ornamentals), which greatly benefits producers and consumers, also facilitates the spread of pests into new areas. These new arrivals can disrupt existing biological control programs. At worst, they can make biological control almost impossible. Some recent examples include the silverleaf whitefly, *B. argentifolii*, and the leafminer *Liriomyza huidobrensis* Blanchard. Perhaps the most serious arrival in most areas is the western flower thrips (*F. occidentalis*). The spread of western flower thrips has made biological control very difficult in all situations where this pest occurs, primarily due to the absence of effective natural enemies for this pest. Greenhouses in cold climates have a slight advantage in effectively managing new introductions because the insects are not active outdoors during part of the year. However, the worldwide transport of plant material ensures that thrips and other pests will move internationally with relative ease.

References Cited

Albajes, R. M. Lodovica Gullino, J. C. van Lenteren, and Y. Elad. 1999. *Integrated Pest and Disease Management in Greenhouse Crops.* Norwell, MA: Kluwer Academic Publishers.

Alebeek, F. A. N., and J. C. van Lenteren. 1992. Integrated pest management for protected vegetable cultivation in the Near East. *FAO Plant Production and Protection Paper,* no. 114:148.

Berlinger, M. J., S. L. Mordechi, D. Fridja, and N. Mor. 1993. The effect of types of greenhouse screens on the presence of western flower thrips: A preliminary study. *IOBC/WPRS Bulletin* 16 (2):13–6.

Bethke, J. A., and T. D. Paine. 1991. Screen hole size and barriers for exclusion of insect pests of glasshouse crops. *Journal of Entomological Science* 26:169–77.

Burnett, T. 1949. The effect of temperature on an insect host-parasite population. *Ecology* 30:113–34.

Clarke, N. D., J. L. Shipp, W. R. Jarvis, A. P. Papadopoulos, and T. J. Jewett. 1994. Integrated management of greenhouse crops – a conceptual and potentially practical model. *HortScience* 29:846-849.

Dole, J. M., and H. F. Wilkins. 1999. *Floriculture: Principles and Species.* Upper Saddle River, N.J.: Prentice-Hall.

Dik, A. J., and R. Albajes. 1999. Principles of epidemiology, population biology, damage relationships and integrated control of diseases and pests. In *Integrated Pest and Disease Management in Greenhouse Crops,* eds. R. Albajes, M. Lodovica Gullino, J. C. van Lenteren and Y. Elad, 69-81. Boston: Kluwer Academic Publishers.

Elad, Y., and D. Shtienberg. 1997. Integrated management of foliar diseases in greenhouse vegetables according to principles of a decision support system. *IOBC Bulletin Integrated Control in Protected Crops "Mediterranean Climate"* 20 (4):71–6.

Fransen, J. 1992. Development of integrated crop protection in glasshouse ornamentals. *Pesticide Science* 36:329–33.

Garcia, F., R. M. Greatrex, and J. Gomez. 1997. Development of integrated crop management systems for sweet peppers in southern Spain. *IOBC Bulletin Integrated Control in Protected Crops "Mediterranean Climate"* 20 (4):8–15.

Greatrex, R. M. 1997. Biological control in Europe: An industry view. In *Proceedings for the 13th Conference on Insect and Disease Management on Ornamentals,* ed. A. Chase, 1–11. Alexandria, Virg.: Society of American Florists.

Hara, A. H. 1994. Ornamentals and flowers. In *Insect Pests and Fresh Horticultural Products: Treatments and Responses,* eds. R. E. Paull and J. W. Armstrong, 329–347. Wallingford, U.K.: CAB International.

Hao, X., J. L. Shipp, K. Wang, A. P. Papadopoulos and M. R. Binns. 2002. Impact of western flower thrips on growth, photosynthesis and productivity of greenhouse cucumber. *Scientia Horticulturae* 92:187-203.

Heinz, K. M. 1998. Dispersal and dispersion of aphids (Homoptera: Aphididae) and selected natural enemies in spatially subdivided greenhouse environments. *Environmental Entomology* 27:1029–38.

Heinz, K. M., L. Nunney, and M. P. Parrella. 1993. Toward predictable biological control of *Liriomyza trifolii* (Diptera: Agromyzidae) infesting greenhouse cut chrysanthemums. *Environmental Entomology* 22:1217–33.

Helgesen, R. G., and M. J. Tauber. 1974. Biological control of greenhouse whitefly, *Trialeurodes vaporariorum* (Homoptera: Aleyrodidae), on short term crops by manipulating biotic and abiotic factors. *Canadian Entomologist* 106:1175–88.

Helyer, N., G. Gill, A. Bywater, and R. Chambers. 1992. Elevated humidities for control of chrysanthemum pests with *Verticillium lecanii. Pesticide Science* 36:373–8.

Hoddle, M. S., R. G. Van Driesche, and J. P. Sanderson. 1997a. Biological control of *Bemisia argentifolii* (Homoptera: Aleyrodidae) on poinsettia with inundative releases of *Encarsia formosa* Beltsville strain (Hymenoptera: Aphelinidae): Can parasitoid reproduction augment inundative releases? *Journal of Economic Entomology* 90:910–24.

———. 1997b. Biological control of *Bemisia argentifolii* (Homoptera: Aleyrodidae) on poinsettia with inundative releases of *Eretmocerus* sp. nr. *californicus* (strain AZ) (Hymenoptera: Aphelinidae): Do release rates and plant growth affect parasitism? *Bulletin of Entomological Research* 88:47–58.

Hussey, N. W., and N. E. A. Scopes, eds. 1985. *Biological Pest Control: The Glasshouse Experience.* Poole, Dorset, U.K.: Blandford Press (Ithaca, N.Y.: Princeton University Press).

Jarvis, W. R. 1992. *Managing Diseases in Greenhouse Crops.* St. Paul, Minn.: APS Press.

Kacira, M., T. H. Short, and R. R. Stowell. 1998. A CFD evaluation on naturally ventilated multi-span sawtooth greenhouses. *Transactions ASAE* 41:833–6.

Morandin, L. A., T. M. Laverty, P. G. Kevan, S. Khosla, and L. Shipp. 2001. Bumble bee (Hymenoptera: Apidae) activity and loss in commercial tomato greenhouses. *The Canadian Entomologist* 133:883-893.

Mumford, J. W. 1992. Economics of integrated pest control in protected crops. *Pesticide Science* 36:379–83.

Murphy, B. C., T. A. Morisawa, J. P. Newman, S. A. Tjosvold, and M. P. Parrella. 1998. Fungal pathogen controls thrips in greenhouse flowers. *California Agriculture* 52:32–6.

Murphy, G. 1997. Biological control experiences—an Ontario perspective. *GrowerTalks,* September, 94–6.

Nelson, P. V. 1991. *Greenhouse Operation and Management.* Englewood Cliffs, N. J.: Prentice-Hall.

Nicoli, G., and G. Burgio. 1997. Mediterranean biodiversity as source of new entomophagous species for biological control in protected crops. *IOBC Bulletin Integrated Control in Protected Crops "Mediterranean Climate"* 20 (4):27–37.

Osborne, L. S. 1982. Temperature-dependent development of greenhouse whitefly and its parasite *Encarsia formosa. Environmental Entomology* 11:483–5.

Osborne, L. S., and Z. Landa. 1992. Biological control of whiteflies with entomopathogenic fungi. *Florida Entomologist* 75:456–71.

Osborne, L. S., J. Peña, F. L. Petit, and Y. Q. Fan. 1995. Biological control of mites. In *Proceedings for the 11th Conference on Insect and Disease Management on Ornamentals,* ed. A. Bishop, M. Hausbeck, and R. Lindquist, 41–9. Alexandria, Virg.: Society of American Florists.

Osborne, L. S., and J. Peña. 1997. More than you want to know about mites and their biological control on ornamentals. In *Proceedings for the 13th Conference on Insect and Disease Management on Ornamentals,* ed. A. Chase, 53–85. Alexandria, Virg.: Society of American Florists.

Parrella, M. P. 1995. Thrips management guide—Part I: Prevention and control. *GrowerTalks,* April, 30–8.

Parrella, M. P., B. Murphy, and E. Fogg. 1997. Do biological controls have a future in greenhouse production? *Greenhouse Product News,* December, 22–4.

Pellett, G. R., R. Furguson, and K. Zary. 1998. *Rosa* (Rose). In *Ball RedBook,* 16th ed., ed. V. Ball, 705–26. Batavia, Ill.: Ball Publishing.

PPC has uses in pest control too. 1994. *Greenhouse Manager,* April, 60.

Ramakers, P. M. J., and J. M. Rabasse. 1995. Integrated pest management in protected cultivation. In *Novel Approaches to Integrated Pest Management,* ed. R. Reuveni, 198–229. Boca Raton, Fla.: Lewis Publishers.

Robb, K. L. 1989. Analysis of *Frankliniella occidentalis* (Pergande) as a part of floricultural crops in California greenhouses. Ph.D. diss., University of California, Riverside.

———. 1995. Controlling thrips and the use of exclusion devices. In *Proceedings for the 11th Conference on Insect and Disease Management on Ornamentals,* ed. A. Bishop, M. Hausbeck, and R. Lindquist, 113–20. Alexandria: Virg.: Society of American Florists.

Sabelis, M. W. 1981. Biological control of two-spotted spider mites using phytoseiid predators. Part 1: Modeling the predator-prey interaction at the individual level. *Agricultural Research Reports* 910:226–42.

Sanderson, J., P. Davis, and R. Ferrentino. 1994. A better, easier way to sample for whiteflies on poinsettias. *Greenhouse Manager,* August, 71–6.

Sekeroglu, E., and C. Kazak. 1993. First record of *Phytoseiulus persimilis* (Athias-Henriot) in Turkey. *Entomophaga* 38:343–5.

Shipp, J. L., M. R. Binns, X. Hao, and K. Wang. 1998. Economic injury levels for western flower thrips (Thysanoptera: Thripidae) on greenhouse sweet pepper. *Journal of Economic Entomology* 91:671-677.

Shipp, J. L., G. J. Boland, and L. A. Shaw. 1991. Integrated pest management of disease and arthropod pests of greenhouse vegetable crops in Ontario: Current status and future possibilities. *Canadian Journal of Plant Science* 71:887–914.

Shipp, J. L., and T. J. Gillespie. 1993. Influence of temperature and water vapor pressure deficit on survival of *Frankliniella occidentalis* (Thysanoptera: Thripidae). *Environmental Entomology* 22:726–32.

Shipp, J. L., and Y. M. van Houten. 1997. Effects of temperature and vapor pressure deficit on the survival of the predatory mite *Amblyseius cucumeris. Environmental Entomology* 26:106–13.

Shipp, J. L., K. I. Ward, and T. J. Gillespie. 1996. Influence of temperature and vapor pressure deficit on the rate of predation by the predatory mite *Amblyseius cucumeris* on *Frankliniella occidentalis. Entomologia Experimentalis et Applicata.* 78:31–8.

Shipp, J. L., Y. Zhang, D. W. A. Hunt, and G. Ferguson. 2003. Influence of humidity and greenhouse microclimate on the efficacy of *Beauveria bassiana* (Balsamo) for control of greenhouse arthropod pests. *Environmental Entomology* 32:1154-1163.

Short, T. H. 1998. Aerodynamic design improves ventilation. *GrowerTalks,* July, 90–8.

———. 1999. Building a better greenhouse—A new era for natural ventilation. In *Proceedings for the 15th Conference on Insect and Disease Management on Ornamentals,* ed. K. M. Heinz, 5–10. Alexandria, Virg.: Society of American Florists.

Short, T. H., and G.V. Duyne. 1996. Naturally ventilated greenhouses for Mediterranean climates. *Acta Horticulturae* 434:229–35.

Stenseth, C. 1976. Some aspects of the practical application of the parasite *Encarsia formosa* for control of *Trialeurodes vaporariorum. IOBC/WPRS Bulletin* 4:104–14.

van Houten, Y. M., and M. M. van Lier. 1995. Influence of temperature and humidity on the survival of eggs of the thrips predator *Amblyseius cucumeris. Mededelingen Faculteit Landbouwwetenschappen, Rijksuniversitiet Gent* 60:879–84.

van Lenteren, J. C. 1995. Integrated pest management in protected crops. In *Integrated Pest Management,* ed. David Dent, 311–43. London: Chapman and Hall.

van Lenteren, J. C. 2000. A greenhouse without pesticides: fact or fantasy? *Crop Protection* 19:375-384.

van Lenteren, J. C., and J. Woets. 1988. Biological and integrated pest control in greenhouses. *Annual Review of Entomology* 33:239–69.

van Oosten, H. J. 1992. IPM in protected crops: Concerns, challenges and opportunities. *Pesticide Science* 36:365–71.

van Roermund, H. J. W., and J. C. van Lenteren. 1992. Life-history parameters of the greenhouse whitefly *Trialeurodes vaporariorum* and the parasitoid *Encarsia formosa.* Wageningen University papers, 92–3.

Wardlow, L. R., and T. M. O'Neil. 1992. Management strategies for controlling pests and diseases in glasshouse crops. *Pesticide Science* 36:341–7.

Wardlow, L. R. 1998. Integrated pest management in ornamental crops. *FloraCulture International,* April, 27–31.

Zhang, Y., and J. L. Shipp. 2002. Manipulating plant moisture conditions using greenhouse high-pressure fogging. *HortTechnology* 12:261-267.

4

THE INSECTARY BUSINESS: DEVELOPING CUSTOMERS, PRODUCTS, AND MARKETS

R. J. P. Valentin
Foliera Inc., Beamsville, Ontario, Canada
and
J. L. Shipp
Agriculture and Agri-Food Canada, Greenhouse and Processing Crops
Research Centre, Harrow, Ontario, Canada

Commercial insectaries (producers of natural enemies), by providing quality natural enemies when needed, are an essential component for the success of augmentation biological control in protected cultures. As businesses, their existence depends upon the development, marketing, and successful use of natural enemies for biological pest control. To be profitable, insectaries must satisfy their customers' needs, maintain the supply and quality of their existing products and develop new ones as needed, and successfully negotiate legislative requirements imposed by governments for the public good. To develop and maintain a customer base, insectaries need growers to be successful when they use a company's natural enemies. Consequently, product advice or advisory services are important tools used by insectaries to make sure their natural enemies are used correctly and to develop satisfied customers.

Information exchange between producers, distributors, and growers is essential to achieve successful biological control and, consequently, will be the first topic we address in this chapter. We will then cover some basic issues of how producers maintain the quality of the natural enemies they produce and develop new ones, as needed, for new pests. Finally, we examine the role of regulations in the production and sale of natural enemies used for pest control. These topics collectively provide a view of how the insectary business functions. Knowledge of this topic can (1) help growers and extension agents maintain realistic expectations of this essential support industry, (2) identify areas where cooperative partnerships need to be developed or strengthened, and (3) maximize the numbers of opportunities for successful augmentative biological control.

Satisfied Customers: Information Exchanges between Producers and Growers

Growers using augmentative biological control usually purchase the natural enemies they release from a commercial source, either a producer or a distributor. In Europe and Canada, producers often employ advisors who work directly with growers to diagnose pest problems, select agents, and determine release rates. When making recommendations, the advisors take into account the level of the pest infestation at the grower's site, as well as any features of construction or management that might influence the outcome of a release. Advisors help troubleshoot and correct pest control programs in difficult cases in which initial efforts have been unsuccessful. In the United States and most other areas outside Europe and Canada, the advisory service provided by producers and distributors to growers is much less. Rather, growers must make their own decisions, perhaps with limited information provided by producers, distributors, or public agricultural advisory services. In many cases, advice is given without an advisor making an on-site visit. In this chapter, we describe biological control practiced in European vegetable greenhouses and use it as a model producer-based advisory system. From this model, we suggest ways in which growers and cooperative extension services may adapt this scheme to other production systems or to regions where this level of insectary-based advisory service is unavailable.

The First Generation of Natural-Enemy Producers in Europe

The practice of biological control in commercially grown greenhouse vegetable crops expanded dramatically in Europe during the 1990s, but the foundation for this expansion was laid many years earlier. Before World War II, an entomologist at the Cheshunt Experimental Station in England named E. R. Speyer was mass-producing *Encarsia formosa* (Gahan) for control of greenhouse whitefly (*Trialeurodes vaporariorum* [Westwood]) and distributing the parasitoids to seven countries (Hussey 1985). Soon after Speyer's initial efforts, several growers also started producing *E. formosa*, and later they became the founders of biological control companies (e.g., Bunting and Sons Ltd., which was purchased by CIBA [later Novartis and then became Syngenta Bio-Line]). The discovery of DDT and other synthetic pesticides after 1945 dealt a crippling blow to this newfound industry. Production of *E. formosa* was curtailed greatly in 1949 and virtually ceased in 1956 due to competition from the newly developed insecticides.

In the 1950s, some growers began searching again for alternatives to chemical control to avoid health risks from spraying harmful chemicals. At the same time, many growers had experienced complete failure of the pesticides to control their pests. In 1960, Bravenboer published an important paper documenting the temporary relief provided by organophosphorous compounds to two-spotted spider mite outbreaks due to the resistance that had developed to DDT during the late 1940s; but by the early 1950s, *Tetranychus urticae* (Koch) populations were also resistant to organophosphorous compounds. With the discovery of the predatory mite *Phytoseiulus persimilis* Athias-Henriot for use in controlling *T. urticae*, interest in biological control was renewed (Bravenboer and Dosse 1962).

Some growers in England and the Netherlands started to produce *P. persimilis* for sale to other growers. Koppert Biological Systems N.V., located in the Netherlands, is a biological control company that started because of this demand for alternative control measures to chemicals. The company is a family business, led by Jan Koppert and his sons Peter and Paul Koppert. Mr. Jan Koppert started the company after he successfully used *P. persimilis* for control of a serious spider mite infestation on his cucumber crop. In 1970, Mr. Koppert started to mass-rear *P. persimilis*; he sold the predatory mites to four distributors. Each distributor had one specialist who provided advice about the biological control agent's use under the guidance of Koppert Biological Systems N.V. (Koppert 1978). Following Koppert's lead, other commercial companies mass-producing *P. persimilis* sprouted throughout the United Kingdom and the rest of Europe.

Initially, the biological control industry supplied only a few species of natural enemies. Most companies started by supplying *E. formosa* and *P. persimilis*. Today, approximately 125 species of natural enemies are commercially available from more than eighty-five companies worldwide. Greenhouse growers can use about ninety of these species for biological control of greenhouse crops (Bolckmans 2003). As a result, many companies have been formed over the last thirty years, such as Biobest N.V. (Belgium), Syngenta Bio-Line (England), Biological Crop Protection Ltd. (England), Applied Bionomics Ltd. (Canada), The Bug Factory (previously Nature's Alternative) (Canada), Beneficial Insectaries (United States and Canada), Zonda Resources Ltd. (New Zealand), and Bio Bee (previously BCI) (Israel). Also, trade associations have been founded, such as the Association of National Biological Control Producers (ANBP) and the International Biocontrol Manufacturers Association (IBMA), which provide information on biological control companies and natural enemies, and represent the industry to national and international authorities.

The beginning of Biobest N.V., a company that specialized in the rearing of natural pollinators, also resulted in a major step toward large-scale adoption of biological control. Dr. Roland de Jonghe, a veterinarian in Belgium, was raising bumblebees as a hobby and discovered that bumblebees were excellent pollinators of greenhouse tomatoes (P. Couwels, Biobest Canada Ltd., Leamington, Ontario, Canada, pers. comm.). The use of bumblebees for pollination is a tremendous labor savings for the greenhouse vegetable industry, in comparison with the traditional method of hand pollination, and also substantially increases fruit quality and yield. Due to bumblebees' sensitivity to pesticides, the use of bumblebees for pollination severely limits the number of chemicals that can be used by the grower. Dr. de Jonghe started Biobest N.V., which is located in Westerlo, Belgium, to supply bumblebees to the growers. Shortly afterward, Biobest N.V. started to produce biological control agents as well and became an important supplier of bumblebees and beneficial species. Like biological control agents, bumblebee colonies are now mass-produced by several companies in North America and Europe.

The Role of the Producer

Companies producing natural enemies can vary greatly in size and in their focus (mass-market versus niche-market species). This strongly influences their capacity and willingness to advise growers on the use of natural enemies. We will describe several aspects of the insectary business and examine the importance of each to achieving successful biological control.

Producer size and product line

Some companies specialize in producing selected species of natural enemies, while other companies produce a wider range of species. Small producers may specialize in the production and marketing of less widely used species for niche markets such as indoor plantscapes, botanical gardens, and zoos. Such companies may purchase more common species from larger producers, acting as distributors in this capacity. Conversely, large companies may concentrate on producing large quantities of the most extensively used natural enemies. These companies either do not sell natural enemies associated with minor pests or crops, or they obtain these species from the niche-market producers and act as distributors for such species.

Degree of grower-support services

Currently, most producers of natural enemies recognize that technical support to the customer is critical to successful implementation of biological control. In the past, when growers were disappointed with the results of biological control, they quickly reverted to chemical control. In most of these situations, technical support was not available or was of poor quality.

The degree of technical support provided to growers often varies substantially among companies. Some biological control compa-

nies strictly mass-produce natural enemies, and advice is based on testimonial data obtained from their clientele or on data in published research reports. Others not only produce biological control agents (and have access to client testimonials and published research reports), but also conduct applied research on the natural enemies that they produce and transfer this technical information too to the growers.

Because IPM systems based on biological control are subject to abrupt changes in pests, quick, effective adaptations by producers and growers are often needed. New pests may emerge (via invasions or release from chemical control) and can quickly become major problems if neither biological solutions nor selective chemicals compatible with the biological control–based IPM program are available. In addition, because chemical residues can severely affect introductions of many biological control agents (Koppert Biological Systems 1999), growers may need specific advice on compatibility of particular agents and pesticides. (See chapter 7 for useful information on this subject.) Which type of producer of natural enemies may be better able to develop an effective response to changes in crop production systems is probably influenced by the areas of specialization within each company and the linkages each company maintains with the various research and regulatory agencies.

As has been demonstrated through historical example, biological control programs within protected culture will fail if the industry does not adjust rapidly to changes in pest problems by the development and information transfer of natural enemy–compatible pesticides or by the discovery and marketing of new natural enemies. It is the role of the primary producers of natural enemies, working together with researchers in universities and government agencies, to find and develop new natural enemies and to develop needed information on pesticide compatibility. Listening to growers' (and customers') pest problems and trying to quickly find solutions has become an expanding responsibility for natural-enemy producers.

Functions and examples of grower-support services

Technical support is needed not only to educate growers and their staff, but also to plan a control strategy for the crop season. Early detection of pest infestations is essential to obtaining economically feasible biological pest control. A grower's staff must be active participants in this detection process by possessing the skills necessary for recognizing the different stages of pests and symptoms of their damage. Some producers provide technical support and training to growers in order to accomplish this task. For example, Koppert Biological Systems and some other companies have specific departments that develop educational programs for growers and their staff.

Grower education in the use of biological control can also be promoted by the use of computerized decision-support systems. These are available for cucumber and tomato (Shipp and Clarke 1999a). These decision-support systems use a combination of decision tools such as expert systems, database systems, simulation, and other computer models. Koppert Biological Systems developed a program called Crop-It to assist the grower in monitoring the development of pests and natural enemies and in evaluating the cost of crop protection (including the use of IPM-compatible pesticides). Syngenta Bio-Line has developed a similar program (Alica) for use in southern Spain (Boonekampe 1999). This program evaluates the potential for all measures of pest control; emphasis is placed on the use of pesticides because biological control programs are not as well developed for southern Europe as they are for northern Europe and Canada. In Canada, a commercially available decision-support system, Harrow Greenhouse Manager, takes a more holistic approach to integrated crop management of greenhouse vegetable crops (Shipp and Clarke 1999a).

The Role of the Distributor

The need for distributors arose as biological control spread across northern Europe, but individual producers remained located in one geographic location for economic efficiency. Early in insectary-business history, the distributor visited the growers and took orders for natural enemies. The distributor also provided a large variety of other greenhouse supplies, including pesticides and fertilizers. It was later recognized that along with the sale of biological control agents, there was a need for transferring technical information on the use of natural enemies from the producer to the grower. Because the distributors needed to be well versed on their entire product line, their abilities to provide the highly specialized information about natural enemies was usually inadequate for the growers' needs. In addition, conflicts of interest arose as distributors often sold both chemicals and biological control agents to the same grower.

Distributors that were most successful in selling biological control products often had specialized departments, with specialized employees, housed within a larger distribution firm. These specialized units maintained close contact with the producers of the natural enemies they sold and were familiar with issues posed by the growers concerning the use of these natural enemies. This two-way flow of information not only facilitated dispersal of quality advice to the growers, but also alerted producers to new problems. Technical information important to the grower moved from the producer through the distributor, and information on field conditions and grower needs was relayed through the distributor to the producer.

Because some producers only sell natural enemies and do not provide direct support to the grower, technical support from distributors is essential for such products. Other producers, such as Koppert Biological Systems, Biobest, and Applied Bionomics, sell both through distributors and directly to growers. These companies often market through distributors, where available, if the distributors can provide adequate technical support. In areas where qualified distributors are lacking, producers may sell directly to growers and use their own technical staff in the field to support growers. Distributors enhance the value of the products they sell by providing advice on their effective use.

The Role of the Advisor

Successful biological control in protected crops depends on the technical training and experience of both the technical advisor and the grower. During the 1990s, the insectary industry realized that it needed people in the field who were capable of transferring the results of basic research, as well as basic concepts in entomology and insect ecology, to the growers. Even though standard guidelines exist for the application of biological control to most common vegetable crops, it is often necessary for an advisor to adjust these guidelines to specific conditions or to adapt them to crops on which biological control is not commonly used. For example, a technical advisor with knowledge of the side effects of various pesticides can alert growers to the negative effects of a pesticide on particular natural enemies.

The technical advisor may also have experience with pesticide–natural enemy conflicts in different crops or crop stages. Using their knowledge, the advisor can prevent potential problems. For example, if it is necessary to apply a pesticide, the advisor may suggest ways to conserve the existing biological control agents in the crop by selecting the least-damaging materials. In anticipation of a pest problem, the advisor may have to convince a grower to introduce natural enemies before the pest is detected within the crop, as growers often feel they are expending resources on a problem that does not exist. In other cases, the advisor has to tell the grower to abandon biological control in favor of chemical control. From these several examples, the technical advisor becomes an integral part of the grower operation in cases where there is a commitment to biological control.

In addition to technical skills, quality technical advisors must have common sense and an intuitive feel for the industry. Advisors must learn the language of the industry and communicate with growers effectively. From a business perspective, it is equally important that technical support people be good sales-people who are able to sell the product. However, sales usually come with quality technical support. Technical support must be realistically priced and sold to the grower. Maintaining technical advisors is expensive for producers and distributors, especially when advisors must make regular visits to remote greenhouses or nurseries. The service provided by advisors can be expensive, especially for small grower operations and those in less-intensive production regions.

Training technical advisors is extremely important. The technical advisor needs to have knowledge of greenhouse crops, their pests, and various control strategies; however, training of new advisors is not accomplished through classroom education alone. Most important to the process is the direct learning gained by accompanying experienced technical advisors when they are doing their field-work. Producers such as Koppert Biological Systems offer company employees and distributors a course in basic entomology, followed by training on field situations by a senior advisor.

Companies also use the Internet to transfer information and educate growers about company products and their use (Shipp and Clarke 1999b). The advantages of the Internet are that it is easy to update information and to quickly disseminate that information to users worldwide. Caution should be exercised, though, when using this information, in that, unlike books and journal articles, Web documents may not be peer reviewed. Thus, there is no guarantee that the information is accurate. However, due to the high cost of publication today, the majority of the scientific journals are moving to on-line publication and many provide free access to their articles. The Internet can also serve as a "chat room" through list servers (e.g., http://www.agrsci.dk/plb/iobc/good-bugs-l.htm is the Internet address for the International Organization for Biological and Integrated Control of Noxious Animals and Plants, West Palaearctic Regional Section, Integrated Control in Protected Crops, Temperature Climate Working Group) for anyone who wants information about a pest or its control. Open communication among growers, technical support advisors, extension advisors, and researchers is an important method for transferring and implementing new technology about biological control.

Biological control frequently uses a systems approach to crop and pest management. In the past, technical support consisted of advising the grower to introduce a certain biological control agent and then selling it. Today, the insectary business does much more than just selling natural enemies. It also includes explaining to growers the reasons for introducing a specific natural enemy against certain pests at a certain time and rate, and detailing how biological control is part of an overall IPM program for a specific crop. Growers want to be informed and to understand why they are making introductions of various natural enemies. With good technical support, the success rate for biological control will increase, and today's customers will continue to be customers in the future.

Issues Growers Must Address When No Advice Is Available

The above scenario is typified most closely by the grower-advisor relationship in northern European and Canadian greenhouses producing vegetable crops. In other parts of the world or on other commodities, biological control programs are not as clearly defined (see chapter 3 for a discussion on this topic), and growers may have little or no direct access to industry advisors or government-supported advisory services with sufficient training and experience. In such cases, growers must often extrapolate information obtained from experts and resources partially or entirely unrelated to their local context. Growers in such circumstances can increase their chances for success by paying attention to the following points:

1. **Pest identification.** A biological control program directed against a missidentified pest is very likely to fail because the information used in choosing which natural enemy to release will be incorrect. To obtain accurate pest identification of species, growers should send specimens to the appropriate institutions or authorities.

2. **Other pests that need to be controlled in the crop.** The supplier cannot accurately advise growers if they do not give a complete picture of the crop, pest complex, and pest control measures that they plan to implement. This information is needed to spot incompatibilities between control measures for other pests and any biological control agents that growers may plan to use.

3. **The source of plant material.** Plants purchased from suppliers may come with residues that can kill natural enemies. To protect the natural enemies, growers must determine if the plants that they ordered will arrive free of damaging residues by asking the supplier of the plant material which pesticides have been used. As a safeguard, growers should expose the natural enemy to a few of the purchased plants and compare mortality rates on these plants to those on plants known to be pesticide free.

4. **Temperature and humidity typical in the crop.** These variables are determined by the local climate and greenhouse structure (see chapter 3) and can vary greatly. Temperature and humidity strongly influence the efficacy of natural enemies and must be considered when choosing which species to release. Growers need to provide their supplier with detailed information about these variables by using recording devices inside the production areas and obtaining complete data sets typical of entire production cycles.

5. **Shipping times.** When talking with a distributor, growers must determine if natural enemies produced elsewhere will reach their location within the length of time that is safe for release of the natural enemies that they are purchasing. Most agents require priority or overnight shipping (one to three days). This may not be available for some locations. Long shipping times will lead to reduced survival and fecundity of the agents, and thus biological control may not be possible in areas too isolated for quick receipt of

natural enemies. In such situations, it will be more effective to seek a local producer, if possible.

6. **Quality upon receipt of product.** Even if material is received quickly, it still may suffer from desiccation or extreme temperatures in transit or in storage after receipt. Growers need to ask producers what the parameters are of a healthy shipment and how they can make the counts or observations needed to determine the quality of the natural enemies that they have received. Growers should also ask specific questions about what temperatures or other conditions are needed for successful storage and how long agents can be stored under such conditions.

7. **Release methods.** Growers need to be sure that they understand how to make the necessary releases. Exposing healthy natural enemies to wet or hot conditions after release can kill many parasitoids or predators before they have time to have any effect. Growers should also explain their irrigation or misting system to the producer to ensure that it does not conflict with the release method.

8. **Monitoring of results.** Biological control programs need to be checked frequently and adjustments made as necessary. This is especially true for growers who lack experience with biological control. They need to ask the producer or distributor what type of monitoring needs to be done after the releases are started, how often such observations are needed, and how to interpret the results. Advice for monitoring pest and natural enemy populations is also given in chapter 5.

The above steps do not cover all possible issues, but they do provide an entry-level set of checks that need to be addressed when initiating a biological control program or when changing agronomic practices within an existing program.

Quality Control for Existing Products

For success, producers of natural enemies must offer customers effective products that meet their pest control needs. This entails ensuring that the quality of parasitoids and predators as purchased is adequate to provide effective pest control under typical crop conditions. It also means having an evolving suite of natural enemies, which will keep pace with changes in the pest complex that growers must control in the crop. Pest complexes can change rapidly through pest invasions from foreign locations (often spread by interchange of plant material among growers) or by release from chemical control of local species that are normally not considered pests because they are controlled by regular pesticide applications. Such species may become more damaging once broad-spectrum pesticide applications are ended and biological control methods are adopted for the essential pests of the crop.

Over eighty-five companies worldwide produce natural enemies. In 1996, thirty-four companies in Europe alone were mass-producing biological control agents (van Lenteren et al. 1997). With this many companies involved in mass production of biological control agents, a great deal of variation can occur in the quality of the biological control agents received by growers (Glenister et al. 2003). Thus, the IOBC has developed guidelines for quality control of biological control agents that are commercially supplied by producers (see chapter 31 for more detailed information). These quality control tests are conducted by the producers on representative samples before the biological control agents are shipped to distributors or growers.

Conducting quality control tests is a very time-consuming process. Some producers, such as Koppert Biological Systems, are trying to improve the efficiency of the tests by computerizing them wherever possible. For example, a computerized image analysis system is used to monitor the appropriate numbers of whitefly nymphs parasitized by *E. formosa* or *Eretmocerus eremicus* Rose and Zolnerowich or for eggs of *Trichogramma* attached to cards prior to shipping. A similar system is being developed to count predatory mites. Quality control goes beyond just checking the quantity provided; IOBC guidelines also call for monitoring the sex ratio, fecundity, longevity, predation or parasitism rate, and flight activity of natural enemies.

Upon receipt of each shipment, growers should also check the quality of the biological control agents that they purchase. However, standardized guidelines are not currently in place for growers to use. It is difficult and time consuming for growers to use the producers' guidelines developed by IOBC. In Canada, a partnership has been formed among users, producers and scientists to develop simple ways for growers to assess shipment numbers and performance criteria for certain biological control agents (Glenister et al. 2003). The grower, however,

can currently determine if the natural enemies purchased are still alive and if the quantity ordered is present. The necessary tools for obtaining this information are a 10x hand lens or, in some cases, a microscope.

As an example, *E. formosa* is a product whose quality can be easily determined by the grower. Most producers supply this parasitoid as parasitized whitefly nymphs on cards. Some producers also supply parasitized nymphs loose in a carrier material such as sawdust. Nymphs on cards are relatively easy to count with a hand lens. The number of nymphs on each card should be mentioned on the package and may vary among producers. Applied Bionomics ships cards with one hundred nymphs per card, while Koppert Biological Systems, Biobest N. V. and Biological Crop Protection produce cards with lower numbers of parasitized nymphs to improve disbursement of introduced cards. Some companies, such as Syngenta Bio-line, sell both cards with high and low numbers of parasitized nymphs.

The number of adult parasitoids that emerge from parasitized nymphs on cards can also be measured. To monitor emergence, randomly select a small number of cards from the shipment and individually place the cards in glass jars containing a small piece of a sticky trap. Cover the opening with paper toweling and a rubber band to hold the toweling in place. Then place the jars in the greenhouse underneath the crop (fig. 4.1). Never place the jars in an office, boiler room, or in full sunshine in the greenhouse, as these conditions do not accurately reflect those experienced by the parasitized pupae on cards that are correctly hung from plants within the greenhouse. The jars should be placed in conditions similar to which the cards are exposed when distributed throughout the crop.

Two weeks after the cards have been introduced, count the number of live and dead parasitoids in the jar and on the sticky card. This number should match the number of emerged adults that the producer specifies in the shipments. This test will also tell the grower if any whiteflies have also emerged from the cards. To get a good idea of the quality of a shipment, it is important to sample a representative number of cards from each shipment. Because the number of cards in a package varies, it is important for the grower to sample enough cards so that they feel confident that the quality and the quantity have been adequately represented.

The same tests can also be used to check the quality of other parasitoids such as *E. eremicus, Trichogramma* spp., and *Aphidius* spp. If the parasitized hosts are shipped as a loose product, samples need to be taken from the bottle. In addition, the total number of parasitized hosts in the bottle should be counted to check the quantity shipped. The tests in these cases are more time consuming than they are for *E. formosa* because the individuals must be located from within a representative sample of the carrier.

Another product whose quality can be easily checked is the predatory mite *P. persimilis.* Most producers supply this product in loose carrier material such as vermiculite. The bottle needs to be mixed well and be at room temperature. Take a small sample from the bottle, and sprinkle it on a white piece of paper. As the *P. persimilis* leave the vermiculite, count and crush them (to prevent duplicate counts). Repeat this procedure until 5 to 10 percent of the volume

Figure 4.1. Monitoring the emergence of *Encarsia formosa* (Gahan) from commercially supplied cards in the greenhouse.
Photo: R. Valentin.

of the bottle has been checked. This test will give the grower an idea of the number of predatory mites in the bottle. Not every bottle ordered needs to be checked.

The predatory mite *Neoseiulus cucumeris* (Oudemans) is often supplied in breeder packages (e.g., Thripex-Plus, Amblypack CRS, or ABS System). These products continuously release predatory mites for thrips control over a number of weeks. To monitor the release rate, a few breeder bags can be placed individually over sticky cards. Place each bag over the middle of a sticky card, and every week count the number of predatory mites on the card. Replace the cards after each count. This test will show how many predators emerge each week and how long the mite cultures in the bags remain alive. Again, remember to place the bags over the sticky cards under conditions similar to those where the bags will be hung in the greenhouse.

Another factor that can affect the quality of biological control agents is the shipping conditions for the products. Natural enemies are shipped all over the world. Some products must be shipped separately due to species incompatibility if contamination occurs or due to differences in the conditions under which the products must be shipped. A food source may also be required. Products usually need to be kept cool during transport to minimize mortality and some companies use climate controlled trucks or air cargo to ship products (Bolckmans 2003). Many companies routinely include data loggers with the shipments to measure temperature and humidity during transport and to determine whether packaging is adequate for safe transport of the product.

Producers realize that their storage facilities for holding natural enemies must also meet certain criteria in order to obtain an optimal shelf life for the natural enemies. Many companies place the production date on their products, and Biological Crop Protection puts an expiration date on its packages. Many natural enemies can be stored for up to two weeks at 39 to 57°F (4 to 14°C), depending upon the species and stage (Ravensberg 1992). Temperature and humidity need to be controlled to facilitate storage of some natural enemies for limited periods as insurance against emergencies or to meet peak demands. There are times during the year when it is difficult for a supplier to produce enough beneficial agents for users, and short-term storage helps the supplier meet these periods of increased material demand.

Producers recognize the importance of product quality control standards to the viability of their industry. Consequently, they have organized their own internal quality control meetings at an international level to deal with this issue. Commercial biological producers may have to consider adopting quality standards similar to other food product industries, such as Hazard Analysis Critical Control Point or International Organization for Standardization, to guarantee the end user that high quality standards are used throughout the production, storage, and shipping processes. Bio Bee Biological Systems (Sde Eliyahu, Israel) became the first producer of natural enemies to obtain an ISO 9000 certificate in 2002 (Bolckmans 2003).

Development of New Products

As growers transitioned to using biological control to suppress their major pests, new arthropod pests, previously controlled by broad-spectrum insecticides, were frequently noticed in the greenhouse. It became obvious that if biological control is to be a success, producers would need to diversify their products. Also, as biological control in protected crops was adopted worldwide, needs developed for new biological control agents to control local pests. Time is required, however, for producers and researchers to acquire the knowledge needed to expand the range of natural enemies to solve such problems. The new pests and their natural enemies need to be collected, identified, and studied. Tests must be conducted (1) to evaluate the ability of a new natural enemy to control the target pest and (2) to assess commercial viability for mass production of the natural enemy. Side effects to the new natural enemy from chemicals typically applied to the target crops must also be determined.

Economic forces dictate that existing products be re-examined whenever possible to determine if packaging or delivery can be improved. For example, the Syngenta Bioline CRS pack for *N. cucumeris* illustrates how improved packaging can increase the efficacy of an existing agent. Opportunities may also exist to make better use of an already commercialized species by finding different biotypes that are more effective. Currently, only a few biotypes, or strains, of each natural enemy are produced for use in greenhouses for a variety of climates worldwide. For example, Koppert Biological Systems discovered a Greek strain of *E. formosa* capable of producing 40% more eggs per female and being more mobile at low-temperature conditions than the strain that was being mass-produced in their facilities. Similarly, a non-diapausing strain of *N. cucumeris* and a pesticide-tolerant strain of *P. persimilis* have been discovered and are currently mass-produced (Gilkeson 1992, van Houten et al. 1995). These and other ideas will form the basis for new pest control options to meet the needs identified by growers.

Developing Markets

Insectary production and sale of natural enemies is a business subject to regulation by government and market forces. To be successful in the marketplace, insectaries must address concerns posed by both forces. These concerns include government-imposed product registration, the sale of natural enemies in geographic regions to which they are not native, and timely delivery of quality natural enemies in the quantities demanded by growers.

Product registration for natural enemies

The registration of natural enemies is currently a very controversial subject among producers, extension advisors, growers, researchers, and government regulatory agencies. This subject will be discussed in more detail in chapter 31, but here we would like to discuss it briefly from an insectary viewpoint. Some countries require all biological control agents to be registered before they can be used in a country (e.g., Japan). Other countries, such as Canada, the United States, and the United Kingdom, do not presently require registration but are considering how to register these organisms. Generally, most countries do not import biological control agents that are not found in their countries, with the exception of the biological control agents that have been commercially available for a considerable period. Still, in other countries (e.g., Israel), mass importation of any natural enemy is prohibited, but registration of natural enemies is not necessary.

The registration of biological control agents can have both a positive and a negative effect. Growers would consider registration to be negative if the number of available biological control agents decreased or if it took longer for new natural enemies to become available. Conversely, positive effects may be felt if regulations required demonstration of efficacy or forced local production of agents and, as a result, the quality of natural enemies that growers purchased was improved.

Many governments do not require efficacy data for natural enemies before allowing their use in a country. However, when such data are required, as in Japan, the cost and time (two years) to secure registration can be considerable. The result is a lag period between the occurrence of a new pest problem and the availability of effective new natural enemies. However, a benefit of this requirement may be that release rates and introduction timing can be tailored to the specific conditions of that country.

Use of non-native species

Government policies regarding importation of non-indigenous species of natural enemies vary greatly among countries. In Canada, Agriculture and Agri-Food Canada regulates the importation and use of non-indigenous species on a case-by-case basis. It is the responsibility of the importer to prove that the species will not be harmful to indigenous ecosystems. In Japan, where the registration process is strict, indigenous species are preferred. However, it is felt wasteful to search for new natural enemies if already commercialized species, such as *E. formosa*, are available and provide good control. Of course, it is important to protect the natural ecosystems of any country, and due diligence must be practiced by those individuals concerned with the importation and use of non-indigenous species. However, if countries were to rely solely on indigenous species, many countries would be unable to control their pests biologically to the same extent as is practiced today. New pests occur much faster than do new species of biological control agents introduced for their control.

Planning, production, and sale of biological control agents

Production planning is an important issue in the management of a biological control company. It is very difficult to maintain a positive relationship with growers without production levels that meet grower demands. One of the most critical factors affecting the success of biological control programs in vegetable crops is the timing of releases of biological control agents. Timing is critical in establishing a biological balance in the crop. Poorly timed releases may result in pest-infestation levels so high that it may be uneconomical to use biological control or a more rapid control method may be needed.

Schedules for mass production of biological control agents are usually based on a company's experience with its markets and current information from clients. In some areas, such as northern Europe, field information is obtained from the technical advisors who regularly visit the growers. On-site visits allow technical advisors to predict current and future demands for natural enemies, and this information is subsequently communicated back to the mass-production facilities of the producer. This flow of information is essential for insuring a proper supply of natural enemies to meet grower demands.

Another important issue is timing of production cycles. The mass production of biological control agents is a very time-consuming process, and producers must anticipate needs two to four months into the future. Predicting the future is risky, but to avoid being caught short of supply, insectaries often produce increased numbers of natural enemies for an anticipated demand that may or may not materialize. Timing is also critical because the shelf life of biological control agents is short (measured in terms of days). Consequently, constraints on natural-enemy production schedules differ greatly from those of chemical companies whose products can be stored for much longer periods of time.

Conclusion

The market potential for sales of biological control products has increased dramatically over the last decade. Producers are becoming more efficient at rearing large numbers of natural enemies, and some companies are investing substantial resources in the facilities and personnel needed for continued expansion of the industry. Total sales of natural enemies worldwide was estimated at US$25 million in 1997 and doubled by 2000. Annual growth in sales is expected to be 15 to 20% per annun for the near future (van Lenteren 2003). The greenhouse vegetable acreage in North America has increased greatly over the last five years, and growers in many Asian countries (e.g., Korea, China, and Japan) have expressed an interest in switching from chemical to biological control. Thus, the future market potential for producers of biological control products looks excellent.

Most sales of natural enemies are generated by visits of technical advisors to growers. The advisor meets with growers to discuss their needs and develops a pest management program for the crop season. For most greenhouse vegetables, along with some ornamental crops, standard guidelines exist that give a range of introduction rates for the different biological control agents.

However, no two greenhouses are exactly the same when it comes to pests. Each greenhouse operation must be treated as a unique situation, with biological control guidelines providing the framework for development of a pest management program that works for that particular situation.

Both producers and advisors play essential roles in augmentative biological control of protected crops. Understanding how such businesses operate allows growers to better interact with producers, distributors, and advisors. This should be encouraged as a basis for helping growers be more effective in managing their choices about the use of biological control.

References Cited

Bolckmans, K. J. F. 2003. State of affairs and future directions of product quality assurance in Europe. In *Quality Control and Production of Biological Control Agents*, ed. J. C. van Lenteren, 215-224. Cambridge, USA:CABI Publishing.

Boonekampe, D. G. 1999. Spaanse coöperatie investeert in menselijke kapitaal. *Groenten en Fruit*, February 12:4–6.

Bravenboer, L. 1960. De chemische en biologische bestrijding van de spintmijt *Tetranychus urticae* Koch. *Publikatie Proefstn Groenten-en Fruiteelt onder Glas te Naaldwijk* no. 75.

Bravenboer, L., and G. Dosse. 1962. *Phytoseiulus riegeli* Dosse als predator einiger schadmilben aus der *Tetranychus urticae* gruppe. *Entomologia Experimentalis et Applicata* 5: 291–304.

Glenister, C. S., A. Hale, and A. Luczynski. 2003. Quality assurance in North America: Merging customer and producer needs. In *Quality Control and Production of Biological Control Agents*, ed. J. C. van Lenteren, 205-214. Cambridge, USA:CABI Publishing.

Gilkeson, L. 1992. Mass rearing of phytoseiid mites for testing and commercial application. In *Advances in Insect Rearing for Research and Pest Management*, ed. T. E. Anderson and N. C. Leppla, 489–506. San Francisco: Westview Press.

Hussey, N. W. 1985. History of biological control in protected culture: Western Europe. In *Biological Pest Control: The Glasshouse Experience*, ed. N. W. Hussey and N. E. A. Scopes, 11–22. Ithaca, N.Y.: Cornell University Press (Poole, U.K.: Blandford Press).

Koppert, J. P. 1978. Ten years of biological control in glasshouses in the Netherlands. *Mededelingen van de Faculteit Landbouwwetenschappen, Rijksuniversiteit Gent* 43:373–8.

Koppert Biological Systems. 1999. *Side Effects Guide.* Koppert B.V.

Ravensberg, W. J. 1992. Production and utilization of natural enemies in western European glasshouse crops. In *Advances in Insect Rearing for Research and Pest Management,* ed. T. E. Anderson and N. C. Leppla, 465–87. San Francisco: Westview Press.

Shipp, J. L., and N. D. Clarke. 1999a. Decision tools for integrated pest management. In *Integrated Pest and Disease Management in Greenhouse Crops,* ed. R. Albajes, M. L. Gullino, J. C. van Lenteren, and Y. Elad, 168–82. Dordrecht, the Netherlands: Kluwer Academic Publisher.

———. 1999b. The information highway and the need for decision support. *Acta Horticulturae* 481(2):663–9.

van Houten, Y. M., P. van Stratum, J. Bruin, and A. Veerman. 1995. Selection for non-diapause in *Amblyseius cucumeris* and *Amblyseius barkeri* and exploration of the effectiveness of selected strains for thrips control. *Entomologia Experimentalis et Applicata* 77:289–95.

van Lenteren, J. C. 2003. Need for quality control of mass-produced biological control agents. In *Quality Control and Production of Biological Control Agents,* ed. J. C. van Lenteren, 1-18. Cambridge, USA:CABI Publishing.

van Lenteren, J. C., M. M. Roskam, and R. Timmer. 1997. Commercial mass production and pricing of organisms for biological control of pests in Europe. *Biological Control* 10:143–49.

5

Sampling Protocols for Pre- and Post-release Evaluations of Natural Enemies in Protected Culture

E. Yano

National Agricultural Research Center, Tsukuba, Ibaraki, Japan

Monitoring of pests and their natural enemies is often perceived to be difficult and costly, but it is the foundation upon which successful implementation of an integrated pest management program depends. Monitoring programs allow pest managers to develop accurate historical records of pest problems and control strategies; assess the current status of crops, pests, and natural enemies; and determine if and when suppression measures should be initiated or modified (Steiner 1990; Shipp and Zariffa 1991; Shipp 1995). Most monitoring programs have concentrated primarily on pest species (Parrella and Jones 1985; Gillespie and Quiring 1987; Shipp and Zariffa 1991; Sanderson and Zhang 1995; Shipp 1995), and little effort has been expended on natural enemy monitoring techniques (Shipp, Zariffa, and Ferguson 1992) or on the use of a single technique to monitor a pest and natural enemy complex (Heinz. Parrella, and Newman 1992). Because biological control programs in protected culture are most effective and economical when initiated when pest densities are low, monitoring methods must be capable of detecting pests at these low

levels (Gillespie and Quiring 1987). This necessity to accurately estimate low population densities presents special challenges to the development and adoption of appropriate sampling procedures.

In this chapter, the bases for sampling greenhouse pests are developed and the tradeoffs that exist between the cost of sampling and the level of accuracy needed to make sound pest management decisions are discussed. This material is divided into two tracks. In the regular text, the key concepts are discussed and developed in a nonmathematical manner. Second, this discussion is supported with interspersed boxed material in which formulae and discussion are used to develop the material more rigorously. Individuals interested in designing sampling plans may find the more technical information in these boxes to be of value. Persons whose primary interest is simply to utilize the methods discussed in the chapter may wish to read only the text and appreciate the ideas, leaving the details up to the mathematically inclined. Also reviewed is the current status of sampling schemes for the major groups of insect pests in greenhouse crops. In the last section of the chapter, methods are developed for sampling natural enemies as well as pests that can support the effective use of biological control.

Approaches for Sampling Greenhouse Pests

The size of a whitefly population in a greenhouse crop, for example, is frequently expressed as the number of whiteflies caught on a sticky trap and number of immature whiteflies counted on leaves, but these two measures are very different in their precision and value in pest management. In general terms, these are examples of *relative estimates* and *absolute estimates* (Southwood and Henderson 2000). Absolute estimates, such as whitefly counts on leaves, quantify a population in terms of number per unit area. More precisely, numbers of whitefly on leaves are *population intensity estimates* (Morris 1955), which are expressions of arthropod numbers per unit of the insect's available food supply (the plant). Expressions such as number per leaf or number per plant are common population intensity measures. These, however, are easily converted to absolute measures (numbers per unit area) by multiplying the number of insects per leaf by the number of leaves per plant and the number of plants per bench, bay, or greenhouse. Population intensity estimates are discussed in depth later in this chapter.

Trap counts, in contrast, are relative estimates that have no relationship to land surface area. Counts per unit effort, such as data from sweep net sampling, vacuum sampling, timed counts, or counts per trap, are commonly used methods that are examples of relative estimates. Relative estimates are less expensive and easier to use than most absolute estimates, and hence are popular with growers and scouts. However, these methods do not provide real estimates of pest numbers and tend to be less accurate. Also, relative estimates are influenced by many variables in addition to actual pest density. Trap catches, for example, can easily be influenced by where traps are placed (especially in relation to the canopy and the air circulation pattern), the behavior of a given species, and the temperature.

The accuracy of population density estimation may be increased greatly by counting numbers of insects per plant part (such as number per leaf) on a sufficient number of plant parts. Various sampling methods may be utilized to make these population counts, but all tend to require relatively few samples when populations are dense and increasingly greater numbers of samples as populations become sparse. Pest densities in protected cultures tend to be low, even when considered to be at unacceptable levels. As a result, large numbers of samples must frequently be collected and processed, which is both labor-intensive and expensive.

To reduce the costs associated with making population counts, several techniques have been invented that allow more information to be obtained from either fewer samples (sequential sampling) or samples that are merely scored for the presence of pests rather than the actual number of pests (presence/absence sampling) (Zehnder and Trumble 1985, Pedigo and Buntin 1994). Each of these can be useful, and they may be combined. Sequential and presence/absence sampling plans are broadly based on mathematical analyses of the distributions and mean/variable relationships of pests in samples. Selection of an appropriate sampling unit and statistical description of the pest's spatial distribution is necessary to develop these sampling plans (Ekbom and Xu 1990, Shelton and Trumble 1991). While the math can be daunting to pest managers, the use of computerized spreadsheets with the mathematical formulas built in can make the methodology readily available to all. Details of their use are developed later in this chapter.

Traps as Sampling Tools for Greenhouse Pests

Attraction of greenhouse pests to color and odor

Some greenhouse pests show strong phototactic responses to various wavelengths of colors or lights. For example, landing of greenhouse whitefly, *Trialeurodes vaporariorum* (Westwood), is strongly elicited by yellow light with wavelengths of 500 to 600 nm, with peak response occurring at 540 to 550 nm (Macdowall 1972). The same response was evoked by solid surfaces that had their maximum reflectance or transmittance in the yellow-green region (520 to 610 nm) (Vaishampayan et al. 1975; Vaishampayan, Waldbauer, and Kogan 1975). This response to yellow appears to be generalizable to many whitefly species; thus, most adult whiteflies of economic importance can be sampled using yellow sticky traps (Ekbom and Xu 1990).

Adult leafminer flies, *Liriomyza* spp., are attracted to wavelengths in the green region (500 to 540 nm) and the yellow region (540 to 600 nm) of the visible spectrum (Affeldt et al. 1983). Tryon, Poe, and Cromroy (1980) and Yudin, Mitchell, and Cho (1987) collected significantly more adult flies on yellow cards than on yellow-green, orange, green, or blue cards. As a result, yellow sticky traps have been used for monitoring *Liriomyza* spp. adults in tomato in the field (Zehnder and Trumble 1985; Zoebisch, Stimac, and Schuster 1993) and *Liriomyza trifolii* (Burgess) on marigold (Parrella et al. 1989) and on chrysanthemum (Parrella and Jones 1985) in greenhouses.

In contrast to whiteflies and leafminers, western flower thrips, *Frankliniella occidentalis* (Pergande), can be monitored using white, yellow, or blue sticky traps. Higher numbers of western flower thrips were caught on white sticky traps than on yellow traps or those of other colors in a pear orchard (Moffitt 1964), in an orange grove (Beavers, Shaw, and Hampton 1971), and on lettuce farms (Yudin, Mitchell, and Cho 1987). Blue traps were found best for attracting western flower thrips on African violet, *Saintpaulia ionantha* Wendl., in greenhouses (Brødsgaard 1989). In greenhouse cucumbers, blue and yellow were the best colors for attracting western flower thrips (Brødsgaard 1993). Vernon and Gillespie (1990) found that male and female thrips alighted preferentially on traps of bright blue, violet, yellow, or white. Adults of two other species of economic importance, *Thrips palmi* Karny and *Frankliniella intonsa* (Trybom), are also attracted to white or blue colors, and sticky traps of these colors can be used for monitoring in greenhouses (Kawai 1986, Murai 1988).

The use of chemical attractants to enhance attractiveness of traps for thrips has been suggested (Teulon and Ramakers 1990). Several aldehydes occur as volatile components of flower odors, and these are attractive to thrips. In outdoor experiments in the Netherlands, traps baited with anisaldehyde, benzaldehyde, and ethyl nicotiate increased the number of *F. occidentalis* and *Thrips tabaci* Lindeman trapped four- to tenfold compared with controls (ibid.). Benzaldehyde increased the number of *F. intonsa* caught thirty-fivefold. The addition of p-anisaldehyde to sticky boards for mass trapping of western flower thrips in greenhouses increased capture of adult females 1.8- to 6-fold (Teulon, Penman, and Ramakers 1993). Brødsgaard (1990) found that anisaldehyde increased catches of western flower thrips on blue sticky traps. Frey, Cortada, and Helbling (1994) found that in laboratory trials, geraniol and ethylnicothianate significantly increased attractancy compared with unbaited visual traps. However, these results could not be reproduced in greenhouses, possibly due to the diffusion properties of these compounds.

Factors affecting efficiency of traps

Since trapping by use of colored sticky traps depends on the flight activity of winged adult pests, trap efficiency can be strongly affected by environmental factors, pest biology, and by the design of the traps themselves. The color, shape, orientation, and placement of sticky traps can affect trapping efficiency. The importance of trap color has already been discussed in the previous section, so other factors are addressed here.

Yano and Koshihara (1984) found that temperature strongly affects catches of *T. vaporariorum* on yellow sticky traps, with the trapping rate per day being almost zero when the maximum temperature was below 68°F (20°C). In geographic regions or at times of the year where average daily temperatures fluctuate greatly, sticky traps should be changed and counted more frequently if they are to be used effectively to monitor population densities. Similar issues should be taken into consideration when attempting to compare trap catches among greenhouses with different temperature regimes.

Studies in four vegetable greenhouses revealed a significant positive correlation between density and the proportion of female western flower thrips caught on sticky traps (Higgins and Myers 1992). At low densities, 80 to 100% of western flower thrips adults on traps were males. As density of thrips within a greenhouse increased, the proportion of females on traps also increased to 60 to 90%. Predictions about future population dynamics of western flower thrips can be made based on the sex ratio of adults caught on traps. This shift in adult sex ratio can have important consequences with respect to outbreak potential of thrips and damage to greenhouse crops. Higher proportions of female thrips locate mates when thrips densities are high, which may be one mechanism permitting rapid generation of thrips outbreaks.

Studies on the relation of sticky trap size to the number of insects caught indicate that trap catches usually increase with size, but the increase is not proportional to size. Small-sized traps tend to catch more insects per unit area than larger traps (Heathcote 1957, Staples and Allington 1959). Trap size is also important in presence/absence sampling because larger traps are likely to catch a greater diversity of species than smaller traps.

For whiteflies, vertically oriented flat traps in various shapes and sizes have been most commonly used, but cylindrical models and ribbons are also effective (Ekbom and Xu 1990). Vertically oriented flat traps are also commonly used for trapping thrips and leafminers, while flat traps positioned horizontally have been used to monitor fungus gnats. The relative height of traps in the canopy also strongly affects trap catch. In greenhouse cucumbers, the largest catches of western flower thrips were on blue traps just above the canopy (Gillespie and Vernon 1990, Brødsgaard 1993).

The major cost of sampling lies not in the capital outlay of traps, but in the time associated with sorting and identifying the insects caught. Techniques that reduce the amount of time spent monitoring may facilitate full integration of monitoring practices into efficient pest management programs in protected culture. Heinz, Parrella, and Newman (1992) examined the distribution of trapped insects on yellow sticky boards in commercial greenhouses and found that *F. occidentalis, L. trifolii,* and *T. vaporariorum* were clustered along the vertical dimension of the trap, but each uniformly distributed along the horizontal dimension. Based on this result, they suggested that the number of insects caught on a trap could be estimated accurately by counting a 0.9-in.- (2.3-cm-) wide vertical strip of the trap, which could significantly reduce the amount of time spent counting insects.

Density estimation by trap catches

Trap catches on colored sticky traps are considered a relative population estimate (Southwood and Henderson 2000). However,

attempts have been made to correlate trap catches to absolute numbers of insects within a crop. For example, Shipp and Zariffa (1991) found blue sticky trap catches of *F. occidentalis* and whole plant counts to be well correlated in greenhouse sweet pepper. Brødsgaard (1993) found a moderate correlation between the number of *F. occidentalis* caught on blue sticky traps and the number found on leaves. Trap catches, however, did not accurately estimate the number of adult thrips on flowers. Kawai, Kitamura, and Yoshihara (1985) found that the number of adult females of *T. palmi* on white sticky traps was significantly correlated with the density of adults on leaves of sweet peppers, eggplants, cucumbers, and watermelons in commercial greenhouses. Gillespie and Quiring (1987) found a slight correlation between the number of adult whiteflies (*T. vaporariorum*) seen on tomato plants and number caught on sticky traps in a greenhouse.

More sophisticated techniques for estimating densities of adults based on trap catches have been developed for *L. trifolii* adults in chrysanthemum. Studies conducted by Jones and Parrella (1986) on the movements of adult flies demonstrated that sticky traps should be spaced a minimum of 85 ft. (26 m) apart for gathering information on population trends and 154 ft. (47 m) apart for evaluation of treatment effects within plots (e.g., pesticide evaluation).

This information was also used to develop constant precision sampling plans for yellow sticky traps (Parrella and Jones 1985). When traps were positioned over homogeneous blocks of chrysanthemum (i.e., chrysanthemum planted less than thirty days apart) the variance-to-mean relationship of catches was consistent from year to year, location to location, and trap type to trap type. Variance-to-mean relationships are simple indices often used to describe the distribution patterns of animal populations (Southwood and Henderson 2000). The type of work conducted by Parrella and Jones (1985) can be useful to growers and scouts in that it demonstrated that only 18% of the traps (as positioned in the study) throughout the season needed to be counted. Similar sequential sampling plans for *L. trifolii* and *Liriomyza sativae* Blanchard in tomato fields were also developed (Zehnder and Trumble 1985). In this study, variance-to-mean relationships were similar for the two leafminer species for two growing seasons, and these relationships were similar to that of *L. trifolii* in chrysanthemum greenhouses (Parrella and Jones 1985). Therefore, the use of yellow sticky traps may prove appropriate for sampling *Liriomyza* species in a variety of cropping systems.

Taylor, Lindquist and Shipp (1998) analyzed data of catches of *F. occidentalis* by yellow sticky cards based on Taylor's power law. They found a consistency of spatial distribution measured by Taylor's power law in six greenhouses despite differences in crop and in thrips population growth and development. They gave tables for optimum sample size for sampling *F. occidentalis* in greenhouses using yellow sticky cards.

How Math Can Help Make Sampling More Precise

An objective common to all sampling is to get a reliable measure of pest (or natural enemy) density. Reliability increases as the uncer-tainty associated with the density measure decreases. Mathematically, uncertainty is reflected in a measure called the variance (the spread of measurements) around the estimated mean density. The smaller the variance, the more reliable the estimate. To get the best estimates possible, with a given amount of work, one must first determine how the pest (or natural enemy) is distributed among sample units. A sample unit is the element from which a count is made and recorded; it is often a leaf, a branch, a plant, an area of space, or a period of time. While these concepts may often become confusing, a thorough understanding of them is essential to scouts and others involved in IPM. If these concepts are ignored, estimates will be needlessly faulty, and growers will be less successful in making pest suppression decisions (when to release natural enemies, when to spray, etc.). Basing these decisions on information obtained from inappropriate or weak sampling methods may result in a grower paying too much (by applying controls when none are needed) or taking dangerous risks in the production of crops (by doing nothing when controls are actually needed). Math, while a bit scary, can be useful for IPM.

How is the pest distributed?

Pests that are counted in samples are grouped in various ways because of their biology. Colonial animals, such as aphids, occur in clumps because offspring remain near mothers and numbers accumulate locally. Other species, like thrips, are more mobile and may be distributed without any connection to the occurrence of other thrips. The former case is a *clumped* distribution and the latter a *random* distribution. Mathematical formulas exist that are good numerical describers of the number of insects with each of these distribution patterns. The accuracy of sampling estimates can be improved if these relationships are used (see boxes 1 and 2 for formulas).

The occurrence in samples of randomly distributed pests can often be described mathematically by the Poisson distribution (see box 1). It is important to realize that a random distribution does not mean an even or uniform distribution, but that there is equal chance of an organism occurring in any sample and that the presence of one individual does not influence the distribution of another. Mathematically, the Poisson distribution is very simple because it depends on only one parameter, the mean.

Recall from above that the variance-to-mean relationship is frequently used as a simple index to describe the distribution patterns. If I is this index, then

$$I = \frac{\text{variance } (= \sigma^2)}{\text{mean } (= \mu)}$$

In the theoretical world of the Poisson distribution, the variance equals the mean (Southwood and Henderson 2000, Davis 1994), and the expected value of I is always 1.0. If in reality organisms are aggregated, the observed variance will be greater than the mean and I will be much larger than 1.0. On the other hand, if organisms are uniformly spaced, the variance will be much less than the mean and I will be close to zero.

In contrast, many organisms live in clumps, where they are found in dense clusters separated by areas of low densities. Insects like aphids, mealybugs, and whiteflies possess biologies that cause them to produce colonies that are likely to be clumped or aggregated. Clumping within insect and mite populations may also result from the type of structure used to protect the plants (see chapter 3), the arrangements of preferred plant types and cultivars, and the size and spacing of benches within greenhouses. Although a variety of mathematical equations have been used to describe aggregated spatial patterns in biological populations (Patil, Pielou, and Walters 1971), the most common one is the negative binomial distribution (see box 2). It is important to know that once the world of random patterns (e.g., the Poisson distribution) is abandoned, Pandora's box is opened to reveal an infinite variety of possibilities. There are many aggregated patterns that cannot be adequately described by the negative binomial.

Box 1: Counts of Randomly Distributed Pests Follow the Poisson Distribution

The probability [$P(x)$] of finding a certain number of individuals (x) in a sample from a pest population that is randomly distributed is given by

$$P(x) = \frac{e^{-\mu}\mu^x}{x!} \quad (5.1)$$

The average number of individuals from all samples of the population (the mean) is symbolized by μ, and e is the base of natural logarithms ($= 2.71828$) raised to this power. The number of individuals observed in a single sample is symbolized by x, and $x!$ is the factorial product [$x! = (x)(x-1)(x-2) \dots (1)$] of this number.

Box 2: Counts of Pests with Clumped Populations Follow the Negative Binomial Distribution

---

This distribution is governed by two parameters, the mean density (μ) of pests in the sampled area, and k, the binomial exponent that describes the degree of clumping in the population. The negative binomial arises by expansion of the expression:

$$(q - p)^{-k}, \text{ where } \mu = kp \text{ and } q = 1 + p.$$

The probability, $P(x)$, of occurrence of samples with a specific number of individuals, x, is given by the expression:

$$P(x) = \left(\frac{(k + x - 1)!}{x!(k - 1)!} \right) \left(\frac{\mu}{\mu + k} \right)^x \left(\frac{k}{\mu + k} \right)^k \qquad (5.2)$$

For the negative binomial distribution, the variance (σ^2) is

$$\sigma^2 = \mu + \frac{\mu^2}{k}.$$

Thus, the variance of the negative binomial is always greater than the mean, and this is a simple hallmark of aggregation in field data. To fit a theoretical negative binomial distribution to some actual data, two parameters must be estimated. The mean (μ) is the easy one, and it is estimated by taking the mean of the samples (x) collected in the field. The value of k is more difficult to estimate since it is influenced greatly by the size of the sample taken (Krebs 1989). A general approximation by be obtained by

$$k = \frac{(\overline{x})}{s^2 + \overline{x}}$$

where s^2 is the variance of the samples collected in the field.

An important feature of these mathematical equations is that they quantitatively describe just how clumped the population actually is. The exponent, k, within the negative binomial describes the degree of aggregation—the larger the value of k, the less the aggregation, and conversely, the smaller the value of k, the greater the clumping. With respect to monitoring programs, the more strongly clumped a population, the more samples need to be taken to accurately estimate its average density.

Several additional methods have been developed to describe the degree of clumping or aggregation occurring in a population. The first, called the *mean crowding value* (first defined by Lloyd, 1967), is defined as the mean number of other individuals sharing a leaf, plant, etc. (a sample unit) with one individual on the same leaf, plant, or sample unit. Dividing this value by the average density of the population gives another index, called the *index of patchiness* (see box 3 for details).

Box 3: Calculating the Mean Crowding Value and the Index of Patchiness

Mean crowding ($\overset{*}{x}$) is defined as the mean number of other individuals sharing a sample unit with one individual in the same unit, and

$$\overset{*}{x} = \bar{x} + \frac{s^2}{\bar{x}} - 1 \qquad (5.3)$$

This value measures the degree of mutual interference or competition among individuals. The ratio of mean crowding to the population mean, $\overset{*}{x}/\bar{x}$, is termed the *index of patchiness*. This index is used as a measure of aggregation. For this index, values less than 1 suggest an evenly spaced populations (i.e., *regular*); a value of 1 is obtained when the population is randomly dispersed; and values over 1 indicate a clumped or aggregated distribution.

Two other methods also frequently used to describe population dispersion are Iwao's patchiness regression and Taylor's power law (see boxes 4 and 5). The value of these mathematical parameters to sampling is that they provide the foundation for the development of sequential and presence/absence sampling methods. Sequential sampling differs from classical statistical methods because sample size is not fixed in advance. Instead, samples are taken, one at a time, and after each sample one determines whether one has enough information to make a management decision. In presence/absence sampling, pest density is inferred from the proportion of sample units containing at least one pest or natural enemy. Both methods tend to minimize the number of samples collected and afford tremendous time-savings, since pest numbers are not actually counted.

How to choose the best number of samples for IPM scouting

The objective of most monitoring programs is to determine the number of pests and/or natural enemies within a prescribed area. A recurrent practical question associated with

monitoring programs is, How much work do I need to do to achieve the stated objective? Naturally, the monitoring program should have the highest accuracy commensurate with the amount of work expended. In terms specific to the monitoring program, the question translates into, How many samples must I take to answer my question with an acceptable degree of confidence? For years, mathematicians have been providing practical advice on how to answer the second question (see box 6 for a general overview). Their answers vary according to information on the pest's distribution in the samples (is it random, clumped, or even?), the mean and variability associated with samples, and the level of sampling accuracy desired (Iwao and Kuno 1968, Karandinos 1976, Ruesink 1980).

Many pests (e.g., mites, aphids, and thrips) and their natural enemies exhibit up to tenfold population changes before they become detectable or between applications of various control strategies. In these cases, a monitoring program capable of estimating the density of pests and natural enemies with a standard error of 25% is acceptable

---

Box 4: Iwao's Patchiness Regression (a method of describing mean/variance relationships)

Iwao (1968) found linear relationships between the mean crowding index, $\overset{*}{x}$, and the mean, $\overline{x}$, (a relationship called Iwao's patchiness regression, given in eq. 5.4)

$$\overset{*}{x} = \alpha + \beta\overline{x} \qquad (5.4)$$

From eq. 5.3 and 5.4, the sample variance (s^2) can be expressed as a function of the sample mean

$$s^2 = (\alpha+1)\overline{x} + (\beta-1)\overline{x}^2 \qquad (5.5)$$

The intercept (α) is termed the *index of basic contagion* and has been interpreted as the average number of other individuals living in the same sample unit with a given individual. When counts consist of number of individuals, the regression passes through the origin. The slope (β) is defined as the *density contagiousness coefficient* and is the measure of the spatial distribution of the clumps. Clump distribution is classified as random when β equals 1. Values of β greater than 1 or less than 1 indicate either aggregated or uniform dispersion patterns of the clumps, respectively. For example, in sampling aphids, it will often be found that the distribution of individual aphids will be clumped and Iwao's patchiness index (α) will have values greater than 1. The aphid colonies, however, may be distributed in various ways. If the β values were found to be 1, it would indicate that, while aphids were clumped in colonies, colonies were randomly distributed.

Box 5: Taylor's Power Law (a method of describing mean/variance relationships)

Taylor (1961, 1984) found that a power law function could be used to express the relationship between the sample mean and the sample variance (Taylor's power law):

$$s^2 = a\overline{x}^b \qquad (5.6)$$

The values of coefficients are easily obtained from linear regression after log transformation of the equation, as

$$\log(s^2) = \log(a) + b\log(\overline{x}) \qquad (5.7)$$

The slope (b) is often used to classify dispersion patterns as random ($b = 1$), aggregated ($b > 1$), or uniform ($b < 1$).

(Southwood and Henderson 2000). In cases where population fluctuations are much lower, a much lower standard error of approximately 10% is advisable (ibid.).

Standard sampling protocols have been developed for some pests occurring within protected culture, but these standard protocols often need to be modified according to local conditions, or new protocols may need to be developed for new pests. To develop these protocols, preliminary samples must be collected and analyzed. In collecting these preliminary samples, biological intuition regarding the pest, crop, sampling objectives, and possible management strategies should be considered. It is also of value to take at least two different-sized sampling units (e.g., a pot and a leaf, or a plant and a flower bud). One sample unit should always be toward the smallest possible limit (e.g., a leaf or a bud), for as a general principle a higher level of reproducibility is obtained (for the same cost) by taking more smaller units than by taking fewer larger ones (ibid.). Samples should be collected at random, meaning that each sample unit in the study area sample has an equal chance of being chosen.

Systems to reduce the cost and effort of sampling: Presence/ absence and sequential methods

From research on a pest's distribution, the mathematical relationship between the proportion of samples with pests present and the average mean density of the pest per sample can be defined. This information can then be used to develop a sampling plan based solely on presence or absence of pests on leaves or other sample units. This eliminates the labor of actually counting pests in samples, which can be considerable.

Box 6: Formulas for Determining the Optimal Number of Samples to Take When Making Counts of the Absolute Numbers of Arthropods (Ruesink 1980)

One approach defines reliability of the sample estimate by the standard error $S_{\bar{x}}$. In this case, the optimal sample size n is obtained by solving the equation $S_{\bar{x}} = \sqrt{s^2/n}$ for n.

$$n = \frac{s^2}{S_{\bar{x}}^2} \quad (5.8)$$

In equation 5.8, s^2 is the population variance and $S_{\bar{x}}$ is the standard error of the mean in a set of samples. When a predetermined *absolute level of sample accuracy* (d) is desired, d can be substituted for $S_{\bar{x}}$, giving

$$n = \frac{s^2}{d^2} \quad (5.9)$$

When the desired level of sampling accuracy is a *fixed percentage* of the sample mean (($D\bar{x}$), the relationship is as given in equation 5.10.

$$n = \frac{s^2}{D^2\bar{x}^2} \quad (5.10)$$

Table 5.1 gives formulas for sample size when reliability is defined in terms of d or D, and the distribution is expressed by the Poisson distribution, the negative binomial distribution, Iwao's patchiness regression, or Taylor's power law.

Table 5.1. Sample size (n) when reliability is defined in terms of the standard error (Ruesink 1980; Iwao and Kuno 1968).

Assumed Distribution	Sampling Accuracy as a Fixed Parameter (d)	Sampling Accuracy as a Proportional Parameter to the Sample Mean (D)
general	$n = \dfrac{s^2}{d^2}$	$n = \dfrac{s^2}{D^2\bar{x}^2}$
Poisson	$n = \dfrac{\bar{x}}{d^2}$	$n = \dfrac{1}{D^2\bar{x}}$
negative binomial	$n = \dfrac{k\bar{x}+\bar{x}^2}{kd^2}$	$n = \dfrac{k+\bar{x}}{D^2k\bar{x}}$
Taylor's power law	$n = \dfrac{a\bar{x}^b}{d^2}$	$n = \dfrac{a\bar{x}^{b-2}}{D^2}$
Iwao's patchiness regression	$n = \dfrac{1}{d^2}\{(\alpha + 1)\bar{x} + (\beta-1)\bar{x}^2\}$	$n = \dfrac{1}{D^2}\left(\dfrac{\alpha+1}{\bar{x}} + \beta-1\right)$

Presence/absence sampling systems

For many small, numerous arthropods—such as thrips, mites, whiteflies, and aphids—actually counting all individuals in a series of samples is too time-consuming for practical use in IPM programs. In such cases, a different approach can be used in which each sample unit (e.g., leaf, flower) is examined and classified only as either infested (present) or pest-free (absent). The density of the arthropod being examined can then be estimated from the proportion of samples that are infested (see box 7). Sample sizes are fixed in advance by the dictates of logistics or money or by forward planning (see box 8).

Sequential classification for binomial counts

Sequential sampling is a procedure whose characteristic feature is that sample size is not fixed in advance. Instead, observations or measurements are made one at a time, and after each observation the sampler determines whether a conclusion can be reached based upon the accumulated data (either absolute counts or presence/absence data). The decisions being made by the sampler fall into three categories: stop sampling and initiate a management strategy, stop sampling and do not initiate a management strategy, or acknowledge uncertainty and take another sample. Sample size is thus minimized, and in some cases only half the number of observations required with classical sampling is needed for sequential sampling. To use this approach, threshold densities upon which treatment decisions can be made are needed. The mathematics of this approach are discussed in box 9.

Box 7: Determining Density from Presence/Absence Data

This sampling technique employs mathematical models that relate density ($\bar{x}$) and the proportion of samples infested (p). Kono and Sugino (1958) used an empirical equation (KS model),

$$p = 1 - \exp(-a\bar{x}^b) \qquad (5.11),$$

which was later proposed independently by Gerrard and Chiang (1970) and Nachman (1984). Another equation, based on the negative binomial distribution (NB model), was proposed by Pielou (1960):

$$p = 1 - \left(1 + \frac{\bar{x}}{k}\right)^{-k} \qquad (5.12).$$

Wilson and Room (1983) generalized the NB model by substituting the variance-mean relationship of Taylor's power law and obtained

$$p = 1 - \exp\left[-\bar{x}\left\{\ln(a\bar{x}^{b-1})(a\bar{x}^{b-1}-1)^{-1}\right\}\right] \qquad (5.13),$$

where a and b are Taylor's coefficients. Kuno (1986) pointed out that this equation is mathematically more complex and much harder to use than the KS model or the NB model. He recommended the KS and NB models for practical use.

Box 8: Determining the Number of Samples for Presence/Absence Sampling

---

Kuno (1986) calculated the variances of the density estimates obtained from the KS and NB models based on a standard procedure and determined the necessary sample sizes at a fixed level of precision. For the NB model, the necessary sample size n at the precision level (in terms of the relative standard error, D) is given by eq. 5.14.

$$n = \frac{1}{D^2} p(1-p)^{-2/k-1}\left[k\left\{(1-p)^{-1/k}-1\right\}\right]^{-2} \qquad (5.14)$$

For the KS model, the sample size needed for a desired precision level (D) is given by eq. 5.15.

$$n = \frac{1}{D^2 b^2} p(1-p)^{-1}\left\{-\ln(1-p)\right\}^{-2} \qquad (5.15)$$

Sampling the Major Groups of Greenhouse Pests

Various methods have been used to obtain relative estimates of populations in support of IPM and biological control programs used in greenhouses. Hassan (1983) recommended monitoring based on noting the presence or absence of pests and natural enemies on plants as a timesaving method. He used this method to monitor *T. vaporariorum, Encarsia formosa* Gahan, *Tetranychus urticae* Koch,

Box 9: Applying Sequential Sampling Methods to Presence/Absence Data

The basis for this type of sampling scheme began with Wald (1945), who proposed a test called the sequential probability ratio test (SPRT), which is the most efficient and elegant method for classifying binomial (e.g., presence/absence) data. Another method based on the confidence intervals of the critical proportion of samples infested has also been developed (Bechinski and Stoltz 1985), but is less efficient and not statistically rigorous (Kuno 1991). In SPRT, two critical densities, m_1 and m_2, are chosen and the thresholds for making sequential decisions are defined in such a way that the probabilities of making wrong decisions (i.e., treating even if $m < m_1$ and not treating when $m > m_2$) are kept below some predetermined levels (denoted as α_1 and α_2). The binomial distribution is assumed to describe the frequency distribution used in SPRT for classifying binomial counts. Decisions are made in SPRT by using a graph such as figure 5.1. Boundary lines divide the graph into three regions—*treat, take more samples,* and *do not treat*—with two parallel lines. The slope and intercepts of these lines are expressed as simple functions of m_1, m_2, α_1, and α_2. In sequential sampling, additional samples are collected until the cumulative plot falls in the regions of either *treat* or *do not treat*.

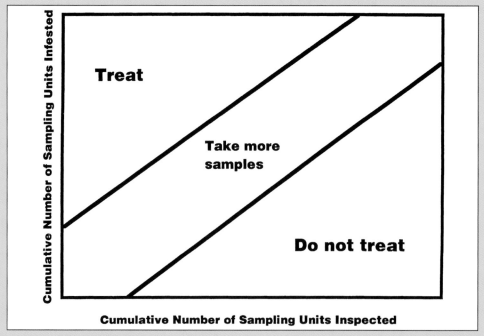

Figure 5.1. Classification of a proportion using bionomial SPRT showing boundary for treat, take more samples, and do not treat.

Phytoseiulus persimilis Athias-Henriot, and *T. tabaci* on cucumber plants. Frijters et al. (1986) compared several sampling methods in commercial tomato greenhouses where *Chrysocharis parksi* J. C. Crawford had been introduced to control *Liriomyza bryoniae* (Kaltenbach) and *L. trifolii*. The sampling methods used included trapping with yellow sticky cards, monitoring of pupae in plastic trays, and systematic counts of empty mines. The authors concluded that counts of empty mines throughout the greenhouse were most accurate and suitable. Schuster and Beck (1983) developed a visual rating system to assess the total number of leaf mines produced by *Liriomyza* spp. on tomato foliage. The number of leaf mines in the visual rating scheme was significantly correlated with the number of leaf mines in actual counts. De Klerk and Ramakers (1986) used the proportion of sample leaves infested with thrips to assess control of *T. tabaci* by *Neoseiulus cucumeris* (Oudemans) on sweet peppers. A 20% level of thrips-infested leaves was suggested as a provisional action threshold.

Whiteflies

The spatial distribution of the whitefly *T. vaporariorum* in greenhouses has been analyzed by fitting theoretical distributions to sample data or by calculating indices of aggregation or the variance-mean relationship. Ekbom (1980) found that both greenhouse whitefly and its parasitoid *E. formosa* have highly aggregated spatial distributions on tomato. Noldus et al. (1986) found this aggregated distribution of whitefly to be constant throughout the cropping season. By contrast, in smaller greenhouses, *T. vaporariorum* was less aggregated (Xu 1982, Yano

1983). This difference in the degree of whitefly aggregation seems to be due to a population-level response to the size of the greenhouses (Yano 1983, Noldus et al. 1986). Table 5.2 shows aggregation indices obtained for *T. vaporariorum* studied in greenhouses of different size. Refer to chapter 3 for other examples of how greenhouse structure and function influence pest populations and strategies used for their control.

Yano (1983) also found that the distributions of whitefly within plants were different among whitefly developmental stages. When populations are aggregated within plants, samples should be collected from various sections (such as top, middle, and bottom leaves) to improve sampling efficiency (Buntin 1994). Taking this into account, Yano (1983) developed an efficient method for sampling whitefly in tomato by using the leaflet as the smallest sampling unit, and by collecting one leaflet from the top, middle, and bottom thirds of the plants.

Yano and Koshihara (1984) calculated the number of tomato plants needed in a binomial sampling scheme to determine the timing of releases of *E. formosa*. The threshold pest density at which parasitoid releases should be started was assumed to be 0.5 adults per plant. This pest density was found, via mathematical models, to be equivalent to 32% of all plants being infested in binomial sampling. To estimate with an accuracy of 20% of the mean percentage of plants infested in a crop, it was calculated that sixty-one plants had to be sampled.

Leafminers

Since leaf mines are readily visible, binomial sampling can easily be applied to this class of

Table 5.2. Aggregation indices for the spatial distribution of the greenhouse whitefly between tomato plants in greenhouses of different size. Parameter values of Iwao's patchiness regression (α, β) or Lloyd's index of patchiness ($\overset{*}{x}/\overline{x}$) are given as aggregation indices.

Area (m^2)	Aggregation Index[a]	Stage	References
10.5	$\alpha = 4.05, \beta = 1.01$	mature larvae	Yano (1983)
	$\alpha = 11.84, \beta = 0.92$	adults	Yano (1983)
32	$\alpha = 2.28, \beta = 4.56$	adults	Xu et al.(1980)
16	$\alpha = -0.26, \beta = 2.32$	adults	Xu et al. (1993)
400–1000	$\beta = 2.09 - 22.7$	larvae	Ekbom (1980)
	$\beta = 4.13 - 17.88$	adults	Ekbom (1980)
6480	$\overset{*}{x}/\overline{x} = 30.2 - 4379.7$	pupae	Noldus et al. (1986)

[a] Parameter values of Iwao's patchiness regression (α, β) or Lloyd's index of patchiness ($\overset{*}{x}/\overline{x}$) are given as aggregation indices.

pests. The population distribution of *L. trifolii* on chrysanthemum leaves was analyzed with Taylor's power law to assist in the development of a binomial sampling plan for this species (Jones and Parrella 1986). An equation developed by Wilson and Room (1983) was used to relate the proportion of leaves infested or damaged to the mean number of larvae or mines per leaf. Development of a mining damage plan was completed so growers or researchers could rapidly assess the final damage to the marketed portion of the chrysanthemum crop. The mean-variance relationships were consistent between different plant strata and between a plot that contained only one chrysanthemum cultivar versus a plot that contained seven different cultivars. A fixed sample size of one hundred leaves collected from the middle parts of plants provided better estimates than a constant precision sample (i.e., a sequential sampling design in which sampling is terminated when a defined level of precision is achieved).

Thrips

Steiner (1990) determined the statistical properties needed to develop binomial sampling plans for *F. occidentalis* and the predatory mite *N. cucumeris* on greenhouse cucumber. The variance-mean relationship, described by Taylor's power law, was found to be the most consistent among adults and larvae of *F. occidentalis* as well as adult *N. cucumeris* collected from leaves in the middle of the plant. The aggregation indices on middle leaves were found to be 1.62 for thrips larvae and 1.31 for both thrips adults and *N. cucumeris*, indicating a clumped distribution. Mean density values were successfully regressed against percentages of middle leaves bearing western flower thrips larvae, western flower thrips adults, and *N. cucumeris* to generate the information necessary for a presence-absence sampling plan. With percentage values of 0 to 80% being the normal limits of reliable use, Steiner (1990) suggested that sampling fifty leaves at low-density and twenty-five leaves at high-density populations of western flower thrips or *N. cucumeris* should be adequate for pest management applications. Further, she reported that fifty middle leaves taken randomly through a 2-acre (2,000-m²) greenhouse could be checked by presence-absence sampling in less than one hour. Unfortunately, there was no relationship between fruit damage and the numbers of thrips on middle leaves.

Shipp and Zariffa (1991) studied spatial patterns of *F. occidentalis* on greenhouse sweet pepper and compared four sampling methods for monitoring densities; i.e., plant tapping, use of blue sticky traps, sampling from leaves, and sampling from blossoms. Sampling of leaves from the middle sections of plants provided the most accurate estimation of adult and larval densities. Aggregation indices were 1.98 for adults and 1.96 for larvae, indicating a very high degree of aggregation. Due to the high level of aggregation, large numbers of leaf samples were necessary, and as a result they concluded that sampling immature thrips is impractical because of time and cost constraints. Sampling blossoms was the most cost-effective sampling method based on time and number of samples for a specific precision level. More recently, Wang and Shipp (2001) developed sequential sampling plans for *F. occidentalis* on greenhouse cucumbers. A fixed-precision sequential sampling plan was designed for estimating thrips adult density using Kuno's (1969) method. Also, a sequential sampling plan for classifying thrips population levels as below or above economic thresholds were developed based on Iwao's model (Iwao 1975).

Kawai (1986) studied interplant distribution of *T. palmi* on cucumbers, eggplants, and sweet peppers using Iwao's patchiness regression. Both adults and larvae showed random distribution on young plants just after planting, but showed aggregated distribution on plants later in the growing period. Both random and sequential sampling plans were developed that calculated the required number of samples to estimate the pest density at a constant precision level. Adult sampling by direct counting was recommended as the most practical approach for monitoring *T. palmi*.

Spider mites

Sanderson and Zhang (1995) examined the effect of abamectin sprays on the dispersion of *T. urticae* and developed fixed-precision-level and binomial sampling plans for this pest on roses. As described by the coefficients within Taylor's power law, dispersion patterns were not significantly different on sprayed and unsprayed canopies, and the aggregation indices were 1.65 to 1.56, indicating that populations of *T. urticae* were clumped. Sample sizes necessary to estimate spider mite density were prohibitively high for fixed precision levels of 15, 20, and 25%. As a result, they developed a binomial sampling plan for practical pest control decision-making. To use their sampling plan, rose beds in infested areas should be divided into sampling areas that are approximately 22 ft.

(6.7 m) long. Regression of mean density (m) on the proportion of sampling units (leaflets) without mites (p_o) resulted in a significant positive relationship between the two parameters [$\ln m = A + B\ln(-\ln p_o)$]. Samples with mean densities of 10.0 and 0.5 mites per leaf correspond to 40.7 and 4.3% infested leaves. Use of these values as action thresholds for upper canopies and lower canopies, respectively, should prevent losses in rose quality (Jesiotr 1978) and yield (Boys and Burbutis 1972).

Nachman (1984) developed a simple model that can be used for binomial sampling of the two-spotted spider mite, *T. urticae*, and its phytoseiid predator *P. persimilis*, occurring on greenhouse cucumbers. The equation he developed is identical to the equations of Kono and Sugino (1958) (the KS model discussed in box 7) and Gerrard and Chiang (1970). Confidence limits for the true mean density were estimated from the proportion of samples without individuals on the assumption that Taylor's power law describes the mean-variance relationship of the species.

Aphids

There are few studies of the spatial distribution of aphids in protected cultivation or of the statistical development of sampling plans for this group. Studies of *Aphis gossypii* Glover and *Myzus persicae* (Sulzer) dispersion among potted chrysanthemums revealed variance to mean ratios ranging between 3.93 and 64.44 for *A. gossypii* and between 3.95 and 62.43 for *M. persicae* (Heinz 1998). The occurrence and rate of aphid clumping significantly affected *M. persicae* population dynamics within individual infested pots. Population growth rates decreased with increasing initial inoculation rates into potted chrysanthemum.

Burgio and Ferrari (1996) analyzed the spatial distribution of *A. gossypii* infesting cucumber and melon crops in greenhouses in northern Italy by Taylor's power law. The aggregation index varied among years and ranged between 1.52 and 1.87. Using the parameters of Taylor's power law and calculating the optimum sample size curves for direct counts by means of Karandinos's (1976) formula, large numbers of leaves (in excess of 500 when $d = 0.3$) needed to be sampled to obtain an accurate estimate of aphid density. Use of a binomial sampling plan according to Gerrard and Chiang's (1970) model cut in half the number of samples to be collected for a given level of accuracy.

Lapchin et al. (1997) used a nonparametric multivariate regression to relate visual classes to precise counts. In this regression, the precise number of cotton aphids, *A. gossypii*, on a cucumber plant was predicted by the visual abundance classes and several environmental factors. The same method was applied to counts of the aphid *Macrosiphum euphorbiae* (Thomas) on tomatoes in greenhouses (Boll and Lapchin 2002). The time for determining the visual classes was approximately 10% of that for the exact counting method.

Does Sampling Make Biological Control Programs More Effective?

Pre- and post-evaluations of biological control releases

The density of the target pest must be estimated to determine the rate and timing of natural enemy releases. To maximize success and minimize costs, it is generally recommended that natural enemies be released as soon as possible after initial detection of a pest infestation. The action threshold triggering such releases is considered to be lower than that for making pesticide treatments, because effects of natural enemies take longer to develop as compared with the action of pesticides. Therefore, a sampling plan capable of providing accurate estimates of low pest densities is essential to the success of biological control.

In contrast, post-release evaluations are made to assess the progress of the biological control program. Density estimates obtained from these evaluations are useful in guiding modifications to natural enemy releases that may be desirable for increasing pest suppres-

sion or for decreasing costs. In a best-case scenario, the biological control may successfully reduce the pests to undetectable levels and releases may be discontinued. In a worst-case scenario, the biological control may fail and an alternate control strategy may need to be implemented. A generalized framework of pre- and post-release evaluations is provided in figure 5.2.

Several methods might be useful for making pre- and post-pest releases in the crop. Most IPM practitioners recommend the use of colored sticky traps for sampling adult thrips, whiteflies, and leafminers. Binomial sampling (presence/absence) is preferred for sampling immature stages or pests for which trapping is not practical, such as spider mites or aphids.

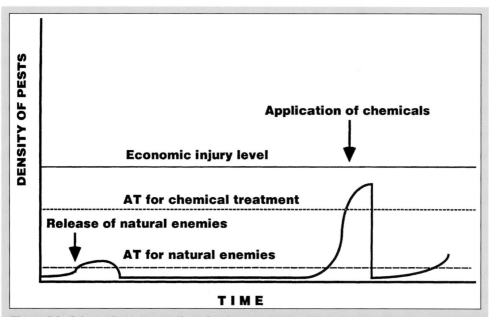

Figure 5.2. Schematic representation of action thresholds (AT) for natural enemies and chemical treatments. The timing of release of natural enemies is determined by sampling of pests as pre-release evaluation. Modification of natural enemy releases or the timing of an insecticide application is determined by sampling of pests as post-release evaluation.

Using damage thresholds that take natural enemies into account

Action thresholds that identify the pest density requiring the beginning of natural enemy releases are not easily determined. Such thresholds must take into account the minimum pest density needed for establishment of a particular natural enemy following its release in a greenhouse. Thresholds are affected by the ratio of the number of natural enemies to the number of pests, the dispersal ability of the natural enemies, the environmental conditions, and the crop. Even with these difficulties, threshold can be estimated empirically by experiments in greenhouses. Development of these thresholds is important from an economic point of view because they allow the grower to calculate the minimum number of the natural enemy that must be released. Studies determining action thresholds marking the initiation of biological control are limited to releases of *E. formosa* for biological control of *T. vaporariorum* (Yano and Koshihara 1984, Gillespie and Quiring 1987). In cases where these biological control thresholds are not established, regular introductions of natural enemies are frequently recommended. The action threshold for post-release evaluation of pests is the same as the action threshold for pesticide treatments, which is estimated based on damage analysis.

Figure 5.3. Use of trained scouts allows personnel to become knowledgeable of various sampling methods and the identification of species associated with each cropping system. *Photo: K. M. Heinz.*

Who Does the Monitoring?

Because of the complexity of designing and executing reliable pest- and natural enemy–sampling plans, it is often a task for a specialist (fig. 5.3). In operations with large areas under protected culture, this specialist may be an employee whose job is to do all of the monitoring throughout the crop for the whole season. This allows for this one person to become knowledgeable of various methods and to determine which approach is satisfactory for the particular greenhouse production system. In smaller greenhouse operations where there is less specialization among employees, hiring a scout or IPM consultant to conduct the monitoring program is a preferred option. Scouts can advance their knowledge of sampling by attending courses and meetings sponsored by public extension and research institutions and spread the cost of such training over many customers. Ultimately, such monitoring will be necessary if greenhouse IPM is to become reliable and based on biological control.

References Cited

Affeldt, H. A., R. W. Thimijan, F. F. Smith, and R. E. Webb. 1983. Response of the greenhouse whitefly (Homoptera: Aleyrodidae) and the vegetable leafminer (Diptera: Agromyzidae) to photospectra. *Journal of Economic Entomology* 76:1405–9.

Beavers, J. B., J. G. Shaw, and R. B. Hampton. 1971. Color and height preference of the citrus thrips in a navel orange grove. *Journal of Economic Entomology* 64:1112–3.

Bechinski, E. J., and R. L. Stoltz. 1985. Presence-absence sequential decision plans for *Tetranychus urticae* (Acari: Tetranychidae) in garden-seed beans, *Phaseolus vulgaris. Journal of Economic Entomology* 78:1475–80.

Boll, R. and L. Lapchin. 2002. Projection pursuit nonparametric regression applied to field counts of the aphid *Macrosiphum euphorbiae* (Homoptera: Aphididae) on tomato crops in greenhouses. *Journal of Economic Entomology* 95:493-8.

Boys, F. E., and P. P. Burbutis. 1972. Influence of *Phytoseiulus persimilis* on populations of *Tetranychus turkestani* at the economic threshold on roses. *Journal of Economic Entomology* 65:114–6.

Brødsgaard, H. F. 1989. Coloured sticky traps for *Frankliniella occidentalis* (Pergande) (Thysanoptera: Thripidae) in glasshouses. *Journal of Applied Entomology* 107:136–40.

———. 1990. The effect of anisaldehyde as a scent attractant for *Frankliniella occidentalis* (Thysanoptera: Thripidae) and the response mechanism involved. *IOBC/WPRS Bulletin* 13 (5):36–8.

———. 1993. Coloured sticky traps for thrips (Thysanoptera: Thripidae) monitoring on glasshouse cucumbers. *IOBC/WPRS Bulletin* 16 (2):19–22.

Buntin, G. D. 1994. Developing a primary sampling program. In *CRC Handbook of Sampling Methods for Arthropods in Agriculture*, ed. L. P. Pedigo and G. D. Buntin, 99–115. Boca Raton, Fla.: CRC Press.

Burgio, G., and R. Ferrari. 1996. Binomial sampling of *Aphis gossypii* Glover (Homoptera: Aphididae) infesting watermelon in open field in northern Italy. *IOBC/WPRS Bulletin*19 (1):27–30.

Davis, P. M. 1994. Statistics for describing populations. In *CRC Handbook of Sampling Methods for Arthropods in Agriculture*, ed. L. P. Pedigo and G. D. Buntin, 33–54. Boca Raton, Fla.: CRC Press.

De Klerk, M. L., and P. M. J. Ramakers. 1986. Monitoring population densities of the phytoseiid predator *Amblyseius cucumeris* and its prey after large-scale introduction to control *Thrips tabaci* on sweet pepper. *Mededelingen Faculteit Landbouwwetenschappen Rijksuniversiteit Gent* 51 (3a):1045–8.

Ekbom, B. S. 1980. Some aspects of the population dynamics of *Trialeurodes vaporariorum* and *Encarsia formosa* and their importance for biological control. *IOBC/WPRS Bulletin* 3 (3):25–34.

Ekbom, B. S., and R. Xu. 1990. Sampling and spatial patterns of whiteflies. In *Whiteflies: Their Bionomics, Pest Status and Management*, ed. D. Gerling, 107–21. Andover, U.K.: Intercept.

Frey, J. E., R. V. Cortada, and H. Helbling. 1994. The potential of flower odours for use in population monitoring of western flower thrips *Frankliniella occidentalis* (Perg.) (Thysanoptera: Thripidae). *Biocontrol Science and Technology* 4:177–86.

Frijters, A. J. M., O. P. J. M. Minkenberg, J. Woets, and W. J. Ravensberg. 1986. *Chrysocharis parksi* in commercial greenhouse for the biological control of leafminers, *Liriomyza bryoniae* and *L. trifolii*, on tomatoes: Case studies and sampling techniques. *Mededelingen Faculteit Landbouwwetenschappen Rijksuniversiteit* 51 (3a):987–97.

Gerrard, D. G., and H. C. Chiang. 1970. Density estimation of corn rootworm egg populations based on frequency of occurrence. *Ecology* 51:237–45.

Gillespie, D. R., and D. Quiring. 1987. Yellow sticky traps for detecting and monitoring greenhouse whitefly (Homoptera: Aleyrodidae) adults on greenhouse tomato crops. *Journal of Economic Entomology* 80:675–9.

Gillespie, D. R., and R. S. Vernon. 1990. Trap catch of western flower thrips (Thysanoptera: Thripidae) as affected by color and height of sticky traps in mature greenhouse cucumber crops. *Journal of Economic Entomology* 83:971–5.

Hassan, S. A. 1983. A practical method to monitor pests and natural enemies in integrated control experiments under glass. *IOBC/WPRS Bulletin* 6 (6):186–93.

Heathcote, G. D. 1957. The optimum size of sticky aphid traps. *Plant Pathology* 6:104–7.

Heinz, K. M. 1998. Dispersal and dispersion of aphids (Homoptera: Aphididae) and selected natural enemies in spatially subdivided greenhouse environments. *Environmental Entomology* 27:1029–38.

Heinz, K. M., M. P. Parrella, and J. P. Newman. 1992. Time-efficient use of yellow sticky traps in monitoring insect populations. *Journal of Economic Entomology* 85:2263–9.

Higgins, C. J., and J. H. Myers. 1992. Sex ratio patterns and population dynamics of western flower thrips (Thysanoptera: Thripidae). *Environmental Entomology* 21:322–30.

Iwao, S. 1968. A new regression method for analyzing the aggregation pattern of animal populations. *Researches on Population Ecology* 10:1–20.

———. 1975. A new method of sequential sampling to classify population relative to a critical density. *Researches on Population Ecology* 16:281–8.

Iwao, S., and E. Kuno. 1968. Use of the regression of mean crowding on mean density for estimating sample size and the transformation of data for the analysis of variance. *Researches on Population Ecology* 10:210–14.

Jesiotr, L. J. 1978. The injurious effects of the two-spotted spider mite (*Tetranychus urticae* Koch) on greenhouse roses. *Polish Journal of Ecology* 26:311–8.

Jones, V. P., and M. P. Parrella. 1986. Development of sampling strategies for larvae of *Liriomyza trifolii* (Diptera: Agromyzidae) in chrysanthemums. *Environmental Entomology* 15:268–73.

Karandinos, M. G. 1976. Optimum sample size and comments on some published formulae. *Bulletin of the Entomological Society of America* 22:417–21.

Kawai, A. 1986. Studies on population ecology and population management of *Thrips palmi* Karny. *Bulletin of the Vegetable and Ornamental Crops Research Station of Japan* (Series C) 9:69–135.

Kawai, A., C. Kitamura, and T. Yoshihara. 1985. Studies on population ecology of *Thrips palmi* Karny. VIII. Population trends examined by the direct count and the sticky trap method. *Bulletin of the Vegetable and Ornamental Crops Research Station of Japan* (Series C) 8:81–6.

Kono, T., and T. Sugino. 1958. On the estimation of the density of rice stem infested by the rice stem borer. *Japanese Journal of Applied Entomology and Zoology* 2:184–7.

Krebs, C. J. 1989. *Ecological Methodology*. New York: Harper Collins.

Kuno, E. 1969. A new method of sequential sampling to obtain the population estimates with a fixed level of precision. *Researches on Population Ecology* 11:127–36.

———.1986. Evaluation of statistical precision and design of efficient sampling for the population estimation based on frequency of occurrence. *Researches on Population Ecology* 28:305–19.

———. 1991. Sampling and analysis of insect populations. *Annual Review of Entomology* 36:285–304.

Lapchin, L., R. Boll, J. Rochant, A.M. Geria and E. Franco. 1997. Projection pursuit nonparametric regression used for predicting insect densities from visual abundance classes. *Environmental Entomology* 26:736–44.

Lloyd, M. 1967. Mean crowding. *Journal of Animal Ecology* 36:1–30.

Macdowall, F. D. H. 1972. Phototactic action spectrum for whitefly and the question of colour vision. *Canadian Entomologist* 104:299–307.

Moffitt, H. R. 1964. A color preference of the western flower thrips, *Frankliniella occidentalis*. *Journal of Economic Entomology* 57:604–5.

Morris, R. F. 1955. The development of sampling techniques for forest insect defoliators with particular reference to the spruce budworm. *Canadian Journal of Zoology* 33:225–94.

Murai, T. 1988. Studies on the ecology and control of flower thrips, *Frankliniella intonsa* (Trybom). *Bulletin of the Shimane Agricultural Experiment Station* 23:1–73.

Nachman, G. 1984. Estimates of mean population density and spatial distribution of *Tetranychus urticae* (Acarina: Tetranychidae) and *Phytoseiulus persimilis* (Acarina: Phytoseiidae) based upon the proportion of empty sampling units. *Journal of Applied Ecology* 21:903–13.

Noldus, L. P. J. J., R. Xu, M. H. Eggenkamp-Rotteveel Mansveld, and J. C. van Lenteren. 1986. The parasite-host relationship between *Encarsia formosa* Gahan (Hymenoptera, Aphelinidae) and *Trialeurodes vaporariorum* (Westwood) (Homoptera, Aleyrodidae). XX. Analysis of the spatial distribution of greenhouse whitefly in a large glasshouse. *Journal of Applied Entomology* 102:484–98.

Parrella, M. P., and V. P. Jones. 1985. Yellow traps as monitoring tools *for Liriomyza trifolii* (Diptera: Agromyzidae) in chrysanthemum greenhouses. *Journal of Economic Entomology* 78:53–6.

Parrella, M. P., V. P. Jones, M. S. Malais, and K. M. Heinz. 1989. Advances in sampling in ornamentals. *Florida Entomologist* 72:394–403.

Patil, G. P., E. C. Pielou, and W. W. Walters, eds. 1971. *Spatial Patterns and Statistical Distributions*. University Park, Penn.: Pennsylvania State University Press.

Pedigo, L. P., and G. D. Buntin, eds. 1994. *Handbook of Sampling Methods for Arthropods in Agriculture*. Boca Raton, Fla.: CRC Press.

Pielou, D. P. 1960. Contagious distribution in the European red mite, *Panonychus ulmi* (Koch), and a method of grading population densities from a count of mite-free leaves. *Canadian Journal of Zoology* 38:645–53.

Ruesink, W. G. 1980. Introduction to sampling theory. In *Sampling Methods in Soybean Entomology*, ed. M. Kogan and D.C. Herzog, 61–78. New York: Springer-Verlag.

Sanderson, J. P., and Z. Q. Zhang. 1995. Dispersion, sampling, and potential for integrated control of twospotted spider mite (Acari: Tetranychidae) on greenhouse roses. *Journal of Economic Entomology* 88:343–51.

Schuster, D. J., and H. W. Beck. 1983. Visual rating system for *assessing Liriomyza* spp. (Diptera: Agromyzidae) leafmining on tomatoes. *Journal of Economic Entomology* 76:1465–6.

Shelton, A. M., and J. T. Trumble. 1991. Monitoring insect populations. In *CRC Handbook of Pest Management of Agriculture Vol. II*, ed. D. B. R. Pimentel, 45–62. Boca Raton, Fla.: CRC Press.

Shipp, J. L. 1995. Monitoring of western flower thrips on glasshouse and vegetable crops. In *Thrips Biology and Management*, ed. B.L. Parker, M. Skinner, and T. Lewis, 547–55. New York: Plenum Press.

Shipp, J. L., and N. Zariffa. 1991. Spatial patterns and sampling methods for western flower thrips (Thysanoptera: Thripidae) on greenhouse sweet pepper. *Canadian Entomologist* 123:989–1000.

Shipp, J. L., N. Zariffa, and G. Ferguson. 1992. Spatial patterns and sampling methods for *Orius* spp. (Hemiptera: Anthocoridae) on greenhouse sweet pepper. *Canadian Entomologist* 124:887–94.

Southwood, T. R. E. and P. A. Henderson. 2000. *Ecological Methods*. Oxford:Blackwell.

Staples, R., and W. B. Allington. 1959. The efficiency of sticky traps in sampling endemic populations of the eriophyid mite *Aceria tulipae* (K.) vector of wheat streak mosaic virus. *Annals of the Entomological Society of America* 52:159–64.

Steiner, M. Y. 1990. Determining population characteristics and sampling procedures for the western flower thrips (Thysanoptera: Thripidae) and the predatory mite *Amblyseius cucumeris* (Acari: Phytoseiidae) on greenhouse cucumber. *Environmental Entomology* 19:1605–13.

Taylor, L. R. 1961. Aggregation, variance and the mean. *Nature* 189:732–5.

———. 1984. Assessing and interpreting the spatial distribution of insect populations. *Annual Review of Entomology* 29:321–57.

Taylor, R. A. J., R. K. Lindquist, and J. L. Shipp. 1998. Variation and consistency in spatial distribution as measured by Taylor's power law. *Environmental Entomology* 27:191-201.

Teulon, D. A. J., D. R. Penman, and P. M. J. Ramakers. 1993. Volatile chemicals for thrips (Thysanoptera: Thripidae) host-finding and application for thrips pest management. *Journal of Economic Entomology* 86:1405–15.

Teulon, D. A. J., and P. M. J. Ramakers. 1990. A review of attractants for trapping thrips with particular reference to glasshouses. *IOBC/WPRS Bulletin* 13 (5):212–4.

Tryon, E. H., Jr., S. L. Poe, and H. L. Cromroy. 1980. Dispersal of vegetable leafminer onto a transplant production range. *Florida Entomologist* 63:292–6.

Vaishampayan, S. M., M. Kogan, G. P. Waldbauer, and J. T. Woolley. 1975. Spectral specific responses in the visual behavior of the greenhouse whitefly, *Trialeurodes vaporariorum* (Homoptera: Aleyrodidae). *Entomologia Experimentalis et Applicata* 18:344–56.

Vaishampayan, S. M., G. P. Waldbauer, and M. Kogan. 1975. Visual and olfactory responses in orientation to plants by the greenhouse whitefly, *Trialeurodes vaporariorum* (Homoptera: Aleyrodidae). *Entomologia Experimentalis et Applicata* 18:412–22.

Vernon, R. S., and D. R. Gillespie. 1990. Spectral responsiveness of *Frankliniella occidentalis* (Thysanoptera: Thripidae) determined by trap catches in greenhouses. *Environmental Entomology* 19:1229–41.

Wald, A. 1945. Sequential tests of statistical hypothesis. *Annals of Mathematics and Statistics* 16:117–86.

Wang, K., and J. L. Shipp. 2001. Sequential sampling plans for western flower thrips (Thysanoptera: Thripidae) on greenhouse cucumbers. *Journal of Economic Entomology* 94:579-85.

Wilson, L. T., and P. M. Room. 1983. Clumping patterns of fruit and arthropods in cotton, with implications for binomial sampling. *Environmental Entomology* 12:50–4.

Xu, R. 1982. Population dynamics of *Trialeurodes vaporariorum* (greenhouse whitefly): Some comments on sampling techniques and prediction of population developments. *Zeitschrift für Angewandte Entomologie* 94:452–65.

Xu, R., C. Chuo, and J. C. van Lenteren. 1993. The parasite-host relationship between *Encarsia formosa* Gahan (Hym., Aphelinidae) and *Trialeurodes vaporariorum* (Westwood) (Hom., Aleyrodidae) XXIII. Application of different sampling methods on spatially stratified whitefly adult populations. *Journal of Applied Entomology* 116:199–211.

Xu, R., L. Liu, and Y. Ding. 1980. Spatial patterns of adults of greenhouse whiteflies *Trialeurodes vaporariorum* Westw. in greenhouses. *Acta Entomologica Sinica* 23:265–75.

Yano, E. 1983. Spatial distribution of greenhouse whitefly (*Trialeurodes vaporariorum* [Westwood]) and a suggested sampling plan for estimating its density in greenhouses. *Researches on Population Ecology* 25:309–20.

Yano, E., and T. Koshihara. 1984. Monitoring techniques for adults of the greenhouse whitefly, *Trialeurodes vaporariorum* (Westwood). *Bulletin of the Vegetable and Ornamental Crops Research Station of Japan (Series A)* 12:85–96.

Yudin, L. S., W. C. Mitchell, and J. J. Cho. 1987. Color preference of thrips (Thysanoptera: Thripidae) with reference to aphids (Homoptera: Aphididae) and leafminers in Hawaiian lettuce farms. *Journal of Economic Entomology* 80:51–5.

Zehnder, G. W., and J. T. Trumble. 1985. Sequential sampling plans with fixed levels of precision for *Liriomyza* species (Diptera: Agromyzidae) in fresh market tomatoes. *Journal of Economic Entomology* 78:138–42.

Zoebisch, T. G., J. L. Stimac, and D. J. Schuster. 1993. Methods for estimating adult densities of *Liriomyza trifolii* (Diptera: Agromyzidae) in staked tomato fields. *Journal of Economic Entomology* 86:523–8.

6

KINDS OF NATURAL ENEMIES

L. S. Osborne
University of Florida, IFAS, Mid-Florida Research and Education Center,
Apopka, Florida

K. Bolckmans
Koppert Biological Systems, Berkel en Rodenrijs,
The Netherlands

Z. Landa
Department of Plant Sciences, University of South Bohemia, Ceske Budejovice,
Czech Republic

and

J. Peña
University of Florida, IFAS, Tropical Research and Education Center.
Homestead, Florida

Successful biological control requires knowledge of the organisms used and their biology. Growers, scouts, and consultants can use such information to choose which natural enemy to use for a particular situation and to predict the level of control possible to achieve. A variety of predators, parasitoids, pathogens, and entomopathogenic nematodes are used to manage pest arthropods. In this chapter, we list the principal species in current use and describe their biologies. Basic references for further reading on natural enemies include Burges and Hussey (1971), Huffaker (1971), Van den Bosch, Messenger, and Guitierrez (1982), and Van Driesche and Bellows (1996) and can be helpful to developing a broader knowledge of the topic.

Predators

How they work

Predators are free-living organisms for which the adults and most of the immature stages must kill and eat prey for their survival. Predators are usually larger than their prey, and many prey are often needed for complete development. Commercially available predators include predatory insects and mites (see tables 6.1 and 6.2), such as thrips (Thysanoptera), true bugs (Hemiptera, *Orius* spp.), green lacewings (Neuroptera, *Chrysoperla* spp.), beetles (Coleoptera, various ladybird beetles), flies (Diptera), and phytoseiid mites.

The biologies of predators are quite diverse. Some feed by chewing up the prey's tissue with their mandibles; others pierce the prey's body and suck out body fluids. A visible sign of the action of predators may be dead prey, particularly in the case of sucking predators, which often leave remnants of prey attacked on plants. Others, such as *Delphastus* spp., may deposit brightly colored frass droplets on the foliage as signals of their activity.

Predators are generally released when pest densities are relatively high, because low densities of prey are not sufficient for predators to sustain themselves. For example, two coccinellid predators of whiteflies, *Nephaspis oculatus* (Blatchley) and *Delphastus catalinae* (Horn), feed on all stages of *Bemisia argentifolii* Bellows and Perring, but both species must eat many whiteflies to be able to lay eggs. Adult female *D. catalinae*, for example, must find and eat a minimum of 167 *B. argentifolii* eggs per day (Hoelmer, Osborne, and Yokomi 1993), whereas adult females of *N. oculatus* need to find and eat only 78 eggs per day (Liu et al. 1997) to maintain oviposition. Immature *N. oculatus* must consume 700 whitefly eggs to develop from a second instar to an adult (Ibid.), but *D. catalinae* requires 1,000 eggs for complete larval development (Hoelmer, Osborne, and Yokomi 1993).

Issues of prey density occur both in the mass production of predators and in their subsequent release into protected crops. Because predators have large food requirements, they are often expensive to mass rear, and these costs are passed on to the end user. In addition, some predators are cannibalistic if underfed, making their mass rearing more difficult and costlier because they must be reared individually. In an attempt to reduce production costs, numerous research projects have focused on the development of artificial diets to feed to predators during the mass-rearing process in place of normal prey (Thompson 1999). Unfortunately, the demand for this technology still far outweighs the successes made by researchers.

Once released, some predators can sustain themselves on alternate foods such as pollen or by feeding on the crop if prey is scarce. Many predatory mites eat pollen, and some species can develop on a diet of pollen alone. Green lacewing adults (*Chrysoperla* spp.) will lay eggs if fed on honeydew (sugars produced by aphids and other homopteran insects). Pollen and sugars are used in some mass-rearing systems to lower production costs.

The selection of predators for release is often based on the target crop and pest species. For example, the predatory mite *Neoseiulus californicus* (McGregor) is used for crops typically infested with the pest mites *Tetranychus urticae* Koch and *Polyphagotarsonemus latus* (Banks). In contrast, *Phytoseiulus persimilis* Athias-Henriot is the preferred predatory mite for release onto palms because *T. urticae* is often the only important pest mite. Occasionally, a release of *Neoseiulus fallacis* (Garman) will be made on palms to manage species such as *Tetranychus tumidus* Banks, which *P. persimilis* will not eat.

Knowledge of predator mobility is important to obtain maximum benefit in terms of pest suppression from a natural-enemy release, especially when pest outbreaks are distributed as isolated patches within a crop. Predator mobility is a function of development stage as well as of the species in question. The immature stages of most predators used in protected culture are mobile, but their abilities to locate prey over large distances are limited. For insects, the adults fly and can search larger areas to find patches of prey and lay their eggs. Their offspring, then, need to search only the local area for prey. Wingless predators, in contrast, must search plants by walking in both immature and adult stages, limiting their ability to cross barriers between plants and benches. Insects such as the fly *Feltiella acarisuga* (Vallot) can easily move through an entire crop after its release. It feeds on several species of mites, and it does so under high temperature and low humidity, which are unfavorable to *P. persimilis*. Other anecdotes prevail, but in at least one case the importance of movement to biological control has been demonstrated experimentally. The parasitoid *Aphidius colemani* Viereck is capable of dispersing almost 150 ft. (46 m) per day due to its ability to fly. As a result, this wasp is capable of locating and parasitizing many more green peach aphids (*Myzus persicae* [Sulzer]) infesting potted chrysanthemums than are larvae of the green lacewing, *Chrysoperla rufilabris* (Burmeister), which is incapable of dispersing to pots located 1 ft. (0.3 m) from their point of release (Heinz 1998). Spacing *A. colemani* release points within greenhouses appropriately greatly increases the level of aphid suppression obtainable (see chapter 16).

The food requirements of a natural enemy can also affect the release strategy employed. If the goal of a release is establishment, then most predators need dense prey populations to reproduce successfully. If, however, the aim is to utilize multiple releases of a predator as a biological insecticide, then any pest population density can be targeted. If the predators are relatively inexpensive, as with predatory mites, releases are often initiated early within a crop cycle and continue until harvest to prevent pest outbreaks. If the predators are relatively expensive, as with beetles, mirids, and anthocorids, then predators may be used locally to reduce high-density host patches, or they may be used temporarily throughout a crop to reduce a pest outbreak to an acceptably low density (Heinz and Parrella 1994a).

Predatory mites vary in their biologies, most importantly in their choices of food or prey (McMurtry and Croft 1997), which may significantly influence their effectiveness as biological control agents. Several species are highly specialized predators of select pest species. As examples, *P. persimilis* feed only on *T. urticae* and a few other tetranychids. *Neoseiulus californicus, N. fallacis*, and *Galendromus occidentalis* (Nesbitt) feed on *Tetranychus* spp. that produce webbing. Other species, such as *Iphiseius degenerans* (Berlese), *Neoseiulus cucumeris* (Oudemans), and *Neoseiulus barkeri* Hughes, are generalist predators and feed on mites, thrips, whiteflies, mealybugs, and scale crawlers, although the last three groups are not preferred prey. These predatory mites can also develop if fed only pollen. A final group of predators, *Euseius* spp., are specialized pollen feeders that also act as generalist predators, but none are currently being used in protected culture. Releasing predators with different dietary specializations in combination, such as *P. persimilis* and *Neoseiulus longispinosus* (Evans), can provide better control than either species used alone (Mori, Saito, and Nakao 1990). In contrast, combining two species with the same dietary specialization (*N. fallacis* and *G. occidentalis*) may provide the same level of pest suppression as releasing either alone (Strong and Croft 1995).

Predators Sold for Use in Protected Culture

Species of predators sold commercially vary between countries. Tables 6.1 and 6.2 list thirty-three species that are currently available in North America and are recommended for use in greenhouses (Hunter 1997). Although commercially available, many of these species have not been critically evaluated for efficacy, and few experiments are available to support claims made by some retailers.

Predators of aphids

Adalia bipunctata *(two-spotted ladybird beetle)*

This species of ladybird beetle occurs naturally in both Europe and North America. Both adults and larvae are voracious predators of more than 50 aphid species. The adults are 0.5 to 0.8 in. (3.5 to 5.5 mm) in length. There

Table 6.1.   Common Predatory Mites Sold for Control of Greenhouse Pests.

Predator Species (all Phytoseiidae)	Prey
Galendromus (= *Metaseiulus* = *Typhlodromus*) *occidentalis* (Nesbitt)	spider mites
Hypoaspis aculeifer Canestrini	fungus gnats and western flower thrips
Hypoaspis (= *Geolaelaps*) *miles* (Berlese)	fungus gnats and western flower thrips
Iphiseius (= *Amblyseius*) *degenerans* (Berlese)	western flower thrips and pest mites
Mesoseiulus (= *Phytoseiulus*) *longipes* (Evans)	spider mites
Neoseiulus (= *Amblyseius*, = *Phytoseiulus*) *barkeri* (= *mckenziei)* Hughes	Thrips
Neoseiulus (= *Amblyseius*) *californicus* (McGregor)	spider mites
Neoseiulus (= *Amblyseius*) *cucumeris* (Oudemans)	thrips, cyclamen, and broad mites
Neoseiulus (= *Amblyseius*) *fallacis* (Garman)	European red and two-spotted spider mites
Phytoseiulus macropilis (Banks)	spider mites
Phytoseiulus persimilis Athias-Henriot	spider mites

Table 6.2.   Common Predatory Insects Sold for Control of Greenhouse Pests.

Predator Species	Prey
Adalia bipunctata (Linnaeus), Coccinellidae (two-spotted ladybird beetle)	Predator for aphids
Aphidoletes aphidimyza (Rondani), Cecidomyiidae (gall midge)	Predator for aphids
Chrysoperla (= *Chrysopa*) *carnea* (Stephens), Chrysopidae (common green lacewing)	General predator
Chrysoperla (= *Chrysopa*) *comanche* Banks, Chrysopidae (Comanche lacewing)	General predator
Chrysoperla (= *Chrysopa*) *rufilabris* (Burmeister), Chrysopidae (green lacewing)	General predator
Coleomegilla maculata (De Geer), Coccinellidae (pink-spotted ladybeetle)	Predator for aphids
Cryptolaemus montrouzieri Mulsant, Coccinellidae (mealybug destroyer)	Predator for various scales and mealybugs
Delphastus catalinae (Horn), Coccinellidae	Predator for whiteflies
Deraeocoris brevis (Uhler), Miridae (true bug)	Predator for whiteflies
Feltiella acarisuga (Vallot)(= *Therodiplosis persicae* Kieffer), Cecidomyiidae (gall midge)	Predator for mites
Geocoris punctipes (Say), Lygaeidae (big-eyed bug)	General predator
Harmonia axyridis (Pallas), Coccinellidae (ladybeetle)	Predator for aphids
Hippodamia convergens Guérin-Méneville, Coccinellidae (convergent ladybeetle)	General predator
Macrolophus caliginosus Wagner, Miridae	Predator of whiteflies
Orius insidiosus (Say), Anthocoridae (insidious flower bug)	General predator
Orius majusculus (Reuter), Anthocoridae (minute pirate bug)	General predator
Orius laevigatus (Fieber), Anthocoridae (minute pirate bug)	General predator
Orius tristicolor (White), Anthocoridae (minute pirate bug)	General predator
Podisus maculiventris (Say), Pentatomidae (spined soldier bug)	Predator for caterpillars
Rhyzobius (= *Lindorus*) *lophanthae* (Blaisdell), Coccinellidae	Predator for various scales
Rhyzobius (= *Lindorus*) *ventralis* (Erichson), Coccinellidae	Predator for various scales
Scolothrips sexmaculatus (Pergande), Thripidae (six-spotted thrips)	Predator for mites and thrips
Stethorus punctillum Weise, Coccinellidae	Predator for mites

are at least 2 color forms, shiny black with red spots or red to yellowish-orange with one black spot on each side of the body. The eggs are 0.015 to 0.2 in. (1 to 1.5 mm) long, orange-yellow in color and laid in groups near aphids. Eggs hatch in about 4 to 8 days depending on temperature. Larvae are 0.08 to 0.09 in. (5 to 6 mm) long, brown to blackish-grey with black, yellow, or orange spots (Malais and Ravensberg 2003).

Hippodamia convergens *(convergent lady beetle)*

Both adults and larvae (fig. 6.1) are general-ists that feed on aphids, mites, mealybugs, and scales. Beetles may consume twenty-five to 170 melon aphids (*Aphis gossypii* Glover) per day when on potted chrysanthemum (Dreistadt and Flint 1996). This species may either be mass reared or collected from large natural aggregations occurring within the field. Unless physically confined by a green-house structure, aggregation-collected beetles disperse from plants one to three days after release. This tendency to disperse can be reduced by prefeeding and preflying beetles for seven to ten days prior to their release (Ibid.). Also, insectary-reared beetles disperse more slowly than aggregation-collected beetles stored at 39 to 50°F (4 to 10°C) until their release. A single release of thirty-four to forty-two beetles per pot (of chrysanthemums) can result in 25 to 84% melon aphid control (Ibid.).

Coleomegilla maculata *(the pink-spotted lady beetle)*

This beetle is able to efficiently reduce aphid populations in corn (Wright and Laing 1982) and wheat (Rice and Wilde 1991). Until

Figure 6.1. Convergent lady beetle adults (left) and larvae (right) are generalists that feed on aphids, mites, mealybugs, and scales. Beetles may consume large numbers of prey per day, but they may also be prone to disperse unless confined by a well-sealed greenhouse.
Photos: M. P. Parrella.

recently it was obtainable from commercial insectaries, where it was produced on artificial diet. At the present, its abilities to control aphids infesting crops within protected culture have not been evaluated.

Harmonia axyridis *(Asian multicolored lady beetle)*

The larvae and adults of this species are semi-arboreal in nature and feed on a wide range of aphid species (Lamana and Miller 1998). Eggs of this predator occur in groups of ten to fifty on the bottoms of aphid-infested leaves. Larvae are black with orange-yellow spots, and development from egg to the last (fourth) larval stage takes two to three weeks. Larvae are the stage usually sold by commercial insectaries. They may eat 150 aphids per day, and because they can tolerate low temperatures, they may be useful in unheated greenhouses located in temperate climates. Larvae pupate on the foliage. Adults can live for months and lay more than 3,000 eggs during their life. This natural enemy has been best evaluated for biological control of arboreal pests (McClure 1987, LaRock and Ellington 1996), and thus it may prove useful in controlling aphids and mites infesting interiorscape trees. Evaluations of its effectiveness at controlling pests occurring on plants grown in protected culture are still needed. This species was introduced into the United States as part of a classical biological control program for aphids. It has also gained entry by accidental introductions. It is now considered an invasive species. *Harmonia axyridis* (Pallas) adults aggregate to overwinter. As a result of this behavior, it becomes a serious nuisance each winter when many individuals enter buildings. Secondly, losses have been reported in the Canadian and northeastern United States wine industries because the beetles contaminate grapes with materials they excrete in the bunches. These compounds give the wine a significant off flavor or odor (Koch 2003).

Aphidoletes aphidimyza *(gall midge)*

Adults of this fly are not predacious, but rather feed on plant nectars and aphid honeydew. Adults will use spider webs as a substrate on which to mate. The adults resemble fungus gnats, but are smaller (0.08 to 0.12 in. [2 to 3 mm]). They are weak fliers and are most active at dawn and dusk. A female can lay 100 to 300 eggs during her life, the actual number depending on the number and types of prey consumed by the larva. Eggs are laid near aphids, and in two to three days (at 70°F [21°C]) hatch into small reddish larvae that feed on aphids. Larvae eat three to fifty aphids per day and kill more aphids than they consume. After seven to fourteen days at 70°F (21°C), larvae drop to the soil and pupate. Fourteen days later, adults emerge and then mate. *Aphidoletes aphidimyza* (Rondani) work well in combination with parasitoids, and use of this species is important for control of *A. gossypii*. These flies are used in pepper, tomato, cucumber, and ornamental crops. They are sold as pupae, which are sprinkled on moist substrates. *A. aphidimyza* do poorly in greenhouses with plastic or concrete on the floor because there is little substrate for pupation. Repeated releases are necessary when establishment is not possible (as is the case in Florida). These predators are released in three different ways: trickle, inundative, and use of banker plants. Some strains enter diapause under short, cool days. The optimum temperature for this species is 64 to 77°F [18 to 25°C].

Chrysoperla carnea, C. comanche, *and* C. rufilabris *(green lacewings)*

Lacewing larvae eat aphids, mealybugs, thrips and whiteflies and will attack other species of beneficial organisms. Adults are delicate, light-green insects with golden eyes and long, transparent wings with very fine venation. Adults feed on honeydew, nectar, and pollen (Hagen 1964). The larvae consume over 400 aphids during their development; older larvae consume 30 to 50 aphids per day. Green lacewings have given excellent control of mealybugs in interior landscapes. High release rates for control of *Bemisia* sp. infesting poinsettia have yielded promising results in small-scale greenhouse trials (Nordlund and Legaspi 1996). Because reproduction and establishment within the crop are seldom achieved, inundative releases are necessary for achieving biological control. Lacewing eggs are produced and sold cheaply, and equipment has been developed for mechanical application of eggs to plants. Lacewings are also sold as young larvae that have been given some food before release (prefed larvae). These have performed better than eggs in interior landscapes but are more expensive to rear because larvae are cannibalistic. Larvae of *C. rufilabris* can sustain themselves in the absence of insect prey by limited feeding on plants. Developmental times depend on both temperature and prey. Development from egg to adult requires twenty-eight days at 75°F (24°C) and eighteen days at 81°F (27°C). With the development of artificial diets on which larvae can be reared, adult releases have become more economical. No data have been published to indicate how effective this tactic is.

Predators of mites

Of the natural enemies known to attack mites, most are other predatory mites. More than 1,000 species of predacious mites have been described, and many have potential for use in plant protection. During the period of 1970 to 1985, about 500 scientific papers were published on the role of one group of mites, the phytoseiids, as predators of spider mites (Chant 1985). Consequently, most of our attention will be directed toward the biologies of predacious mites important to biological control within protected crops. Many species of predatory mites are commercially available but we will concentrate on a few common species here (Osborne et al. 1998). Several insect species (in the taxonomic groups containing beetles, flies, and thrips) may also be important predators of pest mites (see chapters 10 and 11).

Phytoseiulus persimilis

This is the most widely used predatory mite. It was the first commercially available beneficial species used in greenhouse crops, first sold in 1968 (chapter 1). *Phytoseiulus persimilis* is a voracious predator of the two-spotted spider mite, *T. urticae*, and it cannot survive without *T. urticae*. Consequently, fluctuations in these predator and prey populations require multiple applications of *P. persimilis* to be made throughout the season to achieve biological control. In ornamental crops, biweekly applications are made even when no mites have been detected. Scouting is used to concentrate releases in and around dense patches of mites (areas with 1.9 mites per ft.^{2} [20 mites per m^2]). This predator does not perform well at relative humidities below 50% or temperatures above 90°F (32°C). Of critical importance are these values at the leaf surfaces (the area occupied by the mites), which can often have higher relative humidities and different temperatures than the ambient values. Strains may be purchased that tolerate higher temperatures or some pesticides. Growers that produce crops susceptible to broad mites (*P. latus*) should consider using *N. californicus* instead *P. persimilis* or use either *N. californicus* or *N. cucumeris* in addition to *P. persimilis*. *P. persimilis* will not feed on broad mites.

Neoseiulus *(= Amblyseius)* californicus

This species is very mobile and is used to control spider mites in peppers, roses, strawberries, and ornamental crops. Relative to *P. persimilis*, it tolerates lower relative humidity (Osborne et al. 1998), and it can survive longer without food, making preventive releases possible. Even though it attacks all stages of prey mites and it develops twice as fast as *T. urticae* at some temperatures, *N. californicus* reduces dense populations of spider mites more slowly than *P. persimilis*. Many growers use both mites together, *N. californicus* as the primary control agent and *P. persimilis* applied to plants with high mite densities. In Florida, it is also an effective predator of broad mite, *P. latus* (Peña and Osborne 1996).

Neoseiulus *(= Amblyseius)* cucumeris

This species is the most commonly used agent for control of western flower thrips (*Frankliniella occidentalis* [Pergande]), but will also feed on other mite species, including *Phytonemus pallidus* (Banks) (cyclamen mite) and broad mite. For additional information on this species and *N. barkeri*, see the section on predators of thrips.

Stethorus punctillum

Little is known about the ability of *Stethorus punctillum* Weise to control mites in greenhouses. It is a small (0.1-in. [2-mm]), dark brown to black beetle. Eggs are laid individually near mite infestations and hatch in 5-7 days. The larva has four stages and is gray to blackish in color. After approximately 12 to 14 days the larva will find a suitable site and pupate. The adult will emerge 5 to 7 days later. It commonly feeds on mites outdoors and should be evaluated further (see chapter 11).

Feltiella acarisuga

This species is similar in appearance to *A. aphidimyza*. Larvae feed on all stages of *T. urticae*, but information is lacking on its full host range. For details on the biology of this species, see chapter 11. Larvae are parasitized by *Aphanogmus parvulus* Roberti, which may reduce the ability of this fly to establish and suppress mites. The degree of mortality caused by this predator depends on mite density. Larvae kill more prey than they eat. Adults are excellent searchers, and in Florida are often among the first species to find mite infestations on plants grown outdoors. The optimum relative humidity for this species is around 90%. Development rate increases with increasing temperature to a maximum of 81°F (27°C). *Feltiella acarisuga* requires at least a few high-density patches of mites to establish successfully. Commercial use of this predator has been limited, and results have been inconsistent.

Scolothrips sexmaculatus

Both larvae and adults of this species are predacious, and they attack all stages of spider mites. In Florida, this predator is among the first predator species to colonize heavily mite-infested plants outdoors. Palm growers in south Florida have found that *Scolothrips sexmaculatus* (Pergande) can help control *T. urticae* on plants grown under shade cloth. Limited numbers of this thrips are commercially available. Adults lay eggs in plant tissue, but no plant damage has been noted.

Predators of thrips

Orius *spp.*

These bugs feed on mites, aphids, whiteflies, lepidopteran eggs, pollen, and on plant sap. Nymphs can develop to adults on a diet of pollen, and the adults can sustain themselves on pollen but need animal prey in order to reproduce. *Orius* spp. are sold as adults, primarily for the control of thrips. These bugs attack all stages of thrips, in contrast to predatory mites that mainly attack the very young larvae. All stages feed by inserting their piercing–sucking mouthparts into a prey and removing body fluids. At high prey densities, *Orius* bugs will kill more prey than they consume. Adults fly well and easily find new pest infestations. Eggs are laid in plant tissue and hatch in twelve to twenty days. Nymphs (0.02 to 0.07 in. [0.4 to 1.8 mm] in length) are pear-shaped, yellow to red-brown, and have red eyes and no wings. Adults (0.08 to 0.12 in. [2 to 3 mm] long) are dark purple with white markings, and live three to four weeks. Development from egg to adult takes under three weeks at 77°F (25°C). For *Orius insidiosus* (Say), development does not occur below 59°F (15°C). Often recommended minimum release rates for *Orius* spp. are 0.05 per ft.^{2} (0.5 per m^2) as a preventive measure if pollen is available and to 0.09 to 0.93 ft.^{2} (1 to 10 per m^2) for control of light to heavy infestations.

Neoseiulus *(=Amblyseius)* cucumeris

This species is used against thrips, but also feeds on various mites. It is light brown, about 0.04 in. (1 mm) long, very mobile, and quite easy to see. Development (egg to adult) takes eight to eleven days at 77 and 68°F (25 and 20°C, respectively). Adults live three weeks if adequate food is available. Adults eat larval stages of thrips and are used in peppers, cucumbers, eggplants, melons, and several ornamental crops. A controlled release formulation (sachet bags hung in crop canopy) allows for continuous release of this predator in the crop for four to six weeks. Sachet bags contain bran and grain mites (which feed on the bran). The predators feed on grain mites, later moving into the crop in search of other prey as predator numbers increase. Control of thrips with this predator has been erratic.

Iphiseius *(=Amblyseius)* degenerans

Adults are dark brown and slightly larger than *A. cucumeris* (fig. 6.2). They are very active and easily seen foraging on flowers or undersides of leaves. Eggs are laid in groups along veins on the undersides of leaves. The larva is brown with an x-shaped marking on its back; it is not very active and does not feed. Adults and nymphs search actively for thrips larvae and spider mites, consuming their body fluids. Pollen is also eaten and can support mite populations even if thrips are absent. Mite colonies can be reared on a diet of castor bean (*Ricinus communis* L.) pollen alone. *Iphiseius degenerans* is used primarily for control of thrips in peppers. It is introduced as a preventive application as soon as flowers produce pollen, allowing populations to increase and spread throughout the entire crop and be present when thrips invade the greenhouse. *I. degenerans* can tolerate environments with low relative humidities, and it does not enter diapause. Therefore, it has been successfully used in both summer and winter crops.

Figure 6.2. ***Iphiseius degenerans*, characterized by their dark brown coloration and relatively large size as adults, are used primarily for control of thrips in peppers. Adults are very active and easily seen foraging on flowers or undersides of leaves.** *Photo: J. L. Shipp.*

Hypoaspis aculeifer *and* Hypoaspis miles

Hypoaspis spp. are soil-dwelling predatory mites that feed on insects found in the top 1.6 in. (4 cm) of soil. Adults (0.04 in. [1 mm] in length) are brown and lay their eggs in soil; egg to adult developmental time is twelve to thirteen days at 77°F (25°C). *Hypoaspis* spp. are active above 10°C (50°F), and their optimum temperature range is 60 to 72°F (16 to 22°C). The influences of warm temperatures on mite biology and effectiveness are unknown. Optimal habitats are moist but not water-logged soils. *Hypoaspis (= Geolaelaps) miles* (Berlese) can live for several weeks without prey. The rates recommended for fungus gnat management (9.3 mites per ft.^{2} [100 mites per m^2] as a preventative to 23 per ft.^{2} [250 per m^2] as a curative) are also the rates used to suppress thrips.

In greenhouses, *Hypoaspis* spp. eat collembolans, thrips pupae, and fungus gnat larvae. They reduce survival of thrips pupating in the soil, but the level of control is insufficient by itself (Gillespie and Quiring 1990; Lindquist, Buxton, and Piatkowski 1994; Brødsgaard, Sardar, and Enkegaard 1996). *Hypoaspis* spp. are best used in combination with other controls. Mites are released onto the moistened soil surface before planting or potting. Mites feed on organic matter or other prey if fungus gnats or thrips are absent, but are compatible with entomopathogenic nematodes. *Hypoaspis aculeifer* Canestrini, which is sold primarily in Europe, has been reported to be better than *H. miles* for thrips control (see chapter 20), and is used for control of bulb mites during bulb storage. Diapause has not been reported in either species, and both can be used all year.

Predators of whiteflies

Delphastus catalinae

There has been some confusion concerning the name of the beetle most commonly used in augmentative biological control programs. According to Hoelmer and Pickett (2003), most of the published studies of *Delphastus pusillus* biology and behavior on *Bemisia* spp. actually refer to *D. catalinae*. Similarly, *Delphastus* species in commercial insectary cultures are probably *D. catalinae* and not *D. pusillus*. This shiny black beetle (fig. 6.3) is 0.05 to 0.06 in. [1.2 to 1.4 mm] long. Females lay about three eggs per day (about 183 over their lifetime). There are four to five larval instars and a pupa. Development (egg to adult) requires about twenty-one days. This beetle is used against locally dense patches of whiteflies or where parasitoids have been unsuccessful (Heinz and Parrella 1994a), or in crops with high whitefly tolerances. Beetle larvae and adults consume many whitefly eggs, nymphs, and pupae. Adults require one hundred whitefly eggs per day to produce eggs. This beetle is compatible with the use of whitefly parasitoids.

Macrolophus caliginosus

This predacous bug is widely used and referred to as *M. caliginosus*. However, this name appears to be incorrect, being a junior synonym of *Macrolophus melanotoma* (Costa), (Carapezza 1995). However, in this book we refer to this bug as *M. caliginosus* throughout. This bright green bug (0.11 to 0.14 in. [2.9 to 3.6 mm] in length) inserts eggs into plant tissue. The bugs develop through five nymphal stages, requiring twenty-nine to ninety-five days at 77 to 59°F (25 to 15°C) before becoming adults with red eyes and long legs and antennae. Adults and nymphs move rapidly in search of prey, feeding on spider mites, whiteflies, and other insects. Adults lay 100 to 250 eggs in their lifetime, depending on temperature and availability of food. When prey are unavailable and *Macrolophus caliginosus* Wagner densities high, some tomato varieties are damaged when these predators feed on plant sap. Because this insect can cause damage to plants, it probably will not be approved for importation into some countries, including the United States.

Inoculative releases of this predator are common in Holland, France, Belgium, Scandinavia, Poland, and Germany. A seasonal inoculative approach is typically

Figure 6.3. *Delphastus catalinae* **adults (left) and larvae (right) feed primarily on whitefly immatures. Because they are relatively compatible with the use of whitefly parasitoids, they have been used successfully to control localized outbreaks of whitefly (in patches where parasitoids have failed). They may also be used alone in crops with high damage thresholds to whitefly.** *Photos: M. P. Parrella.*

employed, whereby two releases are made two weeks apart. Sometimes moth eggs (*Ephestia* sp.) are provided as food to facilitate establishment. Release rates vary greatly depending on the crop and expected pest pressure. For example, recommended release rates range from 0.05 to 0.5 predators per ft.^{2} [0.5 to 5.0 per m^2]; at higher rates, predators should be concentrated in whitefly-infested areas. *Macrolophus caliginosus* are often used together with *Encarsia formosa* Gahan when greenhouse whitefly is the most important pest within a complex of pests attacking a crop. In these cases, *E. formosa* release rates often need to be increased to achieve the desired level of biological control, since *M. caliginosus* does not distinguish between parasitized or unparasitized whitefly nymphs as does *D. catalinae*. Populations of this predator may become infected in late summer by a naturally occurring *Entomophthora* sp. fungus, thus greatly reducing their densities. For more information see chapters 8 and 9.

Chrysoperla carnea, C. comanche, *and* C. rufilabris

These green lacewings are sold as aphid predators, but they also eat whiteflies. See the section Predators of Aphids for details on the biology and use of these species.

Predators of other pests
Cryptolaemus montrouzieri
This predator (fig. 6.4) is often used for control of the citrus mealybug, *Planococcus citri* (Risso), or the longtailed mealybug, *Pseudococcus longispinus* (Targioni-Tozzetti), infesting interior landscapes. *Cryptolaemus montrouzieri* Mulsant does not reproduce well on species of mealybugs that

do not produce masses of eggs protected by waxy filaments. Both larvae and adults of this predator feed on all mealybug stages but require large prey populations to sustain a population. Consequently, releases are often made in combination with parasitoids (see the section Other Parasitoids) to achieve the greatest level of success.

Eggs (about 500 per female per lifetime) are laid in mealybug aggregations and hatch in about five to six days. The larvae (up to 0.5 in. [13 mm] long) are covered with copious amounts of white wax, and to the uneducated eye look like large, active mealybugs. Larvae eat about 250 young mealybugs before pupating. Adults (0.2 in. [4 mm] in length) are brownish black, with an orange-brown head and thorax. The life cycle requires thirty-one to forty-five days at 81 to 70°F (27 to 21°C). This beetle is not active below 61°F (16°C) or above 91°F (33°C), and it may enter diapause in winter.

Parasitoids
General biology of parasitoids
Insect parasitoids (a term frequently but incorrectly interchanged with *parasites*) develop inside (endoparasitoids) or outside (ectoparasitoids) their hosts, depending on the parasitoid species. Immature parasitoids are closely associated with their hosts and do not move from one host to another. Parasitoids are generally smaller than their hosts and are free-living only as adults. Parasitoids used most commonly in greenhouses are wasps (Hymenoptera), including *E. formosa*, *Eretmocerus eremicus* Rose and Zolnerowich, *Aphelinus abdominalis* (Dalman), *A. colemani*, *Aphidius ervi* Haliday, *Dacnusa sibirica* Telenga,

Figure 6.4. *Cryptolaemus montrouzieri* **is often used to control mealybugs infesting interior landscapes, and hence has the common name mealybug destroyer. The larvae are covered with copious amounts of white wax and hence are often mistaken as active mealybugs rather than mealybug predators. Adults are brownish black, with an orange-brown head and thorax.** (*Photo: M. P. Parrella*)

Diglyphus isaea (Walker), and *Leptomastix dactylopii* Howard (table 6.3).

Adult parasitoids have wings and are active fliers. Some kill hosts by puncturing them with an ovipositor and feeding on body fluids. This process is called host-feeding and can be very important in pest population suppression. When adults parasitize a host rather than feed on it, they lay one or more eggs near, on, or within the host insect (fig. 6.5). These eggs hatch, and the wormlike larvae feed on the host. Because parasitoid eggs are placed within or very near to hosts, which are often immobilized during the attack by the adult wasp, imma-

ture parasitoids do not forage for prey, as do immature predators. Parasitoid larvae pupate near the host (as in the case of *D. isaea* on leafminers) or inside of the host (as in the case of parasitoids of aphids and whiteflies).

Parasitoids have evolved many specialized characteristics due to their close associations with their hosts. Many of these characteristics are associated with parasitoid reproduction and host location, which are directly associated with the abilities of parasitoids to establish or to suppress a target pest after their release. In the following sections, we discuss several of these characteristics

Table 6.3.   Common Parasitoids Sold for Control of Greenhouse Pests.

Parasitoid	Host
Aphelinus abdominalis (Dalman), Aphelinidae	Aphids
Aphidius colemani Viereck, Braconidae	Aphids
Aphidius ervi Haliday, Braconidae	Aphids
Dacnusa sibirica Telenga, Braconidae	Leafminers
Diglyphus isaea (Walker), Eulophidae	Leafminers
Encarsia formosa Gahan, Aphelinidae	Greenhouse whitefly
Eretmocerus eremicus Rose and Zolnerowich, Aphelinidae	Silverleaf and greenhouse whiteflies
Eretmocerus mundus Mercet, Aphelinidae	Silverleaf and tobacco whiteflies
Leptomastix dactylopii Howard, Encyrtidae	Citrus mealybug

and relate the importance of each to the implementation of biological control.

Parasitoid reproduction

Parasitoids are described as egg, larval, nymphal, pupal, or adult parasitoids, depending on which life stage of the host they attack. Due to these host-stage specializations, parasitoid releases should be synchronized with the availability of hosts suitable for parasitoid attack. The occurrences of host stages tend to change dramatically with time within a pest infestation cycle. Early within an infestation cycle, one life stage of the pest tends to predominate at a time. But if the pest population persists, then all life stages tend to be available. Thus, the abundances of parasitoid-suitable hosts need to be monitored and parasitoid releases carefully coordinated to achieve success.

The patterns of egg production and deposition within the lives of parasitoids may vary significantly. Female wasps of *proovigenic* species emerge from their pupae with their full complement of mature or nearly mature eggs. Consequently, proovigenic wasps begin ovipositing eggs almost immediately after emerging. The number of eggs they oviposit is determined by the conditions experienced by the preceding larval stage rather than the conditions experienced by the ovipositing wasps (Jervis and Kidd 1996). Proovigenic wasps tend to be short-lived, surviving for only a few days, and they may feed for maintenance purposes (Ibid.). *Synovigenic* parasitoids emerge with none or part of their total mature egg complement and develop eggs throughout their adult life. These wasps need to feed (on hosts, honeydew, or flowers) to maintain and maxi-

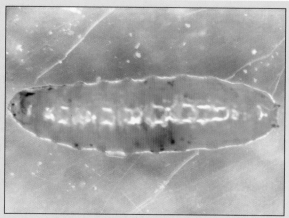

Figure 6.5. Parasitoids may oviposit directly into their hosts, as in the case of *Hyposoter exiguae* (Viereck) in its beet armyworm host (left); or they oviposit outside their hosts, usually placing the egg on or near the host as in the case of the egg of *Diglyphus begini* (Ashmead) on its leafminer host (right). *Photos: M. P. Parrella (left) and K. M. Heinz (right).*

mize egg production, but they also tend to be relatively long-lived.

Few parasitoids have been shown to be proovigenic. One such group consists of the whitefly parasitoids in the genus *Amitus*. Several releases of these species, or high synchronization of each release with their susceptible host stage, may be needed to obtain their establishment. Because they can lay eggs rapidly without having to wait for more to mature, they may be best used in inundative approaches. The majority of parasitoids, including species within the genera *Diglyphus* and *Encarsia* (Heimpel and Rosenheim 1998), appear to be synovigenic (Jervis and Kidd 1986). To achieve the maximum benefit from releases of synovigenic species, sufficient food supplies must be available to reach maximum egg production and reproduction. Parasitoids with this method of egg production can be used in all forms of biological control, but they may be

particularly well suited to situations where long-term control is desired.

Hymenopteran parasitoids exhibit several modes of reproduction important to the ratio of male to female offspring produced by a single wasp. Because female wasps are the only sex capable of attacking pestiferous hosts, parasitoid sex ratios are critical to biological control. Most parasitoids reproduce through *arrhenotoky*, in which unfertilized eggs become males and fertilized eggs produce females. The female controls the sex of her offspring when ovipositing by selectively controlling fertilization of each egg passing through her reproductive tract. Such species are termed *biparental* since both a mother and father are necessary for the production of daughters. A minority of parasitic Hymenoptera reproduces in other, entirely parthenogenic ways termed *thelytoky* and *deuterotoky*. With thelytoky, there are no males, and unfertilized eggs give rise to daughters. With deuterotoky, either male or female progeny may be produced from unfertilized eggs, but the males are nonfunctional. In both of these latter cases of parthenogenic reproduction, these species are referred to as *uniparental*, and all functional wasps are female. Mass rearings and releases of thelytokous and deuterotokous species are simpler and less expensive than those of arrhenotokous species, since only females must be included in all facets of biological control when using completely parthenogenic forms.

Knowing which natural enemies attack which hosts is essential to manipulating parasitoid complexes within biological control programs. Parasitoids can be grouped based on the kind of hosts they attack; some kinds of natural enemies may not be beneficial to biological control. A *primary parasitoid* attacks hosts that are not parasitoids themselves. Provided they target the pest species as their host, primary parasitoids are frequently used in biological control programs. In selecting an appropriate parasitoid for release, it should be remembered that some parasitoids may attack and kill other nonpestiferous insects. In these cases, releases of natural enemies may not provide the level of biological control desired, or they may draw the ire of other groups with special interests in nonpestiferous species affected by the releases.

Parasitoids that attack other parasitoids are termed *hyperparasitoids* or *secondary parasitoids*. Yet another type of parasitism, called *adelphoparasitism* or *autoparasitism*, occurs when a species is parasitic on individuals of its own species. Some whitefly parasitoids, for example, lay unfertilized eggs (destined to become males) in or on female larvae of their own species inside parasitized whiteflies. Male eggs hatch and larvae feed on females within the body of the whitefly host. Fertilized eggs, destined to become females, are laid within the unparasitized whitefly. Typically, hyperparasitoids and autoparasitoids are not used in biological control programs aimed at protected culture. However, parasitoids with these lifestyles commonly occur in nature and may invade greenhouses and interfere with ongoing biological control programs. There is some evidence from Spain to suggest that the autoparasitoid *Encarsia pergandiella* (Howard) may invade tomato greenhouses and interfere with the primary parasitoid *E. formosa* released for control of greenhouse whitefly (Gabarra et al. 1999).

One additional form of parasitoid-to-parasitoid interaction occurs most commonly in mass-rearing systems and hence may influence augmentation biological control programs. If more than one egg is laid in a host by a single species of parasitoid, and if not all of the eggs are able to develop to maturity, competition for the host results. This condition is called *superparasitism*. Superparasitism may lead to the production of small-sized parasitoids of inferior quality, the overproduction of male wasps, and a general decline in the supply of wasps available for an augmentation biological control project.

Host finding and selection

The methods parasitoids use to find and choose hosts to attack are important in understanding their effectiveness (see Van Driesche and Bellows 1996 for an overview). These mechanisms can be complex, and often involve behavioral responses to a series of odors, tastes, or other cues. In augmentative biological control, we release natural enemies into the pest's habitat (i.e., the crop), but the parasitoid must still find the individual pests. A few species of parasitoids find hosts by chance encounter, but most species use airborne or contact chemicals, visual features, or vibrations to detect hosts. These stimuli can be produced by the host, the plant eaten by the host, or the interaction of pest and plant. Once a parasitoid locates a host, similar or other stimuli (e.g., size of the host, chemicals on its body, and whether or not it is already parasitized) may elicit oviposition, host-feeding, or host rejection behaviors (Van Driesche and Bellows 1996). Pesticide applications, cultivar selections, and cultural practices that influence plant or environmental characteristics can modify these host-finding and host-acceptance stimuli.

E. formosa, once released into a greenhouse, searches randomly for whiteflies (van Lenteren, van Roermund, and Sütterlin 1996; Hoddle et al. 1998). When *E. formosa* wasps detect a host, honeydew, or other whitefly remains, they are stimulated to stay in a local patch and search longer for more hosts. Encounters with whitefly nymphs or waste products can stimulate wasps to increase the length of time on a patch two- to tenfold. Some natural enemies find host patches by following physical trails formed by excrement, webbing, cast skins, or feeding marks on the plant caused by the host (Turlings et al. 1993).

Encounters with hosts by searching parasitoids can be influenced by many environmental factors. Light, temperature, host plant architecture, and presence of honeydew can affect the walking speed of some parasitoids, which in turn has a marked influence on the rate and efficiency of host location. *E. formosa*, for example, prefers to walk rather than fly at temperatures below 64°F (18°C), and does not remain long in patches with copious amounts of honeydew, which interferes with the wasps' searching and causes them to spend more time cleaning their legs. Many studies have demonstrated that high densities of leaf trichomes reduce searching parasitoid efficiency (Heinz and Parrella 1994b, van Lenteren et al. 1995, Sütterlin and van Lenteren 1996).

Once a host is found, the natural enemy must decide what to do with it. Depending on the stage of whitefly encountered and the nutritional state of the adult, *E. formosa* may oviposit in it or may pierce the nymph with its ovipositor and feed on the host's body fluids to obtain nutrition to develop additional eggs. Such host-feeding is a significant source of mortality in many pest populations (Debach 1943). Sometimes a wasp will use its ovipositor to pierce a potential host, but will neither oviposit nor host-feed on it. Depending on the amount of damage caused by this probing, the host may die. If neither host-feeding nor death from probing occur, the host is likely to receive an egg, and a new parasitoid will develop on the host and eventually emerge, increasing the population of parasitoids in the greenhouse. Superparasitism occurs infrequently within biological control programs since hosts that have previously been parasitized are often rejected. *E. formosa*, for example, rejects parasitized whitefly nymphs (van Roermund and van Lenteren 1992).

Species of parasitoids sold commercially vary between countries. Table 6.3 lists eight species that are currently available in North America and are commonly used in greenhouses (Hunter 1997). Although commercially available, several of these species have not been critically evaluated for efficacy, and experiments may be lacking to support or refute claims made by some retailers.

Parasitoids of aphids

Aphelinus abdominalis

This synovigenic parasitoid attacks large-sized aphids such as *Macrosiphum euphorbiae* (Thomas) (potato aphid) and *Aulacorthum solani* (Kaltenbach) (glasshouse and potato aphid). The adult (0.12 in. [3 mm] long) is black with a yellow abdomen. The female oviposits inside aphids. Larvae grow through four instars and, after one week, pupate inside mummified aphids, which turn black. Upon emergence, mating occurs within the first twenty-four hours. It takes about two weeks to complete the entire life cycle. Wasps parasitize ten to fifteen aphids per day, and they will kill other aphids not accepted for oviposition by host-feeding. Previously parasitized hosts are not attacked. Hyperparasitoids of *A. abdominalis* are known to occur. Although this species does best in well-lighted, warm greenhouses, release of *A. abdominalis* alone does not result in successful biological control. To achieve satisfactory levels of aphid suppression in sweet pepper, tomato, eggplant, beans, gerbera, rose, chrysanthemums, and *Lisianthus*, aphid predators must also be released.

Aphidius colemani

This species has replaced *Aphidius matricariae* Haliday as the most commonly used aphid parasitoid in many southern greenhouses. This parasitoid will attack *M. persicae*, *Myzus nicotianae* Blackman, and, most importantly, the melon aphid, *A. gossypii*. In contrast, *A. matricariae* can only be used against *Myzus* spp. The adult (0.08 inch [2 mm] long) is black with brown legs. Because the adult is not long-lived, this species is shipped as pupae (inside mummies). Most of the female's eggs are laid in four to five days, inserted inside aphids or nymphs. After seven days (at 70°F [21°C]), the parasitoid larva attaches the aphid to the leaf and pupates in the dead aphid, forming a cocoon that makes the aphid swell and become brown and leathery. At this stage, the dead aphid is often called a mummy. After three to four days, the adult parasitoid chews a round circular hole in the mummy and emerges.

Adults of *A. colemani* can find aphid colonies from a long distance by using odors from honeydew (an adult food source) and possibly odors produced by aphid-infested plants. In some situations, this wasp eradicates the aphid population and thus fails to establish. When long-term control is desired, the failure of the parasitoid to establish leaves the crop unprotected against future aphid infestations. Therefore, continuous releases of *A. colemani* may be achieved using a banker plant system (based on the use of barley plants infested with a nonpest aphid *Rhopalosiphum padi* [L.]). Alternatively, *A. colemani* may be released weekly in low numbers. Other release strategies used include seasonal inoculative, preventive, and inundative releases. Typical release rates are 0.01 wasps per ft.^{2} [0.15 per m^2] each week (preventive), 0.05 wasps per ft.^{2} [0.5 per m^2] each week for at least three weeks (curative), and 0.05 wasps per ft.² [0.5 per m²] twice weekly for six weeks (for infestations). Dense infestations should be managed with other tactics (compatible pesticides, predators) either in combination with or before releasing this wasp.

Aphidius ervi

This parasitoid resembles *A. colemani*, but is much larger and attacks different species of aphids. This species is used against *M. euphorbiae* and *A. solani* on such crops as tomato, pepper, eggplant, gerbera, rose, cucumber, strawberry, and *Lisianthus*. *Aphidius ervi* develops from egg to adult in twelve to twenty-six days at 75.5 and 57°F (24 and 14°C, respectively). The mummy is yellowish brown in color. One female wasp can lay over 300 eggs. This species is most frequently used as a preventative measure by making weekly introductions of less than one wasp per 108 ft.² [1 per 10 m²] or by using a banker plant system of barley plants infested with the nonpest aphid *Metopolophium dirhodum* (Walker). In suppressing existing aphid infestations, this species is recommended for use with *A. aphidimyza* and *H. axyridis*.

Parasitoids of whiteflies

Encarsia formosa

This is the most commonly used and best-studied parasitoid in protected culture. In this thelytokous species, virtually all individuals are females (0.02 in. [0.6 mm] long) with black bodies and yellow abdomens. Eggs are laid preferentially in third- and early fourth–instar whiteflies. At 73.4°F (23°C), the larva pupates inside the host in ten days, and the adult emerges twenty days after oviposition by chewing a circular hole in the dead whitefly. The duration of this life cycle varies from fifteen to thirty-two days at 79 to 64°F (26 to 18°C). Parasitized *Trialeurodes vaporariorum* (Westwood) (greenhouse whitefly) last-instar nymphs become melanized and turn black. In *B. argentifolii*, however, parasitized nymphs remain transparent enough to allow one to see the parasitoid inside. *E. formosa* prefers to attack *T. vaporariorum* rather than *B. argentifolii*. Adults of *E. formosa* eat honeydew and host-feed on first and second instars. *E. formosa* can parasitize between 250 and 400 whiteflies and host-feed on thirty to seventy nymphs in a lifetime. Additional details on the biology and use of this species are reviewed by Hoddle, Van Driesche and Sanderson (1998).

Eretmocerus eremicus

This wasp, formally referred to as *Eretmocerus* sp. near *californicus* Howard, is a common, lemon-colored parasitoid of *B. argentifolii* and *T. vaporariorum* in the southern United States. *Eretmocerus* spp. differ from *Encarsia* spp. in several ways. In contrast to *Encarsia* wasps, which lay eggs inside hosts, *Eretmocerus* species lay their eggs underneath the whitefly nymph. The first instar larva of *E. eremicus* burrows into the host, where it completes its development. *E. eremicus* will develop on younger instars than *E. formosa* will. Second- and early third–instars are *E. eremicus*'s preferred hosts for oviposition. The egg hatches three days after oviposition; two weeks later, a yellow pupa is visible inside the host. The total life cycle takes seventeen to twenty days, depending on temperature and the stage of whitefly attacked. *E. eremicus* kills many whiteflies by host-feeding, and in commercial poinsettia, most host suppression is due to host-feeding, not parasitization. In this arrhenotokous species, males comprise about 50% of pupae received from commercial producers.

Eretmocerus mundus

Eretmocerus mundus Mercet is a parasitoid of *Bemisia* species that it occurs naturally in the Mediterranean region. The biology of this species is quite similar to *E. eremicus*. However, producers claim that it may be better suited to manage *Bemisia* in areas with significant temperature fluctuations such as in Spain. This species has been commercially available in Europe since 2002 and is now available in North America. An adult female lays between 80 and 250 eggs. *E. mundus* parasitizes all instars of its host but prefers to attack second-instar whiteflies (Jones and Greenberg 1998). The adult female will also kill a significant number of immature whiteflies by host feeding (Malais and Ravensberg 2003).

Parasitoids of leafminers

Dacnusa sibirica

This endoparasitoid parasitizes all larval stages of its *Liriomyza* hosts. Adults (0.08 in. [2 mm] long) are dark brown to black, with long antennae (in contrast to *D. isaea*, which has short antennae). Eggs are laid preferentially in young host larvae (first or second instars), which continue to feed and to pupate. The parasitoid larva develops within the later developmental stages of the leafminer and the wasp emerges from the leafminer pupa. The developmental time (egg to adult) varies from seventeen to twenty days at 68°F (20°C), but it also varies according to the leafminer instar parasitized by the wasp. This species does not host-feed, and adults do not attack parasitized larvae. As the tempera-

ture increases from 59 to 77°F (15 to 25°C, respectively), the average number of eggs laid per female declines from more than two hundred to less than fifty. Consequently, both inundative and inoculative releases of this species are used predominantly during the winter season or in northern climates to suppress early infestations of leafminers (Minkenberg and van Lenteren 1986). This wasp will parasitize *Liriomyza bryoniae* (Kaltenbach), *Liriomyza huidobrensis* (Blanchard), *Liriomyza trifolii* (Burgess), and *Phytomyza syngenesiae* (Hardy).

Diglyphus isaea

This synovigenic ectoparasitoid causes significant mortality by host-feeding, which the female must do to support the production of her eggs. The adult (0.08 to 0.12 in. [2 to 3 mm] long) is slightly larger and has shorter antennae than *D. sibirica*. Female wasps are larger than males, and both are black and metallic green. When attacking a leafminer larva, a female first paralyzes the second or third instar with her ovipositor and then reinserts it into the mine to lay an individual egg on or near the host. The parasitoid larva feeds externally on the paralyzed leafminer larva, eventually pupating inside the leaf mine. Upon emergence, the adult wasp escapes the leaf mine by chewing a small exit hole through the leaf cuticle. The optimum temperature for oviposition by this species is 77°F (25°C), and the developmental time (egg to adult) ranges from thirteen to thirty-three days at 77 and 61°F (25 and 16°C). Under laboratory conditions, the female may lay between 200 and 300 eggs during her life span, which ranges from between ten to thirty-two days at 77 to 68°F (25 to 20°C). Oviposition rates and adult life spans are likely to be significantly lower in conditions typical of protected culture (Heinz 1996, Heinz and Parrella 1990a). The abilities of this parasitoid to increase rapidly and to be effective at warm temperatures are its most important advantages compared to *D. sibirica*. Inundative or seasonal inoculative releases of this species have been used to manage *L. bryoniae*, *L. huidobrensis*, *L. trifolii*, and *P. syngenesiae* (Minkenberg and van Lenteren 1986, Johnson and Hara 1987, Heinz and Parrella 1990b).

Other parasitoids

Leptomastix dactylopii

This encyrtid parasitoid can be used to manage citrus mealybug, *P. citri*. This wasp does not parasitize other mealybugs commonly found in protected culture. The adult wasp (0.12 in. [3 mm] long) is yellow-brown and parasitizes large female citrus mealybug nymphs and adults. One egg is usually laid inside each host, and the larva develops through four instars before pupating. Once the parasitoid pupates, the mealybug mummy becomes brown and swollen, resembling a grain of brown rice. To emerge, the parasitoid adult chews a circular hole in the mummy. Each wasp can parasitize fifty to one hundred mealybugs and can live relatively long if given food and high humidity. The life cycle ranges from twelve to forty-five days at 95 to 64°F (35 to 18°C), respectively. *Leptomastix dactylopii* is most effective when the mealybug density is very low, provided it is released directly into areas where mealybugs occur (due to the parasitoid's poor dispersal ability). Dense mealybug populations should be treated with selective pesticides prior to making parasitoid releases, or *L. dactylopii* should be used in conjunction with other mealybug natural enemies such as *C. montrouzieri*, *Anagyrus pseudococci* (Girault), and *Leptomastidea abnormis* (Girault).

Trichogramma spp.

Various species of *Trichogramma* (e.g. *Trichogramma evanescens* [Westwood], *T. brassicae* Bezdenko, *T. pretiosum* Riley and *T. voegelei* Pintureau) are used against moth and butterfly species damaging greenhouse vegetable crops like *Chrysodeixis chalcites* Esper, *Lacanobia oleracea* (L.), *Mamestra brassicae* (L.), *Spodoptera exigua* Hübner, *Autographa gamma* (L.) and *Keiferia lycopersicella* (Walshingham), or to protect ornamental plants against various tortricids (e.g. *Clepsis spectrana* Treitschke and *Cacoecimorpha pronubana* [Hübner]). The adult females are extremely small and lay their eggs in the host moth's egg. One egg is laid per moth egg and the *Trichogramma* larva hatches from the egg 24 to 48 hours after being laid. *Trichogramma* are sold as parasitized moth eggs that are either loosely packaged or glued to pieces of cardboard. Adults emerge 2 to 3 days after shipment. A relative humidity above 60% and temperatures between 68 to 81°F (20 to 27 °C) are required for optimum hatching. Adult wasps will feed on nectar, honeydew, and pollen. Both preventive and curative inundative releases of parasitoids are used. Usually, repeated releases are needed (5-8, weekly) with doses ranging from 5 (preventive releases) to 20 parasitoids (curative releases) per m². Very little has been published on using *Trichogramma* spp. in protected culture (see chapter 18).

Pathogens

Insect pathogens, generally applied as commercially formulated biopesticides in protected culture, include bacteria, fungi, viruses, and protozoa. These biopesticides contain either the living microbe or its chemical byproducts, and they are regulated as pesticides in most countries. Such products must meet criteria concerning safety, purity, and, in some countries, efficacy. Because of the cost of such registrations, the number of products available for use in protected culture is limited (see tables 6.4, 6.5, and 6.6). Consequently, we discuss only species that are commercially available. We will discuss nematodes separately.

Bacteria

Many bacteria are associated with insects; however, very little is known about many of them and only a few have been commercialized. The most important, *Bacillus thuringiensis* Berliner (Bt), was first commercialized in 1938. This bacterium has been widely used by gardeners and commercial growers for the control of certain caterpillars. However, commercial Bt products are not truly biological control agents because their activity is the result of a toxin the bacteria produce during the fermentation process. The formulated material contains a protein called a delta endotoxin, which is sprayed on plants or the soil surface to kill worms, beetles, and fly larvae. The toxin must be ingested to

Table 6.4. Commercially Available Bacterial Pathogens and Their Target Pests.

Bacterial Pathogen	Target Pests
Bacillus thuringiensis Berliner *kurstaki*	Lepidopteran larvae
B. thuringiensis aizawai	Lepidopteran larvae, especially those that are not susceptible to *B. thuringiensis* var. *kurstaki*
B. thuringiensis israelensis	Diptera larvae (mosquitoes, black flies, and fungus gnats)
B. thuringiensis tenebrionis	Coleoptera (esp. the Colorado potato beetle, *Leptinotarsa decemlineata*) (Say)
B. thuringiensis japonensis strain *buibui*	Soil-inhabiting beetles
B. thuringiensis aizawai encapsulated delta-endotoxins	Lepidopteran larvae
B. thuringiensis kurstaki encapsulated delta-endotoxins	Lepidopteran larvae and some beetles
Bacillus sphaericus Neide	Mosquito larvae

Table 6.5. Commercially Available Viral Pathogens (All Baculoviridae) and Their Target Pests.

Viral Pathogen	Target Pests
Adoxophyes orana granulovirus	Summerfruit tortrix (*Adoxophyes orana* Fischer von Röslarstamm)
Anagrapha falcifera NPV	Lepidopteran larvae, celery looper (*Anagrapha falcifera* [Kirby])
Anticarsia gemmatalis NPV	*Anticarsia gemmatalis* Hübner and *Diatreae saccharalis* (Speyer)
Autographa californica NPV	Lepidopteran larvae
Cydia pomonella granulovirus	*Cydia pomonella* (L.)
Helicoverpa zea NPV	*Heliothis* and *Helicoverpa* species
Lymantria dispar NPV	*Lymantria dispar* L.
Mamestra brassicae NPV	Lepidopteran larvae
Neodiprion lecontei, NPV	Sawflies
Spodoptera exigua NPV	Beet armyworm (*Spodoptera exigua* [Hübner])
Syngrapha falcifera NPV	*Heliothis* and *Heliocoverpa* spp.

poison the target pest. Labels of commercial products indicate the toxin concentration (in international units) and describe how best to use the product.

Products may contain any of several Bt strains: *kurstaki*, *tenebrionis*, *san diego*, *israelensis*, or *aizawai*. Strains differ in the pests they kill. Most strains kill caterpillars, or fly larvae, or some beetles. For example, *B. thuringiensis* var. *kurstaki* kills over one hundred species of caterpillars (Lepidoptera). Disease outbreaks do not occur when these products are applied because transmission between hosts is poor. Genetic engineering of *B. thuringiensis* has added new genes to this

species, resulting in products with several toxins. In addition, genes to express Bt toxins have been genetically engineered into many crop plants. This is a very active area of research, as well as a catalyst for debate on the utility and ethics of transforming agricultural plants and animals.

Bacterial products sold commercially for insect control that do not contain live bacteria are not considered to be biological control agents. Rather, these are chemical pesticides based on the endotoxin as the active ingredient. Other biopesticides contain the bacteria *Bacillus papilliae* Dutky, *Bacillus sphaericus* Neide, or *Serratia entomophila* (Grimont et

Table 6.6. Commercially Available Fungal Pathogens (All Deuteromycetes) and Their Target Pests.

Fungal Pathogen	Target Pests
Beauveria bassiana (Balsamo) Vuillemin	Whiteflies, thrips, and soil-inhabiting beetles
Beauveria brongniartii (Saccardo) Petch	Soil-inhabiting beetles
Metarhizium anisopliae (Metschnikow) Sorokin	Coleoptera, Lepidoptera, cockroaches, and termites
Metarhizium flavoviride Gams and Rozsypa	Grasshoppers and locusts
Paecilomyces fumosoroseus (Wize) Brown and Smith	Whiteflies, thrips, and spider mites
Verticillium lecanii (Zimmerman) Viégas	Aphids, thrips, and whiteflies

al. 1988). These products, however, are not useful against pests in protected culture.

Viruses

Viruses have not been as widely accepted as bacterial biopesticides, even though insect viruses are highly host-specific and significantly different from those that cause disease in vertebrates and plants. Economically, their high host specificity is a limiting factor because the returns of costs associated with product registrations are low. A product that has activity on a single host or at best a very limited number of hosts will, in general, offer limited economic incentives for its commercialization. However, there are some viral pesticides registered in the United States for control of Lepidoptera. Each product contains a nuclear polyhedrosis virus (NPV), consisting of rod-shaped, elongated particles that are enclosed in crystalline protein matrices (called occlusion bodies) that protect virus particles from environmental adversities. Potency of a particular product is expressed in OBs/ml (occlusion bodies/milliliter). In Europe, two products exist that contain members of another group, the granulosis viruses.

Insect viruses attack and multiply within cells located in the hemolymph, trachea, fat bodies, and epithelium. Gypchek (*Lymantria dispar* nuclear polyhedrosis virus) is registered for the control of gypsy moth (*Lymantria dispar* [L.]), and Spod-X LC (*S. exigua* nuclear polyhedrosis virus) for the control of beet armyworm (*Spodoptera exigua*). These products must be ingested to kill the host insect, but they are somewhat slow to act compared with conventional pesticides (killing in one to seven days, depending on the size of larva attacked). Infected insects often crawl to an upper portion of the plant and die, where they rupture and release virus particles onto the foliage or soil, potentially starting a viral epidemic throughout the pest population.

Fungi

Fungal products have had less commercial acceptance than bacterial products. Because fungal biopesticides contain living cells, conditions such as humidity, temperature, and ultraviolet light levels must be within certain limits if acceptable results are to be achieved (Burges and Hussey 1971). Of hundreds of known entomopathogenic fungi, only a dozen species have been seriously considered for development as biopesticides.

There are several benefits, however, to using fungi. First, some fungi have limited host ranges, allowing them to be used with little harm to beneficial insects. Fungi are considered safer than chemical pesticides for the environment because they do not damage wildlife or contaminate food, soil, or water, as many conventional insecticides do. Second, fungi have the ability, if conditions are favorable, to multiply and cause an epidemic throughout the pest population (Burges and Hussey 1971). Greenhouse crops, which are grown under conditions with controlled temperature, high relative humidity and reduced solar radiation, offer a good physical environment for pest control using entomogenous fungi (van Lenteren and Woets 1988), especially with several species of Deuteromycetes.

Currently, many species of fungi are unsuitable for mass production or formulation into biopesticides, yet the prospect of using other fungi as biopesticides is good. In greenhouses, fungi are primarily used to suppress whiteflies and perhaps thrips. Both *Aschersonia aleyrodis* Webber and *Verticillium lecanii* (Zimmerman) Viégas are common pathogens of whiteflies (fig. 6.6). Products containing spores of these fungi either have been registered as biopesticides or are currently being evaluated for commercialization. Recent data indicate that *Paecilomyces fumosoroseus* (Wize) Brown and Smith and *B. bassiana* might also play important roles in control of whiteflies and other major pests of vegetable and ornamental plants in greenhouses (Fransen 1990; Osborne 1990; Osborne and Hoelmer 1990; Osborne, Hoelmer, and Gerling 1990; Osborne et al. 1990; Landa et al. 1994; Bolckmans et al. 1995).

Figure 6.6. Fungi, as the *Aschersonia* sp. shown here, reproduce by emitting spores that are typically positioned atop stemlike mycelia (white ring in photograph). Sporulation, which only occurs if environmental conditions are favorable, is a prerequisite to causing an epidemic. *Photo: Z. Landa.*

Aschersonia aleyrodis

This fungus is specific to whiteflies and occurs naturally in the subtropical region of the Western Hemisphere, causing natural insect epidemics (Berger 1921, Petch 1921, Mains 1959, Fransen 1987).

Verticillium lecanii

This fungus is a common pathogen of aphids, whiteflies, and coccids (Gams 1971, Hall 1976, 1980). It occurs less commonly in Orthoptera, Hemiptera, Thysanoptera, Coleoptera, Lepidoptera, Hymenoptera (Gams 1971; Hall 1980; McCoy, Samson, and Boucias 1988), and mites (e.g., tetranychids and eryiophids) (Gams 1971, Kanagaratnam , Hall, and Burges 1981).

Paecilomyces fumosoroseus

This species (fig. 6.7) is widespread throughout nature and is a pathogen of many different insect hosts. It is most commonly found infecting Lepidoptera, Coleoptera, and Diptera (Poprawski, Marchal, and Robert 1985). A Florida isolate of *P. fumosoroseus* is highly virulent to whiteflies and many other pests, and it causes epidemics that severely reduce whitefly populations in both greenhouses and open shade cloth–protected structures. This strain (PFR 97) is currently registered for use in the United States and Europe and has been evaluated in the laboratory and under greenhouse conditions (Osborne 1990; Osborne and Hoelmer 1990; Osborne, Hoelmer, and Gerling 1990; Osborne et al. 1990; Landa et al. 1994, Bolckmans et al. 1995).

Beauveria bassiana

This fungus is reported as a pathogen of many different insect hosts. Most of the host records for *B. bassiana* are from Lepidoptera

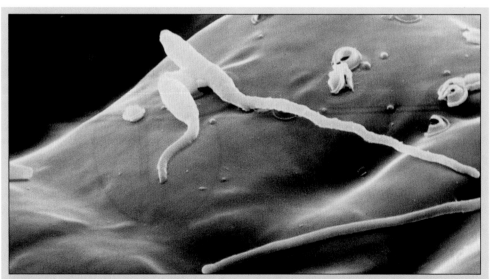

Figure 6.7. Germination tubes of *Paecilomyces fumosoroseus* penetrate the cuticle of a *Bemisia tabaci* (Gennadius). Contact with the host is necessary for this mechanical and chemical process of penetration to occur and to initiate whitefly mortality. *Photo: L. S. Osborne.*

and Coleoptera, but this pathogen has also been isolated from true bugs (Hemiptera), termites (Isoptera), and ants (Hymenoptera). After the emergence of *B. argentifolii* as a new pest problem in greenhouses in late 1986, isolates of *B. bassiana* able to infect this whitefly were identified and commercialized in the United States. At least one isolate has shown promise for the management of whiteflies. Infection and control of western flower thrips by *B. bassiana* has also been reported, but the levels of control vary substantially by geographic region, season, and crop.

Entomopathogenic Nematodes

Nematode biology

Entomopathogenic nematodes are small, colorless, and unsegmented cylindrical worms classified into nine taxonomic families, but only those in three—the Steinernematidae, Heterorhabditidae, and Rhabditidae—are reared commercially (or are in development) for use as biopesticides. Many species in these families have wide host ranges, and the infective stages of some species can be easily and economically produced and stored. Their microscopic size makes them very susceptible to desiccation, and consequently they show the most promise for controlling pests residing in soil or inside plant tissues (e.g., borers, leafminers).

Some nematodes actively seek out and penetrate susceptible hosts. These are called cruiser species and include *Steinernema (= Neoaplectana) glaseri* (Steiner) and *Heterorhabditis bacteriophora (= heliothidis)* Poinar. Other nematodes wait for a host to pass near them and then attack. These are called ambush species; examples are *Steinernema (= Neoaplectana) carpocapsae* (Weiser) and *Steinernema scapterisci* Nguyen and Smart. Once nematodes have penetrated a host, death is certain and occurs within twenty-four to forty-eight hours.

Eleven species of Steinernematidae and three of Heterorhabditidae are commercially available for use in protected culture (see table 6.7 for a list of the principal species used in greenhouses). These species are all obligate parasites of insects or slugs and thus are harmless to vertebrates and plants.

The effectiveness of nematodes in biological control is due to the presence of mutualistic bacteria within their guts. These bacteria in the genera *Xenorhabdus* (for steinernematids) and *Photorhabdus* (for heterorhabditids) produce antibiotics and toxins that assist in the infection process and in converting host tissues to food usable by the nematodes. Two forms of the bacteria exist. The first form promotes increased growth and reproduction by nematodes and is found in the infective stage of the nematode and in the pest insect during the early stages of infection. This form also produces antibiotics that prevent putrefaction of the host cadaver. The other form is more stable and occurs late in the infection process, but its function is unclear. Once the insects are dead, they turn a characteristic color, depending on which type of nematode is responsible: brownish yellow with the steinernematids, and red with the heterorhabditids.

The generalized nematode life cycle consists of an egg, four juvenile stages, and the adult. The third juvenile stage (frequently called a dauer) is the infective stage. All

Table 6.7. Principal Commercially Available Nematode Species and Their Target Pests.

Nematode Species[a]	Target Pests
Heterorhabditis bacteriophora Poinar (H)	Manure flies, caterpillars, weevil larvae, and other soil-dwelling insects
Heterorhabditis megidis Poinar, Jackson,	Various soil-dwelling insects
Phasmarhabditis hermaphrodita (Schneider) (R)	Slugs
Steinernema carpocapsae (Weiser) (S)	Caterpillars, beetle larvae, some flies, and other soil-dwelling insects
Steinernema feltiae (= *bibionis*) (Filipjev) (S)	Various soil-dwelling insects such as fungus gnats and banana moth larvae (*Opogona* spp.)
Steinernema glaseri (Steiner) (S)	Soil-dwelling white grubs
Steinernema riobravis Cabanillas et al. (S)	Corn earworm, mole crickets, and the larvae of citrus weevils

[a] Heterorhabditidae (H), Steinernematidae (S), and Rhabditidae (R)

members of this stage contain living bacteria and are free-living and motile. This stage has stored food reserves, and even though it does not feed, it can survive in an active state for several weeks when conditions are favorable.

Once a host is found, nematodes enter through natural body openings such as the mouth, anus, or spiracles. Heterorhabditids have a dorsal tooth that allows them to enter the host directly by penetrating the softer membranes found between insect segments (Bedding and Molymeux 1982, Poinar 1990). Inside the host's body, nematodes enter the hemocoel and release bacteria. The infected insect dies within twenty-four to forty-eight hours from bacterial growth (septicemia). The nematodes feed and develop on the bacteria cells and host body tissues. More

than one generation of nematodes can develop within the cadaver of a single host. The life cycle typically requires ten to twenty days at 82.2 to 64.4°F (28 to 18°C) (Martin and Miller 1994).

Steinernematids reproduce sexually in all generations. The number of generations, as well as the number and size of individuals within a generation, are thought to depend on host size and the amount of nutrition available to the nematodes. Small insects will die after being attacked, but they may not support a generation of nematodes.

Due to their microscopic size, nematodes are very susceptible to desiccation, and as a result, moisture has the greatest environmental influence on nematode biology. The activity and infectivity of one of the more commonly used nematodes, *Steinernema* (= *Neoaplectana*) *feltiae* (= *bibionis*) (Filipjev), are greatest at 25 to 40% soil moisture. Low moisture levels, rapid desiccation on leaf surfaces, and exposure to ultraviolet light are believed to limit the ability of nematodes to infect foliage-feeding arthropods. These factors can also significantly affect nematodes that are applied to the soil surface if they are not transported into the soil by ample irrigation immediately after the application.

Temperature also influences nematode biology, although the relationship is not quite as direct as with moisture. The relationships between survival, infection, developmental rate, and temperature all vary between species and strains. Some strains have a narrow range of temperatures over which they are effective. The strain selected for use in a given crop should be effective at the temperatures it will encounter in that crop; *Heterorhabditis marelatus* Liu and Berry, for example, is a cool-temperature species, whereas *H. bacteriophora* is a warm-temperature species.

Commercially available nematodes

Heterorhabditis bacteriophora

This species attacks the black vine weevil, *Otiorhynchus sulcatus* (F.), a serious pest of nursery stock. This nematode moves actively through the upper layers of potted soil to find hosts. Several biological factors work against the widespread use of *H. bacteriophora* for biological control within protected culture. The species is sensitive to low temperatures, and control declines when temperatures drop below 68°F (20°C). In addition, it has a poor shelf life,

and the infective stages are short-lived in the soil.

Heterorhabditis megidis

This species has also shown efficacy against black vine weevil larvae and pupae. Dependent upon pest densities, recommended release rates vary between 46,500 and 93,000 nematodes per ft.² (500,000 and 1,000,000 nematodes per m²) of soil surface. *Heterorhabditis megidis* Poinar, Jackson, and Klein is effective in soils where the temperature does not fall below 54°F (12°C) for at least two weeks following treatment. This nematode can remain active for about four weeks, as long as the soil conditions are suitable.

Steinernema carpocapsae

This species has been well studied and is widely used. It has proven effective against many pests, including webworms, cutworms, armyworms, girdlers, and wood-borers. It is an ambush species that waits for its prey to pass by. Therefore, it is most useful against prey that are highly mobile. *Steinernema carpocapsae* products have much better shelf life than do those containing *Heterorhabditis* spp. This is generally the case when comparing *Steinernema* species with *Heterorhabditis* species. *Steinernema carpocapsae* works best at temperatures between 72 and 82°F (22 and 28°C).

Steinernema feltiae

This nematode seeks out its prey in soil and is most often used in greenhouses to control fungus gnats (Sciaridae) and various other flies. It is frequently used in combination with predatory mites (*Hypoaspis* spp.) to control particularly problematic infestations. Effective management programs for sciarid larvae require routine preventative applications of nematodes. *S. feltiae* is most effective in moist soil that is between 59 and 68°F (15 and 20°C). These nematodes become inactive at temperatures below 50°F (10°C) and above 86°F (30°C), and hence applications during these conditions should be avoided. One hindrance to using *Steinernema feltiae* products is their relatively short shelf life.

Other nematodes

Although *Steinernema glaseri* and *Steinernema riobravis* Cabanillas et al. are commercially available, they are currently recommended for managing pests only in turf, citrus, and sugarcane.

References Cited

Bedding, R. A., and R. S. Molymeux. 1982. Penetration of insect cuticle by infective juveniles of *Heterorhabditis* spp. (Heterorhabditidae: Nematoda). *Nematologica* 28:354–9.

Berger, E. W. 1921. Natural enemies of scale insects and whiteflies in Florida. *Florida State Plant Board Quarterly Bulletin* 5:141–54.

Bolckmans, K., G. Sterk, J. Eyal, B. Sels, and W. Stepman. 1995. PreFeRal (*Paecilomyces fumosoroseus*, strain Apopka 97), a new microbial insecticide for the biological control of whiteflies in greenhouses. *Mededelingen Faculteit Landbouwwetenschappen, Rijksuniversiteit Gent* 60:707–11.

Brødsgaard, H. F., M. A. Sardar, and A. Enkegaard. 1996. Prey preference of *Hypoaspis miles* (Berlese) (Acarina: Hypoaspididae): Non-interference with other beneficials in glasshouse crops. *IOBC/WPRS Bulletin* 19 (1):23–6.

Burges, H. D., and N. W. Hussey. 1971. *Microbial Control of Insects and Mites*. London: Academic Press.

Carpezza, A. 1995. The specific identity of *Macyulophus* melanotoma (A. Costa 1853) and *Stenodemg* curticolle (A. Costa 1853) (Insecta Heteroptera, Miridae). *Nat. Sicil.* 19:295-298.

Chant, D. A. 1985. The Phytoseiidae: Systematics and morphology. In *Spider Mites. Their Biology, Natural Enemies, and Control*, Vol. 1B, ed. W. Helle and M. W. Sabelis, 3. New York (Amsterdam): Elsevier.

Debach, P. 1943. The importance of host-feeding by adult parasites in the reduction of host populations. *Journal of Economic Entomology* 36:647–58.

Dreistadt, S. H., and M. L. Flint. 1996. Melon aphid (Homoptera: Aphididae) control by inundative convergent lady beetle (Coleoptera: Coccinellidae) release on chrysanthemum. *Environmental Entomology* 25:688–97.

Fransen, J. J. 1987. *Aschersonia aleyrodis* as a microbial control agent of greenhouse whitefly. Doctoral dissertation. Wageningen, the Netherlands: University of Wageningen.

———. 1990. Natural enemies of whiteflies: Fungi. In *Whiteflies: Their Bionomics, Pest Status, and Management*, ed. D. Gerling, 187–209. Andover, U.K.: Intercept.

Gabarra, R., J. Arnó, O. Alomar, and R. Albajes. 1999. Naturally occurring populations of *Encarsia pergandiella* (Hymenoptera: Aphelinidae) in tomato greenhouses. *IOBC/WPRS Bulletin* 22 (1):85–8.

Gams, W., ed. 1971. *Cephalosporium—artige Schimmelpilze* (Hyphomycetes). Stuttgart, Germany: Gustav Fischer.

Gillespie, D. R., and D. M. J. Quiring. 1990. Biological control of fungus gnats, *Bradysia* spp. (Diptera: Sciaridae), and western flower thrips, *Frankliniella occidentalis* (Pergande) (Thysanoptera: Thripidae), in greenhouses using a soil-dwelling predatory mite, *Geolaelaps* sp. nr. *aculeifer* (Canestrini) (Acari: Laelapidae). *Canadian Entomologist* 122:975–83.

Grimont, P. A. D., T. A. Jackson, E. Ageron, and M.J. Noonan. 1988. *Serratia entomophila* sp. nov. associated with amber disease in the New Zealand grass grub *Costelytra zealandica. International Journal of Systemic Bacteriology.* 38:1-6.

Hagen, K. S. 1964. Nutrition of entomophagous insects and their hosts. In *Biological Control of Insect Pests and Weeds*, ed. P. DeBach, 356–80. London: Chapman and Hall.

Hall, R. A. 1976. A bioassay of the pathogenicity of *Verticillium lecanii* on the aphid *Macrosiphoniella sanborni. Journal of Invertebrate Pathology* 27:41–8.

———. 1980. Comparison of laboratory infection of aphids by *Metarhizium anisopliae* and *Verticillium lecanii. Annals of Applied Biology* 95:159–62.

Heimpel, G. E., and J. A. Rosenheim. 1998. Egg limitation in parasitoids: A review of the evidence and a case study. *Biological Control* 11:160–8.

Heinz, K. M. 1996. Space- and cohort-dependent longevity in adult *Liriomyza trifolii* (Burgess) (Diptera: Agromyzidae) mass-rearing cultures. *Canadian Entomologist* 128:1225–7.

———. 1998. Dispersal and dispersion of aphids (Homoptera: Aphididae) and selected natural enemies in spatially subdivided greenhouse environments. *Environmental Entomology* 27(4):1029–38.

Heinz, K. M., and M. P. Parrella. 1989. Attack behavior and host size selection by *Diglyphus begini* on *Liriomyza trifolii* in chrysanthemum. *Entomologia Experimentalis et Applicata* 53:147–56.

———. 1990a. Holarctic distribution of the leafminer parasitoid *Diglyphus begini* (Hymenoptera: Eulophidae) and notes on its life history attacking *Liriomyza trifolii* (Diptera: Agromyzidae) in Chrysanthemum. *Annals of the Entomological Society of America* 83:916–24.

———. 1990b. Biological control of insect pests on greenhouse marigolds. *Environmental Entomology* 19 (4):825–35.

———. 1994a. Biological control of *Bemisia argentifolii* (Homoptera: Aleyrodidae) infesting *Euphorbia pulcherrima*: Evaluations of releases of *Encarsia luteola* (Hymenoptera: Aphelinidae) and *Delphastus pusillus* (Coleoptera: Coccinellidae). *Environmental Entomology* 23:1346–53.

———. 1994b. Poinsettia (*Euphorbia pulcherrima* Willd. ex Klotz) cultivar mediated differences in performance of five natural enemies of *Bemisia argentifolii* Bellows and Perring n. sp. (Homoptera: Aleyrodidae). *Biological Control* 4:305–18.

Hoddle, M. S., R. G. Van Driesche, J. S. Elkinton, and J. P. Sanderson. 1998a. Discovery and utilization of *Bemisia argentifolii* patches by *Eretmocerus eremicus* and *Encarsia formosa* (Beltsville strain) in greenhouses. *Entomologia Experimentalis et Applicata* 87:15–28.

Hoddle, M. S., R. G. Van Driesche, and J. P. Sanderson. 1998. Biology and utilization of the whitefly parasitoid *Encarsia formosa*. Annual Review of Entomology. 43:645–49.

Hoelmer, K.A. and C.H. Pickett. 2003. Geographic origin and taxonomic history of *Delphastus* spp. (Coleoptera: Coccinellidae) in commercial culture. *Biocontrol Science and Technology* 13:529–535.

Hoelmer, K. A., L. S. Osborne, and R. K. Yokomi. 1993. Reproduction and feeding behavior of *Delphastus pusillus* (Coleoptera: Coccinellidae), a predator of *Bemisia tabaci* (Homoptera: Aleyrodidae). *Journal of Economic Entomology* 86:322–9.

Huffaker, C. B., ed. 1971. *Biological Control*. New York: Plenum Press.

Hunter, C. D. 1997. *Suppliers of Beneficial Organisms in North America.* Sacramento, Calif.: California Environmental Protection Agency.

Jervis, M. A., and N. A. C. Kidd. 1986. Host feeding strategies in hymenopteran parasitoids. *Biological Reviews* 61:395–434.

———. 1996. *Insect Natural Enemies: Practical Approaches to Their Study and Evaluation.* London: Chapman and Hall.

Johnson, M. W., and A. H. Hara. 1987. Influence of host crop on parasitoids (Hymenoptera) of *Liriomyza* spp. (Diptera: Agromyzidae). *Environmental Entomology* 16:339–44.

Jones, W.A. and S.M. Greenberg. 1998. Suitability of *Bemisia argentifolii* (Homoptera: Aleyrodidae) instars for the parasitoid *Eretmocerus mundus* (Hymenoptera: Aphelinidae). *Environmental Entomology* 27:1569–1573.

Kanagaratnam, P., R. A. Hall, and H. D. Burges. 1981. New or unusual records of plant diseases and pests. *Plant Pathology* 30:117–8.

Koch, R.L. 2003. The multicolored Asian lady beetle, *Harmonia axyridis*: A review of its biology, uses in biological control, and non-target impacts. 16pp. *Journal of Insect Science*, 3:32.

Lamana, M. L., and J. C. Miller. 1998. Temperature-dependent development in an Oregon population of *Harmonia axyridis* (Coleoptera: Coccinellidae). *Environmental Entomology* 27:1001–5.

Landa, Z., L. S. Osborne, F. Lopez, and J. Eyal. 1994. A bioassay for determining pathogenicity of entomogenous fungi on whiteflies. *Biological Control* 4:341–50.

LaRock, D. R., and J. J. Ellington. 1996. An integrated pest management approach, emphasizing biological control, for pecan aphids. *Southwestern Entomologist* 21 (2):153–66.

Lindquist, R., J. Buxton, and J. Piatkowski. 1994. Biological control of sciarid flies and shore flies in glasshouses. *Brighton Crop Protection Conference on Pests and Diseases 1994: Proceedings of an International Conference*, Vol. 3, British Crop Protection Council, 1067–72. Farnham, U.K.: British Crop Protection Council.

Liu, T. X., P. A. Stansly, K. A. Hoelmer, and L. S. Osborne. 1997. Life history of *Nephaspis oculatus* (Coleoptera: Coccinellidae), a predator of *Bemisia argentifolii* (Homoptera: Aleyrodidae). *Annals of the Entomological Society of America* 6:776–82.

Mains, E. B. 1959. North American species of *Aschersonia* parasitic on Aleyrodidae. *Journal of Invertebrate Pathology* 1:43–7.

Malais, M.H., and W.J. Ravensberg. 2003. *Knowing and recognizing, the biology of glasshouse pests and their natural enemies*. Reed Business Information, BA Doetinchem, The Netherlands.

Martin, W. R., and R. W. Miller. 1994. Commercialization of entomopathogenic nematodes in Florida. In *Pest Management in the Subtropics: Biological Control—A Florida Perspective*, eds. D. Rosen, F. D. Bennett, and J. L. Capinera, 207–18. Andover, U.K.: Intercept.

McCoy, C. W., R. A. Samson, and D. G. Boucias. 1988. Entomogenous fungi. In *CRC Handbook of Natural Pesticides,* Vol. 5A, ed. C. M. Ignoffo, 151–236. Boca Raton, Fla.: CRC Press.

McClure, M. S. 1987. Potential of the Asian predator, *Harmonia axyridis* Pallas (Coleoptera: Coccinellidae), to control *Matsucoccus resinosae* Beau and Godwin (Homoptera: Margarodidae) in the United States. *Environmental Entomology* 16:224–30.

McMurtry, J. A., and B. A. Croft. 1997. Life-styles of phytoseiid mites and their roles in biological control. *Annual Review of Entomology* 42:291–321.

Minkenberg, O. P. J. M., and J. C. van Lenteren. 1986. *The Leaf Miners* Liriomyza trifolii *and* L. Bryoniae *(Diptera: Agromyzidae), Their Parasites and Host Plants: A Review.* Wageningen, Netherlands: Agricultural University Wageningen Press.

Mori, H., Y. Saito, and H. Nakao. 1990. Use of predatory mites to control spider mites (Acarina, Tetranychidae) in Japan. In *The Use of Natural Enemies to Control Agricultural Pests*, ed. J. Bay-Petersen, 142–56. Taipei, Taiwan: Food and Fertilizer Technology Center for the Asian and Pacific Region.

Nordlund, D. A., and J. C. Legaspi. 1996. Whitefly predators and their potential for use in biological control. In *Bemisia: 1995 Taxonomy, Biology, Damage, Control, and Management*, ed. D. Gerling and R. T. Mayer, 499–513. Andover, U.K.: Intercept.

Osborne, L. S. 1990. Biological control of whiteflies and other pests with a fungal pathogen. *United States Patent No. 4,942,030.*

Osborne, L. S., and K. A. Hoelmer. 1990. Potential for using *Paecilomyces fumosoroseus* to control sweetpotato white-fly, *Bemisia tabaci*. In *Sweetpotato Whitefly-Mediated Vegetable Disorders in Florida: Proceedings of a Workshop Held at the Tropical Research and Education Center of the University of Florida, Homestead, Florida, February 1–2, 1990*, ed. R. K. Yokomi, K. R. Narayanan, and D. J. Schuster, 79–80. Homestead, Fla.: Institute of Food and Agricultural Sciences of the University of Florida in cooperation with the Florida Tomato Committee.

Osborne, L. S., K. A. Hoelmer, and D. Gerling. 1990. Prospects for biological control of *Bemisia tabaci*. *IOBC/WPRS Bulletin* 13 (5):153–60.

Osborne, L. S., G. K. Storey, C. W. McCoy, and J. F. Walter. 1990. Potential for controlling the sweetpotato whitefly, *Bemisia tabaci*, with the fungus *Paecilomyces fumosoroseus*. In *Proceedings of the 5th International Colloquium on Invertebrate Pathology and Biological Control*, Adelaide, Australia, August 20-24. Society of Invertebrate Pathology, Knoxville, TN, USA. Proceedings and Abstracts p. 386.

Osborne, L. S., J. E. Peña, R. L. Ridgway, and W. Klassen. 1998. Predaceous mites for mite management on ornamentals in protected cultures. In *Mass Reared Natural Enemies: Application, Regulation, and Needs*, ed. R. L. Ridgway, M. P. Hoffmann, M. N. Inscoe, and C. Glenister, 116–38. Lanham, Md.: Entomological Society of America.

Peña, J. E., and L. Osborne. 1996. Biological control of *Polyphagotarsonemus latus* (Acarina: Tarsonemidae) in greenhouses and field trials using introductions of predacious mites (Acarina: Phytoseiidae). *Entomophaga* 41:279–85.

Petch, T. 1921. Studies in entomogenous fungi: II. The genera *Hypocrella* and *Aschersonia*. *Royal Botanical Garden, Peradeniya Annals* 7:167–278.

Poinar, G. O. 1990 Taxonomy and biology of Steinernematidae and Heterorhabditidae. In *Entomopathogenic Nematodes in Biological Control*, ed. R. Gaugle and H. Kaya, 23–61. Boca Raton, Fla.: CRC Press.

Poprawski, T. J., M. Marchal, and P. H. Robert. 1985. Comparative susceptibility of *Otiorhynchus sulcatus* and *Sitona lineatus* (Coleoptera: Curculionidae) early stages to five entomopathogenic Hyphomycetes. *Environmental Entomology* 14:247–253.

Rice, M. E., and G. E. Wilde. 1991. Aphid predators associated with conventional and conservation-tillage winter wheat. *Journal of the Kansas Entomological Society* 64 (3):245–50.

Strong, W. B., and B. A. Croft. 1995. Inoculative release of phytoseiid mites (Acarina: Phytoseiidae) into the rapidly expanding canopy of hops for control of *Tetranychus urticae* (Acarina: Tetranychidae). *Environmental Entomology* 24:446–53.

Sütterlin, S., and J. C. van Lenteren. 1996. Hairiness of *Gerbera jamesonii* leaves and the walking speed of the parasitoid *Encarsia formosa*. *IOBC/WPRS Bulletin* 19:171–4.

Thompson, S. N. 1999. Nutrition and culture of entomophagous insects. *Annual Review of Entomology* 44:561–92.

Turlings, T. C. J., P. J. McCall, H. T. Alborn, and J. H. Tumlinson. 1993. An elicitor in caterpillar oral secretions that induces corn seedlings to emit chemical signals attractive to parasitic wasps. *Journal of Chemical Ecology* 19:411–25.

Van den Bosch, R., P. S. Messenger, and A. P. Gutierrez. 1982. *An Introduction to Biological Control*. New York: Plenum Press.

Van Driesche, R. G., and T. S. Bellows Jr. 1996. *Biological Control*. New York: Chapman and Hall.

van Lenteren, J. C., and J. Woets. 1988. Biological and integrated pest control in greenhouses. *Annual Review of Entomology* 33:239–69.

van Lenteren, J. C., L. Z. Hua, J. W. Kamerman, and X. Rumei. 1995. The parasite-host relationship between *Encarsia formosa* (Hym., Aphelinidae) and *Trialeurodes vaporariorum* (Hom., Aleyrodidae). XXVI. Leaf hairs reduce the capacity of *Encarsia* to control greenhouse whitefly on cucumber. *Journal of Applied Entomology* 119:553–9.

van Lenteren, J. C., H. J. B. van Roermund, and S. Sütterlin. 1996. Biological control of greenhouse whitefly (*Trialeurodes vaporariorum*) with the parasitoid *Encarsia formosa*: How does it work? *Biological Control* 6:1–10.

van Roermund, H. J. W., and J. C. van Lenteren. 1992. Life-history parameters of the greenhouse whitefly, *Trialeurodes vaporariorum*, and the parasitoid *Encarsia formosa*. Wageningen, the Netherlands: University of Wageningen.

Wright, E. J., and J. E. Laing. 1982. Stage-specific mortality of *Coleomegilla maculata lengi* Timberlake on corn in southern Ontario, Canada, a predator of the corn leaf aphid, *Rhopalosiphum maidis*. *Environmental Entomology* 11:32–7.

7

COMPATIBILITY OF PESTICIDES WITH BIOLOGICAL CONTROL AGENTS

S. A. Hassan
Federal Research Centre, Institute for Biological Control,
Darmstadt, Germany

and
M. Van de Veire
Faculty of Agricultural and Applied Biological Sciences, Ghent University,
Ghent, Belgium

The high efficacy, easy accessibility, and consistent performance of chemical control methods often make them the tool of choice for pest managers operating within protected cultures. Biological control is practiced on approximately 7% of the area covered by greenhouses (van Lenteren 1995). Further incorporation of biological control into standard pest management strategies will most likely involve the combined use of natural enemies and pesticides to manage pests, a concept initially proposed by Stern et al. (1959) as integrated pest management (IPM). Natural enemies and pesticides can be effectively integrated through knowledge of the pesticide to be used and its effect on natural-enemy populations (Bartlett 1964; Newsom, Smith, and Whitcomb 1976, Croft 1990). The simplest and most readily available means of integrating pesticides with natural enemies involves the use of two methods: temporal or spatial separation of pesticides from the natural enemies, or use of selective pesticides or rates. These two methods are addressed separately below.

Separating Natural Enemies from Pesticides in Time or Space

Temporal separation of pesticides and natural enemies can be accomplished in several ways. Applying pesticides with low residual effects prior to initiating natural-enemy releases is the simplest and easiest method for achieving integration. Natural-enemy releases follow the final pesticide application, after residual toxicity has declined to levels that will not adversely affect natural-enemy efficacy. Short-residual pesticides may also be applied when important natural enemies are in their most tolerant life stages. The pupae of natural enemies, compared to their eggs or soft-bodied larval stages, often represent the developmental stage most tolerant to pesticides. Examples include aphids mummified by *Aphidius colemani* Viereck, *Encarsia formosa* Gahan within the cuticle of fourth-instar whiteflies located on the undersurfaces of leaves, *Dacnusa sibirica* (Telenga) within leaf mines, and *Delphastus* spp. pupae located on the bottoms of pots.

Successful targeting of pesticide applications to the most-tolerant life stages of natural enemies and to the least-tolerant stages of the pest relies on accurate monitoring of both pest and natural-enemy populations by life stages. In many cut flower crops, temporal separation may be easily obtained by permitting natural enemies to operate prior to the growth of the harvested portion of the plant. Should the harvested portions possess near-zero damage tolerances, pesticides may need to be applied to achieve the desired level of crop protection. Using this approach, pesticides should be able to be applied with much less frequency because they are applied only during the latter portion of the crop cycle and after pest populations have been greatly suppressed by the activities of natural enemies.

Spatial separation of natural enemies and pesticides may be achieved by using several techniques. Spot treatments only in pest-infested areas greatly reduce the adverse effects to natural enemies, compared to treating the entire plant production area. Similarly, treating only the portions of continuous cropping systems containing plant material with near-zero damage tolerances will conserve natural enemies. Adoption of new technologies such as Global Positioning System (GPS) and site-specific pesticide-application equipment may provide the necessary tools for specifically targeting pest infestations in an economically feasible manner (Weisz, Fleischer, and Smilowitz 1995). Another practice that minimizes spatial overlap of pesticides and natural enemies may include applications of systemic versus foliar drenches of contact pesticides. Use of this method delivers specific toxins to the pest-infested plant parts rather than the entire surface of the plant.

Use of pesticide-resistant natural enemies represents an additional means of integrating chemical and biological control methods. Success in this area is limited to only a few natural enemy species, but there are opportunities for expansion (Beckendorf and Hoy 1985; Hoy 1990; Narang, Bartlett, and Faust 1994). Full implementation of this method will be limited until the release of resistant natural enemies is demonstrated to be consistently cost effective.

Identification of selective insecticides relies heavily on the availability of valid information on the effects of pesticides on natural enemies. This information is often a challenge to obtain because test results may vary significantly among crop species, varieties, cropping practices, and pest and natural-enemy genotypes. Further, the number of insecticides to be tested is virtually limitless. Interregional Research Project No. 4 (IR-4 Project)—a federal program within the U.S. that helps the producers of minor crops obtain registration for pest control materials—has assisted in obtaining 3,600 ornamental registrations for ornamental crops alone over the last thirty years. Nevertheless, such information is vital for development of effective IPM programs.

In the next section we will describe a testing program used for identifying selective pesticides. We also will summarize some of the results obtained to date from the use of this testing program. Finally, we will discuss some of the selective pesticides that are available for use in greenhouse IPM programs.

Methods to Assess Compatibility of Pesticides and Natural Enemies

No single test can provide enough information to fully assess the side effects of a pesticide on a beneficial organism. Rather, a series of tests are needed to examine various aspects of the overall effect of the pesticide. The process is conducted under increasing degrees of complexity that include laboratory, cage, and field tests. Pesticides found to be harmless to a particular beneficial species in laboratory tests are likely to be harmless to the same organism in the field (or greenhouse), but the converse is not necessarily true. Thus, materials that are harmless under the close confinement in a petri-dish test can be assumed to be harmless in the crop, and further testing under cage or field conditions is not needed. Materials that are harmful in the laboratory, however, might be less harmful in the crop due to rapid breakdown or dissipation of the material in the field by sun, rain, or other factors excluded from laboratory tests. For such materials, cage and field tests are important.

Development of standardized testing methods reduces duplicate testing of the same compounds and natural enemies in each country, and standardized tests facilitate the rapid exchange of results among researchers, regulatory agencies, and pest management specialists. Such methods have been developed and published by members of the Working Group "Pesticides and Beneficial Organisms" of the International Organisation for Biological Control (IOBC), West Palaearctic Regional Section (WPRS) (Hassan 1992, Vogt 1994). Specific descriptions of testing methods have been published for several natural enemies, including *Trichogramma cacoeciae* Marchal (Hassan 1977, 1980), *E. formosa* (Oomen 1985), *Chrysoperla carnea* (Stephens) (Vogt 1992), *Aphidoletes aphidimyza* (Rondani) (Helyer 1991), *Phytoseiulus persimilis* Athias-Henriot (Stolz 1990), and *Verticillium lecanii* (Zimmerman) Viégas (Tuset 1988). Results from tests conducted on twenty species of natural enemies by scientists located in thirteen different countries have been published previously (Franz et al. 1980; Hassan et al. 1983, 1987, 1988, 1991, 1994).

Laboratory tests

In laboratory tests, natural enemies receive a maximum challenge of the possible adverse effects associated with direct contact with a pesticide. Changes in survival and/or fecundity due to pesticide contact are measured in both the active life stages (the free-living adults, etc.) and the protected stages (such as parasitoids inside hosts, cocoons, or mummies). In separate tests, these different life stages are exposed to various residues from a pesticide to determine how long any harmful effects caused by fresh residues might persist.

Susceptible life stage test

Natural enemy life stages that by virtue of their small body size or feeding habits might be exposed to proportionately more pesticide are also tested. Such stages might include adult parasitoids and predators or the immature stages of mites and insect predators. Natural enemies are exposed to fresh pesticide deposits on glass plates, leaves, sand, or soil. Fungi and nematodes are exposed to pesticide residues by placing them in a broth, on agar, or on soil contaminated with the pesticide. Laboratory-reared or field-collected natural enemies may be used in the tests, provided each test uses natural enemies of the same sex and age. Natural enemies are tested against the highest recommended application rate of each pesticide. Adverse effects are measured for significant reductions in egg-laying capacity, lower parasitism rates, or increased mortality relative to a water-treated control. Results are categorized, using a relative scale from 1 to 4, with 4 denoting greatest harm: (1 for less than 30% of organisms adversely affected; 2 for 30 to 79% affected; 3 for 80 to 99% affected; and 4 for more than 99% affected).

Less-susceptible life stage test

Natural enemy life stages likely to be either less exposed to pesticides (those, such as cocoons or leafminers, found within hosts or in other protective structures), or to have larger body size relative to the quantity of pesticide they contact (e.g., adult mites and insect predators) are tested. Test methods and conditions are the same as described above.

Duration of harmful activity (persistence)

In this test, the intent is to determine how long pesticide residues remain toxic to natural enemies that contact a sprayed surface. Crop foliage or soils are treated, following standard field protocols and the Good Agricultural Practices (guidelines established to ensure a clean and safe working environment for all employees) used by growers. The surface on which the pesticide residue is created may be either the foliage of the crop or the soil. The treated foliage or soil are then aged in the field or

greenhouse where they are exposed to temperatures and lighting conditions typical of the crop. Natural enemies are exposed to the treated surfaces periodically until no harmful effects on test groups can be observed. Tests are terminated after one month if harmful effects are still detected after that time period. Other experimental design aspects described previously are also used in the current tests. Results are categorized, using a relative scale from A to D, with D denoting greatest harm: A, short lived (less than five days); B, slightly persistent (five to fifteen days); C, moderately persistent (sixteen to thirty days); D, persistent (longer than thirty days).

Cage tests

For materials found to be harmful in laboratory tests, subsequent tests are run on plants within cages placed in the field or held at field-simulated conditions. Tests are conducted on crop plants grown using standard practices and on which the chemical might commonly be used. Tests are commonly conducted in several regions or in conditions that reflect the climatic and cropping-practice variability commonly present. Tests are conducted on natural enemies already on the crop at the time of testing or on laboratory-reared or field-collected organisms of uniform age placed on plants as soon as possible after spraying.

The highest recommended application rate of pesticide is used, and applications are made according to the Good Agricultural Practices used by growers. Natural-enemy exposure to the pesticide-treated plants should be sufficiently long to permit occurrence of pesticide-induced effects prior to conducting evaluations. The experiments include both a water-treated control and a chemical standard as reference points. Natural enemy egg-laying and death rates, parasitism or predation rates, and population changes are compared among the various treatments. Reductions in the various life history variables due to pesticide exposure are scored on a relative scale, with 4 denoting greatest harm: 1, less than 25% reduction; 2, 25 to 50% reduction; 3, 51 to 75% reduction; and 4, greater than 75% reduction.

Field tests

Field tests may be run either by applying pesticides to populations of natural enemies that occur naturally in a crop or to natural enemies released into a crop after an application has been made.

Tests using naturally occurring organisms

In this approach, crops or soil populated by the native natural enemies of interest are sprayed with the test chemical at the highest recommended dose and recommended number of treatments, following Good Agricultural Practices. Tests are conducted at the appropriate time and season for normal use of the chemical and repeated at several locations. Releases of the target beneficial species into the test locations at other times during the test year are not permitted.

After a sufficient amount of time has passed for the natural enemy population to become well exposed to the pesticide, changes in population sizes of natural enemies are determined by measuring differences between pre- and post-treatment population density and mortality counts. Both a water-treatment control and a chemical stan-

dard are included as reference points. Experiments must be sufficiently replicated to permit statistical analysis. Test results are used to assign a compatibility score reflective of an increasing degree of mortality or population reduction: 1, less than 25%; 2, 25 to 50%; 3, 51 to 75%; and 4, greater than 75%.

Tests using released organisms

Most aspects of these tests are identical to the cage tests populated by native natural enemies. The key difference in these tests is the release of laboratory mass-reared natural enemies into the test plots just prior to the pesticide application. This ensures the presence of a large number of the species in the plot.

Selection of species for the tests

A dilemma facing any attempt to understand the effects of a pesticide on natural enemies is that it is not possible to test all species that may be exposed to pesticides. Since natural enemies vary in their response to pesticides, use of a mutually agreed-upon set of species as standard index organisms is a key feature in creating a standardized international testing system. The natural enemies chosen are intended to represent a cross section of biologies and to be relevant to the crops on which the particular pesticide is used.

Species selected by the IOBC Working Group as standard test species for various crops include five parasitic wasps (*T. cacoeciae, E. formosa, Leptomastix dactylopii* Howard, *Cales noacki* Howard, *Aphidius matricariae* Haliday), three predatory mites (*P. persimilis, Amblyseius andersoni* [Chant], *Amblyseius finlandicus* [Oudemans]), one green lacewing (*C. carnea*), two predatory bugs (*Orius laevigatus* [Fieber] and *Macrolophus caligi-*

nosus Wagner), one gall midge (*A. aphidimyza*), one coccinellid beetle (*Coccinella septempunctata* L.), three fungal entomopathogens (*V. lecanii, Beauveria bassiana* [Balsamo] Vuilemin, and *Beauveria brongniartii* [Saccardo] Petch), and one nematode (*Steinernema feltiae* [Filipjev]) (Hassan 1992).

Results of IOBC/WPRS testing of pesticides

International programs to test the effects of pesticides on natural enemies were started by the IOBC Working Group in 1978. Approximately 124 pesticides have since been tested, with each test pesticide being registered in at least one of the IOBC member countries. A number of fungicides, herbicides, and insecticides have been found to be compatible with the use of

several important natural enemies of major pests. These pesticides are recommended for use in integrated control programs (table 7.1).

Selective Pesticides for IPM in Greenhouses

Although the use of natural enemies of pests has priority in greenhouse IPM programs, biological control alone is often difficult or impossible to implement (van Lenteren 1987). The outcome of biological control is sometimes difficult to predict, and pesticides are important tools to remedy any deficiencies that may occur. In greenhouse vegetables, pest control programs depend primarily on the use of natural enemies combined with selective pesticides or selectively used pesticides. In ornamentals, controls are based

Table 7.1. Pesticides Found Compatible with Natural Enemies in IOBC Testing Programs.

Insecticides and Acaricides	*Bacillus thuringiensis*, buprofezin, benzoximate, diflubenzuron, clofentezine, dicofol, fenbutatin oxide, hexythiazox, pirimicarb, pyrethrum, piperonylbutoxide, pyriproxyfen, tetradifon
Fungicides	Anilazine, bitertanol, bupirimate, captafol, captan, carbendazim, chlorothalonil, copper-oxychlorid, ditalimfos, dithianon, flutriafol, hexaconazole, iprodion, mancozeb, procymidone, thiram, thiophanate-methyl, triadimefon, triadimenol, tridemorph, triforine, vinclozolin
Herbicides	Bentazone chlormequat, 2,4-D aminesalt, desmetryn, diclofop-methyl, metsulfuron-methyl, phenmedipham, propyzamid, tralkoxydim
Plant Growth Regulators	Alphanaphthyl-acetamid, naphthyl acetic acid

more on use of chemical pesticides, but selective pesticides support efforts to implement biological control methods.

For example, the success of biological control of the two-spotted spider mite, *Tetranychus urticae* Koch, encouraged greenhouse vegetable growers in European countries to extend the use of biological control to other pests in their crops, such as aphids. A variety of beneficial arthropods are being used commercially to control aphids in greenhouses, but often are not completely successful when used alone. Selective pesticides (such as pirimicarb, used in Europe but not currently available in North America) are often needed to correct poor biological control of aphids. This selective pesticide plays an important role in greenhouse vegetable IPM in Europe.

In recent years, pesticides with new modes of action have been developed that are useful as selective or partially selective materials in IPM programs. These include (1) microbial pesticides, (2) botanical pesticides, (3) insect growth regulators, and (4) other compounds of miscellaneous origin. The compounds of miscellaneous origin include abamectin, a fermentation product; diafenthiuron, a pro-insecticide that interferes with insect and mite respiration after the pesticide's photoconversion; pymetrozine, a feeding inhibitor affecting nervous control of the salivary pump of aphids and whiteflies; and several new compounds, such as pyridaben (use on aphids, whitefly, leafhoppers, and mites) and two pyrazole miticides, tebufenpyrad and fenpyroximate. In the following section, we will discuss various pesticides that may be useful in greenhouse IPM programs that include the use of natural enemies. Some of the compounds have widespread compatibility with natural enemies and hence are listed in table 7.1. The compatibility of compounds with natural enemies may be dependent upon various conditions. Comments reflect testing done in Europe by the IOBC Working Group, as well as results from tests conducted by scientists elsewhere.

Microbial pesticides

Microbial pesticides (based on bacteria, fungi, or viruses that attack insects) can be effective against their target pests, are harmless to humans, and, if used appropriately, have few adverse impacts on natural enemies. These pesticides are not persistent, act slowly, and have a narrow host range. In many cases, it is the lack of persistence (temporal and spatial separation from natural enemies) that confers compatibility with natural enemies. Control may be influenced by factors at the application site and so results may be variable. Monitoring and incorporation of additional controls into the IPM program are often important for successful use of microbial pesticides. Reliability of pest control provided by microbial pesticides may be enhanced when these materials are used together with natural enemy releases.

Bacteria

The bacterium *Bacillus thuringiensis* Berliner is marketed as a wettable powder that can be applied to plants using commonly available spray equipment. It is most efficacious when applied to young caterpillars, including *Mamestra brassicae* L., *Mamestra oleracea* L., and *Chrysodeixis chalcites* Esper, which often invade greenhouses. Early detection of these Lepidoptera species is possible with the use of pheromone traps placed within the greenhouses. The compound has very low residual activity, so repeated applications may be necessary if infestations are continuous. This low residual activity and high host specificity permit applications shortly before harvesting tomatoes. *B. thuringiensis* does not kill the beet armyworm, *Spodoptera exigua* Hübner or late larval stages of *M. oleracea*. Applications of this bacterium do not adversely affect natural enemies or pollinators currently used in greenhouses.

Fungal insecticides

Three fungal species are currently available for use as mycoinsecticides: *Beauveria bassiana, Verticillium lecanii,* and *Paecilomyces fumosoroseus.* Most efforts to commercialize the first material have taken place in North America, and those efforts are not considered here.

Verticillium lecanii is an insect pathogen that is particularly active against aphids and whiteflies (Hall 1980). *V. lecanii* has been shown to provide some control of spider mites (Rombach and Gillespie 1988, Helyer 1993) and only moderate control of western flower thrips (Vestergaard et al. 1995). It has often been used as a part of IPM programs in cucumbers and ornamentals (Osborne and Landa 1992). The *V. lecanii* strain 198499 was effective against several common pests of cucumber, but it was also able to infect the many parasitoids and predators associated with these pests. However, the pests are more susceptible than the natural enemies are, so sublethal doses could be used to minimize the pathogen's impact on natural enemies while still killing the pests (Askary et al. 1998).

Paecilomyces fumosoroseus (Wize) Brown and Smith, strain Apopka 97 was isolated from the mealybug *Phenacoccus solani* (Targioni-Tozzetti) (Bolckmans et al. 1995). In contrast to *V. lecanii, P. fumosoroseus* has a broader host range and, in addition to having pathogenicity to aphids and whiteflies, it can also infect the larvae of flies, moths, and beetles (Osborne and Landa 1992). The relative humidity requirements for *P. fumosoroseus* are less restrictive than those for *V. lecanii.* High RH (ca. 100%) is only required for the first twelve hours after treatment to stimulate germination of the spores and penetration into the insect body. Published research results suggest that its compatibility with natural enemies is highly variable. First-instar-convergent ladybeetle larvae, *Hippodamia convergens* Guérin-Méneville, exposed to *P. fumosoroseus* preparations in the laboratory experienced up to 56% mortality (James and Lighthart 1994). The larval development time of *Serangium parcesetosum* Sicard, a predator of whiteflies, increased when exposed to *P. fumosoroseus,* but adult longevity and feeding activities were unaffected (Poprawski, Legaspi, and Parker 1998). Conversely, acute and sublethal effects from the fungus were observed on the aphid parasitoid *Aphelinus asychis* Walker under conditions of low (approximately 55% RH) but not high (greater than or equal to 95% RH) humidity at 75°F (24°C) (Lacey et al. 1997).

Botanical pesticides

A variety of chemicals have been extracted from plants or microbial organisms for use as chemical pesticides. Of greatest interest for use in greenhouse IPM programs have been neem extracts (azadirachtin), nicotine, pyrethrin, and the microbial extracts avermectin and spinosad.

Azadirachtin

Azadirachtin is a pesticide made from the oil extracted from the seeds of the neem tree (*Azadirachta indica* A. Juss.), which has properties compatible with the use of natural enemies. The extracted oil is a mixture of triglycerides, organic sulfur compounds, and limonoids. One of these limonoids, called azadirachtin, is found in abundance in neem extracts. The extract disrupts mating and sexual communication, repels both larvae and adults, deters females from laying eggs, disrupts or inhibits the development of eggs, larvae, or pupae, sterilizes adults, deters feeding and inhibits chitin formation. At present, blocking larval molting appears to be neem's most important insecticidal property (Anon. 1992). Azadirachtin formulations are registered in the United States for the control of aphids, armyworms, caterpillars, gypsy moths, leafhoppers, leafminers, psyllids, thrips, and whiteflies on outdoor ornamentals, trees, and shrubs (Agridyne 1993).

Compatibility of this compound varies substantially among the species tested. Direct exposure to the pesticide significantly reduced or completely eliminated oviposition in the adult seven-spotted lady beetle, *C. septempunctata* (Banken and Stark 1998). Other symptoms of exposure included delay or prevention of pupation, blackening of the pupal case, formation of pupal/adult intermediates, and deformation of wings and elytra in adults (Ibid.). Few to no adverse effects were detected in laboratory assays with two predatory mites, *P. persimilis* and *Neoseiulus cucumeris* (Oudemans), and

the predatory midge of aphids, *A. aphidimyza* (Spollen and Isman 1996). When applied at recommended rates, infectivity rates of three entomopathogenic nematode species—*Steinernema carpocapsae* (Steiner), *S. glaseri* (Steiner), and *S. feltiae*—were not adversely affected by applications of a commercial neem product (Stark 1996). When applied after an application of nuclear polyhedrosis virus, mortality to second-instar Lepidoptera larvae was reduced (relative to use of the virus alone), presumably because of a reduction in feeding by the insects after ingestion of the compound (Cook et al. 1997).

Nicotine

Nicotine is a pure chemical isolated from the tobacco plant (*Nicotiana tabacum* L.). The compound is no longer sold in Belgium, the Netherlands, or the U.S.A. due to its toxicity, but it is still available in the United Kingdom, where it is used for aphid control. Nicotine is a toxic, broad-spectrum insecticide, but is not persistent because the compound is rapidly decomposed by sunlight or by microbes (Olkowski, Daar and Olkowski 1991). As such, it can be integrated into an IPM program based on repeated natural enemy releases. It is less suitable for use in programs of seasonal inoculative release—in which long-term growth of a natural-enemy population is important—because fumigation and spray formulations of nicotine are toxic to nymphs and adults of most beneficial organisms up to one week after application.

Pyrethrin

Extracts of the plant *Tanacetum cinerariifolium* de Visiani are called pyrethrins or pyrethrum. These materials are broad-spectrum contact insecticides with a rapid paralytic effect ("knockdown"). But these compounds are very susceptible to decomposition by sunlight and hence are not persistent. Like nicotine, pyrethrin products are toxic to nymphs and adults of most beneficial arthropods. However, due to their fast decomposition, the compounds can possibly be used in IPM programs, if a safety period of a couple of weeks is observed.

Avermectins

Abamectin, a mixture of 80% avermectine B1a and 20% avermectine B1b, is a macrocyclic lactone fermentation product produced by the soil microorganism *Streptomyces avermitilis* Burg. It is toxic to phytophagous mites, thrips, and leafminers. Abamectin acts by stimulating the release of gamma aminobutyric acid, an inhibitory neurotransmitter in arthropods. The product photodegrades rapidly (Dybas 1989). Field experiments conducted under high light intensity indicate that abamectin can be used selectively for the control of leafminers since it does not affect development of *D. isaea* (Weintraub and Horowitz 1998). In greenhouse experiments, combined treatment of abamectin and *E. formosa* maintained significantly lower densities of whiteflies on poinsettia throughout the season, with fewer abamectin applications than needed when using abamectin alone. Moreover, the percentage of parasitism did not differ significantly between plants treated with or without abamectin (Zchori-Fein, Roush, and Sanderson 1994). The mummy stage of *Aphelinus semiflavus* Howard and *Diaeretiella rapae* (McIntosh) are resistant to abamectin in concentrations that are lethal to green peach aphid, *Myzus persicae* Sulzer (Shean and Cranshaw 1991). In laboratory experiments, conducted in unknown light

conditions, abamectin was toxic to the larvae and adults of the coccinellid mite predator, *Stethorus punctum* (LeConte) (Biddinger and Hull 1995).

Spinosad

Spinosad is a recently developed insecticide derived from the fermentation products of *Saccaropolyspora spinosa*, a natural occurring bacteria. The product is highly active on western flower thrips and on caterpillars and leafminers to some extent. Spinosad uniquely alters the function of nicotinic and GABA-gated ion channels (Salgado, 1998) in a manner consistent with the observed neuronal excitation. The compound displays a high level of selectivity towards important beneficial organisms (*O. laevigatus, M. caliginosus, Neoseiulus californicus* [McGregor]). Spinosad is toxic to the parasitic wasp *E. formosa*, and the predatory bug *O. laevigatus*, when they are exposed shortly after treatment, but their populations are not seriously affected when they are exposed to 2 to 3 week old residues (Van de Veire and Tirry 2003).

Insect growth regulators (IGRs)

IGRs are chemicals that kill insects by interfering with the mechanisms controlling their growth. Some IGRs are juvenile-hormone mimics or juvenile-hormone analogues (Rudolph 1988). Such products do not kill within larval stages and thus do not provide rapid control of caterpillars or leafminers. They can, however, be used effectively to manage whitefly populations. IGRs discussed below include pyriproxifen, buprofezin, cyromazine, benzoylphenyl urea, and tebufenozide.

Pyriproxyfen

This synthetic juvenile hormone affects the physiology of molting and egg production in insects. The compound is effective against the whiteflies *T. vaporariorum* (Van de Veire 1995) and *Bemisia tabaci* Gennadius (= *Bemisia argentifolii* Bellows and Perring) (Ishaaya and Horowitz 1992, 1995), the aphid *M. persicae* (Hatakoshi et al. 1991), and *Thrips palmi* Karny (Nagai 1990). The product has strong translaminar activity and is able to reach and affect insects — in appropriate developmental stages — located on the underside of the leaves (Ishaaya, De Cock, and Degheele 1994). With the exception of *E. formosa*, this compound can be used effectively in combination with natural enemies for whitefly control. Laboratory tests of the effects of pyriproxyfen on the larvae, pupae, and adults of the three endoparasitoids of the silverleaf whitefly, *B. argentifolii*, revealed that the compound was safe to *Encarsia pergandiella* Howard, relatively safe to *Encarsia transvena* (Timberlake), but relatively toxic to *E. formosa* pupae (Liu and Stansly 1997). Hoddle et al. (2001) were unable to detect elevated levels of mortality in *Eretmocerus eremicus* Rose and Zolnerowich adults exposed to twenty-four-hour-old pyriproxyfen residues on poinsettia leaves.

Buprofezin

Buprofezin suppresses insect populations by inhibiting molting of nymphs and oviposition of adults (Anon. 1987). It strongly affects the brown planthopper, *Nilaparvata lugens* (Stål), (Asai et al. 1983), whiteflies such as *T. vaporariorum* and *B. tabaci* (Ishaaya, Mendelson, and Melamed-Madjer 1988; Ishaaya, Blumberg, and Yarom 1989), and scales such as *Aonidiella aurantii* (Maskell) and *Saissetia oleae* Bernard (Yarom, Blumberg, and Ishaaya 1988). Buprofezin should be applied against immature stages,

especially the first and second instars. Buprofezin is highly selective and does not affect Lepidoptera, Diptera, or Hymenoptera. It is safe to most parasitoids and predators used in greenhouses for biological control. The compound is now registered in many countries.

Cyromazine

Cyromazine interferes with molting and puparium formation (Binnington et al. 1987). Treated larvae develop into malformed pupae. Emergence of adults is either suppressed or incomplete. Adult flies that contact the material are not killed, but a reduction in egg number and egg hatch has been observed as a result. Cyromazine is very effective against fly larvae, including species resistant to other insecticides (Friedel and McDonell 1985). It is very toxic to larvae of the genus *Liriomyza* (Parrella et al. 1982; Parrella, Robb, and Morishita 1982; Price 1983; Schuster and Everett 1983; Yathom et al. 1986). Cyromazine is highly systemic and can be applied to the leaves or drenched at the stem base or put in the irrigation tank on rock-wool cultures.

Benzoylphenyl urea

Benzoylphenyl urea compounds act as stomach poisons against larval stages of Lepidoptera, Coleoptera, and Diptera and prevent the next molt. Death is mainly caused by malformation of the cuticle, which causes a failure to molt correctly. Benzoylphenyl urea compounds include diflubenzuron and its analogues: triflumuron, chlorfluazuron, teflubenzuron, hexaflumuron, flufenoxuron, flucycloxuron, lufenuron, and novaluron. Teflubenzuron and hexaflumuron also affect psyllids and whiteflies. Flufenoxuron and flucycloxuron have both insecticidal and acaricidal action. These compounds have limited effect on beneficial arthropods, which makes them suitable for use in IPM programs.

Tebufenozide

Tebufenozide mimics the activity of insect-molting hormones such as 20-hydroxy ecdyson. Treated larvae show signs of premature molting within twelve to twenty-four hours after treatment, leading to double-head capsule formation and cessation of feeding; larvae die trapped within a double cuticle (Wing and Ramsay 1989, Wing and Aller 1990, Hsu 1991, Rohm and Haas 1994, Carlson 2000). Tebufenozide is important for the control of pest Lepidoptera in vegetables, cotton, and cereals (Smagghe and Degheele 1994). The safety to various important predatory beneficial insects and mites has been demonstrated (Brown 1994, Rohm and Haas 1994, Shimizu 1994, Smagghe and Degheele 1995, Jacas, Gonzalez, and Vinuela 1995, Carlson 2000). The selectivity of tebufenozide makes this compound suitable for controlling lepidopterous pests in IPM programs.

Miscellaneous new pesticides

New pesticides that have new modes of action and are found in novel chemical families are rapidly being developed for registration and will increasingly replace materials in current use. As growers adopt these materials, information on their compatibility with natural enemies will be required. This places a continuous and even increasing burden on researchers to conduct such compatibility tests. Examples of new materials include (1) new fungicides derived from natural products (e.g. strobilurins), (2) chloronicotinyl insecti-

cides such as imidacloprid (already widely used for whitefly and aphid control in greenhouses), thiacloprid, acetamiprid, thiamethoxam, (3) pyridine azomethin insecticides such as pymetrozine, , (4) mitochondrial electron transport inhibitors (such as pyridaben, tebufenpyrad, fenpyroximate, chlorfenapyr [Perrior 1993]) and (5) new acaricides such as bifenazate, a carbazate with unique mode of action; spiromesifen, an insecticide/acaricide, a new chemical class belonging to spirocyclyc phenyl substituted tetronic acids.

For most of these new materials, relatively little is known about their potential for use as selective pesticides in IPM programs. Exceptions are (1) pymetrozine, which is effective on whiteflies, aphids, and planthoppers (Fuog, Fergusson, and Fluckiger 1998) and is selective with respect to the currently used beneficial organisms, including the bumblebee *B. terrestris*, (2) bifenazate, and (3) spiromesifen. The last two compounds are effective on the two-spotted spider mite and are also very selective pesticides.

The Use of Pesticides in IPM in Greenhouses

In this section, we summarize current views about which materials (of those tested to date by the Working Group) are likely to be most useful as selective pesticides in greenhouse IPM programs. We have organized this material first by crop (for tomatoes, cucumbers, and sweet peppers only) and then by pest. Growers using this information should consult with extension authorities, as local conditions may vary. Also, information presented here is likely to become outdated as the registration status of materials changes.

Tomato

Greenhouse whitefly

The greenhouse whitefly, *T. vaporariorum*, is the main pest of protected tomatoes. Biological control with the wasp *E. formosa* is generally successful, but at low or high temperatures may be insufficient. The correction of poor biological control can be done with other biological control agents, such as the parasitic wasp *E. eremicus* or the predatory bug *M. caliginosus*, or with selective chemicals such as buprofezin or pyriproxyfen.

Buprofezin acts slowly. At a concentration of 75 mg active ingredient per liter, it efficiently controls the nymphal stages of the greenhouse whitefly, while pupae and adults are not affected (Van de Veire 1995). One or two treatments with this concentration efficiently control the greenhouse whitefly without adversely affecting *E. formosa* or the braconids *D. sibirica* and *Praon volucre* Haliday. Buprofezin may be used alone or in combination with parasitic wasps. However, the product should be used as a "corrective" agent rather than as the primary means of control, as whiteflies may develop resistance to this product (De Cock et al. 1995). Buprofezin is toxic to some beetles, including the ladybird *C. septempunctata*.

Pyriproxyfen causes young nymphs of greenhouse whitefly to stop developing at the prepupal stage and die (Yamomoto and Kasamatsu 1990). It also kills whitefly eggs (Ascher and Eliyahu 1988). Two treatments, fourteen days apart, at 100 mg active ingredient per liter gave excellent control of the greenhouse whitefly. Pyriproxyfen is toxic to nymphs parasitized by *E. formosa*, but this does not affect the success of biological control.

Pymetrozine is also a promising compound for greenhouse whitefly control when used at a concentration of 200 mg active ingredient per liter.

Leafminers

Leafminers of the genus *Liriomyza* can destroy a commercial tomato crop. Cyromazine provides excellent control of these pests. One application at 75 mg active ingredient per liter efficiently controls larvae of *Liriomyza trifolii* Burgess, *Liriomyza bryoniae* Kaltenbach, and *Liriomyza huidobrensis* Blanchard without harming the parasitoids *D. sibirica, P. volucre, E. formosa* or the predatory bug *O. laevigatus* (Van de Veire 1995; Van de Veire, Smagghe, and Degheele 1996). Because of this, cyromazine can be used to correct poor biological control of leafminers. Applications made as soil drenches (20 mg per plant) or through addition to the irrigation tank (for rock wool cultures) are also very efficient, but more insecticide is needed. Cyromazine has been used in greenhouse lettuce (*Lactuca sativa* L.) in Belgium with great success to control the *L. huidobrensis* (Van de Veire and Bleyaert 1990).

Spinosad can reduce leafminer populations substantially when sprayed at 125 mg active ingredient per liter. The product has a high level of selectivity to most beneficial species used in IPM in glasshouses.

Caterpillars

Some moth species may occur in tomatoes, including *Spodptera exigua;* the cabbage moth, *M. brassicae;* the vegetable moth, *M. oleracea;* and the turnip moth, *Agrotis segetum* (Denis and Schiffermüller). Larvae of these species are difficult to control with *B. thuringiensis* spp. (Moar, Osbrink, and Trumble 1986). Good control can be achieved with teflubenzuron (Nomolt) at 150 mg active ingredient per liter without adverse effects on the parasitic wasp *E. formosa.*

The moth *C. chalcites* can also be efficiently controlled with cyromazine, when sprayed at 150 mg active ingredient per liter (Van de Veire 1994) without harming *E. formosa* or *A. matricariae.* Tebufenozide is very promising for use in IPM programs on tomatoes. Spinosad controls *C. chalcites* when applied twice at 60 mg active ingredient per liter as a foliar spray.

Two-spotted spider mite

The two-spotted spider mite is an important pest of greenhouse tomatoes, but biological control with *P. persimilis* is very difficult. Selective chemical control of the spider mite can be achieved without adversely affecting the beneficial organisms used in the crop by applying a mixture of the ovicide hexythiazox with a larvicide such as fenbutatin oxide, bifenazate, or spiromesifen. Tebufenpyrad, applied at a dosage of 100 mg active ingredient per liter, efficiently controls *T. urticae* by contact and/or oral toxicity and does not harm the parasitic wasp *E. formosa* (Van de Veire 1995). Other promising compounds used in IPM programs on greenhouse vegetables for control of the two-spotted spider mite are fenpyroximate and chlorfenapyr. Fenpyroximate was slightly toxic to the predatory bug *O. laevigatus* (Van de Veire, Smagghe, and Degheele 1996) and the wasp *E. formosa* in laboratory tests. Chlorfenapyr, however, is moderately toxic to the preda-

tory bug *O. laevigatus* (Ibid.) and persistently toxic (more than twenty-seven days) to nymphs of the predatory bug *M. caliginosus,* a species used for whitefly control. It is doubtful whether this compound can be incorporated in IPM programs. Tebufenpyrad, fenpyroximate, bifenazate, and spiromesifen seem the most appropriate compounds for use against spider mites in IPM programs.

Aphids

When biological control of aphids (*M. persicae, M. euphorbiae, Aulacorthum solani* Kaltenbach) fails in tomato crops, selective chemical control can be achieved with pirimicarb or heptenophos without much harm to *E. formosa* or *M. caliginosus.* Imidacloprid (Elbert et al. 1990) and pymetrozine (Flückiger et al. 1992) are very effective aphicides; both compounds are also very toxic to whiteflies (Esters 1992, Flückiger et al. 1992). When systemically applied, imidacloprid can be used on tomato, where whiteflies are controlled with *E. formosa* — since the wasp does not feed on plant sap — but not together with *M. caliginosus,* which does feed on plant sap. Because imidacloprid also kills bumblebees, it can only be used on tomatoes if the flowers are pollinated manually. Pymetrozine is the most promising new chemical for aphid control. It efficiently controls all the aphids common on tomatoes without adversely affecting the beneficial species on the crop.

Fungal diseases

Fungal diseases in tomatoes are still being controlled with chemicals. Fungicides with few toxic effects on beneficial agents are available to control *Botrytis cinerea* Micheli,

Cladosporium fulvum Cooke, *Phytophtora infestans* de Bari, *Fusarium oxysporum* Gemend. Snyd. and Hans., and *Oidium* spp.

Sweet pepper and cucumber

Western flower thrips

Frankliniella occidentalis (Pergande) has become a major pest in sweet peppers and cucumbers in many European countries. Biological control of western flower thrips with species of *Orius* or predatory mites is sometimes difficult because of high initial thrips densities. In this case, the population can be reduced with a short-lived insecticide such as dichlorvos. One week after treatment, the biological control program can start.

Lufenuron at a rate of 100 mg active ingredient per liter and chlorfenapyr at a rate of 200 mg active ingredient per liter (applied two times with an interval of two weeks) efficiently controls western flower thrips in cucumber and sweet pepper in large greenhouses. However, in laboratory tests, lufenuron caused 80 to 90% mortality to the predatory bug *M. caliginosus,* and its effects persisted more than fourteen days. Greenhouse tests showed that lufenuron was toxic to *O. laevigatus* and *E. formosa* and was not compatible with the use of these beneficial species. In laboratory tests, chlorfenapyr was very toxic to *E. formosa* and *M. caliginosus* and moderately toxic to *O. laevigatus* (Van de Veire. Unpub. 1998). Lufenuron and chlorfenapyr can thus best be used either as spot treatments or to eradicate pest organisms at the end of the season. Spinosad efficiently controls the western flower thrips, when sprayed twice at 7 days intervals, with a concentration of 125 mg active ingredient per liter.

Two-spotted spider mite

The two-spotted spider mite, *T. urticae*, is a serious pest in greenhouse sweet peppers and cucumbers. Under normal abiotic conditions the predatory mite, *P. persimilis* efficiently controls this pest organism, but at high temperatures and/or low RHs mites can rapidly develop huge populations which cannot be controlled biologically anymore. Efficient selective chemical control can be achieved with hexythiazox, fenbutatin oxide, bifenazate or spiromesifen.

Aphids

If biological control of *M. persicae, A. gossypii, A. solani,* or *M. euphorbiae* fails, selective chemical control with pirimicarb or heptenophos can be carried out without much harm to the beneficial species used against these aphids. Imidacloprid, applied systemically at 2 mg active ingredient per sweet pepper plant, effectively controls *M. persicae* and *A. gossypii* without adversely affecting the biological control agent *O. laevigatus* (Van de Veire. Unpub. 1998).

Pymetrozine, applied at a dose of 10 mg per plant as a drench to the base of stems of sweet peppers grown in rock wool, efficiently controls *M. persicae*. When sprayed at 200 mg active ingredient per liter on cucumber plants, pymetrozine was also very effective against *A. gossypii*. It did not affect *O. laevigatus* nymphs, even when second-instar nymphs were continuously exposed to the pesticide spray deposit. When sprayed at 200 mg active ingredient per liter, pymetrozine is safe for the parasitoid *E. formosa* and relativele safe for the predatory bug *M. caliginosus* (Van de Veire. Unpub. 2002). Pymetrozine is selective, and this makes it very suitable for IPM programs, especially in greenhouse crops (Sechser 1996).

Caterpillars

The biological control of moth pests in sweet pepper with the predatory bug *Podisus maculiventris* (Say) or various species of *Trichogramma* wasps is still experimental. Caterpillars often occur locally in the greenhouse and can be controlled with spot applications of *B. thuringiensis,* teflubenzuron, or tebufenozide, without harming the beneficial agents used on these crops. Spinosad also controls a number of caterpillar species, when sprayed twice at 7 day intervals with a concentration of 60 mg active ingredient per liter.

Fungal diseases

The main diseases (gray mold and mildew) of sweet pepper and cucumber can be controlled with fungicides that are safe to the beneficial arthropods commonly used on these crops.

References Cited

Agridyne Technologies. 1993. EPA label restrictions and directions for use of azatin. *The IPM Practitioner* 15 (9):8.

Anon. 1987. Applaud, new pesticide (insect growth regulator), technical information. Tokyo: Nihon Nohyaku Company.

Anon. 1992. *Neem: A Tree for Solving Global Problems.* Washington, D.C.: National Academy Press.

Asai, T., M. Fukada, S. Maekawa, K. Ikeda, and H. Kanno. 1983. Studies on the mode of action of buprofezin. I. Nymphicidal and ovicidal activities on the brown rice plant hopper, *Nilaparvata lugens* (Stål) (Homoptera: Delphacidae). *Applied Entomology and Zoology* 18:550–2.

Ascher, K. R. S., and M. Eliyahu. 1988. The ovicidal properties of the juvenile hormone mimic Sumitomo S-31183 (SK-591) to insects. *Phytoparasitica* 16:15–21.

Askary, H., Y. Carriere, R. R. Belanger, and J. Brodeur. 1998. Pathogenicity of the fungus *Verticillium lecanii* to aphids and powdery mildew. *Biocontrol Science and Technology* 8:23–32.

Banken, J.A.O., and J. D. Stark. 1998. Multiple routes of pesticide exposure and the risk of pesticides to biological controls: a study of neem and sevenspotted lady beetle (Coleoptera: Corrinellidae). *Journal of Economic Entomology* 91:1–6.

Bartlett, B. R. 1964. Integration of chemical and biological control. In *Biological Control of Insect Pests and Weeds*, ed. P. Debach, 489–511. New York: Chapman and Hall.

Beckendorf, S. K., and M. A. Hoy. 1985. Genetic improvement of arthropod natural enemies through selection, hybridization, or genetic engineering techniques. In *Biological Control in Agricultural IPM Systems*, ed. M. A. Hoy and D. C. Herzog, 167–87. Orlando, Fla.: Academic Press.

Biddinger, D. J., and L. A. Hull. 1995. Effects of several types of insecticides on the mite predator, *Stethorus punctum* (Coleoptera: Coccinellidae), including insect growth regulators and abamectin. *Journal of Economic Entomology* 88:358–66.

Binnington, K. C., A. Retnakaran, S. Stone, and P. Skelly. 1987. Studies on cyromazine and diflubenzuron in the sheep blowfly, *Lucilia cuprina:* Inhibition of vertebrate and bacterial dihydrofolate reductase by cyromazine. *Pesticide Biochemistry and Physiology* 27:201–10.

Bolckmans, K., G. Sterk, J. Eyal, B. Sels, and W. Stepman. 1995. PreFeRal (*Paecilomyces fumosoroseus*, strain Apopka 97) a new microbial insecticide for the biological control of whiteflies in greenhouses. *Mededelingen Faculteit Landbouwwetenschappen, Rijksuniversiteit Gent* 60 (3a):707–11.

Brown, J. J. 1994. Effects of a nonsteroidal ecdysone agonist, tebufenozide, on host/parasitoid interactions. *Archives of Insect Biochemistry and Physiology* 26:235–48.

Carlson, G. R. 2000.Tebufenozide: a novel caterpillar control agent with unusually high target selectivity. In *Symposium Series 767, Green Chemical Synthesis and Processes*, ed. P.T. Anastas, L.G. Heine, and T.C. Williamson, 8–17. Washington, DC: American Chemical Society.

Cook, S. P., R. E. Webb, K. W. Thorpe, J. D. Podgwaite, and G. B. White. 1997. Field examination of the influence of azadirachtin on gypsy moth (Lepidoptera: Lymantriidae) nuclear polyhedrosis virus. *Journal of Economic Entomology* 90:1267–72.

Croft, B. A. 1990. *Arthropod Biological Control Agents and Pesticides.* New York: John Wiley and Sons.

De Cock, A., I. Ishaaya, M. Van De Veire, and D. Degheele. 1995. Response of buprofezin-susceptible and resistant strains of *Trialeurodes vaporariorum* (Homoptera: Aleyrodidae) to pyriproxyfen and diafenthiuron. *Journal of Economic Entomology* 88:763–7.

Dybas, R. A. 1989. Abamectin use in crop protection. In *Ivermectin and Abamectin*, ed. W. C. Campbell, 287–310. New York: Springer.

Elbert, A., H. Overbeck, K. Iwaya, and S. Tsuboi. 1990. Imidacloprid, a novel systemic nitromethylene analogue insecticide for crop protection. *Brighton Crop Protection Conference—Pests and Diseases 1990* 1–2:21–8.

Esters, M., ed. 1992. Symposium: Papers on the mechanism and mode of action of imidacloprid. *Pflanzenschutz Nachrichten Bayer* 45 (63):325–546.

Flückiger, C. R., H. Kristinsson, R. Senn, H. Rindlisbacher, H. Buholzer, and G. Voss. 1992. CGA 215944—A novel agent to control aphids and whiteflies. *Brighton Crop Protection Conference—Pests and Diseases 1992* 2–3:43–50.

Franz, J. M., H. Bogenschutz, S. A. Hassan, P. Huang, E. Naton, H. Suter, and G. Viggiani. 1980. Results of a joint pesticide test programme by the Working Group "Pesticides and Beneficial Arthropods." *Entomophaga* 25:231–6.

Friedel, T., and P. A. McDonnell. 1985. Cyromazine inhibits reproduction and larval development of the Australian sheep blow fly (Dipt.: Calliphoridae). *Journal of Economic Entomology* 78:868–73.

Fuog, D., S. J. Fergusson, and C. Fluckiger. 1998. Pymetrozine: A novel insecticide affecting aphids and whiteflies. In *Insecticides with Novel Modes of Action*, ed. I. Ishaaya and D. Degheele, 40-49. New York: Springer-Verlag.

Hall, R. A. 1980. Comparison of laboratory infection of aphids by *Metarhizium anisopliae* and *Verticillium lecanii*. *Annals of Applied Biology* 95:149–62.

Hassan, S. A.1977. Standardized techniques for testing side-effects of pesticides on beneficial arthropods in the laboratory. *Zeitschrift für Pflanzenkrankheiten und Pflanzenschutz* 84:158–63.

———.1980. Reproduzierbare Laborverfahren zur Prüfung der Schadwirkungsdauer von Pflanzenschutzmitteln auf Eiparasiten der Gattung Trichogramma (Hymenoptera: Trichogrammatidae). *Zeitschrift für Angewandte Entomologie* 89:282–9.

———, ed. 1992. Guidelines for testing the effects of pesticides on beneficial organisms. *IOBC/WPRS Bulletin* 15 (3):1–186.

Hassan, S. A., F. Bigler, H. Bogenschütz, J. U. Brown, S. I. Firth, P. Huang, M. S. Ledieu, et al. 1983. Results of the second joint pesticide testing programme by the IOBC/WPRS Working Group "Pesticides and Beneficial Arthropods." *Zeitschrift für Angewandte Entomologie* 95:151–8.

Hassan, S. A., R. Albert, F. Bigler, P. Blaisinger, H. Bogenschütz, E. Boller, J. Brun, et al. 1987. Results of the third joint pesticide testing programme by the IOBC/WPRS Working Group "Pesticides and Beneficial Organisms." *Zeitschrift für Angewandte Entomologie* 103:92–107.

Hassan, S. A., F. Bigler, H. Bogenschütz, E. Boller, J. Brun, P. Chiverton, P. Edwards, et al. 1988. Results of the fourth joint pesticide testing programme carried out by the IOBC/WPRS Working Group "Pesticides and Beneficial Organisms." *Zeitschrift für Angewandte Entomologie* 105:321–329.

Hassan, S.A., F. Bigler, H. Bogenschütz, E. Boller, J. Brun, J. N. M. Calis, P. Chiverton, et al. 1991. Results of the fifth joint pesticide testing programme carried out by the IOBC/WPRS Working Group "Pesticides and Beneficial Organisms." *Entomophaga* 36:55–67.

Hassan, S.A., F. Bigler, H. Bogenschütz, E. Boller, J. Brun, J. N. M. Calis, J. Coremans-Pelseneer, et al. 1994. Results of the sixth joint pesticide testing programme of the IOBC/WPRS Working Group "Pesticides and Beneficial Organisms." *Entomophaga* 39:107–19.

Hatakoshi, M., Y. Shono, H. Yamamoto, and M. Hirano. 1991. Effects of the juvenile hormone analog pyriproxyfen, on *Myzus persicae* and *Unaspis yanonensis*. *Applied Entomology and Zoology* 26:412–14.

Helyer, N. 1991. Laboratory pesticide screening method for the aphid predatory midge *Aphidoletes aphidimyza* (Rondani) (Diptera: Cecidomyiidae). *Biocontrol Science and Technology* 1:53–8.

———. 1993. *Verticillium lecanii* for control of aphids and thrips on cucumber. *IOBC/WPRS Bulletin* 16:63–6.

Hoddle, M. S., R. G. Van Driesche, S. Lyon, and J. P. Sanderson. 2001. Compatibility of insect growth regulators with *Eretmocerus eremicus* (Hymenoptera: Apelinidae) for whitefly (Homoptera: Aleyrodidae) control on poinsettias. II. Trials in commercial poinsettia crops. *Biological Control* 20 (2):122–146.

Hoy, M. A. 1990. Genetic improvement of arthropod natural enemies: becoming a conventional tactic? In *New Directions in Biological Control*, ed. R. R. Baker and P. E. Dunn, 405–17. New York: Alan R. Liss.

Hsu, A.C.-T., 1991. 1,2-Diacyl-1-alkylhydrazines: A new class of insect growth regulators. In *ACS Symposium Series 443—Synthesis and Chemistry of Agrochemicals II*, ed. D. R. Baker, J. G. Fenyes, and W. K. Molberg, 478–90. Washington, D.C.: American Chemical Society.

Ishaaya, I., D. Blumberg, and I. Yarom. 1989. Buprofezin, a novel IGR for controlling whiteflies and scale insects. *Mededelingen Faculteit Landbouwwetenschappen, Rijksuniversiteit Gent* 54:1003–8.

Ishaaya, I., A. De Cock, and D. Degheele. 1994. Pyriproxyfen, a potent suppressor of egg hatch and adult formation of the greenhouse whitefly (Homoptera: Aleyrodidae). *Journal of Economic Entomology* 87:1185–89.

Ishaaya, I., and R. A. Horowitz. 1992. A novel phenoxy juvenile hormone analog (pyriproxyfen) suppresses embryogenesis and adult emergence of the sweetpotato whitefly (Homoptera: Aleyrodidae). *Journal of Economic Entomology* 85:2113–17.

———. 1995. Pyriproxyfen, a novel insect growth regulator for controlling whiteflies: Mechanisms and resistance management. *Pesticide Science* 43:227–32.

Ishaaya, I., Z. Mendelson, and V. Melamed-Madjar. 1988. Effect of buprofezin on embryogenesis and progeny formation of sweetpotato whitefly (Homoptera: Aleyrodidae). *Journal of Economic Entomology* 81:781–4.

Jacas, J., M. Gonzalez, and A. Vinuela. 1995. Influence of the application method on the toxicity of the moulting accelerating compound tebufenozide on adults of the parasitic wasp *Opius concolor* Szèpl. *Mededelingen Faculteit Landbouwwetenschappen, Rijksuniversiteit Gent* 60/3b : 935–9.

James, R. R., and B. Lighthart. 1994. Susceptibility of the convergent lady beetle (Coleoptera: Coccinellidae) to four entomogenous fungi. *Environmental Entomology* 23:190–2.

Lacey, L. A., A. L. M. Mesquita, G. Mercadier, R. Debire, D. J. Kazmer, and F. Leclant. 1997. Acute and sublethal activity of the entomopathogenic fungus *Paecilomyces fumosoroseus* (Deuteromycotina: Hyphomycetes) on adult *Aphelinus asychis* (Hymenoptera: Aphelinidae). *Environmental Entomology* 26:1452–60.

Liu, T. X., and P. A. Stansly. 1997. Effects of pyriproxyfen on three species of *Encarsia* (Hymenoptera: Aphelinidae), endoparasitoids of *Bemisia argentifolii* (Homoptera: Aleyrodidae). *Journal of Economic Entomology* 90:404–11.

Moar, W. J., W. L. A. Osbrink, and T. Trumble. 1986. Potentiation of *Bacillus thuringiensis* var. *kurstaki* with Thuringiensin on beet armyworm (Lepidoptera: Noctuidae). *Journal of Economic Entomology* 79:1443–6.

Nagai, K., 1990. Effects of a juvenile hormone mimic material, 4-phenoxyphenyl (RS)-82-(2-pyridyloxy) propyl ether, on *Thrips palmi* Karny (Thysanoptera: Thripidae) and its predator, *Orius* spp. (Hemiptera: Anthocoridae). *Applied Entomology and Zoology* 25:199–204.

Narang, S. K., A. C. Bartlett, and R. M. Faust. 1994. *Applications of Genetics to Arthropods of Biological Control Significance.* Boca Raton, Fla.: CRC Press.

Newsom, L. D., R. F. Smith, and W. H. Whitcomb. 1976. Selective pesticides and selective use of pesticides. In *Theory and Practice of Biological Control*, ed. C. B. Huffaker and P. S. Messenger, 565–92. New York: Academic Press.

Olkowski, W., S. Daar, and H. Olkowski, eds. 1991. *Common-Sense Pest Control Handbook.* Newtown, Conn.: Taunton Press.

Oomen, P. 1985. Guideline for the evaluation of side-effects of pesticides: *Encarsia formosa. Bulletin OEPP/EPPO* 15:257–65.

Osborne, L., and Z. Landa. 1992. Biological control of whiteflies with entomopathogenic fungi. *Florida Entomologist* 75:456–71.

Parrella, M. P., K. L. Robb, G. D. Christie, and J. A. Bethke. 1982. Control of *Liriomyza trifolii* with biological agents and insect growth regulators. *California Agriculture* 36 (11/12):17–19.

Parrella, M. P., K. L. Robb, and P. Morishita. 1982. Response of *Liriomyza trifolii* (Diptera: Agromyzidae) larvae to insecticides, with notes about efficacy testing. *Journal of Economic Entomology* 75:1104–8.

Perrior, T. R. 1993. Chemical insecticides for the 21st century. *Chemistry and Industry* 15:883–7.

Poprawski, T. J., J. C. Legaspi, and P. E. Parker. 1998. Influence of entomopathogenic fungi on *Serangium parcesetosum* (Coleoptera: Coccinellidae), an important predator of whiteflies (Homoptera: Aleyrodidae). *Environmental Entomology* 27:785–95.

Price, J. F. 1983. Field evaluations of new pesticides for the control of leafminers, mites and aphids on flower crops. *Proceedings of the Florida State Horticultural Society* 96:287–91.

Rohm and Haas. 1994. Technical bulletin, Mimic®-Confirm®, tebufenozide (RH-5992). Philadelphia: Rohm and Haas Company.

Rombach, M.C., and A. T. Gillespie. 1988. Entomogenous hyphomycetes for insect and mite control on greenhouse crops. *Biocontrol News and Information* 9:7–18.

Rudolph, R. 1988. Developing the insect growth regulators. In *Boletin de Sanidad Vegetal Parasitis 88.* Proceedings of a scientific congress, ed. R. Cavallor and V. Delucchi, 271–82, Barcelona, Spain, 25–28 October.

Salgado, V.L. 1998. Studies on the mode of action of Spinosad: insect symptoms and physiological correlates. *Pesticide Biochemistry and Physiology* 60:91-102.

Schuster, D. J., and P. H. Everett. 1983. Response of *Liriomyza trifolii* (Diptera: Agromyzidae) to insecticides on tomato. *Journal of Economic Entomology* 76:1170–4.

Sechser, B. 1996. IPM fitness and selectivity. Chess, Plenum (active ingredient = pymetrozine), 7–25. Novartis Basle, Switzerland: Group IPM Services, Novartis.

Shean, B., and W. S. Cranshaw. 1991. Differential susceptibilities of green peach aphid (Homoptera: Aphididae) and two endoparasitoids (Hymenoptera: Encyrtidae and Braconidae) to pesticides. *Journal of Economic Entomology* 84:844–50.

Shimizu, T. 1994. Effect of RH-5849 on the emergence of *Apanteles kariyai* parasitoid from the common armyworm larvae, *Leucania sperarata. International Pest Control* 36:131–3.

Smagghe, G., and D. Degheele. 1994. The significance of pharmacokinetics and metabolism to the biological activity of RH-5992 (tebufenozide) in *Spodoptera exempta*, *Spodoptera exigua*, and *Leptinotarsa decemlineata. Pesticide Biochemistry and Physiology* 49:224–34.

———. 1995. Selectivity of nonsteroidal ecdysteroid agonists RH 5849 and RH 5992 to nymphs and adults of the predatory soldier bugs *Podisus nigrispinus* and *Podisus maculiventris* (Hemiptera: Pentatomidae). *Journal of Economic Entomology* 88:408–45.

Spollen, K. M., and M. B. Isman. 1996. Acute and sublethal effects of a neem insecticide on the commercial biological control agents *Phytoseiulus persimilis* and *Amblyseius cucumeris* (Acari: Phytoseiidae) and *Aphidoletes aphidimyza* (Diptera: Cecidomyiidae). *Journal of Economic Entomology* 89:1379–86.

Stark, J. D. 1996. Entomopathogenic nematodes (Rhabditida: Steinernematidae): Toxicity of neem. *Journal of Economic Entomology* 89:68–73.

Stern, V. M., R. F. Smith, R. van den Bosch, and K. S. Hagen. 1959. The integrated control concept. *Hilgardia* 29:81–101.

Stolz, M. 1990. Testing side effects of various pesticides on the predatory mite *Phytoseiulus persimilis* Athias-Henriot (Acarina: Phytoseiidae) in laboratory. *Pflanzenschutzberichte* 51 (3):127–38.

Tuset, J. J. 1988. *Verticillium lecanii*, hongo entomopatógeno que combate en los agrios al coccido "caparreta" (*Saissetia oleae*). *Phytoma Espana* 4:31–5.

Van de Veire, M. 1994. Toxicity of the insect growth regulator cyromazine on the tomato looper *Chrysodeixis chalcites* (Esper) (Lep.: Plusiinae). *Parasitica* 50:95–102.

———. 1995. Integrated pest management in glasshouse tomatoes, sweet peppers and cucumbers in Belgium. Ph.D. diss., Faculty of Agricultural and Applied Biological Sciences, Coupure Links, Ghent, Belgium.

———. 1998. Internal report

Van de Veire, M., and P. Bleyaert. 1990. Control of the leafminer *Liriomyza huidobrensis* (Blanchard) on glasshouse lettuce with the IGR cyromazine. *Mededelingen Faculteit Landbouwwetenschappen, Rijksuniversiteit Gent* 55 (2b):661–6.

Van de Veire, M., G. Smagghe, and D. Degheele. 1996. Laboratory test method to evaluate the effect of 31 pesticides on the predatory bug, *Orius laevigatus* (Het.: Anthocoridae). *Entomophaga* 41:235–43.

Van de Veire, M., and L. Tirry. 2003. Side-effects of pesticides on four species of beneficials used in IPM in glasshouse vegetable crops: "worst case" laboratory tests. *IOBC/wprs Bulletin,* 26 (5):41-50.

van Lenteren, J. C. 1987. World situation of biological control in greenhouses and factors limiting use of biological control. *IOBC/WPRS Bulletin* 10 (2):78–81.

———. 1995. Integrated pest management in protected crops. In *Integrated Pest Management,* ed. D. R. Dent, 311–43. London: Chapman and Hall.

Vestergaard, S., A. T. Gillespie, T. M. Butt, G. Schreiter, and J. Eilenberg. 1995. Pathogenicity of the hyphomycete fungi *Verticillium lecanii* and *Metarhizium anisopliae* to the western flower thrips, *Frankliniella occidentalis. Planta Medica* 5 (2):185–92.

Vogt, H. 1992. Untersuchungen zu Nebenwirkungen von Insektiziden und Akariziden auf *Chrysoperla carnea* Steph. (Neuroptera, Chrysopidae). *Mededelingen Faculteit Landbouwwetenschappen, Rijksuniversiteit Gent* 57 (2b):559–67.

———, ed. 1994. Side-effects of pesticides on beneficial organisms: Comparison of laboratory, semi-field and field results. *IOBC/WPRS Bulletin* 17 (10):1–157.

Weintraub, P. G., and A. R. Horowitz. 1998. Effects of translaminar versus conventional insecticides on *Liriomyza huidobrensis* (Diptera: Agromyzidae) and *Diglyphus isaea* (Hymenoptera: Eulophidae) populations in celery. *Journal of Economic Entomology* 91:1180–5.

Weisz, R., S. Fleischer, and Z. Smilowitz. 1995. Site-specific integrated pest management for high-value crops: Sample units for map generation using the Colorado potato beetle (Coleoptera: Chrysomelidae) as a model system. *Journal of Economic Entomology* 88:1069–80.

Wing, K. D., and H. E. Aller. 1990. Ecdysteroid agonists as novel insect growth regulators. In *Pesticides and Alternatives,* ed. J. E. Casida, 251–7. Amsterdam: Elsevier Science Publishers.

Wing, K. D., and J. R. Ramsay. 1989. Other hormonal agents: Ecdysone agonists. *Brighton Crop Protection Conference Monograph* no. 43. *Progress and Prospects in Insect Control,* 107–17.

Yamomoto, H. and K. Kasamatsu. 1990. Effects of a juvenile hormone mimic, S-71639 on the greenhouse whitefly, *Trialeurodes vaporariorum,* and the green peach aphid, *Myzus persicae,* in a greenhouse. In *Advances in Invertebrate Reproduction,* vol. 5, ed. M. Hoshi and O. Yamashita, 393–8. Amsterdam: Elsevier Science Publishers.

Yarom, I., D. Blumberg, and I. Ishaaya. 1988. Effects of buprofezin on California red scale (Homoptera: Diaspididae) and Mediterranean black scale (Homoptera: Coccidae). *Journal of Economic Entomology* 81:1581–5.

Yathom, S., K. R. S. Ascher, S. Tal, and N. E. Nemny. 1986. The effect of cyromazine on different stages of *Liriomyza trifolii* (Burgess). *Israel Journal of Entomology* 20:85–93.

Zchori-Fein, E., R. T. Roush, and J. P. Sanderson. 1994. Potential for integration of biological and chemical control of greenhouse whitefly (Homoptera: Aleyrodidae) using *Encarsia formosa* (Hymenoptera: Aphelinidae) and abamectin. *Environmental Entomology* 23:1277–82.

8

BIOLOGICAL CONTROL OF
WHITEFLIES ON ORNAMENTAL CROPS

M. S. Hoddle
Department of Entomology, University of California, Riverside, California

Whitefly Biology

Life stages

Whiteflies (Homoptera: Aleyrodidae) are small plant-feeding insects with piercing-sucking mouthparts, and both immature and adult whiteflies feed on the undersides of leaves. Adult whiteflies have the ability to both walk and fly, and females lay eggs either singly in a haphazard manner or in spirals or circles on the undersides of leaves. Whitefly eggs are ovoid and have a peglike pedicel that is inserted into a slit made by the female's ovipositor in the leaf surface. Alternatively, eggs may be laid directly into stomatal openings. A gluelike substance deposited at the base of the pedicel cements eggs in place (Byrne and Bellows 1991). The pedicel draws water into the egg from the leaf, thereby preventing desiccation before hatching (Byrne, Cohen, and Draeger 1990).

Most whitefly species are arrhenotokous—males are haploid and eclose from unfertilized eggs, and females are produced from fertilized eggs. The ratio of male and female whiteflies in a population changes over time and is affected by both temperature (Enkegaard 1993) and male longevity. Males tend to live for shorter periods, and popula-tions appear female-biased as a result (Byrne and Bellows 1991).

First-instar nymphs, which hatch from eggs, are mobile and walk a short distance before selecting sites where they settle to commence feeding. This ambulatory first instar is referred to as the crawler, and crawlers may walk for several hours and cover distances up to 1.2 in. (30 mm) before settling (Ibid.). After settling, crawlers insert their mouthparts into leaf tissue, and the stylet passes between host cells until the phloem is penetrated and sap extraction begins. A modified alimentary system concentrates sugars in the anterior midgut while excess fluids are diverted to the hindgut and excreted (Cicero, Hiebert, and Webb 1995). The subsequent developmental stages (the second, third, fourth, and pupal [the last, nonfeeding portion of the fourth instar]) (Nechols and Tauber 1977) are sessile and do not move from the feeding site originally selected by the crawler.

Honeydew

Whitefly waste products resulting from feeding are referred to as honeydew. These viscous liquids contain high concentrations of various sugars (Hendrix and Wei 1994).

149

Intracellular symbiotic bacteria in the whitefly gut convert the sucrose found in plant sap into a variety of sugars, which are excreted (Davidson et al. 1994). Nymphs on well-fertilized plants produce less honeydew, as nymphs on poor-quality hosts must feed more to satisfy their dietary requirements (Blua and Toscano 1994). Adult female whiteflies produce the most honeydew of any life stage (Hong and Rumei 1993), and honeydew excretion is continuous and not restricted to certain periods of the day (Ibid., Yee et al. 1996). Whiteflies have a unique method for disposing of honeydew (Byrne and Bellows 1991). The anus of a whitefly nymph opens into a depression on the dorsal surface called the vasiform orifice. A mobile structure known as the lingula dips into honeydew as it pools in the vasiform orifice, and, upon release, the lingula flicks the honeydew off the nymph.

Much of what is known about whitefly biology comes from research on pest species such as sweetpotato whitefly, *Bemisia tabaci* (Gennadius), greenhouse whitefly, *Trialeurodes vaporariorum* (Westwood), and silverleaf whitefly, *Bemisia argentifolii* Bellows and Perring (also referred to as the B strain or biotype B of *B. tabaci* [Brown, Frohlich, and Rosell 1995]). The remainder of this chapter will focus on the biology and biological control of *T. vaporariorum* and *B. argentifolii*, which are the two most important pests of greenhouse-grown ornamentals worldwide.

Host Plants and Feeding Damage

Bemisia argentifolii and *Trialeurodes vaporariorum* are cosmopolitan in distribution and are extremely polyphagous, having been recorded from over sixty different plant families (Russel 1963, Mound and Halsey 1978, Roditakis 1990). *T. vaporariorum* has been recorded as a pest from greenhouse-grown *Arum* spp., *Begonia* sp., *Coleus* sp., *Fuchsia* sp., *Pelargonium* sp., *Primula* sp., *Verbena* sp., and *Euphorbia* spp. (e.g., poinsettias) (Byrne, Bellows, and Parrella 1990). *Bemisia argentifolii* infests a variety of greenhouse ornamentals, including poinsettias, *Pelargonium* sp., *Impatiens* sp., *Gerbera* sp., *Hibiscus* sp., and *Begonia* sp. (Fransen 1994). Different host plant species can significantly affect whitefly survivorship and reproductive rates For example, at 77°F (25°C), egg to adult development for *B. argentifolii* is fastest on begonia (twenty days), slowest on gerbera (twenty-nine days), and intermediate on hibiscus (twenty-five days) and poinsettia (twenty-three days) (Fransen 1990a).

Direct feeding damage

Whiteflies can cause direct damage to plants as a result of feeding. *B. argentifolii* vectors geminiviruses that cause yellowing and leaf curling in several vegetable crops (Duffus 1996), and feeding by nymphs can induce physiological disorders such as irregular ripening in tomatoes and silverleaf in cucurbits (Shapiro 1996). Vein clearing of foliage and induction of white stems on poinsettia and other ornamentals can occur as a result of feeding by *B. argentifolii*. However, the ability of this whitefly to vector viral diseases affecting ornamentals is not a generally recognized problem (Brown, Frohlich, and Rosell 1995, Oetting and Buntin 1996). *T. vaporariorum* vectors closteroviruses that affect cucurbitaceous species (Coffin and

Coutts 1995, Duffus 1996), and documented economic losses from viruses vectored by *T. vaporariorum* in ornamental crops are lacking. Feeding by *B. argentifolii* on poinsettias can reduce plant height, leaf number, leaf size, and dry weight yields (Oetting and Buntin 1996).

Indirect feeding damage

Honeydew deposition on leaves produces a shiny, sticky sheen and provides an ideal substrate for sooty mold growth (e.g., *Cladosporium* and *Alternaria* spp.). Declines in the aesthetic quality of ornamental plants in greenhouses because of honeydew, black sooty mold contamination, or flying adults are problems associated with high-density whitefly populations (Helgesen and Tauber 1974). Disfigurement of plants in this manner by whiteflies is referred to as indirect damage, as it has not resulted from physical damage caused by whitefly feeding. Consumer acceptance of ornamental plants with indirect damage is low (Oetting and Buntin 1996).

Whitefly Distribution within Plants and Interspecific Competition

All developmental stages of *T. vaporariorum* and *B. tabaci* exhibit aggregation within and between ornamental plants in greenhouses (Liu, Oetting, and Buntin 1993). Whitefly life stages are vertically stratified in a plant with respect to leaf age. Adults, eggs, and first-instar nymphs are found predominantly on young leaves, second- and third-instar nymphs on middle-aged leaves, and fourth instars, pupae, and pupal cases on middle-

aged and old leaves. Consequently, population estimates can be based on whitefly counts made from leaves in these three age categories (Ibid.). Adult whiteflies can be monitored in greenhouses with yellow sticky cards. Placement of cards 2 in. (5 cm) above the crop canopy produces the most abundant adult catches (Liu, Oetting, and Buntin 1994a). Adults of *B. tabaci* and *T. vaporariorum* tend to exhibit peak flight activity in the morning and afternoon, respectively (Ibid.).

On poinsettias, *B. tabaci* outcompetes and may displace *T. vaporariorum* within two generations when these species coexist simultaneously over the temperature range 68 to 86°F (20 to 30°C) (Liu, Oetting, and Buntin 1994b). Displacement of *T. vaporariorum* by *B. tabaci* may be related to host plant suitability, with poinsettias favoring increased oviposition and immature survivorship of *B. tabaci*. Aggregations of adult *B. tabaci* on leaves initiate avoidance behavior in adult *T. vaporariorum*, which rarely settle in close proximity to *B. tabaci* (Ibid.).

Identification of Pest Whiteflies

An important first step in any pest management program is the accurate identification of the pests. This is particularly important for biological control programs because natural enemies are often specific to just one pest species or group of pests (e.g., whiteflies). Adults and pupae of *B. argentifolii* are readily distinguishable from *T. vaporariorum*. Adults of *B. argentifolii* are smaller than those of *T. vaporariorum*, are more active, and hold their wings in a tentlike manner against the sides of the abdomen (fig. 8.1). In comparison, adult *T. vaporariorum* hold their wings flat over the top of the abdomen (fig. 8.2).

Nymphs and pupae of *B. argentifolii* are dorsoventrally compressed, yellow in color,

Figure 8.1. The adult silverleaf whitefly, *Bemisia argentifolii* Bellows and Perring, is approximately 16 mm in length. A key characteristic to identifying these adults in the field is their holding of their wings down toward the leaf at a greater than a 45 degree angle when at rest. *Photo: Jack Kelly Clark, UC Regents.*

and generally lack long wax filaments on the dorsal surface (fig. 8.3). Red eyespots and white wing pads are readily visible. In contrast, the nymphs and pupae of *T. vaporariorum* are white. The body wall of the pupa is composed of an elevated palisade layer and is ornamented with long wax filaments (fig. 8.4).

Photographs of all life stages for both species are available on the World Wide Web (www.ipm.ucdavis.edu/PMG/PEST-NOTES/pn002.html). Important aspects of the developmental and reproductive biology of *B. argentifolii* and *T. vaporariorum* are presented in tables 8.1 and 8.2, respectively. A life cycle diagram for *B. argentifolii* is presented in figure 8.5.

Whitefly Natural Enemies

Natural enemies (predators, pathogens, and parasitoids) debilitate organisms either by

Figure 8.2. Adult *Trialeurodes vaporariorum* (Westwood) whitefly are approximately 10 mm long, pale yellow in color, with two pairs of wings covered with a white powdery wax. At rest, wings are held flat, virtually parallel to the surface atop they are standing. *Photo: Jack Kelly Clark, UC Regents.*

Figure 8.3. The *Bemisia argentifolii* Nymph is flat, oval, pale green, and nearly transparent. The pupa is yellow with reddish colored eyes, oval in shape, and lacks long waxy spines. *Photo: Jack Kelly Clark, UC Regents.*

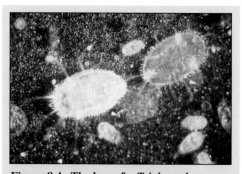

Figure 8.4. The legs of a *Trialeurodes vaporariorum* nymph are nonfunctional; thus, the nymphs are sedentary, remaining at the feeding site selected by the mobile crawler. These stages become flattened on the leaf surface and are very difficult to see because of their transparent green color. Except for size, the second through early fourth instars are similar in appearance. The pupa is white; it has an elevated straight-sided body wall with a fringe of waxy spines. The body of this instar is thicker than other stages and possesses characteristic long wax filaments along the outer margin. *Photo: J. L. Shipp.*

prematurely killing the target (i.e., the pest) through predation, disease, or parasitism, or by reducing the reproductive output or competitiveness of the pest. Predators, pathogens, and parasitoids are commercially available for use in greenhouses against *T. vaporariorum* and *B. argentifolii* infesting ornamentals. Chapter 6 provides a review on the biology and use of natural enemies in greenhouses.

Predators

Predators are free-living mobile organisms that obtain energy as food by consuming more than one individual prey over the course of their lifetime. Often, both immature and adult stages are predatory. A notable exception are some species of adult green lacewings (e.g., *Chrysoperla carnea* [Stephens]), in which the adults feed on plant exudates or honeydew (Hagen 1964).

B. argentifolii is attacked by predatory species representing eight arthropod orders, including members of the families

Table 8.1. Biology of *Bemisia argentifolii* Reared on the Poinsettia (*Euphorbia pulcherrima* Willd.) Cultivar 'Angelica' at Three Constant Temperatures in the Laboratory. Data are from Enkegaard (1993). Means are presented with standard errors (±SE) where possible.

Biological Attribute	Temperature 61°F (16°C)	Temperature 72°F (22°C)	Temperature 82°F (28°C)
Mean adult longevity (days)	50.8 ± 3.9	21.8 ± 1.6	16.0 ± 0.8
No. eggs laid per female (fecundity)	60.2	90.9	96.3
Egg to adult emergence (days)	168.1 ± 4.1	49.9 ± 0.35	29.9 ± 0.23
Mean no. days to egg hatch	45.5 ± 0.4	16.9 ± 0.16	10.4 ± 0.08
Proportion of females in progeny	—	0.63 ± 0.03	0.76 ± 0.02

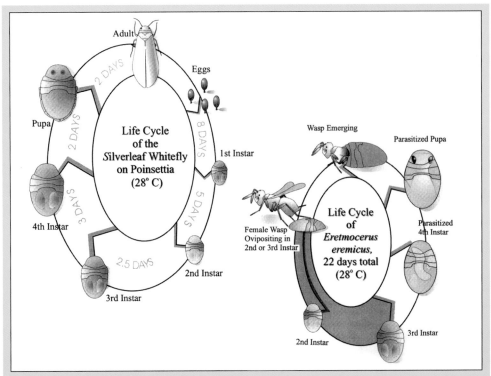

Figure 8.5. Schematic illustrating the lifecycle of *Bemisia argentifolii* and its parasitoid *Eretmocerus eremicus*. *Artwork: Vincent D'Amico III, Bean's Art Ink.*

Table 8.2. Biology of *Trialeurodes vaporariorum* Reared on Tomato (*Lycopersicon lycopersicum* [Linnaeus] Karsten ex Farwell) Cultivar 'Bonnie Best' at Three Different Temperatures in the Laboratory. Data are from Burnett (1949). Means are presented with standard errors (±SE) where possible.

Biological Attribute	Temperature 59°F (15°C)	Temperature 70°F (21°C)	Temperature 81°F (27°C)
Mean adult longevity (days)	50.5	28.5	8.3
Mean no. eggs laid per female (fecundity)	93.6 ± 6.9	209.4 ± 14.3	29.5 ± 4.4
Egg to adult emergence (days)	—	27.9 ± 0.06	21.3 ± 0.07
Mean daily oviposition rate	2.2 ± 0.1	8.4 ± 0.3	5.1 ± 0.5

Phytoseiidae (Acari); Coccinellidae (Coleoptera); Syrphidae (Diptera); Anthocoridae, Nabidae, and Miridae (all Hemiptera); and Chrysopidae and Coniopterygidae (both Neuroptera) (Nordlund and Legaspi 1996). At least four species of predators that are commercially available have been evaluated for their ability to control *B. argentifolii* on greenhouse-grown crops: *Delphastus pusillus* LeConte, *Macrolophus caliginosus* Wagner, *C. carnea*, and *Chrysoperla rufilabris* (Burmeister).

Delphastus pusillus *and* D. catalinae *(Coleoptera: Coccinellidae)*

Delphastus pusillus is often associated with high-density populations of whiteflies and feeds readily on *B. argentifolii* (Hoelmer, Osborne, and Yokomi 1993, 1994). Adult *D. pusillus* are small, shiny black beetles 0.05 to 0.06 in. (1.3 to 1.4 mm) in length, and larvae and pupae are pale yellow. Beetles pupate in groups on the undersides of lower leaves or in crevices (Hoelmer, Osborne, and Yokomi 1993). Adults and immature beetles feed by piercing the whitefly integument and extracting the contents, resulting in a flattened, empty whitefly cuticle (Hoelmer, Osborne, and Yokomi 1994). Adults and all larval stages will feed on whitefly eggs, nymphs, and adults (K. M. Heinz, pers. comm. 1998). In artificial arenas, female fecundity is greatest on a diet of eggs (Hoelmer, Osborne, and Yokomi 1993), but in cage studies with small poinsettia plants, *B. argentifolii* nymphs were preferred over eggs (Heinz and Parrella 1994a).

Leaf hairs can affect life-history traits and searching ability of *D. pusillus* (Heinz and Zalom 1996). For example, leaf trichome densities on poinsettia vary depending on cultivar. The cultivar 'Annette Hegg Brilliant Diamond' has trichome densities 15% lower than 'Lilo'. On the least hairy variety, prey consumption and oviposition rates by *D. pusillus* are significantly higher than more hirsute varieties (Heinz and Parrella 1994b).

D. pusillus larvae and adults avoid feeding on whiteflies with late-stage developing parasitoids (Hymenoptera: Aphelinidae) (i.e., parasitoid immatures at least seven days of age) (e.g., *Encarsia transvena* (Timberlake), *Encarsia luteola* Howard, and *Eretmocerus* sp. nr. *californicus* Howard) and preferentially attack unparasitized prey (Heinz and Parrella 1994a; Heinz et al. 1994; Hoelmer, Osborne, and Yokomi 1994; Heinz and Nelson 1996). Biological control with *D. pusillus* is most effective when this predator is combined with one or more species of aphelinid parasitoids (Heinz 1996, Heinz and Nelson 1996). For example, *D. pusillus* combined with *E. luteola* at a weekly release rate of one beetle and one parasitoid per plant can control *B. argentifolii* to levels attained with insecticides (Heinz and Parrella 1994b). Recently, there has been some confusion as to the true identity of *D. pusillus*. Holmer and Pickett (2003) suggest that most of published studies referring to *D. pusillus* and current insectary cultures are most likely *D. catalinae*.

Macrolophus caliginosus *(Hemiptera: Miridae)*

This predatory bug is polyphagous and feeds on spider mites (Acari: Tetranychidae), aphids (Homoptera: Aphididae), whitefly nymphs and eggs, leafminers (Diptera: Agromyzidae), and lepidopterous pests (Fauvel, Malausa, and Kasper 1987; Foglar, Malusa, and Wajnberg 1990; Sampson and

King 1996; van Schelt et al. 1996). *Macrolophus caliginosus* is a partial predator and needs to supplement its diet by feeding on plant material to complete its life cycle (Ferran et al. 1996), and damage to plants can occur in some ornamental crops as a result of phytophagy when there is a lack of prey (van Schelt et al. 1996). Phytophagy, however, allows *M. caliginosus* to establish early in greenhouses when prey densities are low and to persist if pest densities decline. Three releases of this predator at a rate of 0.05 to 0.09 per ft.^{2} (0.5 to 1.0 per m^2) at two-week intervals in combination with weekly releases of *Encarsia formosa* Gahan (Hymenoptera: Aphelinidae) has provided successful biological control of low- and high-density populations of *T. vaporariorum* in tomatoes. Release of two *M. caliginosus* per 10.8 ft.^{2} (2 per m^2) is recommended if whitefly densities are close to economically damaging levels (Sampson and King 1996, van Schelt et al. 1996).

Chrysoperla spp. (Neuroptera: Chrysopidae)

Ten species of lacewings have been reported to feed on whitefly nymphs, including the commercially available species *C. carnea* and *C. rufilabris* (Nordlund and Legaspi 1996). The three larval stages of *C. carnea* will feed on *B. tabaci* and *T. vaporariorum* eggs, nymphs, and pupae (Butler and Henneberry 1988, Senior and McEwen 1998). However, *C. carnea* is unable to develop to adulthood on a diet consisting only of *T. vaporariorum* (Senior and McEwen 1998). Similarly, *C. rufilabris* larvae will feed on all immature stages of *B. tabaci*, but they are unable to reach adulthood on this diet alone. Also, larval developmental times on whiteflies are substantially longer than those of lacewing larvae reared on lepidopteran hosts or on a diet composed of several types of food (Legaspi, Carruthers, and Nordlund 1994). In the absence of prey, *C. rufilabris* can sustain itself on nutrients extracted from leaves for six to seven days (Ibid.).

Despite being an unsuitable host, *B. tabaci* infesting greenhouse-grown hibiscus plants (*Hibiscus rosa-sinensis* Linnaeus) can be controlled to commercially acceptable levels with inundative releases of *C. rufilabris* (Breene et al. 1992). Two releases two weeks apart of either twenty-five or fifty larvae per plant consistently produced marketable plants. Releases of five *C. rufilabris* larvae per plant produced inconsistent levels of control (Ibid.). Releases of *C. carnea* larvae in combination with *E. formosa* have suppressed *T. vaporariorum* on marigolds (*Tagetes erecta* L.) (Heinz and Parrella 1990).

Pathogens

Insect pathogens are disease-causing organisms that either kill or debilitate the host, and include bacteria, viruses, protozoa, and fungi. Owing to the feeding mechanisms of whiteflies, only pathogenic organisms with the ability to penetrate the cuticle (e.g., fungi) have potential as microbial control agents (Lacey, Fransen, and Carruthers 1996). The most commonly observed fungal pathogens of whiteflies are *Paecilomyces fumosoroseus* (Wize) Brown and Smith, *Aschersonia aleyrodis* Webber, *Verticillium lecanii* (Zimmerman) Viegas, and *Beauveria bassiana* (Balsamo) Vuillemin (Fransen 1990b; Lacey, Fransen, and Carruthers 1996). Of these, *V. lecanii*, *B. bassiana,* and *P. fumosoroseus* are commercially available.

Verticillium lecanii *(Deuteromycotina: Hyphomycetes)*

This pathogen attacks aphids, scales, thrips, whiteflies, and other fungi, and it also has the ability to act as a saprophyte and feed upon nonliving organic substrates (Lacey, Fransen, and Carruthers 1996). Epidemics of *V. lecanii* can occur naturally in greenhouses, and the inoculum for initial infection is probably present in some potting media (Samson and Rombach 1985). *Verticillium lecanii* develops at temperatures ranging from 59 to 77°F (15 to 25°C) and relative humidities of 85 to 90%, which must exist for ten to twelve hours each day (Ibid.). Spore solutions of *V. lecanii* sprayed onto poinsettia leaves with eggs and first-, second-, and third-instar nymphs of *B. tabaci* or *T. vaporariorum* caused mortality ranging from 89 to 96% for *B. tabaci* and 79 to 96% for *T. vaporariorum*. Eggs of both whitefly species exhibited low rates of infection (less than 1%) (Meade and Byrne 1991), and adult whiteflies are also relatively immune to infection (Hall 1982). Certain fungicides are harmful to *V. lecanii* and should not be used simultaneously with this pathogen (Ravensberg, Van Buysen, and Berns 1994).

Beauveria bassiana *(Deuteromycotina: Hyphomycetes)*

Beauveria bassiana is not a natural regulator of whitefly populations and is only occasionally found infesting whiteflies in agroecosystems (Wraight et al. 1998). In comparison to other fungal pathogens, little work has been done to evaluate the efficacy of this natural enemy against whiteflies (Osborne and Landa 1992), and results from greenhouse trials against *B. argentifolii* have not been encouraging (Olson and Oetting, 1999).

Commercially available strains of *B. bassiana* exhibit high levels of pathogenicity in laboratory studies, and *B. tabaci* nymphs and adults are susceptible to infection (Zaki 1998). Temperature and humidity levels affect *B. bassiana* pathogenicity; maximum mortality is inflicted at low temperatures (no greater than 68°F [20°C]) and high humidity (greater than 96%) when these conditions persist for at least twenty-four hours (James et al. 1998). Whitefly nymphs infected with *B. bassiana* display a pronounced red pigmentation. Oosporein, a dibenzquinone, is responsible for the red color, and its antibiotic properties aid the infection process (Wraight et al. 1998).

The efficacy of *B. bassiana* can be enhanced if this pathogen is used in combination with insecticides that stress the target pest. Sublethal doses of imidacloprid (a chloronicotinyl insecticide commonly used against whiteflies) in combination with *B. bassiana* have a synergistic effect and cause higher levels of mortality than using either compound alone for pest control (Quintela and McCoy 1997). Imidacloprid applications increase the rate and amount of *B. bassiana* conidial germination on the insect cuticle (Quintela and McCoy 1998). Similarly, combining *B. bassiana* with diflubenzuron (an insect growth regulator) has an additive effect for grasshopper control as this IGR enhances the pathogen's infection process (Delgado et al. 1999). Similar data investigating the efficacy of combining *B. bassiana* with insecticides for whitefly control are currently unavailable, and research in this area is warranted. Commercially available fungicides (e.g., maneb, mancozeb, and thiophanate-methyl) inhibit mycelial growth and sporulation by *B. bassiana*, and careful consideration should be given when using these chemicals with entomopathogenic fungi (Todorova et al. 1998).

Paecilomyces fumosoroseus (Deuteromycotina: Hyphomycetes)

Paecilomyces fumosoroseus has a broad host range and have been recorded from over forty different insect species (Smith 1993). Hosts for this fungus include whiteflies, mealybugs, beetles, caterpillars, and flies (Osborne and Landa 1992). Natural epizootics of *P. fumosoroseus* infesting *B. tabaci* in greenhouses and shade houses have been recorded (Ibid.).

The range of whitefly life stages infected by *P. fumosoroseus* is broader than most entomopathogenic fungi; it is able to attack eggs, nymphs, pupae, and adults of *B. tabaci* and *T. vaporariorum* (Osborne and Landa 1992; Vidal, Lacey, and Fargues 1997). Conditions that favor infection of whiteflies by sporulating *P. fumosoroseus* conidia are temperatures ranging from 72 to 91°F (22 to 33°C) and relative humidities from 68 to 100% (Vidal et al. 1998). The susceptibility of *B. tabaci* to infection by *P. fumosoroseus* is not affected by the host plant being used by the whitefly. In greenhouses, second-instar *B. tabaci* nymphs were equally susceptible to *P. fumosoroseus* infection on cucumbers (*Cucumis sativus* L.), cabbage (*Brassica olerácea* L.), and three cultivars of tomato under optimal environmental conditions (Ibid.).

Foliar applications of *P. fumosoroseus* conidia have been successfully combined with *E. formosa* in commercial greenhouses for control of *T. vaporariorum* on tomatoes. *Trialeurodes vaporariorum* nymphs that have been parasitized by *E. formosa* and have turned black are immune from infection by *P. fumosoroseus*, making simultaneous use of these two natural enemies compatible (van de Vrie and Degheele 1996). Compatibility of *P. fumosoroseus* with *Eretmocerus* sp. and *D. pusillus* has been observed (Osborne and Landa 1992). *Paecilomyces fumosoroseus* has been used as the sole control strategy for *B. tabaci* on greenhouse-grown poinsettias and hibiscus. To produce plants of the same quality as those protected by *P. fumosoroseus*, poinsettias required eighteen insecticide treatments for *B. tabaci* control, while hibiscus plants were treated twenty-one times (Osborne and Landa 1994). Laboratory tests indicate that *P. fumosoroseus* has a high tolerance to a broad range of fungicides that are frequently used to protect ornamental plants in greenhouses (Osborne and Landa 1992).

Aschersonia aleyrodis (Deuteromycotina: Coelomycetes)

Members of the genus *Aschersonia* are highly specific to whiteflies (Fransen 1990b). On poinsettia and cucumber, *A. aleyrodis* infects and kills nymphs and pupae, but not eggs, of *T. vaporariorum* and nymphs of *B. argentifolii* (Meekes, Fransen, and van Lenteren 1996, Fransen 1995). Trials in vegetable crops indicate that ultralow volume sprays of conidial suspensions can cause 75% mortality to *T. vaporariorum* under varying climatic conditions (Samson and Rombach 1985, Fransen 1990b). Spores can germinate at temperatures ranging from 59 to 86°F (15 to 30°C) if relative humidities are between 98 and 100% (Fransen 1990b). *A. aleyrodis* can be combined with the parasitoid *E. formosa* for *T. vaporariorum* control (Fransen and van Lenteren 1993, 1994). Parasitized whitefly nymphs in which immature parasitoids are greater than four days old are immune to infection by *A. aleyrodis*. The developing wasp larva induces physical or physiological changes in the host that reduce its susceptibility to fungal infection (Fransen and van Lenteren 1994). Similarly, *E. formosa* is able to discriminate and reject whitefly hosts that have been infected with *A. aleyrodis* for at least seven days. If hosts are parasitized before this seven-day period, *A. aleyrodis* inhibits parasitoid development (Fransen and van Lenteren 1993). *Aschersonia aleyrodis* and *E. formosa* appear to be highly compatible natural enemies for combined use against *T. vaporariorum* in greenhouses.

Parasitoids

Parasitoids are distinguished by the fact that the immature stages develop at the expense of a single individual, which is referred to as the host. Parasitoids differ from parasites in that they kill their host upon completing development. Whitefly parasitoids belong to just three hymenopterous families: Platygasteridae (e.g., *Amitus* spp.), Aphelinidae (e.g., *Eretmocerus* and *Encarsia* spp.), and Eulophidae (e.g., *Euderomphale* spp.) (Gerling 1990). The best-studied of these whitefly parasitoids are *E. formosa* and *Eretmocerus eremicus* Rose and Zolnerowich, both of which are commercially available.

Encarsia formosa *(Hymenoptera: Aphelinidae)*

E. formosa (fig. 8.6) is used globally for the control of *T. vaporariorum* on greenhouse-grown vegetable crops, and to a lesser extent on ornamental crops (Hoddle, Van Driesche, and Sanderson 1998). This parasitoid is a

solitary, thelytokous (unfertilized eggs produce female offspring) endoparasitoid (parasitoid develops inside the body of the host). Females preferentially deposit single eggs in third- and fourth-instar whitefly nymphs (fig. 8.7). Adult wasps obtain energy and nutrients by piercing the integument of nymphs with the ovipositor and feeding on hemolymph that seeps from the wound. Killing hosts for adult nutritional purposes is termed host-feeding (Jervis and Kidd 1986). On some plants, high trichome densities reduce the searching efficacy of *E. formosa*, and this has made whitefly control on some crops such as gerbera more difficult to achieve (Sütterlin and van Lenteren 1996)

B. argentifolii on poinsettia is an unsuitable host for *E. formosa* because parasitoid development is slower, more immature parasitoids die, and adults are less fecund in comparison to wasps reared in *T. vaporariorum* on the same host plant (Szabo, van Lenteren, and Huisman 1993). In small experimental greenhouses, *E. formosa* and a

Figure 8.6. Adult *Encarsia formosa* Gahan females are small (~0.6mm in length), have a black head and thorax and a yellow abdomen. Males are rare and dark in color. *Photo: Jack Kelly Clark, UC Regents.*

Figure 8.7. Female *Encarsia formosa* Gahan lay a single egg in the young whitefly (healthy late-instar whitefly on the right). The parasite larva subsequently destroys the internal contents of the host so that all that remains is the exoskeleton. A reliable and conspicuous sign that a parasite is developing within a greenhouse whitefly is a color change that takes place about two weeks after deposition of the parasite's egg. At this time the skin of the last nymphal stage turns black (center). When fully developed, the adult wasp splits the whitefly exoskeleton and emerges (left). *Photo: Jack Kelly Clark, UC Regents.*

Bemisia-adapted strain of *E. formosa* appeared to be promising biological control agents of *B. argentifolii* (Hoddle, Van Driesche, and Sanderson 1997a, 1997b). However, in commercial greenhouses, weekly releases of three or more *E. formosa* failed to control pure populations of *B. argentifolii* on poinsettia stock plants or colored poinsettias (Parrella et al. 1991, Hoddle and Van Driesche 1996, 1999a,b). Consequently, use of this parasitoid for control of *B. argentifolii* is not recommended. Improved control of *B. argentifolii* may be achieved when *T. vaporariorum* (the preferred host) is present

in the crop (Heinz 1996). Aspects of the biology of *E. formosa* reared on either *B. argentifolii* or *T. vaporariorum* are presented in table 8.3.

Eretmocerus eremicus *(Hymenoptera: Aphelinidae)*

This parasitoid (fig. 8.8) was formerly known as *Eretmocerus* sp. nr. *californicus* (see Rose and Zolnerowich 1997), and it is a primary, biparental, solitary ecto-endoparasitoid (part of the life cycle is spent feeding on the outside of the host before parasitoid development is completed inside the host) of whiteflies with a one-to-one sex ratio in mass culture (Rose, Zolnerowich, and Hunter 1996; Van Driesche et al. 1999). Females oviposit under suitable hosts, and parasitoid

Figure 8.8. Female *Eretmocerus eremicus* Rose and Zolnerowich (shown left) are pale lemon yellow with green eyes and clubbed antennae. Male wasps have longer, elbowed antennae, and are yellowish brown in color. Whitefly pupae that have been parasitized by *E. eremicus* appear beige in color, whereas healthy whitefly pupae are white or pale yellow. The wasp can only emerge through the upper surface of the host. This is accomplished by chewing a circular exit hole (shown center). *Photo: Jack Kelly Clark, UC Regents*

Table 8.3. Comparison of Biological Attributes of *E. formosa* reared on *T. vaporariorum* or *B. argentifolii* at 70°F (21°C) with Poinsettia as the Host Plant. Data are from Nell et al. (1976), Szabo, van Lenteren, and Huisman (1993), and Enkegaard (1994).

Biological Attributes of *Encarsia formosa*	*T. vaporariorum* as Host	*B. argentifolii* as Host
Mean longevity of adults (days)	11.9	8.7
Mean daily oviposition rate (eggs)	5.0	5.9
Mean lifetime fecundity	59.2 eggs per female	51.3 eggs per female
Daily host feeding rate (nymphs/day)	2.8	2.3
Egg to adult emergence (days)	24.5	29.8
Mortality of *E. formosa* larvae	41.6%	55.9%
Preferred stages for host feeding	2nd-instar nymphs and pupae	all nymphal instars and pupae
Preferred stages for oviposition	3rd-and 4th-instar nymphs	3rd-and 4th-instar nymphs

larvae, after hatching, penetrate the ventral surface of the host and develop as endoparasitoids inside the host (Gerling 1966). *Eretmocerus eremicus* host feeds by inserting its ovipositor in the vasiform orifice of the host (Headrick, Bellows, and Perring 1995). Weekly releases (three female wasps per plant per week) of *E. eremicus* have proven to be more effective than the same release rate of *E. formosa* for controlling *B. argentifolii* on poinsettias (Hoddle et al. 1998b, Hoddle and Van Driesche 1999b). In commercial greenhouses, visual inspections of experimental plants with artificial whitefly patches indicated that *E. eremicus* finds whitefly patches faster and consistently kills more nymphs after discovery than *E. formosa* (Hoddle et al. 1998a).

Biological control of *B. argentifolii* on poinsettias in small greenhouses with *E. eremicus* may be improved by varying the weekly parasitoid release rate to concentrate parasitoid attacks against whiteflies when cuttings are small and there are few leaves to search. With a variable release strategy, six female parasitoids are released per plant per week for the first half of the growing season. This rate is then reduced to one female parasitoid per plant per week for the remainder of the growing season. The assumption is that low-level releases coupled with parasitoid reproduction will maintain whitefly densities at nondamaging levels until harvest because of high levels of mortality inflicted on whiteflies by parasitoids during the high release rate phase (Hoddle, Sanderson, and Van

Driesche, 1998). With this variable release rate strategy, the overall release rate is still three female wasps per plant per week. However, in commercial greenhouses fixed vs. variable release rates of *E. eremicus* did not show significant differences in efficacy for controlling *B. argentifolii* on poinsettias (Van Driesche et al., 2001a). Growers have successfully used *E. eremicus* to control pure populations of either *B. argentifolii* or *T. vaporariorum* in commercial poinsettia ranges (Hoddle et al. 2001). Aspects of the biology of *Eretmocerus* spp. reared on either *B. argentifolii* or *T. vaporariorum* are

presented in table 8.4. The life cycle of *E. eremicus* is shown in figure 8.5.

Initiating a Biological Control Program

When natural enemies are missing from an agricultural setting (e.g., greenhouses immediately after planting), or are too scarce to provide control, making releases of agents purchased from insectaries can increase their numbers. This approach is termed *augmentative biological control*, and either inoculative or inundative approaches are used.

Table 8.4. Comparison of Biological Attributes of *Eretmocerus* sp. from Riverside, California, Reared on *T. vaporariorum* on Tomato at 63°F (17°C) (Vet and van Lenteren 1981) and *Eretmocerus eremicus* Reared on *B. argentifolii* on cotton (*Gossypium hirsutum* Linnaeus) at 82°F (28°C) (Headrick, Bellows, and Perring 1996, 1999). Means are presented with standard errors (±SE) where possible.

Biological Attributes	*Eretmocerus* sp. on *T. vaporariorum* as Host	*Eretmocerus eremicus* on *B. argentifolii* as Host
Mean longevity of adults (days)	[a] 30	5.9 ± 3.0
Mean daily oviposition rate (eggs/day)	≈ 7	≈ 5
Mean lifetime fecundity	149.9 ± 21.8	22.9 ± 6.8
Daily host feeding rate (nymphs/day)	—	≈ 2-3[1]
Egg to adult emergence (days)	27	21.7 ± 2.1
Preferred stages for host feeding	—	1st instars
Preferred stages for oviposition	2nd-and 3rd-instar nymphs	1st- to 3rd-instar nymphs

[1] Data from McAuslane and Nguyen (1996). Host plant was hibiscus and temperature was 75 to 82°F (24 to 28°C).

Inoculative releases are those in which small numbers of natural enemies are introduced into the greenhouse early in the crop production cycle, and subsequent control occurs as natural enemies reproduce and feed on the pest. This approach has been used to control *T. vaporariorum* on greenhouse-grown tomatoes with *E. formosa* (Hoddle, Van Driesche, and Sanderson 1998).

Inundative or mass releases are used when natural-enemy reproduction is expected to be insufficient to suppress pest population growth and control is achieved by released natural enemies and, to a limited extent, their offspring. Inundative biological control is the approach used for rapid pest suppression on ornamentals because of low tolerances for aesthetic damage and arthropod contamination of the saleable product (Hoddle, Van Driesche, and Sanderson 1997a). Preventative inundative natural enemy releases are started early in the growing season, when pest densities are well below those that cause economic damage and pest population growth is prevented from reaching damaging levels. Inundative natural enemy releases cannot be used in "curative" manner to reduce pest populations to nondamaging levels once they have reached economically injurious densities. The steps recommended for initiating a preventative inundative biological control program with *E. eremicus* for *B. argentifolii* on poinsettias are outlined below.

Case Study: Biological Control of *Bemisia tabaci* Strain B on Poinsettias

If whitefly populations are *T. vaporariorum*, *B. argentifolii*, or a mixture of both,

E. eremicus is recommended as a biological control agent. Success can be further enhanced by developing an effective scouting program and using either trained staff or hiring a professional IPM scout to identify whitefly species and monitor pest and parasitoid population growth (see chapter 5 for more details on sampling).

Prerelease crop inspection

Before releases of *E. eremicus* are made, cuttings need to be inspected for the presence of whitefly nymphs and adults. To determine initial infestation levels, whitefly nymphs on every leaf of fifty randomly selected cuttings should be recorded. If mean densities of whitefly nymphs are two or less per cutting, initial infestation levels are low enough to commence weekly parasitoid releases (Hoddle and Van Driesche 1999b, Van Driesche et al. 1999). If nymph densities are greater than two per cutting, alternative control measures should be taken. One approach is the use of insecticides that may leave persistent residues. Long-lived residues may prevent the use of natural enemies for several weeks, thereby making a biological control program impractical to implement. Alternatively, the use of chemicals compatible with parasitoids to reduce densities of whitefly nymphs to levels less than two per leaf may be used. Insecticides compatible with natural enemy use are reviewed in chapter 7.

Ordering and deploying natural enemies

A weekly release rate of three female *E. eremicus* per plant per week for the duration of the growing period can be used. At this release rate, *E. eremicus* provides effective control by itself. However, the total cost of purchasing parasitoids can be reduced by employing a lower weekly release rate (i.e., one female parasitoid per plant per week) in combination with two applications of an effective insect growth regulator (IGR) (e.g., buprofezin) made one week apart at the midpoint of the growing season. Parasitoid releases are then resumed following IGR applications (Hoddle et al. 2001; Van Driesche et al., 2001b).

After shipment, *E. eremicus* emergence from parasitized *T. vaporariorum* nymphs placed in greenhouses averages 60% (Van Driesche et al. 1999). When an order is placed, commercial insectaries may over-supply parasitoids to compensate for reduced parasitoid emergence. For example, Koppert Biological Systems supplies approximately 142% of the number of *E. eremicus* requested by the client because adult emergence is esti-mated to be 70% (Ibid.).

E. eremicus are shipped as parasitized *T. vaporariorum* nymphs and may be either packaged in sawdust or glued to release cards that are placed in the greenhouse. Material in sawdust can be placed in release cups and distributed at a rate of one cup per 194 ft.^{2} (18 m^2) of greenhouse. *E. eremicus* is highly vagile and disperses readily within green-houses, thereby making large numbers of release sites unnecessary (Ibid.). Samples of recently purchased material should be exam-ined to ensure that parasitoids are arriving in good condition and are emerging success-fully. This can be done by placing fifty to one hundred parasitized whitefly nymphs in a clear glass jar and counting the number of parasitoids that have emerged after five to seven days. If a high number of yellow para-sitoids are seen, the shipment can be assumed to have arrived in good condition. If few para-sitoids are observed, inform the supplier that shipment quality was poor and negotiate for a replacement order or change suppliers. Chapter 4 provides more details on purchasing natural enemies.

Monitoring whitefly populations and determining parasitoid efficacy

Once releases of *E. eremicus* begin, plants should be inspected weekly to measure the effectiveness of parasitoid releases. Records of the numbers of live whitefly nymphs, pupae, and adults should be kept. These records will indicate whether whitefly popu-lations are increasing, decreasing, or remaining stable. Should whitefly numbers begin to increase to levels that are unaccept-able, use of an insecticide that is compatible with *E. eremicus* (e.g., use of IGRs such as buprofezin) should be used to reduce whitefly numbers, and parasitoid releases should be reinitiated. At time of harvest, densities of live nymphs and pupae should average 0.55 to 1.5 per leaf, and this level of control has been achieved with weekly releases of *E. eremicus*. Final nymph densities within this range are acceptable to consumers and are similar to those attained with insecticides (Hoddle et al. 1998b; Hoddle and Van Driesche 1999b; Van Driesche et al. 1999, 2001b).

Economics of Whitefly Biological Control and Future Prospects

Presently, control of whiteflies with natural enemies alone is more expensive than using insecticides (Stevens et al., 2000). The combined use of *E. luteola* and *D. pusillus* provided acceptable control of whiteflies in comparison to insecticide applications but was five times more expensive (Heinz and Parrella 1994a). Similarly, the use of *E. eremicus* alone at a rate of three females per week per plant is twenty-seven to forty-four times more expensive than using insecticides. However, it is possible to totally eliminate the use of insecticide applications through the use of *E. eremicus* for whitefly control on poinsettia stock plants and colored plants grown for sale at Christmas (Hoddle and Van Driesche 1999a,b, Van Driesche et al. 1999). Furthermore, when releases of natural enemies are used in combination with insecticides, spray applications can be reduced by 75% and control costs can become comparable to those of foliage-applied insecticides (Hoddle and Van Driesche 1996, Van Driesche et al. 1999, 2002).

To be economically feasible, either lower release rates of *E. eremicus* need to be used or the cost of the parasitoid needs to be reduced. In 1994, *E. eremicus* (list as *E. californicus*) was offered commercially for the first time at a cost of $76.00 per thousand parasitized nymphs (Crenshaw, Sclar, and Cooper 1996). In 1995, the price per thousand dropped to $22.00, and in 1998 the cost fell further to $8.30, a decrease of 89% from the original 1994 retail price (Hoddle and Van Driesche 1999b). Further price reduction for *E. eremicus* and other natural enemies can be expected to continue as production efficiency improves and demand increases.

Lower release rates of *E. eremicus* (as low as 0.5 female parasitoids per plant per week) can provide adequate whitefly control in commercial poinsettia crops if supplemented with limited use of compatible IGRs (Van Driesche et al. 2002, Van Driesche and Lyon 2003). Results indicate that an *E. eremicus*–IGR combination is more effective than use of either an IGR or *E. eremicus* alone (Van Driesche et al. 2001b), and IGRs compatible with *E. eremicus* have been identified from laboratory studies (Hoddle et al. 2001).

Resistance development by *B. argentifolii* to imidacloprid, the main pesticide used for control of this pest on poinsettias, is expected, as it has been detected in Europe on vegetable crops (Cahill et al. 1996). However, greenhouse surveys in the United Kingdom have failed to detect resistant *B. tabaci* and *T. vaporariorum* populations (Gorman et al., 2002). Resistant *B. argentifolii* populations, once present, are predicted to become widespread within a short period, given the extensive exchange of poinsettia cuttings and plants nationally and internationally (Fransen 1994). Van Driesche and Lyon (2003) have demonstrated that it is possible for commercial poinsettia growers to successfully integrate scouting, releases of *E. eremicus* and carefully time applications of insect growth regulators for control of *B. argentifolii* in commercially grown poinsettia crops and for such programs to be as efficacious and economically competitive and with imidacloprid-based programs in the northeast U.S.A. Research driven problem solving has resulted in the development of a biologically-based IPM program for whitefly pests of greenhouse grown poinsettias and this new technology deserves greater adoption. Incorporation of *E. eremicus* into an

IPM program diversifies whitefly control options, reduces reliance on insecticides, and when combined with a compatible IGR enhances cost-effectiveness of biological control, thereby providing sustainable whitefly control programs for greenhouse poinsettia production.

References Cited

Blua, M. J., and N. C. Toscano. 1994. *Bemisia argentifolii* (Homoptera: Aleyrodidae) development and honeydew production as a function of cotton nitrogen status. *Environmental Entomology* 23:316–21.

Breene, R. G., R. L. Meagher Jr., D. A. Nordlund, and Y. T. Wang. 1992. Biological control of *Bemisia tabaci* (Homoptera: Aleyrodidae) in a greenhouse using *Chrysoperla rufilabris* (Neuroptera: Chrysopidae). *Biological Control* 2:9–14.

Brown, J. K., D. R. Frohlich, and R. C. Rosell. 1995. The sweet-potato or silverleaf whiteflies: Biotypes of *Bemisia tabaci* or a species complex? *Annual Review of Entomology* 40:511–34.

Burnett, T. 1949. The effect of temperature on an insect host–parasite population. *Ecology* 30:113–34.

Butler, G. D., and T. J. Henneberry. 1988. Laboratory studies of *Chrysoperla carnea* predation on *Bemisia tabaci*. *Southwestern Entomologist* 13:165–70.

Byrne, D. N., and T. S. Bellows Jr. 1991. Whitefly biology. *Annual Review of Entomology* 36:431–57.

Byrne, D. N., A. C. Cohen, and E. A. Draeger. 1990. Water uptake from plant tissue by the egg pedicel of the greenhouse whitefly, *Trialeurodes vaporariorum* (Westwood) (Homoptera: Aleyrodidae). *Canadian Journal of Zoology* 68:1193–5.

Byrne, D. N., T. S. Bellows Jr., and M. P. Parrella. 1990. Whiteflies in agricultural systems. In *Whiteflies: Their Bionomics, Pest Status, and Management*, ed. D. Gerling, 227–61. Andover, U.K.: Intercept.

Cahill, M., I. Deholm, K. Gorman, S. Day, A. Elbert, and R. Nuen. 1996. Baseline determination and detection of resistance to imidacloprid in *Bemisia tabaci* (Hemiptera: Aleyrodidae). *Bulletin of Entomological Research* 85:343–9.

Cicero, J. M., E. Hiebert, and S. E. Webb. 1995. The alimentary canal of *Bemisia tabaci* and *Trialeurodes abutilonea* (Homoptera: Sternorrhyncha): Histology, ultrastructure, and correlations to function. *Zoomorphology* 115:31–9.

Coffin, R. S., and R. H. A. Coutts. 1995. Relationships among *Trialeurodes vaporariorum*—transmitted yellowing viruses from Europe and North America. *Journal of Phytopathology* 143:375–80.

Crenshaw, W., D. C. Sclar, and D. Cooper. 1996. A review of 1994 pricing and marketing by suppliers of organisms for biological control of arthropods in the United States. *Biological Control* 6:291–6.

Davidson, E. W., B. J. Segura, T. Steele, D. L. Hendrix. 1994. Microorganisms influence the composition of honeydew produced by the silverleaf whitefly, *Bemisia argentifolii*. *Journal of Insect Physiology* 40:1069–76.

Delgado, F. X., J. H. Britton, J. A. Onsager, W. Swearingen. 1999. Field assessment of *Beauveria bassiana* (Balsamo) Vuillemin and potential synergism with diflubenzuron for control of savanna grasshopper complex (Orthoptera) in Mali. *Journal of Invertebrate Pathology* 73:34–9.

Duffus, J. E. 1996. Whitefly-borne viruses. In *Bemisia: 1995 Taxonomy, Biology, Damage, Control, and Management*, ed. D. Gerling and R. T. Mayer, 255–63. Andover, U.K.: Intercept.

Enkegaard, A. 1993. The poinsettia strain of the cotton whitefly, *Bemisia tabaci* (Homoptera: Aleyrodidae), biological and demographic parameters on poinsettia (*Euphorbia pulcherrima*) in relation to temperature. *Bulletin of Entomological Research* 83:535–46.

———. 1994. Temperature dependent functional response of *Encarsia formosa* parasitizing the poinsettia-strain of the cotton whitefly, *Bemisia tabaci*, on poinsettia. *Entomologia Experimentalis et Applicata* 73:19–29.

Fauvel, G., J. C. Malausa, and B. Kaspar. 1987. Etude en laboratoire des principles caracteristiques biologiques de *Macrolophus caliginosus* (Heteroptera: Miridae). *Entomophaga* 32:529–43.

Ferran, A, A. Rortais, J. C. Malausa, and J. Gambier. 1996. Ovipositional behavior of *Macrolophus caliginosus* (Heteroptera: Miridae) on tobacco leaves. *Bulletin of Entomological Research* 86:123–8.

Foglar, H., J. C. Malusa, and E. Wajnberg. 1990. The functional response and preference of *Macrolophus caliginosus* (Heteroptera: Miridae) for two of its prey: *Myzus persicae* and *Tetranychus urticae*. *Entomophaga* 35:465–74.

Fransen, J. J. 1990a. Development of *Bemisia tabaci* (Gennadius) (Homoptera: Aleyrodidae) on poinsettia and other pot plants grown under glass. *IOBC/WPRS Bulletin* 13:61–3.

———. 1990b. Natural enemies of whiteflies: Fungi. In *Whiteflies: Their Bionomics, Pest Status, and Management*, ed. D. Gerling, 187–210. Andover, U.K.: Intercept.

———. 1994. *Bemisia tabaci* in the Netherlands: Here to stay? *Pesticide Science* 42:129–34.

———. 1995. Survival of spores on the entomopathogenic fungus *Aschersonia aleyrodis* (Deuteromycotina: Coelomycetes) on leaf surfaces. *Journal of Invertebrate Pathology* 65:73–5.

Fransen, J. J., and J. C. van Lenteren. 1993. Host selection and survival of the parasitoid *Encarsia formosa* on greenhouse whitefly, *Trialeurodes vaporariorum*, in the presence of hosts infected with the fungus *Aschersonia aleyrodis*. *Entomologia Experimentalis et Applicata* 69:239–49.

———. 1994. Survival of the parasitoid *Encarsia formosa* after treatment of parasitized greenhouse whitefly larvae with fungal spores of *Aschersonia aleyrodis*. *Entomologia Experimentalis et Applicata* 71:235–43.

Gerling, D. 1966. Studies with whitefly parasites of southern California. II. *Eretmocerus californicus* Howard (Hymenoptera: Aphelinidae). *Canadian Entomologist* 98:1316–29.

———. 1990. Natural enemies of whiteflies: Predators and parasitoids. In *Whiteflies: Their Bionomics, Pest Status, and Management*, ed. D. Gerling, 147–85. Andover, U.K.: Intercept.

Gorman, K., F. Hewitt, I. Denholm and G. J. Devine. 2002. New developments in insecticide resistance in the glasshouse whitefly (*Trialeurodes vaporariorum*) and two spotted spider mite (*Tetranychus uriticae*) in the U.K. *Pest Management Science* 58:123-130.

Hagen, K. S. 1964. Nutrition of entomophagous insects and their hosts. In *Biological Control of Insect Pests and Weeds*, ed. P. DeBach, 356–80. New York: Chapman and Hall.

Hall, R. A. 1982. Control of whitefly, *Trialeurodes vaporariorum,* and cotton aphid, *Aphis gossypii,* in glasshouses by two isolates of the fungus *Verticillium lecanii. Annals of Applied Biology* 101:1–11.

Headrick, D. H., T. S. Bellows Jr., and T. M. Perring. 1995. Behaviors of female *Eretmocerus* sp. nr. *californicus* (Hymenoptera: Aphelinidae) attacking *Bemisia argentifolii* (Homoptera: Aleyrodidae) on sweetpotato. *Environmental Entomology* 24:412–22.

———. 1996. Behaviors of female *Eretmocerus* sp. nr. *californicus* (Hymenoptera: Aphelinidae) attacking *Bemisia argentifolii* (Homoptera: Aleyrodidae) on cotton, *Gossypium hirsutum* (Malavaceae), and melon, *Cucumis melo* (Cucurbitaceae). *Biological Control* 6:64–75.

———. 1999. Development and reproduction of a population of *Eretmocerus eremicus* (Hymenoptera: Aphelinidae) on *Bemisia argentifolii* (Homoptera: Aleyrodidae). *Environmental Entomology* 28:300–6.

Heinz, K. M. 1996. Predators and parasitoids as biological control agents of *Bemisia* in greenhouses. In *Bemisia: 1995 Taxonomy, Biology, Damage, Control, and Management*, ed. D. Gerling and R. T. Mayer, 435–49. Andover, U.K.: Intercept.

Heinz, K. M., J. R. Brazzle, C. H. Pickett, E. T. Natwick, J. M. Nelson, and M. P. Parrella. 1994. *Delphastus pusillus* as a potential biological control agent for sweetpotato (silverleaf) whitefly. *California Agriculture* 48:35–40.

Heinz, K. M., and J. M. Nelson. 1996. Interspecific interactions among natural enemies of *Bemisia* in an inundative biological control program. *Biological Control* 6:384–93.

Heinz, K. M., and M. P. Parrella. 1990. Biological control of insect pests on greenhouse marigolds. *Environmental Entomology* 19 (4):825–35.

———. 1994a. Poinsettia (*Euphorbia pulcherrima* Willd. ex Klotz) cultivar mediated differences in performance of five natural enemies of *Bemisia argentifolii* Bellows and Perring n. sp. (Homoptera: Aleyrodidae). *Biological Control* 4:305–18.

———. 1994b. Biological control of *Bemisia argentifolii* (Homoptera: Aleyrodidae) infesting *Euphorbia pulcherrima*: Evaluations of releases of *Encarsia luteola* (Hymenoptera: Aphelinidae) and *Delphastus pusillus* (Coleoptera: Coccinellidae). *Environmental Entomology* 23:1346–53.

Heinz, K. M., and F. G. Zalom. 1996. Performance of the predator *Delphastus pusillus* on *Bemisia* resistant and susceptible tomato lines. *Entomologia Experimentalis et Applicata* 81:345–52.

Helgesen, R. G., and M. J. Tauber. 1974. Biological control of greenhouse whitefly, *Trialeurodes vaporariorum* (Aleyrodidae: Homoptera), on short-term crops by manipulating biotic and abiotic factors. *Canadian Entomologist* 106:1175–88.

Hendrix, D. L., and Y. Wei. 1994. Bemisiose: An unusual trisaccharide in *Bemisia* honeydew. *Carbohydrate Research* 253:329–34.

Hoddle, M. S., J. P. Sanderson, and R. G. Van Driesche. 1998. Biological control of *Bemisia argentifolii* (Hemiptera: Aleyrodidae) on poinsettia with inundative releases of *Eretmocerus eremicus* (Hymenoptera: Aphelinidae): Does varying the weekly release rate affect control? *Bulletin of Entomological Research* 89:41–51.

Hoddle, M. S., and R. G. Van Driesche. 1996. Evaluation of *Encarsia formosa* (Hymenoptera: Aphelinidae) to control *Bemisia argentifolii* (Homoptera: Aleyrodidae) on poinsettia (Euphorbia pulcherrima): A lifetable analysis. *Florida Entomologist* 79:1–12.

———. 1999a. Evaluation of inundative releases of *Eretmocerus eremicus* and *Encarsia formosa* Beltsville strain in commercial greenhouses for control of *Bemisia argentifolii* on poinsettia stock plants. *Journal of Economic Entomology* 92:811–24.

———.1999b. Evaluation of *Eretmocerus eremicus* and *Encarsia formosa* (Hymenoptera: Aphelinidae) Beltsville strain in commercial greenhouses for biological control of *Bemisia argentifolii* (Homoptera: Aleyrodidae) on colored poinsettia plants. *Florida Entomologist* 82:556-569.

Hoddle, M. S., R. G. Van Driesche, and J. P. Sanderson. 1997a. Biological control of *Bemisia argentifolii* (Homoptera: Aleyrodidae) on poinsettia with inundative releases of *Encarsia formosa* Beltsville strain (Hymenoptera: Aphelinidae): Can parasitoid reproduction augment inundative releases? *Journal of Economic Entomology* 90:910–24.

———. 1997b. Biological control of *Bemisia argentifolii* (Homoptera: Aleyrodidae) on poinsettia with inundative releases of *Encarsia formosa* (Hymenoptera: Aphelinidae): Are higher release rates necessarily better? *Biological Control* 10:166–79.

———. 1998. Biology and use of the whitefly parasitoid *Encarsia formosa. Annual Review of Entomology* 43:645–69.

Hoddle, M. S., R. G. Van Driesche, J. S. Elkinton, and J. P. Sanderson. 1998a. Discovery and utilization of *Bemisia argentifolii* patches by *Eretmocerus eremicus* and *Encarsia formosa* (Beltsville strain) in greenhouses. *Entomologia Experimentalis et Applicata* 87:15–28.

Hoddle, M. S., R. G. Van Driesche, S. Lyon, and J. P. Sanderson. 2001. Compatibility of insect growth regulators with *Eretmocerus eremicus* (Hymenoptera: Apelinidae) for whitefly (Homoptera: Aleyrodidae) control on poinsettias. I. Laboratory Assays. *Biological Control* 20 (2):122–131.

Hoddle, M. S., R. G. Van Driesche, J. P. Sanderson, and O. P. J. M. Minkenberg. 1998b. Biological control of *Bemisia argentifolii* on poinsettia with inundative releases of *Eretmocerus eremicus* (Hymenoptera: Aphelinidae): Do release rates affect parasitism? *Bulletin of Entomological Research* 88:47–58.

Hoelmer, K. A., L. S. Osborne, and R. K. Yokomi. 1993. Reproduction and feeding behavior of *Delphastus pusillus* (Coleoptera: Coccinellidae), a predator of *Bemisia tabaci* (Homoptera: Aleyrodidae). *Journal of Economic Entomology* 86:322–9.

———. 1994. Interactions of the whitefly predator *Delphastus pusillus* (Coleoptera: Coccinellidae) with parasitized sweetpotato whitefly (Homoptera: Aleyrodidae). *Environmental Entomology* 23:136–9.

Hoelmer K. A. and C. H. Pickett. 2003. Geographic origin and taxonomic history of *Delphastus* spp. (Coleoptera: Coccinellidae) in commercial culture. *Biocontrol Science and Technology* 13:529-535.

Hong, L., and X. Rumei. 1993. Studies on honeydew excretion by greenhouse whitefly, *Trialeurodes vaporariorum* (Westw.) on its host plant *Cucumis sativus*. *Journal of Applied Entomology* 115:43–51.

James, R. R., B. A. Croft, B. T. Shaffer, and B. Lighthart. 1998. Impact of temperature and humidity on host-pathogen interactions between *Beauveria bassiana* and a coccinellid. *Environmental Entomology* 27:1506–13.

Jervis, M. A., and N. A. C. Kidd. 1986. Host feeding strategies in hymenopteran parasitoids. *Biological Reviews* 61:395–443.

Lacey, L. A, J. J. Fransen, and R. Carruthers. 1996. Global distribution of naturally occurring fungi of *Bemisia*, their biologies and use as biological control agents. In *Bemisia: 1995 Taxonomy, Biology, Damage, Control, and Management*, ed. D. Gerling and R. T. Mayer, 401–33. Andover, U.K.: Intercept.

Legaspi, J. C., R. I. Carruthers, and D. A. Nordlund. 1994. Life history of *Chrysoperla rufilabris* (Neuroptera: Chrysopidae) provided sweetpotato whitefly *Bemisia tabaci* (Homoptera: Aleyrodidae) and other food. *Biological Control* 4:178–84.

Liu, T. X., R. D. Oetting, and G. D. Buntin. 1993. Distribution of *Trialeurodes vaporariorum* and *Bemisia tabaci* (Homoptera: Aleyrodidae) on some greenhouse-grown ornamental plants. *Journal of Entomological Science* 28:102–12.

———. 1994a. Temperature and diel catches of *Trialeurodes vaporariorum* and *Bemisia tabaci* (Homoptera: Aleyrodidae) adults on sticky traps in the greenhouse. *Journal of Entomological Science* 29:222–30.

———. 1994b. Evidence of interspecific competition between *Trialeurodes vaporariorum* (Westwood) and *Bemisia tabaci* (Gennadius) (Homoptera: Aleyrodidae) on some greenhouse-grown plants. *Journal of Entomological Science* 29:55–65.

Meade, D. L., and D. N. Byrne. 1991. The use of *Verticillium lecanii* against subimaginal instars of *Bemisia tabaci*. *Journal of Invertebrate Pathology* 57:296–8.

Meekes, E. T. M., J. J. Fransen, and J. C. van Lenteren. 1996. Pathogenicity of entomopathogenic fungi of the genus *Aschersonia* against whitefly. *IOBC/WPRS Bulletin* 19:103–6.

McAuslane, H. J., and R. Nguyen. 1996. Reproductive biology and behavior of a thelytokous species of *Eretmocerus* (Hymenoptera: Aphelinidae) parasitizing *Bemisia argentifolii* (Homoptera: Aleyrodidae). *Annals of the Entomological Society of America* 89:686–93.

Mound, L. A., and S. H. Halsey. 1978. *Whitefly of the World: A Systematic Catalogue of the Aleyrodidae (Homoptera) with Host Plant and Natural Enemy Data*. Chichester, U.K.: British Museum of Natural History and John Wiley and Sons.

Nechols, J. R., and M. J. Tauber. 1977. Age-specific interaction between the greenhouse whitefly and *Encarsia formosa*: Influence of host on the parasite's oviposition and development. *Environmental Entomology* 6:143–9.

Nell, H. W., L. A. Sevenster-van de Lelie, J. Woets, and J. C. van Lenteren. 1976. The host-parasite relationship between *Encarsia formosa* (Hymenoptera: Aphelinidae) and *Trialeurodes vaporariorum* (Homoptera: Aleyrodidae). II. Selection of host stages for oviposition and feeding by the parasite. *Zeitschrift für Angewandte Entomologie*. 81:372–6.

Nordlund, D. A., and J. C. Legaspi. 1996. Whitefly predators and their potential for use in biological control. In *Bemisia: 1995 Taxonomy, Biology, Damage, Control, and Management*, ed. D. Gerling and R. T. Mayer, 499–513. Andover, U.K.: Intercept.

Oetting, R. D., and G. D. Buntin. 1996. *Bemisia* damage expression in commercial greenhouse production. In Bemisia: *1995 Taxonomy, Biology, Damage, Control, and Management*, ed. D. Gerling and R. T. Mayer, 201–8. Andover, U.K.: Intercept.

Olson, D. L. and R. D. Oetting. 1999. The efficacy of mycoinsecticides of *Beauveria bassiana* against silverleaf whitefly (Homoptera: Aleyrodidae) on poinsettia. *Journal of Agricultural and Urban Entomology* 16:179-185.

Osborne, L. S., and Z. Landa. 1992. Biological control of whiteflies with entomopathogenic fungi. *Florida Entomologist* 75:456–71.

———. 1994. Utilization of entomogenous fungus *Paecilomyces fumosoroseus* against sweetpotato whitefly, *Bemisia tabaci*. *IOBC/WPRS Bulletin* 17:201–6.

Parrella, M. P., T. D. Paine, J. A. Bethke, K. L. Robb, and J. Hall. 1991. Evaluation of *Encarsia formosa* (Hymenoptera: Aphelinidae) for biological control of sweetpotato whitefly (Homoptera: Aleyrodidae) on poinsettia. *Journal of Economic Entomology* 20:713–9.

Quintela, E. D., and C. W. McCoy. 1997. Pathogenicity enhancement of *Metarhizium anisopliae* and *Beauveria bassiana* to first instars of *Diaprepes abbreviatus* (Coleoptera: Curculionidae) with sublethal doses of imidacloprid. *Environmental Entomology* 26:1173–82.

———. 1998. Conidial attachment of *Metarhizium anisopliae* and *Beauveria bassiana* to the larval cuticle of *Diaprepes abbreviatus* (Coleoptera: Curculionidae) treated with imidacloprid. *Journal of Invertebrate Pathology* 72:220–30.

Ravensberg, W. J., A. C. Van Buysen, and R. Berns. 1994. Side-effects of pesticides on *Verticillium lecanii*: In vivo tests on whiteflies and aphids. *IOBC/WPRS Bulletin* 17:234–8.

Roditakis, N. E. 1990. Host plants of greenhouse whitefly *Trialeurodes vaporariorum* Westwood (Homoptera; Aleyrodidae) in Crete. Attractiveness and impact on whitefly lifestages. *Agriculture, Ecosystems and Environment* 31:217–24.

Rose, M., and G. Zolnerowich. 1997. *Eretmocerus* Haldeman (Hymenoptera: Aphelinidae) in the United States, with descriptions of new species attacking *Bemisia* (*tabaci* complex) (Homoptera: Aleyrodidae). *Proceedings of the Entomological Society of Washington* 99:1–27.

Rose, M., G. Zolnerowich, and M. S. Hunter. 1996. Systematics, *Eretmocerus*, and biological control. In *Bemisia: 1995 Taxonomy, Biology, Damage, Control, and Management*, ed. D. Gerling and R. T. Mayer, 477–97. Andover, U.K.: Intercept.

Russel, L. M. 1963. Hosts and distribution of live species of *Trialeurodes*. *Annals of the Entomological Society of America* 56:149–53.

Sampson, A. C., and V. J. King. 1996. *Macrolophus caliginosus*, field establishment, and pest control effect in protected tomatoes. *IOBC/WPRS Bulletin* 19:143–6.

Samson, R. A., and M. C. Rombach. 1985. Biology of the fungi *Verticillium* and *Aschersonia*. In *Biological Pest Control: The Glasshouse Experience*, ed. N. W. Hussey and N. E.A. Scopes, 34–42. Poole, U.K.: Blandford Press (Ithaca, N.Y.: Cornell University Press).

Senior, L. J., and P. K. McEwen. 1998. Laboratory study of *Chrysoperla carnea* (Stephens) (Neuropt., Chrysopidae) predation on *Trialeurodes vaporariorum* (Westwood) (Hom., Aleyrodidae). *Journal of Applied Entomology* 122:99–101.

Shapiro, J. P. 1996. Insect-plant interactions and expression of disorders induced by the silverleaf whitefly, *Bemisia argentifolii*. In *Bemisia: 1995 Taxonomy, Biology, Damage, Control, and Management*, ed. D. Gerling and R. T. Mayer, 167–77. Andover, U.K.: Intercept.

Smith, P. 1993. Control of *Bemisia tabaci* and the potential of *Paecilomyces fumosoroseus* as a biopesticide. *Biocontrol News and Information* 14:71N–78N.

Stevens III, T. J., R. L. Kilmer, and S. J. Glenn. 2000. An economic comparison of biological and conventional control strategies for whiteflies (Homoptera: Aleyrodidae) in greenhouse poinsettias. *Journal of Economic Entomology* 93:623-629.

Sütterlin, S., and J. C. van Lenteren. 1996. Hairiness of *Gerbera jamesonii* leaves and the walking speed of the parasitoid *Encarsia formosa*. *IOBC/WPRS Bulletin* 19:171–4.

Szabo, P., J. C. van Lenteren, and P. W. T. Huisman. 1993. Development time, survival, and fecundity of *Encarsia formosa* on *Bemisia tabaci* and *Trialeurodes vaporariorum*. *IOBC/WPRS Bulletin* 16:173–6.

Todorova, S. I., D. Coderre, R. M. Duchesne, and J. C. Côté. 1998. Compatibility of *Beauveria bassiana* with selected fungicides and herbicides. *Environmental Entomology* 27:427–33.

van de Vrie, M., and D. Degheele. 1996. Toxicity of the fungal pathogen *Paecilomyces fumosoroseus* strain Apopka 97 to the greenhouse whitefly *Trialeurodes vaporariorum* and the parasitoid *Encarsia formosa*, and first results of a control experiment in glasshouse tomatoes. *IOBC/WPRS Bulletin* 19:191–4.

Van Driesche, R. G. and S. Lyon. 2003. Commercial adoption of biological control-based IPM for whiteflies in poinsettia. *Florida Entomologist* 86:481–3.

Van Driesche, R. G., S. M. Lyon, M. S. Hoddle, S. Roy, and J. P. Sanderson. 1999. Assessment of cost and reliability of *Eretmocerus eremicus* (Hymenoptera: Aphelinidae) for whitefly (Homoptera: Aleyrodidae) control in commercial poinsettia crops. *Florida Entomologist* 82 (4):570–95.

Van Driesche, R. G., M. S. Hoddle, S. Roy, S. Lyon and J. P. Sanderson. 2001a. Effect of parasitoid release pattern on whitefly (Homoptera: Alerodidae) control in commercial poinsettia. *Florida Entomologist* 84:63-69.

Van Driesche, R.G., M. S. Hoddle, S. Lyon, and J. P. Sanderson. 2001b. Compatibility of insect growth regulators with *Eretmocerus eremicus* (Hymenoptera: Aphelinidae) for whitefly (Homoptera: Aleyrodidae) control on poinsettias. II. Trials in commercial poinsettia crops. *Biological Control* 20: 132-146.

Van Driesche, R. G., S. Lyon, K. Jacques, T. Smith, and P. Lopes. 2002. Comparative cost of chemical and biological whitefly control in poinsettia: is there a gap? *Florida Entomologist* 85:488-493.

van Schelt J., J. Klapwik, M. Letard, and C. Aucouturier. 1996. The use of *Macrolophus* as a whitefly predator in protected crops. In *Bemisia: 1995 Taxonomy, Biology, Damage, Control, and Management*, ed. D. Gerling and R. T. Mayer, 515–21. Andover, U.K.: Intercept.

Vet, L. E. M., and J. C. van Lenteren. 1981. The parasite–host relationships between *Encarsia formosa* Gah. (Hymenoptera: Aphelinidae) and *Trialeurodes vaporariorum* (Westw.) (Homoptera: Aleyrodidae). X. A comparison of three *Encarsia* spp. and one *Eretmocerus* sp. to estimate their potentialities in controlling whitefly on tomatoes in greenhouses with a low temperature regime. *Zeitschrift für Angewandte Entomologie* 91:327–48.

Vidal, C., L. A. Lacey, and J. Fargues. 1997. Pathogenicity of *Paecilomyces fumosoroseus* (Deuteromycotina: Hyphomycetes) against *Bemisia argentifolii* (Homoptera: Aleyrodidae) with a description of a bioassay method. *Journal of Economic Entomology* 90:765–72.

Vidal, C., L. S. Osborne, L. A. Lacey, and J. Fargues. 1998. Effect of host plant on the potential of *Paecilomyces fumosoroseus* (Deuteromycotina: Hyphomycetes) for controlling the silverleaf whitefly, *Bemisia argentifolii* (Homoptera: Aleyrodidae) in greenhouses. *Biological Control* 12:191–9.

Wraight, S. P., R. I. Carruthers, C. A. Bradley, S. T. Jaronski, L. A. Lacey, P. Wood, and S. Galaini-Wraight. 1998. Pathogenicity of the entomopathogenic fungi *Paecilomyces* spp. and *Beauveria bassiana* against the silverleaf whitefly, *Bemisia argentifolii*. *Journal of Invertebrate Pathology* 71:217–26.

Yee, W., D. L. Hendrix, N. C. Toscano, C. C. Chu, and T. J. Henneberry. 1996. Diurnal field patterns of honeydew sugar secretion by *Bemisia argentifolii* (Homoptera: Aleyrodidae) nymphs on cotton. *Environmental Entomology* 25:776–82.

Zaki, F. N. 1998. Efficiency of the entomopathogenic fungus *Beauveria bassiana* (Bals), against *Aphis crassivora* Koch and *Bemisia tabaci* Gennadius. *Journal of Applied Entomology* 122:397–9.

9

BIOLOGICAL CONTROL OF
WHITEFLIES ON VEGETABLE CROPS

J. Avilla
Universitat de Lleida, Centre UdL-IRTA
Lleida, Spain

R. Albajes
Universitat de Lleida, Centre UdL-IRTA
Lleida, Spain

O. Alomar
IRTA, Centre de Cabrils, Departament de Protecció Vegetal
Cabrils, Spain

C. Castañé
IRTA, Centre de Cabrils, Departament de Protecció Vegetal
Cabrils, Spain

and

R. Gabarra
IRTA, Centre de Cabrils, Departament de Protecció Vegetal
Cabrils, Spain

Whiteflies (Homoptera: Aleyrodidae) are among the most harmful pests of protected vegetable crops. Although several dozen species of whiteflies have been reported to feed on vegetables (Mound and Halsey 1978), only two species cause economically important problems in greenhouse vegetables: the greenhouse whitefly, *Trialeurodes vaporariorum* (Westwood), and the tobacco or sweetpotato whitefly, *Bemisia tabaci* (Gennadius). The cabbage whitefly, *Aleyrodes proletella* (L.), has been identified more recently as causing problems in some greenhouse crops in The Netherlands (Loomans et al. 2002). Based on genomic,

behavioral, and morphological studies, one *B. tabaci* biotype, referred to as B-biotype, was proposed as a new species called silverleaf whitefly, *Bemisia argentifolii* Bellows and Perring (Bellows et al. 1994). Since then, several *B. tabaci* biotypes have been identified around the world showing differences in host ranges, biological parameters, and virus transmission capacity (Frohlich et al. 2001; Moya et al. 2001; Perring 2001). In this chapter, we use the name *B. tabaci* to refer to this complex of biotypes.

Whitefly nymphs and adults feed on phloem sap, and the consequent debilitating effect on the plant may cause significant reductions in crop yield. Like other homopterans, they produce honeydew that falls on leaves and fruits, on which sooty mold develops quickly under suitable temperature and relative humidity conditions. Sooty mold hampers photosynthesis and respiration and renders fruits unmarketable if they are not washed. A third kind of damage caused by whiteflies is related to their ability to act as virus vectors. Several viruses that severely affect protected vegetable crops worldwide are transmitted by *B. tabaci* and, to a far lesser extent, by *T. vaporariorum* (Rubio et al. 1999; Lecoq et al. 2000; Moriones and Navas-Castillo 2000). Several phytotoxic effects on vegetables (e.g., the silverleaf syndrome) may be caused by some biotypes of *B. tabaci* (Shapiro 1996).

The relationship between whitefly density and yield loss depends on the type of damage, and a wide range of tolerance levels is found in the literature. If a large primary inoculum of virus is available, plant diseases are rapidly introduced into the crop. Damage resulting from the transmission of plant viruses can occur at low whitefly densities, damage from honeydew deposition at relatively intermediate whitefly densities, and damage resulting from direct feeding occurs only at high densities. For example, 18 adults per leaf or 60 nymphs per leaf can produce sufficient honeydew to induce sooty mold development on tomatoes if the relative humidity reaches at least 80% for eight hours. By contrast, a density of 2,500 greenhouse whitefly nymphs per leaf is typically necessary to cause yield reduction on tomatoes (Hussey and Scopes 1977). A density of 45 greenhouse whitefly nymphs per in.^{2} (7 per cm^2) on younger leaflets has been suggested as a threshold for sooty mold development on tomato fruit (Hussey, Read, and Hesling 1969). Under long day conditions, when plants produce more assimilates, higher whitefly densities are needed to reduce yield, and losses are mainly due to sooty mold development (Johnson et al. 1992).

Several traits of the biology of *T. vaporariorum* and *B. tabaci* may explain their success in exploiting so many crops worldwide grown under different conditions, from greenhouses in northern temperate areas to open field crops in warmer tropical and subtropical regions. Only the most significant traits related to protected vegetable crops are mentioned here (see chapter 8, Byrne and Bellows 1991, and several chapters in Gerling 1990a for more information). *T. vaporariorum* and *B. tabaci* feed on most of the vegetables grown in greenhouses, as well as on many ornamental plants and common weeds. Each plant species is affected somewhat differently, depending on whitefly preference and performance. Eggplant and cucurbits are more affected by greenhouse whitefly than tomato and French bean, while sweet pepper is the least affected of all (van Lenteren and Noldus 1990). The B-biotype of *B. tabaci* is found in high numbers on several *Brassica* species on which other biotypes are seldom found (Perring 1996). Within plant species, strong differences in susceptibility to whiteflies have been observed among cultivars (Heinz and Zalom 1995). On suitable host plants and under favorable environmental conditions, greenhouse whitefly and *B. tabaci* have high population growth rates, mainly due to their short developmental time, high fecundity, and low mortality rate of immatures (van Roermund and van Lenteren 1992; Zalom, Castañé, and Gabarra 1995). Nitrogen fertilization can also affect their population growth rate through an increase in female fecundity (Jauset et al. 1998). In addition to this high potential of population increase, in areas with different cropping cycles, whitefly adults may move among crops and build up high-density populations almost year-round when uninterrupted by prolonged cold temperatures (Alomar et al. 1989).

Two approaches are available to growers for managing whitefly populations in greenhouses: regular use of insecticides or biological control. Because whiteflies develop quickly within greenhouses and because no insecticides are able to kill all development stages, applications have to be repeated frequently, sometimes more than once a week. Frequent pesticide use often leads to development of insecticide resistance (Denholm et al. 1996; Elbert and Nauen 2000), and greatly increases production costs, residues on fruit, and environmental pollution. Biological control of *T. vaporariorum* by the aphelinid wasp *Encarsia formosa* Gahan has been successfully applied in many hectares of protected crops (van Lenteren and Woets 1988; van Lenteren, van Roermund, and Sütterlin 1996). In recent years, an increasing number of parasitoids and predators are being used to control *T. vaporariorum* and *B. tabaci* (Gabarra and Besri, 1999). Other pest control techniques, such as plant resistance and cultural practices, can be used to supplement chemical and biological control for whitefly management in greenhouses.

Whitefly Natural Enemies as Biological Control Agents in Protected Vegetable Crops

Natural enemies (predators, parasitoids, and pathogens) can be used for biological control in three different ways: (a) inoculative releases of relatively few individuals, (b) inundative releases of many individuals to quickly lower the pest population density, and (c) conservation and augmentation of natural enemies already established in the area. Natural enemies used on vegetable crops in greenhouses are seasonally inoculated, with populations reproducing in the greenhouse for six to fifteen months, depending on the length of time required to produce a particular crop. Rarely is cropping so continuous that periodic releases become unnecessary. Little attention, however, has been paid to biological control by conserving and augmenting resident predator, parasitoid, and entomopathogen populations. This is probably because biological control in protected vegetable crops has been primarily used in northern European areas where indoor and outdoor populations of greenhouse pests have few interactions and native natural enemies are scarce. By contrast, the sides of greenhouses are frequently open, and the surrounding environment is a major source of pests and natural enemies (fig. 9.1) in warmer areas such as the Mediterranean region (Gabarra et al. 2004). In these regions, conservation and augmentation of natural enemies is an approach that may reduce, or even sometimes eliminate, the need for inoculative releases of expensive natural enemies (Alomar et al. 1991, Nicoli and Burgio 1997).

Candidate natural enemies used in conservation and augmentation programs are likely to require a suite of biological traits to facilitate their ability to produce successful biological control. The suite of traits, which are somewhat different than those associated with inoculative release programs, includes high dispersal capacity, fast response to sudden increases in prey numbers, ability to switch to the most abundant prey and ability to survive at low prey densities (Albajes and Alomar 1999). Within the context of whitefly conservation or augmentation biological control programs, more extensive research on local whitefly natural enemies is required to find species that are efficient under the regional climate and the cropping pattern.

The taxonomies, life histories, and bionomics of the parasitoids, predators, and entomopathogens associated with greenhouse

Figure 9.1. In many of the growing regions throughout the Mediterranean (Catalonia, Spain shown above), greenhouses are usually surrounded by areas of outdoor crop production and wild vegetation. These areas of vegetation are frequent sources of natural enemies and pest species commonly found in the greenhouses. *Photo: O. Alomar.*

and tobacco whiteflies have been reviewed in the works of Fransen (1990); Gerling (1990b); Polaszek, Evans, and Bennett (1992); Cock (1993); Gerling and Mayer (1996); Faria and Wraight (2001); and Gerling, Alomar, and Arnó (2001) and references within. Below, we will refer mainly to the most relevant natural enemies that have been used in biological control in protected vegetable crops according to the above-mentioned strategies and to those that have been tested in semifield trials.

Parasitoids

E. formosa is the most widely studied and used *T. vaporariorum* parasitoid in greenhouses. In the 1990s, it was released in about 12,355 acres (5,000 ha) of greenhouses (van Lenteren, van Roermund, and Sütterlin 1996), accounting for 25% of the total market for natural enemies in greenhouses (Bolckmans 1999). Van Roermund and van Lenteren (1992); van Lenteren, van Roermund, and Sütterlin (1996); Hoddle, Van Driesche, and Sanderson (1998); and van Lenteren and Martin (1999) have reviewed its biology and use. In the following paragraphs, only the most critical issues for biological control of whiteflies on protected vegetable crops are summarized (see chapter 8 for details on its use in protected ornamental crops).

Releases of *E. formosa* are initiated when greenhouse whitefly population density is low (less than one whitefly adult per plant). Since females lay eggs mostly in third- and fourth-instar nymphs and whiteflies rarely develop synchronously, more than one release is needed. The efficacy of the parasitoid depends on many factors—such as temperature and the host plant—that can limit its use in certain moments, areas, and crops.

Temperature is one of the most critical factors affecting *E. formosa* use. Too low or too high temperatures can affect development, fecundity, longevity, and behavior of *E. formosa* and decrease its biocontrol efficiency. Van Roermund and van Lenteren (1992) reviewed the influence of the temperature on the parasitoid biology and performance.

Crop species also influence the dynamics of the *E. formosa*–greenhouse whitefly relationship, and therefore the success of biological control. Crop species affects the rate of increase of greenhouse whitefly, and biological control is less efficient on crops that are particularly suitable for pest population increase, such as eggplant and cucurbits. Crop plant structure, especially the degree of leaf pubescence, can change the efficiency of parasitoid searching behavior (De Ponti and van Lenteren 1981). Vegetable breeding programs need to consider plant effects on both the pest and the parasitoid when choosing breeding objectives. For example, breeding a very hairy-leafed variety to reduce the rate of increase of whiteflies may be counterproductive because it will make *E. formosa* inefficient and limit its use on the crop (De Ponti, Romanov, and Berlinger 1990).

Other greenhouse whitefly parasitoids have been studied and tested, including *Encarsia tricolor* Förster (Albajes et al. 1980; Onillon, Geria, and Vallier 1989; Avilla et al. 1990), *Encarsia meritoria* Gahan (Avilla et al. 1991), and *Encarsia pergandiella* Howard (Onillon, Maignet, and Cocquempot 1994). *E. tricolor* and *E. pergandiella* are autoparasitoids; females develop on whiteflies, and

males develop as hyperparasitoids of their own or other *Encarsia* species. *E. tricolor* is commonly found in the Mediterranean area, where it develops outdoors on *Aleyrodes* spp. and *T. vaporariorum*. Its rate of increase is higher than the rate of increase of *T. vaporariorum* at temperatures above 59°F (15°C) (Avilla and Copland 1988), and results from field experiments suggest that it may significantly suppress whitefly populations (Albajes et al. 1980; Onillon, Geria, and Vallier 1989). *E. pergandiella* was introduced in Italy from America in the late 1970s (Viggiani and Mazzone 1980) to control greenhouse whitefly. Since its introduction, it has established in many parts of the Mediterranean area, and may interfere with the use of *E. formosa* in greenhouses by hyperparasitizing whitefly nymphs already parasitized by the latter (Onillon, Maignet, and Cocquempot 1994; Gabarra et al. 1999; Giorgini and Viggiani 2000; Gabarra, Arnó, and Albajes 2003). *E. formosa* remains the most useful parasitoid for biological control of greenhouse whitefly on vegetables grown within protected culture.

When *B. tabaci* expanded worldwide beginning in 1986–1987 and became a serious pest in several greenhouse growing areas, *E. formosa* was tested as a control agent of the new pest to avoid interrupting the successful biological control programs already in place for vegetable crops. Most trials against *B. tabaci* have been conducted on poinsettia (see chapter 8 and Hoddle, Van Driesche, and Sanderson 1998), whereas very few results of trials on protected vegetable crops have been reported. In fall greenhouse tomatoes infested by both *T. vaporariorum* and *B. tabaci*, *E. formosa* preferred to parasitize *T. vaporariorum*, even though it was far less abundant than *B. tabaci* (Arnó and Gabarra 1996).

Several species of *Encarsia* (*E. bimaculata* Heraty and Polaszek, *E. lutea* [Masi], *E. nigricephala* Dozier, *E. hispida* De Santis, and *E. sophia* [Girault and Dodd]) and of *Eretmocerus* (*E. emiratus* Zolnerovich and Rose, *E. eremicus* Rose and Zolnerovich, *E. hayati* Zolnerovich and Rose, *E. melanoscutus* Zolnerovich and Rose, *E. mundus* Mercet, and *E. staufferi* Rose and Zolnerovich) have been studied as biocontrol agents of *B. tabaci* (Gerling, Alomar, and Arnó 2001; Hoelmer and Goolsby 2003). *E. pergandiella* was tested for controlling *B. tabaci* in a tomato glasshouse, but autoparasitism was responsible for low parasitism rates in the second parasitoid generation after release (Onillon, Maignet, and Cocquempot 1994). *E. hispida* showed slightly better results (Onillon and Maignet 2000). *E. eremicus* was first tested in poinsettia with good results (Heinz and Parrella 1994) and it was introduced into Europe as a biocontrol agent for vegetable crops. Since it can parasitise both whitefly species, *E. eremicus* is mass reared on *T. vaporariorum* on which rearing is more cost effective than on *B. tabaci*. *E. eremicus* is used for the control of mixed populations of both whitefly species. *E. mundus* is native to the Mediterranean area, and although it is unable to parasitise *T. vaporariorum*, it is more efficient than *E. eremicus* for *B. tabaci* control (Stansly et al. 2004). These authors observed that when *E. mundus* and *E. eremicus* are released in tomato greenhouses, only the former is recovered from the crop at the end of the season; the interaction between the two whitefly parasitoids should be thus studied to evaluate the real efficacy of *E. eremicus* in areas where *E. mundus* is native and can naturally enter greenhouses.

Predators

B. tabaci and greenhouse whitefly predators include beetles (e.g., coccinellids), true bugs (e.g., anthocorids and mirids), lacewings (e.g., chrysopids) and mites (e.g., phytoseiids). Many whitefly predators are polyphagous and have been found associated with outbreaks, but only a few have been extensively studied for use in seasonal inoculative releases, and even fewer are reared commercially.

Predaceous bugs

Several Miridae (Heteroptera) have been incorporated into biological control programs of whiteflies in protected vegetable crops, i.e., *Macrolophus caliginosus* Wagner (*Macrolophus melanotoma* [Costa], according to Carapezza [1995]) (fig. 9.2) and *Dicyphus tamaninii* Wagner (Alomar et al. 1991, Malausa 1994) (fig. 9.3). These species are polyphagous predators that prey on several soft-bodied arthropods, including whiteflies, aphids, mites, thrips, leafminer larvae, and lepidopteran eggs; occasionally, they may feed on plants (Alomar and Albajes 1996). This feeding behavior has been considered a disadvantage to the use of mirids for biological control, particularly on ornamental and flower crops, where feeding damage may reduce the aesthetic appeal of the crop. However, the ability to survive on a plant diet in the absence of prey may help these predators to establish on the crop (Naranjo and Gibson 1996).

Mirid females insert their eggs in plant

Figure 9.2. *Macrolophus caliginosus* **Wagner (adult shown in photograph) are often released into vegetable greenhouses for biological control of whiteflies.**
Photo: O. Alomar.

tissues. Their fecundity, which is influenced by plant and prey species, ranges from 88 to 268 eggs. At 77°F (25°C), eggs take ten to twelve days to hatch, nymphs complete their development in about twenty days, and adults live up to thirty days (Fauvel, Malausa, and Kaspar 1987; Albajes et al. 1996). Fresh plant material is needed for oviposition and subsequent development of eggs, which is one of the main constraints on their mass rearing. *M. caliginosus* readily lays eggs on some artificial substrates with no reduction in fecundity; however, the egg mortality is high due to desiccation (Constant, Grenier, and Bonnot 1996). Although *M. caliginosus* prey preferences are poorly known, *B. tabaci* eggs, nymphs, and to a lesser extent, adults, are frequently used as prey in field and greenhouse conditions (Gabarra, Castañé, and Albajes 1995; Barnadas, Gabarra, and Albajes 1998). Consumption rates are relatively high. Adults of *D. tamaninii* consume 15.0 and 12.1 nymphs of greenhouse and tobacco whitefly per day, respectively, and adults of *M. caliginosus* consume 8.5 and 5.0

nymphs of greenhouse and tobacco whitefly per day, respectively (Barnadas, Gabarra, and Albajes 1998).

In Canada, *Dicyphus hesperus* Knight has been used in recent years to control greenhouse whitefly in greenhouse tomato (Gillespie et al. 2001) and it is expected to play a similar role in biological control of greenhouse vegetables than *M. caliginosus* in Europe. Another native mirid bug, *Macrolophus pygmaeus* Rambur, is sold in Europe to control whiteflies in protected tomato and its use has been recommended in German greenhouses for control at low temperature regimes (Hommes and Horst 2002). Other mirids, such as *Macrolophus costalis* Fieber (Brzezinski 1982), *Campylomma* sp. (Kajita 1984), *Dicyphus errans* (Wolff), and *Nesidiocoris tenuis* (Reuter), could be of interest in the future. The latter species not only naturally colonizes greenhouses, but it is also commercially released.

Figure 9.3. *Dicyphus tamaninii* **Wagner (adult shown in photograph) is a polyphagous predator that naturally enters into vegetable production greenhouses and preys on various pests.**
Photo: O. Alomar.

Mirids that are resident in the Mediterranean area often enter greenhouses and prey on mite and insect pests (Alomar et al. 1991). When used in inoculative biological control, the releases are done when prey populations are low, although sometimes they do not establish on the crop for reasons that remain largely unknown. Factors involved in predator switching to plant feeding and consequences of potential intraguild predation (i.e., predators eating other biological control organisms) are still in need of investigation to define the optimal use of these mirids for biological control in protected vegetable crops (Albajes and Alomar 1999).

In addition to mirids, predaceous anthocorids (pirate bugs) and lygaeids (seed bugs) have been investigated for use as biological control agents in greenhouses. Anthocorids in the genus *Orius* have been studied for potential use against thrips, but they also prey on whiteflies. For example, *Orius sauteri* Poppius feeds on *T. vaporariorum* nymphs and eggs (Kajita 1982), and may help prevent outbreaks of whiteflies in the field. Anthocorids, however, are rarely able to reduce densities of greenhouse whitefly in greenhouses. Among lygaeids, *Geocoris punctipes* (Say) has been evaluated in laboratory tests for control of whiteflies, and its potential as a biological control agent of *B. tabaci* in programs of conservation and augmentation of native natural enemies has been suggested (Cohen and Byrne 1992).

Other predators

Many coccinellids (Coleoptera) have been identified as predators of *B. tabaci* (Nordlund and Legaspi 1996). Among these, *Delphastus*

catalinae (Horn) (most, if not all, of the published studies on *Delphastes pusillus* [LeConte] biology and behavior on *B. tabaci* actually refer to *D. catalinae*, according to Hoelmer and Pickett [2003]) is a very voracious predator whose larvae and adults can consume as many as 10,000 whitefly eggs or 700 fourth-instar nymphs during their life span (Hoelmer, Osborne, and Yokomi 1993). However, this high food requirement of *D. catalinae* for its development and oviposition may hamper the beetle's establishment in the crop when whitefly populations are low. In the review by Gerling, Alomar, and Annó (2001), many other *B. tabaci* predators are listed and their potential use in biological control is discussed.

Entomopathogens

Only fungi have been reported as Aleyrodidae pathogens. *Aschersonia aleyrodis* Webber, *Lecanicillium* (formerly *Verticillium*) *lecanii* (Zimm.) Zare & W. Gams, *Paecilomyces fumosoroseus* (Wize) Brown and Smith, and *Beauveria bassiana* (Balsamo) Vuillemin have been tested for control of greenhouse and tobacco whiteflies (Fransen 1990; Faria and Wraight 2001). Infection rates are highly, although differentially, dependent on temperature and humidity of the microclimate in the phyllosphere (the plant-air interface), and this environmental dependence is a major constraint on their use in warm areas. However, the management of the greenhouse environment and suitable formulations of the active ingredient may enhance the potential for their application. Several mycoinsecticides for whitefly control in greenhouses are available.

Programs of Biological Control of Whiteflies in Protected Vegetable Crops

Problems caused by whiteflies and their biological control in protected vegetable crops are strongly influenced by climate and cropping patterns. Biological control of protected vegetable crops has developed mainly in northern Europe, where the climate is cool and crops are grown within closed glasshouses. In the Mediterranean area, the climate is warm and crops are grown in plastic greenhouses that are frequently open on the sides. By contrasting biological control between these two regions, we aim to present a working template upon which whitefly biological control programs may be adapted to other parts of the world.

In northern Europe (e.g., the Netherlands, Germany, the United Kingdom), there are 106,000 acres (43,000 ha) (Wittwer and Castilla 1995) of crops that are produced primarily in glasshouses (Robertson and Hoxey 1992) that are heated almost year-round and are closed most of the time. Tomato and cucumber are the major vegetable crops grown in glasshouses in these regions, and *T. vaporariorum* is the major pest of these crops. Because it is difficult for whitefly adults to survive outdoors during northern winters, whitefly populations develop entirely inside glasshouses at this time of the year. Only during the few warm summer months can whiteflies enter glasshouses from outdoor crops or weeds. A similar picture can be described in the protected vegetables in Canada.

By contrast, vegetable crops produced in warmer regions (e.g., the Mediterranean basin, parts of Asia) are grown in approximately 603,000 acres (244,000 ha) (Wittwer and Castilla 1995; acreage of protected culture in China is largely unknown) of unheated plastic tunnels and greenhouses. In these regions, greenhouses are usually open from spring through fall to improve ventilation. Warm temperatures allow whiteflies to reproduce year-round both inside and outside of greenhouses, and this leads to a continuous exchange of pest populations between old and young crops, between fields and greenhouses, and among greenhouse crops. High temperatures also allow a greater number of whitefly generations per year. Whitefly problems differ among three regions within this geographic area. In the mild area of southern France, northern Italy, and northern Spain, the main whitefly species on vegetable crops is *T. vaporariorum*. In the warm area of Israel, northern Africa, southern Spain and southern Italy, *B. tabaci* is the main pest species. In the transition area between these two regions, *T. vaporariorum* and *B. tabaci* are present on the same crop but at different ratios throughout the year.

Whitefly biological control programs for protected vegetable crops were initially developed for *T. vaporariorum*. Worldwide expansion of *B. tabaci* in protected culture restricted the use of biological control to those areas where only *T. vaporariorum* was present. More recently, however, biological control programs for *B. tabaci* control are being implemented at a commercial scale.

Biocontrol of *T. vaporariorum* is based on early detection of initial whitefly populations and prompt release of parasitoids and/or predators (Gabarra and Besri 1999). The decision to initiate the release of natural enemies is based on visual counts of whiteflies on plants (with a maximum of one adult greenhouse whitefly per tomato or cucumber plant) or catches of whitefly adults on yellow sticky traps (with presence of whiteflies on traps being the signal to begin parasitoid releases). Once releases begin, natural enemies are introduced periodically throughout the cropping season. Most of the biological control programs currently used against greenhouse whitefly on protected vegetable crops employ inoculative releases of *E. formosa*, although complementary releases of the predatory mirid bug *M. caliginosus* are increasingly being included. The IPM program for the whole crop may also include introductions of other natural enemies against additional pests and/or the use of compatible pesticides.

Current biological whitefly control programs in the cold production area are based upon experiments performed in the 1970s at the Glasshouse Crops Research Institute (U.K.) (Hussey and Scopes 1985) and experiments performed in the Mediterranean area with native mirid bugs. *E. formosa* release rates that have been used range from one to eight parasitized whiteflies per plant made over several releases (Onillon 1990). Release rates recommended for use in cucumber are higher than those recommended in tomato because *E. formosa* is less effective on cucumber due to the trichomes on its leaves. In most greenhouses where biocontrol is applied in the cold production area, *E. formosa* is complemented with *M. caliginosus*—which is usually released at the rate of 0.09 adults per ft.^{2} (1 per m^2) — or with *E. eremicus*, which gives better results when temperatures in glasshouses are lower.

In the mild climates of southern France, northern Italy, and northern Spain, *E. formosa* is being increasingly replaced by other natural enemies due to the interference of the naturally occurring populations of the hyperparasitoid *E. pergandiella*, or the presence of *B. tabaci*. In southern France, *M. caliginosus* (at least 0.18 adults per ft.^{2} [2 adults/m^2]) is used in combination with *E. formosa*, *E. eremicus*, or *E. mundus* to control *B. tabaci* and *T. vaporariorum* (Trottin-Caudal and Capy 2003). In Catalonia (NE Spain), only *M. caliginosus* is used to control *T. vaporariorum* in protected tomatoes; in this case, an inoculative rate of 0.14 adults per ft.^{2} (1.5 adults per m^2) is used (Gabarra, Arnó, and Albajes 2003).

In the warm areas of Israel, northern Africa and southern Spain, *B. tabaci* is the predominant whitefly species. Its capacity to transmit plant viruses is the major constraint to use of biological control. Biological control is mostly applied in sweet peppers on which virus pressure is less than on tomato. In this crop, *E. eremicus* was initially used to control *B. tabaci* (Castañé 2002), but the native *E. mundus* is increasingly used in commercial programs. In tomato, availability of TYLCV-resistant varieties may favor whitefly biological control. *E. mundus* appears to be as well adapted to tomato as it is to pepper, although higher release rates seem to be necessary in tomato (Stansly et al. 2004). Nevertheless, the role of naturally occurring predators and parasitoids in decreasing the pest population and in reducing crop damage in these conditions can still be spectacular. In Israel, populations of

B. tabaci in field crops have been decreasing over the last twenty years, partly due to a reduction in pesticide use, which has permitted conservation of indigenous natural enemies. Some of these locally adapted natural enemies may be then suitable candidates for inoculative releases into greenhouses. The use of banker plants is again being considered, as this approach may help maintain native natural enemies in greenhouses and eliminate several releases. Judicious use of insecticides and augmentation of indigenous natural enemies will be the key for preventing pest population buildup in surrounding crops, rather than the reduction of already high populations in the target crop (Gerling 1996).

In the climatically mild production areas, it is important to use proper cultural control practices to make biological control effective and feasible. For example, it is important to start with clean transplants, to minimize the sources of whitefly infestations within the planting area, and to reduce whitefly immigration from outside. Cultural practices capable of accomplishing these goals include removing weeds from borders close to greenhouses, using screening greenhouse intake vents, and managing neighboring crops to reduce whitefly populations (Alomar et al. 1989; Berlinger and Lebiush-Mordechi 1996; Hanafi et al. 2003).

Concluding Remarks

Biological control of *T. vaporariorum* in greenhouses with inoculative releases of *E. formosa* and/or *M. caliginosus* is effective and widely used in cooler climates with tightly sealed glasshouses, and in some warm areas where *T. vaporariorum* is the most common whitefly pest. However, most protected vegetable crop production occurs in regions where greenhouses are open and linkage exists between field and greenhouse crops, where *B. tabaci* is the most common whitefly pest, or both. The success of biological control programs in these regions depends on managing of pest and natural enemy populations surrounding the greenhouses as well as populations within the greenhouses. Frequently, the dynamics of these pest–natural enemy interactions are poorly understood, and a greater research effort should be exerted on this issue. In addition, strict sanitation of incoming plant material and adherence to good cultural practices (e.g., weed control , sometimes the use of insect screening over vents) are required. Biological control programs based solely on the release of beneficials in these regions are likely to be expensive and ineffective.

References Cited

Albajes, R., and O. Alomar. 1999. Current and potential use of polyphagous predators. In *Integrated Pest and Disease Management in Greenhouse Crops*, ed. R. Albajes, M. L. Gullino, J. C. van Lenteren, and Y. Elad, 265-75. Dordrecht, the Netherlands: Kluwer Academic Publisher.

Albajes, R., O. Alomar, J. Riudavets, C. Castañé, J. Arnó, and R. Gabarra. 1996. The mirid bug *Dicyphus tamaninii:* An effective predator for vegetable crops. *IOBC/WPRS Bulletin* 19 (1):1–4.

Albajes, R., M. Casadevall, E. Bordas, R. Gabarra, and O. Alomar. 1980. La mosca blanca de los invernaderos, *Trialeurodes vaporariorum*, en El Maresme. II. Utilización de *Encarsia tricolor* en un invernadero de tomate temprano. *Anales del Instituto Nacional de Investigaciones Agrarias. Serie Agrícola* 13:191–203.

Alomar, O. and R. Albajes. 1996. Greenhouse whitefly (Homoptera: Aleyrodidae) predation and tomato fruit injury by the zoophytophagous predator *Dicyphus tamaninii* (Heteroptera: Miridae). In *Zoophytophagous Heteroptera: Implications for Life History and Integrated Pest Management*, ed. O. Alomar and R. N. Wiedenmann, 155–77. Lanham, Md.: Entomological Society of America.

Alomar, O., C. Castañé, R. Gabarra, J. Arnó, J. Ariño, and R. Albajes. 1991. Conservation of mirid bugs for biological control in protected and outdoor tomato crops. *IOBC/WPRS Bulletin* 14 (5):33–42.

Alomar, O., C. Castañé, R. Gabarra, E. Bordas, and J. Adillon. 1989. Cultural practices for IPM in protected crops in Catalonia. In *Integrated Pest Management in Protected Vegetable Crops*, ed. R. Cavalloro and C. Pelerents, 347–54. Rotterdam, the Netherlands: Balkema.

Arnó, J., and R. Gabarra.. 1996. Potential for biological control of mixed *Trialeurodes vaporariorum* and *Bemisia tabaci* populations in winter tomato crops grown in greenhouses. In *Bemisia: 1995 Taxonomy, Biology, Damage, Control, and Management*, ed. D. Gerling and R. T. Mayer, 523–6. Andover, U.K.: Intercept.

Avilla, J., M. Artigues, M. J. Sarasúa, and R. Albajes. 1990. A review of the biological characteristics of *Encarsia tricolor* and their implications for biological control. *IOBC/WPRS Bulletin* 13 (5):14–8.

Avilla, J., and M. J. W. Copland. 1988. Development rate, number of mature oocytes at emergence, and adult size of *Encarsia tricolor* at constant and variable temperatures. *Entomophaga* 33:289–98.

Avilla, J., G. Viggiani, X. Díaz, and M. J. Sarasúa. 1991. Morphological and biological notes on *Encarsia meritoria* Gahan (Hymenoptera, Aphelinidae), a new parasitoid in Europe of *Trialeurodes vaporariorum* (Westwood) (Homoptera: Aleyrodidae). *Biocontrol Science and Technology* 1:289–95.

Barnadas, I., R. Gabarra, and R. Albajes. 1998. Predatory capacity of two mirid bugs preying on *Bemisia tabaci*. *Entomologia Experimentalis et Applicata* 86:215–9.

Bellows, T. S., T. M. Perring, R. J. Gill, and D. H. Headrick. 1994. Description of a species of *Bemisia* (Homoptera: Aleyrodidae). *Annals of the Entomological Society of America* 87:195–206.

Berlinger, M. J., and S. Lebiush-Mordechi. 1996. Physical methods for the control of *Bemisia*. In *Bemisia: 1995 Taxonomy, Biology, Damage, Control, and Management*, ed. D. Gerling and R. T. Mayer, 617–34. Andover, U.K.: Intercept.

Bolckmans, K. J. F. 1999. Commercial aspects of biological pest control in greenhouses. In *Integrated Pest and Disease Management in Greenhouse Crops*, ed. R. Albajes, M. L. Gullino, J. C. van Lenteren, and Y. Elad, 310-18. Dordrecht, the Netherlands: Kluwer Academic Publishers.

Brzezinski, K. 1982. Report of investigations on the morphology, biology, and ecology of the heteropteran *Macrolophus costalis* and its predation in relation to *Trialeurodes vaporariorum*. *Materialy Sesji Instytutu Ochrony Roslin* 22/23:285–92.

Byrne, D. N., and T. S. Bellows. 1991. Whitefly biology. *Annual Review of Entomology* 36:431–57.

Carapezza, A. 1995. The specific identities of *Macrolophus melanotoma* (A. Costa, 1853) and *Stenodema curticolle* (A. Costa, 1853) (Insecta, Heteroptera, Miridae). *Naturalista Siciliano S. IV* 19:295–8.

Castañé, C. 2002. Status of biological and integrated control in greenhouse vegetables in Spain: successes and challenges. *IOBC/WPRS Bulletin* 25(1):59-62.

Cock, M. J. W., ed. 1993. Bemisia tabaci: *An Update, 1986–1992, on the Cotton Whitefly with an Annotated Bibliography*. Wallingford, U.K.: CAB International.

Cohen, A. C., and D. N. Byrne. 1992. *Geocoris punctipes* as a predator of *Bemisia tabaci*: A laboratory evaluation. *Entomologia Experimentalis et Applicata* 64:195–202.

Constant, B., S. Grenier, and G. Bonnot. 1996. Artificial substrate for egg laying and embryonic development by the predatory bug *Macrolophus caliginosus* (Heteroptera: Miridae). *Biological Control* 7:140–7.

Denholm, I., M. Cahill, F. J. Byrne, and A. L. Devonshire. 1996. Progress with documenting and combating insecticide resistance in *Bemisia*. In *Bemisia: 1995 Taxonomy, Biology, Damage, Control and Management*, ed. D. Gerling and R. T. Mayer, 577–603. Andover, U.K.: Intercept.

De Ponti, O. M. B., L. R. Romanov, and M. J. Berlinger. 1990. Whitefly-plant relationships: Plant resistance. In *Whiteflies: Their Bionomics, Pest Status, and Management*, ed. D. Gerling, 91–106. Andover, U.K.: Intercept.

De Ponti, O. M. B., and J. C. van Lenteren. 1981. Resistance and glabrousness: Different approaches to biological control of two cucumber pests, *Tetranychus urticae* and *Trialeurodes vaporariorum*. *IOBC/WPRS Bulletin* 6:109–13.

Elbert, A., and R. Nauen. 2000. Resistance of *Bemisia tabaci* (Homoptera: Aleyrodidae) to insecticides in southern Spain with special reference to neonicotinoids. *Pest Management Science* 56: 60-4.

Faria, F., and S. P. Wraight. 2001. Biological control of *Bemisia tabaci* with fungi. *Crop Protection* 20:767-78.

Fauvel, G., J. C. Malausa, and B. Kaspar. 1987. Etude en laboratoire des principales caracteristiques biologiques de *Macrolophus caliginosus* (Heteroptera: Miridae). *Entomophaga* 32:529–43.

Fransen, J. J. 1990. Natural enemies of whiteflies: Fungi. In *Whiteflies: Their Bionomics, Pest Status, and Management*, ed. D. Gerling, 187–209. Andover, U.K.: Intercept.

Frohlich, D. R., I. Torres-Jerez, I. D. Bedford, P. G. Markham, and J. K. Brown. 2001. A phylogeographical analysis of the *Bemisia tabaci* species complex based on mitochondrial DNA markers. *Molecular Ecology* 8:1683-91.

Gabarra, R., J. Arnó, and R. Albajes. 2003. Integrated pest management in greenhouse tomatoes in Spain. In *Actes colloque international*, 198-202. Avignon, France.

Gabarra, R., J. Arnó, O. Alomar, and R. Albajes. 1999. Naturally occurring populations of *Encarsia pergandiella* (Hymenoptera: Aphelinidae) in tomato greenhouses. *IOBC/WPRS Bulletin* 22 (1):85–8.

Gabarra, R., and M. Besri. 1999. Tomatoes. In *Integrated Pest and Disease Management in Greenhouse Crops*, ed. R. Albajes, M. L. Gullino, J. C. van Lenteren, and Y. Elad, 420-34. Dordrecht, the Netherlands: Kluwer Academic Publisher.

Gabarra, R., C. Castañé, and R. Albajes. 1995. The mirid bug *Dicyphus tamaninii* as a greenhouse whitefly and western flower thrips predator on cucumber. *Biocontrol Science and Technology* 5:475–88.

Gabarra, R., O. Alomar, C. Castañé, M. Goula, and R. Albajes. 2004. Movement of greenhouse whitefly and its predators between in- and outside of Mediterranean greenhouses. *Agriculture, Ecosystems and Environment*, in press.

Gerling, D., ed. 1990a. *Whiteflies: Their Bionomics, Pest Status, and Management*. Andover, U.K.: Intercept.

———. 1990b. Natural enemies of whiteflies: Predators and parasitoids. In *Whiteflies: Their Bionomics, Pest Status, and Management*, ed. D. Gerling, 147–85. Andover, U.K.: Intercept.

———. 1996. Status of *Bemisia tabaci* in the Mediterranean countries: Opportunities for biological control. *Biological Control* 6:11–22.

Gerling, D., O. Alomar, and J. Arnó. 2001. Biological control of *Bemisia tabaci* using predators and parasitoids. *Crop Protection* 20:779-99.

Gerling, D., and R. T. Mayer, eds. 1996. *Bemisia: 1995 Taxonomy, Biology, Damage Control, and Management*. Andover, U.K.: Intercept.

Gillespie, D. R., J. A. Sánchez, R. McGregor, and D. Quiring. 2001. *Dicyphus hesperus: Life history, biology and application in tomato greenhouses*. Technical Report # 166. Canada: Agriculture and Agri Food Canada.

Giorgini, M., and G. Viggiani 2000. A compared evaluation of *Encarsia formosa* Gahan and *Encarsia pergandiella* Howard (Hymenoptera: Aphelinidae) as biological control agents of *Trialeurodes vaporariorum* (Westwood) (Homoptera: Aleyrodidae) on tomato under greenhouse in southern Italy. *IOBC/WPRS Bulletin* 23(1):109-116.

Hanafi, A., R. Bouharroud, S. Miftah, and S. Amouat. 2003. Performances of two types of insect screens as a physical barrier against *Bemisia tabaci* and their impact on TYLCV incidence in greenhouse tomato in Souss Valley of Morocco. *IOBC/WPRS Bulletin* 26(10):39-42

Heinz, K. M., and M. P. Parrella. 1994. Poinsettia (*Euphorbia pulcherrima* Willd. ex Koltz.) cultivar-mediated differences in performance of five natural enemies of *Bemisia argentifolii* Bellows and Perring, n. sp. (Homoptera: Aleyrodidae). *Biological Control* 4:305–18.

Heinz, K. M., and F. G. Zalom. 1995. Variation in trichome-based resistance to *Bemisia argentifolii* (Homoptera: Aleyrodidae) oviposition on tomato. *Journal of Economic Entomology* 88:1494–502.

Hoddle, M. S., R. G. Van Driesche, and J. P. Sanderson. 1998. Biology and use of the whitefly parasitoid *Encarsia formosa*. *Annual Review of Entomology* 43:645–69.

Hoelmer, K. A., L. S. Osborne, and R. K. Yokomi. 1993. Reproduction and feeding behavior of *Delphastus pusillus* a predator of sweetpotato whitefly *Bemisia tabaci*. *Journal of Economic Entomology* 86:322–9.

Hoelmer, K. A., and J. A. Goolsby. 2003. Releases, stablishment, and monitoring of *Bemisia tabaci* natural enemies in the United States. In *1st International Symposium on Biological Control of Arthropods*, 58-65. Forest Service Publication FHTET-03-05 USDA,.

Hoelmer, K. A., and C. H.Pickett. 2003. Geographic origin and taxonomic history of *Delphastus* spp. (Coleoptera: Coccinellidae) in commercial culture. *Biocontrol Science and Technology* 13:529-535.

Hommes, M., and S. T. Horst. 2002. Development and life-span of *Macrolophus pygmaeus* Rambur at different temperatures and influence of host plants and prey. *IOBC/WPRS Bulletin* 25(1):103-106.

Hussey, N. W., W. H. Read, and J. J. Hesling. 1969. *The Pests of Protected Cultivation*. London: Edward Arnold.

Hussey, N. W., and N. Scopes. 1977. The introduction of natural enemies for pest control in glasshouses: Ecological considerations. In *Biological Control by Augmentation of Natural Enemies*, ed. R. L. Ridgway and S. B. Vinson, 349–77. New York: Plenum Press.

———, eds. 1985. *Biological Pest Control: The Glasshouse Experience*. Poole, U.K.: Blandford Press (Ithaca, N.Y.: Cornell University Press).

Jauset, A. M., M. J. Sarasúa, J. Avilla, and R. Albajes. 1998. The impact of nitrogen fertilization of tomato on feeding site selection and oviposition by *Trialeurodes vaporariorum*. *Entomologia Experimentalis et Applicata* 86:175–82.

Johnson, M. W., L. C. Caprio, J. A. Coughlin, B. E. Tabashnik, J. A. Rosenheim, and S. C. Welter. 1992. Effect of *Trialeurodes vaporariorum* (Homoptera: Aleyrodidae) on yield of fresh market tomatoes. *Journal of Economic Entomology* 85:2370–6.

Kajita, H. 1982. Predation by adult *Orius sauteri* Poppius (Hemiptera: Anthocoridae) on the greenhouse whitefly *Trialeurodes vaporariorum* (Westwood) (Homoptera: Aleyrodidae). *Applied Entomology and Zoology* 17:424–5.

———. 1984. Predation by the greenhouse whitefly, *Trialeurodes vaporariorum* (Westwood) (Homoptera: Aleyrodidae) by *Campylomma* sp. (Hemiptera: Miridae). *Applied Entomology and Zoology* 19:67–74.

Lecoq, H., C. Desvíes, B. Delecolle, S. Cohen, and A. Manssur. 2000. Cytological and molecular evidence that the whitefly-transmitted *Cucumber Vein Yellowing Virus* is a tentative member of the family Potyviridae. *Journal of General Virology* 81:2289-93.

Loomans, A. J. M., I. Staneva, Y. Huang, G. Bukovinszkiné-Kiss, and J. C. van Lenteren. 2002. When native non-target species go indoors: a new challenge to biocontrol of whiteflies in European greenhouses. *IOBC/WPRS Bulletin* 25(1):139-42

Malausa, J. C. 1994. Le ricerche svolte in Francia sull'impiego dei Miridi predatori nella lotta biologica in colture ortive di serra. In *Strategie di Lotta Biologica Integrata*, ed. Anonymous, 75–94. Cagliari, Italy: Ente Regionale di Sviluppo e Assistenza Tecnica in Agricoltura.

Moriones, E., and J. Navas-Castillo. 2000. *Tomato Yellow Leaf Curl Virus*, an emerging virus complex causing epidemics worldwide. *Virus Research* 71: 123-34.

Mound, L. A., and S. H. Halsey. 1978. *Whitefly of the World: A Systematic Catalogue of the Aleyodidae (Homoptera) with Host Plant and Natural Enemy Data*. Chichester, U.K.: British Museum of natural History and John Wiley and Sons.

Moya, A., P. Guirao, D. Cifuentes, F. Beitia, and J. L. Cenis. 2001. Genetic diversity of Iberian populations of *Bemisia tabaci* (Hemiptera: Aleyrodidae) based on random amplified polymorphic DNA-polymerase chain reaction. *Molecular Ecology*: 10: 891-7.

Naranjo, S. E., and R. L. Gibson. 1996. Phytophagy in predaceous Heteroptera: Effects on life history and population dynamics. In *Zoophytophagous Heteroptera: Implications for Life History and Integrated Pest Management*, ed. O. Alomar and R. N. Wiedenmann, 57–93. Lanham, Md.: Entomological Society of America.

Nicoli, G., and G. Burgio. 1997. Mediterranean biodiversity as source of new entomophagous species for biological control in protected crops. *IOBC/WPRS Bulletin* 20 (4):27–38.

Nordlund, D. A., and J. C. Legaspi. 1996. Whitefly predators and their potential for use in biological control. In *Bemisia: 1995 Taxonomy, Biology, Damage, Control, and Management*, ed. D. Gerling and R. T. Mayer, 499–513. Andover, U.K.: Intercept.

Onillon, J. C. 1990. The use of natural enemies for the biological control of whiteflies. In *Whiteflies: Their Bionomics, Pest Status, and Management*, ed. D. Gerling, 287–314. Andover, U.K.: Intercept.

Onillon, J. C., A. M. Geria, and A. Vallier. 1989. Observations préliminaires sur l'efficacité comparée de *Encarsia formosa* et *Encarsia tricolor* (Hymenoptera, Aphelinidae) dans le contrôle biologique de l'aleurode des serres *Trialeurodes vaporariorum* (Homoptera, Aleyrodidae). In *Integrated Pest Management in Protected Vegetable Crops*, ed. R. Cavalloro and C. Pelerents, 39–54. Rotterdam, the Netherlands: Balkema.

Onillon, J. C., and P. Maignet. 2000. Les parasitoids indigenes du biotype 'B' de *Bemisia tabaci* (Gennadius) (Homoptera: Aleyrodidae). Que peut-on en attendre pour le contrôle biologique de ce ravageur? *IOBC/WPRS Bulletin* 23(1):101-7.

Onillon, J. C., P. Maignet, and C. Cocquempot. 1994. Premiers résultats sur l'efficacité *d'Encarsia pergandiella* (Hymenoptera: Aphelinidae) dans le contrôle de *Bemisia tabaci* (Homoptera: Aleyrodidae) en serres de tomate. *IOBC/WPRS Bulletin* 17 (5):71–80.

Perring, T. M. 1996. Biological differences of two species of *Bemisia* that contribute to adaptive advantage. In *Bemisia: 1995 Taxonomy, Biology, Damage, Control, and Management*, ed. D. Gerling and R. T. Mayer, 3–16. Andover, U.K.: Intercept.

Perring, T. M. 2001. The *Bemisia tabaci* species complex. *Crop Protection* 20:725-737.

Polaszek, A., G. Evans, and F. D. Bennett. 1992. *Encarsia* species (Hymenoptera: Aphelinidae) parasitoids of *Bemisia tabaci* (Homoptera: Aleyrodidae): A preliminary guide to identification. *Bulletin of Entomological Research* 82:375–92.

Robertson, A. P., and R. P. Hoxey. 1992. Structural design of greenhouses with an emphasis on wind loading. *FAO REUR Technical Series* 25:17–41.

Rubio, L., J. Soong, J. Kao, and B. W. Falk. 1999. Geographic distribution and molecular variation of isolates of three whitefly-borne closteroviruses of cucurbits: *Lettuce Infectious Yellows Virus, Cucurbit Yellow Stunting Disorder Virus,* and *Beet Pseudo-Yellows Virus. Phytopathology* 89 (8): 707-711.

Shapiro, J. P. 1996. Insect-plant interactions and expression of disorders induced by the silverleaf whitefly, *Bemisia argentifolii*. In *Bemisia: 1995 Taxonomy, Biology, Damage, Control, and Management*, ed. D. Gerling and R. T. Mayer, 167–77. Andover, U.K.: Intercept.

Stansly, P.A., P. A. Sánchez, J. M. Rodríguez, F. Cañizares, A. Nieta, M. J. López-Leyva, M. Fajardo, V. Suárez, and A. Urbaneja. 2004. Prospects for biological control of *Bemisia tabaci* (Homoptera; Aleyrodidae) in greenhouse tomatoes of southern Spain. *Crop Protection* in press.

Trottin-Caudal, Y, and A. Capy. 2003. Protection integrée de la tomate sous serre en France. Situation actuelle et perspectives. In *Actes colloque international*, 208-12. Avignon,France. .

van Lenteren, J. C., and N. Martin. 1999. Biological control of whiteflies. In *Integrated Pest and Disease Management in Greenhouse Crops*, ed. R. Albajes, M. L. Gullino, J. C. van Lenteren, and Y. Elad, 202-216. Dordrecht, the Netherlands: Kluwer.

van Lenteren, J. C., and L. P. J. J. Noldus. 1990. Whitefly-plant relationships: Behavioural and ecological aspects. In *Whiteflies: Their Bionomics, Pest Status, and Management*, ed. D. Gerling, 47–89. Andover, U.K.: Intercept.

van Lenteren, J. C., H. J. van Roermund, and S. Sütterlin. 1996. Biological control of greenhouse whitefly (*Trialeurodes vaporariorum*) with the parasitoid *Encarsia formosa*: How does it work? *Biological Control* 6:1–10.

van Lenteren, J. C., and J. Woets. 1988. Biological and integrated pest control in greenhouses. *Annual Review of Entomology* 33:239–69.

van Roermund, H. J., and J. C. van Lenteren. 1992. *Life-History Parameters of the Greenhouse Whitefly* Trialeurodes vaporariorum *and the Parasitoid* Encarsia formosa. Wageningen, the Netherlands: Wageningen University Press.

Viggiani, G., and P. Mazzone. 1980. Sull'introduzione in Italia de *Encarsia pergandiella* Howard (Hymenoptera: Aphelinidae), parassita di *Trialeurodes vaporariorum* (Westw.) (Homoptera: Aleyrodidae). *Bolletino del Laboratorio di Entomologia Agraria "Filippo Silvestri"* 37:39–43.

Wittwer, S. H., and N. Castilla. 1995. Protected cultivation of horticultural crops worldwide. *HortTech* 5:6–23.

Zalom, F. G., C. Castañé, and R. Gabarra. 1995. Selection of some winter-spring vegetable crop hosts by *Bemisia argentifolii* (Homoptera: Aleyrodidae). *Journal of Economic Entomology* 88:70–6.

10

BIOLOGICAL CONTROL OF SPIDER MITES ON ORNAMENTAL CROPS

Lynell K. Tanigoshi
Department of Entomology
Washington State University, Vancouver Research and Extension Unit

N. A. Martin
New Zealand Institute of Crop and Food Research, Auckland, New Zealand

Lance S. Osborne
University of Florida, MFREC, Apopka, Florida

and
Jorge E. Peña
University of Florida, TREC, Homestead, Florida

What are spider mites, and why have they become major pests of floriculture and ornamental plants since the 1950s? First, spider mites are mites, not spiders or insects. Unlike insects, adult mites possess two, not three, body regions, eight rather than six legs, and lack both antennae and wings. Spider mites are placed in the family Tetranychidae, which has undergone considerable taxonomic revision. Like their sister order, the "true" spiders, some spider mites (subfamily Tetranychinae) have evolved silk glands. Silk, a proteinaceous secretion, is produced by modified mouthparts in mites. Spider mites feed on plants and are serious pests of man's domesticated food and fiber crops and ornamental plants grown in nurseries, greenhouses, and home landscapes.

In the natural environment, severe spider mite damage to plants is uncommon (van de Vrie, McMurtry, and Huffaker 1972).

Outbreaks of mite populations large enough to cause serious plant damage (i.e., plant death and yield loss) have increased during the last fifty years (Rabbinge 1985). This increase is associated with the development of modern agriculture. Severe mite outbreaks tend to occur in simplified habitats, such as greenhouses and outdoor monocultures, and where pesticides are used to control these and other organisms. Serious plant damage by tetranychid mites is associated with two factors: first, growing crop plants at near-optimal conditions, which enhances tetranychid mite population increase; second, lack of or reduced numbers and diversity of natural enemies (Ibid.). However, the recent successful practice of biological control of tetranychid mites as part of integrated pest management in many crops implies that natural enemies are a key factor for tetranychid control.

The realization that spider mites and other pests can rapidly develop resistance to pesticides has increased the interest in using natural enemies of the mites to provide biological control (Croft and Brown 1975, Hoy 1985). Furthermore, pesticides may be phytotoxic to crops or leave visible residues on foliage. High labor costs associated with frequent pesticide applications and observance of re-entry periods for treated areas have made pesticides less economical and biological control more attractive. Biological control is now a viable alternative to chemicals for spider mite control on greenhouse crops of strawberry, tomato, cucumber, and sweet pepper.

While ornamental plants must meet high aesthetic standards and often have a near-zero tolerance for spider mite injury, an increasing number of flower and ornamental growers are successfully using biological control. Biological control of tetranychid mites for protected crops initially focused on control of the two-spotted spider mite, *Tetranychus urticae* Koch (Acari: Tetranychidae) with a predatory mite, *Phytoseiulus persimilis* Athias-Henriot (Acari: Phytoseiidae) (van Lenteren and Woets 1988). It was soon realized that successful use of biological control of the two-spotted spider mite in greenhouse crops required the integration of biological control with the control of other pests and diseases of the crops, usually requiring integration of selective pesticides. This has been difficult in ornamental crops. In this industry, it has also taken a long time for growers to accept that a few pests on a crop might be acceptable. Now that biological control is established as an acceptable solution for some ornamental crops (Enkegaard et al.

1999), there is interest in use of other natural enemies for control of two-spotted spider mite and other tetranychid mites in greenhouse crops.

There are several excellent reviews on the biology and ecology of spider mites and predatory phytoseiid mites and the latter's role in biological mite control (Huffaker, van de Vrie, and McMurtry 1969; McMurtry, Huffaker, and van de Vrie 1970; Hussey and Huffaker 1976; Hoy 1982; McMurtry 1982, 1992; Tanigoshi 1982; McMurtry and Croft 1997). Other valuable reviews and updates of biological control in greenhouse-grown vegetables and ornamentals in Europe and North America include Chambers (1996), Hussey and Scopes (1985), Osborne and Oetting (1989), Osborne et al. (1994), van de Vrie (1985), and van Lenteren and Woets (1988).

This chapter covers the identification and recognition of pest tetranychid mites, their biology, and the damage they cause. Also presented are the natural enemies of tetranychid mites, the use of some of these as biological control agents, and how to develop a new biological control agent. Finally, the success of and prospects for biological control in ornamentals is discussed. Two papers on biological control in greenhouses were used as the foundation for this chapter (Osborne, Ehler and Nechols 1985, Osborne et al. 1994).

Identification

Two-spotted spider mite is the main tetranychid mite pest of protected crops, and most biological controls for these crops have been developed for this species (van Lenteren and Woets 1988). However, commercial ornamental plants may be attacked by other species of tetranychid mite, some of which are not controlled by natural enemies of *T. urticae*. Even mites that look similar to two-spotted spider mite (e.g., six-spotted spider mite, *Eotetranychus sexmaculatus* ([Riley]), may not be controlled by natural enemies specializing in *Tetranychus* species. For this reason, it is important to know the identity of pest mites. A guide to the identification and biology of pest and benefical mites in greenhouse crops is provided by Zhang (2003). The name of the pest is also the key to information on its biology, host range, and methods of control.

Two-spotted spider mite varies in appearance and may be difficult for a nonspecialist to distinguish from other *Tetranychus* species. In practice this may not matter, as the same biological control agents are effective across the *Tetranychus* genus, at least in temperate regions, though *P. persimilis* does not control all populations of *Tetranychus ludeni* Zacher.

Adult two-spotted spider mites have an oval body with four pairs of legs. The mites may be pale yellow-green, or red with pale legs, but all have a dark spot on each side of the body (fig. 10.1), hence their name. The two dark spots may be small or fill most of the body, the size of which may depend on the host plant (e.g., small spots on mites feeding on cymbidium orchids and large spots on mites feeding on beans). A distinctive feature of *Tetranychus* mites is the web they spin over plants on which they feed. The webbing and the small, pale, spherical eggs can be seen with a 10x hand lens. Juvenile mites look like small adults, though paler and with less prominent spots. Two-spotted spider mite overwinters as a nonfeeding female that has a distinctive orange-red color and two red eyespots. *T. cinnabarinus* has a red body with black spots and white or yellowish legs (fig. 10.2), while a species common in trop-

Figure 10.1. Two-spotted spider mite (*Tetranychus urticae*), summer-form female, eggs and nymph. Diagnostic features include the two distinct dark spots on the body of the mites, the shiny spherical eggs, and webbing. *Photo: New Zealand Institute For Crop and Food Research.*

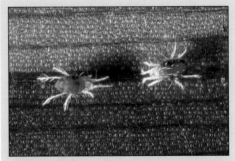

Figure 10.2. Carmine mite (*Tetranychus cinnabarinus*), two female mites on *Heliconia* leaf. Diagnostic features include the white legs, long white dorsal hairs, and red body usually with dark spots. This species is not controlled by the predator, *Phytoseiulus persimilis*. *Photo: New Zealand Institute For Crop and Food Research.*

ical areas, *Tetranychus ludeni* Zacher, has white or red legs and a red body with no dark spots.

Six-spotted spider mite looks like a pale two-spotted spider mite with three pairs of dark spots. It damages greenhouse grapes and a variety of ornamental shrubs (Jeppson, Keifer, and Baker 1975). A common pest on outdoor trees and shrubs that may be found in some greenhouse crops is European red mite, *Panonychus ulmi* (Koch). This mite has distinctive white marks at the base of the long dorsal seta. European red mite overwinters as "distinctive" red eggs. *Bryobia* species are also spider mites that are pests of ornamental plants. They have flat tops to their bodies and short, flat setae, and they usually lay red eggs.

Two-Spotted Spider Mite Biology

Developmental biology

Female mites lay eggs, usually on the underside of leaves. Larvae, which hatch from the egg, look like small adults, but have only three pairs of legs. The larva is followed by two nymphal stages, which also look like small adults but have four pairs of legs. The juvenile feeding stages are each followed by quiescent (resting) stages referred to as nymphochrysalis, deutochrysalis, and teliochrysalis, respectively (Laing 1969; van de Vrie, McMurtry, and Huffaker 1972). Most species of tetranychid mites produce males and females, which usually mate before eggs are laid.

Developmental times for the two-spotted spider mite vary with temperature, humidity, host plant, and leaf age. The rate of development increases with increasing temperature,

causing the time from egg to adult to decrease, although there is an upper lethal temperature. The lower threshold for development is about 54°F (12°C), whereas the maximum upper limit for development is about 104°F (40°C) (Jeppson, Keifer, and Baker 1975). Sabelis (1981) reported the developmental time from egg to adult females for *T. urticae* on detached rose leaves under two alternating day/night temperature regimes of 77 to 95°F (25 to 35°C) and 50 to 68°F (10 to 20°C), for which the developmental times were 8.3 and 28.2 days, respectively. Also note that mites tend to develop more slowly, die sooner, and lay fewer eggs on less favored plants (De Ponti 1985).

In a two-spotted spider mite colony, females are about three times more abundant than males. Males are usually found in close association with quiescent female deutonymphs, which may release a sex pheromone to attract males and keep them in close proximity (Cone et al. 1971, Cone, Predki, and Klostermeyer 1971, Penman and Cone 1972, 1974) to mate with the emergent female. When more than one male attempts to "guard" a developing female, fighting among the males often occurs; usually, larger males win these encounters (Potter, Wrensch, and Johnston 1976ab). Such fights involve pushing and grappling with the forelegs, jousting with the mouthparts, and entangling the opponent with silk.

The life span of the adult female is divided into the preovipositional period and the ovipositional period, the former being the time between emergence from the teliochrysalis to the deposition of the first egg. The preovipositional period is 9% of the time required to develop from egg to egg (less than 0.5 days to 3 days, depending on temperature). The ovipositional period lasts from 10 days at 95°F (35°C) to 40 days at 59° F (15°C) (Sabelis 1981). An individual two-spotted spider mite female can deposit over one hundred eggs in her lifetime (Shih, Poe, and Cromroy 1976; Carey and Bradley 1982). The total number of eggs laid per female and the number of eggs laid per female per day will vary with age, temperature, species of host plant, relative humidity, nutrition of host plant, and exposure to pesticides (Watson 1964; van de Vrie, McMurtry, and Huffaker 1972; Karban and Carey 1984). Temperature and age of the female are especially important determinants of egg production, or fecundity. Sabelis (1981) found that temperatures between 68 to 95°F (20 to 35°C) had little effect on fecundity. At 77°F (25°C), peak oviposition was 161 eggs per female, with a maximum of 12 eggs per female per day occurring two days after the first eggs were laid. The effect of higher temperatures is particularly evident in greenhouses, where spider mite populations often develop rapidly soon after the onset of summer.

According to Helle (1967), a single mating will provide a female with enough sperm to produce diploid eggs for her entire ovipositional period. Sex determination of *T. urticae* is arrhenotokous (Helle and Pijnacker 1985), i.e., females develop from fertilized eggs and have the normal two sets of chromosomes (diploid), while males develop from unfertilized eggs and have only one set of chromosomes (haploid). Unmated females give rise only to males; mated females can produce either female or male progeny. Because the male has only one set of chromosomes, new genetic features arising from mutations will be immediately expressed. Through natural selection, these characteristics can be quickly expressed throughout the population (Helle and Overmeer 1973). This latter feature, considered together with the frequent use of miticides, the high reproductive rate of *T. urticae*, and their fast generation time, may generate miticide-resistant populations of mites in a comparatively short time.

Overwintering behavior

T. urticae can overwinter as inseminated, nonfeeding, and diapausing females. Short daylength, low temperatures, and unfavorable food supply induce diapause (Parr and Hussey 1966, Jeppson, Keifer, and Baker 1975). Diapausing females turn reddish orange and hibernate in cracks and crevices. Diapause terminates in the spring when favorable environmental conditions return. In greenhouses with winter host plants and subtropical climates such as Florida, two-spotted spider mites are active throughout the year.

Damage and Dispersal

Damage to crops

Spider mites damage leaf surfaces of both grasses and higher plant species by inserting their "piercing-sucking" mouthparts, or cheliceral stylets, into plant tissues and removing plant juices (Tanigoshi and Davis 1978, Linquist 1985). They can also expel salivary toxins, enzymes, and hormone-like substances into the feeding puncture (Avery and Briggs 1968; Hislop and Jeppson 1976; Sances, Wyman, and Ting 1979). Host plant responses to spider mite feeding include chlorotic (yellow or white) stippling on leaf surfaces, reduced flower bud formation, reduced yields, abscission of leaves, and even death of the plant (van de Vrie, McMurtry, and Huffaker 1972; De Angelis, Berry, and Krantz 1983; Tomczyk, Kropczynska, and van de Vrie 1991). Although most feeding is on the underside of leaves, the pale damaged areas can often be seen from the top. On older leaves or thick leaves, such as those of cymbidium orchids, the underside of the leaf must be inspected for damage symptoms. Feeding by high densities of mites can result in defoliation, and plants become covered in dense webbing. Some species and strains of mites inject toxic saliva into plants, which causes more severe damage (Hussey and Scopes 1985, Tomczyk and Kropczynska 1985). Unlike most other tetranychids, some *Bryobia* feed on the upper surface of leaves.

The marketable quality of cut flowers and ornamental plants can be reduced by visible signs of mite damage on the flowers or leaves, and this is often used to justify a zero threshold for mites in the crops. However, the recent adoption of IPM and increased demand from buyers for the use of biological control has led to an increased tolerance of some spider mite damage.

Dispersal and distribution in crops

Hussey and Parr (1963) indicated that two-spotted spider mites disperse using four different methods: walking of newly emerged and presumably mated females to oviposition sites, dispersal from infested plants by attaching and dropping from silken thread, aerial displacement on silken thread carried by air currents, and movement over soil surfaces by orientating with the plane of polarized light.

Spider mites are also commonly dispersed on the clothing of greenhouse personnel or through the movement of infested plant material. However, in sprayed crops, patchy infestations in the greenhouse are characteristic of two-spotted spider mites, which often infest the same parts of a greenhouse throughout the season and even from season to season. Pest patchiness may be due to poor spray coverage in hard-to-reach areas or physical effects from ventilators, air-conditioning ducts, and greenhouse orientation to the sun.

Biological Control of Spider Mites

Natural enemies

In natural ecosystems, severe outbreaks of tetranychid mites are uncommon, whereas in crops, severe damage can be caused by mite outbreaks. Severe damage is associated with the reduced occurrence or absence of natural enemies. Natural enemies of tetranychid mites include predators and pathogens; no parasitoids of this group are known.

The most widely used tetranychid predators for biological control in commercial crops are predatory mites of the family Phytoseiidae, especially *P. persimilis* (fig. 10.3), a specialist predator of *Tetranychus* spp. and generalist predators such as *Neoseiulus californicus* (McGregor).

Where pesticides are not used, predatory mites from other families may also be found attacking tetranychid mites (Gerson 1985, Santos and Laing 1985). Outdoors, small, black, lady beetles in the genus *Stethorus* (Coleoptera: Coccinellidae) can control tetranychid mites. Other insect predators that feed on tetranychid mites include *Oligota* spp. (Coleoptera:

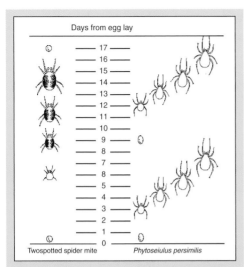

Days from egg lay

17
16
15
14
13
12
11
10
9
8
7
8
5
4
3
2
1
0

Twospotted spider mite   *Phytoseiulus persimilis*

Figure 10.3. Life cycle of two-spotted spider mite and its predator, *Phytoseiulus persimilis*. Six legged larvae hatch from eggs. The mites pass through two nymphal stages with eight legs and become eight-legged adults. At 68°F (20°C) the predator breeds twice as fast as the pest mite.
Illustration: N. Martin, New Zealand Institute For Crop and Food Research.

Staphylinidae), thrips (Thysanoptera), true bugs (Hemiptera), flies (Diptera) of the families Cecidomyiidae and Syrphidae, lacewings (Neuroptera), and earwigs (Dermaptera) (Chazeau 1985). Of these insects, only the cecidomyiid fly *Feltiella acarisuga* Vallot (= *Theridoplosis persicae*) is used specifically for mite control in commercial greenhouses (Wardlow 1985). Other predators such as *Orius* spp. may assist in mite control, but they are not released into greenhouses with spider mites as their intended target.

There are few known pathogens of tetranychid mites; they include alpha Proteobacteria (Breeuwer and Jacobs

1996), viruses, and fungi (Poinar and Poinar 1998). Fungi from three genera—*Beauveria, Entomophora,* and *Hirsutella*—infect tetranychid mites, and *Hirsutella thompsonii* Fisher was commercially available for mite control in greenhouses from 1976 to 1985 (Ibid.), but no pathogen is currently sold specifically for control of tetranychid mites.

Finding new natural enemies

Nearly a thousand species of phytoseiid predatory mites of tetranychid mites are known, yet only a few of the potential species are in commercial use (Hunter 1997). Natural enemies for use in protected crops were developed in temperate climates and primarily for control of two-spotted spider mite. Additional species of natural enemies are required for protected crops in tropical climates where different pest mites may be present and the climate may not be suitable for "temperate" natural enemies. Importation of natural enemies is becoming increasingly scrutinized, due to the potential of such exotic species to harm indigenous faunas. As a result, it is becoming increasingly important to discover local species as possible candidates for use in biological control programs. Candidates must provide satisfactory control of the pest mite on targeted crops, and they must be easy to mass-produce if they are to be reared and sold commercially. The discovery and selection of effective natural enemies can be a long one, but the categorization of phytoseiid lifestyles by McMurtry and Croft (1997) and de Moraes, McMurtry, and Denmark (1986) can assist in the process.

Biology of natural enemies

Details of the biology of the main predators of two-spotted spider mite are given in chapter 11 and are not repeated here. The main predators used on ornamental plants are the phytoseiid predators, *P. persimilis* and *N. californicus*. The predatory response of *P. persimilis* to control *T. urticae* has been demonstrated on many plants, including ornamental ivy (Gould and Light 1971), rose (Boys and Burbutis 1972, Simmonds 1972), dahlia (Harris 1971), and dieffenbachia and schefflera (Hamlen and Lindquist 1981). *P. persimilis* can also be an effective natural enemy in some outdoor crops, such as commercial strawberry plantings (McMurtry et al. 1978, Trumble and Morse 1993, Decou 1994), and on ornamentals in commercial interior plantings (Lindquist 1981).

Various problems and costs of chemical control in greenhouses have also stimulated research on biological control of *T. urticae* on greenhouse-grown ornamentals, including work in Australia (Gough 1991, Goodwin and Wellham 1992), Canada (Burnett 1979), Europe (Gould and Light 1971, Simmonds 1972, Stenseth 1976, Sabelis 1981, Scopes 1985, Buxton 1999, Kropczynska et al. 1999), Japan (Mori, Saito, and Nakao 1990), New Zealand (Burgess 1984, Martin 1987), and the U.S. (Boys and Burbutis 1972; Hamlen 1978, 1980; Hamlen and Poole 1980; Hamlen and Lindquist 1981; Lindquist 1981; Field and Hoy 1984, 1986; Osborne and Petitt 1985).

Guidelines and Tactics of Introduction Methods

In protected ornamental crops, two-spotted spider mite is most effectively controlled by either inoculative or inundative releases of predators. The releases can be made in response to crop monitoring or timed by crop phenology or calendar. Relying on predator populations to persist or to arrive by themselves is not practical for most ornamental crops.

Monitoring for pests and natural enemies in crops

Monitoring of pest mite populations is necessary for most IPM programs. When biological control is used, both pest mites and predators must be monitored. Predators may frequently be associated with mite colonies, thus the methods for sampling tetranychid mites in crops (Sabelis 1985) can also be applied to their predators, but their distribution on plants may be different (Nachman 1985). Monitoring systems vary according to the crop and target market, but comprehensive systems needed to detect the early stages of a pest outbreak must be frequent and are usually time-consuming and expensive. Thus, most release strategies for spider mite control are based on season or crop stage, with supplementary releases in response to monitoring.

Monitoring can vary from casual inspection of crops, which may give a false sense of security, to elaborate schemes in which leaves are collected at random and all mites present are counted either directly on the leaves or after removing the mites from the leaves (Sabelis 1985). To save time, growers may regularly inspect only the most vulnerable cultivars or plant species, as these are usually first to show signs of pests. Another time-saving mechanism is to locate pest mites by first searching for the leaf discoloration damage caused by their feeding (Hussey and

Scopes 1985). Rather than counting numbers of mites, foliage may simply be scored according to the presence or absence of the pest mite and the predators to yield reliable population density information (Beck, Workman, and Martin 1993). Monitoring should be combined with training of staff to recognize and report signs of pests while performing routine tasks in the crop. This training can be especially important when spider mites colonize mature leaves or plants with thick leaves, since the damage and mites can only be seen on the undersides of such leaves.

Predator release strategies

The diversity of ornamental crops, which includes both annuals and perennials with their diverse climatic and horticultural needs, and the market requirement to prevent cosmetic damage to foliage and flowers, all make biological control of spider mites on ornamentals more difficult than on vegetable crops. Osborne et al. (1994) indicated that biological control of spider mites with *P. persimilis* on ornamental plants is most feasible on stock plantings that are grown for multiple years and that are spaced close together. These conditions favor increased searching efficiency and aggregation at high-density prey patches by the predators (Zhang and Sanderson 1995). For most ornamental crops, more effective techniques are regular inoculative or inundative releases of predators (Wardlow 1985, Martin 1993). Releases of large numbers of predatory mites may be expensive, but the practice can provide short-term control and be cost effective on high-value ornamentals like rose, chrysanthemum, and gerbera.

Attempts to use the pest-in-first method of release commonly practiced in vegetable crops has not been embraced by growers of cut flowers, pot plants, and bedding plants. Particularly when these crops are grown for export, the temporary introduction of a pest species may result in unacceptable levels of damage or numbers of two-spotted spider mites. The pest-in-first method for releases of *N. californicus* for two-spotted spider mite control yielded unacceptable results and prompted the suggestion that preventative predator releases were required to avoid unacceptable plant damage (Kropczynska et al. 1999). Preventative, inoculative releases of natural enemies is becoming particularly popular for local-market flowers, certain foliage plants, botanical gardens, conservatories, and interior landscapes (van Lenteren and Woets 1988).

A second method of release may be through the use of banker plants that act as field insectaries of natural enemies. These plants are typically infested with a nonpestiferous mite species and the natural enemy of interest, and the plants are subsequently placed uniformly or at local infestations throughout a mite-susceptible crop, such as roses. Unfortunately, few critical studies have been conducted in ornamental greenhouses that have tested this release methodology.

Probably the most common method for releasing *P. persimilis* is by directly sprinkling them from their shipping container, which contains a nonpestiferous mite species as a food source and bran or sawdust as a carrier. Releases of *P. persimilis* at 16,200 females/acre (40,000 females/ha) every ten to twelve weeks gave excellent mite control in cymbidium orchids (Beck, Workman, and Martin 1993), while in spring, summer, and autumn, releases in greenhouse roses are recommended every six weeks (Martin 1994). In mixed ornamental crops, *P. persimilis* is released every one to two weeks on crops susceptible to two-spotted spider mite infestations or infestations of another mite species (e.g., cyclamen mite on hydrangeas). Although *P. persimilis* reduces two-spotted spider mite populations to very low densities, pest populations on susceptible ornamental crops often rebound after an initial decline. While pest numbers are still low, the predators should be redistributed to assist their finding two-spotted spider mite colonies while the populations are still well below the economic threshold.

Post-release assessment and evaluation

The same methods for monitoring pest mite densities can be used to evaluate the effectiveness of biological mite control. Growers need to be aware that with inoculative releases of predators, pest numbers increase for a few weeks while predator numbers build up and before populations of both decline. In most cases, growers must observe one or two successes with natural enemy releases before they gain confidence in a biological control product. Researchers and consultants need to monitor crops closely so that they can relate the success of predator releases to prerelease pest mite population densities and subsequent events that may influence pest mite–predator mite population dynamics.

Evaluation of success and levels of adoption

Biological control of two-spotted spider mites in a protected crop has to be part of an integrated pest and disease management program for the crop. Growers need a complete crop protection package, and the methods they choose to control diseases and other pests must be compatible with the use of spider mite biological control. There is an increasing amount of published information on the methodology for biological control of two-spotted mite and IPM for ornamental crops, but there is little information evaluating the success of these approaches.

Despite an extensive worldwide literature review, there were few examples found of the use of other phytoseiid mites or predatory insects such as *F. acarisuga*, *Stethorus* spp., and *Orius* spp. for biological control of two-spotted spider mite on ornamentals. Osborne et al. (1994) estimated that less than 5% of all ornamental plants produced in Florida utilize biological control for their arthropod pests. Although biological control of two-spotted mite is rarely used on cut flowers in Europe, it is most successful on gerberas and cymbidium orchids. An integrated pest management approach works well in bedding and pot plants, where plants prone to two-spotted mite are treated weekly with a low dose of *P. persimilis* (1 per 10.8 ft.^{2} [1 per m^2]) and the predatory mites used to treat western flower thrips (*Frankliniella occidentalis* [Pergande]). In addition to phytoseiid mites, release of gall midge larvae, *Feltiella* sp., provide good control of two-spotted mites in hydrangea, datura, and roses.

New Zealand growers have experienced many successes and failures associated with their use of biological control of two-spotted spider mites in cut flower crops. A review of their experiences may provide useful guidelines for others attempting to implement similar biological control programs.

Carnations

P. persimilis has provided inconsistent control of the two-spotted spider mite, a key pest of this crop (Lindquist, Frost, and Wolgamott 1980; Dunman 1992). The predator often fails to establish and spread among spider mite colonies, even though the predator persists on greenhouse weeds. Laboratory studies have shown this predator to have great difficulty climbing the vertical leaves of carnations (Workman and Martin 2000), which may explain its poor dispersal capabilities. Thus, the physical properties of the plant rather than the greenhouse environment or incompatible use of pesticides, are the greatest contributors to the failure of *P. persimilis* to control two-spotted spider mite in this crop.

Cymbidium *orchids*

P. persimilis provides acceptable control of two-spotted spider mites infesting cymbidium orchids grown for export (Beck, Workman, and Martin 1993). Some growers use biological control, even though it is more expensive than pesticides (Martin and Workman 1988). Phytotoxic effects associated with applications of pesticide sprays occur more frequently during the hot summer weather, and this risk is not associated with the use of biological control. Further, the levels of discomfort are high during the summer months for growers who must apply pesticide sprays while wearing appropriate protective gear. Even though biological control may be effective and is the method of choice for some greenhouse growers, the level of adoption by cymbidium orchid growers is relatively low compared with New Zealand's greenhouse vegetable industry. Many orchid growers are more unwilling to pay for the advisory service

that is necessary to make biological control a success than are most vegetable growers. For those orchid growers, a manual is available that may guide them through the methodology (Martin 1993).

Important factors for success

Successful biological control of tetranychid mites in protected crops depends on several elements being in place. It is essential that suitable natural enemies be available to the grower whenever they are needed. The plant species or cultivar should favor the natural enemy more than the pest mite (e.g., carnations are not suitable for *P. persimilis*), and, where possible, cultivars particularly susceptible to the pest should not be grown. The greenhouse environment should also be suitable for the natural enemy (e.g., temperatures should not exceed 86°F [30°C], and low humidity should be avoided for *P. persimilis*). Control of diseases and other pests should cause minimal harm to the natural enemy. Growers must also have access to essential information, and if possible during the first year, have one-to-one contact with an advisor.

Economic competitiveness of biological control

It is difficult to compare the costs of biological control of tetranychid mites with pesticides due to the large amount of variability among pesticide programs used by greenhouse flower crops. However, growers are prepared to pay more for biological control if it gives satisfactory results, especially during the hot summer months. Also, some growers report that when they stop using miticides and insecticides, the plants look healthier and grow more strongly (Teerling and Murphy 1999). Growers sometimes use biological control when the pest mites are resistant to pesticides because it is the only effective option. Some retailers prefer to buy plants produced using IPM, since this allows them to handle flowers with reduced pesticide residues.

Prospects for Future Research and Implementation

The continued development of pesticide resistance in *T. urticae* (Cranham and Helle 1985; Campos, Dybas, and Krupa 1995), increased difficulty in reregistering old miticides, and the high cost of new products means that biological control is increasingly the only practical option for tetranychid mites. The existing biological control products for two-spotted spider mite do not give adequate control in all circumstances. There is a need for new biological control agents and for ways to improve the performance of existing agents. There is increasing concern about the potential adverse effects of introducing new biological control agents to a country, so the emphasis should be on discovering local agents and making known species such as *P. persimilis* work more effectively. Contemporary greenhouse designs with sophisticated environmental controls provide growers with the means to simulate climatic conditions favorable to predators (chapter 3, van Lenteren 1992). In addition, insect screening reduces pest immigration, which further assists biological control. The challenge for the future is to combine academic rigor with a holistic and practical approach that will produce robust and economic crop protection systems for growers.

References Cited

Avery, D. J., and J. B. Briggs. 1968. The aetiology and development of damage in young fruit trees infested with fruit tree red spider mite, *Panonychus ulmi* (Koch). *Annals of Applied Biology* 61:227–8.

Beck, N. G., P. Workman, and N. Martin. 1993. IPM for cymbidium orchids in New Zealand. *IOBC/WPRS Bulletin* 16:12–5.

Boys, F. E., and P. P. Burbutis. 1972. Influence of *Phytoseiulus persimilis* on populations of *Tetranychus turkestani* at the economic threshold on roses. *Journal of Economic Entomology* 65:114–7.

Breeuwer, J. A. J., and G. Jacobs. 1996. *Wolbachia*: Intracellular manipulators of mite reproduction. *Experimental and Applied Acarology* 20:421–34.

Burgess, E. P. 1984. Integrated control of two-spotted spider mite on glasshouse roses. *Proceedings of the Thirty-seventh New Zealand Weed and Pest Control Conference, Russley Hotel, Christchurch, August 14–16, 1984*, 257–61. Wellington, New Zealand: New Zealand Weed and Pest Control Society.

Burnett, T. 1979. An acarine predator-prey population infesting roses. *Researches in Population Ecology* 20:227–34.

Buxton, J. 1999. Biological control of the two-spotted spider mite, *Tetranychus urticae*, on hardy nursery stock. *IOBC/WPRS Bulletin* 22:25–7.

Campos, F., R. A. Dybas, and D. A. Krupa. 1995. Susceptibility of two-spotted spider mite (Acari: Tetranychidae) populations in California to abamectin. *Journal of Economic Entomology* 88:225–31.

Carey, J. R., and J. W. Bradley. 1982. Developmental rates, vital schedules, sex ratios, and life tables for *Tetranychus urticae, T. turkestani*, and *T. pacificus* (Acarina: Tetranychidae) on cotton. *Acarologia* 23:333–45.

Chambers, R. J. 1996. Biological control of insect pests in glasshouse crops: Some recent developments. In *Individuals, Populations and Patterns in Ecology*, ed. S. R. Leather, A. D. Watt, N. J. Mills, and K. F. A. Walters, 223–32. Andover, U.K.: Intercept.

Chazeau, J. 1985. Predaceous insects. In *Spider Mites: Their Biology, Natural Enemies, and Control*, Vol. 1B, ed. W. Helle and M. W. Sabelis, 211–46. New York (Amsterdam): Elsevier.

Cone, W. W., L. M. McDonough, J. C. Maitlen, and S. Burdajewicz. 1971. Pheromone studies of the two-spotted spider mite. 1. Evidence of a sex pheromone. *Journal of Economic Entomology* 64:355–8.

Cone, W. W., S. Predki, and E. C. Klostermeyer. 1971. Pheromone studies of the two-spotted spider mite. 2. Behavioral response of males to quiescent deutonymphs. *Journal of Economic Entomology* 64:379–82.

Cranham, J. E., and W. Helle. 1985. Pesticide resistance in Tetranychidae. In *Spider Mites: Their Biology, Natural Enemies, and Control*, Vol. 1B, ed. W. Helle and M. W. Sabelis, 405–23. New York (Amsterdam): Elsevier.

Croft, B. A., and A. W. A. Brown. 1975. Responses of arthropod natural enemies to insecticides. *Annual Review of Entomology* 20:285–336.

De Angelis, J. D., R. E. Berry, and G. W. Krantz. 1983. Photosynthesis, leaf conductance and leaf chlorophyll content in spider mite (Acari: Tetranychidae) injured peppermint leaves. *Environmental Entomologist* 12:345–9.

de Moraes, G. J., J. A. McMurtry, and H. A. Denmark. 1986. *A Catalog of the Mite Family Phytoseiidae: References to Taxonomy, Synonymy, Distribution, and Habitat.* Brasilia, Brazil: EMBRAPA-DDT.

De Ponti, O. M. B. 1985. Host plant resistance and its manipulation through plant breeding. In *Spider Mites: Their Biology, Natural Enemies, and Control,* Vol. 1B, ed. W. Helle and M. W. Sabelis, 395–403. New York (Amsterdam): Elsevier.

Decou, G. C. 1994. Biological control of the two-spotted spider mite (Acarina: Tetranychidae) on commercial strawberries in Florida with *Phytoseiulus persimilis* (Acarina: Phytoseiidae). *Florida Entomologist* 77:33–41.

Dunman, J. 1992. Mixed results from California study. *Greenhouse Grower,* February, 50–1.

Enkegaard, A., D. F. Jensen, P. Folker-Hansen, and J. Eilenberg. 1999. Present and future potential for biological control of pests and diseases in Danish glasshouses. *IOBC/WPRS Bulletin* 22 (1):65–8.

Field, R. P., and M. A. Hoy. 1984. Biological control of spider mites on greenhouse roses. *California Agriculture* 38:29–32.

Field, R. P., and M. A. Hoy. 1986. Evaluation of genetically improved strains of *Metaseiulus occidentalis* (Nesbitt) (Acarina: Phytoseiidae) for integrated control of spider mites on roses in greenhouses. *Hilgardia* 54:1–32.

Gerson, U. 1985. Other predaceous mites and spiders. In *Spider Mites: Their Biology, Natural Enemies, and Control,* Vol. 1B, ed. W. Helle and M. W. Sabelis, 205–10. New York (Amsterdam): Elsevier.

Goodwin, S., and T. M. Wellham. 1992. Comparison of dimethoate and methidathion tolerance in four strains of *Phytoseiulus persimilis* (Athias-Henriot) (Acarina: Phytoseiidae) in Australia. *Experimental and Applied Acarology* 16:255–61.

Gough, N. 1991. Long-term stability in the interaction between *Tetranychus urticae* and *Phytoseiulus persimilis* producing successful integrated control on roses in southeast Queensland (Australia). *Experimental and Applied Acarology* 12:83–102.

Gould, H. J., and W. I. S. G. Light. 1971. Biological control of *Tetranychus urticae* on stock plants of ornamental ivy. *Plant Pathology* 20:18–20.

Hamlen, R. A. 1978. Biological control of spider mites on greenhouse ornamentals using predaceous mites. *Proceedings Florida State Horticultural Society* 91:247–9.

———. 1980. Report of *Phytoseiulus persimilis* management of *Tetranychus urticae* on greenhouse-grown dieffenbachia. *IOBC/WPRS Bulletin* 3:65–74.

Hamlen, R. A., and R. K. Lindquist. 1981. Comparison of two *Phytoseiulus* species as predators of two-spotted spider mites on greenhouse ornamentals. *Environmental Entomologist* 10:524–7.

Hamlen, R. A., and R. T. Poole. 1980. Effects of a predaceous mite on spider mite populations of *Dieffenbachia* under greenhouse and interior environments. *Hortscience* 15:611–2.

Harris, K. M. 1971. A new approach to pest control in the Dahlia Trail at Wisley. *Journal of the Royal Horticultural Society* 96:200–6.

Helle, W. 1967. Fertilization in the two-spotted spider mite (*Tetranychus urticae*: Acari). *Entomologia Experimentalis et Applicata* 10:103–10.

Helle, W., and W. P. J. Overmeer. 1973. Variability in tetranychid mites. *Annual Review of Entomology* 18:97–120.

Helle, W., and L. P. Pijnacker. 1985. Parthenogenesis, chromosomes, and sex. In *Spider Mites: Their Biology, Natural Enemies, and Control,* Vol. 1A, ed. W. Helle and M. W. Sabelis, 129-39. New York (Amsterdam): Elsevier.

Hislop, R. G., and L. R. Jeppson. 1976. Morphology of the mouthparts of several species of phytophagous mites. *Annals Entomological Society of America* 69:1125–35.

Hoy, M. A. 1982. Genetics and genetic improvement of the Phytoseiidae. In *Recent Advances in Knowledge of the Phytoseiidae,* ed. M. A. Hoy, 72–89. Div. Agricultural Sciences Special Publication 3284. Berkeley, Calif.: University of California.

———. 1985. Recent advances in genetics and genetic improvement of the Phytoseiidae. *Annual Review of Entomology* 30:345–70.

Huffaker, C. B., M. van de Vrie, and J. A. McMurtry. 1969. The ecology of tetranychid mites and their natural control. *Annual Review of Entomology* 14:125–74.

Hunter, C. D. 1997. *Suppliers of beneficial organisms in North America.* Sacramento, Calif.: California Environmental Protection Agency.

Hussey, N. W., and C. B. Huffaker. 1976. Spider mites. In *Studies in Biological Control. International Program No. 9,* ed. V. L. Delucchi, 179–228. Cambridge, U.K.: Cambridge University Press.

Hussey, N. W., and W. J. Parr. 1963. Dispersal of the glasshouse red spider mite *Tetranychus urticae* Koch (Acarina: Tetranychidae*). Entomologia Experimentalis et Applicata* 6:207–14.

Hussey, N. W., and N. Scopes, eds. 1985. *Biological Pest Control: The Glasshouse Experience.* Poole, U.K.: Blandford Press (Ithaca, N.Y.: Cornell University Press).

Jeppson, L. R., H. H. Keifer, and E. W. Baker. 1975. *Mites Injurious to Economic Plants.* Berkeley, Calif.: University of California Press.

Karban, R., and J. R. Carey. 1984. Induced resistance of cotton seedlings to mites. *Science* 225:53–4.

Kropczynska, D., A. Pilko, A. Witul and A. Al.-Mabrouk. 1999. Control of two-spotted spider mite with *Amblyseius californicus* (Oud.) on croton. *IOBC/WPRS Bulletin* 22:133–6.

Laing, J. E. 1969. Life history and life table of *Tetranychus urticae* Koch. *Acarologia* 11:32–42.

Lindquist, R. K. 1981. Introduction of predators for insect and mite control on commercial interior plantings. *Ohio Florists Association Bulletin* 622:5, 8.

Lindquist, R. K., C. Frost, and M. Wolgamott. 1980. Integrated control of insects and mites on Ohio greenhouse crops. *IOBC/WPRS Bulletin* 3:119–26.

Linquist, E. E. 1985. External anatomy. In *Spider Mites: Their Biology, Natural Enemies, and Control*, Vol. 1A, ed. W. Helle and M. W. Sabelis, 3–28. New York (Amsterdam): Elsevier.

Martin, N. A. 1987. Progress towards integrated pest management for greenhouse crops in New Zealand. *IOBC/WPRS Bulletin* 10 (2):111–5.

———. 1993. Integrated pest management for cymbidium orchids. *Crop and Food Research IPM Manual No. 4*, ed. N. A. Martin. Christchurch, New Zealand: NZ Institute for Crop and Food Research. Paging various

———. 1994. Integrated pest management for greenhouse roses. In *Crop and Food Research IPM Manual No. 8*, ed. N. A. Martin. Christchurch, New Zealand: NZ Institute for Crop and Food Research. Paging various

Martin, N. A. and P. Workman. 1988. The cost of integrated pest management for cymbidium orchids. *Proceedings of the Forty-first New Zealand Weed and Pest Control Conference*, 77–80. Wellington, New Zealand: New Zealand Weed and Pest Control Society.

McMurtry, J. A. 1982. The use of phytoseiids for biological control: Progress and future prospects. In *Recent Advances in Knowledge of the Phytoseiidae*, ed. M. A. Hoy, 23–48. Div. Agricultural Sciences Special Publication 3284. Berkeley, Calif.: University of California.

———. 1992. Dynamics and potential impact of "generalist" phytoseiids in agroecosystems and possibilities for establishment of exotic species. *Experimental and Applied Acarology* 14:371–82.

McMurtry, J. A., and B. A. Croft. 1997. Life-styles of phytoseiid mites and their roles in biological control. *Annual Review of Entomology* 42:291–321.

McMurtry, J. A., C. B. Huffaker, and M. van de Vrie. 1970. Ecology of tetranychid mites and their natural enemies: A review. I. Tetranychid enemies: Their biological characters and the impact of spray practices. *Hilgardia* 40:331–90.

McMurtry, J. A., E. R. Oatman, P. A. Phillips, and C. W. Wood. 1978. Establishment of *Phytoseiulus persimilis* (Acari: Phytoseiidae) in southern California. *Entomophaga* 23:175–9.

Mori, H., Y. Saito, and H. Nakao. 1990. Use of predatory mites to control spider mites (Acarina, Tetranychidae) in Japan. In *The Use of Natural Enemies to Control Agricultural Pests*, ed. J. Bay-Petersen, 142–56. Taipei, Taiwan: Food and Fertilizer Technology Center for the Asian and Pacific Region.

Nachman, G. 1985. Sampling techniques. In *Spider Mites: Their Biology, Natural Enemies, and Control*, Vol. 1B, ed. W. Helle and M. W. Sabelis, 175–82. New York (Amsterdam): Elsevier.

Osborne, L. S., and R. D. Oetting. 1989. Biological control of pests attacking greenhouse-grown ornamentals. *Florida Entomologist* 72:408–13.

Osborne, L. S., and F. L. Petitt. 1985. Insecticidal soap and the predatory mite *Phytoseiulus persimilis* (Acari: Phytoseiidae), used in management of two-spotted spider mite (Acari: Tetranychidae) on greenhouse-grown foliage plants. *Journal of Economic Entomology* 78:687–91.

Osborne, L. S., L. E. Ehler, and J. R. Nechols. 1985. Biological control of the two-spotted spider mite in greenhouses. *Florida Agriculture Experiment Station Bulletin*, 853. Pp. 40. Gainesville, Fla.: University of Florida.

Osborne, L. S., F. L. Petitt, Z. Landa, and K. A. Hoelmer. 1994. Biological control of pests attacking crops grown in protected cultivation: The Florida experience. In *Pest Management in the Subtropics: Biological Control—A Florida Perspective*, ed. D. Rosen, F. D. Bennett, and J. L. Capinera, 327–42. Andover, U.K.: Intercept.

Parr, W. J., and N. W. Hussey. 1966. Diapause in the glasshouse red spider mite (*Tetranychus urticae* Koch): A synthesis of present knowledge. *Horticultural Research* 6:1–21.

Penman, D. R., and W. W. Cone. 1972. Behavior of male two-spotted spider mites in response to quiescent female deutonymphs and to web. *Annals Entomological Society of America* 65:1289–93.

———. 1974. Role of web, tactile stimuli, and female sex pheromone in attraction of male two-spotted spider mites to quiescent female deutonymphs. *Annals Entomological Society of America* 67:179–82.

Poinar, G., Jr., and R. Poinar. 1998. Parasites and pathogens of mites. *Annual Review of Entomology* 43:449–69.

Potter, D. A., D. L. Wrensch, and D. R. Johnston. 1976a. Aggression and mating success in spider mites. *Science* 193:160–1.

———. 1976b. Guarding, aggressive behavior, and mating success in male two-spotted spider mites. *Annals Entomological Society of America* 69:707–11.

Rabbinge, R. 1985. Aspects of damage assessment. In *Spider Mites: Their Biology, Natural Enemies, and Control*, Vol. 1B, ed. W. Helle and M. W. Sabelis, 261–72. New York (Amsterdam): Elsevier.

Santos, M. A. and J. E. Laing. 1985. Stigmaeid predators. In *Spider Mites: Their Biology, Natural Enemies, and Control*, Vol. 1B, ed. W. Helle and M. W. Sabelis, 197–203. New York (Amsterdam): Elsevier.

Sabelis, M. W. 1981. Biological control of two-spotted spider mites using phytoseiid predators. Part 1: Modeling the predator-prey interaction at the individual level. *Agricultural Research Reports* 910:226–42.

Sabelis, M. W. 1985. Sampling techniques. In *Spider Mites: Their Biology, Natural Enemies, and Control*, Vol. 1B, ed. W. Helle and M. W. Sabelis, 337–50. New York (Amsterdam): Elsevier.

Sances, F. V., J. A. Wyman, and I. P. Ting. 1979. Morphological responses of strawberry leaves to infestations of two-spotted spider mite. *Journal of Economic Entomology* 72:710–3.

Scopes, N. E. A. 1985. Red spider mite and the predator *Phytoseiulus persimilis*. In *Biological Pest Control: The Glasshouse Experience*, ed. N. W. Hussey and N. E. A. Scopes, 43–52. Poole, U.K.: Blandford Press (Ithaca, N.Y.: Cornell University Press).

Shih, C. I., S. L. Poe, and H. L. Cromroy. 1976. Biology, life table, and intrinsic rate of increase of *Tetranychus urticae*. *Annals Entomological Society of America* 69:362–4.

Simmonds, S. P. 1972. Observations on the control of *Tetranychus urticae* on roses by *Phytoseiulus persimilis*. *Plant Pathology* 21:163–5.

Stenseth, C. 1976. Rovmidd for bekjempelse av veksthusspin-midd pa morplanter av kroton og dieffenbachia. *Gartneryrket* 66:780–2.

Tanigoshi, L. K. 1982. Advances in knowledge of the Phytoseiidae. In *Recent Advances in Knowledge of the Phytoseiidae*, ed. M. A. Hoy, 1–22. Div. Agricultural Sciences Special Publication 3284. Berkeley, Calif.: University of California.

Tanigoshi, L. K., and R. W. Davis. 1978. An ultrastructural study of *Tetranychus mcdanieli* feeding injury to the leaves of 'Red Delicious' apple (Acari: Tetranychidae). *International Journal of Acarology* 4:47–56.

Teerling, C. R., and G. Murphy. 1999. Experience with insect exclusion screening of greenhouse vents in Ontario, Canada. *IOBC/WPRS Bulletin* 22:247–50.

Tomczyk, A., and D. Kropczynska. 1985. Effects on the host plant. In *Spider Mites: Their Biology, Natural Enemies, and Control*, Vol. 1B, ed. W. Helle and M. W. Sabelis, 317–29. New York (Amsterdam): Elsevier.

Tomczyk, A., D. Kropczynska, and M. van de Vrie. 1991. The effects of spider-mite feeding on plant performance in relation to biological control. In *The Acari: Reproduction, Development and Life-History Strategies*, ed. R. Schuster and P. W. Murphy, 405–11. New York: Chapman and Hall.

Trumble, J. T., and J. P. Morse. 1993. Economics of integrating the predaceous mite *Phytoseiulus persimilis* (Acari: Phytoseiidae) with pesticides in strawberries. *Journal of Economic Entomology* 86:879–85.

van Lenteren, J. C. 1992. Biological control in protected crops: Where do we go? *Pesticide Science* 36:321–7.

van Lenteren, J. C. and J. Woets. 1988. Biological and integrated pest control in greenhouses. *Annual Review of Entomology* 33:239–69.

van de Vrie, M. 1985. Greenhouse ornamentals. In *Spider Mites: Their Biology, Natural Enemies, and Control*, Vol. 1B, ed. W. Helle and M. W. Sabelis, 239–83. New York (Amsterdam): Elsevier.

van de Vrie, M., J. A. McMurtry, and C. B. Huffaker. 1972. Ecology of tetranychid mites and their natural enemies: A review. III. Biology, ecology, and pest status, and host-plant relations of tetranychids. *Hilgardia* 4:343–432.

Wardlow, L. 1985. Chrysanthemums. In *Biological Pest Control: The Glasshouse Experience*, ed. N. W. Hussey and N. E. A. Scopes, 180–5. Poole, U.K.: Blandford Press (Ithaca, N.Y.: Cornell University Press).

Watson, T. F. 1964. Influence of host plant condition on population increase of *Tetranychus telarius* (Linnaeus) (Acarina: Tetranychidae) *Hilgardia* 35:273–322.

Workman, P. J., and N. A. Martin. 2000. Movement of *Phytoseiulus persimilis* (Acari: Phytoseiidae) on leaves of greenhouse carnations and other cut flowers. *New Zealand Journal of Crop and Horticultural Science* 28: 9-15.

Zhang, Z. O., and J. P. Sanderson. 1995. Two-spotted spider mite (Acari: Tetranychidae) and *Phytoseiulus persimilis* (*Acari: Phytoseiidae*) on greenhouse roses: Spatial distribution and predator efficacy. *Journal of Economic Entomology* 88:352–7.

Zhang, Z. Q. 2003. Mites of greenhouses: identification, biology and control. Wallingford, UK.: CABI Publishing.

11

BIOLOGICAL CONTROL OF TWO-SPOTTED SPIDER MITES ON GREENHOUSE VEGETABLE CROPS

D. R. Gillespie
Pacific Agri-Food Research Centre,
Agriculture and Agri-Food Canada, Agassiz, British Columbia, Canada

and

D. A. Raworth
Pacific Agri-Food Research Centre,
Agriculture and Agri-Food Canada, Agassiz, British Columbia, Canada

Biological control of the two-spotted spider mite, *Tetranychus urticae* Koch (Acari: Tetranychidae), is one of the cornerstones of biological control in greenhouse vegetable crops around the world. In all countries where *T. urticae* is controlled biologically, the mite *Phytoseiulus persimilis* Athias-Henriot is the most frequently used predator. Hussey and Scopes (1985a,b) reviewed the use of *P. persimilis* against spider mites on greenhouse vegetable crops. The biology of spider mites, their natural enemies, and control and management on a variety of crops were reviewed in Helle and Sabelis (1985a,b). This chapter discusses the current practice of biological control of spider mites on greenhouse vegetable crops, especially the changes since these mid-1980s reviews.

Biology of Spider Mites

Appearance

The most important spider mite in the greenhouse vegetable system is *T. urticae* other-wise known as the two-spotted spider mite or the red spider mite. This species is cosmopolitan (Gutierrez 1985). The only other species of widespread significance in the greenhouse vegetable industry is the carmine spider mite, *Tetranychus cinnabarinus* (Boisduval). This species may be a red-colored variant of the two-spotted spider mite (Foster and Barker 1978, Veerman 1985) but for consistency is referred to as a species herein. *Tetranychus cinnabarinus* is widely distributed in regions of the world with mild, dry climates, and in northern areas is found only in greenhouses (Veerman 1985).

Adult *T. urticae* are light yellow-green or red, with two distinct dorsolateral dark patches on the abdomen; their legs are yellowish. The overwintering form, seen in the autumn, winter, and early spring in northern temperate regions, is an orange-red color. *T. cinnabarinus* has white legs and a plum-red body without spots (Hussey and Scopes 1985a). Males and immatures lack the plum-red coloration and appear identical to *T. urticae*. The external appearance of *T. urticae* developmental stages is covered in chapter 10.

Development and reproduction

Development of *T. urticae* from egg to adult requires approximately thirteen days at 70°F (21°C) (Herbert 1981). Adult females mate, then mature for two to five more days before laying eggs (Crooker 1985). Females lay about fifty eggs at 70°F (21°C) and live for about thirty days. Females of *T. cinnabarinus* lay from 50 to 150 eggs over ten to thirty

days, depending on temperature and relative humidity, with a maximum at 40% RH and 75°F (24°C) (Hazan, Gerson, and Tahori 1973). As for all arthropods, temperature affects population growth rate (fig. 11.1).

Relative humidity also affects the development rate of spider mites. *T. urticae* develops faster, and adults produce more eggs at 25 to 30% RH than at 85 to 95% RH (Nickel 1960). Low RH increases evaporation from the mite's body, consequently increasing food consumption as mites feed on plant tissues to compensate for water loss (Crooker 1985). Hot, dry greenhouse

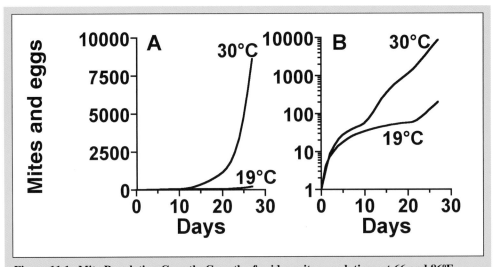

Figure 11.1. Mite Population Growth. Growth of spider mite populations at 66 and 86°F (19 and 30°C) (38% RH), starting with one immigrant female. Based on a simple model with life-history traits abstracted from Hazan, Gerson, and Tahori (1973). At 66°F (19°C), development time from egg to adult = 18 days; prereproductive period = 2 days; survival to reproductive age = 1.0; adult age-specific reproduction and survival; sex ratio, 1.5 females:1 male. At 86°F (30°C), development time, egg to adult = 7 days; prereproductive period = 1 day; survival to reproductive age = 1.0; adult age-specific reproduction and survival; sex ratio, 1.5 females:1 male. Numbers of eggs and actives on an arithmetic scale (A) and a logarithmic scale (B).

conditions therefore encourage mite outbreaks. Conte et al. (2001) report controlling spider mites on cucumber with mist blowers alone.

Drought stress affects injury to plants, as well as reproduction and development of spider mites (Oloumi-Sadeghi et al. 1988; English-Loeb 1990; Wermelinger et al. 1990; McNab, Williams, and Jerie 1994). Water stress sufficient to produce wilting will also produce increases in spider mite population growth rates. Wilting occurs often on greenhouse vegetable crops during transitions from cloudy to sunny weather, and these wilts may play a role in periodic outbreaks of spider mites.

Development and oviposition rates are positively correlated with increasing leaf nitrogen in tomato (van de Vrie, McMurtry, and Huffaker 1972; Wermelinger, Oertli, and Baumgärtner 1991). Increases in leaf nitrogen may lead to increases in spider mite population densities. Carbon dioxide enrichment has also been shown to increase reproduction in *T. urticae* on white clover (Heagle et al. 2002). This may be a factor in the reported biological control problems on tomato in the last 10-15 years.

Plant damage

On tomato, leaf area damage of about 10% results in a loss of yield of about 9%, and there appears to be no damage level below which losses do not occur (Stacey, Wyatt, and Chambers 1985). Cucumbers are more resistant to damage, and moderate spider mite infestation levels do not cause yield losses (Hussey and Parr 1963, van der Werf et al. 1996a). There are no similar estimates for sweet peppers.

The saliva of a European strain of *T. cinnabarinus* induces a hypertoxic response in the plant, and as a result, damage is not strongly related to mite feeding or mite numbers (Tomczyk and Kropczynska 1985, Kielkiewicz 1990, Hussey and Scopes 1985b). Symptoms on tomato leaves resemble magnesium deficiency; they include chlorosis and transparent lesions (Foster and Barker 1978). Lower leaves die prematurely, and whole plants may die if the infestation is severe. Similar responses have been observed for *Tetranychus turkestani* Ugarov and Nikolski in other crop species (Tomczyk and Kropczynska 1985; Brito, Stern, and Sances 1986).

Another form of spider mite damage within greenhouse systems is the pest's potential influence on employee health and health-related losses. Italian farm workers reported allergic responses to spider mites that included rhinitis, bronchial asthma (Astarita et al. 1994), and contact dermatitis (Astarita et al. 1996).

Biology of *Phytoseiulus persimilis*

The predatory mite *P. persimilis* (fig. 11.2) is the natural enemy most widely applied for biological control of two-spotted spider mites in greenhouse crops. It is used on cucumber, tomatoes, and sweet peppers in North America and Europe (van Lenteren and Woets 1988), the former U.S.S.R. (Luk'Yanova and Veremeev 1993, Khloptseva 1991), Moldavia (Bogach 1989), Turkey (Kilincer, Cobanoglu, and Has 1992), much of the Mediterranean region (Vacante and Nucifora 1987), the former Czechoslovakia

(Bartos, Landa, and Taborsky 1990), Egypt (El-Laithy 1992), and Israel (Berlinger, Dahan, and Mordechi 1988). It has also been used to control spider mites on protected strawberry crops in Great Britain (Cross 1984), Italy (Spicciarelli, Battaglia, and Tranfaglia 1992), Japan (Shibao, Negoro, and Tanaka 1995), and Taiwan (Ho 1990), and on field strawberry crops in California (McMurtry et al. 1978) and Australia (Waite 1988).

Description and life history

The adult *P. persimilis* is reddish-orange in color, long-legged, and somewhat larger than the adult *T. urticae* (fig. 11.2, left). Mature females, viewed from above, are distinctly pear-shaped, broadening strongly from anterior to posterior. The body is about 0.02 in. (0.4 mm) long and 0.01 in. (0.3 mm) wide. The eggs (fig. 11.2, right) are slightly pale pink in color, ovoid, and about 0.01 in.

(0.2 mm) long by 0.01 in. (0.15 mm) wide or about three times the size of spider mite eggs. A pale white, six-legged larva hatches from the egg and subsequently molts to an eight-legged, pale pink protonymph and deutonymph before becoming an adult.

From a developmental threshold of 52°F (11°C), *P. persimilis*'s development rates increase by 0.011 per day per degree C (Sabelis 1981). At 90°F (32°C), the development rate reaches its maximum (Sabelis 1985), and it subsequently declines at temperatures above 90°F (32°C). *P. persimilis* population growth rates are unable to keep pace with spider mite population growth rates above 86°F (30°C) (Hussey and Scopes 1985a), thus frequently dooming biological control to failure at warm temperatures. Also, *P. persimilis* eggs die below 60% RH (Pralavorio and Rojas 1980), which limits the use of this predatory mite in dry environments.

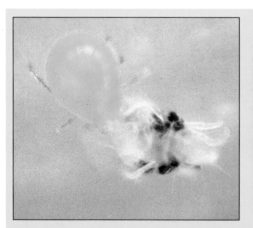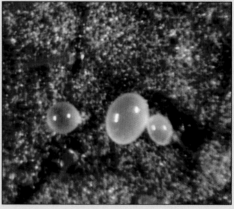

Figure 11.2. Appearance of the predatory mite *Phytoseiulus persimilis* Athias-Henriot (Acari: Phytoseiidae). Left: Adult feeding on two spotted spider mite. *Photo: M. P. Parrella.* **Right: Egg.** *Photo: D. Gillespie.*

Predators require a suitable number of prey for reproduction and development of their offspring. Immature *P. persimilis* require about ten eggs or young spider mites to complete development (Hussey and Scopes 1985a). *P. persimilis* completes development from protonymph to adult with a prey density of two or more juvenile spider mites per 0.6 in.^{2} (4 cm^2), but at one juvenile spider mite per 0.6 in.^{2} (4 cm^2), predators die (Eveleigh and Chant 1982a). Females require an additional ten to fourteen spider mites to begin egg production. The oviposition period is about twenty-two days at 20°C (69°F), and females lay 2.4 eggs per day (Laing 1968). Under unrestricted prey conditions the sex ratio of offspring is 80% female, whereas under restricted prey conditions the sex ratio is 50% females (Toyoshima and Amano 1998).

As predators forage on one prey mite colony, they must be capable of moving to new mite colonies for biological control to be successful. Phytoseiid mites float on breezes of 0.4 to 1.9 ft./second (0.1 to 0.5 m/second) to move from one location to another (Sabelis and Afman 1994, Coop and Croft 1995). Wind speeds greater than 0.4 ft./second (0.1 m/second) are common in the plant canopy of passively vented houses, and speeds up to 3.3 ft./second (1 m/second) are common in fan-vented houses (chapter 3). Adult females of *P. persimilis* orient their movements (floating or walking) to chemical odors produced by plants attacked by spider mites (synomones), and to odors produced by spider mites (kairomones) (Sabelis, Vermaat, and Groenveld 1984; Dicke 1994). *P. persimilis* is not attracted to odours from moderate to heavy infestations of *T. cinnabarinus* on tomato but is attracted to odors from similar infestations of *T. urticae* (Takabayashi et al. 2000). These authors hypothesize that this is due to differences in the way that the tomato plant responds to the saliva of the two mites (Ibid.)

Application in biological control

Phytoseiulus persimilis is sold worldwide to growers by commercial insectaries in a variety of package types and "formulations." The most common formulation is a cardboard tube or plastic bottle that contains one to several thousand adult mites in a vermiculite carrier. Mites are mixed into the vermiculite before application by gently turning (not shaking) the package a few times. Small quantities of vermiculite containing predator mites are tipped from the container onto leaves; shaking them out of the container will injure predators. The major issues with this sort of packaging are risk of injury, the accuracy of the number of mites in the container, and the effects of starvation on the fecundity and survival of predators – although some producers add frozen *T. urticae* eggs for food.

Another common formulation of *P. persimilis* contains adults, immatures, and eggs on pieces of bean leaf in plastic containers. There usually are some spider mites on the leaf pieces. This formulation is not commonly shipped internationally because the phytosanitary regulations of most countries prohibit the importation of pest species, whether or not they already exist in the country. Where permitted, this formulation has advantages because predators can be supplied with prey during shipping, and the leaf material maintains humidity, protecting the predator against desiccation.

Predator mites are released either using the pest-in-first method, or they are released in response to detection of a naturally occurring infestation. In cucumber, the pest-in-first method is initiated with an intentional release of ten nondiapausing female spider mite adults per plant. Ten days after this inoculation, one predator is introduced on every fifth plant (Hussey and Scopes 1985b, Woets 1985). Lindquist (1981) reported the pest-in-first method yields better control than use of inoculative release approaches. However, Blümel (1989) found that simultaneous introductions of *P. persimilis* and *T. urticae* at a ratio of one predator to ten prey did not produce better or more stable control than reactive releases after sighting pests (Blümel 1989). Nachman (1991) produced a predator-prey interaction that was stable over six months by introducing *P. persimilis* and *T. urticae* in low numbers on alternate plants in each row. Dispersal of spider mites among plants stabilized the interactions between predators and prey, even though there were fluctuations in spider mite numbers and extinctions of predators occurred on individual plants.

Initiating releases after detection of a natural infestation requires fewer predators because introductions are targeted only to those places where pests are present (Markkula and Tiittanen 1976). However, in the absence of sampling programs that can detect low densities of spider mites, mite infestations may increase to levels that cause yield losses before they are detected and brought under control. With the pest-in-first approach, more predators are used initially because the pest is widely and uniformly distributed. Considering all the available information, the pest-in-first approach may be used successfully to control spider mite, but the details must be carefully considered. Use of a computer simulation model has demonstrated that relatively small changes in the timing of predator introductions and the numbers of predator releases have large effects on the outcome of the biological control program (fig. 11.3).

A slightly different approach to the pest-in-first method is used on tomatoes. Spider mites and predators are introduced onto plants while they are still on the propagation bench, before planting in the greenhouse (Hussey and Scopes 1985b). Obtaining a uniform spread of spider mites and predators provides better long-term regulation of the spider mite populations, and fewer predators are required for obtaining control (Nihoul 1993a).

Two methods are used to determine rate of *P. persimilis* release for control of natural infestations of spider mites. Either a predetermined, fixed number of predators per unit area are released at the first sign of spider mite infestation, or pest densities are estimated and enough predators are released to achieve a desired predator-to-prey ratio. The first approach has the advantage of simplicity, but releases are made with little to no knowledge of prey density. Typical introduction rates of *P. persimilis* in fixed-release plans are five to twenty predators per plant. Depending on crop and planting density, this is the equivalent of 20,000 to 81,000 per acre (50,000 to 200,000 per ha) (table 11.1).

In fixed-rate release plans, releases are initiated upon first detection of spider mites. Methods for monitoring for spider mite presence vary greatly among growers. Con-

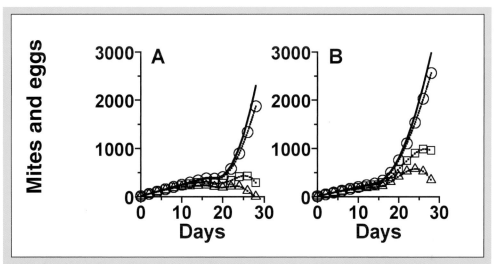

Figure 11.3. Results of a simple predator-prey model where life-history variables for *Tetranychus urticae* **(development time, pre-reproductive period, reproductive period, fecundity, and sex ratio) are from Laing (1969) (A) and from Herbert (1981) (B), and values for** *Phytoseiulus persimilis* **are from Laing (1968). Thompson's (1924) random search model was used to calculate survival (survival** $= e^{(-k\,b/a)}$**, where:** *k* **is the demand for prey by a given predator age class, expressed as** *T. urticae* **eggs;** *b* **is the number of predators in the age class; and** *a* **is the number of prey, expressed as** *T. urticae* **eggs). Solid line, start with 10** *T. urticae* **females per plant and impose no predation; circles, add one predator to every fifth plant 10 days after adding** *T. urticae***; squares, add one predator per plant 10 days after adding** *T. urticae***; triangles, add one predator to every fifth plant two days after adding** *T. urticae*.

sequently, some growers fail to detect spider mites until their numbers exceed what can be suppressed by the recommended predator release rate on the crop. Recommendations that prescribe a release rate (number per unit area or per plant) when spider mites reach a predetermined density offer a solution to this problem (e.g., Nicoli and Benuzzi 1988); however, crop monitoring efforts must be increased when using this method. There are several drawbacks associated with fixed-rate release programs that do not consider pest density. First, these programs generate and reinforce an attitude that equates the applica-

tion of biological control with the application of pesticides. Second, if too few predators are released, spider mite densities may increase and cause unacceptable levels of damage before being controlled. Third, inexperienced growers often experience crop damage due to the general unpredictability associated with the method.

An improvement over fixed-release methods is the establishment of an optimal predator-prey ratio; i.e., a predator release rate relative to the density of pest mites that reduces pest densities below an economic injury level. Predator-prey ratios that are

Table 11.1. Area-based release rates. These rates are based on releases of fixed numbers per unit area or per plant. Some address spider mite density as a qualitative variable.

Crop	Rate	Notes	Reference
Tomato	16/plant	—	Kilincer, Cobanolgu, and Has 1992
Cucumbers	10/plant	Damage resulted under hot and dry conditions	El-Laithy 1992
	15/plant	No damage under hot and dry conditions	ibid
Cucumber	5–10/plant	—	Kilincer, Cobanolgu, and Has 1992
Cucumber	0.5–0.7/ft.^{2} (5–8/m^2)	*T. urticae* not less than 0.1 and not more than 0.5 per leaf	Nicoli and Benuzzi 1988
Cucumber	10/plant	At first sign	Rasmy and El-Laithy 1988
Cucumber	0.5/ft.^{2} (5.5/m^2)	At first sign	Celli, Nicoli, and Benuzzi 1987
Cucumber	1/plant	At first sign, then 1,600 to 4,500/acre (4,000 to 11,000/ha) weekly or biweekly until predators are present on all leaves	Elliott, Gilkeson, and Gillespie 1987
Cucumber	20,000– 40,000/acre	In first infestation foci	Popov 1988
	50,000– 100,000/ha)		ibid
Pepper	2–5/plant	At first sign	Buxton et al. 1990

effective on various crops and under different conditions are summarized in table 11.2. When using this method, predator release rates must be estimated for the number of spider mites that will be in the crop at the time the predator mites are received from the insectary and actually released into the target crop. When making this estimation, one should remember that spider mite populations could increase tenfold during the typical seven- to ten-day

Table 11.2. Pedator-prey ratio-based release rates. These introduction rates are based on the number of predators per prey. The density of spider mites determines the number of *P. persimilis* to introduce.

Crop	Predator-prey \ratio	Notes	Reference
Aubergine	1:10	—	Chermeti 1991, 1992
Strawberry	1:10	When spider mites reach 1–2/leaf	Bonomo et al. 1991
Cucumber	1:20	Minimum	Adam 1986
	1:5	Rapid elimination	ibid
Cucumber	1:20	Up to 5–6 tetranychids/leaf, <20% leaf damage	Loginova, Atanasson, and Georgiev 1987
Tomato, Pepper	1:10	Up to 2-3 tetranychids/leaf	Loginova, Atanasson, and Georgiev 1987

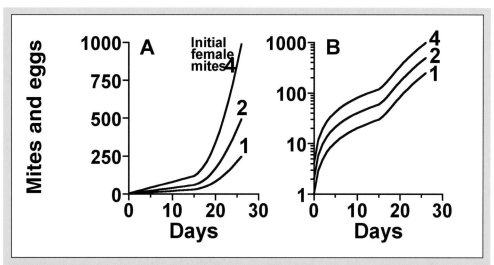

Figure 11.4. Growth of spider mite populations starting from one, two, or four immigrant female mites on a plant. Data based on a simple model with development time from egg to adult equaling 13 days; prereproductive period equaling 1 day; reproduction equaling 1.9 eggs per female per day; females dying after reproducing for 26 days; and a sex ratio of 4.4 females to 1 male (Herbert, 1981). Numbers of eggs and actives on an arithmetic scale (A) and a logarithmic scale (B).

interval between ordering and receiving the predators (See figs.11.3 and 11.4).

An advantage of basing predator release rates on an intended predator-prey ratio is that the outcome is theoretically more predictable than the fixed-rate method. The major disadvantage is that routine sampling must be done to estimate spider mite density, which adds to the cost of control. Estimates of spider mite density have inherently low precision because the mites have a clumped (negative binomial) distribution (e.g., Raworth 1986). Better precision can be obtained by increasing sample size, but this increases sample time and cost. The alternative is a combination of sampling and risk analysis. In an analysis of risk, probabilities are assigned for each set of possible outcomes (success, partial success, failure, etc.) given a particular sample precision and set of specific pest management actions. Based on these probabilities, a grower may decide what course of action to take based upon an acceptable level of risk. Van der Werf et al. (1996b) took this approach for monitoring mites on apple, but thus far, no such analysis has been used by the greenhouse vegetable industry.

Sampling spider mite infestations

There are several approaches to sampling spider mites on greenhouse crops, each with a particular set of strengths and weaknesses. The most direct approach is to count mites on plants or plant structures. Leaves or leaflets are generally the best sample unit, and samples should be obtained at random. However, spider mites tend to be distributed on the upper part of tomato plants (Nihoul 1993a) and other crops, which makes effective sampling difficult if facilities for

reaching the tops of plants are not available. In addition, there is evidence that spider mites move up and down the plant during a twenty-four-hour period (Pralavorio, Fournier, and Millot 1989). This means that the time of day that sampling is performed could affect the results.

A second approach is to indirectly estimate spider mite numbers by the damage they cause to plants. Systems for estimating numbers based on the damage to whole cucumber or tomato leaves (Hussey and Scopes 1985b) and tomato leaflets (Nihoul and Hance 1993; Nihoul, van Impe, and Hance 1991) have been developed. No damage-based approaches have been reported for sampling spider mite numbers on pepper crops. Plant varieties and species vary in their responses to injury, and damage indices must be determined for each.

Knowledge of the number of spider mites and of the state of the population (increasing or decreasing) is necessary to decide whether to do nothing, continue with biological control, apply pesticides, or take other action. This information can only be obtained through observations of pest and natural-enemy populations on the crop through time. Use of any other approach results in introduction of natural enemies in an ad hoc fashion, often too late or in insufficient or excessive numbers.

Effects of temperature and relative humidity on biological control by *P. persimilis*

The rates of development and reproduction of *T. urticae* increase with increasing temperature and decreasing relative humidity. The development rate of *P. persimilis* increases with increasing temperature to a threshold of 86°F (30°C), but relative humidity below 60% prevents development and results in mortality of eggs and immature stages. These biological features provide opportunities for populations of *T. urticae* to escape suppression by predation and to increase to damaging levels. On tomatoes grown at high temperature and low relative humidity, *T. urticae* is concentrated on the upper part of the plant, whereas *P. persimilis* is restricted to the lower part, leading to outbreaks of spider mites (Nihoul 1992). On cucumbers in Egypt, El-Laithy (1992) found that release of fifteen *P. persimilis* per plant provided adequate control under low relative humidity. Applying mist to the greenhouse atmosphere makes the environment less favorable for *T. urticae*, but not more favorable for *P. persimilis* (Lindquist et al. 1987).

Strategies that enhance biological control of spider mite by *P. persimilis* under hot, dry conditions include reducing greenhouse temperature, increasing relative humidity and increasing release rates. However, greenhouse climate should not be manipulated at the expense of crop production. Leaf wetness from excessive misting promotes foliar plant disease, and high (greater than 95%) relative humidity can interfere with transpiration and uptake of nutrients.

Effects of plants on *P. persimilis*

Shoots of modern tomato cultivars have glandular hairs that form a significant part of the plant's defenses (Carter and Snyder 1985, Good and Snyder 1988). Entrapment on these glandular hairs significantly reduces the dispersal of *P. persimilis* between leaves (van Haren et al. 1987). Gillespie and Quiring

(1994) showed that reproduction and survival of *P. persimilis* were reduced when feeding on spider mites on tomato leaves compared with spider mites on bean leaves. The density of glandular hairs on tomato increases with temperature and light intensity, especially in the spring (Nihoul 1993b). This may contribute to outbreaks of spider mites by limiting dispersal of *P. persimilis* to new spider mite patches (Ibid.). As a result, local spider mite outbreaks are probable unless monitoring is extensive and special care is taken to ensure predatory mite releases are made uniformly throughout the greenhouse. At low spider mite densities on leaves, predation by *P. persimilis* is negatively affected by hair density, but at high prey densities there is no effect of plant hairs (Krips et al. 1999). Paradoxically, plant hairs, as well as spider mite webbing, protect predator mites and their eggs from intra-guild predation (Roda et al. (2000).

Interactions of *P. persimilis* with other natural enemies

P. persimilis outcompetes most other phytoseiid predators in experimental systems that contain only spider mites and phytoseiid predators of spider mites. The high dispersal rate of *P. persimilis* relative to other phytoseiids allows it to rapidly locate and exploit patches of spider mites (Eveleigh and Chant 1982b,c,d,e). In a laboratory system, Cloutier and Johnson (1993) demonstrated that the predatory bug *Orius tristicolor* (White) (Hemiptera: Anthocoridae) feeds preferentially on *P. persimilis*, even in the presence of spider mites. However, when western flower thrips (*Frankliniella occidentalis* [Pergande]) were also present, *O. tristicolor* did not exhibit a clear prey preference. There appear to be no recorded instances of reduction of *P. persimilis* populations in greenhouses caused by other predators.

Integration of *P. persimilis* with pesticides

Pesticides may be applied to greenhouse vegetable crops in the presence of *P. persimilis* for the control of spider mites, other pest insects and mites, and plant diseases. Selection of pesticides that do the least harm to natural-enemy populations is one of the basic principles of IPM. Most companies that produce *P. persimilis* also provide lists indicating which pesticides are safe for use with natural enemies, including *P. persimilis*. Oomen, Romeihn, and Wiegers (1991) evaluated the effects of one-hundred pesticides on *P. persimilis*. Growers should compare such information to pesticides registered for use on greenhouse vegetables in their country. The role of insecticides and miticides in the generation of spider mite outbreaks through elimination of natural-enemy populations has been repeatedly demonstrated in a wide variety of crops. As a general rule, growers should assume, unless experience dictates otherwise, that application of any product that is not explicitly compatible with natural enemies will generate an outbreak of spider mites.

Quality of insectary-produced *P. persimilis*

The quality of *P. persimilis* produced in insectaries is currently a controversial issue. Markkula, Tittanen, and Hokkanen (1987) presented evidence that mass-produced *P. persimilis* shipped long distances in bran laid fewer eggs and fed less than *P. persimilis* that

were produced locally in smaller production facilities. Steiner and Bjørnson (1996) demonstrated a high degree of variability in reproduction and survivorship among *P. persimilis* produced in various insectaries. These differences may be due to effects of pathogens and nutritional disorders of *P. persimilis* (Bjørnson, Steiner, and Keddie 1997). *Microsporidium phytoseiuli* Bjørnson, Steiner and Keddie (Microsporidia) reduces fecundity and lifespan and reduces predation rate on *T. urticae* in *P. persimilis* (Bjørnson and Keddie 1999). Similarly, frequency of a white-gut symptom of unknown origin was negatively associated with decreased fecundity and predation rate in *P. persimilis*, but the effect could not be detected on receipt of predators from a producer (Bjørnson, Raworth and Bédard 2000). Later experimental work showed that frequency of white abdominal symptoms increased in an asymptotic curvilinear fashion with increased fertilizer concentration applied to the host plants of the spider mite prey, but none of the life-history traits (fecundity, oviposition period or survival) were affected (Bjørnson and Raworth 2003). The authors consider white abdominal symptoms an expression of normal excretory function that may be affected by other factors. However, biological control may be affected by plant nutrition in that *T. urticae* is affected positively by increased nitrogen, but *P. persimilis* is not. The differences noted by Steiner and Bjørnson (1996) could also be due to poor production methods, physical and physiological trauma suffered in shipping, or to genetic differences among populations. Fecundity and survival on receipt of *P. persimilis* from a producer are typically low, 1.6 eggs per day and 74% survival to Day 5, but age-specific fecundity and survival of the progeny are high, 4 eggs per day from Day 2-14 and 100% survival to Day 6 (Raworth and Bjørnson 2002). If the quality of *P. persimilis* on receipt could be improved it would make a considerable difference to control efforts (ibid.), but as it stands, introductions should be considered as a way of initiating predation with a week time lag before the full potential of the predator is realized. Quality standards for mass produced *P. persimilis* and methods for evaluating quality of *P. persimilis* can be found in van Lenteren et al. (2003).

Biological Control Using Other Predatory Mites

Predatory mites other than *P. persimilis* cannot be recommended for biological control of spider mites at present due to the lack of scientific evidence verifying their effectiveness in crop production systems. Helle and Sabelis (1985b) discuss the role of other species of predatory mites in the regulation and management of spider mite populations; however, *P. persimilis* is still the predominant biological control agent for spider mites on greenhouse vegetable crops.

Neoseiulus barkeri (Hughes), which is commercially available for biological control of thrips, has been released for biological control of spider mites. Karg and Mack (1986) and Karg, Mack, and Baier (1987) reported that releases of *N. barkeri* at 1:10 predator-prey ratios resulted in complete elimination of spider mites under laboratory conditions. They obtained similar results on a cucumber crop. Hance et al. (1991) introduced *Amblyseius andersoni* (Chant) in combination with *P. persimilis* on a tomato crop, but were

unable to assess the contribution of the former to the regulation of spider mites on the crop.

Neoseiulus fallacis (Garman) is now reared by commercial insectaries in North America. Initial use of this predator was on field crops such as strawberry, in cool climates that were unfavorable for *P. persimilis* (Raworth 1990). In greenhouses, experimental introductions of the predator into pepper crops in British Columbia, Canada, were made from October through November 1995 and February through March 1996 (Luczynski, Matys, and Raworth 1996). The predator established after each release, responded numerically to spider mite density, and contributed to spider mite control. Releases of *N. fallacis* on raspberry and sweet pepper in greenhouses in the Netherlands have resulted in establishment and good control of *T. urticae*.

Neoseiulus californicus (McGregor) has been investigated as a biological control for twospotted spider mites by several authors. Rott and Ponsonby (2000) reported that *N. californicus* in combination with *P. persimilis* and either *Stethorus punctillum* Weise or *Feltiella acarisuga* (Vallot) contributed to better mite control on tomato, pepper, cucumber and aubergine in cages than *P. persimilis* alone. Castagnoli, Liguori and Simoni (1999) found that reproduction of *N. californicus* was initially poor on tomato, but that this improved dramatically after several generations on that crop.

Biological Control of Spider Mites Using Predacious Insects

The natural enemies of spider mites were reviewed previously by Chazeau (1985),

Santos and Laing (1985), and Gerson (1985). Some of the natural enemies used in greenhouses for biological control of thrips, whiteflies, or aphids will also attack spider mites and have been credited with spider mite control in isolated reports.

Orius insidiosus

Orius insidiosus (Say) (Hemiptera: Anthocoridae), used for biological control of thrips on greenhouse vegetables (van de Veire and Degheele 1993), is a key predator of spider mites on cotton (e.g., Leigh 1985). It and other *Orius* species introduced for biological control of thrips can contribute to biological control of spider mites on greenhouse vegetable crops. A European pirate bug, *Orius majusculus* (Reuter), controlled spider mites following natural invasions into a pepper crop in the former Czechoslovakia (Jindra, Taborsky, and Skoda 1991).

Macrolophus caliginosus

Macrolophus caliginosus Wagner (Hemiptera: Miridae) is a predatory bug introduced into European greenhouses for whitefly biological control (Sampson and King 1996). It and related species of mirids have reduced spider mites on greenhouse vegetable crops (Kajita 1984; Kimsanbaev, Rashidov, and Akhanov 1991a,b). *M. caliginosus* is not native to North America, and will likely not be permitted into North America because of its omnivorous feeding habits. *Dicyphus hesperus* Knight (Hemiptera: Miridae), a North American species that fills a similar niche to *M. caliginosus*, is currently being investigated as a biological control agent in greenhouses (McGregor et al. 1999, Sanchez, Gillespie and McGregor 2003).

Stethorus punctillum

Stethorus punctillum Weise (Coleoptera: Coccinellidae) is a small (0.1-in. [2-mm]), black ladybird beetle now being mass-reared commercially and used to reduce early-season infestations of *T. urticae*. Recent work by Congdon, Shanks, and Antonelli (1993) demonstrated the ability of a closely related species, *Stethorus punctum picipes* Casey [possibly *S. punctillum;* see Raworth and Robertson 2002], to find and control small spider mite infestations. They suggest that dispersal and searching ability at low prey density contribute to the ability of this predator to suppress spider mite populations. February releases of 400 *S. punctillum* beetles per commercial greenhouse resulted in establishment on pepper and cucumber but not on tomato (Raworth, 2001). Adult beetles moved throughout the pepper and cucumber crops, and the beetles reproduced on cucumber through the season. The contribution of *S. punctillum* to biological control of spider mites was not determined; however, 1,000 *T. urticae* eggs were eaten per larva during development. The numbers of beetles released per unit area was not determined in these inoculative releases. In a cage trial, releases of 3 first-instar *S. punctillum* larvae in combination with *P. perimilis* and either *N. californicus* or *F. acarisuga* provided better control than *P. persimilis* alone on plants with high densities of spider mites (Rott and Ponsonby (2000). The biology of *Stethorus* spp. is discussed in Chazeau (1985). Development from egg to adult requires 217DD above 11.6°C (Raworth 2001). Activity of larvae and adults increases with increasing temperature, and adults and larvae searched more efficiently on tomato and pepper than on cucumber or aubergine leaves (Rott and Ponsonby 2000).

Further work is necessary to determine how to best integrate *Stethorus* species with other available predators in an economically feasible manner. Given the ongoing problems of spider mite control that are often associated with the seasonal changes in climate in a greenhouse, this multipredator approach may be a reasonable strategy.

Feltiella acarisuga

Feltiella acarisuga is a predatory gall midge that feeds on tetranychid mites, including two-spotted spider mites. The North American *F. acarisuga* and the European *Therodiplosis persicae* Kieffer have recently been recognized to be the same species and synonymized as *F. acarisuga* (Gagné 1995).

Roberti (1954) described the biology of *F. acarisuga*. Additional studies on the effects of temperature and relative humidity on the biology of this predator have been conducted by Gillespie et al. (1994) and Gillespie and Quiring (1996). Cylindrical translucent eggs, 0.01 in. (0.2 mm) long, are laid either directly on leaves near spider mite colonies or on the webbing produced by the mites. The eggs hatch after two days at 68 to 77°F (20 to 25°C), and larvae begin feeding immediately on all stages of spider mites. After four to six days of feeding, larvae spin cocoons on the leaves and pupate, often in crevices or beside veins. Adults emerge at a 1:1 sex ratio from these cocoons after an additional four to six days. Adults are delicate flies; they live for only a few days, and females lay about thirty eggs. Development rate, survival, and oviposition are their greatest at a relative humidity of 90% and they decrease with decreasing relative humidity. Development rate increases with increasing temperature to a maximum of 81°F (27°C). Opit, Roitberg, and Gillespie (1997) showed that *F. acarisuga* larvae respond to prey availability in much the same way as *P. persimilis* in that the rate at which prey are killed increases with increasing numbers of prey. Wardlow and Tobin (1990) released *F. acarisuga* as cocoons at a rate of 81 per acre (200 per ha) per week in a tomato crop. The predator established and appeared to play a role in reducing spider mite populations. Pijnakker (2002) recommends introduction of 1000 cocoons per ha per week. *F. acarisuga* requires a moderately large prey population for successful establishment and is sensitive to elemental sulfur used for management of powdery mildews. Vacante (1985) found that *F. acarisuga* could only be used in the winter and spring in Italy. During the summer and fall months, the presence of *Aphanogmus fulmeki* Szelényi (Hymenoptera: Ceraphronidae) inhibits the ability of the predatory midge populations to control spider mites by parasitizing *F. acarisuga* larvae.

References Cited

Adam, H. 1986. Effective yield achievement through new phytosanitary measures with biological control methodsas an example. *Wissenschaftliche Zeitschrift der Humboldt Universitat zu Berlin, Mathematisch Naturwissenschaftliche Reihe* 35:600–2.

Astarita, C., P. Di Martino, G. Scala, A. Franzese, and S. Sproviero. 1996. Contact allergy: Another occupational risk to *Tetranychus urticae*. *Journal of Allergy and Clinical Immunology* 98:732–8.

Astarita, C., A. Franzese, G. Scala, S. Sproviero, and G. Raucci. 1994. Farm workers' occupational allergy to *Tetranychus urticae*: Clinical and immunologic aspects. *Allergy* 49:466–71.

Bartos, J., Z. Landa, and V. Taborsky. 1990. Integrated protection of greenhouse plants. *Metodiky pro Zavadeni Vysledku Vyzkumu do Zemedelske Praxe* 11:40.

Berlinger, M. J., R. Dahan, and S. Mordechi. 1988. Integrated pest management of organically grown greenhouse tomatoes in Israel. *Applied Agricultural Research* 3:233–8.

Bjørnson, S., and D. A. Raworth. 2003. Effects of plant nutrition on the expression of abdominal discoloration in *Phytoseiulus persimilis* (Acari: Phytoseiidae). *The Canadian Entomologist* 135:129-138.

Bjørnson, S., M. Y. Steiner, and B. A. Keddie. 1997. Birefringent crystals and abdominal discoloration in the predatory mite *Phytoseiulus persimilis* (Acari: Phytoseiidae). *Journal of Invertebrate Pathology* 69:85–91.

Bjørnson, S. and B. A. Keddie. 1999. Effects of *Microsporidium phytoseiuli* (Microsporidia) on the performance of the predatory mite, *Phytoseiulus persimilis* (Acari: Phytoseiidae). *Biological Control* 15:153-161.

Bjørnson, S., D. A. Raworth, and C. Bédard. 2000. Abdominal discoloration and the predatory mite *Phytoseiulus persimilis* Athias-Henriot: prevalence of symptoms and their correlation with short-term performance. *Biological Control* 19:17-27.

Blümel, S. 1989. The use of *Encarsia formosa* (Gah.) and *Phytoseiulus persimilis* (A.H.) for the control of *Trialeurodes vaporariorum* Westw. (Aleyrodidae) and *Tetranychus urticae* (Koch) on tomato and cucumber under glass. *Pflanzenschutzberichte* 50(1):9–18.

Bogach, G. I. 1989. The biological method in the greenhouse. *Zashchita Rastenii Moskva* 2:9–13.

Bonomo, G., G. Catalano, V. Maltese, and S. Sparta. 1991. Biological and integrated control experiments in Maralese strawberry crops. *Informatore Agrario* 47:97–100.

Brito, R. M., V. M. Stern, and F. V. Sances. 1986. Physiological response of cotton plants to feeding of three *Tetranychus* spider mite species (Acari: Tetranychidae*). Journal of Economic Entomology* 79:1217–20.

Buxton, J. H., R. Jacobsen, M. Saynor, R. Storer, and L. Wardlow. 1990. An integrated pest management programme for peppers: Three years trial experience. *IOBC/WPRS Bulletin* 13 (5):45–50.

Carter, C. D. and J. C. Snyder. 1985. Mite response in relation to trichomes of *Lycopersicon esculentum* x *L. hirsutum* F{-2} hybrids. *Euphytica* 34, 177-185.

Castagnoli, M., M. Liguori, and S. Simoni. 1999. Effect of two different host plants on biological features of *Neoseiulus californicus* (McGregor). *International Journal of Acarology* 25:145-150.

Celli, G., G. Nicoli, and M. Benuzzi. 1987. Biological control in protected crops in northern Italy's Po Valley. *IOBC/WPRS Bulletin* 10 (2):37–40.

Chazeau, J. 1985. Predaceous insects. In *Spider Mites: Their Biology, Natural Enemies, and Control*, Vol. 1B, ed. W. Helle and M. W. Sabelis, 211–46. New York (Amsterdam): Elsevier.

Chermiti, B. 1991. Lutte biologique: -1-. Essai d'utilisation de *Phytoseiulus persimilis* Athias-Henriot (Acarina, Phytoseiidae) contre *Tetranychus urticae* Koch (Acarina, Tetranychidae) sur une culture protegee d'aubergine. *IOBC/WPRS Bulletin* 14 (5):134-139.

Chermiti, B. 1992. Biological control II: biological control of an artificial infestation of Tetranychus urticae Koch. using *Phytoseiulus persimilis* Athias-Henriot in a protected aubergine crop. *International Symposium on Crop Protection. Mededelingen van de Faculteit Landbouwwetenschappen, Rijksuniversiteit Gent* 57[3A]:959-964.

Cloutier, C., and S. G. Johnson. 1993. Predation by *Orius tristicolor* (Hemiptera: Anthocoridae) on *Phytoseiulus persimilis* (Acarina: Phytoseiidae): Testing for compatibility between biocontrol agents. *Environmental Entomology* 22 (2):477–82.

Congdon, B. D., C. H. Shanks Jr., and A. L. Antonelli. 1993. Population interaction between *Stethorus punctum picipes* (Coleoptera: Coccinellidae) and *Tetranychus urticae* (Acari: Tetranychidae) in red raspberries at low predator and prey densities. *Environmental Entomology* 22:1302–7.

Conte, L., F. Chiarini, L. D. Montà, and C. Duso. 2001. Water as a means of controlling the red spider mite in greenhouses. *Informatore Agrario* 57(45), 65-68.

Coop, L. B., and B. A. Croft. 1995. *Neoseiulus fallacis*: Dispersal and biological control of *Tetranychus urticae* following minimal inoculations into a strawberry field. *Experimental and Applied Acarology* 19:31–43.

Crooker, A. 1985. Embryonic and juvenile development. In *Spider Mites: Their Biology, Natural Enemies, and Control, Volume 1.* ed. W. Helle and M.W. Sabelis, 149–64. New York (Amsterdam): Elsevier.

Cross, J. V. 1984. Biological control of two-spotted spider mite (*Tetranychus urticae*) by *Phytoseiulus persimilis* on strawberries grown in "walk-in" plastic tunnels, and a simplified method of spider mite population assessment. *Plant Pathology* 33:417–23.

Dicke, M. 1994. Local and systemic production of volatile herbivore-induced terpenoids: Their role in plant-carnivore mutualism. *Journal of Plant Physiology* 143:465–72.

El-Laithy, A. Y. M. 1992. Some aspects on the use of the predaceous mite *Phytoseiulus persimilis* Athias-Henriot for biological control of the two-spotted spider mite *Tetranychus urticae* Koch in greenhouses in Egypt. *Zeitschrift für Pflanzenkrankheiten und Pflanzenschutz* 99:93–100.

Elliott, D., L. A. Gilkeson, and D. Gillespie. 1987. The development of greenhouse biological control in western Canadian vegetable greenhouses and plantscapes. *IOBC/WPRS Bulletin* 10:52–6.

English-Loeb, G. M. 1990. Drought stress and outbreaks of spider mites: A field test. *Ecology* 71:1401–11.

Eveleigh, E. S., and D. A. Chant. 1982a. Experimental studies on acarine predator-prey interactions: The numerical response of immature and adult predators (Acarina: Phytoseiidae). *Canadian Journal of Zoology* 60:630–8.

———. 1982b. Experimental studies on acarine predator-prey interactions: The response of predators to prey distribution in a homogeneous arena. *Canadian Journal of Zoology* 60:639–47.

————. 1982c. The searching behaviour of two species of phytoseiid mites, *Phytoseiulus persimilis* Athias-Henriot and *Amblyseius degenerans* (Berlese), in relation to the density and distribution of prey in a homogeneous area (Acarina: Phytoseiidae). *Canadian Journal of Zoology* 60:648–58.

————. 1982d. Experimental studies on acarine predator-prey interactions: Distribution of search effort and the functional and numerical responses of predators in a patchy environment (Acarina: Phytoseiidae). *Canadian Journal of Zoology* 60:2979–91.

————. 1982e. Experimental studies on acarine predator-prey interactions: Distribution of search effort and predation rates of predator populations in a patchy environment (Acarina: Phytoseiidae). *Canadian Journal of Zoology* 60:3001–9.

Foster, G. N., and E. Barker. 1978. A new biotype of red spider mite causing atypical damage on tomatoes. *Plant Pathology* 27:47–8.

Gagné, R. J. 1995. Revision of the tetranychid (Acarina) mite predators of the genus *Feltiella* (Diptera: Cecidomyiidae). *Annals of the Entomological Society of America* 88:16–30.

Gerson, U. 1985. Other predaceous mites and spiders. In *Spider Mites: Their Biology, Natural Enemies, and Control*, Vol. 1B, ed. W. Helle and M.W. Sabelis, 203–10. New York (Amsterdam): Elsevier.

Gillespie, D. R., and D. M. J. Quiring. 1994. Reproduction and longevity of the predatory mite *Phytoseiulus persimilis* (Acari: Phytoseiidae) and its prey *Tetranychus urticae* on different host plants. *Journal of the Entomological Society of British Columbia* 91:3–8.

————. 1996. Rearing the predatory gall midge, *Feltiella acarisuga* (Vallot) (Diptera: Cecidomyiidae). *Pacific Agriculture Research Centre, Agassiz*. Technical Report no. 118, February. 21 p.

Gillespie, D. R., D. M. J. Quiring, G. Opit, and M. Greenwood. 1994. Biological control of two-spotted spider mites on greenhouse tomato. *Pacific Agriculture Research Centre, Agassiz* Technical Report no. 105, November. 18 p.

Good, D. E. J., and J. C. Snyder. 1988. Seasonal variation of leaves and mite resistance of *Lycopersicon* interspecific hybrids. *HortScience* 25:891–4.

Gutierrez, J. 1985. Systematics. In *Spider Mites: Their Biology, Natural Enemies, and Control, Volume 1*. ed. W. Helle and M.W. Sabelis, 75–90. New York (Amsterdam): Elsevier.

Hance, T., G. van Impe, P. Lebrun, P. Nihoul, F. Benoit, and N. Ceustermans. 1991. Comparison of the efficacy of a chemical control technique and biological control technique for protection of the cultivation of tomato against the spider mite *Tetranychus urticae* (Acari: Tetranychidae). *Agronomie* 11:799–806.

Hazan, A., U. Gerson, and A. S. Tahori. 1973. Life history and life tables of the carmine spider mite. *Acarologia* 15:414–40.

Heagle, A. S., J. C. Burns, D. S. Fisher, and J. E. Miller. 2002. Effects of carbon dioxide enrichment on leaf chemistry and reproduction by twospotted spider mites (Acari: Tetranychidae) on white clover. *Environmental Entomology* 31:594-601.

Helle, W., and M. W. Sabelis, eds. 1985a. *Spider Mites: Their Biology, Natural Enemies, and Control, Vol. 1A*. New York (Amsterdam): Elsevier.

————, eds. 1985b. *Spider Mites: Their Biology, Natural Enemies, and Control, Vol. 1B*. New York (Amsterdam): Elsevier.

Herbert, J. 1981. Biology, lifetables, and innate capacity for increase of the two-spotted spider mite, *Tetranychus urticae* (Acarina: Tetranychidae). *The Canadian Entomologist* 113:371–8.

Ho, C. C. 1990. A preliminary study on the biological control of *Tetranychus kanzawai* in tea field by *Amblyseius fallacis* and *Phytoseiulus persimilis* (Acarina: Tetranychidae, Phytoseiidae). *Journal of Agricultural Research of China* 39:133–40.

Hussey, N. W., and W. J. Parr. 1963. The effect of glasshouse red spider mite (*Tetranychus urticae*) on the yield of cucumbers. *Journal of Horticultural Science* 38:255–66.

Hussey, N. W., and N. E. A. Scopes. 1985a. *Biological Pest Control: The Glasshouse Experience*. Poole, U.K.: Blandford Press (Ithaca, N.Y.: Cornell University Press).

————. 1985b. Greenhouse vegetables (Britain). In *Spider Mites: Their Biology, Natural Enemies, and Control Volume 2*. ed. W. Helle and M. W. Sabelis, 285–97. New York (Amsterdam): Elsevier.

Jindra, Z., V. Taborsky, and P. Skoda. 1991. Spontaneous occurrence of a predatory bug *Orius majusculus* (Reut.) in glasshouses. *Ochrana Rostlin* 27:207–9.

Kajita, H. 1984. Predation of the greenhouse whitefly, *Trialeurodes vaporariorum* (Westwood) (Homoptera: Aleyrodidae) by *Campylomma* sp. (Hemiptera: Miridae). *Applied Entomology and Zoology* 19:67–74.

Karg, W., and S. Mack. 1986. Mass production and introduction of the oligophagous predator *Amblyseius mckenziei* Schuster et Pritchard in greenhouse crops. *Nachrichtenblatt für den Pflanzenschutz in der DDR* 40:227–30.

Karg, W., S. Mack, and B. Baier. 1987. Advantages of oligophagous predatory mites for biological control. *IOBC/WPRS Bulletin* 10:66–73.

Khloptseva, R. I. 1991. The use of entomophages in biological pest control in the USSR. *Biocontrol News and Information* 12:243–6.

Kielkiewicz, M. 1990. Metabolic consequences of stress induced by the feeding of *Tetranychus cinnabarinus* on tomato plants. *Symposium Biologica Hungarica* 39:485–6.

Kilincer, N., S. Cobanoglu, and A. Has. 1992. Studies on the potential of the predatory mite *Phytoseiulus persimilis* Athias-Henriot (Acarina: Phytoseiidae) as a biological control agent on various crops in the greenhouse. In *Proceedings of the Second Turkish National Congress of Entomology: 28–31 January 1992*, 109–22. Adama, Turkey: Cukaroa Üniversitesi Ziraat Fakültesi Bitki Koruma Bölümü.

Kimsanbaev, K. K., M. I. Rashidov, and D. D. Akhanov. 1991a. Use of the predatory bug *Macrolophus nubilus* H.S. in Uzbekistan. *Doklady Vzesoyuznoi Ordena Lenina i Ordena Trudovogo Kranogo Znameni Akademii Sel'sk okhozyaistvennykh Nauk im V.I. Lenina* 6:18–20.

———. 1991b. The role of predatory Hemiptera in reducing the numbers of sucking pests. *Zashchita Rastenii* 11:27.

Krips, O.E., P.W. Kleijn, P.E.L. Willems, G.J.Z. Gols, and M. Dicke. 1999. Leaf hairs influence searching efficiency and predation rate of the predatory mite *Phytoseiulus persimilis* (Acari: Phytoseiidae). *Experimental and Applied Acarology* 23:119-131.

Laing, J. E. 1968. Life history and life table of *Phytoseiulus persimilis* Athias-Henriot. *Acarologia* 10:578–88.

———. 1969. Life history and life table of *Tetranychus urticae* Koch. *Acarologia* 11:32–42.

Leigh, T. F. 1985. Cotton. In *Spider Mites: Their Biology, Natural Enemies, and Control, Volume 2.* ed. W. Helle and M. W. Sabelis, 349–58. Amsterdam: Elsevier.

Lindquist, R. K. 1981. Introduction of *Phytoseiulus persimilis* for two-spotted spider mite control on greenhouse cucumber. *Ohio Agricultural Research and Development Center Research Circular No.* 264, pages 8–10.

Lindquist, R. K., M. L. Casey, W. L. Bauerle, and T. L. Short. 1987. Effects of an overhead misting system on thrips populations and spider mite–predator interactions on greenhouse cucumber. *IOBC/WPRS Bulletin* 10:97–100.

Loginova, E., N. Atanasson and G. Georgiev. 1987. Biological control of pests and diseases in glasshouses in Bulgaria—today and in the future. *IOBC/WPRS Bulletin* 10 (2):101–5.

Luk'Yanova, T. G., and N. I. Veremeev. 1993. Biological protection has become routine technique. *Zashchita Tastenii Moskva* 12:42.

Luczynski, A., D. Matys, and D. Raworth. 1996. Assessing the potential of *Amblyseius fallacis* as a biocontrol agent of the two-spotted spider mite on indoor pepper during late fall and early spring. *Report to the British Columbia Western Greenhouse Growers' Society.* 10 p.

Markkula, M., and K. Tiittanen. 1976. "Pest in first" and "natural infestation" methods in the control of *Tetranychus urticae* Koch with *Phytoseiulus persimilis* A-H on glasshouse cucumbers. *Annales Agriculture Fenniae* 15:81–5.

Markkula, M., K. Tittanen, and H. M. T. Hokkanen. 1987. Failures in biological control of spider mites—due to predatory mites or their users. *IOBC/WPRS Bulletin* 10 (2):108–10.

McGregor, R. R., D. R. Gillespie, D. M. J. Quiring, and M. R. J. Foisy. 1999. Potential use of *Dicyphus hesperus* Knight (Heteroptera: Miridae) for biological control of pests of greenhouse tomatoes. *Biological Control* 16:104-110.

McMurtry, J. A., E. R. Oatman, P. A. Phillips, and C. W. Wood. 1978. Establishment of *Phytoseiulus persimilis* [Acari: Phytoseiidae] in Southern California. *Entomophaga* 23:175–9.

McNab, S. C., D. G. Williams, and P. H. Jerie. 1994. Effect of intensity and duration of two-spotted spider mite (Acarina: Tetranychidae) infestation and water stress on leaf scorch damage of 'Bartlett' pears. *Journal of Economic Entomology* 87:1608–15.

Nachman, G. 1991. An acarine predator-prey metapopulation system inhabiting greenhouse cucumbers. *Biological Journal of the Linnean Society* 42:285–303.

Nickel, J. L. 1960. Temperature and humidity relationships of *Tetranychus desertorum* Banks with special reference to distribution. *Hilgardia* 30:41–100.

Nicoli, G., and M. Benuzzi. 1988. Experiments in biological control of *Tetranychus urticae* Koch with *Phytoseiulus persimilis* Athias-Henriot on cucumber in greenhouses. *Informatore Fitopatologico* 38:53–9.

Nihoul, P. 1992. Effect of temperature and relative humidity on successful control of *Tetranychus urticae* Koch by *Phytoseiulus persimilis* Athias-Henriot (Acari: Tetranychidae Phytoseiidae) in tomato crops under glasshouse conditions. *Mededelingen Faculteit Landbouwwetenschappen, Rijksuniversiteit Gent* 57:949–57.

———. 1993a. Spatial distribution of spider mites and predatory mites on the plant related to biological control effectiveness on glasshouse tomatoes. *Mededelingen van de Faculteit Landbouwwetenschappen, Rijksuniversiteit Gent* 58:497–504.

———. 1993b. Controlling glasshouse climate influences the interaction between tomato glandular trichome, spider mite, and predatory mite. *Crop Protection* 12:443–7.

Nihoul, P., and T. Hance. 1993. Use of a damage index to evaluate the biological control of the two-spotted spider mite *Tetranychus urticae* Koch (Acari: Tetranychidae) on tomato crops. *Journal of Horticultural Science* 68:575–80.

Nihoul, P., G. van Impe, and T. Hance. 1991. Characterizing indices of damage to tomato by the two-spotted spider mite, *Tetranychus urticae* Koch (Acari: Tetranychidae) to achieve biological control. *Journal of Horticultural Science* 66:643–8.

Oloumi-Sadeghi, H., C. G. Helm, M. Kogan, and D. F. Schoeneweiss. 1988. Effect of water stress on abundance of two-spotted spider mite on soybeans under greenhouse conditions. *Entomologia Experimentalis et Applicata* 48:85–90.

Oomen, P. A., G. Romeihn and G. L. Wiegers. 1991. Side effects of 100 pesticides on the predatory mite *Phytoseiulus persimilis* collected and evaluated according to the EPPO guideline. *Bulletin OEPP/EPPO* 21:701–12.

Opit, G., B. Roitberg, and D. R. Gillespie. 1997. The functional response and prey preference of *Feltiella acarisuga* (Vallot) (Diptera: Cecidomyiidae) for two of its prey: Male and female two-spotted spider mites, *Tetranychus urticae* (Koch) (Acari: Tetranychidae). *Canadian Entomologist* 129:221–7.

Pijnakker, J. 2002. *Feltiella acarisuga*: a promising predator of mites. *PHM Revue Horticole* No.432:46-48.

Popov, S. Y. 1988. Phytophagous mites in the greenhouse. *Zashchita Rastenii Moskva* 1:46–8.

Pralavorio, M., and A. Rojas. 1980. Influence de température et de l'humidité relative sur le developpment et la reproduction de *Phytoseiulus persimilis. IOBC/WPRS Bulletin* 3:157–62.

Pralavorio, M., D. Fournier, and P. Millot. 1989. Migratory activity of tetranychids: Evidence of a rhythm. *Entomophaga* 34:129–34.

Rasmy, A. H., and Y. M. El-Laithy. 1988. Introduction of *Phytoseiulus persimilis* for two-spotted spider mite control in greenhouses in Egypt (Acari: Phytoseiidae, Tetranychidae). *Entomophaga* 33:435–8.

Raworth, D. A. 1986. Sampling statistics and a sampling scheme for the two-spotted spider mite, *Tetranychus urticae* (Acari: Tetranychidae), on strawberries. *Canadian Entomologist* 118:807–14.

Raworth, D. A. 1990. Predators associated with the twospotted spider mite, *Tetranychus urticae*, on strawberry at Abbotsford, B.C., and development of non-chemical mite control. *Journal of the Entomological Society of British Columbia*. 87:59–67.

Raworth, D. A. 2001. Development, larval voracity, and greenhouse releases of *Stethorus punctillum* (Coleoptera: Coccinellidae). *The Canadian Entomologist* 133:721-724 [*Note Erratum, The Canadian Entomologist* 133:895.].

Raworth, D. A., and S. Bjørnson. 2002. Fecundity and survival of mass reared *Phytoseiulus persimilis* (Acari: Phytoseiidae). *IOBC/WPRS Bulletin* 25 (1):233-236.

Raworth, D.A. and M.C. Robertson. 2002. Occurrence of the spider mite predator *Stethorus punctillum* (Coleoptera: Coccinellidae) in the Pacific northwest. *Journal of Entomological Society of British Columbia* 99:81–82

Roberti, D. 1954. I simbianti degli acari fitofage. 1. *Therodiplosis persicae* Kieffer. *Bolletino del Laboratorio di Entomologia Agraria* 8:1–19.

Roda, A., J. Nyrop, M. Dicke, and G. English-Loeb. 2000. Trichomes and spider-mite webbing protect predatory mite eggs from intraguild predation. *Oecologia* 125:428-435.

Rott, A. S. and D. J. Ponsonby. 2000. Improving the control of *Tetranychus urticae* on edible glasshouse crops using a specialist coccinellid (*Stethorus punctillum* Weise) and a generalist mite (*Amblyseius californicus* McGregor) as biocontrol agents. *Biocontrol Science and Technology* 10:487-498.

Sabelis, M. W. 1981. Biological control of two-spotted spider mites using phytoseiid predators. Part I. Modelling the predator-prey interaction at the individual level. *Agricultural Research Reports* No. 910:226–42.

———. 1985. Development. In *Spider Mites: Their Biology, Natural Enemies, and Control, Volume 1*, ed. W. Helle and M. W. Sabelis, 43–54. New York (Amsterdam): Elsevier.

Sabelis, M. W., and B. P. Afman. 1994. Synomone-induced suppression of take-off in the phytoseiid mite *Phytoseiulus persimilis* Athias-Henriot. *Experimental and Applied Acarology* 18:711–21.

Sabelis, M. W., J. E. Vermaat, and A. Groenveld. 1984. Arrestment responses of the predatory mite, *Phytoseilus persimilis*, to steep odour gradients of a kairomone. *Physiological Entomology* 9:437–46.

Sampson, A. C., and V. J. King. 1996. *Macrolophus caliginosus*: Field establishment and pest control effect in protected tomatoes. *IOBC/WPRS Bulletin* 19 (1):143–6.

Sanchez, J. A., D. R. Gillespie, and R. R. McGregor. 2003.The effects of mullein plants (*Verbascum thapsus*) on the population dynamics of *Dicyphus hesperus* (Heteroptera: Miridae) in tomato greenhouses. *Biological Control* 28:313-319.

Santos, M. A. and J. E. Laing. 1985. Stigmaeid predators. In *Spider Mites: Their Biology, Natural Enemies, and Control*, Vol. 1B, ed. W. Helle and M. W. Sabelis, 197–203. New York (Amsterdam): Elsevier.

Shibao, M., M. Negoro, and H. Tanaka. 1995. Control of Kanzawa spider mite, *Tetranychus kanzawai* Kishida, on strawberry by *Phytoseiulus persimilis* Athias-Henriot, and effects of smoking agents on both species. *Proceedings of the Kansai Plant Protection Society* 37:5–8.

Spicciarelli, R., D. Battaglia, and A. Tranfaglia. 1992. Biological control of *Tetranychus urticae* with *Phytoseiulus persimilis* on strawberry. *Informatore Agrario* 48:59–62.

Stacey, D. L., I. J. Wyatt, and R. J. Chambers. 1985. The effect of glasshouse red spider mite damage on the yield of tomatoes. *Journal of Horticultural Science* 57:93–101.

Steiner, M.Y., and S. Bjørnson. 1996. Performance of *Phytoseiulus persimilis* and other biological control agents—On what are we basing our standards? *IOBC/WPRS Bulletin* 19:163–6.

Takabayashi, J., T. Shimoda, M. Dicke, W. Ashihara, and A. Takafuji. 2000. Induced response of tomato plants to injury by green and red strains of *Tetranychus urticae*. *Experimental & Applied Acarology* 24:377–83.

Thompson, W. R. 1924. La théorie mathématique de l'action des parasites entomophages et le facteur du hasard. *Annales Faculté des Sciences de Marseille* 2:69–89.

Tomczyk, A., and D. Kropczynska. 1985. Effects on the host plant. In *Spider Mites: Their Biology, Natural Enemies, and Control*, ed. W. Helle and M. W. Sabelis, Vol. 1B, 317–30. New York (Amsterdam): Elsevier.

Toyoshima, S. and H. Amano. 1998. Effect of prey density on sex ratio of two predacious mites, *Phytoseiulus persimilis* and *Amblyseius womersleyi* (Acari: Phytoseiidae). *Experimental & Applied Acarology* 22:709–23.

Vacante, V. 1985. The current state of control of phytophagous mites in protected crops in Sicily. *IOBC/WPRS Bulletin* 8:43–50.

Vacante, V., and A. Nucifora. 1987. Possibilities and perspectives of the biological and integrated control of the two-spotted spider mites in the Mediterranean greenhouse crops. *IOBC/WPRS Bulletin* 10 (2):170–3.

van der Werf, W., H. Gijzen, W. A. H. Rossing, R. T. Dierkx, A. Tomczyk, and J. C. van Lenteren. 1996a. Calculation of the influence of the vertical distribution of feeding injury by two-spotted spider mite (*Tetranychus urticae*) on photosynthesis and respiration of cucumber. *IOBC/WPRS Bulletin* 19:199–202.

van der Werf, W., J. P. Nyrop, M. R. Binns, J. Kovach, and J. C. van Lenteren. 1996b. Methodology for developing and evaluating monitoring programs for crop pests and diseases. *IOBC/WPRS Bulletin* 19:195–8.

van de Veire, M., and D. Degheele. 1993. Control of western flower thrips, *Frankliniella occidentalis*, with the predator *Orius insidiosus* on sweet peppers. *IOBC/WPRS Bulletin* 16 (2):185–8.

van de Vrie, M., J. A. McMurtry, and C. B. Huffaker. 1972. Ecology of tetranychid mites and their natural enemies. A review. III. Biology, ecology, and pest status, and host-plant relations of tetranychids. *Hilgardia* 41:343–432.

van Haren, R. J. F., M. M. Steenhuis, M. W. Sabelis, and A. M. B. de Ponti. 1987. Tomato stem trichomes and dispersal success of *Phytoseiulus persimilis* relative to its prey *Tetranychus urticae*. *Experimental and Applied Acarology* 3:115–21.

van Lenteren, J. C., A. Hale, J. N. Klapwijk, J. van Schelt, and S. Steinberg. 2003. Guidelines for quality control of commercially produced natural enemies, In *Quality Control and Production of Biological Control Agents. Theory and Testing Procedures.* ed. J.C. van Lenteren, 265–303. (Wallingford, Oxon UK): CAB.

van Lenteren, J. C., and J. Woets. 1988. Biological and integrated control in greenhouses. *Annual Review of Entomology* 33:239–69.

Veerman, A. 1985. Diapause. In *Spider Mites: Their Biology, Natural Enemies, and Control, Vol. 1B*, ed. W. Helle and M. W. Sabelis, 279–316. New York (Amsterdam): Elsevier.

Waite, G. K. 1988. Integrated control of *Tetranychus urticae* in strawberries in southeast Queensland. *Experimental and Applied Acarology* 5:23–32.

Wardlow, L. R., and A. Tobin. 1990. Potential new additions to the armoury of natural enemies for protected tomatoes. *IOBC/WPRS Bulletin* 13 (5):225–7.

Wermelinger, B., J. J. Oertli, and J. Baumgärtner. 1991. Environmental factors affecting the life tables of *Tetranychus urticae* (Acarina: Tetranychidae). III. Host-plant nutrition. *Experimental and Applied Acarology* 12:259–74.

Wermelinger, B., F. Schnider, J. J. Oertli, and J. Baumgärtner. 1990. Environmental factors affecting the life tables of *Tetranychus urticae* (Acarina). II. Host plant water stress. *Mitteilungen der Schweizerischen Entomologischen Gesellschaft* 63:347–57.

Woets, J. 1985. Tomatoes. In *Biological Pest Control: The Glasshouse Experience*, ed. N. W. Hussey and N. E. A. Scopes, 166–74. Poole, U.K.: Blandford Press (Ithaca, N.Y.: Cornell University Press).

12

BIOLOGICAL CONTROL OF LEAFMINERS ON ORNAMENTAL CROPS

A. Chow
Biological Control Laboratory, Department of Entomology
Texas A&M University, College Station, Texas

and
K. M. Heinz
Biological Control Laboratory, Department of Entomology
Texas A&M University, College Station, Texas

Introduction

Greenhouse production of ornamentals is worldwide and consists of products ranging from cut flowers to potted flowering and foliage plants, landscape, and bulb crops. The diversity of ornamental crops and international movement of plant material have resulted in wide-ranging and diverse pest complexes. A recent example of this phenomenon is the group of pests collectively referred to as leafminers. Larvae from several families of flies and moths mine leaves of flower and nursery crops. The most common and damaging species are small flies (Diptera: Agromyzidae), particularly a number of polyphagous species that attack many host plants throughout the world (Spencer 1989).

The importance of agromyzid leafminers as agricultural pests has prompted extensive research. Onillon (1999) reviewed the biology of the most important agromyzid leafminers in greenhouse crops, the biology of their natural enemies, and the efficacy of

biological control. In chapter 13, van der Linden provides a more recent and focused review on biological control of leafminers infesting greenhouse vegetables. Both of these reviews have been written from largely a European perspective. Biological control of leafminers is more widely practiced on greenhouse crops in Europe than in the United States (van Lenteren 2000).

In this chapter, we review the origin, spread and reasons for the pest status of the most important agromyzid leafminers that attack ornamentals. We also discuss aspects of leafminer biology and crop characteristics that influence economic damage thresholds. Finally, we examine the state of biological control for leafminers in greenhouse ornamentals and factors that may influence management strategies.

Pest Status

Although the Agromyzidae contains many serious and potentially serious pest species (Spencer 1973, 1989; Spencer and Steyskal

1986), three are major pests of greenhouse ornamentals. Two are New World *Liriomyza* species: *Liriomyza trifolii* (Burgess) (Figure 12.1D), the American serpentine leafminer, and *Liriomyza huidobrensis* (Blanchard) (Figure 12.1B), the pea leafminer. The third, *Chromatomyia syngenesiae* (Hardy) (Figure 12-1A) is an Old World species commonly referred to as the chrysanthemum leafminer.

All three of these leafminers, particularly the two New World species, are characterized by their polyphagous feeding habits, ability to develop insecticide resistance, and by their invasive nature (Murphy and LaSalle 1999). The host ranges of

L. huidobrensis and *L. trifolii* each encompass over 400 species of plants in some twelve families, and there is considerable overlap in the ranges of the two species (Spencer 1973, Morgan et al. 2000). These two *Liriomyza* species attack a wide range of ornamentals (Table 12.1). However, they have always been a more serious problem on chrysanthemum (*Dendranthemum grandiflora* Kitam), gerbera (*Gerbera jamesonii* Adlam) and gypsophila (*Gypsophila paniculata* L.) (Parrella, von Damm, and Costamagna 2000).

Chromatomyia syngenesiae is normally oligophagous on Asteraceae (= Compositae), but it has also been recorded on species from Leguminosae, Apiaceae (= Umbelliferae),

Figure 12.1. Adult leaf miner flies of economic importance to ornamentals: (A) *Liriomyza bryoniae* **(Kaltenbach)** (*photo: Anton van der Linden*), **(B)** *Liriomyza huidobrensis* **(Blanchard)** (*photo: Michael P. Parrella*), **(C)** *Liriomyza sativae* **Blanchard** (*photo: Michael P. Parrella*), **and (D)** *Liriomyza trifolii* **(Burgess)** (*photo: Michael P. Parrella*).

Malvaceae and Labiatae (Spencer 1973). This leafminer has been a frequent pest of chrysanthemums and gerbera in England and throughout Europe, but it is relatively uncommon in the United States (Parrella, Hanse, and van Lenteren 1999; Driestadt 2001; Calvarin and Langlois 2001). Other agromyzid leafminer species of minor importance are *Liriomyza sativae* Blanchard (Figure 12.1C) on chrysanthemums and aster (*Aster* spp.); *Liriomyza strigata* (Meigen) on chrysanthemums; *Chromatomyia horticola* (Goureau) on chrysanthemums, gerbera, and petunia (*Petunia x hybrida* Vilm); *Amauromyza maculosa* (Malloch) on chrysanthemums; *Amauromyza flavifrons* (Meigen) on carnation (*Dianthus caryophyllus* L.) and gypsophila.

Spencer (1989) suggested that some dispersal of *L. trifolii* and *L. huidobrensis* within the New World was natural. However, Parrella and Keil (1984) listed several factors that contributed to their extensive range expansion: (1) development of extensive horticulture and ornamental flower production throughout the world; (2) increase in international trade of plant material; (3) difficulties with maintaining quarantine within the horticultural industry (particularly in chrysanthemum cuttings). It is important for management efforts that the identification, status, and distribution of agromyzid pests are kept up to date. The two *Liriomyza* species and *C. syngenesiae* have distinct biological characteristics that may affect pest management responses and strategies.

Liriomyza huidobrensis

This important pest has a rather complex history. First described from Brazil in 1926 as *Agromyza huidobrensis* Blanchard, the leafminer was later described in California as *Liriomyza langei* Frick (Frick 1951). Spencer (1973) synonymized *L. langei* with *L. huidobrensis* because the two species appeared to be morphologically identical. However, recent phylogenetic evidence has shown that these two groups are genetically distinct and represent morphologically cryptic species (Scheffer 2000, Scheffer and Lewis 2001). The name *L. langei* was revived for the cryptic species found in California and Hawaii, but *L. huidobrensis* was reserved for the cryptic species endemic to South and Central America (Scheffer and Lewis 2001).

Since 1989, *L. huidobrensis* has spread to Europe (Hume, Dunne, and O'Connor 1990; Cheek, MacDonald, and Bartlett 1993; Weintraub and Horowitz 1995), the Middle East (Weintraub and Horowitz 1995), Asia (Shepard, Samsudin, and Braun 1998; Rauf, Shepard, and Johnson 2000), several Pacific Islands (Johnson 1993), Sri Lanka (Scheffer et al. 2001), Canada (Ibid.), and South Africa (Ibid.). Throughout its range, *L. huidobrensis* has evolved resistance to numerous insecticides and its status as a relatively unimportant secondary pest has changed to that of a highly damaging threat to both vegetable and ornamental crops (Weintraub and Horowitz 1995; Rauf, Shepard, and Johnson 2000). Presently, *L. langei* has not been detected in any location other than North America and Hawaii (Scheffer et al. 2001).

Liriomyza langei is becoming a more important agricultural pest in California (Chaney 1995, Morgan et al. 2000). Parrella and Bethke (1984) reported that *L. langei* (as *L. huidobrensis*) was commonly found on flower crops in California, but it was not as serious a pest as *L. trifolii* and relatively easier to control. During the 1990s, *L. langei* began to displace *L. trifolii* along the central coast of California and is now the predominant *Liriomyza* species in central California (Reitz and Trumble 2002). Invasive populations of *L. langei* may be present in other areas. Since *L. huidobrensis* and *L. langei* are suspected to differ in crop preference and in insecticide resistance (Bartlett 1993, Weintraub and Horowitz 1995, Sheffer et al. 2001), it is important that newly introduced populations be identified.

Liriomyza trifolii

This species' endemic focus appears to be Florida but it has spread throughout the eastern and southern United States and invaded other regions of the world including the Caribbean, Hawaii, Europe, Japan, Africa, Central America, and South America (Spencer 1989, Saito 1994, Murphy and LaSalle 1999). During the 1980s, *L. trifolii* developed resistance to many insecticides and became a worldwide threat to the chrysanthemum industry and other agricultural crops (Parrella and Keil 1984; Parrella and Trumble 1989; Keil and Parrella 1990; Parrella, von Damm, and Costamagna 2000). From 1981 through 1985, the chrysanthemum industry was estimated to have lost US $93 million to this pest alone (Newman and Parrella 1986). However by the 1990s, new insecticides, effective natural enemies and tighter quarantines reduced *L. trifolii* to the status of a secondary pest (Parrella, von Damm, and Costamagna 2000).

Liriomyza trifolii was recently displaced by *L. langei* in central California, but *L. trifolii* remains the predominant species in southern California (Reitz and Trumble 2002). The host range of *L. trifolii* in central California seems to be restricted to hosts on which *L. langei* does poorly. Differences in host plant performance and genetic data suggest that central and southern California populations of *L. trifolii* are distinct biotypes and possibly cryptic species (Ibid.).

Chromatomyia syngenesiae

The chrysanthemum leafminer is native to Europe and introduced to North America, Japan, and Australasia (Spencer 1973, Spencer and Steyskal 1986). Damage to chrysanthemums in Western Europe was first reported for this species in 1930 (Spencer 1973), and it is still a problem on chrysanthemums in England and Europe (Parrella, Hanse, and van Lenteren 1999; Martinez 2001). In the United States, *C. syngenesiae* is rarely found on chrysanthemums but has been reported on *Cineraria* and other ornamentals (Table 12.1).

Biology and Damage

Parrella (1987) has reviewed the biology of *Liriomyza* species, while Ibrahim and Madge (1977) described the biology of *C. syngenesiae*. The adult and all larval stages of *L. trifolii*, *L. huidobrensis*, *L. langei* and *C. syngenesiae* can seriously damage ornamentals. Only some important details relating to the pest status of these four species will be highlighted here.

Oviposition and feeding damage

Adult female leafminers use their ovipositors to puncture leaf or petal surfaces for feeding on sap or for laying eggs. These punctures usually turn white and damaged foliage take

Table 12.1. Flower and nursery crops recorded as host plants for *Liriomyza trifolii*, *Liriomyza huidobrensis*, and *Chromatomyia syngenesiae*[a]

	Liriomyza trifolii (Burgess)	*Liriomyza huidobrensis* (Blanchard)	*Chromatomyia syngenesiae* (Hardy)
Aster (*Aster* spp. L.)	X	X	
Calendula *Calendula officinalis* L. Pot marigolds	X		
Carnation *Dianthus caryophyllus* L.	X	X	
Chrysanthemum *Dendranthema grandiflorum* Kitam *Chrysanthemum morifolium* Ramat.	X	X	X
Cineraria *Pericallis cruenta* (Masson ex *L'Hér.*) Bolle .	X	X	X
Dahlia *Dahlia* X *hybrida*	X	X	
English Daisy *Bellis perennis* L.	X		
Gerbera *Gerbera jamesonii* Adlam Gerbera daisy	X	X	X
Gypsophila *Gypsophila paniculata* L. Baby's breath	X	X	
Impatiens *Impatiens walleriana* Hook New Guinea impatiens	X		
Marguerite Daisy *Argyanthemum frutescens* (L.)	X		X

(continued)

Table 12.1. *(continued)*

	Liriomyza trifolii (Burgess)	Liriomyza huidobrensis (Blanchard)	Chromatomyia syngenesiae (Hardy)
Marigold *Tagetes* spp.	X		
Nasturtium *Tropaeolum* spp.		X	
Petunia *Petunia* X *hybrida* (Hook) Vilm	X	X	
Primrose (*Primula* spp.)	X	X	
Shasta Daisy *Leucanthemum superbum* (J. Ingram)	X		X
Snapdragon *Antirrhinum majus* L.	X		
Sweet William *Dianthus barbatus* L.	X	X	
Verbena *Verbena* spp.	X		
Violet *Viola* spp. L.		X	

[a](Spencer 1973, 1990; Stanton, Clement, and Dutky 1999; Gullino and Wardlow 1999; Rauf, Shepard, and Johnson 2000; Dreistadt 2001)

on a stippled appearance. Stippling by *L. trifolii* can reduce photosynthetic rates and stomatal and mesophyll conductance in greenhouse chrysanthemums (Parrella et al. 1985). Stippling also provides entry sites for infection by plant pathogens (Matteoni and Broadbent 1988, Broadbent and Matteoni 1990). *Liriomyza trifolii* females seem to randomly deposit their eggs on the upper leaf surface, whereas *L. huidobrensis* females normally lay eggs towards the base of the leaf, on or near the midrib (Spencer 1989).

Extensive aesthetic damage to ornamentals can result from larval feeding within the leaves, which form distinct mines. Larvae of *C. syngenesiae*, *L. trifolii* and *L. langei* prefer different leaf tissue. *Chromatomyia syngenesiae* larvae feed mainly in the palisade tissues

(Smith and Jones 1998). Parrella et al. (1985) found that *Liriomyza trifolii* prefers the palisade mesophyll and *L. langei* (as *L. huidobrensis*) the spongy mesophyll. On chrysanthemums, mining in the spongy mesophyll by *L. langei* reduces photosynthesis rates and tissue conductance more than mining in the palisade mesophyll by *L. trifolii* (Ibid.). Light infestations by *L. langei* can be more damaging to plant growth than similar infestations by *L. trifolii*, but there is no difference in damage at heavy infestations. Interestingly, marigolds grown for seed can compensate for herbivore damage and yield more viable seeds if subjected to some leafminer damage (Heinz and Parrella 1992).

Life history

Liriomyza trifolii, *L. huidobrensis*, *L. langei*, and *C. syngenesiae* share a number of attributes that combine to make them serious pests: polyphagous habit, relatively short developmental period, high dispersal capability, high reproductive rate, and immature stages that are concealed from conventional pesticide sprays. However, there are some interesting differences between them. Larvae of *C. syngenesiae* pupate inside leaves, while larvae of the three *Liriomyza* species tend to drop to the soil to pupate (Spencer 1989, Dreistadt 2001). Populations of both *L. trifolii* and *L. huidobrensis* have repeatedly developed resistance to various insecticides (Parrella 1984, Weintraub and Horowitz 1995). In greenhouse trials on chrysanthemums, *C. syngenesiae* consistently show less tolerance to insecticides than either *L. trifolii* or *L. huidobrensis* (Parella and Lindquist 1983, Lindquist et al 1984).

Parrella, Allen, and Morishita (1981) reported that in California, the reproductive potential of female *L. trifolii* is approximately three times greater than that of *L. langei* (as *L. huidobrensis*). Lanzoni et al. (2002) compared the development time and mortality of a European strain of *L. huidobrensis* and *L. trifolii* on beans (*Phaseolus vulagris* L.) at different temperatures. *Liriomyza huidobrensis* developed faster than *L. trifolii* at both 68°F (20°C) and 59°F (15°C). Although the pupal development time of *L. huidobrensis* was generally shorter than that of *L. trifolii*, larval development time was longer. Estimated lower threshold temperatures for each developmental stage and total development of *L. huidobrensis* was always less than *L. trifolii* thresholds, which suggests that *L. huidobrensis* can colonize cooler regions than *L. trifolii*. Conversely, *L. trifolii* may do better in warmer regions because pre-imaginal mortality for this species was always lower than for *L. huidobrensis* from 68° to 86°F (20 to 30°C).

Natural Enemies

Agromyzid leafminers are reported to have extensive communities of natural enemies, particularly insect parasitoids in both their native and invaded ranges (Murphy and LaSalle 1999; Rauf, Shepard, and Johnson 2000). Surprisingly, the number of natural enemies commercially available is rather small and has not increased since the 1980s. Biological control studies have focused primarily on insect parasitoids and nematodes, but some predators have been reported.

Parasitoids

As a group, leaf-mining insects have the most species of parasitoids per host of any feeding guild (Connor and Taverner 1997). Murphy and LaSalle (1999) listed seventy-four genera of parasitic Hymenoptera that attack agromyzid leafminers. Cornelius and Godfray (1984) and Bene (1989) identified parasitoid species attacking *C. syngenesiae* in Europe. Reviews for parasitoids attacking important *Liriomyza* species are available for North America (LaSalle and Parrella 1991), the Pacific Basin (Johnson and Hara 1987, Waterhouse and Norris 1987, Johnson 1993), Asia (Murphy and LaSalle 1999; Rauf, Shepard, and Johnson 2000), the Middle East (Al-Ghabeish and Allawi 2001; Civelek, Yoldas, and Weintraub 2002) and Europe (Minkenberg and van Lenteren 1986). Parasitoids of the genera *Opius* (Braconidae), *Chrysocharis* and *Diglyphus* (Eulophidae) and *Halticoptera* (Pteromalidae) are globally distributed and have species that attack *L. trifolii* and *L. huidobrensis* in almost all invaded regions (Murphy and LaSalle 1999).

Classical biological control programs against *L. trifolii* and *L. huidobrensis* in open field systems or in partly covered ornamental crops have yielded mixed results throughout the Pacific Basin, Asia, and Senegal (Johnson 1993, Murphy and LaSalle 1999). Natural control of leafminers by indigenous populations of parasitoids that move into greenhouses is important for pest management in both the Mediterranean region and Northern Europe (van Lenteren and Manzaroli 1999). Biological control of agromyzid leafminers on ornamentals under glass has focused on augmentative methods for reasons discussed later.

Two parasitoid species are commercially available and used for control of leafminers on greenhouse ornamentals, *Diglyphus isaea* (Walker) (Eulophidae) and *Dacnusa sibirica* Telenga (Braconidae). Both parasitoid species are indigenous to Europe and have been used as biological control agents against a wide range of agromyzid leafminers including *L. trifolii, L. huidobrensis, L. langei,* and C. *syngenesiae. Diglyphus isaea* is a solitary ectoparasitoid that attacks the larvae of agromyzid leafminers. Females of *D. isaea* paralyze their host with venom and oviposit on or near larger hosts but reject or host feed on smaller hosts (Ode and Heinz 2002). *Diglyphus isaea* larvae feed externally on their hosts and complete development within the leaf mines. *Dacnusa sibirica* is an endoparasitoid of agromyzid larvae and eclose as adults from the pupal stage of their hosts (Croft and Copland 1994).

Other parasitoids can potentially control leafminers on ornamentals. *Diglyphus begini* (Ashmead), a congener of *D. isaea*, was extensively evaluated for biological control of *L. trifolii* on greenhouse chrysanthemum and marigolds (Heinz, Newman, and Parrella 1988; Heinz and Parrella 1990; Heinz, Nunney, and Parrella 1993) but is not commercially available. Similarly, *Diglyphus intermedius* (Girault) has been used in research trials to control *L. trifolii* on commercial chrysanthemums grown for cut flowers (Jones et al 1986, Hara and Matayoshi 1990). *Opius pallipes* Wesmael (Braconidae) will attack *L. huidobrensis* (van der Linden 1991) and *L. trifolii* (Scholz-Dobelin 1997); however, it was primarily used against *Liriomyza bryoniae* (Kaltenbach) on vegetables during the 1980s in Europe. *Opius pallipes* has not been widely produced or used since 1988 (van Lenteren 1995).

Predators

Many different predators have been cited for use against pest insects of protected crops (Hussey and Scopes 1985, Parrella, Hanse, and van Lenteren 1999). Generalist predators are often ideal for seasonal inoculative or augmentative releases when short-term control of pests is required (Albajes and Alomar 1999). Yet, there is relatively little information on predators of agromyzid leafminers.

Mirid bugs

Mirid bugs (Hemiptera: Miridae) have been studied for release or conservation in biocontrol for *Liriomyza* leafminers. Parrella et al. (1982) evaluated *Cyrtopeltis modestus* (Distant), a common mirid species in southern California. Later instars and adults of *C. modestus* attack larvae of *L. trifolii* within chrysanthemum leaves. *C. modestus* will also attack the third-instar larvae of *L. trifolii* as the latter emerge from leaves to drop to the ground to pupate. Carvalho and Mexia (2000) reported that *Dicyphus cerastii* Wagner, a common mirid bug in Portuguese greenhouses, is a potential predator of *L. huidobrensis* larvae. *Dicyphus tamaninii* Wagner is also an important natural enemy of *Liriomyza* species on greenhouse crops in the Mediterranean region (Albajes et al. 1996; Salamero, Gabarra, and Albajes 1987). Local populations of Dicyphinae species quickly colonize Mediterranean greenhouses and contribute to the natural control of leafminers and other pests on vegetables and ornamentals (Alomar and Albajes 1999). However, only one Dicyphinae species, *Macrolophus costalis* Fieber, has been commercially reared

and it is primarily supplied for inoculative releases against whiteflies on greenhouse tomato in northern Europe and France (van Schelt et al. 1996, Albajes and Alomar 1999).

Predatory mirids feed facultatively on plants, which may limit their use in ornamental crops. There are few studies on the susceptibility of ornamental crops and cultivars to mirid feeding and more importantly the risk for commercial loss. Damage to gerbera flower buds was reported for *M. costalis* when prey was depleted at the end of the crop (Sampson 1996, van Schelt et al. 1996). *Cyrtopeltis modestus* does not feed on chrysanthemum but is considered a secondary pest of tomatoes in California (Parrella et al. 1982). Possible movement of *C. modestus* from chrysanthemum to tomato crops may limit the regions where it is used.

Predatory thrips

Adults and larvae of *Franklinothrips vespiformis* (Crawford) (Thysanoptera: Thripidae), a predatory thrips, have been reported to prey upon larvae of *L. trifolii* in kidney bean (Arakaki and Okajima 1998). In South America, *F. vespiformis* has both sexes but it appears to be thelytokous (producing only female offspring) throughout Southeast Asia and Japan (Ibid.). Females lay their eggs into leaf veins and other plant tissue, but do not appear to feed facultatively on plants.

Predators of adult Liriomyza

Predatory Diptera of the families Dolichopodidae, Empididae, and Muscuidae prey on adult *Liriomyza*. A muscid fly, *Coenosia exigua* Stein, attacks *L. huidobrensis* adults among vegetable crops in Malaysia (Rauf, Shepard, and Johnson 2000).

Freidberg and Gijswijt (1983) observed emphidid and muscid flies attacking adult *L. trifolii* in Israel. Rauf, Shepard, and Johnson (2000) also noted that emphidid and dolichopodid flies attack *Liriomyza* species in Indonesia. Predatory wasps can also attack adult leafminers. Leite et al. (2001) has studied the predatory behavior of *Protonectarian sylveriare* (Saussure), a vespid wasp, on adult *Liriomyza* in mustard fields.

Control of the adult stage has been largely overlooked in biological control for leafminers. The distribution of damage throughout a crop is largely dependent on the movement and oviposition behavior of adult female flies (Jones and Parrella 1986). However, little is known about the impact of adult mortality on the dynamics of leafminer outbreaks on agricultural crops. Predators of adult *Liriomyza* and their potential role in biological control programs deserve additional attention.

Entomopathogenic nematodes

Entomopathogenic nematodes in the families Steinernematidae and Heterorhabditidae have been investigated for biological leafminer control. Under the right conditions, several nematode species can successfully infect leafminer larvae within plant tissue. *Steinernema feltiae* (Filipjev) can infect and kill all larval instar stages of *L. bryoniae*, *L. huidobrensis* and *C. syngenesiae* (Williams and MacDonald 1995, Williams and Walter 2000). Second larval instars of *L. huidobrensis* were more susceptible to infection by *S. feltiae* than first or third larval instars and the two *Liriomyza* species were more susceptible than *C. syngenesiae*. Williams and

Walter (2000) suggested that *C. syngenesiae* may have better defenses or emit less attractive cues than *Liriomyza* species. *Steinernema carpocapsae* (Weiser) can also infect *L. trifolii* larvae in chrysanthemum (Harris, Begley, and Warkentin 1990; Broadbent and Olthof 1995). Williams (1993) reported that initial attempts to use *Heterorhabditis megidis* Poinar against *L. huidobrensis* were promising.

Entomopathogenic nematodes are applied to the crop as infective juveniles in foliar sprays. Juveniles enter infested plants primarily through oviposition sites and feeding scars made by adult leafminers (Harris, Begley, and Warkentin 1990; Kaya and Gaugler 1993; Lebeck et al. 1993). Within a mine, nematodes may locate leafminer larvae by following various chemical trails (Schmidt and All 1978, 1979; Gaugler et al. 1980). They penetrate larvae and release symbiotic bacterium that kill and break down the host for consumption (Kaya and Gaugler 1993). Commercial nematode formulations are marketed for application primarily against soil-dwelling insects, but entomopathogenic nematodes are ineffective against the pupal stage of *L. trifolii* (Colombo and Locatelli 1985, Finney-Crawley and Smith 1985).

Despite this body of supporting literature and the availability of commercial formulations, few growers in the United States or Europe use nematodes for biological leafminer control on ornamentals. The effectiveness of nematodes is primarily limited by their requirements for extremely high levels of humidity ($\geq 80\%$) to prevent desiccation before they enter the leaf tissue and moderate temperatures 68° to 79°F (20° to 26°C) for optimal activity (Hara et al. 1993, Broadbent and Olthof 1995, Williams and MacDonald 1995, Dreistadt 2001). The use of antidesiccants to retard desiccation of nematodes did not increase leafminer mortality in a greenhouse study with potted chrysanthemums (Broadbent and Olthof 1995). Entomopathogenic nematodes may be most effective for leafminer control in cuttings during rooting on mist tables, but their efficacy under other conditions is questionable.

Foliar applications of entomopathogenic nematodes for leafminers on ornamentals have not compared well to chemical alternatives. Calvarin and Langlois (2001) found that applications of *S. felatiae* on gerbera reduced the incidence of *Liriomyza* and *Chromatomyia* mines by 24%, while cyromazine gave a 73% reduction. Similarly, Broadbent and Olthof (1995) found that abamectin provided significantly higher mortality of *L. trifolii* than applications of *S. carpocapsae*, with or without antidesiccants, on chrysanthemums.

Sher, Parrella, and Kaya (2000) suggested that entomopathogenic nematodes and parasitoid wasps could act in a complementary fashion to provide more acceptable and affordable leafminer control in floricultural crops. Under laboratory conditions, they found few antagonist interactions between *S. carpocapsae* and *D. begini* on *L. trifolii* in chrysanthemums. However, applications of *S. carpocapsae* in a gerbera greenhouse, where *D. isaea* was providing successful control, increased leafminer mortality only slightly and was not cost effective (Parrella, von Damm, and Costamagna 2000).

Strategies and Obstacles
Augmentative releases of natural enemies

Periodic release of natural enemies is a common approach to biological control in greenhouses. Debach (1964) divided periodic releases into two categories: (1) inundative releases where the natural enemies released rather than their progeny actually control the pest and (2) inoculative release where control is dependent on progeny from following generations. Augmentative release falls between these two categories because large numbers of natural enemies are released on a regular basis, yet control by the offspring of those released is vital to obtaining successful control (Parrella, Heinz, and Nunney 1992).

Theoretical simulation models (Ibid.; Heinz, Nunney, and Parrella 1993) suggest that augmentative release strategies can significantly reduce pest outbreaks on ornamentals. Parrella, Heinz, and Nunney (1992) argued that augmentative release of natural enemies was the only means of effective biological control on most ornamental crops. This approach offers the best chances of success when growers have low tolerance for the presence of insects and damage on their crop. Augmentative releases of natural enemies have been successfully applied in greenhouses for control of many vegetable pests (van Lenteren 2000). In comparison, successful cases of biological control for leafminers on ornamental crops are few.

Ornamental versus vegetable crops

Biological control of leafminers on ornamental crops is more challenging than for vegetables. First, damage thresholds for leafminers on vegetables are usually much higher than on floriculture crops. Leafminers do not directly attack marketable portions of many greenhouse vegetables. Grower tolerance for foliar damage by pests can be relatively high for crops such as tomatoes, peppers, or cucurbits.

In comparison, ornamental crops are frequently sold as whole plants, so foliar damage significantly reduces aesthetic value. Damage thresholds for the same leafminer species can vary dramatically between vegetable and ornamental crops. A tomato plant may tolerate several dozens mines with no significant yield loss, whereas one to two mines on a potted chrysanthemum could constitute unacceptable damage. For European growers, zero tolerance on pest damage or presence applies to most flowers and potted plants sold to export markets (Ibid.).

Second, leafminers also attack a wide range of ornamental species and cultivars that support extensive pest complexes (Gullino and Wardlow 1999, Driestadt 2001). For biological control to succeed, reliable natural enemies of all key pests are often required because chemical treatment for even one pest can disrupt biological control for other pests. The wide range of crops and pests in many floriculture operations complicate development and implementation of biological control for leafminers.

Windows of Opportunity in Floriculture Crops

At first glance, augmentative biological control would not appear to be a feasible strategy for controlling leafminers on susceptible ornamentals. Augmentative tactics always result in some plant damage because of the delay between introductions of the natural enemies and reduction in pest populations. Flowering plant crops are grown for seed, or sold as cut flowers, potted flowering plants, or bedding plants. Biological control is not suitable for the last two categories because the entire plant is sold and leafminer damage to any part is unacceptable. However, the crop cycle of cut flowers and seed crops may allow for some mining damage without loss in aesthetic or economic value.

Jones, Parrella, and Hodel (1986) first proposed a biological control program for agromyzid leafminers based on a "window of opportunity" during crop production. In cut flowers or seed crops, only the upper portion of the plant or flowering stalk is harvested and sold while the lower portion of the plant is disposed. Leafminer damage to the lower portion of the plant is acceptable since it is not sold. The lower foliage contributes to photosynthesis and thus flower or seed production, but some damage is acceptable if there is no economic loss.

With this approach, a feasible management goal is to restrict damage to the non-marketed portion of the crop by suppressing leafminer populations before development of the marketable product. Early in the crop cycle, augmentative releases of natural enemies are used to eliminate the pest and maintain suppression until harvest. In the United

States, this approach has been validated on two ornamental crops at scales characteristic of commercial production—chrysanthemums grown for cut flowers and marigolds grown for seed.

Seed crops: Marigolds

Certain characteristics of floral seed crops make them ideal for augmentative biological control of leafminers (Heinz and Parrella 1990). Leafminers do not directly attack the marketed product; therefore, some damage to the foliage is sustained without economic loss. Repeated insecticide sprays are not desirable in marigolds and other floral crops grown for seed. Wet spray can shatter seed heads and result in seed loss, or the spray can clump pollen and interfere with fertilization. Often, manual pollination and harvesting of the crop also restricts insecticide usage. Seed crops are also held for long periods, several months to several years. This makes them vulnerable to repeated attacks. Natural enemies will not disrupt either the development of seed heads or labor-intensive procedures and can provide long-term control of pests.

Liriomyza leafminers can be serious pests of greenhouse marigolds, *Tagetes erecta* L., grown for seed in California (Heinz et al. 1988). In commercial greenhouse trials, Heinz and Parrella (1990) used augmentative releases of *D. begini* to suppress large *L. trifolii* populations on thousands of greenhouse marigolds grown for seed. The leafminer populations were practically eradicated within eight weeks of the first release and remained at that this suppressed level for the duration of the crop, an additional nine weeks. Released *D. begini* and their progeny

were responsible for 97% of parasitism. Two other parasitoid species, which moved into the greenhouses, accounted for only 3% of parasitism. High leafminer populations early in the crop cycle led to high damage in the expendable lower foliage of all plants. However, the upper foliage of the plants under biological control had an average of only 0-1.2 mines per leaf, a damage level acceptable to the cooperating grower.

Cut flowers: Chrysanthemums

Biological control of leafminers can be quite feasible on greenhouse cut flowers. In some cut flowers like chrysanthemums, only the top portion of the plant is harvested. For others like gerbera daisies, the harvested flower stalk totally lacks foliage. Consequently, leafminer damage is tolerated during production if the damaged foliage will not be included in the finished cut flower.

In the United States, several studies evaluated the utility of augmentative releases of eulophid wasps for biological control of *L. trifolii* on chrysanthemums grown for cut flowers. Jones, Parrella, and Hodel (1986) estimated that the foliage that developed during the first four to six weeks of crop growth was the difference between the length of the flowers sold to retailers and the height of the crop at harvest. In trials with commercial plantings of greenhouse chrysanthmums, they used repeated releases of *Diglyphus intermedius* (Girault) and *Chrysocharis parksi* Crawford to control *L. trifolii* during this period. Although they achieved a reduction in the leafminer population, an insecticide application was required eleven days before harvest to keep damage at an acceptable level.

A computer model was developed to predict augmentative releases of *D. begini* for control of *L. trifolii* on cut chrysanthemums (Parrella, Heinz, and Nunney 1992; Heinz, Nunney, and Parrella 1993). The model attempted to determine the appropriate release rate for reducing leafminer densities below one larva per 1000 chrysanthemum leaves within forty days after planting, after which time marketable foliage develops. Testing of the model in a commercial cut chrysanthemum greenhouse resulted in the production, harvest, and sale of the crop without the use of any pesticides. However, economic costs associated with biological control on cut chrysanthemums were still significantly greater than those based on conventional insecticides. This predictive model was further refined to improve biological realism and then made available to California greenhouse growers.

Augmentative releases of parasitoids against European populations of leafminers on cut flower crops have yielded similar results. Bene (1990) conducted trials with *D. isaea* to control *L. trifolii*, *C. horticola* and *C. syngenesiae* on chrysanthemums and gerbera in commercial greenhouses in Tuscany, Italy. They found that *D. isaea* gave adequate control when released at a rate of five to thirty adults per 108 ft.^{2} (10 m^2) in newly established greenhouses. Indigenous parasitoid species recovered in the greenhouses may have provided additional natural control of the leafminers. At harvest, gerbera flowers were similar in terms of quality and quantity to that obtained with chemical treatments. On chrysanthemums, the parasitoids provided adequate protection during the early phase of crop development, but insecticides were required before harvest to protect the leaves that would be sold with the flowers. Landi (1993) also used releases of *D. isaea* and *D. sibirica* to control *L. trifolii* on chrysanthemums in greenhouses in Pescia, Italy. They did not apply insecticides to the plants under biological control. At the time of harvest, they reported that 30% of the plants had mined leaves, which was slightly higher than on plants treated with insecticides.

Natural control may be just as effective as augmentative releases if natural enemies are abundant and able to quickly establish. In Hawaii, Hara and Matayoshi (1990) reported that natural populations of *D. intermedius* and *Ganaspidium utilis* Beardsley (Eucoilidae) provided adequate control of *L. trifolii* in a commercial cut-chrysanthemum nursery before the marketable portion of the chrysanthemum foliage began development. Additional pesticides were also required to protect the marketable portion of the crop from leafminer damage.

For some situations, inoculative releases provide adequate control. In England, infestations of *C. syngenesiae* on chrysanthemum can be controlled with inoculative releases of both *D. sibrica* and *D. isaea*. Wardlow (1985, 1986) recommended that *D. sibrica* should be released at the rate of three adults per 1000 plants approximately one week after planting. A release of *D. isaea* at the same rate approximately six weeks after planting follows the first release.

Summary

There are several good reasons for the use of natural enemies for control of leafminers on greenhouse ornamentals. Ongoing concerns include development of insecticide resistance in the two invasive species of *Liriomyza* and interference with IPM programs for other pests. Phytotoxic and physical spray damage to sensitive crops and worker safety are also issues. Social and economic concerns over growing consumer demand for products produced in an environmentally conscientious manner cannot be ignored in regional markets such as Europe (Hamrick 2000).

The use of augmentative biological control with parasitoids is particularly feasible for control of agromyzid leafminers in cut flower crops that can tolerate some damage early in the production cycle. However, there are presently three major reasons for the limited use of this approach even for ornamental crops that meet the criteria for damage tolerance. First, parasitoids are too expensive for growers to use except when leafminers are present at low densities. In 1997, retailers charged up to US $0.35 per wasp for *D. isaea* (van Lenteren, Roskan, and Timmer 1997). Current mass rearing of *D. isaea* and *D. sibricia* are inefficient and costly, in part because of male-biased sex ratios (Heimpel and Lundgren 2000, Ode and Heinz 2002).

Second, potent leafminer insecticides are still available and effective when properly rotated. *Liriomyza trifolii* and *L. huidobrensis* have yet to develop widespread resistance to abamectin, cyromazine, or spinosad. Commercial formulations provide control of leafminers that is less expensive than augmentative parasitoid releases and requires less monitoring and expertise for success.

Third, broad-spectrum insecticides for western flower thrips, *Frankliniella occidentalis* (Pergande) (Thysanoptera: Thripidae), are incompatible with leafminer parasitoids

(Parrella, Hanse, and van Lenteren 1999). *Frankliniella occidentalis* is one of the primary pests of greenhouse chrysanthemums in the United States and difficult to control using only natural enemies.

These three issues need addressing for biological control of leafminers to be more widely used in IPM programs of greenhouse ornamentals. Development of rearing systems that maximize female wasp production could reduce overall mass-rearing costs and increase the attractiveness of using these parasitoids to control leafminers in commercial operations. Better education and support for growers interested in alternatives to chemical control of pests should increase the chances of biological control succeeding and becoming more widely adopted.

References Cited

Albajes, R. and O. Alomar. 1999. Current and potential use of polyphagous predators. In *Integrated Pest and Disease Management in Greenhouse Crops,* ed. R. Albajes, M. L. Gullino, J. C. van Lenteren, and Y. Elad, 265–75. Dordrecht, the Netherlands: Kluwer Academic Publishers.

Albajes, R., O. Alomar, J. Riudavets, C. Castañé, J. Amó, and R. Gabarra. 1996. The mirid bug *Dicyphus tamaninii:* An effective predator for vegetable crops. *IOBC/WPRS Bulletin* 19 (1):1–4.

Al-Ghabeish, I., and T.F. Allawi. 2001. Agromyzid leaf miners and their parasitoids in Jordan. *Dirasat Agricultural Sciences* 28:172–7.

Arakaki, N., and S. Okajima. 1998. Notes on the biology and morphology of a predatory thrips, *Franklinothrips vespiformis* (Crawford) (Thysanoptera: Aeolothripidae): First record from Japan. *Entomological Science* 1:359–63.

Bartlett, P. W. 1993. Plant quarantine experience of *Liriomyza* spp. in England and Wales. *Liriomyza Conference on Leafmining Flies in Cultivated Plants.* Centre de Cooperation Internationale en Recherche Agronomique pour le Developpement (CIRAD), Montpellier, France. (24-26 March, 1993), 23–30.

Bene, G. del. 1989. Natural enemies of *Liriomyza trifolii* (Burgess), *Chromatomyia horticola* (Goureau) and *Chromatomyia syngenesiae* (Hardy) (Diptera: Agromyzidae) in Tuscany. *Redia* 72:529–44.

————. 1990. Use of *Diglyphus isaea* (Wlk.) (Hym:. Eulophidae) for the control of *Liriomyza trifolii* (Burgess), *Chromatomyia horticola* (Goureau) and *Chromatomyia syngenesiae* (Hardy) (Dipt.: Agromyzidae) in greenhouses of chrysanthemum and gerbera. *Redia* 73:63–78.

Broadbent, A. B., and J. A. Matteoni. 1990. Acquisition and transmission of *Pseudomonas chichorii* by *Liriomyza trifolii* (Diptera: Agromyzidae). *Proceedings of the Entomological Society of Ontario* 121:79–84.

Broadbent, A. B., and T. H. A. Olthof. 1995. Foliar application of *Steinernema carpocapsae* (Rhabditidae, Steinernematidae) to control *Liriomyza trifolii* (Diptera: Agromyzidae) larvae in chrysanthemums. *Environmental Entomology* 24:431–5.

Calvarin, V., and A. Langlois. 2001. Integrated biological protection against mining flies in ornamental horticulture. *Revue Horticole* 430:14–7.

Carvalho, P., and A. Mexia. 2000. First approach on the potential role of *Dicyphus cerastii* Wagner (Hemiptera: Miridae), as natural control agent in Portuguese greenhouses. *IOBC/WPRS Bulletin* 23:261–4.

Chaney, W. E. 1995. The pea as a pest of vegetable crops. *Crop Notes*, October, 4.

Cheek, S., O. C. MacDonald, and P. W. Bartlett. 1993. Statutory action against *Liriomyza huidobrensis* (Blanchard) in the United Kingdom. *Liriomyza Conference on Leaf-mining Flies in Cultivated Plants*. Centre de Cooperation Internationale en Recherche Agronomique pour le Developpement (CIRAD), Montpellier, France. (24-26 March, 1993):79–86.

Civelek, H. S., Z. Yoldas, and P. Weintraub. 2002. The parasitoid complex of *Liriomyza huidobrensis* in cucumber greenhouses in Izmir Province, western Turkey. *Phytoparasitica* 30:285–7.

Colombo, M., and D. P. Locatelli. 1985. Laboratory evaluation of the activity of *Steinernema feltiae* (Filip.) and *Heterorhabditis* spp. on *Liriomyza trifolii* (Burgess) and *Opogona sacchari* (Bojer) infesting cultivated flowering plants. *Difesa Delle Piante* 8:263–9.

Connor, E.F., and M. P. Taverner. 1997. The evolution and adaptive significance of the leaf-mining habit. *Oikos* 79:6–25.

Cornelius, S. J., and H. C. Godfray. 1984. Natural parasitism of the chrysanthemum leafminer, *Chromatomyia syngenesiae* [Diptera: Agromyzidae]. *Entomophaga* 29:341-5.

Croft, P., and M. J. W. Copland. 1994. Larval morphology and development of the parasitoid *Dacnusa sibirica* (Hym.: Braconidae) in the leaf miner host *Chromatomyia syngenesiae*. *Entomophaga* 39:85–93.

DeBach, P., ed. 1964. *Biological Control of Insect Pests and Weeds*. London: Chapman and Hall.

Dreistadt, S. H. 2001. *Integrated Pest Management for Floriculture and Nurseries*. Div. of Agriculture and Natural Resources Publication 3402. Oakland California. Berkeley, Calif.: University of California.

Finney-Crawley, J. R., and R. Smith. 1985. Feasibility of using nematodes for the control of the chrysanthemum leaf miner, *Liriomyza trifolii*. Agri-Food Development Agreement Project Report 1986-89. Truro, Canada: Agriculture Canada.

Freidberg, A., and M. J. Gijswijt. 1983. A list and preliminary observations on natural enemies of the leaf miner, *Liriomyza trifolii* (Burgess) (Diptera: Agromyzidae). *Israel Journal of Entomology* 17:115–6.

Frick, K. E. 1951. *Liriomyza langei*, a new species of leaf miner of economic importance in California. *Pan Pacific Entomologist* 27:81–8.

Gaugler, R., L. Lebeck, B. Nakagaki, and G. M. Boush. 1980. Orientation of the entomogenous nematode *Neoaplectana carpocapsae* to carbon dioxide. *Environmental Entomology* 9:649–52.

Gullino, M. L., and L. R. Wardlow. 1999. Ornamentals. In *Integrated Pest and Disease Management in Greenhouse Crops*, ed. R. Albajes, M. L. Gullino, J. C. van Lenteren, and Y. Elad, 486–504. Dordrecht, the Netherlands: Kluwer Academic Publishers.

Hamrick, D. 2000. MPS: Documenting effects on the environment. *GrowerTalks*, July, 112–4.

Hara, A. H., H. K. Kaya, R. Gaugler, L. M. Lebeck, and C. L. Mello. 1993. Entomopathogenic nematodes for biological control of the leaf miner, *Liriomyza trifolii* (Dipt: Agromyzidae). *Entomophaga* 38:359–69.

Hara, A. H., and S. Matayoshi. 1990. Parasitoids and predators of insect pests on chrysanthemums in Hawaii. *Proceedings of the Hawaiian Entomological Society* 30:53–8.

Harris, M. A., J. W. Begley, and D. L. Warkentin. 1990. *Liriomyza trifolii* (Diptera: Agromyzidae) suppression with foliar applications of *Steinernema carpocapsae* (Rhabditidae, Steinernematidae) and abamectin. *Journal of Economic Entomology* 83:2380–4.

Heimpel, G. E., and J. G. Lundgren. 2000. Sex ratios of commercially reared biological control agents. *Biological Control* 19:77–99.

Heinz, K. M., J. P. Newman, and M. P. Parrella. 1988. Biological control of leaf miners on greenhouse marigolds. *California Agriculture* 42:10–2.

Heinz, K. M., L. Nunney, and M. P. Parrella. 1993. Toward predictable biological control of *Liriomyza trifolii* (Diptera: Agromyzidae) infesting greenhouse cut chrysanthemums. *Environmental Entomology* 22 (6):1217–33.

Heinz, K. M., and M. P. Parrella. 1990. Biological control of insect pests on greenhouse marigolds. *Environmental Entomology* 19 (4):825–35.

Heinz, K. M., and M. P. Parrella. 1992. The effect of leaf-mining by *Liriomyza trifolii* on seed set in greenhouse marigolds. *Ecological Applications* 2:139–46.

Hume, H., R. Dunne, and J. P. O'Connor. 1990. *Liriomyza huidobrensis* new record (*Blanchard*) (Diptera: Agromyzidae) an imported pest new to Ireland. *Irish Naturalists' Journal* 23:325–6.

Hussey, N. W., and N. E. A. Scopes, eds. 1985. *Biological Pest Control: The Glasshouse Experience*. Ithaca, N.Y.: Cornell University Press (Poole, U.K.: Blandford Press).

Ibrahim, A. G., and D. S. Madge. 1977. The life cycle of the chrysanthemum leaf miner, *Phytomyza syngenesiae* (Hardy), with reference to its larval development and behavior. *Entomologist's Monthly Magazine* 113:1–7.

Johnson, M. W. 1993. Biological control of *Liriomyza* leaf miners in the Pacific Basin. *Micronesica Supplement* 4:81–92.

Johnson, M. W., and A. H. Hara. 1987. Influence of host crop on parasitoids (Hymenoptera) of *Liriomyza* spp. (Diptera: Agromyzidae). *Environmental Entomology* 16:339–44.

Jones, V. P. and M. P. Parrella. 1986. The movement and dispersal of *Liriomyza trifolii* (Diptera: Agromyzidae) in a chrysanthemum greenhouse. *Annals of Applied Biology* 109:33-39.

Jones, V. P., M. P. Parrella, and D. R. Hodel. 1986. Biological control of leaf miners in greenhouse chrysanthemums. *California Agriculture* 40:10–2.

Kaya, H. K., and R. Gaugler. 1993. Entomopathogenic nematodes. *Annual Review of Entomology* 38:181–206.

Keil, C. B., and M. P. Parrella. 1990. Characterization of insecticide resistance in two colonies of *Liriomyza trifolii* (Diptera: Agromyzidae). *Journal of Economic Entomology* 83:18–26.

Landi, S. 1993. Biological control of *Liriomyza trifolii* on chrysanthemum. *Colture Protette* 22:43–6.

Lanzoni, A., G. G. Bazzocchi, G. Burgio, and M. R. Fiacconi. 2002. Comparative life history of *Liriomyza trifolii* and *Liriomyza huidobrensis* (Diptera: Agromyzidae) on beans: effect of temperature on development. *Environmental Entomology* 31:797–803.

LaSalle, J., and M. P. Parrella. 1991. The chalcidoid parasites (Hymenoptera, Chalcidoidea) of economically important *Liriomyza* species (Diptera, Agromyzidae) in North America. *Proceedings of the Entomological Society of Washington* 93:571–91.

Lebeck, L. M., R. Gaugler, H. K. Kaya, A. H. Hara, and M. W. Johnson.1993. Host stage suitability of the leaf miner *Liriomyza trifolii* (Diptera, Agromyzidae) to the entomopathogenic nematode *Steinernema carpocapsae* (Rhabditida, Steinernematidae). *Journal of Invertebrate Pathology* 62:58–63.

Leite, G. L. D., I. R. de Oliveira, R. N. C. Guedes and M. Picanço. 2001. Predatory behaviour of *Protonectarina sylveirae* (Saussure) (Hymenoptera: Vespidae) in mustard. *Agro-Ciencia* 17:93-96.

Lindquist, R. K., M. L. Casey, N. Helyer, and N. E. A. Scopes. 1984. Leaf miners on greenhouse chrysanthemum: control of *Chromatomyia syngenesiae* and *Liriomyza trifolii*. *Journal of Agricultural Entomology* 1:256–63.

Martinez, M. 2001. Agromyzid mining flies injurious to ornamental and market-garden crops under glass. *Revue Horticole*. 430:9–13.

Matteoni, J. A., and A. B. Broadbent. 1988. Wounds caused by *Liriomyza trifolii* (Diptera: Agromyzidae) as sites for infection of chrysanthemum by *Pseudomonas cichorii*. *Canadian Journal of Plant Pathology* 10:47–52.

Minkenberg, O. P. J. M., and J. C. van Lenteren. 1986. The leaf miners *Liriomyza bryoniae* and *L. trifolii* (Diptera: Agromyzidae), their parasites and host plants: a review. *Agricultural University of Wageningen papers* 86 (2):1-50.

Morgan, D. J. W., S. R. Reitz, P. W. Atkinson, and J. T. Trumble. 2000. The resolution of California populations of *Liriomyza huidobrensis* and *Liriomyza trifolii* (Diptera: Agromyzidae) using PCR. *Heredity* 85:53–61.

Murphy, S. T., and J. LaSalle. 1999. Balancing biological control strategies in the IPM of New World invasive *Liriomyza* leaf miners in field vegetable crops. *Biocontrol News and Information* 20:91–104.

Newman, J. P., and M. P. Parrella. 1986. A license to kill. *Greenhouse Manager* 5:86–92.

Ode, P. J., and K. M. Heinz. 2002. Host-size-dependent sex ratio theory and improving mass-reared parasitoid sex ratios. *Biological Control* 24:31–41.

Onillon, J.C. 1999. Biological control of leaf miners. In *Integrated Pest and Disease Management in Greenhouse Crops*, ed. R. Albajes, M. L. Gullino, J. C. van Lenteren, and Y. Elad, 254–62. Dordrecht, the Netherlands: Kluwer Academic Publishers.

Parrella, M. P. 1984. Insect pest management: The lesson of *Liriomyza*. *Bulletin of the Entomological Society of America* 30:22–5.

———. 1987. Biology of *Liriomyza*. *Annual Review of Entomology* 32:201–24.

Parrella, M. P., and J. A. Bethke. 1984. Biological studies of *Liriomyza huidobrensis* (Diptera, Agromyzidae) on chrysanthemum, aster, and pea. *Journal of Economic Entomology* 77:342–5.

Parrella, M.P., W. W. Allen, and P. Morishita. 1981. Leafminer species causes California mum growers new problems. *California Agriculture* 116: 28-30.

Parrella, M. P., L. S. Hanse, and J. C. van Lenteren. 1999. Glasshouse environments. In *Handbook of Biological Control: Principles and Applications of Biological Control*, ed. T. S. Bellows and T. S. Fisher, 819–39. San Diego, Calif.: Academic Press.

Parrella, M. P., K. M. Heinz, and L. Nunney. 1992. Biological control through augmentative releases of natural enemies: A strategy whose time has come. *American Entomologist* 38:172–9.

Parrella, M. P., G. D. Christie, K. L. Robb and J. A. Bethke. 1982. Control of *Liriomyza trifolii* with biological agents and insect growth regulators. *California Agriculture* 36: 17-19.

Parrella, M. P., V. P. Jones, R. R. Youngman, and L. M. Lebeck. 1985. Effect of leaf-mining and leaf-stippling of *Liriomyza* spp. on photosynthetic rates of chrysanthemum. *Annals of the Entomological Society of America* 78:90–3.

Parrella, M. P., and C. B. Keil. 1984. Insect pest management: The lesson of *Liriomyza*. *Bulletin of the Entomological Society of America* 30:22–5.

Parrella, M. P., and R. K. Lindquist. 1983. Research on biology and control of leaf miners (Diptera: Agromyzidae) in the genus *Liriomyza* Mik. *10th International Congress of Plant Protection 1983: Plant Protection for Human Welfare. Proceedings of a Conference Held in Brighton, England, 20–25 November 1983, Vol. 3*, 1117. Croydon, U.K.: British Crop Protection Council.

Parrella, M. P., and J. T. Trumble. 1989. Decline of resistance in *Liriomyza trifolii* (Diptera: Agromyzidae) in the absence of insecticide selection pressure. *Journal of Economic Entomology* 82:365–8.

Parrella, M. P., G. K. von Damm, and T. Costamagna. 2000. Mining for compatibility. *GrowerTalks* 64 (6):60–8.

Rauf, A., B. M. Shepard, and M. W. Johnson. 2000. Leaf miners in vegetables, ornamental plants and weeds in Indonesia: Surveys of host crops, species composition and parasitoids. *International Journal of Pest Management* 46:257–66.

Reitz, S. R., and J. T. Trumble. 2002. Interspecific and intraspecific differences in two *Liriomyza* leaf miner species in California. *Entomologia Experimentalis et Applicata* 102:101–13.

Saito, T. 1994. Occurrence of the leafminer, *Liriomyza trifolii* (Burgess), and its control in Japan. *Agrochemicals Japan* 62:1-3.

Salamero, A., R. Gabarra, and R. Albajes. 1987. Observations on the predatory and phytophagous habits of *Dicyphus tamaninii* Wagner (Heteroptera: Miridae). *IOBC/WPRS Bulletin* 10:165–9.

Sampson, C. 1996. Macrolophus pros and cons. *Grower* 26:9.

Scheffer, S. J. 2000. Molecular evidence of cryptic species within the *Liriomyza huidobrensis* (Diptera: Agromyzidae). *Journal of Economic Entomology* 93:1146–51.

Scheffer, S. J., and M. L. Lewis. 2001. Two nuclear genes confirm mitochondrial evidence of cryptic species within *Liriomyza huidobrensis* (Diptera: Agromyzidae). *Annals of the Entomological Society of America* 94:648–53.

Scheffer, S. J., A. Wijesekara, D. Visser, and R. B. Hallett. 2001. Polymerase chain reaction-restriction fragment-length polymorphism method to distinguish *Liriomyza huidobrensis* from *L. langei* (Diptera: Agromyzidae) applied to three recent leafminer invasions[1]. *Journal of Economic Entomology* 94 (5):1177–82.

Schmidt, J., and J. N. All. 1978. Chemical attraction of *Neoaplectana carpocapsae* (Nematoda: Steinernematidae) to insect larvae. *Environmental Entomology* 7:605–7.

———. 1979. Attraction of *Neoaplectana carpocapsae* (Nematoda: Steinernematidae) to common excretory products of insects. *Environmental Entomology* 8:55–61.

Scholz-Dobelin, H. 1997. Experiences with natural enemies. *Gemuse* 33:246–8.

Shepard, B., M. Samsudin, and A. Braun. 1998. Seasonal incidence of *Liriomyza huidobrensis* (Diptera: Agromyzidae) and its parasitoids on vegetables in Indonesia. *International Journal of Pest Management*. 44 (1): 43-47.

Sher, R. B., M. P. Parrella, and H. K. Kaya. 2000. Biological control of the leaf miner *Liriomyza trifolii* (Burgess): Implications for intraguild predation between *Diglyphus begini* (Ashmead) and *Steinernema carpocapsae* (Weiser). *Biological Control* 17:155–63.

Smith, P. H. D., and T. H. Jones. 1998. Effects of elevated CO_2 on the chrysanthemum leaf miner, *Chromatomyia syngenesiae*: A greenhouse study. *Global Change Biology* 4 (3):287–91.

Spencer, K. A. 1973. *Agromyzidae (Diptera) of Economic Importance*. Series Entomologica, Vol. 9, ed. E. S. Gottingen.. The Hague: Dr. W. Junk B. V

———. 1989. Leaf miners. In *Plant Protection and Quarantine, Vol. II. Selected Pests and Pathogens of Quarantine Significance,* ed. P. R. Kahn, 77–98. Boca Raton, Florida: CRC Press.

Spencer, K. A. 1990. *Host specialization in the world Agromyzidae (Diptera).* Dordrecht, the Netherlands: Kluwer Academic Publishers.

Spencer, K. A., and G. C. Steyskal. 1986. *Manual of the Agromyzidae (Diptera) of the United States.* United States Department of Agriculture, Agriculture Handbook No. 638.

Stanton, G., D. L. Clement, and E. Dutky. 1999. *Pests & Diseases of Herbaceous Perennials: The Biological Approach.* Batavia, Illinois: Ball Publishing.

van der Linden, A. 1991. Biological control of the leafminer *Liriomyza huidobrensis* (Blanchard) in Dutch glasshouse tomatoes. *Mededelingen van de Faculteit Landbouwwetenschappen Rijksuniversiteit Gent* 56:265-271.

van Lenteren, J. C. 1995. Integrated pest management in protected crops. In *Integrated Pest Management*, ed. D. Dent, 311-43. London: Chapman and Hall.

van Lenteren, J. C. 2000. A greenhouse without pesticides: Fact or fantasy? *Crop Protection* 19:375–84.

van Lenteren, J. C., and G. Manzaroli. 1999. Evaluation and use of predators and parasitoids for biological control of pests in greenhouses. In *Integrated Pest and Disease Management in Greenhouse Crops*, ed. R. Albajes, M. L. Gullino, J. C. van Lenteren, and Y. Elad, 183–99. Dordrecht, the Netherlands: Kluwer Academic Publishers.

van Lenteren, J.C., M. M. Roskan, and R. Timmer. 1997. Commercial mass production and pricing of organisms for biological control of pests in Europe. *Biological Control* 10:143–9.

van Schelt, J., J. Klapwijk, M. Letard, and C. Aucouturier. 1996. The use of *Macrolophus caliginosus* as a whitefly predator in protected crops. In *Bemisia: 1995 Taxonomy, Biology, Damages, Control, and Management*, ed. D. Gerling and R. T. Mayer, 515–21. Andover, U.K.: Intercept.

Wardlow, L. R. 1985. Chrysanthemums. In *Biological Pest Control: The Glasshouse Experience.* ed. N. W. Hussey and N. E. A. Scopes, 180–5. Ithaca, N.Y.: Cornell University Press (Poole, U.K.: Blandford Press).

Wardlow, L. R. 1986. Adapting integrated pest control to work for ornamentals. *Grower* 6:26-29.

Waterhouse, D. F., and K. R. Norris. 1987. *Biological Control: Pacific Prospects.* Melbourne: Inkata Press.

Weintraub, P. G., and A. R. Horowitz. 1995. The newest leaf miner pest in Israel, *Liriomyza huidobrensis*. *Phytopharasitica* 23:177–84.

Williams, E.C. 1993. Entomophatogenic nematodes for leaf miner control. *IOBC/WPRS Bulletin* 16:158–62.

Williams, E. C., and O. C. MacDonald. 1995. Critical factors required by the nematode *Steinernema feltiae* for the control of the leafminers *Liriomyza huidobrensis*, *Liriomyza bryoniae* and *Chromatomyia syngenesiae*. *Annals of Applied Biology* 127:329–41.

Williams, E. C., and K. F. A. Walter. 2000. Foliar application of the entomopathogenic nematode *Steinernema feltiae* on vegetables. *Biocontrol Science and Technology* 10:61–70.

13

BIOLOGICAL CONTROL OF
LEAFMINERS ON VEGETABLE CROPS

A. van der Linden
Applied Plant Research, Wageningen University and Research Centre
Boskoop, The Netherlands

Leafminer Species and Host Plants

Vegetable growing in greenhouses is of great economic importance, particularly in Europe. Several leafminers in the genus *Liriomyza* (Diptera: Agromyzidae) cause problems in these crops, especially species with resistance to chemical pesticides. Some species have also become pests outside their original area of distribution. The fact that these species are polyphagous may also contribute to their success as agricultural pests. Since tomatoes, cucumbers, and sweet peppers are now grown on rockwool, soil sterilization is not applied between crops, as was the normal practice when these crops were grown in soil. Therefore, pupae in and on the ground easily survive periods between crops. The following *Liriomyza* species are considered quarantine pests in Europe.

Liriomyza trifolii (Burgess)

This species was originally distributed in the eastern United States (Spencer and Steyskal 1986), with its greatest abundance occurring in Florida. In the 1970s and early 1980s, this species developed from a secondary to a serious pest, and it spread to many other countries around the world (Minkenberg 1988a). By 1980, *L. trifolii* had developed resistance to at least ten important insecticides, with about a twentyfold resistance against permethrin and a sixteenfold resistance against methamidophos in areas where control failures were noticed (Parrella 1984). *L. trifolii* attack some thirty-nine herbs and vegetables (Spencer 1973, 1990; table 13.1).

Liriomyza sativae (Blanchard)

This species is closely related to *L. trifolii*, and in the past, proper identification of these species was often lacking. *Liriomyza sativae* is believed to have originated in the southern United States, but it is also recorded from California, Hawaii, Ohio, Texas, Argentina, the Bahamas, Barbados, Brazil, Chile, Jamaica, Peru, Tahiti, and Venezuela (Spencer 1973, Spencer and Steyskal 1986). This species was collected in Oman in 1990 and in Yemen in 1991 (Deeming 1992), Jordan (Al-Ghabeish and Allawi 2001), Sudan and Cameroon (Martinez and Bordat 1996), West Africa (Deeming and Mann 1999), China (Zhuang-BingLiang 1998), Vietnam (Andersen et al. 2002), Indonesia (Rauf et al. 2000), Japan (Ishida et al. 2003) and it is still spreading. Problems with resistance to pesticides are not as serious as with *L. trifolii*. *L. sativae* is polyphagous, and the range of host plants are listed by Spencer (1973, 1990) and Spencer and Steyskal (1986) (table 13.1).

Liriomyza huidobrensis (Blanchard)

This leafminer is native to the western United States, including California, Washington, and Utah. It is also widespread in the temperate areas in South America (Spencer 1973, Spencer and Steyskal 1986). In 1989, this species first appeared, in very high numbers, on different crops in several countries in Europe. In the Netherlands, many hectares of lettuce (*Lactuca sativa* L.) both in greenhouses and outdoors have been completely lost from the damage caused by this leafminer. The usual pesticides failed to control the pest. The origins of these infestations are unknown, but it is likely that the pest was imported on plant material. These problems coincided with serious infestations and the development of resistance against insecticides in Costa Rica (Zúñiga, Zoebisch, and Carballo 1991). *Liriomyza huidobrensis* is still spreading and has reached also Turkey (Civelek et al. 2002), Israel (Weintraub and Horowitz 1998), Jordan (Al-Ghabeish and Allawi 2001), Arabia (Dawah and Deeming 2002), China (Wang-Jian Wen, Szhangzhi-Ying, and She-Yu Ping 1998), Vietnam (Andersen et al. 2002) and Indonesia (Shepard et al. 1998).

Earlier instances of resistance to pesticides by *L. huidobrensis* were recorded in Peru, where *L. huidobrensis* developed into a primary pest of potato as a result of indiscriminate spraying against the potato moth *Scrobipalpuloides (Scrobipalpula) absoluta*

(Meyrik) (Raman 1988). In the Netherlands, few pesticides were effective against *L. huidobrensis* larvae when the first outbreaks occurred. Only oxamyl, abamectin, cyromazine, and thiocyclamhydrogenoxalate gave adequate control (van der Staay 1992). But these chemicals were not registered for use on most of the affected crops. Eighteen other agents, including pyrazophos and triazophos, were not effective against *L. huidobrensis*, even though they were still effective against *L. trifolii*. *L. huidobrensis* is a polyphagous species (Spencer 1973, 1990; de Goffau 1991), attacking many species of vegetables and herbs (table 13.1).

Liriomyza bryoniae (Kaltenbach)

This insect is native to the Palearctic region: Europe, North Africa (Spencer 1973), and Asia (Safjanov and Skripnik 1968, Kamijo 1978, Wang and Lin 1988). This species has not yet developed resistance against pesticides. *Liriomyza bryoniae* is closely related to the polyphagous Palearctic species *Liriomyza strigata* Meigen (Spencer 1973), which is generally not a pest of cultivated plants, and to the Neotropical and Nearctic species *L. huidobrensis*. This relatedness is demonstrated by the similarity of male genitalia among these species, and by the production of progeny resulting from forced laboratory crossings of *L. bryoniae* females with *L. huidobrensis* males and *L. strigata* females with *L. bryoniae* males. Such hybridization, however, does not occur in nature or in horticultural environments. Moreover, since the reciprocal crosses (*L. bryoniae* males with *L. huidobrensis* females and *L. strigata* males with *L. bryoniae* females) did not occur in the laboratory, there is only a small chance of genetic introgression among these species. *L. bryoniae* is considered to be primarily a pest of tomato, but in fact it is a polyphagous species (Spencer 1973, 1990; table 13.1).

Other leafminer species of minor importance that occur in greenhouse vegetables are *Chromatomyia syngenesiae* Hardy on lettuce and carrot (*Daucus carota* L.), *Phytomyza rufipes* Meigen on *Brassica* spp., and *Scaptomyza flava* (Fallén) (Diptera: Drosophilidae) on *Brassica* spp. and radish (*Raphanus sativus* L.).

Biology and Damage

After mating, a female leafminer lays its eggs in leaf tissue. Females also make holes with their ovipositors in the leaf surface and feed on fluids from the wounded leaf. These wounds are visible and are known as feeding marks or punctures. The larvae cause the characteristic mines in the leaves, starting as a narrow line and widening as the larvae grow. There are three larval stages in all species discussed here. Mature larvae exit the leaves by making a hole in the epidermis and fall to the ground or onto other plant structures. The nature of the leaf can affect the ability of larvae to reach the soil. Exiting larvae and pupae are frequently found on the leaves of common bean, *Phaseolus vulgaris* L., as they appear to be held there by the trichomes. Larvae of *L. trifolii, L. sativae,* and *L. bryoniae* feed primarily in the upper side of the leaf blade, while *L. huidobrensis* larvae often feed in the leaf veins and on the underside of the leaf. Larvae of *L. bryoniae* can be found in the upper side or in the underside of the leaf, as well as in the leaf veins. All *Liriomyza* species mentioned can penetrate

leafstalks and even the stamen of a plant, particularly when leafminer densities are high.

Quantification of damage

Leaf mining results in a loss of chlorophyll, which significantly reduces photosynthesis and stomatal conductance rates in leaves (Johnson et al. 1983; Trumble, Ting, and Bates 1985). In tomato, there exists a negative linear correlation between these physiological rates and the percentages of tomato leaflets damaged by leaf mining (Johnson et al. 1983). Further, effects of *L. sativae* mining upon leaflet photosynthesis are not limited to the specific areas damaged by larval feeding; low levels of mining activity may greatly reduce photosynthesis for the entire leaflet.

Attempts have been made to quantify the relationship between leafminer damage and yield loss. Results from these studies are difficult to interpret because it is difficult to tell what the damage is caused by the leaf miners and what damage might have been caused by pesticides. Several authors have suggested that pesticides may adversely affect the physiology, growth, and yield of plants (LaPre et al. 1982, Toscano et al. 1982, Jones et al. 1986, Heinz and Parrella 1992). As a result, it is difficult to separate the influences of leafminer damage on changes in crop yield from plant responses to insecticides. It is, therefore, not surprising to find reports suggesting that yields of tomato plants increase, do not change, or decrease with decreasing levels of leafminer damage (Lindquist 1974; Levins et al. 1975; Schuster, Jones, and Everett 1976; Johnson, Oatman, and Wyman 1980a, 1980b).

The position and timing of damage influence crop yields as much as does the total

Table 13.1. Herbs and Vegetables Recorded as Host Plants[a] of *Liriomyza trifolii* (Burgess), *Liriomyza sativae* (Blanchard), *Liriomyza huidobrensis* (Blanchard), and *Liriomyza bryoniae* (Kaltenbach)

	Species of *Liriomyza*			
	trifolii	sativae	huidobrensis	bryoniae
Allium cepa L.	x		x	
Allium sativum L.			x	
Allium schoenoprasum L.	x			
Amaranthus sp.	x			x
Apium graveolens L.[b]	x		x	x
Arachis sp.	x			
Atriplex sp.				x
Basella alba L.	x			
Beta vulgaris L.[b]	x		x	x
Brassica sp.		x		
Brassica oleracea L.[b]			x	
Brassica pekinensis L.[b]	x		x	x
Cajanus cajan (L.) Millsp.		x		
Capsicum annuum L.[b]	x	x	x	x
Chenopodium sp.	x			x
Citrullus vulgaris L.	x	x		x
Coriandrum sativum L.				x
Cucumis melo L.[b]	x	x	x	x
Cucumis sativus L.[b]	x	x	x	x
Cucurbita pepo L.[b]	x	x	x	x
Daucus carota L.[b]	x		x	
Glycine sp.	x			
Hibiscus esculentus L.	x	x	x	
Lactuca sativa L.[b]	x	x	x	x
Levisticum officinale Koch				x
Lycopersicon esculentum L. Mill.[b]	x	x	x	x
Petroselinum crispum L.[b]			x	x
Phaseolus lunatus L.	x	x		
Phaseolus vulgaris L.[b]	x	x	x	x
Physalis sp.	x	x		
Pisum sativum L.	x	x	x	x
Raphanus sativus L.[b]		x	x	x
Solanum melongena L.[b]	x	x	x	x
Solanum tuberosum L.	x	x	x	x
Spinacia oleracea L.[b]	x	x	x	x
Taraxacum sp.	x			
Valerianella locusta (L.) Betcke [b]				x
Vicia faba L.	x		x	x
Vigna sinensis L. (V. *unguiculata* [L.] Walp)	x	x		

[a](Spencer 1973 as cited in 1990, Spencer and Steyskal 1986, de Goffau 1991)
[b]Greenhouse crops

amount of damage to foliage. Stacey (1983) reported that removing a quarter of each leaflet on leaves from the lower half of the plant or one leaf between each truss caused no loss in yield. It appears that plants can tolerate considerable defoliation by pests such as leafminers, particularly on the lower leaves, without serious crop loss. Ledieu (1981) reported that only the yield from the first two trusses was significantly reduced by leafminer infestation. Yield was not reduced at any other time because damage was mostly confined to the lower leaves, which probably do not contribute significantly to swelling of the fruit.

Wolk, Kretchman, and Ortega (1983) found that severe defoliation from the transplanting stage up to within about four weeks of harvest could significantly reduce fruit production. However, it also appears that tomato may have the capacity to compensate for foliar damage through an increase in the photosynthetic rate in the remaining leaves. Ledieu and Helyer (1982) indicated that yields from plants with a high infestation level (where individual mines eventually could no longer be identified) were up to 17% lower than in the control without mines. Timing of the development of an infestation was a major factor in determining whether yield was reduced. Damage levels as low as fifteen mines per leaf were sufficient to reduce yield if the leaves were adjacent to fruit at an early to intermediate stage of swelling. More mature fruit developed normally. Wyatt et al. (1984) found that the best correlation was between the yield of a truss and the leaf miner infestation on the six leaves surrounding that truss twenty days before picking or when the fruit were half

grown. Under these conditions, the loss was directly proportional to the number of mines, such that thirty mines per leaf caused a 10% loss, sixty mines per leaf a 20% loss, etc. The location of damage was of utmost importance, and it appeared that even the most severe damage to the lower leaves caused no appreciable loss of yield.

Effects of Crop and Climate on Leaf Miner Biology

Greenhouse environments are conducive to the development and maintenance of *Liriomyza* outbreaks. Further, winter heating in temperate climates extends the growing season for both crops and pests. The optimum temperature for *L. bryoniae* development and reproduction is 77°F (25°C), with a lower development threshold of 46°F (8°C) and an 52°F (11°C) threshold for oviposition (Minkenberg and Helderman 1990). *Liriomyza bryoniae* is able to reproduce all year in heated greenhouses, but the length of the life cycle increases during winter as temperatures approach the minimum thresholds (Helyer and Ledieu 1990). By comparison, temperatures above 60°F (16°C) are necessary for populations of *L. trifolii* to increase (Minkenberg 1988b), and this species may completely disappear from tomato greenhouses during winter, probably because of low temperatures (van der Linden 1986).

L. bryoniae forms dark-colored pupae during the winter, and adults take longer to emerge from dark-colored pupae than from light-colored pupae. *Liriomyza huidobrensis* is a species characteristically found in cooler areas in the Neotropics, and it shows a seasonal dimorphism similar to *L. bryoniae*. In the Netherlands, adult *L. huidobrensis* commonly infest outdoor crops such as broad bean (*Vicia faba* L.) and lettuce beginning in early April until their populations are killed by the night time frosts that occur in November. Both *L. bryoniae* and *L. huido-brensis* were able to overwinter as pupae outdoors in the Netherlands (van der Linden 1993a). Despite the species' ability to live outdoors, leafminer-infested neighboring greenhouses or plants brought in from other infested greenhouses are the most common sources of new infestations.

Once an infestation has established, leafminers are able to quickly infest subsequent plantings placed within the same greenhouse. Because all *Liriomyza* leafminers are polyphagous, they may also easily move between different types of crops. Given such characteristics, the practice of proper sanitation between crops is essential in controlling this pest. Practices should consider the ability of pupae to survive the winter months in or on the soil or on various structures within the greenhouse. These pupae are the source of new, emerging leafminer flies that can later infest subsequent young plantings.

Natural Enemies
Commercialized parasitoids

Important factors that have encouraged the use of natural enemies for control of leafminers are their development of resistance against pesticides and the interference of chemical control with biological control of other pests. Many different species, depending on the geographical region, have been recorded as natural enemies of

Liriomyza spp. (Minkenberg and van Lenteren 1986; Johnson and Hara 1987; van der Linden 1990a; Grenouillet, Martinez, and Rasplus 1993; Iannacone-Oliver 1998; Arakaki and Kinjo 1998; Shepard et al. 1998; Rauf et al. 2000; Al-Ghabeish and Allawi 2001), and the occurrence of each is influenced by the leafminer species, host plants, greenhouse environment, and local climate. The natural occurrence of natural enemies within a greenhouse is an indication that its environment is suitable for their survival, and such occurrences can provide guidance on which species to choose for release.

The parasitoids that are currently reared on a commercial basis for introduction in greenhouses are *Dacnusa sibirica* Telenga (Hymenoptera: Braconidae) and *Diglyphus isaea* (Walker) (Hymenoptera: Eulophidae), while natural occurrence of *Opius pallipes* Wesmael (Hymenoptera: Braconidae) contributes to biological control. Native to Europe, these species are widely distributed and are released for biological control of leafminers in many parts of the world. *D. sibirica* and *O. pallipes* are larval-pupal endoparasitoids. Females of these species oviposit eggs into leafminer larvae, the young develop within the host larva and pupa, and the parasitoids eventually emerge as wasps from the leafminer pupa. *O. pallipes* is primarily useful for biological control of *L. bryoniae,* as it is not able to reproduce on *L. trifolii*.

Diglyphus isaea is a larval ectoparasitoid; females lay their eggs individually on or near the host inside the mine. Because the larvae feed outside the host, development of *D. isaea* from egg to adult can be easily observed inside the leaf mine with the aid of

Figure 13.1. The braconid *Dacnusa sibirica* Telenga is an internal parasitoid of leafminer larvae and is widely used in greenhouses for control of various leafminer species. *Photo: Koppert Biological Systems Inc.*

backlighting. This species kills 15 to 40% of leafminer larvae attacked simply by feeding on them rather than utilizing these hosts for oviposition (Minkenberg 1989). At times, host feeding is the most important factor responsible for the decrease of the leaf miner population (van der Linden 1991). The high egg-laying potential (209–293 eggs per female lifetime) and host-feeding habits (48–192 host feedings per female lifetime) of *D. isaea* make it especially useful at high leaf miner densities (Minkenberg 1989).

Other parasitoids

The fact that only European species have been commercialized for leafminer control does not imply that there are not other species elsewhere in the world that may be useful. In California, *Diglyphus begini* (Ashmead) might be useful in biological control programs (Heinz and Parrella 1990). In Florida, *Opius dissitus* Muesebeck (Petitt, Turlings, and Wolf 1992; Petitt and Wietlisbach 1993), and in

Ohio, *Opius dimidiatus* Ashmead (Hymenoptera: Braconidae) (Lindquist and Casey 1983) are other prominent species capable of suppressing leafminers within protected cultivation. Another interesting species worth mentioning is *Chrysocharis bedius* (Walker) (Hymenoptera: Eulophidae), which is a larval-pupal endoparasitoid of Neotropical origin (Hansson 1987). This species shows parthenogenetic reproduction, whereby unmated females produce mainly female offspring (thelytoky). So far, only a few other leafminer parasitoids, such as *Neochrysocharis formosa* (Westwood) (Arakaki and Kinjo 1998) and *Gronotoma micromorpha* (Perkins) (Abe, 2001) have shown this feature. Pupae of *Chrysocharis bedius* (Walker), when stored in the refrigerator at 45°F (7°C), are able to survive for more than a year. Similar ability to survive prolonged cold storage was also found for another species of this genus, *Chrysocharis oscinidis* Ashmead (= *Chrysocharis parksi* Crawford) (van der Linden 1990b).

Figure 13.2. The eulophid *Diglyphus isaea* (Walker) is an external parasitoid of leafminer larvae, commonly used in greenhouses for control of various leafminer species. *Photo: Koppert Biological Systems Inc.*

Releases of *C. oscinidis* and *O. dimidiatus* were evaluated for their ability to control *L. trifolii* and *L. bryoniae* in Dutch greenhouses (van der Linden 1986). Several biological characteristics adversely affected the abilities of the two parasitoids to control leafminers. *C. oscinidis* was active only from the end of March to the end of the crop, and *O. dimidiatus* consistently generated extremely male-biased sex ratios. As a result, neither parasitoid species improved leafminer biological control over that provided by the native parasitoid complex in Holland.

Predators and entomopathogenic nematodes

Other natural enemies of leafminers that deserve attention are predatory flies of the genus *Coenosia* (Diptera: Muscidae). *Coenosia* spp. have a wide distribution, and several species regularly appear in greenhouses. These predators are often very abundant in crops that are grown in soil, such as lettuce (van der Linden 1993c). Although believed to be generalist predators (Kühne et al. 1994), they are often observed catching *Liriomyza* flies on the wing. *Coenosia* spp. warrant further study since they may be the most effective natural enemy against leafminer adults. By controlling the adults, leaf stippling and egg laying could be greatly reduced. The larvae of *Coenosia* spp. are predacious on larvae of other insects living in the soil, including fungus gnats (Sciaridae) and shore flies (Ephydridae).

Entomopathogenic nematodes (*Steinernema* spp.) have not received as much attention as parasitoids, but they can also contribute to control of leafminers. Nematodes were more effective against *L. bryoniae* and *L. huidobrensis* than against *C. syngenesiae* (Williams and Walters 2000). Combined application of *D. begini* and *Steinernema carpocapsae (Weiser)* may, however, result in infection of *Diglyphus* larvae (Sher et al. 2000).

Biological Control Programs

Tomato

In its simplest form, biological control makes use of the beneficial species that occur naturally in greenhouses. Combating other pests with methods that do not harm the indigenous natural-enemy fauna conserves these natural enemies. To assess the occurrence and impact of naturally occurring parasitoids and predators, foliage samples should be collected at least twice per leafminer generation and the occurrence of parasitism checked by looking for developing wasps within leaf mines and/or leafminer larvae. Samples for dissection should consist of fifty third-instar leafminer larvae collected from all areas of the greenhouse. The decision to release or not to release parasitoids or to use some other control tactic depends on the severity of the infestation and the natural rate of parasitism. Table 13.2 is a guide for making decisions about the need to release additional leafminer parasitoids.

Sole reliance on indigenous natural enemies can be risky, since they rarely invade tomato greenhouses in sufficient numbers early enough within a pest outbreak to provide sufficient control. A developing infestation of leafminers should never be ignored. Although the absolute number of mines may be low, densities may increase one hundredfold between generations, particu-

Table 13.2. Number of Mines (of One Generation) per Tomato Plant and the Safe Rate of Parasitism to Omit further Control Measures.

Mines per Plant	Required Rate of Parasitism
100	100
50	95
25	80
10	50
5	25
1	10

larly in the warmer months. As soon as an infestation is detected, sampling should be intensified, control options explored, and the best strategy implemented immediately.

Releasing natural enemies for the control of leafminers is conducted on a large scale in tomato crops in some countries. Typically, the natural enemies are released directly from their shipping containers as emerging adults. *D. sibirica* is most commonly introduced against increasing infestations early in the season, sometimes in combination with *D. isaea*. The reproductive rate of *D. sibirica* decreases with increasing temperatures, which is why *D. sibirica* is less effective at high temperatures (Minkenberg 1990). During the cooler months, *D. isaea* development and oviposition rates are reduced to levels that greatly inhibit its ability to effectively control leafminers. *D. isaea* eggs and pupae cease developing when temperatures drop below 49 and 46°F (10 and

8°C), respectively, and oviposition ceases at 46°F (8°C) and below (Minkenberg 1989). As a result, *D. isaea* releases occur most frequently during the warmer portions of the growing season. Sampson and Walker (1998) studied the feasibility of establishing an action threshold for the release of *D. isaea*. They found that the use of an action threshold of one new mine per plant per week to trigger releases of *D. isaea* was practical and effective.

Usually, two to four introductions of the parasitoids are made throughout an infested greenhouse, with some concentration of releases on spots with higher leafminer density. The desired number of introduced parasitoids is approximately 12,500 per acre (5,000 per ha). The numbers of wasps released are frequently adjusted up or down depending on the severity of the infestation, the rate of parasitism, and the age of the crop. *O. pallipes* is likely to provide better control in trellised crops such as tomato because it does not preferentially search one height over the other, whereas *D. sibirica* appears to prefer searching foliage near the ground (van der Linden 1988, 1994). *D. isaea* has shown promising results against *L. trifolii* (Lyon 1986) and is the only parasitoid released for biological control of leafminers in France. In the United Kingdom and the Netherlands, *D. isaea* dominates during the warm summer months (Wardlow 1984, Woets 1985, van der Linden 1991), while *D. sibirica* or *O. pallipes* are most common and effective in the early spring and fall. Should leaf miner populations escape biological control, oxamyl can be applied as a selective systemic chemical by means of drip irrigation in some countries (van der Linden 1986).

Other crops

In lettuce, where any amount of leafminer damage reduces the value of the crop, problems with *L. huidobrensis* can be severe. Similar low damage thresholds occur for celery and radish. Banker plant systems are used in these crops to create a constant supply of parasitoids on a factitious host that is not harmful to the crop. *Phytomyza caulinaris* Hering and *Phytomyza ranunculi* (Schrank) are closely related species (Spencer 1990) that can be reared in large numbers on the buttercup *Ranunculus asiaticus* L. This host and host plant combination is suitable for use in a banker plant system since it produces large numbers of both *D. sibirica* and *D. isaea* (van der Linden 1992). However, *R. asiaticus* becomes dormant during the hot summer months and thus is limited in use. Other buttercup species, such as *Ranunculus repens* L. or *Ranunculus acris* L., are preferred for use in most temperate regions because they remain green longer. *D. sibirica* reliably parasitizes leafminers infesting lettuce, but *D. isaea* does not (van der Linden 1993b). Although the exact reason for this difference is not known, observations suggest that both *D. sibirica* and *O. pallipes* are successful in detecting spot infestations of leaf miners and *D. isaea* is not (van der Linden 1988).

In lettuce, radish, and celery, biological control may also be accomplished by introducing *D. sibirica* or *O. pallipes* as parasitized *P. caulinaris* (or *P. ranunculi*) pupae. Emerging *P. caulinaris* adults from incidental unparasitized pupae are not a threat to the crop. Parasitoids reared on *P. caulinaris* are larger and of potentially greater quality than those reared on *Liriomyza* spp. Two para-

meters important to biological control—the numbers of eggs at emergence and offspring produced by female *D. sibirica*—are correlated with wasp size (Croft and Copland 1993).

In recent years, the incidence of leafminers in sweet pepper and cucumber has also become problematic. In Germany, researchers have reported some success at biological control of the leafminer *L. huidobrensis* in cucumber, beans, and eggplant (*Solanum melongena* L.) (Leuprecht 1992). While *D. sibirica, O. pallipes,* and *D. isaea* frequently invade greenhouses to effect biological control, use of banker plants provides greater reliability.

Economic Competitiveness with Insecticides

The application of natural enemies against leafminers is necessary when the leafminers show resistance against chemical agents and when the biological control of other pests must not be jeopardized. Moreover, current public policy in many countries is to reduce the use of pesticides in agriculture and horticulture, both for environmental protection and because of increased demand for organic produce from buyers. Biological control requires less labor than the use of pesticides, with the exception of systemic materials like oxamyl, which can be applied through irrigation systems when the plants are grown on rockwool. The cost of crop protection is only a minor part of the total cost of crop production within protected culture. In Dutch tomato production, crop protection represents about 4% of the total costs (Kwantitatieve Informatie 1995).

Biological controls for leafminers and other pests are used in the majority of greenhouses located in western Europe. Natural enemies are being used in nearly 100% of round tomato, beef tomato, cherry tomato, sweet pepper, and cucumber crops. Growers who have gained experience with biological control easily adapt to the use of new natural enemies or release techniques. Application of biological control in crops other than tomato, sweet pepper, and cucumber, or in other countries may be hindered because growers lack experience with natural enemies, not because biological control is too costly.

Acknowledgments

The author wishes to thank Pierre Ramakers and Wim van Winden for reviewing a previous draft of this chapter.

References Cited

Abe, Y. 2001. Egg-pupal and larval-pupal parasitism in the parasitoid *Gronotoma micromorpha* (Hymenoptera: Eucoilidae). *Applied Entomology and Zoology* 36 (4): 479-482.

Al-Ghabeish, I., and T. F. Allawi. 2001. Agromyzid leafminers and their parasitoids in Jordan. *Dirasat. –Agricultural Sciences* 28 (2-3):172-177.

Andersen, A., E. Nordhus, Vu-Thi-Thang, Tran-Thi-Thien-An, Ha-Quang-Hung, and T. Hofsvang. 2002. Polyphagous *Liriomyza* species (Diptera: Agromyzidae) in Vietnam. *Tropical Agriculture.* 79 (4):241-246.

Arakaki, N., and L. Kinjo. 1998. Notes on the parasitoid fauna of the serpentine leafminer *Liriomyza trifolii* (Diptera: Agromyzidae) in Okinawa, southern Japan. *Applied Entomology and Zoology.* 33 (4):577-581.

Civelek, H. S., Z. Yoldas, and P. Weintraub. 2002. The parasitoid complex of *Liriomyza huidobrensis* in cucumber greenhouses in Izmir Province, Western Turkey. *Phytoparasitica.* 30 (3):285-287.

Croft, P., and M. J. W. Copland. 1993. Size and fecundity in *Dacnusa sibirica* Telenga. *IOBC/WPRS Bulletin* 16 (8):53–6.

Dawah, H. A., and J. C. Deeming. 2002. *Liriomyza huidobrensis* (Blanchard) (Dipt.: Agromyzidae) in Arabia. *Entomologist's Monthly Magazine.* 138:1656-1659.

Deeming, J. C. 1992. *Liriomyza sativae* Blanchard (Diptera: Agromyzidae) established in the Old World. *Tropical Pest Management* 38:218–9.

Deeming, J. C., and D. J. Mann. 1999. Distributional notes on two economically important Agromyzidae (Dipt.) in West Africa. *Entomologist's Monthly Magazine.* 135:1624-7, 205-206.

de Goffau, L. J. W. 1991. *Liriomyza huidobrensis* (Blanchard) (Diptera: Agromyzidae): A new economically important leafminer in the Netherlands. *Proceedings of the Section Experimental and Applied Entomology of the Netherlands Entomological Society* 2:41–5.

Grenouillet, C., M. Martinez, and J. Y. Rasplus. 1993. Liste des parasitoides et des predateurs des *Liriomyza* d'importance economique dans le monde (Diptera: Agromyzidae). *Liriomyza Conference on Leaf-mining Flies in Cultivated Plants.* Centre de Cooperation Internationale en Recherche Agronomique pour le Development (CIRAD), Montpellier, France. (March, 1993), pp. 143–56.

Hansson, C. 1987. Revision of the New World species of *Chrysocharis* Förster (Hymenoptera: Eulophidae). *Entomologica Scandinavia* Suppl. 29: 1-86. Lund, Sweden 15 November 1987. ISSN 0105-3574.

Heinz, K. M., and M. P. Parrella. 1990. Holarctic distribution of the leafminer parasitoid *Diglyphus begini* (Hymenoptera: Eulophidae) and notes on its life history attacking *Liriomyza trifolii* (Diptera: Agromyzidae) in chrysanthemum. *Annals of the Entomological Society of America* 83:916–24.

———. 1992. The effect of leaf-mining by *Liriomyza trifolii* on seed set in greenhouse marigolds. *Ecological Applications* 2 (2):139–46.

Helyer, N. L., and M. Ledieu. 1990. The seasonal variability in tomato leafminer (*Liriomyza bryoniae* [Kaltenbach]) life cycle. *IOBC/WPRS Bulletin* 13 (5):83–6.

Iannacone-Oliver, J. A. 1998. Diversity of parasitoid fauna of the leafminer fly, *Liriomyza huidobrensis* (Diptera: Agromyzidae) on beans in the Lima area of Peru (in Spanish). *Revista Colombiana de Entomologia* 24 (3-4):103-107.

Ishida, T., M. Yoneda, and M. Odahara. 2003. A field survey of the vegetable leafminer, *Liriomyza sativae* Blanchard (Diptera: Agromyzidae) in Okinawa (in Japanese). *Research of the Plant Protection Service, -Japan.* 29: 71-74.

Johnson, M. W., and A. H. Hara. 1987. Influence of host crop on parasitoids (Hymenoptera) of *Liriomyza* spp. (Diptera: Agromyzidae). *Environmental Entomology* 16:339–44.

Johnson, M. W., E. R. Oatman, and J. A. Wyman. 1980a. Effects of insecticides on populations of the vegetable leafminer and associated parasites on summer pole tomatoes. *Journal of Economic Entomology* 73:61–6.

———. 1980b. Effects of insecticides on populations of the vegetable leafminer and associated parasites on fall pole tomatoes. *Journal of Economic Entomology* 73:67–71.

Johnson, M. W., S. C. Welter, N. Toscano, I. P. Ting, and J. T. Trumble. 1983. Reduction of tomato leaflet photosynthesis rates by mining activity of *Liriomyza sativae* (Diptera: Agromyzidae). *Journal of Economic Entomology* 76:1061–3.

Jones, V. P., N. C. Toscano, M. W. Johnson, S. C. Welter, and R. R. Youngman. 1986. Pesticide effects on plant physiology: Integration into a pest management program. *Bulletin of the Entomological Society of America* 32:103–8.

Kamijo, K. 1978. Chalcidoid parasites (Hymenoptera) of agromyzidae in Japan, with description of a new species. *Kontyû* 46:455–69.

Kühne, S., K. Schrameyer. 1994. Räuberische Fliegen ein bisher wenig beachteter Nützlingskomplex in Gewächshäusern. *Mitteilungen aus der Biologischen Bundesanstalt für Land und Forstwirtschaft, Heft*, no. 301: 347.

Kwantitatieve Informatie voor de Glastuinbouw 1995–1996. Groenten Snijbloemen Potplanten. 1995. *Ministerie van Landbouw, Natuurbeheer en Visserij. Informatie en Kennis Centrum Landbouw. Afdeling Glasgroente en Bloemisterij, Aalsmeer/Naaldwijk*, 130 pp. + Tables [Facts and Figures of Dutch Glasshouse Horticulture].

LaPre, L. F., F. V. Sances, N. C. Toscano, E. R. Oatman, V. Voth, and M. W. Johnson. 1982. The effects of acaricides on the physiology, growth, and yield of strawberries. *Journal of Economic Entomology* 75:616–9.

Ledieu, M. S. 1981. Effect of tomato leafminer on yield. *Glasshouse Crops Research Institute Annual Report 1980*:109.

Ledieu, M. S. and N. L. Helyer. 1982. Effect of tomato leafminer on yield of tomatoes. *Glasshouse Crops Research Institute Annual Report 1981*:106–107.

Leuprecht, B. 1992. Biologische Bekämpfung von *Liriomyza huidobrensis* in Gemüsekulturen im Gewächshaus. *Gesunde Pflanzen* 44:222–9.

Levins, R. A., S. L. Poe, R. C. Littell, and J. P. Jones. 1975. Effectiveness of a leafminer control program for Florida tomato production. *Journal of Economic Entomology* 68:772–4.

Lindquist, R. K. 1974. Effects of leafminer larvae on yields of greenhouse tomatoes: A preliminary report. *Ohio Agricultural Research and Development Center, Wooster, Ohio. Research Summary* 73:25–9.

Lindquist, R. K., and M. L. Casey. 1983. Introduction of parasites for control of *Liriomyza* leafminers on greenhouse tomato. *IOBC/WPRS Bulletin* 6 (3):108–15.

Lyon, J. P. 1986. Problèmes particuliers posés par *Liriomyza trifolii* Burgess (Diptera: Agromyzidae) et lutte biologique contre ce nouveau ravageur des cultures protégées. L'emploi d'ennemis naturels dans la protection des cultures. *Les Colloques de l'INRA* 34:85–97.

Martinez, M. and D. Bordat. 1996. Note on the occurrence of *Liriomyza sativae* Blanchard in Sudan and Cameroon (Diptera: Agromyzidae) (in French). *Bulletin de la Societé Entomologique de France*. 101 (1):71-73.

Minkenberg, O. P. J. M. 1988a. Dispersal of *Liriomyza trifolii*. *Bulletin OEPP/EPPO* 18:173–82.

———. 1988b. Life history of the agromyzid fly *Liriomyza trifolii* on tomato at different temperatures. *Entomologia Experimentalis et Applicata* 48:73–84.

———. 1989. Temperature effects on the life history of the eulophid wasp *Diglyphus isaea*, an ectoparasitoid of leafminers (*Liriomyza* spp.), on tomatoes. *Annals of Applied Biology* 115:381–97.

———. 1990. Reproduction of *Dacnusa sibirica* (Hymenoptera: Braconidae), an endoparasitoid of the leafminer *Liriomyza bryoniae* (Diptera: Agromyzidae), on tomatoes, at constant temperatures. *Environmental Entomology* 19:625–9.

Minkenberg, O. P. J. M., and C. A. J. Helderman. 1990. Effects of temperature on the life history of *Liriomyza bryoniae* (Diptera: Agromyzidae) on tomato. *Journal of Economic Entomology* 83:117–25.

Minkenberg, O. P. J. M., and J. C. van Lenteren. 1986. The leaf miners *Liriomyza bryoniae* and *L. trifolii* (Diptera: Agromyzidae), their parasites and host plants: A review. *University of Wageningen papers*, 86(2):1-50.

Parrella, M. P. 1984. Insect pest management: The lesson of *Liriomyza*. *Bulletin of the Entomological Society of America* 30:22–5.

Petitt, F. L., and D. O. Wietlisbach. 1993. Effects of host instar and size on parasitization efficiency and life history parameters of *Opius dissutus*. *Entomologia Experimentalis et Applicata* 66:227–36.

Petitt, F. L., T. C. J. Turlings, and S. P. Wolf. 1992. Adult experience modifies attraction of the leafminer parasitoid *Opius dissitus* (Hymenoptera: Braconidae) to volatile semiochemicals. *Journal of Insect Behavior* 5:623–34.

Raman, K. V. 1988. Integrated insect management for potatoes in developing countries. *Centro Internacional de la Papa (C.I.P.) Circular* 16:1–8.

Rauf, A., B. M. Shepard, and M. W. Johnson. 2000. Leafminers in vegetables, ornamental plants and weeds in Indonesia: surveys of host crops, species composition and parasitoids. *International Journal of Pest Mangagement* 46 (4): 257-266.

Safjanov, S. P., and J. J. Skripnik. 1968. The solanaceous miner (in Russian). *Zaschita Rastenii* 13:51.

Sampson, C., and P. Walker. 1998. Improved control of *Liriomyza bryoniae* using an action threshold for the release of *Diglyphus isaea* in protected tomato crops. *Mededelingen van de Faculteit Landbouwwetenschappen Rijksuniversiteit Gewt*, 63(2b):415-422.

Schuster, D. J., J. P. Jones, and P. H. Everett. 1976. Effect of leafminer control on tomato yield. *Proceedings of the Florida State Horticultural Society* 89:154–6.

Shepard, M., Samsudin, and A. R. Braun. 1998. Seasonal incidence of *Liriomyza huidobrensis* (Diptera: Agromyzidae) and its parasitoids on vegetables in Indonesia. *International Journal of Pest Management*. 44 (1): 43-47.

Sher, R. B., M. P. Parrella, and H. K. Kaya. 2000. Biological control of the leafminer *Liriomyza trifolii* (Burgess): implications for intraguild predation between *Diglyphus begini* Ashmead and *Steinernema carpocapsae* (Weiser). *Biologiacal Control*. 17(2):155-163.

Spencer, K. A. 1973. *Agromyzidae (Diptera) of Economic Importance*. Series Entomologica, vol. 9. The Hague, the Netherlands: Dr. W. Junk B.V.

———. 1990. *Host Specialization in the World Agromyzidae (Diptera)*. Series Entomologica, vol. 45. Dordrecht, the Netherlands: Kluwer Academic Publishers.

Spencer, K. A., and G. C. Steyskal. 1986. *Manual of the Agromyzidae (Diptera) of the United States*. U.S. Department of Agriculture Handbook No. 638.

Stacey, D. L. 1983. The effect of artificial defoliation on the yield of tomato plants and its relevance to pest damage. *Journal of Horticultural Science* 58:117–20.

Toscano, N. C., F. V. Sances, M. W. Johnson, and L. F. LaPre. 1982. Effects of various pesticides on lettuce physiology and yield. *Journal of Economic Entomology* 75:738–41.

Trumble, J. T., I. P. Ting, and L. Bates. 1985. Analysis of physiological, growth, and yield responses of celery to *Liriomyza trifolii*. *Entomologia Experimentalis et Applicata* 38:15–21.

van der Linden, A. 1986. Addition of the exotic leafminer parasites *Chrysocharis parksi* and *Opius dimidiatus* to the native Dutch parasite complex on tomato. *Mededelingen Faculteit Landbouwwetenschappen, Rijksuniversiteit Gent* 51 (3a):1009–16.

———. 1988. Searching capacity and seasonal dependency of parasites of *Liriomyza bryoniae* (Kalt.) and *Liriomyza trifolii* (Burgess) (Diptera: Agromyzidae). *Mededelingen Faculteit Landbouwwetenschappen, Rijksuniversiteit Gent* 53 (3a):955–60.

———. 1990a. Prospects for the biological control of *Liriomyza huidobrensis* (Blanchard), a new leafminer for Europe. *IOBC/WPRS Bulletin* 13 (5):100–3.

———. 1990b. Survival of the leafminer parasitoids *Chrysocharis oscinidis* Ashmead and *Opius pallipes* Wesmael after cold storage of host pupae. *Mededelingen Faculteit Landbouwwetenschappen, Rijksuniversiteit Gent* 55 (2a):355–60.

———. 1991. Biological control of the leafminer *Liriomyza huidobrensis* (Blanchard) in Dutch glasshouse tomatoes. *Mededelingen Faculteit Landbouwwetenschappen, Rijksuniversiteit Gent* 56 (2a):265–71.

———. 1992. *Phytomyza caulinaris* Hering, an alternative host for the development of an open rearing system for parasitoids of *Liriomyza* species. *Proceedings of the Section Experimental and Applied Entomology of the Netherlands Entomological Society* 3:31–9.

———. 1993a. Overwintering of *Liriomyza bryoniae* and *Liriomyza huidobrensis* (Diptera: Agromyzidae) in the Netherlands. *Proceedings of the Section Experimental and Applied Entomology of the Netherlands Entomological Society* 4:145–50.

———. 1993b. Biological control of leafminers in glasshouse lettuce. *Liriomyza Conference on Leafmining Flies in Cultivated Plants, Montpellier, France (March 1993), Centre de Cooperation Internationale en Recherche Agronomique pour le Developement (CIRAD)*, 157–62.

———. 1993c. Development of an IPM program in leafy and tuberous crops with *Liriomyza huidobrensis* as a key pest. *IOBC/WPRS Bulletin* 16 (2):93–5.

———. 1994. Can biological control of *Liriomyza* spp. in glasshouse crops be improved? *Mededelingen Faculteit Landbouwwetenschappen, Rijksuniversiteit Gent* 59 (2a):297–303.

van der Staay, M. 1992. Chemical control of the larvae of the leafminer *Liriomyza huidobrensis* (Blanchard) in lettuce. *Mededelingen Faculteit Landbouwwetenschappen, Rijksuniversiteit Gent* 57 (2b):473–8.

Wang, C. L., and F. C. Lin. 1988. A newly invaded insect pest *Liromyza trifolii* (Diptera: Agromyzidae) in Taiwan. *Journal of Agricultural Research of China* 37:453–7.

Wang-Jian Wen, Zhang-Zhi-Ying, She-Yu Ping. 1998. Flight and daily activity of *Liriomyza huidobrensis* (in Chinese). 24 (5):3-4.

Wardlow, L. R. 1984. Monitoring the activity of tomato leaf miner (*Liriomyza bryoniae* Kalt.) and its parasites in commercial glasshouses in southern England. *Mededelingen Faculteit Landbouwwetenschappen, Rijksuniversiteit Gent* 49 (3a):781–91.

Weintraub, P. G., and A. R. Horrowitz. 1998. Effects of translaminar versus conventional insecticides on *Liriomyza huidobrensis* (Diptera: Agromyzidae) and *Diglyphus isaea* (Hymenoptera: Eulophidae) populations in celery. *Journal of Economic Entomology*. 91 (5):1180-1185.

Williams, E. C., and K. F. A. Walters. 2000. Foliar application of the entomopathogenic nematode *Steinernema feltiae* against leafminers on vegetables. *Biocontrol Science and Technology* 10 (1):61-70.

Woets, J. 1985. Tomatoes. In *Biological Pest Control: The Glasshouse Experience*, ed. N.W. Hussey and N.E.A. Scopes, 166–74. Poole, U.K.: Blandford Press (Ithaca, N.Y.: Cornell University Press).

Wolk, J. O., D. W. Kretchman, and D. G. Ortega Jr. 1983. Response of tomato plants to defoliation. *Ohio Report* 68:87–9.

Wyatt, I. J., M. S. Ledieu, D. L. Stacey, and P. F. White. 1984. Crop loss due to pests: Tomato leafminer. *Glasshouse Crops Research Institute Annual Report 1982*: 88–9.

Zhuang-BingLiang. 1998. The preliminary study on the genetic generations and living habit on *Liriomyza sativae* Blanchard (in Chinese). *Journal of Henan Agricultural Sciences*. 9:22.

Zúñiga, H. R., T. Zoebisch, and M. Carballo. 1991. Ciclo de vida y preferencia alimentaria de *Liriomyza huidobrensis* (Blanchard) (Diptera: Agromyzidae) en papa, apio, y cinco malezas importantes en Cartago, Costa Rica. *Manejo Integrado de Plagas (Costa Rica)* 22:1–4.

14

BIOLOGICAL CONTROL OF THRIPS ON ORNAMENTAL CROPS

H. F. Brødsgaard
Department of Crop Protection
Danish Institute of Agricultural Sciences, Research Centre Flakkebjerg
Slagelse, Denmark

Thrips are insects belonging to the family Thysanoptera, which includes more than 5,000 described species, mainly from tropical and subtropical regions. Of these 5,000 species, approximately half are phytophagous, with the other half feeding mainly on fungal hyphae or fungal spores. Of the phytophagous species, approximately 30 species have pest status, and of these, only a handful may cause serious economic damage in protected crops (Mound and Teulon 1995). Despite the limited number of pest species, thrips are the major pest of protected crops in Europe, the United States, and Southeast Asia. The pest status of thrips is mainly due to the spread of insecticide-resistant tropical or subtropical polyphagous species into greenhouse operations worldwide.

The economically important thrips species belong the suborder Terebrantia, and they each develop through six characteristic life stages: egg, two larval instars, prepupa, pupa, and adult. The kidney-shaped eggs are embedded singly in plant tissue by means of the female sawlike ovipositor, and, as a result, are protected from predators or pesticides. The two feeding larval instars live on various parts of their host plants; exactly which parts depends on the species of thrips and host plant. The nonfeeding pupal stages are normally found in the litter or the topsoil layer. The adults of the pest species in protected crops all have a slender body with a length of 0.04 to 0.1 inch (1.0 to 2.5 mm). Adults are winged, but are rather weak fliers, as exemplified by the inability of *Frankliniella occidentalis* (Pergande) to navigate properly in wind speeds above 0.72 ft. per second (0.22 m per second) or to make upwind flights in wind speeds above 1.44 ft. per second (0.44 m per second) (Hollister, Cameron, and Teulon 1995). Depending on species and biotype, adult females may reproduce by thelytoky or by facultative arrhenotoky. Furthermore, most pestiferous thrips species are polyphagous on both flower and leaf tissue, produce many offspring, have a short generation time, reach reproductive maturity early within the adult stage, exhibit parthenogenesis, and lack diapause.

The larvae and adults of all pest thrips use a similar "punch and suck" feeding technique, whereby the single mandible punches a hole in the plant surface, through which the paired maxillary stylets are then inserted and the liquid contents drawn through (Chisholm and Lewis 1984, Heming 1993). The damage to plant tissues resulting directly from this feeding consists of gray or silvery chlorotic spots on infested plant parts. This type of damage can reduce the photosynthetic activity of tissues, distort growth when feeding occurs within the meristematic tissues, or simply reduce the aesthetic value of affected plants. In addition, several of the most damaging pest thrips are vectors of plant viruses of the family Tospoviridae. Several of these viruses are especially devastating to crops grown within protected culture; they include tomato spotted wilt virus (TSWV), impatiens necrotic spot virus (INSV), and peanut bud necrosis virus (PBNV) (Garman, Ullman, and Moyer 1992; Lakshmi et al. 1995).

The interest in biological thrips control among greenhouse growers worldwide has recently increased due to lack of effective pesticides for control of this pest (Immaraju and Morse 1990, Immaraju et al. 1992, Brødsgaard 1994). In addition, there are fewer insecticides registered for use in protected crops, due to decisions by chemical companies to withdraw pesticides with small profit margins and due to legislative restrictions on compounds that may be hazardous to the environment or human health. Furthermore, the availability of potentially effective natural enemies obtainable from commercial insectaries has increased greatly as well.

At present, there are no selective pesticides for chemical thrips control that may be integrated into existing biological control programs. The few active ingredients that are at least partly effective against resistant thrips species such as *F. occidentalis, Thrips palmi* Karny, or *Thrips tabaci* (Lindeman) are disruptive to biological pest control programs using arthropod predators or parasitoids. Hence, effective biological thrips control is essential for biological and IPM programs in crops where thrips are economically important.

The biology and behavior of the economically important thrips make biological control of these species difficult. Eggs are embedded in plant tissues, the two pupal stages normally occur in the litter or soil, and the remaining development stages prefer to inhabit various plant structures. Furthermore, the active larvae and adults normally have a thigmotactic behavior, meaning they prefer to be in tightly enclosed structures. The culmination of these traits makes it difficult for applications of contact chemical insecticides or fungal pathogens to be effective in controlling thrips. Due to the complex life cycle of thrips, it is usually necessary to use several different beneficial agents targeted at different life stages of the pest to achieve successful biological control. As a result, an effective thrips control program is likely to be very complex.

Economically Important Thrips Species

Mound and Kibby (1998) published a taxonomic key for identifying ninety-nine economically important thrips genera and species. While many of the species within the taxonomic key occur as pests in protected ornamental crops, most of them occur only as secondary pests and are easily controlled by insecticides. Biological control of a primary pest could be hampered or destroyed if insecticide sprays targeted against the secondary pest adversely affect the natural enemies acting on the primary pest. Thus, biological control of thrips species that are minor pests may be desirable if a successful biological control program for another key pest is already in place.

Three species of thrips are primary pests of ornamental crops. The western flower thrips, *F. occidentalis*, is the most important thrips pest in protected crops worldwide. Originally, this pest occurred only in the United States west of the Rocky Mountains, but during the 1970s and 1980s, it spread throughout the world to become a cosmopolitan pest of protected crops (Tommasini and Maini 1995). Several characteristics of this species explain why it is such an important pest. *F. occidentalis* is highly polyphagous, with at least 244 plant species from 62 families (EPPO 1989) as suitable hosts. This species is mainly a flower feeder, but it also readily feeds on leaves and stems. In addition, it is probably the most potent vector of tospoviruses (Wijkamp et al. 1995). Attempts to rely on chemical control of western flower thrips have frequently failed due to the pest's success in developing resistance to many insecticides relatively quickly.

The onion thrips, *T. tabaci*, is a cosmopolitan pest both in protected and outdoor crops. It probably originated in the Middle East, but currently there are two biotypes that differ in their method of reproduction. The original type has a 1:1 sex ratio and is found in field crops in the region around Iran (Bournier 1983). By contrast, the biotype infesting protected crops reproduces by thelytokous parthenogenesis only. The two biotypes also differ in relation to their respective host plant range and apparently in the ability to vector tospoviruses. In Poland, where both biotypes are present, only the bisexual type is able to transmit TSWV (Zawirska 1976). *T. tabaci* is mainly a leaf-feeder, but may also feed on flower tissue.

The palm thrips, *T. palmi*, originated in Sumatra, Indonesia, but has spread rapidly throughout the Pacific and Orient. It was first detected in 1978 in protected crops in Japan because of its apparent resistance to the insecticides being applied by growers at the time (Yoshihara 1982). Since that time, its geographic distribution has grown to include Hawaii, the West Indies, and Florida. Although *T. palmi* feeds on leaves of many different host plants, it is also a pest of some flowering ornamentals. In most cases, the severe damage caused by this species results from the scarring caused by its feeding. However, *T. palmi* is also a vector for at least two tospoviruses—peanut bud necrosis virus (Amin, Reddy, and Ghaneker 1981; Reddy et al. 1992) and watermelon silver mottle virus (WSMV) (Honda et al. 1989, Yeh et al. 1992).

Other thrips species may occur as pests of ornamental crops. These include *Echinothrips americanus* Morgan, *Parthenothrips dracaenae* Heeger, *Heliothrips haemorrhoidalis* (Bouché), *Hercinothrips femoralis* (Reuter), *Frankliniella intonsa* Trybom, *Frankliniella schultzei* Trybom, and *Frankliniella tritici* (Fitch). In comparison to *F. occidentalis*, *T. tabaci*, and *T. palmi*, these seven species have a relatively narrow host plant range and are susceptible to a wider range of insecticides. Biological agents can, however, control all of the aforementioned thrips.

Biological Thrips Control Agents

Many different organisms have been examined for biological control of thrips in protected crops, including predacious mites and bugs, parasitic wasps, as well as entomopathogenic nematodes and fungi. Some of them are presently in commercial production and are readily available for use in commercial greenhouse production in many countries, while others are still under investigation.

Predatory mites

The most widely used biological control agents for thrips in protected crops are predatory mites of the families Phytoseiidae and Hypoaspididae. Biological control programs using these mites were first developed for *T. tabaci* infesting vegetables grown in European greenhouses (see chapter 15) and were subsequently adapted to ornamental crops. In ornamentals, biological control efforts have been focused primarily on control of *F. occidentalis* after its introduction into the greenhouse industry in the United States and Europe during the 1980s. The difficulties in controlling this species with insecticides prompted many European growers to examine the use of biological control as an alternative to pesticides. The first attempts to control thrips biologically on ornamentals were made by introducing *Neoseiulus barkeri* (Hughes) or *Neoseiulus cucumeris* Oudemans (Acarina: Phytoseiidae) into greenhouses. These mites are predators mainly of first instar thrips larvae, and to a smaller extent, second instar larvae (Bakker and Sabelis 1989). Both *A. barkeri*

and *A. cucumeris* are easily mass-reared using mold mites, *Tyrophagous putrescentiae* (Schrank), as alternate prey in a substrate of wheat bran (Ramakers 1983). Because this rearing procedure is so inexpensive, releases of large numbers of these predators are cost-effective and compensate for the relatively low predation rates exhibited by these natural enemies.

Another predatory mite, *Iphiseius degenerans* (Berlese), has recently been introduced as a biological control agent for thrips. This species is nondiapausing and is capable of surviving and reproducing within dry environments (van Houten and van Stratum 1993). Because this species is able to survive solely on a diet of pollen, prophylactic introductions of this species are possible in crops where pollen is produced in sufficient supply or where it is augmented by external sources. *I. degenerans*, however, shares the same limited predatory capacity as the other two *Neoseiulus* species discussed previously. As a result, additional predatory species have been sought.

The soil-dwelling mites *Hypoaspis miles* (Berlese) and *Hypoaspis aculeifer* Canestrini are polyphagous and predate on the pupal instars of thrips that normally occur in the soil (Gillespie and Quiring 1990, Brødsgaard et al. 1996). *Hypoaspis* spp. have been commercially available for several years, since they have been shown to contribute to thrips control in protected crops. Because *Hypoaspis* mites are able to survive for very long periods in greenhouses without food, a single preventive introduction may contribute significantly to thrips suppression throughout an entire plant production cycle.

Predatory insects

Many insect species of different families are known to be predators of thrips. The polyphagous anthocorids within the genus *Orius* (Heteroptera: Anthocoridae) have proven to be effective biological control agents for thrips in protected crops. In addition, *Orius* species are rather inexpensive to rear, and, as a result, several Palearctic species (*O. majusculus* [Reuter] and *O. laevigatus* [Fieber]) and Nearctic species (*O. insidiosus* [Say] and *O. tristicolor* [White]) are currently available from commercial insectaries. Though small in size, the minute pirate bugs are larger than the thrips, and the bugs readily attack both thrips larvae and adults. All of the *Orius* species available from commercial insectaries are effective thrips biological control agents, and only small differences in their physiological and behavioral optima regarding environmental factors and host plants exist among them.

Other general predatory insects worth mentioning are lacewings (Chrysopidae), ladybird beetles (Coleoptera), predatory thrips (Thysanoptera), and mirid bugs (Heteroptera). Commercially available lacewing predators include *Chrysoperla carnea* (Stephens), *Chrysoperla comanche* Banks, and *Chrysoperla rufilabris* (Burmeister). Generalist predator beetles include *Hippodamia convergens* Guerin-Meneville and *Stethorus punctillum* Weise. The six-spotted thrips, *Scolothrips sexmaculatus* (Pergande), is a predator of mites and thrips, and the mirids *Dicyphus tamaninii* Wagner and *Macrolophus caliginosus* Wagner are generalist predators frequently associated with thrips. All of these predators are marketed for biological control of many pests, but they may contribute to thrips biological control when they become established in the crops.

Parasitoids and parasites

Parasitoids within the genera *Ceranisus* and *Goetheana* (Eulophidae) contain species known to attack thrips related to western flower thrips at the genus or subfamily level (Van Driesche et al. 1998). Most attention has been directed toward the larval parasitoids *Ceranisus menes* (Walker) and *Ceranisus americensis* (Girault) (Loomans and van Lenteren 1995, 1996; Castineiras, Baranowski, and Glenn 1996) as potential biological control agents. However, developmental times of the immature stages of *Ceranisus* are relatively long—twenty-five to fifty days, depending on the host species, if temperatures are in the 68 to 77°F (20 to 25°C) range, and much longer (up to 130 days) at temperatures below 68°F (20°C). The long developmental time of these parasitoids, relative to that of western flower thrips, limits their effectiveness as biological control agents. Further investigations of new species or races of thrips parasitoids, perhaps subtropical or tropical species, could lead to discovery of wasps with faster developmental rates that might be more effective.

Several species of nematodes in the genus *Steinernema* have been tested to assess their ability to kill developmental stages of western flower thrips in the soil. Results have varied, with 4 to 77% mortality in various tests (Tomalak1994; Helyer et al. 1995; Chyzik, Glazer, and Klein 1996). Tests with *Heterorhabditis bacteriophora* Poinar strain

HP88 have shown 36 to 49% mortality (Chyzik, Glazer, and Klein 1996). Because these nematodes have little or no effect in the habitat where adult and larval thrips are found (the plant's foliage and buds), they must be integrated with other natural enemies to provide effective thrips biological control.

In contrast to *Steinernema* and *Heterorhabditis,* the allantonematid *Thripinema nicklewoodi* Siddiqi infects but does not kill thrips larvae. Rather, thrips larvae live to become sterile adults that vector the nematodes (in their feces) into buds and flowers where thrips congregate. This biology suggests that *T. nicklewoodi* might be effectively transmitted within a western flower thrips population on plants. This nematode was the most common natural enemy associated with western flower thrips in California, the area from which this pest is believed to have originated (Heinz, Heinz, and Parrella 1996). In small-scale laboratory tests, a low-level inoculation of *T. nicklewoodi* reduced thrips populations 3.5-fold relative to an untreated control population within forty days of the inoculation (Mason and Heinz 1999). Greenhouse studies (Lim and Van Driesche 2004) have shown high rates of parasitism of adult female thrips (48 to 52%) and persistence for up to seven generations. This led to a reduction in adult female thrips but not of larval thrips.

Pathogenic fungi

Fungi are the most common microbes recovered from diseased thrips (Butt and Brownbridge 1997), which has prompted interest in their exploitation in biological control programs. Fungi do not have to be ingested to be infective; rather, they infect thrips directly through the cuticle after making contact with the pest (Charnley, Cobb, and Clarkson 1997). Isolates of *Verticillium lecanii* (Zimmerman) Viégas have been available commercially for many years in Europe for control of thrips and other greenhouse pests (Ravensberg, Malais, and van der Schaaf 1990; van der Schaaf, Ravenberg, and Malais 1991; Helyer et al. 1992). More recently, products based on *Beauveria bassiana* (Bals.) Vuill. have been registered for thrips control on ornamental, vegetable, and nursery crops in the United States. Another fungal species, *Paecilomyces fumosoroseus* (Wize) Brown & Smith, is registered (PFR-97) but is not presently available commercially. Among these fungi, *B. bassiana* and *V. lecanii* tend to be more active against western flower thrips than *P. fumosoroseus* (Brownbridge 1995, Vestergaard et al. 1995). Western flower thrips mortality from fungal infection is dose-dependent; the more spores that contact the insect, the more rapid the kill and the higher the rate of infection (Brownbridge et al. 1994, Vestergaard et al. 1995).

V. lecanii has been used to successfully control western flower thrips and several other insect pests on chrysanthemum (Helyer et al. 1992). Control was achieved by applying the pathogen every fourteen days and by artificially raising the relative humidity to above 95% for four consecutive nights following each application. Under these conditions, epizootics developed and controlled the insect population with no adverse effects on the crop. Good control of western flower thrips has also been achieved with a commercial preparation of *P. fumosoroseus* (PFR-97) (Lindquist 1996). Trials carried out in California, Maryland, and Vermont have shown that *B. bassiana* efficiently controlled thrips on rose, carnation, and potted sunflower and suppressed populations in chrysanthemum (Brownbridge et al. 1996, Gill 1997, Murphy et al. 1998). However, trials conducted in Texas on western flower thrips infesting potted chrysanthemum and African violet failed to detect any affect (Thompson, Krauter, and Heinz 1999).

Preparing for Biological Thrips Control

The seriousness of thrips as pests of ornamentals requires biological control practitioners to carefully review several issues that may greatly increase the opportunities for success. First is to consider prevention of pest infestations. In colder areas, thrips often gain entry into greenhouses by means of imported plant material. Many thrips problems could be avoided by establishing quarantine facilities at individual greenhouse operations. In warmer areas or in very dense greenhouse clusters, thrips immigration through open vents is a major problem. Although many trials have been conducted demonstrating the utility of insect screening in reducing pest problems, the small size and cylindrical shape of thrips requires the use of an extraordinarily small mesh size that can create ventilation problems. Should thrips successfully invade a greenhouse, their spread through the various phases of production should be hampered as much as possible. This is effectively done by physically separating the different production phases—mother stock, propagation, production, packing, and, if present, the sales depart-

ment and showroom. A thrips population within a greenhouse may be partially managed by eliminating weedy hosts, thereby reducing the pest's ability to survive and reproduce between crops.

A prerequisite for any successful biological control program is careful monitoring of the thrips population size and distribution in the greenhouse. That is done by scouting the plants for larvae and damage and by suspending blue sticky traps to monitor the adults. Only through reliable estimates of thrips populations can appropriate control actions be decided and release rates of beneficials be determined. Biological control programs based on release rates per unit area of crop are reminiscent of preventative pesticide programs and are not optimal for releases of predators or parasitoids. Natural enemies eat pests, not units of crop area.

Biological Thrips Control Programs

Biological control of thrips has taken longer to be achieved in ornamental crops than in vegetable crops. This is because of the major differences between the two cropping systems—most potted ornamentals have short production times and complex growing procedures—and because ornamentals are sold for their aesthetic value, very little cosmetic damage is tolerated on top-quality plants. Multiple pest species attack most ornamental crops, and hence they are treated frequently with many different pesticides. The number of registered insecticides that provide effective pest control is far greater for ornamental than for vegetable crops. Ornamental greenhouses are normally large, unbroken units containing polycultures with a mixture of plant ages, whereas vegetable greenhouses typically contain a monoculture of one crop of uniform age. Pest introductions into ornamental greenhouses frequently occur via imported plant material or immigration from surrounding areas, whereas the latter is the main avenue of infestation in vegetable greenhouses. Biological control is best used as a management strategy rather than for immediate control of a pest outbreak, because biological control agents do not have the same 'knock-down' effect that most pesticides have. This puts larger demands on growers' knowledge of pests and control agents and makes it necessary that growers include pest management in their overall production planning.

Very low levels of thrips are tolerated in most ornamental crops due to the extraordinarily low tolerance for pest damage in the marketplace. Because of this very low damage tolerance and because thrips occupy habitats from the soil to the apical meristem and everything in between, strategies involving multiple introductions of several different types of natural enemies are often needed for biological thrips control.

Cut flowers

Few examples of biological pest control programs established at commercial cut flower operations have been reported in literature. The reason for this absence stems from the lack of positive results from small-scale research evaluations. For example, Hessein and Parrella (1990) found that releases of *A. cucumeris* and *A. barkeri* were not able to suppress western flower thrips below a level of two to seven per chrysanthemum leaf, a number too high for this crop. In tests of *C. americensis*, Loomans and van Lenteren (1996) found thrips parasitism remained below 10% in a rose greenhouse over five months after an initial release of two thousand wasps. However, applications of commercial formulations of *B. bassiana* have provided promising results for thrips control in rose, carnation, and chrysanthemum (Brownbridge et al. 1996, Gill 1997, Murphy et al. 1998).

Cut gerbera has been the focus of much work, possibly because only the flower stems are harvested, allowing the vegetative part of the crop to be damaged by thrips without hampering the quality of the marketable part of the crop. *Orius* spp. seem to establish well in this crop, aggregate in the flowers, and provide effective thrips control in the flowers (Brødsgaard 1995). *Orius* spp. also establish well in chrysanthemum, but an intolerance of damage to the uppermost leaves in this crop make satisfactory control more difficult.

Biological control programs in chrysanthemum may be enhanced by the occurrence of partial host plant resistance against thrips that exists in certain cultivars (Heinz and Thompson 1997). By selecting for partial host plant resistance, the successful use of biological thrips control in cut chrysanthemum may increase with the agents presently available (de Jager et al. 1995). Selecting optimal crop cultivars for biological control programs is, on the other hand, not only a question of pest resistance, but also of beneficial acceptance. For example, successful establishment of *Orius* spp. varies significantly among rose cultivars and thus represents a serious obstacle to successful thrips control in that crop.

Potted plants

Compared with cut flowers, biological thrips control in potted ornamentals is even more difficult, as whole plants are sold (neither flower damage nor leaf damage is tolerated) and the production time is very short for most potted and bedding plants. For example, Smitley (1992) found that *O. insidiosus* was unable to reduce western flower thrips densities in marigolds below 3.5 thrips per flower, a density that greatly surpasses acceptable levels for this bedding plant. However, Fransen and Tolsma (1992) found that the release of one *O. insidiosus* per chrysanthemum plant every other week reduced thrips damage from 40 to 90% in the untreated controls to 5 to 20% in the *O. insidiosus*–treated plants. Also, Gill (1994) found that releases of *A. cucumeris* in bedding plants reduced the number of pesticide applications needed for western flower thrips control from 5.0 to 0.4 per crop. Trials in Massachusetts and New York (Van Driesche et al. 2002) suggest that *N. cucumeris* releases can suppress thrips in spring bedding plant crops.

Concluding Remarks

Regardless of the type of ornamental crop that is grown, the same assortment of natural enemies is applied to form the biological thrips control program. While different host plants may influence the dynamics of the thrips–natural enemy interactions, for biological control to be effective, growers must avoid taking a passive approach to the problem.

Growers must always be well informed of their pest problems and should utilize the following *keep-down* strategy if attempting to implement biological pest control (Brødsgaard 1995). The strategy includes the following key components: (1) correct identification of the key pests and their anticipated occurrence based on earlier experience; (2) prophylactic introductions of natural enemies targeted against the key pests; and (3) regular monitoring or scouting of the crop so natural enemy releases may be continuously evaluated and adjusted as necessary. The aim of this strategy is to never let thrips populations approach pest levels.

When releases of natural enemies are initiated onto young plants, pest numbers are usually low and natural enemy effectiveness is high since the plant surface area to be searched by the natural enemies is small (compared with later stages in the crop production cycle). As a result, relatively few natural enemies are necessary to achieve satisfactory thrips control, and the price of the biological control program remains comparatively inexpensive. Prophylactic treatments of ornamental crops are often cheaper than curative treatments later in the plant production phase.

A biological control program may start by trying to establish a pest–natural enemy equilibrium in the mother stock to ensure the lowest possible pest pressure in the subsequent potted plant production phases. If available, entomopathogenic fungi (*V. lecanii, P. fumosoroseus,* or *B. bassiana*) may also be applied to the cuttings, since the humidity requirements of the pathogens are usually met in these propagation areas. By starting the biological control program within the propagation area, the young rooted plants can enter the production area of the greenhouse operation virtually free of pests. The young plants are then treated prophylactically with a single augmentation of *Hypoaspis* sp. and/or by applying *Steinernema* spp., either by watering the nematodes into the newly planted pots or by mixing the nematodes with the growth substrate before planting. Then, biweekly prophylactic applications of *N. cucumeris* are made, making sure the mites are thoroughly distributed among all plants. Concurrently, careful monitoring of the thrips population by means of blue sticky traps and scouting of plants must be conducted in order to adjust frequencies or rates of *N. cucumeris* augmentations and to create a basis for eventual introductions of other beneficials. If the mites are not able to suppress the thrips, or if experience suggests that thrips may become especially problematic at a specific point within the crop cycle, *Orius* sp. may be introduced.

Implementation of biological thrips control requires a large education effort to change the attitudes of growers. Biological control is not a simple replacement of insecticides, but rather a wholesale change in the approach to pest management. Using the Danish system as an example, implementation of biological thrips control is possible, effective, and economical. Of the Danish ornamental potted plant growers, 30% have used biological pest control since 1995. In 1992, the average cost was US $0.14 per ft.^{2} ($1.50 per m^2), with a range of US $0.03 to $0.64 per ft.^{2} ($0.36 to $6.86 per m^2), depending on the crop and the effort put into pest scouting and monitoring. The more effort put into pest monitoring, the lower the cost for biological control.

References

Amin, P. W., D .V. R. Reddy, and A. M. Ghanekar. 1981. Transmission of tomato spotted wilt virus, the causal agent of bud necrosis of peanut, by *Scirtothrips dorsalis* and *Frankliniella schultzei*. *Plant Disease* 65:663–5.

Bakker, F. M., and M. W. Sabelis. 1989. How larvae of *Thrips tabaci* reduce the attack success of phytoseiid predators. *Entomologia Experimentalis et Applicata* 50:47–51.

Bournier, A. 1983. Les thrips. Biologie, importance agronomique. INRA, Paris: 128 pp.

Brødsgaard, H. F. 1994. Insecticide resistance in European and African strains of western flower thrips (Thysanoptera: Thripidae) tested in a new residue-on-glass test. *Journal of Economic Entomology* 87:1141–6.

———. 1995. "Keep-down," a concept of thrips biological control in ornamental pot plants. In *Thrips Biology and Management*, ed. B. L. Parker, M. Skinner, and T. Lewis, 221–4. New York: Plenum Press.

Brødsgaard, H. F., M. A. Sardar, and A. Enkegaard. 1996. Prey preference of *Hypoaspis miles* (Berlese) (Acarina: Hypoaspididae): Non-interference with other beneficials in glasshouse crops. *IOBC/WPRS Bulletin* 19 (1) :23–6.

Brownbridge, M. 1995. Prospects for mycopathogens in thrips management. In *Thrips Biology and Management*, ed. B. L. Parker, M. Skinner, and T. Lewis, 281–95. New York: Plenum Press.

Brownbridge, M., A. Adamowicz, M. Skinner, and B. L. Parker. 1996. Management of silverleaf whitefly and western flower thrips with *Beauveria bassiana*: Effect of spray techniques on efficacy. In *Abstracts, Society of Invertebrate Pathology 29*[th] *Annual Meeting,* Cordoba, Spain, 11–2.

Brownbridge, M., D. L. McLean, B. L. Parker, and M. Skinner. 1994. Use of fungal pathogens for insect control in greenhouses. In *Proceedings, Tenth Conference on Insect and Disease Management on Ornamentals*, ed. K. Robb, 7–20. Batavia, Ill.: Ball Publishing.

Butt, T., and M. Brownbridge. 1997. Fungal pathogens of thrips. In *Thrips as Crop Pests*, ed. T. Lewis, 399–433. Wallingford, U.K.: CAB International.

Castineiras, A., R. M. Baranowski, and H. Glenn. 1996. Temperature response of two strains of *Ceranisus menes* (Hymenoptera: Eulophidae) reared on *Thrips palmi* (Thysanoptera: Thripidae). *Florida Entomologist* 79:13–20.

Charnley, A. K., B. Cobb, and J. M. Clarkson. 1997. Towards the improvement of fungal insecticides. In *Microbial Insecticides: Novelty or Necessity? Proceedings of a Symposium Organised by British Crop Protection Council Held at the University of Warwick, Coventry, U.K. 16–18 April 1997*, 115–26. Farnham, U.K.: British Crop Protection Council.

Chisholm, I. F., and T. Lewis. 1984. A new look at thrips (Thysanoptera) mouthparts, their action, and effects of feeding on plant tissue. *Bulletin of Entomological Research* 74:663–75.

Chyzik, R., I. Glazer, and M. Klein. 1996. Virulence and efficacy of different entomopathogenic nematode species against western flower thrips (*Frankliniella occidentalis*). *Phytoparasitica* 24:103–10.

de Jager, C. M., R. P. T. Butôt, P. G. L. Klinkhamer, and E. van der Meijden. 1995. Chemical characteristics of chrysanthemum cause resistance to *Frankliniella occidentalis* (Thysanoptera: Thripidae). *Journal of Economic Entomology* 88:1746–53.

EPPO data sheets on quarantine organisms. 1989. No. 177. *Frankliniella occidentalis* (Pergande). *Bulletin OEPP/EPPO* 19:725–31.

Fransen, J. J., and J. Tolsma. 1992. Releases of the minute pirate bug, *Orius insidiosus* (Say) (Hemiptera: Anthocoridae), against western flower thrips, *Frankliniella occidentalis* (Pergande), on chrysanthemum. *Mededelingen Faculteit Landbouwwetenschappen, Rijksuniversiteit Gent* 57:479–84.

Garman, T. L., D. E. Ullman, and J. W. Moyer. 1992. Tospoviruses: Diagnosis, molecular biology, phylogeny, and vector relationships. *Annual Review of Phytopathology* 30:315–48.

Gill, S. 1994. Thrips management and biological control. *GrowerTalks,* October, 36–40.

———. 1997. You can control thrips biologically. *GrowerTalks,* July, 114–7.

Gillespie, D. R., and D. M. J. Quiring. 1990. Biological control of fungus gnats, *Bradysia* spp. (Diptera: Sciaridae), and western flower thrips, *Frankliniella occidentalis* (Pergande) (Thysanoptera: Thripidae), in greenhouses using a soil-dwelling predatory mite, *Geolaelaps* sp. nr. *aculeifer* (Canestrini) (Acari: Laelapidae). *Canadian Entomologist* 122:975–83.

Heinz, K. M., L. M. Heinz, and M. P. Parrella. 1996. Natural enemies of western flower thrips indigenous to California ornamentals. *IOBC/WPRS Bulletin* 19 (1):51–4.

Heinz, K. M., and S. Thompson. 1997. Using resistant varieties for chrysanthemum pest management. *GrowerTalks,* March, 82–6.

Helyer, N., G. Gill, A. Bywater, and R. Chambers. 1992. Elevated humidities for control of chrysanthemum pests with *Verticillium lecanii. Pesticide Science* 36:373–8.

Helyer, N. L., P. J. Brobyn, P. N. Richardson, and R. N. Edmondson. 1995. Control of western flower thrips (*Frankliniella occidentalis* [Pergande]) pupae in compost. *Annals of Applied Biology* 127:405–12.

Heming, B. S. 1993. Structure, function, ontogeny, and evolution of feeding in thrips (Thysanoptera). In *Proceedings: Functional Morphology of Insect Feeding,* ed. C. W. Schaefer and R. A. B. Leschen, 3–41. Lanham, Md.: Entomological Society of America.

Hessein, N. A., and M. P. Parrella. 1990. Predatory mites help control thrips on floriculture crops. *California Agriculture* 44:19–21.

Hollister, B., A. E. Cameron, and D. A. J. Teulon. 1995. Effect of p-anisaldehyde and yellow color on behavior and capture of western flower thrips. In *Thrips Biology and Management*, ed. B. L. Parker, M. Skinner, and T. Lewis, 571–4. New York: Plenum Press.

Honda, Y., M. Kameya-Iwalky, K. Hananda, H. Tochhara, and I. Tokashiki. 1989. Occurrence of tomato spotted wilt virus in watermelon in Japan. *Technical Bulletin ASPAC* 114:14–9.

Immaraju, J. A., and J. G. Morse. 1990. Selection for pyrethroid resistance, reversion, and cross-resistance with citrus thrips (Thysanoptera: Thripidae). *Journal of Economic Entomology* 83:698–704.

Immaraju, J. A., T. D. Paine, J. A. Bethke, K. L. Robb, and J. P. Newman. 1992. Western flower thrips (Thysanoptera: Thripidae) resistance to insecticides in California greenhouses. *Journal of Economic Entomology* 85:9–14.

Lakshmi, K. V., J. A. Wightman, D. V. R. Reddy, G. V. R. Rao, A. A. M. Buiel, and D. D. R. Reddy. 1995. Transmission of peanut bud necrosis virus by *Thrips palmi* in India. In *Thrips Biology and Management*, ed. B. L. Parker, M. Skinner, and T. Lewis, 179–84. New York: Plenum Press.

Lindquist, R. K. 1996. Microbial control of greenhouse pests using entomopathogenic fungi in the USA. *IOBC/WPRS Bulletin* 19:153–6.

Lim, U. T. and R. G. Van Driesche. 2004. Population dynamics of nematode transmission in western flower thrips in caged impatiens. *Biological Control* in press.

Loomans, A. J. M., and J. C. van Lenteren. 1995. Biological control of thrips pests: A review on thrips parasitoids. *Wageningen Agricultural University Papers* 95–1:89–201.

Loomans, A. J. M., and J. C. van Lenteren. 1996. Prospects of *Ceranisus americensis* (Girault) (Hymenoptera: Eulophidae) as a potential biological control agent of thrips pests in protected crops. *IOBC/WPRS Bulletin* 19 (1):95–8.

Mason, J. M., and K. M. Heinz. 1999. Potential for the biological control of *Frankliniella occidentalis* (Pergande) with a nematode, *Thripinema nicklewoodi* (Siddiqi). *IOBC/WPRS Bulletin* 22 (1):173–6.

Mound, L. A., and G. Kibby. 1998. *Thysanoptera: An Identification Guide*. Wallingford, U.K.: CAB International.

Mound, L. A., and D. A. Teulon. 1995. Thysanoptera as phytophagous opportunists. In *Thrips Biology and Management*, ed. B. L. Parker, M. Skinner, and T. Lewis, 3–19. New York: Plenum Press.

Murphy, B. C., T. A. Morisawa, J. P. Newman, S. A. Tjosvold, and M. P. Parrella. 1998. Fungal pathogen controls thrips in greenhouse flowers. *California Agriculture* 52 (3):32–6.

Ramakers, P. M. J. 1983. Mass production and introduction of *Amblyseius mckenziei* and *A. cucumeris. IOBC/WPRS Bulletin* 3 (3):203–8.

Ravensberg, W. J., M. Malais, and D. A. van der Schaaf. 1990. *Verticillium lecanii* as a microbial insecticide against glasshouse whitefly. In *Brighton Crop Protection Conference—Pest and Diseases 1990,* British Crop Protection Council, 265–8. Lavenham, U.K.: The Lavenham Press, Ltd.

Reddy, D. V. R., A. S. Ratna, M. R. Sundarshana, F. Poul, and I. K. Kumar. 1992. Serological relationships and purification of but necrosis virus, a tospovirus occurring in peanut (*Arachis hypogaea* L.) in India. *Annals of Applied Biology* 120:279–86.

Smitley, D. R. 1992. Biological control of western flower thrips with *Orius*, a predaceous bug. *Roses Incorporated Bulletin,* April, 59–64.

Thompson, S., P. C. Krauter, and K. M. Heinz. 1999. Battling bugs biologically. *Greenhouse Grower,* February, 26–34.

Tomalak, M. 1994. Genetic improvement of *Steinernema feltiae* for integrated control of the western flower thrips, *Frankliniella occidentalis*. *IOBC/WPRS Bulletin* 17 (3):17–20.

Tommasini, M. G., and S. Maini. 1995. *Frankliniella occidentalis* and other thrips harmful to vegetable and ornamental crops in Europe. *University of Wageningen papers* 95–1:89–201.

van der Schaaf, D. A., W. A. Ravenberg, and M. Malais. 1991. *Verticillium lecanii* as a microbial insecticide against whitefly. In *Proceedings of the 3rd European Meeting on Microbial Control of Pests: Meeting at Wageningen, 24–27 February 1991,* ed. R. H. Smits, 120–3. Alassio, Italy: International Organization for Biological and Integrated Control of Noxious Animals and Plants.

van Houten, Y. M., and P. van Stratum. 1993. Biological control of western flower thrips in greenhouse sweet pepper using non-diapausing predatory mites. *IOBC/WPRS Bulletin* 16 (2):77–80.

Van Driesche, R. G., K. M. Heinz, J. C. van Lenteren, A. Loomans,. R. Wick, T. Smith, P. Lopes, J. P. Sanderson, M. Daughtrey, and M. B. Brownbridge. 1998. Western flower thrips in greenhouses: a review of its biologial control and other methods. UMASS Extension Floral Facts, University of Massachusetts, Amherst, Masssachusetts, USA.

Van Driesche, R., S. Lyon, J. Sanderson, T. Smith, P. Lopes, S. MacAvery, T. Rusinek, and G. Couch. 2002. Greenhouse trials in Massachusetts and New York with *Amblyseius cucumeris:* effects of formulation and mechanical application. *IOBC/WPRS Bulletin* 25(1):273-6.

Vestergaard, S., A. T. Gillespie, T. M. Butt, G. Schreiter, and J. Eilenberg. 1995. Pathogenicity of the hyphomycete fungi *Verticillium lecanii* and *Metarhizium anisopliae* to the western flower thrips, *Frankliniella occidentalis*. *Biocontrol Science and Technology* 5 (2):185–92.

Wijkamp, I., N. Almarza, R. Goldbach, and D. Peters. 1995. Distinct levels of specificity in thrips transmission of tospoviruses. *Phytopathology* 85:1069–74.

Yeh, S. D., Y. C. Lin, L. H. Cheng, C. L. Jih, M. J. Chen, and C. C. Chen. 1992. Identification of tomato spotted wilt virus on watermelon in Taiwan. *Plant Disease* 76:835–40.

Yoshihara, T. 1982. An overview of researches on *Thrips palmi* in Japan. *Entomological Laboratory Publications*. Kurume, Japan: Kurume Vegetable Experimental Substation.

Zawirska, I. 1976. Untersuchungen über zwei biologische Typen von *Thrips tabaci* Lind. (Thysanoptera: Thripidae) in der VR Polen. *Archiv Phytopathologie Pflanzenschutz* 12:411–22.

15

BIOLOGICAL CONTROL OF THRIPS ON VEGETABLE CROPS

J. L. Shipp
Agriculture and Agri-Food Canada
Greenhouse and Processing Crops Research Centre
Harrow, Ontario, Canada

and

P. M. J. Ramakers
Applied Plant Research WUR, Division Glasshouse Horticulture
Naaldwijk, The Netherlands

Pest Thrips and Their Damage

Three species of thrips are major pests of greenhouse vegetable crops: western flower thrips (*Frankliniella occidentalis* [Pergande]), onion thrips (*Thrips tabaci* Lindeman), and palm thrips (*Thrips palmi* Karny). Several other species can cause sporadic pest problems, but are generally more of a problem in ornamentals (see chapter 14). For a description of the geographic distribution, basic biology, and host plant range of the major pest thrips, see chapter 14. Populations of *T. tabaci* and *T. palmi* seem to be of one single strain or biotype worldwide. In contrast, there seem to be several biotypes of *F. occidentalis* (Mound 1997). For example, a damaging strain of *F. occidentalis* invaded New Zealand greenhouses in 1993, but for the previous sixty years, a morphologically identical form had been present outdoors, mainly on lupine (Mound and Teulon 1995). In

Canada, populations of *F. occidentalis* in Ontario and Quebec can be serious pests of tomato, but populations of the same species found in British Columbia (and many other tomato-producing regions of the world) are not pests on that crop.

Thrips can cause economic damage to greenhouse crops by feeding or ovipositing in plant tissues (leaves, flowers, or fruit). Thrips can also transmit plant viruses, leading to severe disease outbreaks. All thrips feed by pressing their mouthparts against plant tissue and using their single stylet to puncture epidermal cells. The two maxillary stylets form a food canal through which the liquid contents of the cell are sucked into the thrips' digestive tract (Kirk 1997). Each puncture into the plant tissue results in the destruction of an epidermal cell and several underlying parenchymal cells, all of which are usually killed by a phytotoxic substance that lyses the cell contents (Tommasini and Maini 1995). The result is cell dehydration and discoloration (Kloft and Ehrhardt 1959).

Damage symptoms on leaves resemble streaks or patches that are silvery white or light brown, usually on the undersurface of leaves. In tomatoes, thrips feed on the upper and lower surfaces of the leaves. These spots are accompanied by dark specks of fecal droppings from the thrips feeding. If feeding damage is severe, spots coalesce and the leaf turns brown, withers, and dies. In crops such as sweet pepper, feeding on young developing leaves can result in leaves being deformed when they unfold. Thrips will also feed in the flowers, causing brown spots in sweet peppers, or silvering or white spots in cucumbers. However, it does not seem that feeding in the flowers is correlated to marked or deformed fruit. Thrips, both larvae and adults, will feed on the epidermis of developing fruit. Feeding on the fruit surface results in a bronze or silver discoloration in sweet pepper and silver striations in cucumber. For tomato, bronzing and silvering are less obvious than for sweet pepper. Many growers consider deformation of young cucumber fruits (bending, curling, 'pig tails') as thrips-related.

Oviposition by adult thrips, especially *F. occidentalis,* can also damage the surface of the fruit. In tomato and sweet pepper, a halo-like discoloration develops around oviposition sites as surrounding tissue becomes white. In cucumber, this effect is less pronounced, with a small dark scar surrounded by a lighter green halo (Shipp et al. 1998). In sweet pepper, larval feeding under the calyx can cause the ends of the calyx to turn up, exposing the fruit to bacterial infections. Thrips feeding on developing cucumber fruit can result in curling of fruit (Howard, Garland, and Seaman 1994).

Thrips, particularly *F. occidentalis,* can also be excellent vectors of plant viral diseases of greenhouse vegetable crops. *Frankliniella occidentalis* is a major vector of tospoviruses, including tomato spotted wilt virus (TSWV) (German, Ullman, and Moyer 1992). This virus affects a wide range of host plants, including important solanaceous crops (e.g., tomatoes, sweet peppers, and aubergines). Symptoms of TSWV are bronzing of young leaves, one-sided distortion, severe stunting, and near cessation of growth. Bronzed areas usually roll inward and become necrotic. Fruit may develop spots about 10 mm (0.4 inch) in diameter with concentric, circular markings. Ripe fruit are often distorted with alternate red and yellow bands (Howard, Garland, and Seaman 1994). Another viral disease, watermelon silver mottle virus (WSMV), is transmitted by *T. palmi* and has been isolated from watermelons in Japan and Taiwan (Ullman, Sherwood, and German 1997). Symptoms of this disease include leaf crinkling and mottling, and yellow spotting on the leaves. Infected plants show severe stunting, short internodes, and tip necrosis. Fruit exhibit reduced size, distortion, and necrosis or silver mottling (Yeh et al. 1992).

The economic impact of thrips on greenhouse vegetable crops ranges from slight to complete crop loss, depending upon the level and duration of the thrips infestation. In sweet pepper, 150 to 500 thrips-days per sticky card (i.e., seven to twenty-four thrips per card in a twenty-four–hour period) from Weeks 3 to 5 before harvest will result in economic loss due to lower fruit quality from thrips damage to the fruit. Total marketable yield (kg) decreases when *F. occidentalis* larval-days exceed 1,800 per plant (Shipp et al. 1998). With cucumber, a mean density of sixty-five thrips per sticky card per day or ten adult thrips per flower will result in 5% of the yield being downgraded from grade 1 to 2 (Shipp, Wang, and Binns 2000). In the United Kingdom, *F. occidentalis* can cause up to 90% loss of summer-replanted cucumbers (loss of US $30,000 per acre [US $12,000 per ha] in 1996) (Lewis 1997), although improvements in biological control methods have made this level of loss less common. In tomatoes, fifty to seventy-five adult and larval *F. occidentalis* per plant was determined as the threshold for economic loss in fruit quality (Shipp and Wang 2003). When viral disease outbreaks occur, the whole crop may be lost because the recommended method of control for TSWV and WSMV is to quarantine the crop and destroy it to prevent further spread of the disease.

Thrips Biology in Greenhouse Vegetables

The life cycles for all greenhouse thrips pests are similar and have been described briefly in chapter 14. Median life span of adult females of *F. occidentalis* and *T. tabaci* at 77°F (25°C) on cucumber leaves is 20.5 and 11.9 days, respectively. The time from egg to adult for both species ranges from twelve to fifteen days at 77°F (25°C) (Gaum, Giliomee, and Pringle 1994; van Rijn, Mollema, and Steenhuis-Broers 1995). The oviposition rate for *F. occidentalis* is two to ten eggs per day, depending on the host plant and access to pollen (Howard, Garland, and Seaman 1994).

Certain aspects of the biology and behavior of thrips make these pests difficult to control (see chapter 14). Because the various life stages of thrips are found on different plant parts or on the growing substrate or ground, it is impossible for a single pest management measure to control all stages, especially given that some thrips life stages are found in small crevices or are concealed in plant structures. Studies have also found that certain stages of the thrips are able to withstand high temperatures and low humidities. The pupal stage of *F. occidentalis* is the most resistant of all the stages, and has 100% survival at temperatures between 59° and 86°F (15° and 30°C). At 95°F (35°C), survival for this stage decreases to 60% at a vapor pressure deficit (VPD) greater than 2.78 kPa. It takes a temperature of 104°F (40°C) and a VPD of 4.76 kPa for two to three days to control all stages (Shipp and Gillespie 1993). Lastly, the ability of *F. occidentalis* and *T. palmi* to rapidly develop pesticide resistance makes these two species very difficult to control with any insecticide, especially insecticides that are compatible with other biological control agents (Immaraju et al. 1992). Thus, when managing thrips, it is necessary to use more than one control measure, and sometimes more than one biological control agent.

Thrips Biological Control Agents

In many regions of the world, *F. occidentalis* and *T. palmi* are the most important obstacles to the use of IPM in greenhouses. As a result, considerable effort has been expended in searching for suitable biological control agents to suppress these pests. *Neoseiulus barkeri* (Hughes) was the first species used for thrips control in greenhouses, but *Neoseiulus cucumeris* (Oudemans) is now the most widely used species because it has been found to be more effective than *N. barkeri* on sweet pepper (Ramakers 1988). The rapid spread of western flower thrips throughout greenhouse production regions of the world stimulated researchers to study new kinds of predators, such as anthocorids that feed in flowers, where this thrips is most numerous. Various species of anthocorids in the genus *Orius* have been produced and sold for thrips control. Recently, other generalist predators in the families Miridae, Aeolothripidae, Chrysopidae, Coccinellidae, Nabidae, and Lygaeidae and some species-specific parasitoids have been used with varying success. Entomopathogenic fungi are sometimes recommended for additional control of thrips in cases where the humidity is high enough or can be raised artificially.

Predatory mites

When phytoseiid mites were first suggested as suitable predators for controlling thrips in vegetable crops in greenhouses, there was little scientific support for this idea. The mite species studied were considered to be predators chiefly of spider mites or soil-dwelling Collembola, which only occasionally fed on thrips. The breakthrough for biological control of thrips control came with the development of a mass-rearing method for phytoseiids based on the use of storage mites as substitute prey (Ramakers and van Lieburg 1982). Selection of a non-diapausing strain of this predator has further improved its effec-

tiveness throughout the season (van Houten et al. 1995b). More recently, orchard entomologists confirmed that phytoseiids are more important predators of thrips than was previously assumed, leading to the inclusion of more species in studies and finally the commercialization of *Iphiseius degenerans* (Berlese) (Congdon and McMurtry 1988, van Houten et al. 1995a).

Most predatory mites in the family Phytoseiidae are characterized by a relatively loose relationship with their prey and are considered opportunistic predators, attacking anything that they can physically overpower. Probably, predatory mites became natural enemies of thrips because they occupied the same niche as their prey. Host plant characteristics are of paramount importance in the successful use of predatory mites. The observation that *N. cucumeris* is more successful on sweet pepper than on cucumber is explained by the fact that pollen, which is continuously produced and released by sweet pepper, is used as food by the predator (De Klerk and Ramakers 1986; Ramakers, Dissevelt, and Peeters 1989). Therefore, a population of predators can be established long before thrips are present ("predator-in-first"), which produces more predictable control than curative releases.

Biological control of thrips with *N. cucumeris* was first recommended only for sweet pepper (De Klerk and Ramakers 1986). In this crop, complete colonization of the foliage is usually achieved after a single release. Introduction on a very young crop might be followed by a period without flowering, in which case a second introduction might be required. With progress in mass-rearing efficiency, inundative rather than inoculative releases became an option. Of special importance was the commercialization of "open rearing units" for introducing the predators, in which the last part of the mass-rearing process is done in the greenhouse (Ramakers 1990). In this system, the predator population's growth is supported neither by thrips nor by pollen, but by storage mites within the rearing units. These rearing units, or "sachets," contain bran, storage mites (which feed on the bran), and *N. cucumeris,* which prey on the storage mites. As the population density of *N. cucumeris* increases, the storage mites in the sachets are depleted, and the predatory mites leave the sachet looking for another food source. The potential production capacity of these open rearing units is enormous, and their use has allowed the introduction of predatory mites into crops that are less favorable to the predator than sweet pepper, such as cucumber, eggplant, chrysanthemum, pot plants, and bedding plants. Replacing the storage mite *Acarus siro* L. by 'straw mites' (*Tyrophagus* spp.) increases the productivity of the open rearing units, but creates a certain risk of plant damage , especially on young cucumber plants. Under greenhouse conditions, the life span of the open rearing units varies depending on their original content and the humidity in the greenhouse. Consequently, these units need to be checked regularly for the presence of living predators and replaced as needed. Shipp and Wang (2003) found that *N. cucumeris* dispersed from the slow-release sachets (1000 predatory mites per sachet) over a 4 to 5 week period under greenhouse production conditions for tomatoes.

Another species, *I. degenerans,* was found to be superior to *N. cucumeris* for use in sweet pepper when equal release numbers of the two predators were compared (van Houten and van Stratum 1995). This species benefits more strongly from pollen by actively visiting flowers; a dozen or more of these predators are commonly found in a single pepper flower. It has been demonstrated that the artificial addition of pollen to gynoecious cucumbers (sterile female plants) facilitates the initial establishment of this predator (Ramakers 1995). However, the effect of pollen on the interaction between thrips and *N. cucumeris* is less clear. It may be because cattail pollen is not a good food source for *N. cucumeris* or that this predator is not sufficiently attracted to leaves with pollen (van Rijn 2002). Due to the high cost of using pollen to mass-produce *I. degenerans, N. cucumeris* is still the more popular of the two species. Pepper growers make inoculative releases of *I. degenerans* (e.g., liberating a few thousand per hectare) in combination with the use of a million or so *N. cucumeris.* As a result, pepper crops are usually colonized mainly by *N. cucumeris* in the winter and spring, while in summer *I. degenerans* becomes the dominant species.

There is no reason to believe that the phytoseiids currently available for thrips control are the best possible species. Thus, researchers continue to look for better species or strains adapted to various crops and climatic conditions (van Houten et al. 1995b, Goodwin and Steiner 1996). As a result, an indigenous mite from Australia, *Typhlodromips montdoresis* (Schicha), is now commercially available for control of *F. occidentalis*

(Steiner and Goodwin 2002a). Also, *Amblyseius limonicus* Garman and McGregor, isolated from cucumber in New Zealand, is more effective than *N. cucumeris* if introduced in similar numbers, but has not reach the market yet because of the higher production costs (van Houten and van Lier 1996).

Greenhouse microclimate, especially temperature and humidity, can have a dramatic effect on the survival rate and predation response of predatory mites (Shipp, Ward, and Gillespie 1996; Shipp and van Houten 1997). Failure of biological control of *F. occidentalis* during winter months has often been ascribed to low survival rates and a reduced predation response of *N. cucumeris* under conditions of low humidity. Under controlled temperature and humidity conditions in the laboratory, it has been shown that the larval mite stage is the most sensitive to high temperatures and low humidities (Shipp and van Houten 1997). The critical VPD for 50% egg hatch of *N. cucumeris* varies from 0.8 to 1.3 kPa over a temperature range of 68 to 86°F (20 to 30°C). Because it is drought-resistant, *I. degenerans* is considered more suitable for hot, dry conditions.

Two soil-dwelling mites, *Hypoaspis miles* Berlese and *Hypoaspis aculeifer* Canestrini, and a soil-dwelling staphylinid, *Atheta coriaria* Kraatz, have also shown potential for control of the pupal stage of thrips (Brødsgaard, Sarder, and Enkegaard 1996; Carney et al. 2002). These predatory mites are used primarily for control of sciarid flies (Sabelis and van Rijn 1997; Carney et al. 2002). If used for thrips control, these mite species should be combined with other biological control agents.

Predatory bugs

Among the generalist predatory insects, *Orius* species (Hemiptera: Anthocoridae) demonstrate the greatest preference for thrips as a food source and have the highest effectiveness for biological control. The habit of the adults to search in flowers seems to make them ideal predators for flower thrips. Anthocorids, in contrast to predatory mites, can feed on both immature and adult thrips. These bugs are therefore faster in eliminating an established thrips population. The development time from egg to adult is, however, longer for anthocorids than phytoseiids, so their numerical response to a sudden pest increase is slower. In commercial greenhouses, it has been observed that after natural enemy numbers have been reduced by the use of moderately harmful pesticides, the anthocorid populations need more time to recover.

Orius species are mobile bugs that can move 26 to 43 ft. (8 to 13 m) per day after release in the greenhouse depending upon temperature and VPD (Zhang and Shipp 1998). The major drawback to the use of *Orius* species from northern latitudes (approximately >40° N lat.) is that the adults enter reproductive diapause under short day conditions. In the Mediterranean area, *Orius albidipennis* (Reuter) collected from the Canary Islands does not undergo diapause under short day conditions. However, life table and predation studies in controlled environmental chambers found that *O. albidipennis* would be more effective at high temperatures (95°F [35°C]) and *Orius laevigatus* (Fieber) at cooler ones (59 and 77°F [15 and 25°C]) (Cocuzza et al. 1997). Because many countries now require that all biological control agents used in that country be indigenous to the region, internationally operating biological control companies prefer species with wide geographical distributions such as *O. laevigatus*. Subtropical populations can be selected to avoid problems with diapause.

Thrips control with *Orius* species became popular in crops with pollen-producing flowers, including sweet pepper, eggplant, melon, and strawberry, and to a lesser extent in other crops, such as cucumber. Because of the high cost of the mass rearing, only inoculative releases are economically feasible, and usually a grower has to wait two generations before thrips control is achieved.

When mixed populations of phytoseiids or anthocorids are introduced in uniform ecosystems like greenhouse vegetable monocultures, one species usually dominates and displaces the other. Coexistence of an anthocorid and a phytoseiid species was found to be possible (Gillespie and Quiring 1992; Ramakers 1993), but predation by the *Orius* species on the phytoseiid (as well as cannibalism within the *Orius* sp. population) was very common. Many growers introduce both predators, assuming they will act as complementary control agents. In sweet pepper, *Orius* species are meant to control adult thrips in the flowers and reduce the pest population quickly, whereas the smaller phytoseiids are assumed to be better for removing thrips larvae from their hiding places underneath the calyx and thus to prevent immediate damage to the fruits. In addition, different responses to occasional applications of pesticides may be an advantage in IPM. For example, an application of pirimicarb against aphids affects phytoseiids more than anthocorids, but phyto-seiids survive better after the use of tefluben-zuron for caterpillar control. In either case, one predator species will persist and feed on the pest while the other species is recovering in number.

The search for indigenous natural enemies of greenhouse pests has recently led to the discovery of several new potential biological control agents for thrips. In Spain, many greenhouses are constructed with single-layer plastic and frequently with screened sides that are open during hot weather for ventilation. Under these conditions, many pests (thrips, whiteflies, and aphids) and natural enemies enter the greenhouses. Use of these naturally-occurring natural enemies is a possible strategy in the Mediterranean area. Surveys of outdoor vegetable and ornamental crops outdoors in the main greenhouse production area identified eighteen predatory insect species, of which two mirid species, *Dicyphus tamaninii* Wagner and *Macrolophus caliginosus* Wagner, were the most abundant and most widely distributed (Riudavets and Castañé 1998). Both show good potential as predators of thrips, and greenhouse trials with *D. tamaninii* on cucumber found that this species could control *F. occidentalis* at a predator-to-prey ratio of 3-to-10 (Castañé, Alomar, and Riudavets 1996; Riudavets and Castañé 1998; Montserrat, Albajes, and Castañé 2000). In Asia, *Campylomma chinensis* Schuh and *Campylomma livida* Reuter were recently identified as predators of *T. palmi* (Hirose et al. 1993, Wang 1995).

Pathogenic fungi

Thrips populations in greenhouses may be affected by fungi in the Entomophthoraceae.

Epizootics have been observed on eggplant in the Netherlands (Ramakers 1976), sweet pepper in Italy (Vacante, Cacciola, and Pennisi 1994) and cucumber in Spain (Montserrat, Castañé, and Santamaria 1998). Two species have been identified to date: *Neozygites parvispora* (MacLeod and Carl) Remaudière and Keller and *Entomophthora thripidum* Samson, Ramakers, and Oswald. Both are specialized pathogens not known to attack any hosts other than thrips. Such organisms are usually difficult to mass-produce and manipulate, and it is questionable whether they would be effective beyond the season of their natural occurrence. However, they are sometimes an important natural mortality factor, and IPM advisors should be able to recognize symptoms of infections by these fungi.

Other, less specialized insect fungi are potential control agents for thrips (Butt and Brownbridge 1997). Three fungi (*Verticillium lecanii* [Zimmerman] Viégas, *Beauveria bassiana* [Balsamo] Vuillemin, and *Paecilomyces fumosoroseus* [Wize] Brown and Smith) are registered as pesticides for thrips control in one or more countries. *Verticillium lecanii* was the first fungus to be registered for control of greenhouse insects. Laboratory and greenhouse trials have shown that *V. lecanii* can sometimes successfully control *T. tabaci* and *F. occidentalis* on cucumber (Binns, Hall, and Pickford 1982; van der Schaaf, Ravensberg, and Malais 1991). Its effectiveness, however, has been highly variable when evaluated across the many published trials.

The main reason for high variability in *V. lecanii* efficacy is likely due to variation in levels of humidity. Milner and Lutton (1986) showed that high humidity was critical for germination and multiplication of *V. lecanii* on its host. Manufacturers have made formulation changes to fungal pesticides in an attempt to develop a formulation that will be effective at lower humidities (i.e., use of oil formulations or addition of adjuvents) (Wraight, Jackson, and de Kock 2001). Some fungal pathogens, such *B. bassiana* and *Metarhizium anisopliae* Sorokin, are tolerant of drier conditions (Ramoska 1984; Lomar et al. 1994). Humidity at the plant surface, not ambient humidity, is the condition that most influences the effectiveness of these entomopathogens (Shipp et al. 2003). Fortunately, the humidity within the leaf boundary layer is often high (greater than 80% RH), depending on leaf architecture and conditions in the greenhouse.

The relative susceptibility of the different thrips life stages also affects the efficacy of entomopathogens. The egg stage is protected in the plant tissue and is not exposed to fungal spores on the leaf surface. The susceptibility of the larval instars is low due to molting of the exoskeleton, which can remove many conidia before they have a chance to penetrate the host cuticle (Vestergaard et al. 1995). This is especially important with *V. lecanii*, whose hyphae typically colonize the exterior surface of the insect before penetrating the cuticle (Schreiter et al. 1994). Efficacy is also influenced by the degree of exposure of the pest to the applied fungal spray. Thrips are known to prefer dark, constricted spaces and the undersides of leaves. Thus, it is difficult to get effective coverage in some areas where many thrips congregate, which include growing points, flowers, and the undersides of leaves. In addition, the pupal stage usually falls to the substrate below to complete its development, reducing its contact with spray applications. However, Helyer et al. (1995) found that applications of *M. anisopliae* to the compost or soil to kill the prepupal stage of *F. occidentalis* provided 75% reduction in the population density of *F. occidentalis.*

Entomopathogens should be viewed as "mycoinsecticides," which need to be applied several times for effective control, rather than as biological control agents that can be effective after a single inoculative release. These fungi are unlikely to provide effective control of thrips by themselves and should be integrated with other control strategies. Studies have found that *B. bassiana* is compatible with predatory mites and the immature stages of parasitoids (Jacobson et al. 2001; Ludwig and Oetting 2001; Shipp et al. 2003).

Miscellaneous natural enemies

A number of natural enemies of thrips have been studied that are either not very promising as control agents or require further investigation. Several commercially available species of nematodes (*Steinernema feltiae* [Filipjev] and *Steinernema carpocapsae* [Weiser]) have been shown in trials to cause mortality (75 to 97%) to the pupal stage of thrips when applied to the soil/peat based compost (Helyer et al. 1995). *Heterorhabditis bacteriophora* (Poinar) HK3 strain has also shown potential as a control agent for pupae of *F. occidentalis* (Ebssa et al. 2001). A thorough study of thrips parasitoids has been carried out by Loomans (2003), but the eulophid species studied (*Ceranisus menes* [Walker] and *C. americensis* [Girault]) were found to have limited potential for use in greenhouses. In sweet pepper and cucumber crops receiving reduced input of insecticides,

Echinothrips americanus Morgan (a species normally restricted to ornamentals) can also become a severe problem. Additional observations indicate that other panchaetothripine species such as *Heliothrips haemorrhoidalis* Bouché and *Parthenothrips dracaenae* Heeger may cause similar problems. These thrips species seem to escape predation by both phytoseiids and anthocorids. Hence, greenhouse experiments were initiated with *Franklinothrips* spp. because they were believed to be better-suited predators to these thrips pests (Loomans and Vierbergen 1999). *Franklinothrips vespiformis* (Crawford) was found an effective control agent for *E. americanus* but unable to *control F. occidentalis* (Ramakers, van den Meiracker, and Mulder 2000).

IPM Programs for Greenhouse Vegetables

Biological control programs for thrips on sweet pepper and cucumber are described in detail in chapters 26 and 27. The most common pest species in most regions is *F. occidentalis*. Species of *Orius* bugs and predatory mites (*N. cucumeris* and *I. degenerans*) are the most popular biological control agents used. A new predatory mite species (*T. montdorensis*) is used in Australia for control of *F. occidentalis* and *T. tabaci* on cucumber (Steiner and Goodwin 2002b). In Spain, natural populations of the mirid bugs *D. tamaninii* and *M. caliginosus* can invade the greenhouses and provide effective control of *F. occidentalis* on cucumbers (Montserrat, Albajes, and Castañé 2000). *Dicyphus tamaninii* complements the native *Orius* species because the mirid bug can establish in a crop at low prey densities and does not require pollen as an additional food source as do anthocorids (Castañé, Riudavets, and Yano 1999). In Asian greenhouses, *T. palmi* is the most important pest thrips. The usual control strategy in Asia is chemical control. Recently, studies have found that *Orius sauteri* (Poppius) is an effective control agent for *T. palmi,* and this species has been registered for biological control in Japan (Yano 1999). Japan, Korea, and China are presently making a concerted effort to develop biological control programs using native biological control species.

There have been few published studies detailing the economic cost of biological control versus chemical control in greenhouse crops. This is partly due to the rapidly changing prices of biological control agents (which often decrease as the efficiency of mass production improves) and to the variability in local prices due to supply and demand in different parts of the world (van Lenteren, Roskam, and Timmer 1997). In addition, it is difficult to estimate cost of labor when growers view their own time as free, or the actual economic benefit of increased fruit quality and yield when biological control agents are used. One component that is often not considered is the effect of chemicals on the ecosystem (soil, water, and air). In the Netherlands, a survey in the mid-1990s found that cucumber growers were spending approximately $0.09ft^2 (0.8 Euros per m^2) for control of all pests, of which 34% was spent on biological control. Jacobson (1997) has provided a review of the economics of IPM measures for thrips control on cucumber and sweet pepper in the United Kingdom.

References Cited

Binns, E. S., R. A. Hall, and R. J. J. Pickford. 1982. *Thrips tabaci* Lind. (Thysanoptera: Thripidae)—Distribution and behavior on glasshouse cucumber in relation to chemical and integrated control. *Entomologists Monthly Magazine* 118:55–68.

Brødsgaard, H. F., M. A. Sardar, and A. Enkegaard. 1996. Prey preference of *Hypoaspis miles* (Berlese) (Acarina: Hypoaspidae): Non-interference with other beneficials in glasshouse crops. *IOBC/WPRS Bulletin* 19 (1):23–6.

Butt, T., and M. Brownbridge. 1997. Fungal pathogens of thrips. In *Thrips as Crop Pests*, ed. T. Lewis, 399–433. Wallingford, U.K.: CAB International.

Carney, V. A., J. C. Diamond, G. D. Murphy and D. Marshall. 2002. The potential of *Atheta coriaria* Kraatz (Coleoptera: Staphylinidae), as a biological control agent for use in greenhouse crops. *IOBC/WPRS Bulletin* 25 (1):37-40.

Castañé, C., O. Alomar, and J. Riudavets. 1996. Management of western flower thrips on cucumber with *Dicyphus tamaninii* (Heteroptera: Miridae). *Biological Control* 7:114–20.

Castañé, C., J. Riudavets, and E. Yano. 1999. Biological control of thrips. In *Integrated Pest and Disease Management in Greenhouse Crops,* ed. R. Albajes, M. L. Gullino, J. C. van Lenteren, and Y. Elad, 244–53. Dordrecht, the Netherlands: Kluwer Academic Publisher.

Cocuzza, G. E., P. De Clerq, S. Lizzio, M. van de Veire, L. Tirry, D. Degheele, and V. Vacante. 1997. Life tables and predation activity of *Orius laevigatus* and *O. albidipennis* at three constant temperatures. *Entomologia Experimentalis et Applicata* 85:189–98.

Congdon, B. D., and J. A. McMurtry. 1988. Prey selectivity in *Euseius tularensis* (Acari: Phytoseiidae). *Entomophaga* 33:281–7.

De Klerk, M. L., and P. M. J. Ramakers. 1986. Monitoring population densities of the phytoseiid predator *Amblyseius cucumeris* and its prey after large-scale introduction to control *Thrips tabaci* on sweet pepper. *Mededelingen Faculteit Landbouwwetenschappen, Rijksuniversiteit Gent* 51 (3a):1045–8.

Ebssa, L., C. Borgemeister, O. Berndt, and H-M. Poehling. 2001. Efficacy of entomopathogenic nematodes against soil-dwelling life stages of western flower thrips, *Frankliniella occidentalis* (Thysanoptera: Thripidae). *Journal of Invertebrate Pathology* 78:119-27.

Gaum, W. G., J. H. Giliomee, and K. I. Pringle. 1994. Life history and life tables of western flower thrips, *Frankliniella occidentalis* (Thysanoptera: Thripidae), on English cucumbers. *Bulletin of Entomological Research* 84:219–24.

German, T. L., D. E. Ullman, and J. W. Moyer. 1992. Tospoviruses: Diagnosis, molecular biology, phylogeny, and vector relationships. *Annual Review of Phytopathology* 30:315–48.

Gillespie, D. R., and D. J. M. Quiring. 1992. Competition between *Orius tristicolor* (White) (Hemiptera: Anthocoridae) and *Amblyseius cucumeris* (Oudemans) (Acari: Phytoseiidae) feeding on *Frankliniella occidentalis* (Pergande) (Thysanoptera: Thripidae). *Canadian Entomologist* 124:1123–8.

Goodwin, S., and M. Y. Steiner. 1996. Survey of Australian natural enemies for control of thrips. *IOBC/WPRS Bulletin* 19 (1):47–50.

Helyer, N. L., P. J. Brobyn, P. N. Richardson, and R. N. Edmondson. 1995. Control of western flower thrips (*Frankliniella occidentalis* [Pergande]) pupae in compost. *Annals of Applied Biology* 127:405–12.

Hirose, Y., H. Kajita, M. Takagi, S. Okajima, B. Napompeth, and S. Buranapanichpan. 1993. Natural enemies of *Thrips palmi* and effectiveness in the native habitat, Thailand. *Biological Control* 3:1–5.

Howard, R. J., J. A. Garland, and W. L. Seaman. 1994. *Diseases and Pests of Vegetable Crops in Canada*. Ottawa, Canada: M.O.M. Printing Ltd.

Immaraju, J. A., T. D. Paine, J. A. Bethke, K. L. Robb, and J. P. Newman. 1992. Western flower thrips (Thysanoptera: Thripidae) resistance to insecticides in coastal California greenhouses. *Journal of Economic Entomology* 85:9–14.

Jacobson, R. J. 1997. Integrated pest management (IPM) in glasshouses. In *Thrips as Crop Pests*, ed. T. Lewis, 639–66. Wallingford, U.K.: CAB International.

Jacobson, R. J., D. Chandler, J. Fenlon, and K. M. Russell. 2001. Compatibility of *Beauveria bassiana* (Balsamo) Vuillemin with *Amblyseius cucumeris* Oudemans (Acarina: Phytoseiidae) to control *Frankliniella occidentalis* Pergande (Thysanoptera: Thripidae) on cucumber plants. *Biocontrol Science and Technology* 11:391-400.

Kirk, W. D. J. 1997. Feeding. In *Thrips as Crop Pests*, ed. T. Lewis, 119–74. Wallingford, U.K.: CAB International.

Kloft, W., and P. Ehrhardt. 1959. Zur frage der speichelinjektion beim saugakt von *Thrips tabaci* Lind. (Thysanoptera: Terebrantia). *Naturwissenschaften* 46:586–7.

Lewis, T. 1997. Pest thrips in perspective. In *Thrips as Crop Pests*, ed. T. Lewis, 1–13. Wallingford, U.K.: CAB International.

Lomar, C. J., C. Kooyman, C. Prior, and P. A. Shah. 1994. Influence of climatic factors on field performance of mycoinsecticides in grasshopper and locust control. In *Proceedings, VIth International Colloquium on Invertebrate Pathology and Microbial Control*, 289–91. Montpellier, France: Society for Invertebrate Pathology.

Loomans, A. J. M. 2003. *Parasitoids as Biological Control Agents of Thrips Pests*. Ph.D. Thesis, Wageningen University.

Loomans, A. J. M., and G. Vierbergen. 1999. *Franklinothrips*: Perspectives for greenhouse pest control. *IOBC/WPRS Bulletin* 22 (1):157–60.

Ludwig, S. W., and R. D. Oetting. 2001. Susceptibility of natural enemies to infection by *Beauveria bassiana* and impact of insecticides on *Iphesius degenerans* (Acari: Phytoseiidae). *Journal of Agricultural and Urban Entomology* 18:169-78.

Milner, R. J., and G. G. Lutton. 1986. Dependence of *Verticillium lecanii* (Fungi: Hyphomycetes) on high humidities for infection and sporulation using *Myzus persicae* (Homoptera: Aphidae) as host. *Environmental Entomology* 15:380–2.

Montserrat, M., R. Albajes, and C. Castañé. 2000. Functional response of four heteropteran predators preying on greenhouse whitefly (Homoptera: Aleyrodidae) and western flower thrips (Thysanoptera: Thripidae). *Environmental Entomology* 29:1075-82.

Montserrat, M., C. Castañé, and S. Santamaria. 1998. *Neozygites parvispora* (Zygomycotina: Entomophthorales) causing an epizootic in *Frankliniella occidentalis* (Thysanoptera: Thripidae) on cucumber in Spain. *Journal of Invertebrate Pathology* 71:165–8.

Mound, L. A. 1997. Biological diversity. In *Thrips as Crop Pests*, ed. T. Lewis, 197–215. Wallingford, U.K.: CAB International.

Mound, L. A., and D. A. Teulon. 1995. Thysanoptera as phytophagous opportunists. In *Thrips Biology and Management*, ed. B. L. Parker, M. Skinner, and T. Lewis, 3–19. New York: Plenum Press.

Ramakers, P. M. J. 1976. Preliminary observations on an *Entomophthora* sp. on *Thrips tabaci* Lind. in Dutch glasshouses. *IOBC/WPRS Bulletin* 1976/4:180–2.

———. 1988. Population dynamics of the thrips predators *Amblyseius mckenziei* and *Amblyseius cucumeris* on sweet pepper. *Netherlands Journal of Agricultural Science* 36:247–52.

———. 1990. Manipulation of phytoseiid thrips predators in the absence of thrips. *IOBC/WPRS Bulletin* 13 (5):169–72.

———. 1993. Coexistence of two thrips predators, the anthocorid *Orius insidiosus* and the phytoseiid *Amblyseius cucumeris*, on sweet pepper. *IOBC/WPRS Bulletin* 16 (2):133–6.

———. 1995. Biological control using oligophagous predators. In *Thrips Biology and Management*, ed. B. L. Parker, M. Skinner, and T. Lewis, 225–9. New York: Plenum Press.

Ramakers, P. M. J., M. Dissevelt, and K. Peeters. 1989. Large-scale introductions of phytoseiid predators to control thrips on cucumber. *Mededelingen Faculteit Landbouwwetenschappen, Rijksuniversiteit Gent* 54:923–9.

Ramakers, P. M. J., and M. J. van Lieburg. 1982. Start of commercial production and introduction of *Amblyseius mckenziei* Sch. & Pr. (Acarina: Phytoseiidae) for the control of *Thrips tabaci* Lind. (Thysanoptera: Thripidae) in glasshouses. *Mededelingen Faculteit Landbouwwetenschappen, Rijksuniversiteit Gent* 47:541–5.

Ramakers, P. M. J., R. A. F. van den Meiracker and S. Mulder. 2000. Predatory thrips as thrips predators. *Mededelingen Faculteit Landbouwwetenschappen, Rijksuniversiteit Gent* 65:343-350.

Ramoska, W. A. 1984. The influence of relative humidity on *Beauveria bassiana* infectivity and replication in the chinch bug *Blissus leucopterus*. *Journal of Invertebrate Pathology* 43:389–94.

Riudavets, J., and C. Castañé. 1998. Identification and evaluation of native predators of *Frankliniella occidentalis* (Thysanoptera: Thripidae) in the Mediterranean. *Environmental Entomology* 27:86–93.

Sabelis, M. W., and P. C. J. van Rijn. 1997. Predation by insects and mites. In *Thrips as Crop Pests*, ed. T. Lewis, 259–354. Wallingford, U.K.: CAB International.

Schreiter, G., T. M. Butt, A. Beckett, S. Vestergaard, and G. Moritz. 1994. Invasion and development of *Verticillium lecanii* in the western flower thrips, *Frankliniella occidentalis*. *Mycological Research* 98:1025–34.

Shipp, J. L., and T. J. Gillespie. 1993. Influence of temperature and water vapor pressure deficit on survival of *Frankliniella occidentalis* (Thysanoptera: Thripidae). *Environmental Entomology* 22:726–32.

Shipp, J. L., X. Hao, A. P. Papadoulos, and M. R. Binns. 1998. Impact of western flower thrips (Thysanoptera: Thripidae) on growth, photosynthesis and productivity of greenhouse sweet pepper. *Scientia Horticulturae* 72:87–102.

Shipp, J. L., and Y. M. van Houten. 1997. Influence of temperature and vapor pressure deficit on survival of the predatory mite *Amblyseius cucumeris* (Acari: Phytoseiidae). *Environmental Entomology* 26:106–13.

Shipp, J. L., and K. Wang. 2003. Evaluation of *Amblyseius cucumeris* (Acari: Phytoseiidae) and *Oorius insidiosus* (Hemiptera: Anthocoridae) for control of *Frankliniella occidentalis* (Thysanoptera: Thripidae) on greenhouse tomatoes. *Biological Control* 28: 271-81.

Shipp, J. L., K. Wang, and M. R. Binns. 2000. Economic injury levels for western flower thrips (Thysanoptera: Thripidae) on greenhouse cucumber. *Journal of Economic Entomology* 93:1732-40.

Shipp, J. L., K. I. Ward, and T. J. Gillespie. 1996. Influence of temperature and vapor pressure deficit on the rate of predation by the predatory mite, *Amblyseius cucumeris*, on *Frankliniella occidentalis*. *Entomologia Experimentalis et Applicata* 78:31–8.

Shipp, J. L., Y. Zhang, D. W. A. Hunt, and G. Ferguson. 2003. Influence of humidity and greenhouse microclimate on the efficacy of *Beauveria bassiana* (Balsamo) for control of greenhouse arthropod pests. *Environmental Entomology* 32: 1154-63.

Steiner, M., and S. Goodwin. 2002a. Development of a new thrips predator, *Typhlodromips montdorensis* (Schicha) (Acari: Phytoseiidae) indigenous to Australia. *IOBC/WPRS Bulletin* 25 (1): 245-7.

Steiner, M., and S. Goodwin. 2002b. Management of thrips on cucumbers with *Typhlodromips montdorensis* (Schicha) (Acari: Phytoseiidae). *IOBC/WPRS Bulletin* 25 (1): 249-52.

Tommasini, M. G., and S. Maini. 1995. *Frankliniella occidentalis* and other thrips harmful to vegetable and ornamental crops in Europe. *University of Wageningen papers* 95-1:89–201.

Ullman, D. E., J. L. Sherwood, and T. L. German. 1997. Thrips as vectors of plant pathogens. In *Thrips as Crop Pests*, ed. T. Lewis, 539–65. Wallingford, U.K.: CAB International.

Vacante, V., S. O. Cacciola, and A. M. Pennisi. 1994. Epizootiological study of *Neozygites parvispora* (Zygomycota: Entomophthoraceae) in a population of *Frankliniella occidentalis* (Thysanoptera: Thripidae) on pepper in Sicily. *Entomophaga* 39:123–30.

van der Schaaf, D. A., W. J. Ravensberg, and M. Malais. 1991. *Verticillium lecanii* as a microbial insecticide against whitefly. *IOBC/WPRS Bulletin* 14 (7):120–3.

van Houten, Y. M., P. C. J. van Rijn, L. K. Tanigoshi, P. van Stratum, and J. Bruin. 1995a. Preselection of predatory mites to improve year-round biological control of western flower thrips in greenhouse crops. *Entomologia Experimentalis et Applicata* 74:225–34.

van Houten, Y. M., and P. van Stratum. 1995. Control of western flower thrips on sweet pepper in winter with *Amblyseius cucumeris* (Oudemans) and *A. degenerans* Berlèse. In *Thrips Biology and Management,* ed. B. L. Parker, M. Skinner, and T. Lewis, 245–8. New York: Plenum Press.

van Houten, Y. M., P. van Stratum, J. Bruin, and A. Veerman. 1995b. Selection for non-diapause in *Amblyseius cucumeris* and *Amblyseius barkeri* and exploration of the effectiveness of selected strains for thrips control. *Entomologia Experimentalis et Applicata* 77:289–95.

van Houten, Y. M. and T. van Lier. 1996. Effect of temperature and humidity on survival of the thrips predator *Amblyseius cucumeris* and *A. limonicus* in a cucumber crop. *Proceedings Experimental and Applied Entomology of the Netherlands Entomological Society* 7:95-99.

van Lenteren, J. C., M. M. Roskam, and R. Timmer. 1997. Commercial mass production and pricing of organisms for biological control of pests in Europe. *Biological Control* 10:143–9.

van Rijn, P. C. J. 2002. The impact of supplementary food on a prey – predator interaction. Ph. D. Thesis, University of Amsterdam.

van Rijn, P. C. J., C. Mollema, and G. M. Steenhuis-Broers. 1995. Comparative life history studies of *Frankliniella occidentalis* and *Thrips tabaci* (Thysanoptera: Thripidae) on cucumber. *Bulletin of Entomological Research* 85:285–97.

Vestergaard, S., A. T. Gillespie, T. M. Butt, G. Schreiter, and J. Eilenberg. 1995. Pathogenicity of the hypomycete fungi *Verticillium lecanii* and *Metarhizium anisopliae* to the western flower thrips, *Frankliniella occidentalis*. *Biocontrol Science and Technology* 5:185–92.

Wang, C. L. 1995. Predatory capacity of *Campylomma chinensis* Schuh (Hemiptera: Miridae) and *Orius sauteri* (Poppius) (Hemiptera: Anthocoridae) on *Thrips palmi*. In *Thrips Biology and Management,* ed. B. L. Parker, M. Skinner, and T. Lewis, 259–62. New York: Plenum Press.

Wraight, S. P., M. A. Jackson, and S. L. de Kock. 2001. Production, stabilization and formulation of fungal biocontrol agents. In *Fungi as Biocontrol Agents: Progress, Problems and Potential*, eds. T. M. Butt, C. Jackson, and N. Magan, 253-87. Wallingford, U.K.: CAB International.

Yano, E. 1999. Recent advances in the study of biocontrol with indigenous natural enemies in Japan. *IOBC/WPRS Bulletin* 22 (1):291–4.

Yeh, S. D., Y. C. Lin, L. H. Cheng, C. L. Jih, M. J. Chen, and C. C. Chen. 1992. Identification of tomato spotted wilt-like virus on watermelon in Taiwan. *Plant Disease* 76:835–40.

Zhang, Y., and J. L. Shipp. 1998. Effect of temperature and vapor pressure deficit on the flight activity of *Orius insidiosus* (Hemiptera: Anthocoridae). *Environmental Entomology* 27:736–42.

16

BIOLOGICAL CONTROL OF APHIDS ON ORNAMENTAL CROPS

A. Chau

Biological Control Laboratory, Department of Entomology
Texas A&M University, College Station, Texas

and

K. M. Heinz

Biological Control Laboratory, Department of Entomology
Texas A&M University, College Station, Texas

Aphid Pests on Ornamental Crops

Aphids (Homoptera: Aphididae) are one of the most important pest groups on greenhouse ornamentals and vegetables. Fifteen aphid species are identified to be economically important to greenhouse ornamentals (Table 16.1). The most important aphid pests for ornamental and vegetable crops are melon or cotton aphid, *Aphis gossypii* Glover (Figure 16.1A); green peach aphid, *Myzus persicae* (Sulzer) (Figure 16.1B); and potato aphid, *Macrosiphum euphorbiae* (Thomas). These aphids are extremely polyphagous and vector a large number of plant viruses. Although the majority of the aphids are polyphagous, a few are found only on specific ornamental crops such as rose aphid, *Macrosiphum rosae* (Linnaeus), and chrysanthemum aphid, *Macrosiphoniella sanborni* (Gillette). Seven aphid species listed in Table 16.1 are classified as major pests on orna-

mentals because they are commonly found on high value crops such as chrysanthemum, rose, carnation, begonia, gerbera, and geranium (Table 16.2). The rest of the aphids are classified as minor pests either because they are found on other ornamental crops or they are only occasionally found on ornamentals. The list of aphids found attacking ornamentals is expected to grow as additional species or new cultivars of ornamentals are produced in commercial greenhouses.

Biology of aphids

Aphid control, in the past, relied heavily on the use of insecticides. When aphids such as *A. gossypii* and *M. persicae* developed resistance to numerous insecticides (Anthon 1955, McClanahan and Founk 1983, Furk and Vedjhi 1990, Furk and Hines 1993), biological control became an attractive alternative. For biological control programs to be successful, it is important to match the natural enemies to the pests. We will review two

Figure 16.1. Two of the most important aphid pests of ornamental crops are the green peach aphid, *Myzus persicae* **(Sulzer) (A) and the cotton aphid,** *Aphis gossypii* **Glover (B).** *Photos: Les Shipp.*

important aspects of aphid biology that are essential for evaluating and selecting their natural enemies.

Rapid reproduction

Aphids are important pests of greenhouse crops because of their extremely rapid reproduction. In greenhouses, most aphids are able to reproduce asexually (parthenogenesis) and continuously give birth to live female offspring (viviparous) that quickly contribute to further population growth. Rapid reproduction coupled with short developmental time enable aphids to quickly develop resistance to insecticides.

Guldemond, van den Brink, and den Belder (1998) showed that the growth stage of chrysanthemums influenced the population growth rate (r_m) of both *M. persicae* and *A. gossypii*. Cultivar, aphid species, and plant growth stage can interact to influence population growth rate. Under greenhouse conditions at 68°F (20°C), they found that r_m for the two aphid species were similar but higher on budding and flowering stages (r_m = 0.29 and 0.32, *M. persicae* and *A. gossypii* respectively) than the young vegetative stage (r_m = 0.21 and 0.27, *M. persicae* and *A. gossypii* respectively). Aphid population grew twice as fast during budding versus vegetative plant stages; however, *A. gossypii* had a shorter developmental time (number of days between birth and first reproduction) (7.1 days on vegetative plants and 7.6 days on budding plants) than *M. persicae* (8.4 days on vegetative plants and 9.5 days on budding plants). Information on the population growth rate and developmental time of an aphid species is important for developing predictive models for insect outbreaks. Furthermore, an aphid's population growth rate would provide a useful criterion for evaluating and selecting appropriate natural enemies. As van Lenteren and Woets (1988) and van Steenis (1992) suggested, natural enemies that reproduce and develop as fast as the aphid pest would be expected to provide better control than those that have a lower population growth rate.

Distribution and dispersal of aphids

Aphid species differ in their distribution and dispersal capability. *Aphis gossypii* tends to form obvious dense clumps in the floral terminals but *M. persicae* tends to be less tightly aggregated within the plant (Tamaki and Allen 1969; Vehrs, Walker, and Parrella

Table 16.1 Aphid Pests on Greenhouse Ornamentals: Distribution and Host Range[a]

Aphid species	Distribution	Host Range [b]
Major Pests		
Aphis gossypii Glover	Worldwide	Extremely polyphagous, attacks wide range of agricultural crops and many ornamental plants including *Hibiscus*.
Aulacorthum solani (Kaltenbach)	Worldwide	Extremely polyphagous, colonizing plants in many different families of both dicots and monocots. Found on ornamentals like anemone, arum, calceolaria, carnation, cineraria, dahlia, geranium, gloxinia, nasturtium, and bulbs (especially tulip).
Brachycaudus helichrysi (Kaltenbach)	Worldwide	Primary hosts are various *Prunus* spp. Secondary hosts are numerous species of Compositae (e.g., *Achillea, Chrysanthemum, Matricaria, Senecio, Erigeron, Ageratum*) and Boraginaceae (*Myosotis, Cynoglossum*) and sometimes in other families. Major pest of plum, sunflower, and glasshouse chrysanthemum in Europe.
Macrosiphoniella sanborni (Gillette)	Worldwide	Usually on cultivated florist's chrysanthemum (*Dendranthema indicum, morifolium, frutescens*); can be found on other Compositae like *Artemisia, Aster* in eastern Asia.
Macrosiphum euphorbiae (Thomas)	Worldwide	Primary host *Rosa* spp. Highly polyphagous on secondary hosts. Feeds on over 200 plant species in more than 20 different families. Recorded on many greenhouse ornamentals, such as abutilon, carnation, cineraria, rose, and tulip.
Macrosiphum rosae (Linnaeus)	Almost cosmopolitan except in Eastern Asia	Primary hosts are wild and cultivated *Rosa* spp. Secondary hosts are Dipsacacea (*Dipsacus, Succisa*). Occasional summer hosts include other Rosaceae (*Fragaria, Geum, Pyrus, Malus, Rubus*), Onagraceae (*Chamerion=Epilobium*), and Valerianaceae (*Centranthus, Valerianetta*).

(continued)

Table 16.1 *(continued)*

Aphid species	Distribution	Host Range [b]
Myzus persicae (Sulzer)	Worldwide	Primary host usually *Prunus* spp. Highly polyphagous on secondary hosts. Feeds on over forty different plant families including many economically important plants such as floral crops.
Minor Pests		
Aphis fabae Scopoli	Widespread in temperate regions of the Northern Hemisphere, also in South America and Africa	Very polyphagous on its secondary hosts. Recorded on citrus, carnation, dahlia, nasturtium, and tulip.
Aphis nerii Boyer de Fonscolombe	Widely distributed in the Old and New World tropics and subtropics	Mainly on Asclepiadaceae (*Asclepias, Gomphocarpus, Calotropis*) and Apocynaceae (*Nerium oleander, Vinca*), also occasionally found on other families like Euphorbiaceae, Compositae, Convolvulaceae.
Aphis spiraecola Patch	In North America, Mediterranean region, Africa, Australia, and New Zealand	Very polyphagous with numerous host plants in over 20 families but especially on Caprifoliaceae, Compositae, Rosaceae, Rubiaceae, and Rutaceae. Citrus is probably its most important host.
Aulacorthum circumflexum (Buckton)	Worldwide	Extremely polyphagous, colonizing plants in many different families of both dicots and monocots. Found feeding on ferns and conifers. It is common in glasshouses and a common pest of house plants (*Cineraria, Cyclamen, Fuschia, Zantedeschia*).
Dysaphis tulipae (Boyer de Fonscolombe)	Almost cosmopolitan, except in South America	Hosts include plants in Liliaceae, Iridaceae, Araceae, and Musaceae. *Iris* spp. are perhaps the most common hosts. Also found infesting outer skins of tulip bulbs, corms of gladiolus.

(continued)

Table 16.1 *(continued)*

Aphid species	Distribution	Host Range [b]
Myzus ascalonicus Doncaster	In North and South America, Europe, India, Japan, New Zealand, and Australia	Extremely polyphagous, colonizing plants in over twenty families, mostly on vegetables, also found on potted plants.
Rhodobium porosum (Sanderson)	Worldwide	*Rosa* spp., especially cultivated varieties and *Fragaria vesca*.
Toxoptera aurantii (Boyer de Fonscolombe)	In the tropics and subtropics and in glasshouses in temperate climates	Recorded on more than 120 plant species, especially in the families Anacardiaceae, Annonaceae, Araliaceae, Euphorbiaceae, Lauraceae, Moraceae, Rubiaceae, Rutaceae, Sterculiaceae, and Theaceae. Particularly damaging to citrus, ficus, gardenia, and camellia.

[a] Source information on distribution and host range were from Blackman and Eastop (2000) and Gill and Sanderson (1998).
[b] Host range includes both agricultural and ornamental crops.

1992). This behavioral difference coupled with coloration difference make *A. gossypii* (usually dark green or light yellow) easier to detect and monitor for than *M. persicae* (pale green). Although it has been suggested that *M. persicae* is more mobile than *A. gossypii* (Rabasse and Wyatt 1985; Vehrs, Walker, and Parrella 1992), Heinz (1998) did not find significant differences between the two species in linear displacement distances or planar areas of spread. Heinz (1998) further showed that both *A. gossypii* and *M. persicae* exhibited extreme clumping in space (s^2/mean>>1.0) among potted chrysanthemums in greenhouses. Such information is important when scouting aphid infestations, making efficient releases of natural enemies, or applying spot-treatment of insecticides.

Aphid Damage

Aphids feed by inserting their stylets (mouthpart) directly into the phloem to extract plant sap. When aphid colonies are large, their feeding can greatly reduce plant vigor and even stunt plant growth. Aphids can also cause indirect damage to the plants because they excrete excess plant sap or "honeydew" during feeding. Honeydew promotes the growth of black sooty molds that reduce plant vigor by interfering with photosynthesis. Most of the time aphid feeding does not cause significant damage to plants, but the presence of aphids, their cast skins, and honeydew may greatly reduce the aesthetic quality of ornamentals.

Aphids also vector many plant diseases. Viruses such as cucumber mosaic virus and lettuce mosaic virus, can infect both green-house vegetables and ornamentals and are commonly transmitted by *A. gossypii*, *M. persicae* and *M. euphorbiae* (Moriones and Luis-Arteaga 1999). Among aphid vectors of plant diseases, *M. persicae* is the most important because of its ability to transmit well over one hundred plant viruses (Kennedy, Day, and Eastop 1962).

Natural Enemies of Aphids

Aphids are attacked by numerous natural enemies that include parasitoids, predators, and pathogens. Only a few of these natural enemies have shown potential for controlling aphids in greenhouses because of their ability to locate aphid patches, kill aphids rapidly either by parasitization or consumption, and reproduce and develop as fast as the aphid pests. Even fewer of these natural enemies are available commercially because they may be difficult to mass rear.

Parasitoids

Aphids are attacked by female parasitoids from mainly two families of Hymenoptera: the Aphidiidae and the Aphelinidae. The Aphidiidae are exclusive endoparasitoids and often the most important group of parasitoids in many aphid control programs. This family includes many genera like *Aphidius*, *Ephedrus*, *Lysiphlebus*, *Praon,* and *Trioxys*. The adults are generally 0.08 in. (2 mm) in length and have a slender body shape. The Aphelinidae are parasitoids of many homopterans but only one genus, *Aphelinus*, is important for aphid control. The adults are stout bodied and smaller (0.04 in. [1 mm] in length) than Aphidiidae. *Aphelinus* species are also solitary endoparasitoids but, unlike

Aphidiidae, female wasps also attack and kill aphids by feeding on their haemolymph.

An effective aphid parasitoid should possess characteristics such as high reproductive capacity, short generation time, good dispersal capabilities, and a life cycle well synchronized with their aphid hosts (Mackauer and Way 1976). These characteristics are useful for pre-introduction evaluation of natural enemies (van Lenteren and Woets 1988; van Steenis 1992). For example, Guldemond, van den Brink, and den Belder (1998) showed that the population growth rate (r_m) of *A. gossypii* on greenhouse-grown chrysanthemums was 0.32 at 68°F (20°C); therefore, one would expect parasitoids that have a similar or higher r_m would be good candidates for controlling *A. gossypii*. Numerous studies have examined the development time, intrinsic rate of increase and searching ability of parasitoids; however, almost all these studies were done on greenhouse vegetable crops. Only one study was done on a greenhouse ornamental crop (Heinz 1998). Although the transfer of information generated from vegetable crops to ornamental crops requires caution, the criteria for selecting natural enemies should be similar. Future studies are needed to evaluate the efficacy of aphid parasitoids on greenhouse ornamental crops.

Aphidius *spp. (Hymenoptera: Aphidiidae)*

Van Steenis (1995) compared four aphidiine parasitoids for biological control of *A. gossypii* on cucumber and found *Aphidius colemani* Viereck (Figure 16.2) to be the most effective one. In the laboratory, *A. colemani* parasitized more aphids (72–80%) than *Ephedrus cerasicola* Starý (23%), *Lysiphlebus testaceipes* Cresson (26%), or *Aphidius matricariae*

Haliday (6%) when each species was given a fixed number of aphids. In greenhouses, *A. colemani* found significantly more aphid colonies and parasitized more aphids than *E. cerasicola* or *L. testaceipes*. At 68°F (20°C), *A. colemani* requires approximately thirteen days to complete development, lives for six days and has a lifetime fecundity of 302 eggs per female (van Steenis 1993). The intrinsic rate of increase (r_m) of *A. colemani* increased with temperature from 0.35 at 68°F (20°C) to 0.44 at 77°F (25°C) and was compatible to r_m of *A. gossypii* on greenhouse grown cucumber (0.35) (van Steenis and El-Khawass 1995). One would expect *A. colemani* to be able to match the population growth rate of *A. gossypii* on greenhouse-grown chrysanthemum ($r_m = 0.32$) which was slightly lower than that on cucumber (Guldemond, van den Brink, and den Belder 1998). Finally, Heinz (1998) showed that *A. colemani* was capable of spreading across 14 ft.^{2} (1.3 m^2) of greenhouse space within ten hours of its release and locating 96.9% of aphid-infested chrysanthemum plants.

    Aphidius matricariae is used mainly for biological control of *M. persicae* on sweet pepper and eggplant (Rabasse and Shalaby 1980). At 70°F (21°C), *A. matricariae* takes thirteen to fourteen days to complete development and has a lifetime fecundity of 309 eggs per female (Giri et al. 1982). The intrinsic rate of increase of *A. matricariae* ($r_m = 0.29$) might be comparable to that of *M. persicae* on greenhouse-grown chrysanthemum (0.29) (Guldemond, van den Brink, and den Belder 1998).

Ephedrus cerasicola *(Hymenoptera: Aphidiidae)*

Development time and intrinsic rate of increase (r_m) of *E. cerasicola* was studied on

Figure 16.2. An adult female *Aphidius colemani* Viereck female parasitizing an aphid. *Photo: Les Shipp.*

M. persicae (Hågvar and Hofsvang 1986, 1990). At 70°F (21°C), *E. cerasicola* takes seventeen days to develop and has a lifetime fecundity of 961 eggs per female. Female parasitoids have an average longevity of eighteen days. The intrinsic rate of increase of *E. cerasicola* ($r_m = 0.29$) might be comparable to that of *M. persicae* on greenhouse grown chrysanthemum (0.29) (Guldemond, van den Brink, and den Belder 1998).

Lysiphlebus testaceipes *(Hymenoptera: Aphidiidae)*

This parasitoid has been used for biological control of *A. gossypii* on cucumber. At 68°F (20°C), *L. testaceipes* takes thirteen days to develop from egg to female adult and has a lifetime fecundity of 128 eggs per female (van Steenis 1994). The intrinsic rate of increase (r_m) of *L. testaceipes* was 0.30 and might be comparable to that of *A. gossypii* on greenhouse-grown chrysanthemum (0.32) (Guldemond, van den Brink, and den Belder 1998).

Aphelinus spp. *(Hymenoptera: Aphelinidae)*

Compared to Aphidiidae, *Aphelinus* species have lower population growth rates and longer developmental times. Although adult females tend to lay fewer eggs per day, the potential fecundity of this group of parasitoids can be very high because they live much longer. Jarosik et al. (1996) studied the development of *Aphelinus abdominalis* (Dalman) on *M. euphorbiae* caged on young aubergine plants and found that at 79°F (26°C), female *A. abdominalis* lived twenty-four days and had a lifetime fecundity of 158 eggs per female. Host mortality due to host feeding is insignificant because *A. abdominalis* usually kill one aphid per day for host feeding (Hamilton 1973, Bai and Mackauer 1990).

Predators

Potential predators for aphid control come from five major groups: Anthocoridae (minute pirate bugs), Cecidomyiidae (predatory midges), Chrysopidae (lacewings), Coccinellidae (lady beetles), and Syrphidae (hoverflies). Unlike parasitoids, with the exception of *Aphelinus* species, predators consume more than one prey and their ability to control aphids depends on their predation rate, ability to locate prey, and their ability to increase in numbers as prey numbers increase. Voracity, the maximum biomass or number of prey consumed by a predator, usually sets limits to the predation rate when prey are abundant. However, the ability to locate prey will also influence the predation rate when prey become scarce. Studies on the voracity and developmental rate of potential aphid predators have been done exclusively in greenhouse vegetable crops with the exception of one study by Scopes (1969) on ornamental crops.

Minute pirate bugs (Heteroptera: Anthocoridae)

The two most important genera of anthocorid aphid predators are *Anthocoris* and *Orius* from the subfamily Anthocorinae (Hodgson and Aveling 1988). The most important anthocorids, also known as the minute pirate bugs, in Europe are *Anthocoris nemorum* (Linnaeus), *A. nemoralis* (Fabricius), *A. confusus* Reuter, and *Orius majusculus* (Reuter). Whereas *A. melanocerus* Reuter, *A. nemoralis* (introduced), *Orius insidiousus* (Say) and *O. tristicolor* (White) are the most important anthocorids in North and South America. The anthocorids have many desirable characteristics such as high searching efficiency, ability to increase rapidly when prey are abundant (Dempster 1968), a density-dependent decrease in fecundity resulting from mutual interference (Evans 1976), and a tendency to aggregate in areas of high prey density (Hodgson and Aveling 1988). Both the nymphs and adults feed on aphids. Nymphal development is affected by temperature and both the quantity and quality of food. In general, nymphs require sixteen to twenty-five days to become adults at 68°F (20°C). Meyling, Enkegaard, and Brødsgaard (2002) studied the voracity and prey preference of *A. nemorum* and *A. nemoralis* and found that both anthocorids prefer (in descending order) *M. persicae* to *A. gossypii*, *A. solani*, or *M. euphorbiae*. The number of aphids killed per day varied between one to eleven.

Predatory midges (Diptera: Cecidomyiidae)

Aphidoletes aphidomyza (Rondani), the aphid midge, is highly polyphagous, and preys on sixty-one species of aphids including *A. gossypii*, *M. persicae,* and *M. euphorbiae*

(Harris 1973). Only the larvae are predaceous. The adults (Figure 16.3A) feed on honeydew (Kuo-Sell 1987). Adult females use both olfactory and visual cues to locate aphids and were in a greenhouse study able to find a single infested *Brassica* plant among seventy-five non-infested plants (El-Titi 1974). Adult females (Figure 16.3A) only lay eggs on dense colonies of aphids, minimizing the need for larvae to search for prey (Markkula et al. 1979, Scopes 1981). Using *M. persicae* as prey, Uygun (1971) showed that *A. aphidomyza* took sixteen to seventeen days to develop from egg to adult at 70°F (21°C) and a larva killed an average of twenty-six small *M. persicae* during its development. Although the larval stage of *A. aphidomyza* (Figure 16.3B) requires as few as seven small *M. persicae* to complete its development (Uygun 1971), the number of aphids killed per larva may vary greatly. Nijveldt (1988) showed an average kill of 5.2 large or 14.7 small *M. persicae* per larva while Roberti (1946) and Smith (1966) reported 40 to 80 aphids killed per larva. *Aphidoletes aphidomyza* can control a number of aphids in greenhouses, including *A. gossypii* on cucumber, *M. euphorbiae* and *M. rosae* on commercial rose plantings, and *M. persicae* on tomatoes, capsicum, and sweet pepper (Markkula and Tiittanen 1977, Hansen 1983, Nijveldt 1988).

Lacewings (Neuroptera: Chrysopidae)

The green lacewings *Chrysoperla (=Chrysopa) carnea* (Stephens) (Figure 16.4) and *C. rufilabris* (Burmeister) are the most common Chrysopidae used in aphid control (New 1988). Only the larvae feed on aphids, adults feed on honeydew and pollen. Scopes (1969) used larvae of *C. carnea* to control *M. persicae* on

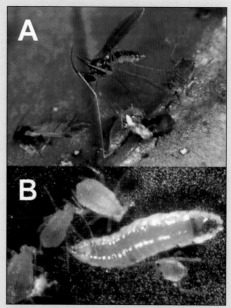

Figure 16.3. The adult aphid midge (A), *Aphidoletes aphidomyza* (Rondani), feeds on aphid honeydew, whereas the larva (B) preys on numerous aphid species. *Photos: Les Shipp.*

chrysanthemums and found that *M. persicae* was controlled by introducing one first-instar larva for up to fifty aphids, or one third-instar larva for up to two hundred aphids. Repeated introductions of eggs at three to four week intervals were necessary to maintain control. Control was not effective when initiated at low aphid densities (<100 aphids per plant). Sundby (1966) found that at 70°F (21°C), development of *C. carnea* from egg to adult took about five weeks and each larva could consume about four hundred aphids. A female laid up to five hundred eggs during an oviposition period of thirty-five days. Like the aphid midge, lacewings tend to lay their eggs in the vicinity of aphids.

Figure 16.4. Green lacewing larvae are chrysopid predators commonly used for aphid biological control. *Photo: Mark Hoddle.*

Lady beetles (Coleoptera: Coccinellidae)

Coccinellids are the most common and intensively studied predators of aphids (Frazer 1988). Both larvae and adults feed on aphids. Adult beetles also feed on pollen, fungi, and nectar but need to feed on aphids for egg production (Hagen 1962). The number of aphids consumed depends on aphid size and species and also on the larval stage of the coccinellid (Olszak 1988). Older larvae are more efficient than younger ones at capturing prey and adult beetles are generally less efficient than fourth-instar larvae (Frazer 1988). Voracity ranges from 200 to 1000 aphids per larva and 65 to 200 aphids per adult (Gurney and Hussey 1970, Olszak 1988). Under average greenhouse conditions, development from egg to adult takes fifteen to twenty-five days.

The convergent lady beetle, *Hippodamia convergens* Guérin-Méneville, and the Asian lady beetle, *Harmonia axyridis* (Pallas), are commonly used in biological control of aphids in greenhouses. One disadvantage of using adult coccinellids in aphid control is their tendency to leave the greenhouse. The dispersal tendency of *H. convergens* females depends upon the state of their ovaries (Rankin and Rankin 1980, Davis and Kirkland 1982). A hungry adult female with immature ovaries is likely to remain in an area if she captures enough prey to become satiated. Although larvae are used in most biological control programs to delay dispersal, repeated introductions of coccinellids are necessary because of their inability to form a self-perpetuating population in the greenhouse (Hämäläinen 1980). Attempts to reduce the dispersal tendency of adult coccinellids include the development of flightless *H. axyridis* adults (Tourniaire et al. 2000) and preflight *H. convergens* collected in mountain aggregations (Flint et al. 1995). However, the efficacy and effectiveness of these approaches to improving aphid control in greenhouses have yet to be tested.

Hoverflies (Diptera: Syrphidae)

Most aphidophagous species of Syrphidae are found in two tribes of the subfamily Syrphinae: Syrphini and Melanostomini (Chambers 1988). The Syrphini includes the common *Metasyrphus (=Syrphus) corollae* (Fabricius) and *Episyrphus balteatus* (DeGeer), both being highly polyphagous. The Melanostomini includes *Platycheirus peltatus* (Meigen), *P. manicatus* (Meigen) and *Melanostoma scalare* (Fabricius), and these species may be of economic importance because of their habit of ovipositing at low aphid, densities (Chambers 1988). The larvae feed on aphids while the adults feed only on pollen and nectar (Schneider 1969). Females may lay up to 400 eggs during an oviposition period of two weeks. Development from egg to adult takes eighteen to twenty-five days at temperatures of 70 to 75°F (21 to 24°C). Larval voracity can be as high as 900 aphids per larva (Barlow 1961, Bombosch 1962, Sundby 1966). In cage studies, Chambers (1986) found that *M. corollae* rapidly suppressed *A. gossypii* on cucumber plants and continuous control was possible with the presence of at least one gravid hoverfly. Hoverflies have great potential for aphid control because both the fecundity of female hoverflies and the substantial voracity of the larvae exceed those of the aphid midge, *A. aphidomyza* (Bondarenko and Asyakin 1981). Repeated introductions are necessary because pre-reproductive female hoverflies tend to disperse from greenhouses.

Other predators

Several mirid bugs (Heteroptera: Miridae), including *Dicyphus tamaninii* Wagner and *Macrolophus caliginosus* Wagner, are native polyphagous predators in Europe and particularly in the Mediterranean basin. These mirids usually colonize greenhouses and are able to control several pests. Although mirids are mainly used to control whiteflies on greenhouse vegetables in Europe, they also have great potential to control aphids such as *A. gossypii* and *M. euphorbiae* (Malausa, Drescher, and Franco 1987; Albajes et al. 1996; Sampson and King 1996; Alvarado, Balta, and Alomar 1997). However, these predatory mirids also feed on plants when prey become scarce and can cause severe plant damage such as distorted growth and premature flower or fruit drop (Salamero, Gabarra, and Albajes 1987; Sampson and Jacobson 1999). It is unlikely that mirids would be a suitable biological control agent to control aphids on greenhouse ornamentals because of the very low tolerance to plant damage.

Entomophagous fungi

Hyphomycete fungi belonging to the fungal subdivision Deuteromycotina are the most important group for aphid control and include *Beauveria bassiana* (Balsamo) Vuillemin, *Metarhizium anisopliae* (Metchnikoff) and *Verticillium lecanii* (Zimmermann) Viégas (Federici 1999, Lipa and Smits 1999). *Beauveria bassiana* and *M. anisopliae* are the two fungal species with the best potential as mycoinsecticides. These two fungi have very broad host ranges and infect insects of most orders. *Verticillium lecanii*, on the other hand, has a relatively narrow host range. Another important group used for aphid control is the Entomophthorales and includes genera such as *Entomophthora*, *Conidiobolous*, *Erynia*, *Zoophthora*, and *Tarichium* (Federici 1999, Lipa and Smits 1999). Relative humidity and temperature requirements differ among fungal species, but in general, relative humidity has to be high (more than 90%) to enable successful germination/sporulation. (van der Geest, Samson, and Wassink 1980; Latgé and Papierok 1988).

Verticillium lecanii (Vertalec) is widely used to control aphids on greenhouse grown chrysanthemums in Europe (Hall and Burges 1979, Hall 1985, Helyer et al. 1992). The aphid pests are usually most severe from April to September. During this period, the chrysanthemum crop is usually covered at night with polythene blackout sheets to restrict daylength and stimulate flower production. Under the blackouts, humidity rises to sufficient levels (>95%), which permits *V. lecanii* spores to germinate. Susceptibility to *V. lecanii* varies among aphid species, with *M. persicae* being the most susceptible to this fungus and

Brachycaudus helichrysi (Kaltenbach), *A. gossypii*, and *M. sanborni* being less susceptible (in descending order). Registration of Vertalec is not likely for aphid control in the United States (Parrella, Hansen, and van Lenteren 1999). However, *B. bassiana* has gained U.S. registration (BotaniGard, Naturalis O) and shown potential for controlling aphids, thrips, and whiteflies (Murphy et al. 1998, Shipp et al. 2002). Unlike *V. lecanii*, *B. bassiana* is active over a much broader range of environmental conditions. Under conditions of 64-81% RH in commercial production greenhouses, Shipp et al. (2002) showed that infection levels of *B. bassiana* (BotaniGard ES) ranged from 65-91% in cage studies for various pest species.

Biological Control Programs for Aphids on Ornamentals Since 1985

Compared to vegetable crops, studies that evaluate biological control of aphids on ornamental crops are few and rare (Chambers 1990; Sopp, Gillespie, and Palmer 1990; Flint et al. 1995; Heinz 1998; Heinz, Thompson, and Krauter 1999). Release rates and strategies for natural enemies based on studies for greenhouse vegetables may not be transferable to ornamental crops. Unlike vegetable crops, multiple ornamental crops are usually grown together in the same greenhouse; thus the number of pests and the strategies for biological control may be very different from vegetable crops. Rabasse and Wyatt (1985) gave an overview of biological control for aphids in greenhouse crops, but they focused almost exclusively on vegetables. We will now review more recent biological control efforts for aphids on greenhouse ornamentals (Table 16.2).

Introduction rates and methods
For aphid midge

The release rate of *A. aphidomyza* for the control of *A. gossypii* was examined in greenhouses on bed grown chrysanthemums (Chambers 1990). Good control was achieved at approximately ten cocoons per 10.8 ft.^{2} (1 m^2) per week, although aphid suppression increased with rate of release (up to thirty cocoons per 10.8 ft.^{2} [1 m^2] per week). Midge cocoons were introduced weekly from the time of planting to three weeks before the crop was due for cutting. The rate and frequency of release were much higher than the recommended rate (two to five cocoons per 10.8 ft.^{2} [1 m^2], repeat treatment in two to four weeks) for greenhouse vegetable crops (Markkula et al. 1979).

Certain cultural practices for ornamental crops may affect the efficacy of *A. aphidomyza*. The practice of "blacking out" to initiate flowering in chrysanthemums can cause *A. aphidomyza* larvae to enter diapause when they descend to the soil to form cocoons. Chambers (1990) further showed that the use of light-selective thermal screen could reduce the number of larvae that entered diapause from 83% under the standard plastic blackout sheet to 24% under the thermal screen, as compared to 14% with no blacking out. Gilkeson and Hill (1986) also showed that the use of low-intensity light averts diapause in *A. aphidomyza*. Another concern is that larvae of *A. aphidomyza* tend to pupate in the soil. If the adults do not emerge before cutting the crop, destruction of the developing cocoons occurs with soil sterilization at the next planting. In the case of potted chrysanthemums that are grown on slatted benching, the larvae might be able to

Table 16.2 Major Ornamental Crops: Their Aphid Pests and Biological Control Related Research Since 1985

Ornamental Crops	Aphid Species	Biological Control Related Research on Natural Enemy (References)
Begonia	*Aphis gossypii* Glover	No information available
	Myzus persicae (Sulzer)	No information available
Carnation	*Aulacorthum solani* (Kaltenbach)	No information available
	Myzus persicae (Sulzer)	No information available
Chrysanthemum	*Aphis gossypii* Glover	Hall and Burges 1979; Chambers 1990; Sopp et al. 1990; Dreistad and Flint 1996; Heinz 1998, 2001; Heinz et al., 1999
	Aulacorthum solani (Kaltenbach)	No information available
	Brachycaudus helichrysi (Kaltenbach)	Hall and Burges 1979
	Macrosiphoniella sanborni (Gillette)	Hall and Burges 1979, Sopp et al. 1990
	Myzus persicae (Sulzer)	Scopes 1969; Hall and Burges 1979; Heinz 1998, 2001; Heinz et al. 1999; Olson and Oetting 1999
Geranium	*Aphis gossypii* Glover	No information available
	Myzus persicae (Sulzer)	No information available
Gerbera	*Aulacorthum solani* (Kaltenbach)	No information available
Rose	*Macrosiphum euphorbiae* (Thomas)	No information available
	Macrosiphum rosae (Linnaeus)	Flint et al. 1995

pupate on the ground below and emerge later. In soilless cultures, the lack of a suitable pupation substrate can limit the population establishment of *A. aphidomyza* in the green- house. "Banker plants" or open rearing units containing predatory midges feeding on an aphid that will not infest the greenhouse crop have been suggested as an augmentative strategy (Hansen 1983, Rabasse and van Steenis 1999). Further research is needed to determine rate, timing, and method of release for effective aphid control on greenhouse ornamental crops.

For lady beetles

Inundative release of the convergent lady beetle for the control of *A. gossypii* and *M. rosae* was examined on outdoor grown potted chrysanthemums and roses (Flint et al. 1995, Dreistad and Flint 1996). The results showed that a single release of 34 to 42 adult *H. convergens* per pot provided 25 to 84% aphid control, although all beetles left the study area within three days of release. Voracity of the beetle ranged from 25 to 170 aphids per day and there was a density-dependent functional response in predation. Beetles consumed more aphids when released on plants with higher aphid densities. Dreistad and Flint (1996) concluded that any control from a single release would likely be temporary given the rapid dispersal and lack of reproduction. They recommended using convergent lady beetle for inundative rather than inoculative release. However, the applicability of this information to greenhouse grown potted chrysanthemums and roses remains to be tested.

For *Verticillium lecanii*

Application methods and rates of *Verticillium lecanii* for the control of *A. gossypii* and *M. sanborni* were compared on greenhouse grown chrysanthemums (Sopp, Gillespie, and Palmer 1990). The study showed that significantly more spores were deposited by the electrostatic ULV rotary atomizer (APE-80), with 36 to 45% of spores being deposited on the abaxial leaf surface and the stem compared with 15 to 23% using the hydraulic sprayer. Infection of aphids occurred earlier on electrostatically treated plots, and aphid populations peaked at significantly lower densities. Unlike *M. persicae*, *A. gossypii* and *M. sanborni* are not as mobile and tend to stay on abaxial leaf surfaces and the stems, respectively. The APE-80 system provided more effective coverage of these parts of the plant and increased the chances of the two aphids coming in contact with the fungal pathogen. Furthermore, a single full-rate (equivalent to 2×10^{13} blastospores per 2.47 acres [per ha]) or 12 one-twelfth-rate treatments resulted in better aphid control than 2 half-rate or 6 one-sixth-rate treatments, regardless of application method.

Strategic release sites

To be an effective biological control agent, parasitoids or predators must be able to locate aphid patches when patches are relatively scarce, respond to a rapidly changing landscape of aphid patches, and inflict some form of density-dependent mortality. For crops grown for their aesthetic value, such as potted chrysanthemums, the issue is not simply whether natural enemies inflict density-dependent aphid mortality but how rapidly they can do so. Dispersal of a the parasitoid *A. colemani* and the predator *C. rufilabris* was studied in a research greenhouse to determine the optimal distance between release sites and the number of release sites needed to provide control of *A. gossypii* and *M. persicae* (Heinz, Thompson, and Krauter 1999). Heinz (1998) showed that displacement distances and diffusion constants were significantly greater for adult *A. colemani* compared with third instars of *C. rufilabris*.

The percentage of *A. colemani* actively searching for aphids was significantly higher than the percentage of *C. rufilabris* larvae doing so. Furthermore, differences in dispersal capability and searching activity may explain why *A. colemani* successfully located 97% of all aphid infested pots compared with the 49% located by *C. rufilabris* within ten hours of their release. Heinz (1998) concluded that aphid biological control in greenhouse grown potted chrysanthemums may be enhanced by releasing sufficient numbers of natural enemies from points approximately twice their displacement distance within ten hours of their release. These distances are 10.75 ft. (3.25 m) apart among benches for *A. colemani* and 2.25 ft. (0.68 m) apart among benches for *C. rufilabris*.

Heinz, Thompson, and Krauter (1999) further examined the influence of *A. colemani* release strategies relative to control of *M. persicae* in a research greenhouse. Wasps were released at the rate of three per pot per week from four release points, 12 ft. (3.7 m) apart, or from one central release point in 1,205 ft.^{2} (112 m^2) greenhouses filled with potted chrysanthemums. The impact of parasitoid releases and the aphid populations were compared between the two release strategies and the control where no parasitoids were released. The results showed that both *A. colemani* releases (from one or from four points) provided significant aphid suppression. However, aphid densities were significantly lower throughout the experiment using four release points. Furthermore, pots grown with such releases ranked higher in quality and their acceptability for purchase as gifts compared to pots grown with one release point. The results showed that biological control is not only an effective method of aphid control but facilitates production of high quality potted chrysanthemums. When the efficacy of release strategies was further tested in commercial greenhouses, use of the optimal release distances (four release points) again resulted in significantly better aphid control than the suboptimal release (one release point) (Heinz 2001). The cost of the optimal release rate is 1.2 to 1.3 times the cost of insecticide applications; whereas the cost of suboptimal releases is 2 to 3 times the cost of insecticide applications.

Compatibility of fungal pathogen and insect growth regulator

Olson and Oetting (1999) examined the efficacy of *B. bassiana* (BotaniGard) against *M. persicae* when applied to greenhouse grown chrysanthemums treated with an insect growth regulator (S-Kinoprene). Under greenhouse conditions, the use of BotaniGard and S-Kinoprene suppressed aphid populations; however, aphid suppression was the same regardless of rates and the use of BotaniGard and S-Kinoprene alone or in combination.

Limitations for Adopting Biological Control of Aphids in Ornamentals

The use of biological control in greenhouse ornamentals is very limited compared to greenhouse vegetables because of a much lower tolerance of insect damage in ornamental crops, a wider range of crop and pest species, and a lack of guidelines for implementing biological control programs specifically for ornamental crops. In some vegetable crops, only the fruits are harvested and any insects that do not damage the fruits are usually tolerated. In contrast, both flowers and leaves of most ornamental crops are valuable. Potted plants are usually sold as whole plants, and cut flowers are sold with branches and leaves. Thus tolerance to insect damage and presence is extremely low. Additionally, the so-called "zero tolerance" export requirement in the Netherlands has been used generally as a "standard" for all products (van Lenteren and Woets 1988). This places serious constraints on biological control agents because they must be used in a way to maintain the crop virtually free of pests.

Large production costs and high crop value of ornamental crops coupled with potentially large losses associated with even moderate insect damage justify indiscriminant use of insecticides for many growers (Parrella, Hansen, and van Lenteren 1999). Toxic residues left by chemical pesticides are of less concern on ornamental crops than on vegetable crops for human consumption; therefore, growers have little incentive to consider using biological control as an alternative. Heavy reliance on chemical pesticides and their harmful effects on natural enemies make it difficult to use biological control in ornamental crops.

Unlike vegetable crops, the diversity of ornamental crops is much greater. In the Netherlands alone, 110 species of cut flowers and 300 species of potted plants are being grown in a range of cultivars in the greenhouse (Fransen 1992, 1993). The wide range of ornamental crops together with the constant turnover in consumer interests multiply the number of potential pests and complicate the implementation of biological control.

Studies on population growth rate of aphids on ornamental crops have provided the basic information needed for the selection of natural enemies. The next steps are to determine the rate of development and reproduction of natural enemies on ornamental crops, to evaluate their efficacy in controlling aphid pests, and to document release methodology and rate versus success within the context of ornamental crops. As Parrella, Heinz, and Nunney (1992) pointed out, vigorous research such as proper replication of field and greenhouse studies, the use of statistically accurate sampling of plants for the pest and natural enemy, and the proper establishment of experimental controls are needed to accurately evaluate the effect of natural enemy releases on pest populations. Information on rate, timing, and method of release would provide guidelines to implement biological control properly and effectively.

Economics of Biological Control

Without accurate assessment of release rates and their successes, it is very difficult to determine the economics of biological control of aphids on ornamentals. The cost of biological control depends mainly on the cost of the natural enemies and the number and frequency of releases needed. An increase in crop yield using biological aphid control versus chemical control could offset costs. Presently, only Heinz (2001) has examined the cost of biological control relative to chemical control in commercial greenhouses. The cost of using *A. colemani* to control *A. gossypii* on greenhouse grown chrysanthemums was 1.2 to 1.3 times the cost of insecticide application when the optimal release rate was used. Although the use of biological control in general is more expensive than chemical control, the benefits of using biological control such as reduced environmental contaminations and worker exposure to hazardous chemicals make it a desirable alternative for some growers.

References Cited

Albajes, R., O. Alomar, J. Riudavets, C. Castañé, J. Arnó, and R. Gabarra. 1996. The mirid bug *Dicyphus tamaninii*: An effective predator for vegetable crops. *IOBC/WPRS* 19 (1):1–4.

Alvarado, P., O. Balta, and O. Alomar. 1997. Efficiency of four Heteroptera as predators of *Aphis gossypii* and *Macrosiphum euphorbiae* (Hom.: Aphididae). *Entomophaga* 42:215–26.

Anthon, E. W. 1955. Evidence for green peach aphid resistance to organophosphorous insecticides. *Journal of Economic Entomology* 48:56–7.

Bai, B., and M. Mackauer. 1990. Oviposition and host-feeding patterns in *Aphelinus asychis* (Hymenoptera: Aphelinidae) at different aphid densities. *Ecological Entomology* 11:9–16.

Barlow, C. A. 1961. On the biology and reproductive capacity of *Syrphus corollae* Fab. (Syrphidae) in the laboratory. *Entomologia Experimentalis et Applicata* 4:91–100.

Blackman, R. L., and V. F. Eastop. 2000. *Aphids on the World's Crop: An Identification and Information Guide*. West Sussex, U.K.: John Wiley & Sons.

Bombosch, S. 1962. Untersuchung über die Auslösung der Eiablage bei *Syrphus corollae* Fabr. (Dipt.: Syrphidae). *Zeitschrift für Angewandte Entomologie* 50:81–8.

Bondarenko, N. V., and B. P. Asyakin. 1981. Behaviour of the predatory midge [*Aphidoletes aphidomyza* (Rond.)] and other aphidivorous insects in relation to population density of the prey. In *Insect Behaviour as a Basis for Developing Control Measures Against Pests of Field Crops and Forests*, ed. V. P. Pristavko, 6–14. New Delhi, India: Oxonian Press.

Chambers, R. J. 1986. Preliminary experiments on the potential of hoverflies (Dipt.: Syrphidae) for the control of aphids under glass. *Entomophaga* 31:197–204.

———. 1988. Syrphidae. In *Aphids: Their Biology, Natural Enemies and Control. Vol. B*, ed. A. K. Minks and P. Harrewijn, 259–70. New York (Amsterdam): Elsevier.

———. 1990. The use of *Aphidoletes aphidomyza* for aphid control under glass. *IOBC/WPRS Bulletin* 13 (5):51–4.

Davis, J. R., and R. L. Kirkland. 1982. Physiological and environmental factors related to the dispersal flight of the convergent lady beetle *Hippodamia convergens*. *Journal of the Kansas Entomological Society* 55:187–96.

Dempster, J. P. 1968. Intra-specific competition and dispersal: As exemplified by psyllid and its anthocorid predator. In *Insect Abundance, Symposia of the Royal Entomological Society of London Vol. 4*, ed. T. R. E. Southwood, 8–17. London: Blackwell Scientific Publications.

Dreistad, S. H. and M. L. Flint. 1996. Melon aphid (Homoptera: Aphididae) control by inundative convergent lady beetle (Coleoptera: Coccinellidae) release on chrysanthemum. *Environmental Entomology* 25:688–97.

El-Titi, A. 1974. Zur Auflösung der eiablage bei der aphidophagen Gallmücke *Aphidoletes aphidomyza* (Diptera: Cecidomyiidae). *Entomologia Experimentalis et Applicata* 17:9–21.

Evans, H. F. 1976. Mutual interference between predatory anthocorids. *Ecological Entomology* 1:283–6.

Federici, B. A. 1999. A perspective on pathogens as biological control agents for insect pests. In *Handbook of Biological Control: Principles and Applications of Biological Control*, ed. T. S. Bellows and T. W. Fisher, 517–48. San Diego, Calif.: Academic Press.

Flint, M. L., S. H. Dreistad, J. Rentner, and M. P. Parrella. 1995. Lady beetle release controls aphids on potted plants. *California Agriculture* 49:5–8.

Fransen, J. J. 1992. Development of integrated protection in glasshouse ornamentals. *Pesticide Science* 36:329–33.

———. 1993. Integrated pest management in glasshouse ornamentals in the Netherlands: A step-by-step policy. *IOBC/WPRS Bulletin* 16 (2):35–8.

Frazer, B. D. 1988. Coccinellidae. In *Aphids: Their Biology, Natural Enemies and Control, Vol. A*, ed. A. K. Minks and P. Harrewijn, 231–47. New York (Amsterdam): Elsevier.

Furk, C., and C. M. Hines. 1993. Aspects of pirimicarb resistance in the cotton and melon aphid, *Aphis gossypii* Glover (Homoptera: Aphididae). *Annals of Applied Biology* 123:9–17.

Furk, C., and S. Vedjhi. 1990. Organophosphorous resistance in *Aphis gossypii* (Homoptera: Aphididae). *Annals of Applied Biology* 116:557–61.

Gilkeson, L. A., and S. B. Hill. 1986. Diapause prevention in *Aphidoletes aphidomyza* (Diptera: Cecidomyiidae) by low-intensity light. *Environmental Entomology* 15:1067–9.

Gill, S., and J. Sanderson. 1998. *Ball Identification Guide to Greenhouse Pests and Beneficials*. Batavia, Illinois: Ball Publishing.

Giri, M. K., B. C. Pass, K. V. Yeargan, and J. C. Parr. 1982. Behavior, net reproduction, longevity, and mummy-stage survival of *Aphidius matricariae* (Hym.: Aphidiidae). *Entomophaga* 27:147–53.

Guldemond, J. A., W. J. van den Brink, and E. den Belder. 1998. Methods of assessing population increase in aphids and the effect of growth stage of the host plant on population growth rates. *Entomologia Experimentalis et Applicata* 86:163–73.

Gurney, B., and N. W. Hussey. 1970. Evaluation of some coccinellid species for the biological control of aphids in protected cropping. *Annals of Applied Biology* 65:451–8.

Hagen, K. S. 1962. Biology and ecology of predaceous Coccinellidae. *Annual Review of Entomology* 7:289–326.

Hågvar, E. B., and T. Hofsvang. 1986. Parasitism by *Ephedrus cerasicola* (Hym.: Aphidiidae) developing in different stages of *Myzus persicae* (Hom.: Aphididae). *Entomophaga* 31:337–46.

———. 1990. Fecundity and intrinsic rate of increase of the aphid parasitoid *Ephedrus cerasicola* Starý (Hym.: Aphidiidae) *Journal of Applied Entomology* 109:262–7.

Hall, R. A. 1985. Aphid control by fungi. In *Biological Pest Control: The Glasshouse Experience*, ed. N. W. Hussey and N. E. A. Scopes, 138–41, Poole, U.K.: Blandford (Ithaca, N.Y.: Cornell University Press).

Hall, R. A., and H. D. Burges. 1979. Control of aphids in glasshouses with the fungus, *Verticillium lecanii*. *Annals of Applied Biology* 93:235–46.

Hämäläinen, M. 1980. Evaluation of two native coccinellids for aphid control in glasshouses. *IOBC/WPRS* 3 (3):59–61.

Hamilton, P. A. 1973. The biology of *Aphelinus flavus* (Hym.: Aphelinidae), a parasite of the sycamore aphid *Drepanosiphum platanoides* (Hom.: Aphididae). *Entomophaga* 18:449–62.

Hansen, L. S. 1983. Introduction of *Aphidoletes aphidomyza* (Rond.) (Diptera: Cecidomyiidae) from an open rearing unit for the control of aphids in glasshouses. *IOBC/WPRS Bulletin* 6 (3):146–50.

Harris, K. M. 1973. Aphidophagous Cecidomyiidae (Diptera): Taxonomy, biology, and assessments of field populations. *Bulletin of Entomological Research* 63:305–25.

Heinz, K. M. 1998. Dispersal and dispersion of aphids (Homoptera: Aphididae) and selected natural enemies in spatially subdivided greenhouse environments. *Environmental Entomology* 27:1029–38.

———. 2001. Optimizing success with aphid parasitoids using strategic release sites. In *Proceedings for the 17th Conference on Insect and Disease Management on Ornamentals,* ed. L. Felter, T. Higgins, and N. Rechcigl, 113–20. Alexandria, Virg.: Society of American Florists.

Heinz, K. M., S. P. Thompson, and P. C. Krauter. 1999. Development of biological control methods for use in Southwestern U.S. greenhouses and nurseries. *IOBC/WPRS Bulletin* 22 (1):101–4.

Helyer, N., G. Gill, A. Bywater, and R. Chambers. 1992. Elevated humidities for control of chrysanthemum pests with *Verticillium lecanii*. *Pesticide Science* 36:373–8.

Hodgson, C., and C. Aveling. 1988. Anthocoridae. In *Aphids: Their Biology, Natural Enemies and Control, Vol. B*, ed. A. K. Minks and P. Harrewijn, 279–92. New York (Amsterdam): Elsevier.

Jarosik, V. A., A. Honek, J. M. Rabasse, and L. Lapchin. 1996. Life history characteristics of the aphid parasitoid *Aphelinus abdominalis* reared on *Macrosiphum euphorbiae*. *Ochrana Rostlin* 32:83–8.

Kennedy, J. S., M. F. Day, and V. F. Eastop. 1962. *A Conspectus of Aphids as Vectors of Plant Viruses*. London: Commonwealth Institute of Entomology.

Kuo-Sell, H. L. 1987. Some bionomics of the predacious aphid midge, *Aphidoletes aphidomyza* (Rond.) (Diptera: Cecidomyiidae), and the possibility of using the rose grain aphid, *Metopolophium dirhodum* (Wlk.), as an alternative prey in an open rearing unit in greenhouses. In *Integrated and Biological Control in Protected Crops: Proceedings of a Meeting of the EC Experts' Group, Heraklion, April 24-26, 1985*, ed. R. Cavalloro, 151–6. Rotterdam, the Netherlands: A.A. Balkema.

Latgé, J. P., and B. Papierok. 1988. Aphid pathogens. In *Aphids: Their Biology, Natural Enemies and Control, Vol. B.*, ed. A. K. Minks and P. Harrewijn, 323–35. New York (Amsterdam): Elsevier.

Lipa, J. J., and P. H. Smits. 1999. Microbial control of pests in greenhouses. In *Integrated Pest and Disease Management in Greenhouse Crops,* ed. R. Albajes, M. L. Gullino, J. C. van Lenteren, and Y. Elad, 295–309. Dordrecht, the Netherlands: Kluwer Academic Publishers.

Mackauer, M., and M. J. Way. 1976. *Myzus persicae*, an aphid of world importance. In *Studies in Biological Control*, ed. V. L. Delucchi, 51–117. Cambridge, U.K.: Cambridge University Press.

Malausa, J. C., J. Drescher, and E. Franco. 1987. Perspectives for the use of predacious bug *Macrolophus caliginosus* Wagner (Heteroptera: Miridae) on glasshouse crops. *IOBC/WPRS Bulletin* 10 (2):106–7.

Markkula, M., and K. Tiittanen. 1977. Use of the predatory midge *Aphidoletes aphidomyza* (Rond.) (Diptera: Cecidomyiidae) against aphids in glasshouse cultures. *Proceedings Symposium XV, International Congress of Entomology, Washington, D.C., United States. Department of Agriculture, Agricultural Research Service ARS-NE* 85:43–4.

Markkula, M., K. Tiittanen, M. Hämäläinen, and A. Forsberg. 1979. The aphid midge *Aphidoletes aphidomyza* (Diptera: Cecidomyiidae) and its use in biological control of aphids. *Annales Entomologici Fennici* 45:89–98.

McClanahan, R. J., and J. Founk. 1983. Toxicity of insecticides to the green peach aphid (Homoptera: Aphididae) in laboratory and field tests. *Journal of Economic Entomology* 76:899–905.

Meyling, N. V., A. Enkegaard, and H. F. Brødsgaard. 2002. The flower bugs, *Anthocoris nemorum* and *Anthocoris nemoralis*, voracity and prey preference for aphids in glasshouses. *IOBC/WPRS Bulletin* 25 (1):185–8.

Moriones, E., and M. Luis-Arteaga. 1999. Viral diseases. In *Integrated Pest and Disease Management in Greenhouse Crops*, ed. R. Albajes, M. L. Gullino, J. C. van Lenteren, and Y. Elad, 16–33. Dordrecht, the Netherlands: Kluwer Academic Publishers.

Murphy, B. C., T. A. Morisawa, J. P. Newman, S. A. Tjosvold, and M. P. Parrella.1998. Fungal pathogen controls of thrips in greenhouse flowers. *California Agriculture* 52 :32–6.

New, T. R. 1988. Neuroptera. In *Aphids: Their Biology, Natural Enemies and Control, Vol. B,* ed. A. K. Minks and P. Harrewijn, 249–58. New York (Amsterdam): Elsevier.

Nijveldt, W. 1988. Cecidomyiidae. In *Aphids: Their Biology, Natural Enemies and Control, Vol. B,* ed. A. K. Minks and P. Harrewijn, 271–7. New York (Amsterdam): Elsevier.

Olson, D. L., and R. D. Oetting. 1999. Compatibility of insect growth regulators and *Beauveria bassiana* (Balsamo) Vuillenin in controlling green peach aphid (Homoptera: Aphididae) on greenhouse chrysanthemums. *Journal of Entomological Science* 34:286–94.

Olszak, R. W. 1988. Voracity and development of three species of Coccinellidae, preying upon different species of aphids. In *Ecology and Effectiveness of Aphidophaga,* ed. E. Niemczyk and A. F. G. Dixon, 47–73. The Hague: the Netherlands: SPB Academic Publishing.

Parrella, M. P., L. S. Hansen, and J. van Lenteren. 1999. Glasshouse environments. In *Handbook of Biological Control: Principles and Applications of Biological Control,* ed. T. S. Bellows and T.W. Fisher, 819–39, San Diego, Calif.: Academic Press.

Parrella, M. P., K. M. Heinz, and L. Nunney. 1992. Biological control through augmentative releases of natural enemies: A strategy whose time has come. *American Entomologist* 38:172–9.

Rabasse, J. M., and F. F. Shalaby. 1980. Laboratory studies on the development of *Myzus persicae* Sulz. (Hom.: Aphididae) and its primary parasite, *Aphidius matricariae* Hal. (Hym.: Aphidiidae) at constant temperatures. *Acta Oecologica, Oecologica Applicata* 1:21–8.

Rabasse, J. M., and M. J. van Steenis. 1999. Biological control of aphids. In *Integrated Pest and Disease Management in Greenhouse Crops*, ed. R. Albajes, M. L. Gullino, J. C. van Lenteren, and Y. Elad, 235–43. Dordrecht, the Netherlands: Kluwer Academic Publishers.

Rabasse, J. M., and I. J. Wyatt. 1985. Biology of aphids and their parasites in greenhouses. In *Biological Pest Control: The Glasshouse Experience*, ed. N. W. Hussey and N. E. A. Scopes, 66–73. Poole, U.K.: Blandford Press (Ithaca, New York: Cornell University Press).

Rankin, M. A., and S. M. Rankin. 1980. Some factors affecting the presumed migratory flight activity of the convergent ladybeetle, *Hippodamia convergens* (Coleoptera: Coccinellidae). *Biological Bulletin* 158:356–69.

Roberti, D. 1946. La *Phenobremia aphidimyza* Ront. (Diptera: Cecidomyiidae) predatrice di *Aphis* (Doralis) *frangulae* Koch. *Bolletino dell'Istituto di Entomologia della Università di Bologna* 15:233-256.

Salamero, A., R. Gabarra, and R. Albajes. 1987. Observations on the predatory and phytophagous habits of *Dicyphus tamaninii* (Heteroptera: Miridae). *IOBC/WPRS Bulletin* 10 (2):165–9.

Sampson, A. C., and V. J. King. 1996. *Macrolophus caliginosus*: Field establishment and pest control effect in protected tomatoes. *IOBC/WPRS Bulletin* 19 (1):143–6.

Sampson, C., and R. J. Jacobson. 1999. *Macrolophus caliginosus* Wagner (Heteroptera: Miridae): A predator causing damage to U.K. tomatoes. *IOBC/WPRS Bulletin* 22 (1):213–6.

Schneider, F. 1969. Biology and physiology of aphidophagous Syrphidae. *Annual Review of Entomology* 14:103–24.

Scopes, N. E. A. 1969. The potential of *Chrysopa carnea* as a biological control agent of *Myzus persicae* on glasshouse chrysanthemums. *Annals of Applied Biology* 64:433–9.

———. 1981. Evaluation of *Aphidoletes aphidomyza*. Littlehampton, United Kingdom: *Glasshouse Crops Research Institute Annual Report 1980*: 105.

Shipp, L., Y. Zhang, D. Hunt, and G. Ferguson. 2002. Influence of greenhouse microclimate on the efficacy of *Beauveria bassiana* (Balsamo) Vuillemin for control of greenhouse pests. *IOBC/WPRS Bulletin* 25 (1):237–40.

Smith, B.D. 1966. Effects of parasites and predators on a natural population of the aphid *Acyrthosiphon spartii* (Koch) on broom (*Sarothamnus scoparius* R.). *Journal of Animal Ecology* 35:255-267.

Sopp, P. I., A. T. Gillespie, and A. Palmer. 1990. Comparison of ultra low-volume electrostatic and high-volume hydraulic application of *Verticillium lecanii* for aphid control on chrysanthemums. *Crop Protection* 9 (3):177–84.

Sundby, R. A. 1966. A comparative study of the efficiency of three predatory insects *Coccinella septempunctata* L. (Coleoptera: Coccinellidae), *Chrysopa carnea* (St.) (Neuroptera: Chrysopidae), and *Syrphus ribesii* L. (Diptera: Syrphidae) at two different temperatures. *Entomophaga* 11:395–404.

Tamaki, G., and W. Allen. 1969. Competition and other factors influencing the population dynamics of *Aphis gossypii* and *Macrosiphoniella sanborni* on greenhouse chrysanthemums. *Hilgardia* 39:447–505.

Tourniaire, R., A. Ferran, J. Gambier, L. Giuge, and F. Bouffault. 2000. Locomotory behavior of flightless *Harmonia axyridis* (Pallas) (Col.: Coccinellidae). *Journal of Insect Physiology* 46:721–6.

Uygun, N. 1971. Der Einflu der Nahrungsmenge auf Fruchtbarkeit und Lebensdauer von *Aphidoletes aphidomyza* (Rond.) (Diptera: Itonididae). *Zeitschrift für Angewandte Entomologie* 69:234–58.

van der Geest, L.P.S., R.A. Samson, and H.J.M. Wassink. 1980. Control of aphids with insect pathogens Entomophthora spp. In *Integrated Control of Insect Pests in The Netherlands*, ed. A.K. Minks and P. Gruys, 271-273. Wageningen, the Netherlands: Center for Agricultural Publishing and Documentation.

van Lenteren, J. C., and J. Woets. 1988. Biological and integrated pest control in greenhouses. *Annual Review of Entomology* 33:239–69.

van Steenis, M. J. 1992. Biological control of the cotton aphid, *Aphis gossypii* Glover (Hom.: Aphididae): pre-introduction evaluation of natural enemies. *Journal of Applied Entomology* 114:362–80.

———. 1993. Intrinsic rate of increase of *Aphidius colemani* Vier. (Hym.: Braconidae), a parasitoid of *Aphis gossypii* Glov. (Hom.: Aphididae), at different temperatures. *Journal of Applied Entomology* 116:192–8.

———. 1994. Intrinsic rate of increase of *Lysiphlebus testaceipes* Cresson (Hym.: Braconidae), a parasitoid of *Aphis gossypii* Glov. (Hom.: Aphididae) at different temperatures. *Journal of Applied Entomology* 118:399–406.

———. 1995. Evaluation of four aphidiine parasitoids for biological control of *Aphis gossypii*. *Entomologia Experimentalis et Applicata* 75:151–7.

van Steenis, M. J., and K. A. M. H. El-Khawass. 1995. Life history of *Aphis gossypii* on cucumber: Influence of temperature, host plant and parasitism. *Entomologia Experimentalis et Applicata* 76:121–31.

Vehrs, S. L. C., G. P. Walker, and M. P. Parrella. 1992. Comparison of population growth rate and within-plant distribution between *Aphis gossypii* and *Myzus persicae* (Homoptera: Aphididae) reared on potted chrysanthemums. *Journal of Economic Entomology* 85:799–807.

17

BIOLOGICAL CONTROL OF APHIDS ON VEGETABLE CROPS

Sylvia Blümel
Austrian Agency of Health and Food Safety
Institute of Plant Health, Vienna, Austria

Major Pest Aphids

Cucumber, tomato, sweet pepper, eggplant, and lettuce are the major greenhouse vegetable crops damaged by one or more aphid species. The principal pest species involved are *Aphis gossypii* Glover, *Myzus persicae* Sulzer, *Macrosiphum euphorbiae* (Thomas), and *Aulacorthum solani* (Kaltenbach) (see Table 17.1 for a list of aphid pests commonly infesting vegetables in greenhouses). In some crops such as tomatoes, yield reduction from aphid infestations can be as high as 40% (Muminov, Askaraliev, and Oripov 1976).

Immature aphids can start aphid infestations on greenhouse vegetables, propagation material, and on weeds; or winged aphids may enter the greenhouse from outdoor crops or from crops in adjacent greenhouses. Host plants are damaged either directly by aphid feeding and honeydew deposits, or indirectly by transmission of viruses (Schepers 1988). Resistance of *A. gossypii* and *M. persicae* to pesticides, especially those selective materials used in IPM strategies, has enhanced grower interest in aphid biological control (Devonshire 1988). *Aphis gossypii* can attack more than fifty families of host plants. It has become one of the most important aphid pests on Cucurbitaceae in protected crops (van Steenis 1995).

Aphid Natural Enemies

Natural enemies used against aphids in greenhouse crops include eight hymenopterous parasitoids from the families Aphelinidae and Braconidae; fifteen predators, including species of Cecidomyiidae, Chrysopidae, Coccinellidae, Syrphidae, Anthocoridae, Miridae; and several insect-pathogenic fungi, such as *Verticillium lecanii* (Zimmermann) Viégas and various species of Entomophthorales (Chambers 1986; Trottin-Caudal, Fournier, and Millott 1996; Albajes et al. 1996). The most widely used species are listed in Table 17.2. These species are available from commercial producers in various countries.

Parasitoids

Aphid parasitoids are small (0.08 in. [2 mm]) wasps that feed on honeydew and host haemolymph. Eggs are laid inside aphids and solitary larvae develop inside their hosts. When larval development is complete, only the hardened aphid body, the so-called

Table 17.1 Occurrence of Pest Aphids on Greenhouse Vegetable Crops

Aphid species	Crop	Country	References
Aphis gossypii (Glover)	cucumber	Austria	Pleininger 1996
		Belgium	van de Veire 1991
		France	Boll et al. 1994, Maisonneuve 1993
		Germany	Lampharter 1992
		Greece	Lykouressis and Roditakis 1994
		Hungary	Hatala-Zseller et al. 1993
		Israel	Steinberg et al. 1993
		Italy	Burgio et al. 1994, Benuzzi and Nicoli 1993
		Netherlands	van Steenis 1993
		U.K.	Bennison 1992, Helyer 1993
	melon	Greece	Lykouressis and Roditakis 1994
		Italy	Burgio et al. 1994
		Portugal	Cecilio et al. 1994
	eggplant	Netherlands	van Steenis 1993
		Italy	Celli et al. 1987
	sweet pepper	Algeria	Guenaoui et al.1994
		Belgium	van de Veire 1991
		France	Boll et al. 1994
	various crops	Russia	Bondarenko 1987
Aphis nasturtii (Kaltenbach)	sweet pepper	Hungary	Hatala-Zseller et al. 1993
Aulacorthum solani (Kaltenbach)	cucumber	Germany	Lampharter 1992
	lettuce	Germany	Quentin et al. 1995
	tomato	Canada	Gilkeson 1990
	various crops	Russia	Bondarenko 1987
Macrosiphum euphorbiae (Thomas)	tomatoes	Italy	Benuzzi and Nicoli 1993, Celli et al. 1991
		Netherlands	van Steenis 1993
		Russia	Popov et al. 1987
		Spain	Alomar et al. 1997
	cucumber	Germany	Lampharter 1992
	lettuce	Germany	Quentin et al. 1995

(continued)

Table 17.1 *(continued)*

Aphid species	Crop	Country	References
Myzus persicae (Sulzer)	sweet pepper	Canada	Gilkeson 1990
		Netherlands	van Steenis 1993
		Russia	Popov et al. 1987
		U.K.	Buxton et al. 1990
		Australia	Spooner-Hart 1993
	tomatoes	Belgium	van de Veire 1991
	various crops	Hungary	Hatala-Zseller et al. 1993
		U.S.A.	Meadow et al. 1985
	lettuce	Germany	Quentin et al. 1995
Nasonovia ribisnigri (Mosley)	lettuce	Germany	Quentin et al. 1995

mummy, remains. The principal species of aphid parasitoids in commercial use in greenhouses are three braconids and one aphelinid: *Aphidius colemani* Viereck, *Aphidius matricariae* (Haliday), *Ephedrus cerasicola* Starý, and *Aphelinus abdominalis* Dalman, respectively.

Aphidius colemani and other species useful against A. gossypii

Aphidius colemani is one of the most important parasitoids for the control of *A. gossypii*; it is also effective against *M. persicae* (van Steenis 1993). Its population growth rates (r_m = the intrinsic rate of natural increase) are comparable to that of the pest aphid, *A. gossypii* (0.35 versus 0.44) under laboratory conditions. Parasitoids whose rate of population growth equals or exceeds that of their host are generally better able to suppress their hosts' densities than parasitoids with lower population growth rates. *Lysiphlebus testaceipes* Cresson and *Aphelinus varipes* (Förster) also have sufficiently high popula-

tion growth rates relative to *A. gossypii*, unlike the relatively low population growth rates recorded for *Ephedrus cerasicola* Starý (van Steenis 1995).

At 77°F (25°C), *A. colemani* and *L. testaceipes* live approximately 4.4 and 2.6 days, respectively, and produce 388 and 180 eggs per female. Fecundity of these species is greatest at this temperature. *Aphidius colemani* is effective at temperatures up to 77°F (25°C), but the population growth rate of *A. colemani* is lower than that of the pest aphid at higher temperatures. By comparison, the fecundity of *A. varipes* is 291 eggs per female and its life span is 10.6 days at 68°F (20°C).

The efficacy of parasitoids as control agents of *A. gossypii* in greenhouse cucumbers is also influenced by their searching efficacy, their host feeding behavior, and the response of the aphid while a parasitoid forages in aphid colonies. For example, *A. varipes* is more efficient in the control of *A. gossypii* than *A. colemani* at 86°F (30°C) due

Table 17.2 Natural Enemies Used for Aphid Control in Greenhouse Vegetables

Parasitoid or Predator	Host aphids	Crops	Country/author	Commercial importance
Aphidius colemani Viereck (Braconidae)	*Aphis gossypii*	cucumber	Austria (Pleininger 1998) Italy (Burgio et al. 1994) the Netherlands (van Steenis 1993) U.K. (Bennison and Corless 1993)	High
	Myzus persicae	sweet pepper	Norway (Hofsvang and Hågvar 1978)	High
	Aphis gossypii	melon	Italy (Burgio et al. 1994),	High
Aphelinus abdominalis Dalman (Aphelinidae)	*Macrosiphum euphorbiae*	tomatoes	Spain (Alomar et al. 1997) France (Trottin-Caudal et al. 1996) Switzerland (Hurni and Stadler 1993)	Moderate
Aphidius matricariae Haliday (Braconidae)	*Myzus persicae*	sweet pepper	Canada (Gilkeson 1990) France (Shalaby and Rabasse 1979) Norway (Hågvar and Hofsvang 1990) the Netherlands (van Steenis 1993) Russia (Popov et al. 1987) U.K. (Buxton et al. 1990)	Moderate
Aphidius ervi Haliday (Braconidae)	*Aulacorthum solani*	sweet pepper	International	Low
Ephedrus cerasicola Starý (Braconidae)	*Myzus persicae*	sweet pepper	Norway (Hågvar and Hofsvang 1990)	Low
Lysiphlebus testaceipes Cresson (Braconidae)	*A. gossypii*	melon	Portugal (Cecilio et al. 1994)	Low
	A. gossypii	cucumber	Israel (Steinberg et al. 1993) the Netherlands (van Steenis 1993)	Low
Aphidoletes aphidomyza (Rondani) (Cecidomyiidae)	*Aphis gossypii*,	cucumber	Germany (Lampharter 1992)	Low
	Macrosiphum euphorbiae	sweet pepper	the Netherlands (van Schelt et al. 1990)	Low

(continued)

Table 17.2 *(continued)*

Parasitoid or Predator	Host aphids	Crops	Country/author	Commercial importance
	Aulacorthum solani	sweet pepper	Russia (Bondarenko 1987)	Low
	A. gossypii	cucumber	U.K. (Bennison and Corless 1993)	Low
	M. persicae	sweet pepper	Norway (Hofsvang and Hågvar 1982)	Low
	M. persicae	tomatoes	U.S.A. (Meadow et. al. 1985)	Low
Chrysoperla carnea (Stephens) (Chrysopidae)	various	cucumber, sweet pepper	Russia (Bondarenko 1987)	Moderate
Chrysoperla rufilabris (Burmeister) (Chrysopidae)	*A. gossypii*	various	International	Low
Harmonia dimidiata (Fabricius) (Coccinillidae)	*A. gossypii, M. persicae, A. nasturtii*	cucumber, sweet pepper, tomatoes	Russia (Lezhneva and Anisimov 1995)	Moderate
Hippodamia convergens Guérin (Coccinellidae)		Various	International	Low

to enhanced host-feeding activity by *A. varipes* at this relatively warm temperature. Due to the sensitivity of various parasitoid characteristics related to efficacy, a combined release of *A. colemani* and *A. varipes* is recommended for providing the most effective biological control of *A. gossypii* (van Steenis 1995).

Aphidius matricariae

This parasitoid is effective for the control of *M. persicae* on sweet pepper and eggplant (Rabasse and Shalaby 1980). *A. matricariae* can parasitize all nymphal stages of *M. persicae*. Hosts parasitized before reaching the third instar do not reproduce. Only 10 to 15% of aphids parasitized as fourth instars or adults are able to produce progeny. On eggplant, development time of *A. matricariae* is longer than that of the pest aphid *M. persicae*. Unparasitized *M. persicae* complete their development from birth to the adult stage in 8.8 days at 68°F (20°C) (Ibid.). *Aphidius matricariae* develops from the egg through four larval instars and a pupa to the adult in 13.5 days at 68°F (20°C). The sex ratio of emerged wasps is 50 to 60% female. Adults can live 14 days and parasitize up to 309 aphids (Shalaby and Rabasse 1979).

Ephedrus cerasicola

At 70°F (21°C) this wasp has a generation time of 10.5 days and a population growth rate of 0.32, compared to a population growth rate of 0.47 and a developmental time of 6.5 days for its host *M. persicae* (Hågvar and Hofsvang 1986). Aphid honeydew on sweet pepper improves the efficiency of the host finding behavior of *E. cerasicola* (Hågvar and Hofsvang 1989). In aphid patches of medium and high density, there may be 500 to 1000 aphids per plant, but a single *E. cerasicola* is only able to parasitize at most about 50 aphids per plant (Hågvar and Hofsvang 1987). In its whole lifetime, *E. cerasicola* can produce about 961 eggs per female (Hågvar and Hofsvang 1990). Oviposition takes place in all four nymphal instars, as well as in adults of *M. persicae.* Parasitization of young aphids leads to nearly complete inhibition of molting, whereas nearly 100% of parasitized third or fourth instars complete their development to the adult stage (Hågvar and Hofsvang 1986).

Aphelinus abdominalis

This aphelinid wasp requires 23.5 days for development from egg to adult on *M. euphorbiae* at 68°F (20°C). At 79°F (26°C), adults live 24 days, and lay about 158 eggs (Jarosik et al. 1996). The size of the host aphid influences the sex ratio of *A. abdominalis,* with males commonly being reared from small aphids and females from larger hosts (Honek et al. 1998).

Predators

Important aphid predators used in greenhouse vegetable crops include the midge *Aphidoletes aphidomyza* (Rondani), the green lacewing *Chrysoperla carnea* (Stephens), and various coccinellid ladybird beetles.

Aphidoletes aphidomyza

This predatory gall midge occurs worldwide and it feeds exclusively on aphids, including the most important pest aphids on greenhouse vegetables. The developmental cycle, which takes 19 to 31 days, includes an egg, three larval instars, pupa and an adult. The orange eggs (0.19 in. long × 0.04 in. wide [0.3 mm × 0.1 mm]) are placed singly or in groups of up to forty near or in aphid colonies. Environmental conditions for successful egg hatch are a relative humidity above 75% and a temperature above 50°F (10°C). During their development, the predacious, orange larvae grow to 0.09 in. (2.4 mm) in length, with the last larval instar having white stripes arranged vertically along its sides and back.

Larvae pierce the aphids with their mandibles and paralyze them with a toxin, and suck the fluids from the aphid's body. The number of prey killed increases with prey density; a larva can consume about eighty aphids during its life. The feeding capacity of *A. aphidomyza* larvae is highest at low relative humidities (less than 55%).

Young larvae search for aphids over very small areas (traveling only 0.1 in. [2.7 cm]), and they may starve during the first two days after emergence if there are no aphids nearby. By contrast, older midge larvae are active in their search for prey. Larvae flip themselves off plants with the help of a special structure in the thorax. They pupate in the substrate below by spinning a cocoon (0.07 in. long × 0.03 in. wide [1.8 mm × 0.7 mm]) that webs together soil particles and feces. About 80% of pupae emerge as adults, of which 50 to 66% are female.

Aphidoletes aphidomyza enters diapause at photoperiods below 15.5 hours. By augmenting day length within the greenhouse using a single 60W bulb, this light-induced diapause can often be avoided. However, declining temperature and host plant quality also promote diapause induction. In Canada, nondiapausing strains of *A. aphidomyza* are available from commercial insectaries (Gilkeson and Hill 1986). This predator is most typically purchased from commercial insectaries and released into infested greenhouses as pupae since this stage is more durable than the adult or egg (Kulp 1989).

Adult gall midges are approximately 0.08 in. long × 0.02 in. wide (2.0 × 0.5 mm), and they are active at night. Adults are attracted to the odor of honeydew, which assists them in locating aphid colonies. During their adult life span, midges may lay up to 200 eggs. Because the strength of these cues increases with the density of aphid colonies, high-density colonies are preferred by adult midges for oviposition. The quality of the nutrition obtained as larvae strongly influences the longevity and egg production of *A. aphidomyza* adults. Larvae that feed on cereal aphids *Sitobion avenae* (F.), *Metopolophium dirhodum* (Walker), and *Rophalosiphum padi* (L.) develop into bigger adult midges that lay more eggs than do midges from larvae feeding on green peach aphid, *M. persicae*.

Cereal aphids are, therefore, the ones recommended for use on banker plants (Kuo-Sell 1989).

Chrysoperla carnea

This species is distributed nearly worldwide and feeds on various aphids, including *A. gossypii*, *M. persicae,* and *M. euphorbiae*. This lacewing develops from the egg through three larval instars and a pupal stage to the adults in thirty-five days. The eggs (0.04 × 0.01 in. [0.9 × 0.4 mm]) are yellowish and laid in groups near aphid colonies. First instar larvae emerge after three to nineteen days, with the shortest duration at high temperatures (82 to 90°F [28 to 32°C]) and high relative humidities (80 to 100%). Larvae increase in size approximately sixteen-fold when developing from a first to third instar, during which time they consume up to 400 aphids. Larval cannibalism is frequent, especially if food is lacking. *Chrysoperla carnea* larvae actively search for prey, which are recognized as prey only after direct contact of the aphid by the lacewing's mouthparts. Lacewing larvae cannot distinguish between parasitized and unparasitized aphids, and as a result they often attack parasitized aphids. To pupate, larvae enter a protected site and spin a cylindrical cocoon (0.32 in. long × 0.16 in. wide [8 mm long × 4 mm wide]). Emerging adults are 38 to 54% male. Adult females can lay several hundred eggs each, and the eggs tend to be distributed randomly on host plants. Adult *C. carnea* live for several months and feed on pollen and nectar, not aphids. As with many other arthropod predators, diapause is induced primarily by short day conditions (Bay 1993).

Ladybird beetles

Polyphagous coccinellids such as *Harmonia axyridis* (Pallas) and *Hippodamia convergens* Guérin are also used for biological aphid control. Developmental stages of the ladybird beetles include an egg, four larval instars, and a pupa. Efficacy of coccinellids as aphid predators is dependent on their density in relation to that of the prey, the voracity of a given species, and its searching behavior (Frazer 1988). In greenhouses, the ability of a coccinellid to reproduce and to build up a self-perpetuating population is important to determine a species' effectiveness. Prey are usually recognized only after direct contact and can often escape without capture. Both larvae and adults are actively feeding stages and need a certain number of aphids for growth or egg production. Coccinellids do not distinguish between parasitized and unparasitized aphids; hence releases of this generalist predator together with parasitoids may not increase the level of aphid biological control obtained.

A number of different coccinellids have been studied in experimental trials. In a comparative study of four aphid predators that included *Adalia bipunctata* L., *Coccinella septempunctata* (L.), *Coleomegilla maculata* (De Geer), and *Cycloneda sanguinea* (L.), only *C. sanguinea* controlled *A. gossypii, M. persicae,* and *Acyrtosiphon pisum* (Harris) on cucumbers when released at a ratio of one predator for every fifty aphids (Gurney and Hussey 1970). Trials with *Harmonia dimidiata* (Fabricius) showed it to be effective in controlling *A. gossypii* on cucumber, and *M. persicae* and *Aphis nasturtii* Kaltenbach on sweet pepper and tomatoes (Lezhneva and Anisimov 1995).

Entomopathogenic Fungi

About twenty different species of entomopathogenic fungi are potential candidates for suppression of aphid populations (Latgé and Papierok 1988). Only *V. lecanii* has been most widely used for biological control of aphids infesting vegetables within greenhouses.

Verticillium lecanii

This species is marketed for the control of aphids, whiteflies, and thrips under the trade names Vertalec, Mycotal and MicroGermin. *Verticillium lecanii* occurs in nature worldwide and infects over twenty-eight species of aphids, including *A. gossypii, M. persicae, M. euphorbiae, A. solani,* and *A. nasturtii.* When suitable environmental conditions occur, sporulating white fluffy mycelium cover the infected aphids on the host plant. Hyphae (conidiophores) that emerge from dead hosts produce asexual conidial spores. The conidia are the infective stage, producing the germination tube that penetrates the cuticle of the host and enters the hemocoel. Penetration of the host integument by the germination tube is achieved by the combined action of enzymes that degrade chitin and by the mechanical pressure exerted by the growing germination tube. In the hemocoel, blastospores are produced that are transported throughout the body. Hosts die from mechanical damage to vital tissues as well as from toxicants released into the hemocoel. After the death of the host, *V. lecanii* develops saprophytically on the host and conidiophores emerge on the surface of the aphids and complete the cycle by producing new conidial spores.

Development and the germination of conidia are dependent on the relative humidity and temperature. Relative humidities above 90% for at least twelve hours are needed in the fungus-host microenvironment for spore germination and host infection. At 68°F (20°C), 100% r.h. and free water for thirty-six hours are required for infection of 95% of the contacted hosts to occur within ninety-six hours after application and for sporulation from *M. persicae* cadavers to occur on sweet pepper. By contrast, no infections or sporulations occur when the relative humidity drops to 80% (Milner and Lutton 1986). The optimal temperature for growth and infection of *V. lecanii* is 68 to 77°F (20 to 25°C). High host densities promote natural fungal epidemics since the conidia, imbedded in mucus, are spread by splashing water and direct contact, rather than in the air.

Trials with *V. lecanii* have documented its ability to provide excellent aphid control in vegetables. Applying a 0.5% spray solution of Vertalec against *M. persicae* on eggplant resulted in a control of the aphid population within three weeks. The infection rate reached 90% and the suppressive effect lasted for four weeks (Zimmermann, 1982). Two application rates and frequencies were tested against *A. gossypii* on cucumber for four weeks under conditions of 85% r.h. and 73°F (23°C) (Pinna 1992). Application of 0.08 oz. (2.5 g) of *V. lecanii* spores per 1.06 qt. (1 l) (= 5×10^{12} spores/l) three times at ten-day intervals, or five applications of 0.04 oz. (1.25 g) of *V. lecanii* spores per 1.06 qt. (1 l) (= 2.5×10^{12} spores/l) at five-day intervals caused 94 and 80% infection, respectively. Aphid density was reduced to 9.6 and 18.5 per plant, respectively, compared to 390 aphids per plant on untreated controls (Ibid.). Six applications of *V. lecanii*, at fourteen-day intervals, successfully controlled

A. gossypii on cucumber, when relative humidity in the greenhouse was manipulated to favor infection (Helyer 1993).

Other entomopathogens

Some Entomophthorales like *Erynia neoaphidis* (Remaudière and Hennebert) and *Conidiobolus obscurus* (Hall and Dunn) have high pathogenicity, wide geographical distributions, and broad host ranges. In addition, these species are relatively easy to mass rear *in vitro* and have favorable storage traits, as either mycelium or spores. However, in greenhouse trials against *M. persicae*, *M. euphorbiae*, and *A. gossypii* on eggplant and lettuce, infection levels were low, varying from 4 to 66%, or in some cases staying below 10% for up to five weeks after application (Latgé et al. 1982).

At least two commercial formulations of the muscardine fungus *Beauveria bassiana* (Balsamo) Vuillemin are available in many areas of the world. Although there has been little published on the use of these mycoinsecticides on pests of greenhouse vegetables, these formulations have been very effective in controlling various aphid species in tests conducted by several different researchers (Feng, Johnson, and Kish 1990; Hayden, Bidochka, and Khachtourians 1992; Wang and Knudsen 1993; Poprawski, Parker, and Tsai 1999). Provided environmental conditions are appropriate for infection, there do not appear to be biological reasons preventing testing of these formulations for aphid control in greenhouses.

Review of Relevant Biological Control Programs

Release programs for the biological control of aphids on greenhouse vegetables include the "pest in first method," the "open-rearing method" (i.e., banker plant system), and the direct release of beneficial agents either preventively or curatively. Most of the reports on the use and effect of biological control agents were derived from trials that were planned as demonstrations rather than for hypothesis testing with appropriate statistical analysis. Only one test used a design that permitted statistical analyses of the data (Gilkeson and Hill 1987). Most studies compared several different biological treatments (Bennison 1992; van Steenis and El-Khawass 1996), but few studies included an untreated or chemically treated control.

Flawed experimental designs force successful control to be defined as an increase of the parasitization rate, eradication of the aphid population, or a reduction in aphid densities below the levels of the infestation present at the start of the trial. In a few studies, the influence of pest control on crop yield was also assessed (Meadow, Kelly, and Shelton 1985; Gilkeson and Hill 1987; Hofsvang and Hågvar 1979). The influence of some other aphid natural enemies on aphid numbers have been described for situations in which these species were not intentionally introduced (Gilkeson 1990, Alomar et al. 1997).

Introduction Rates

Several studies have tried to identify the correct release rate and appropriate release intervals to achieve biological aphid control. In tomatoes, predator/prey ratios of one *A. aphidomyza* to three aphids per plant at infestation levels of fifteen to twenty aphids per plant led to the elimination of the aphids

within four weeks after making two releases seven days apart (Meadow, Kelly, and Shelton 1985). Three different introduction rates (0.09 wasps per ft.^{2} [1/m^2] of greenhouse space every two weeks; 0.05 wasps per ft.^{2} [0.5/m^2] every week or 0.02 wasps per ft.^{2} [0.25/m^2] two times per week) of *A. colemani* were assessed for the control of *A. gossypii* on cucumber plants (van Steenis and El-Khawass 1996). At the start of this test, 7% of the plants were artificially infested with five aphids per plant. Only at the highest *A. colemani* release rate were aphid populations sufficiently controlled, and eventually eliminated, within four weeks after the first introduction. For both of the lower release rate treatments, aphids increased to high levels before eventually being controlled (Ibid.). A single inoculative release of *A. matricariae* was tested for its ability to control *M. persicae* given an initial condition of 5,000 aphids on six eggplants (Tremblay 1974). A parasitoid-to-host ratio of one *A. matricariae* to fifty aphids proved to be effective, whereas a ratio of 1 to 150 was ineffective (Ibid.).

Open-rearing method

An open-rearing method (i.e., banker plant system) was first evaluated by Hansen (1988) in which a natural enemy, *A. aphidomyza*, was reared on a non-pestiferous aphid species, *Megoura viciae* Buckton, using broad bean (*Vicia faba* L.) as the host plant. These small, self-contained rearing systems were placed in greenhouses containing sweet pepper for control of *M. persicae*. Use of this method provided a prolonged release of natural enemies that in turn yielded successful aphid biological control. As a result, the method has been adopted for releasing other natural enemies in other cropping systems.

The banker plant system has been used most effectively in cucumber for the control of *A. gossypii* and other aphid species. Aphid species such as *S. avenae*, *M. dirhodum*, and *R. padi*, which do not infest cucumber, serve as hosts or prey for various beneficial agents. These aphid-infested banker plants allow the establishment of overlapping generations of the parasitoids or predators in the greenhouse, before the pest aphids have invaded the greenhouse (Bennison 1992, Lampharter 1992, Starý 1993). The common host aphids and host plants used are *R. padi* on winter barley (*Hordeum vulgare* L.) or the greenbug, *Schizaphis graminum* (Rondani) on winter wheat (*Triticum* sp.). The suggested numbers of banker plant units to place within the greenhouse vary. Recommendations include four to five banker plant units per 10,800 ft.^{2} (4 to 5/1,000 m^2), or one unit per hundred plants in early season crops (when the threat of an aphid infestation is high), or one unit per thousand plants in late season or replanted crops (when the threat of an aphid infestation is low). Weekly release rates between 0.01 and 0.05 *A. colemani* or *A. aphidomyza* per ft.^{2} (0.1 to 0.5/m^2), six to ten times during the season resulted in persistent control of *A. gossypii* within six weeks of the first release (Lampharter 1992, Bennison and Corless 1993).

Preventive releases

Preventive releases of *A. aphidomyza* at 0.02 to 0.05 pupae per ft.^{2} (0.25 to 0.5/m^2) every fourteen days, increased to 0.05 to 0.09 per ft.^{2} (0.5 to 1.0/m^2) after the first detection of aphids, have been used successfully for the control of *M. persicae* on sweet pepper (van Schelt, Douma, and Ravensberg 1990; Hansen 1988). The same approach has also been used for the control of other aphid species in cucumber. In contrast, releases of higher rates of *A. aphidomyza* (two per plant), at longer intervals (every four weeks), used two times preventively or once in combination with *A. matricariae* after aphids were seen, was unsuccessful, as neither beneficial species established (Buxton et al. 1990).

Seasonal inoculative releases

Tomato

In tomato, *M. euphorbiae* was successfully controlled by two releases of *A. abdominalis* at 0.07 to 0.11 adult wasps per ft.^{2} (0.8 to 1.2/m^2) within an eight to ten week period after the releases. During this period, the percentage of plants with parasitized aphids increased from 50 to 100% resulting in the complete disappearance of aphids (Alomar, Gabarra, and Castané 1997). Two releases of the predatory midge, *A. aphidomyza*, at the rate of 1 or 0.5 *A. aphidomyza* per six plants made seven days apart, eliminated *M. persicae* and *A. solani* four weeks after making the releases (Gilkeson 1990).

Cucumber

Four weekly releases of 0.09 to 0.19 *A. colemani* adults per ft.^{2} (1 to 2/m^2) starting one week after first aphid detection, led to control of *A. gossypii* on cucumber within eight weeks (Burgio, Ferrari, and Nicoli 1994). Release of 9.3 *A. aphidomyza* pupae per ft.^{2} (100/m^2) suppressed infestations of approximately 300 *A. gossypii* per cucumber plant within three weeks (Asyakin 1977). In another study, this predator was effective when released at the rate of one gall midge pupa for every five aphids (Bondarenko 1987).

Eggplant

On eggplant, four to seven releases of second instar *C. carnea* over a period of three to five months resulted in complete elimination of *M. persicae*, given a ratio of one predator for every five aphids. Sufficient control may be attained using a lower ratio of one predator to twenty aphids (Hassan 1977).

Sweet pepper

Predators are more commonly used than are parasitoids for control of aphids infesting sweet pepper. However, Hofsvang and Hågvar (1980) reported that the parasitoid *E. cerasicola* controlled a *M. persicae* infestation for more than four months on sweet pepper when released twice, ten days apart, at a rate of 0.4 adults per ft.^{2} (4/m^2).

Several studies have examined the use of the predatory midge *A. aphidomyza* for aphid biological control in sweet pepper. A release of one *A. aphidomyza* for every ten aphids controlled *M. persicae* for four weeks after the first release, whereas release rates of 1 to 50 and 1 to 100 provided unsatisfactory levels of control (Gilkeson and Hill 1987). Use of *A. aphidomyza*-to-aphid ratios between 1:10 and 1:50 yielded successful aphid control if releases were made three times during the early phases of an aphid infestation (Hofsvang and Hågvar 1980).

Green lacewing, *C. carnea*, successfully controlled *M. euphorbiae,* when ten to twenty second-instar lacewing larvae were released twice soon after detection of the infestation (Celli et al. 1991). Releases of *C. carnea* also controlled *M. persicae* and *A. fabae* when one lacewing larva was released for every three aphids weekly for six weeks, or when 1 lacewing egg was released for every 1.3 aphids, provided there were fewer than 100 aphids/plant and eggs were released every three to four weeks (Tulisalo and Tuivonen 1975; Tulisalo, Tuivonen, and Kurppa 1977). When *C. carnea* was released as second-instar larvae, a release of four lacewing larvae per plant controlled *M. persicae* within two weeks after one release. Three sequential, variable-rate releases of green lacewing larvae were also effective, with release rates of four larvae per plant in week one, one larva per plant in week two, and four larvae per plant in week three (Hassan 1977).

Factors Affecting Adoption of Aphid Biological Control

In many countries, aphid biological control is used on up to 53% of the total greenhouse vegetable area. Commonly used natural enemies are *A. colemani, A. matricariae, A. abdominalis, Praon volucre* (Haliday), *A. aphidomyza, C. carnea, H. convergens, H. axyridis,* and *V. lecanii* (Popov et al. 1987, Maisonneuve 1993, van Steenis 1995, Blümel and Schausberger 1996).

The ability of aphid natural enemies to control the target pest is influenced by factors such as temperature, relative humidity, and photoperiod and by various biotic factors (Gilkeson 1990; Burgio, Ferrari, and Nicoli 1994; Lezhneva and Anisimov 1995). Plant features such as trichomes, or sticky or toxic exudates adversely affect the searching efficiency of parasitoids and larvae of various predators, such as *C. carnea*, some coccinellids, and the predatory midge *A. aphidomyza* (Arzet 1973, Gurney and Hussey 1970,

Lampe 1984). Ants hinder or disturb parasitoids by protecting aphids from attack (while ants are feeding from their honeydew) or by directly removing the larval stages of natural enemies, such as *A. aphidomyza*, from the plant (Tulisalo, Tuivonen, and Kurppa 1977). Some predators (e.g., *Chrysoperla* spp.) are cannibalistic, which means they must be kept physically separated during shipping; and there exists an optimal release rate that will most efficiently bring about biological control (Quilici, Iperti, and Rabasse 1984). Other natural enemies are harmed by cultural practices that include the removal of lower leaves that often carry high numbers of parasitized aphid mummies, or by covering the ground with horticultural foil that interferes with the emergence of gall midge adults from the soil. In addition, all aphid natural enemies can be killed by chemical pesticide treatments (see chapter 7). Finally, the release of inferior quality natural enemies resulting for poor production, storage, or shipping practices can dramatically reduce the probability of achieving biological control (Buxton et al. 1990). Collectively, these problems affect the adoption of biological control by pest managers.

Economics of Aphid Biological Control

In general, the use of biological agents for aphid control on greenhouse vegetables is more expensive than chemical control. However, problems with pre-harvest or reentry intervals required after chemical treatment, loss of flowers and/or fruit caused by the phytotoxicity of some pesticides, the adoption of biocontrol or integrated measures to control other greenhouse crop pests and costs of spraying equipment and labor make the use of biological control of aphids attractive to and necessary for growers.

Within the context of a complete biological control program for cucumbers, the cost of aphid natural enemies represents a minor portion of the overall program costs. In 1996 and 1997, the costs of aphid natural enemies purchased for use in Austrian cucumber greenhouses accounted for 8.5 to 28.7% of all natural enemy purchases if *A. colemani* was the agent used, or 1.0 to 6.6% for locations using *A. aphidomyza*. The costs for materials and labor for aphid biological control, US $0.06 to 0.14 per ft.^{2} ($0.70 to 1.50/m^2) of greenhouse space, compare favorably to the US $0.01 to 0.32 per ft.^{2} ($0.10 to 3.50/m^2) for chemical control (Pleininger 1996, 1998). Yields in greenhouses where biological controls exceeded chemically treated by three to four cucumbers per plant, which more than compensated for the additional costs of purchasing the natural enemies. Gilkeson (1990) calculated the average cost of using *A. aphidomyza* at a release rate of one cocoon per four tomato plants at US $176 per acre ($0.04/m^2), which was acceptable in contrast to the very high expenses of US $5,800 per acre ($1.43/m^2) for use in sweet pepper production.

References Cited

Albajes, R., O. Alomar, J. Ruidavets, C. Castané, J. Arnó, and R. Gabarra. 1996. The mired bug *Dicyphus tamaninii*: An effective predator for vegetable crops. *IOBC/WPRS Bulletin* 19 (1):1–4.

Alomar, O., R. Gabarra, and C. Castané. 1997. The aphid parasitoid *Aphelinus abdominalis* (Hym.: Aphelinidae) for biological control of *Macrosiphum euphorbiae* on tomatoes grown in unheated plastic greenhouses. *IOBC/WPRS Bulletin* 20 (4):203–6.

Arzet, H. R. 1973. Suchverhalten von *Chrysopa carnea* Steph. (Neuroptera: Chrysopidae). *Zeitschrift für Angewandte Entomologie* 74 (1):64–79.

Asyakin, B. P. 1977. The effectiveness of a gall midge *Aphidoletes aphidomyza* Rond. (Diptera: Cecidomyiidae) in control of aphids on vegetable crops in glasshouses. *Vsesoyuznyi Nauchno-issledovatel'skii Institut Zashchity Rastenii* 37:51–5.

Bay, T. 1993. Die Florfliege *Chrysoperla carnea* (Stephens). *Mitteilungen aus der Biologischen Bundesanstalt für Land- und Forstwirtschaft, Berlin-Dahlem*. No. H288: 15-77.

Bennison, J. A. 1992. Biological control of aphids on cucumbers: Use of open rearing systems or "banker plants" to aid establishment of *Aphidius matricariae* and *Aphidoletes aphidomyza*. *Mededelingen Faculteit Landbouwweten-schappen Rijksuniversiteit Gent* 57 (2b):457–66.

Bennison, J. A., and S. P. Corless. 1993. Biological control of aphids on cucumbers: Further development of open rearing units or "banker plants" to aid establishment of aphid natural enemies. *IOBC/WPRS Bulletin* 16 (2):5–8.

Benuzzi, M., and G. Nicoli. 1993. Outlook for IPM in protected crops in Italy. *IOBC/WPRS Bulletin* 16 (2):9–12.

Blümel, S., and P. Schausberger. 1996. Current status of IPM in greenhouses in Austria. *IOBC/WPRS Bulletin* 19 (1):19–22.

Boll, R., J. Rochat, E. Franco, and L. Lapchin. 1994. Variabilité inter-pacellaire de la dynamique des populations de puceron *Aphis gossypii* Glover en serres de concombre. *IOBC/WPRS Bulletin* 17 (5):184–91.

Bondarenko, N.V. 1987. The experience of biological and integrated control of pests on glasshouse crops in the USSR. *IOBC/WPRS Bulletin* 10 (2):33–6.

Burgio, G., R. Ferrari, and G. Nicoli. 1994. Biological and integrated control of *Aphis gossypii* in protected cucumber and melon. *IOBC/WPRS Bulletin* 17 (5):192–7.

Buxton, J. H., R. Jacobsen, M. Saynor, R. Storer, and L. Wardlow. 1990. An integrated pest management programme for peppers: Three years trial experience. *IOBC/WPRS Bulletin* 13 (5):45–50.

Cecilio, A., M. M. Vieira, J. E. Feranades, and A. Neves. 1994. The control of aphids on protected melon crop in Algarve. *IOBC/WPRS Bulletin* 17 (5):170–6.

Celli, G., M. Benuzzi, S. Maini, G. Manzaroli, L. Antoniacci, and G. Nicoli. 1991. Biological and integrated pest control in protected crops of northern Italy's Po Valley: Overview and outlook. *IOBC/WPRS Bulletin* 14 (5):2–12.

Celli, G., G. Nicoli, and M. Benuzzi. 1987. Biological control in protected crops in northern Italy's Po Valley. *IOBC/WPRS Bulletin* 10 (2):37–40.

Chambers, R. J. 1986. Preliminary experiments on the potential of hoverflies (Dipt.: Syrphidae) for the control of aphids under glass. *Entomophaga* 31:197–204.

Devonshire, A. L. 1988. Resistance of aphids to insecticides. In *Aphids: Their Biology, Natural Enemies and Control, Vol. 2C*, ed. A. K. Minks and P. Harrewijn, 123–35. New York (Amsterdam): Elsevier.

Feng, M. G., J. B. Johnson, and L. P. Kish. 1990. Virulence of *Verticillium lecanii* and an aphid-derived isolate of *Beauveria bassiana* (Fungi: Hyphomycetes) for six species of cereal-infesting aphids (Homoptera: Aphidiidae). *Environmental Entomology* 19 (3):815–20.

Frazer, B.D. 1988. Coccinellidae. In *Aphids: Their Biology, Natural Enemies and Control, Vol. 2B*, ed. A. K. Minks and P. Harrewijn, 231–47. New York (Amsterdam): Elsevier.

Gilkeson, L. A. 1990. Biological control of aphids in greenhouse sweet peppers and tomatoes. *IOBC/WPRS Bulletin of* 13 (5):64–70.

Gilkeson, L. A., and S. B. Hill. 1986. Genetic selection for an evaluation of nondiapause lines of predatory midge *Aphidoletes aphidomyza* (Rondani) (Diptera: Cecidomyiidae). *Canadian Entomologist* 118 (9):869–79.

———. 1987 Release rates for control of green peach aphid (Homoptera: Aphidiidae) by the predatory midge *Aphidoletes aphidomyza* (Diptera: Cecidomyiidae) under winter greenhouse conditions. *Journal of Economic Entomology* 80:147–50.

Guenaoui, Y., R. Mahiout, M. Boualem, and R. Kerachi. 1994. Recherches de moyens biologiques pour lutter contre *Aphis gossypii* Glover (Hom.: Aphidiidae) en cultures protegees. Premiere evaluation de l'action parasitaire d'une souche thelytoque de *Lysiphlebus fabarum* Marshall (Hym.: Aphidiidae) d'origine algerienne sur son hôte *Aphis gossypii*. *IOBC/WPRS Bulletin* 17 (5):165–9.

Gurney, B, and N. W. Hussey. 1970. Evaluation of some coccinellid species for the biological control of aphids in protected cropping. *Annals of Applied Biology* 65:451–8.

Hågvar, E. B., and T. Hofsvang. 1986. Parasitism by *Ephedrus cerasicola* (Hym.: Aphidiidae) developing in different stages of *Myzus persicae* (Hom.: Aphidiidae). *Entomophaga* 31:337–46.

———. 1987. Foraging by the aphid parasitoid *Ephedrus cerasicola* for patchily distributed hosts. *Entomologia Experimentalis et Applicata* 44:81–8.

———. 1989. Effect of honeydew and hosts on plant colonization by the aphid parasitoid *Ephedrus cerasicola*. *Entomophaga* 34:495–501.

———. 1990. Fecundity and intrinsic rate of increase of the aphid parasitoid *Ephedrus cerasicola* Starý (Hym.: Aphidiidae). *Journal of Applied Entomology* 109:262–7.

Hansen, L. S. 1988. Introduction of *Aphidoletes aphidomyza* (Rond.) (Diptera: Cecidomyiidae) from an open rearing unit for the control of aphids in glasshouses. *IOBC/WPRS Bulletin* 6 (3):146–50.

Hassan S. A. 1977. Untersuchungen zur Verwendung des Prädators *Chrysoperla carnea* (Steph.) (Neuroptera: Chrysopidae) zur Bekämpfung der Grünen Pfirsichblattlaus *Myzus persicae* (Sulzer) an Paprika im Gewächshaus. *Zeitschrift für Angewandte Entomologie* 82:234–9.

Hatala-Zseller, I., E. Simon, P. Szabó, and E. Ceglarska-Hódi. 1993. Integrated pest and disease management in Hungarian greenhouses. *IOBC/WPRS Bulletin* 16 (2):55–8.

Hayden, T. P., M. J. Bidochka, and G. G. Khachatourians. 1992. Entomopathogenicity of several fungi toward the English grain aphid (Homoptera: Aphidiidae) and enhancement of virulence with host passage of *Paecilomyces farinosus*. *Journal of Economic Entomology* 85 (1):58–64.

Helyer, N. 1993. *Verticillium lecanii* for control of aphids and thrips on cucumber. *IOBC/WPRS Bulletin* 16 (2):63–6.

Hofsvang, T., and E. B. Hågvar. 1978. Effect of parasitism by *Ephedrus cerasicola* Starý on *Myzus persicae* (Sulzer) in small glasshouses: Biological methods to control pests. *Journal of Applied Entomology* 85 (1):11–5.

———. 1979. Different introduction methods of *Ephedrus cerasicola* Starý to control *Myzus persicae* (Sulzer) in small paprika glasshouses. *Journal of Applied Entomology* 88:16–23.

———. 1980. Use of mummies of *Ephedrus cerasicola* Starý to control *Myzus persicae* (Sulzer) in small greenhouses. *Journal of Applied Entomology* 90:220–6.

———. 1982. Comparison between the parasitoid *Ephedrus cerasicola* Starý and the predator *Aphidoletes aphidomyza* (Rondani) in the control of *Myzus persicae*. *Journal of Applied Entomology* 4:412–9.

Honek, A., J. Vojtech, L. Lapchin, and J. M. Rabasse. 1998. The effect of parasitism by *Aphelinus abdominalis* and drought on the walking movements of aphids. *Entomologia Experimentalis et Applicata* 87:191–200.

Hurni, B., and E. Stadler. 1993. The parasitic wasp *Aphelinus abdominalis* against aphids in tomatoes. *Gemüse* 29 (3):196–8.

Jarosik, V. A., A. Honek, J. M. Rabasse, and L. Lapchin. 1996. Life history characteristics of the aphid parasitoid *Aphelinus abdominalis* reared on *Macrosiphum euphorbiae*. *Ochrana Rostlin* 32 (2):83–8.

Kulp, D. 1989. Die räuberische Gallmücke *Aphidoletes aphidomyza* (Rondani) (Diptera: Cecidomyiidae). *Mitteilungen aus der Biologischen Bundesanstalt für Land- und Forstwirtschaft, Berlin-Dahlem*. No. H250, 14-72. Issue Number is H250; relevant pages: 14-72.

Kuo-Sell, H. L. 1989. Cereal aphids as a basis for the biological control of the peach aphid, *Myzus persicae* (Sulz.) with *Aphidoletes aphidomyza* (Rond.) (Dipt.: Cecidomyiidae) in greenhouses. *Journal of Applied Entomology* 107:58–64.

Lampe, U. 1984. Einflüsse unterschiedlicher Tpyen von Pflanzenhaaren auf Blattläuse und räuberische Blattlausfeinde. Dissertation. Universität Göttingen, Germany.

Lampharter, B. 1992. Nützlingseinsatz in der Kultur von Treibgurken–Das Problem Gurkenlaus (*Aphis gossypii*)–ein Erfahrungsbericht von der Insel Reichenau. *Gesunde Pflanzen* 44:229–32.

Latgé, J. P., and B. Papierok. 1988. Aphid pathogens. In *Aphids: Their Biology, Natural Enemies and Control, Vol. 2B*, ed. A. K. Minks and P. Harrewijn, 323–35. New York (Amsterdam): Elsevier.

Latgé, J. P., P. Silvie, B. Papierok, G. Remaudiere, C. A. Dedryvers, and J. M. Rabasse. 1982. Advantages and disadvantages of *Conidiobolus obscurus* and of *Erynia neoaphidis* in the biological control of aphids. In: *Aphid Antagonists*, ed. Cavalloro, R., Rotterdam: A. A. Balkema, 1983, 20-31. Proceedings of a meeting of the EC Experts' Group, Portici, Italy, 23-24 November 1982, 152 pp.

Lezhneva, I. P., and A. I. Anisimov. 1995. Predatory aphidophages for protection of greenhouse crops. *Zashchita-Rastenii-Moskwa* 11:39–40.

Lykouressis, D. P., and N. E. Roditakis. 1994. Aphid monitoring in greenhouse crops by using yellow water traps. *IOBC/WPRS Bulletin* 17 (5):176–80.

Maisonneuve, J. C. 1993. Biological control in protected crops in France in 1992. *IOBC/WPRS Bulletin* 16 (2):105–8.

Meadow, R. H., W. C. Kelly, and A. M. Shelton. 1985. Evaluation of *Aphidoletes aphidomyza* (Dipt.: Cecidomyiidae) for the control of *Myzus persicae* (Hom.: Aphidiidae) in greenhouse and field experiments in the United States. *Entomophaga* 30:385–92.

Milner, R. J., and G. G. Lutton. 1986. Dependence of *Verticillium lecanii* (Fungi: Hyphomycetes) on high humidities for infection and sporulation using *Myzus persicae* (Homoptera: Aphidiidae) as host. *Environmental Entomology* 15 (2):380–2.

Muminov, A., K. Askaraliev, and K. Oripov. 1976. The control of sucking pests of vegetables in glasshouses. *Zashchita Rostalnii* 2:27–8.

Pinna, M. 1992. Use of *Verticillium lecanii* (Zimm.) for the biological control of *Aphis gossypii* (Glover) on cucumber in protected cultivation. *Informatore Fitopatologico* 42:56–8.

Pleininger, S. 1996. Use of beneficials in cucumber. Demonstration project. LWK-Vienna *Die Information*, 2–4.

Pleininger, S. 1998. Demonstration trials in cucumber. *Gärtner and Florist* 11:2–6.

Popov, N. A., Y. V. Belousov, I. A. Zabudskaya, O. A. Khudyakova, V. B. Shevtvchenko, and E. S. Shijko 1987. Biological control of glasshouse crop pests in the south of the U.S.S.R. *IOBC/WPRS Bulletin* 10 (2):155–7.

Poprawski, T. J., P. E. Parker, and J. H. Tsai. 1999. Laboratory and field evaluation of hyphomycete insect pathogenic fungi for control of brown citrus aphid (Homoptera: Aphidiidae). *Environmental Entomology* 28 (2):315–21.

Quentin, U., M. Hommes, and T. Basedow. 1995. Studies on the biological control of aphids (Hom.: Aphidiidae) on lettuce in greenhouses. *Journal of Applied Entomology* 119:227–32.

Quilici, S., G. Iperti, and J. M. Rabasse. 1984. Trials of biological control in greenhouses on aubergine with an aphidophagous predator: *Propylea quatuordecimpunctata* L. (Coleoptera: Coccinellidae). *Frustula Entomologica* 7/8:9–25.

Rabasse, J. M., and F. F. Shalaby. 1980. Laboratory studies on the development of *Myzus persicae* Sulz. (Hom.: Aphidiidae) and its primary parasite, *Aphidius matricariae* Hal. (Hym.: Aphidiidae) at constant temperatures. *Acta Oecologica, Oecologica Applicata* 1:21–8.

Schepers, A. 1988. Chemical control. In *Aphids: Their Biology, NaturalEnemies and Control, Vol. 2C*, ed. A. K. Minks and P. Harrewijn, 89–121. New York (Amsterdam): Elsevier.

Shalaby, F. F., and J. M. Rabasse. 1979. On the biology of *Aphidius matricariae* Hal. (Hym.: Aphidiidae) parasite on *Myzus persicae* (Sulz.) (Hom.: Aphidiidae). *Annals of Agricultural Science Moshtohor* 11:75–96.

Spooner-Hart, R. 1993. Arthropods in the antipodes: Pests and biological control in protected crops in Australia. *IOBC/WPRS Bulletin* 16 (2):153–6.

Starý, P. 1993. Alternative host and parasitoid in first method in aphid pest management in glasshouses. *Journal of Applied Entomology* 116:187–91.

Steinberg, S., H. Prag, and D. Rosen. 1993. Host plant affects fitness and host acceptance in the aphid parasitoid *Lysiphlebus testaceipes* Cresson. *IOBC/WPRS Bulletin* 16 (2):161–4.

Tremblay, E. 1974. Possibilities for utilization of *Aphidius matricariae* (Hymenoptera: Ichneumonidea) against *Myzus persicae* (Sulz.) (Hom.: Aphidiidae) in small greenhouses. *Zeitschrift für Pflanzenkrankheiten und Pflanzenschutz* 10:612–9.

Trottin-Caudal, Y., C. Fournier, and P. Millot. 1996. Tomatoes under greenhouse: methods for controlling aphids. *Infos-Paris* 123:30–5.

Tulisalo, U. and T. Tuivonen. 1975. The green lacewing *Chrysoperla carnea* (Steph.) (Neuroptera: Chrysopidae) used to control the green peach aphid *Myzus persicae* (Sulz.) and the potato aphid *Macrosiphum euphorbiae* (Thomas) (Hom.: Aphidiidae) on greenhouse green peppers. *Annales Entomologici Fennici* 41:94–102.

Tulisalo, U., T. Tuivonen, and S. Kurppa. 1977. Biological control of aphids with *Chrysopa carnea* on parsley and green pepper in the greenhouse. *Annales Entomologici Fennici* 43:97–100.

van de Veire, M. 1991. Progress in IPM in glasshouse vegetables in Belgium. *IOBC/WPRS Bulletin* 14 (5):22–32.

van Schelt, J. 1993. Market driven research and development in biological control. *Pesticide Science* 37:405–9.

van Schelt, J., J. B. Douma, and W. J. Ravensberg. 1990. Recent developments in the control of aphids in sweet peppers and cucumbers. *IOBC/WPRS Bulletin* 13 (5):190–3.

van Steenis, M. J. 1993. Suitability of *Aphis gossypii* Glov., *Macrosiphum euphorbiae* (Thom.), and *Myzus persicae* (Sulz.) (Hom.: Aphidiidae) as host for several aphid parasitoid species (Hym.: Braconidae). *IOBC/WPRS Bulletin* 16 (2):157–60.

———. 1995. Evaluation and application of parasitoids for biological control of *Aphis gossypii* in glasshouse cucumber crops. Ph. D. Thesis, Wageningen, the Netherlands. 217pp.

van Steenis, M. J., and K. A. M. H. El-Khawass. 1996. Different parasitoid introduction schemes determine the success of biological control of *Aphis gossypii* with the parasitoid *Aphidius colemani*. *IOBC/WPRS Bulletin* 19 (1):159–62.

Wang, Z. G., And G. R. Knudsen. 1993. Effect of *Beauveria bassiana* (Fungi: Hyphomycetes) on fecundity of the Russian wheat aphid (Homoptera: Aphidiidae). *Environmental Entomology* 22 (4):847–78.

Zimmermann, G. 1982. Biological control of aphids by entomopathogenic fungi. Present state and prospects. Aphid antagonists. *Proceedings of the European Community Experts Meeting*, Portici, Italy, November, 33–40.

18

BIOLOGICAL CONTROL OF MINOR PESTS

D. R. Gillespie

Pacific Agri-Food Research Centre, Agriculture and Agri-Food Canada
Agassiz, British Columbia, Canada

and

R. A. Costello

British Columbia Ministry of Agriculture, Food and Fisheries
Abbotsford Agriculture Centre
Abbotsford, British Columbia, Canada

In addition to the regularly occurring arthropod pests that almost always cause serious damage to their host crop, there are minor pests of greenhouse crops that include some mites, scales, mealybugs, and many species of caterpillars. While the exact species of concern vary between regions and crops, methods employed for their biological control and the natural enemies used are similar.

Here, we provide information on the biology of these pests and their natural enemies. We do not cover pests of only sporadic or local importance, particularly if no biological control agents are used against them. For example, the pepper weevil, *Anthonomus eugenii* Cano (Coleoptera: Curculionidae), is a pest of field-grown pepper crops in the United States and Mexico that occurs in greenhouses in British Columbia (Riley 1992, Costello and Gillespie 1993). However, no biological control agents are used against this species.

Mirid plant bugs in the genera *Lygus*, *Lygocoris,* and *Liocoris* invade greenhouses and damage crops in North America and Europe. The classical biological control agents used outdoors have not been used in greenhouses (Day 1996; Norton and Welter 1996; Kuhlman, Mason, and Greathead 1998). However, microbial agents such as the entomopathogenic fungus *Beauvaria bassiana* (Balsamo) Vuillemin show promise as biological controls for these pests.

Where a pest is sporadic in occurrence or limited in distribution, the economics of the biocontrol industry generally preclude the production of low-demand specialty products. Generalist natural enemies developed and applied against other pests may be of some value. Integrated use of insecticides, monitoring, exclusion through quarantine and screening, and removal of infested plants remain the best control methods for these sporadic minor pests.

Pest Mites Other Than Spider Mites

Family Eriophyidae: Tomato russet mite

The tomato russet mite, *Aculops lycopersici* (Masse), is an important pest of field and greenhouse tomato crops in many parts of the world (Rice and Strong 1962, Perring and Farrar 1986, Cranshaw 1993). Adult russet mites are dispersed by wind. This is the probable mechanism of movement from field to greenhouse plants. Infestations usually are limited to a relatively small part of the crop and spread slowly, carried on the clothes of workers. Because of their small size (0.006 in. [0.15 mm] in length), infestations are rarely noticed until there are hundreds of mites per leaf and plants are damaged. At greenhouse temperatures, the life cycle is completed in seven days. The most favorable conditions are near 79°F (26°C) and 30% relative humidity, and photoperiod does not affect the life cycle. The tomato russet mite is a warm weather species and has no dormant stage. Subfreezing temperatures kill all stages within a few hours or days.

Damage caused by russet mites

Russet mites first feed on tomato plant stems, especially around the leaf axils, and later spread to the leaves (Keifer et al. 1982). Stems and leaves first bronze, then later turn brown. Leaves dry up and fall off (fig. 18.1). Light to moderate infestations cause a reduction in the photosynthetic activity of damaged leaves (Royalty and Perring 1989) that can lead to a reduction in crop yield. Heavy infestations cause tomato fruit to become russeted and heavily infested tomato plants may die in a few weeks. Pepper, potato, eggplant, and petunia (*Petunia hybrida* Vilm.) are also attacked.

Biological control of tomato russet mite

Commercially available predators that feed on *A. lycopersici* include the predatory mites *Neoseiulus cucumeris* (Oudemans), *Amblyseius fallacis* (Garman), and *Typhlodromus occidentalis* Nesbitt, as well as the minute pirate bug *Orius insidiosus* (Say). None of these have been used successfully to control greenhouse or field infestations. However, *A. fallacis* feeds on all stages of the pest and survives, develops, and reproduces in the presence of *A. lycopersici* (Brodeur, Bouchard, and Turcotte 1997). In addition, the little studied predatory mite *Euseius concordis* (Chant) (Acarina: Phytoseiidae) is also know to prey

Figure 18.1. The tomato russet mite, *Aculops lycopersici* **Masse, causes a characteristic bronzing on tomato leaves.** *Photo by D. Gillespie.*

on tomato russet mites (de Moraes and Lima 1983). Biological control may be enhanced by the use of tomato cultivars resistant to *A. lycopersici* damage (Kamau, Mueke, and Khaemba 1992) but compatible with the use of natural enemies.

Family Tarsonemidae: Cyclamen mite

The cyclamen mite, *Phytonemus pallidus* (Banks), is a tiny (0.005 in. [0.13 mm] long) colorless mite that thrives in cool temperatures and high relative humidity. Development from egg to adult can be completed in as little as eighteen days (Green 1978). Cyclamen mites avoid light and feed mainly on unopened leaflets and buds. Feeding causes wrinkled deformed leaves and buds that do not open or that produce distorted blooms. Preferred host plants include African violets (*Saintpaulia ionantha* Wendl.), cyclamen (*Cyclamen persicum* Miller), fuchsia (*Fuchsia* × hybrida), geranium (*Pelargonium* × hortorum L.H. Bailey), azalea (*Rhododendron* spp.), ivy (*Hedera helix* L.), and snapdragon (*Antirrhinum majus* L.).

There are no biological control agents identified for cyclamen mites, although *N. cucumeris* feeds on tarsonomid mites and may be of some value (Malais and Ravensberg 1992). If only a few plants are affected, it is best to destroy the infested plants. Immersion, pot and all, for fifteen minutes may kill cyclamen mites on non-blooming plants in water heated to 109°F (43°C). Lowering relative humidity can reduce infestation levels.

Family Tarsonemidae: Broad mite

The broad mite, *Polyphagotarsonemus latus* (Banks), is native to the tropics but is estab-

lished in greenhouses in Europe and North America. The adult is very small (0.007 in. [0.2 mm] long) and colorless. Like cyclamen mites, broad mites do best at moderate temperatures and high relative humidity. Under optimum conditions, development from egg to adult requires about seventeen days (Jeppson, Keifer, and Baker 1975). Broad mites feed on buds and growing tips, and as a result infested plants have curled leaves, shortened internodes, and damaged flowers. Toxins secreted by mites when feeding cause these deformations (Ibid.). Leaves become brittle and severe bud-drop occurs. Broad mites feed on impatiens (*Impatiens* x hybrida), ivy, begonia (*Begonia hiemalis* Fotsch), chrysanthemum (*Dendranthema* spp.), sweet pepper, tomato, and cucumber.

Several phytoseiid mites, including *Neoseiulus californicus* (McGregor), *Neoseiulus barkeri* Hughes, and *N. cucumeris* are known to feed on tarsonomid mites (Malais and Ravensberg 1992, Peña and Osborne 1996). Peña and Osborne (1996) were able to suppress broad mites on bean and lime plants in a greenhouse with releases of *N. californicus*, but not *N. barkeri*. However, Fan and Pettit (1994) report the success of augmentative releases of *N. barkeri* to control broad mite on many greenhouse crops in central Florida for more than three years.

Several cultural control methods may be useful in controlling broad mite infestations in addition to or as a substitute for biological control. If only a small number of plants are infested, one option is to remove those few plants from the greenhouse. Alternately, because road mites are sensitive to heat, immersing infested plants in water at 109°F (43°C) for fifteen minutes may kill the mites without damaging the plants.

Pest Scales and Mealybugs

Family Coccidae: Soft scales

Soft scales found in greenhouses include black scale (*Saissetia oleae* [Bernard]), nigra scale (*Saissetia nigra* [Nietner]), hemispherical scale (*Saissetia coffeae* [Walker]), and brown soft scale (*Coccus hesperidium* L.). Males are uncommon in the greenhouse environment, but female scales of some species can lay up to 2,000 eggs, with three to six generations per year (Steiner and Elliott 1983). Time from egg to reproductive adult averages sixty days, but varies with temperature and species. Soft scales are sap feeders, and their feeding on stems and the undersurfaces of leaves can cause stunting, distortion, and yellowing. They secrete copious amounts of honeydew resulting in sooty mold. Plants commonly attacked by soft scales include schefflera (*Schefflera* spp.), ivy, ficus (*Ficus* spp.), and cyclamen.

Family Diaspidae: Armored scales

Armored scales have a hard, waxy, plate-like covering over their bodies. They are less common than soft scales in greenhouses. Important species include the oleander scale (*Aspidiotus nerii* [Bouché]), San José scale (*Quadraspidiotus perniciosus* [Comstock]), oystershell scale (*Lepidosaphes ulmi* [L.]), and fern scale (*Pinnaspis aspidistrae* Signoret). Generation time is as long as ninety days, depending on temperature and species (Ibid.). Armored scales are found on

stems and lower leaf surfaces. They feed on sap but do not secrete honeydew. Feeding by armored scales stunts and distorts plants. Severe infestations may kill plants. Hosts in greenhouses include woody foliage plants such as palms (Palmae), ferns (such as *Nephrolepis exaltata* L.), and aspidistra (*Aspidistra elatior* Blume).

The parasitoid *Aphytis melinus* DeBach is available from commercial insectaries for release against some armored scales. Another parasitoid, *Metaphycus helvolus* (Compere), may be purchased for biological control of the soft scales *S. coffeae* and *C. hesperidium* (Visser and van Alphen 1987). Adult parasitoids are released two or three times at intervals of fourteen to twenty-one days. Release rates are relatively high (at least 0.9 per ft.^{2} [10/m^2]), but control remains variable. Several reasons may contribute to the unsatisfactory results. First, these parasitoids require temperatures of 72°F to 84°F (22 to 29°C) and temperatures below or above this range reduce their ability to locate and attack the scale hosts. Second, honeydew accumulations associated with soft scale infestations must be washed off plants before parasitoid introductions are initiated, as wasps walking on sticky foliage spend time cleaning themselves instead of searching for hosts and laying eggs (Steiner and Elliott 1983). Other parasitoids for control of brown soft scale appear to provide better control (e.g., *Metaphycus alberti* [Howard] [Stauffer and Rose 1997]), but these species are not commercially available.

Some predators can also contribute to scale control. The predatory ladybird beetle *Cryptolaemus montrouzieri* Mulsant, primarily used to control mealybugs, will feed on soft scales if other prey are scarce.

Other commercially available ladybird beetles, such as *Hippodamia convergens* Guerin, may provide some scale control if released in large numbers. Larvae of the green lacewing, *Chrysoperla carnea* (Stephens), feed on immature scales and may contribute to control. Because even dead scales can affect the appearance of a plant, it is best to discard heavily infested plants. In interior plantscapes, where labor costs may not be as important as in a production greenhouse, hand-removal, swabbing with alcohol, or hosing plants vigorously with water can be effective.

Family Pseudococcidae: Mealybugs

Mealybugs (fig. 18.2) are mobile, soft-bodied insects with waxy filaments projecting from the sides of their body. The wingless adult females are 0.20 to 0.31 in. (5 to 8 mm) long, whereas male mealybugs are less than 0.03 in. (1 mm) long and winged. The species most commonly found in greenhouses and plant conservatories are the citrus mealybug, *Planococcus citri* (Risso), and the long-tailed mealybug, *Pseudococcus longispinus* (Targioni-Tozzetti). Clausen (1978) provides discussions of the biology and natural enemies of both of these species. These mealybugs differ in various aspects of their host range and biology, but in particular in their reproductive habits. In contrast to citrus mealybug, whose females lay several hundred orange colored eggs in white cottony ovisacs, long-tailed mealybugs give birth to live young. The presence of ovisacs for one species and their absence for the other affects the resources available for predators, which in turn can affect their

success in establishing populations after their release in a greenhouse or conservatory.

After hatching, nymphs of citrus mealybug disperse to search for suitable feeding sites. Preferred sites include nodes and crotches of the host plant. Large colonies may form. There may be up to six generations per year on some greenhouse crops. Hosts include coleus (*Solenostemon scutellarioides*), cactus (Cactaceae), oleander (*Nerium oleander* L.), fuchsia, and cucumber, among others. Damage to host plants may result from mealybug feeding or mere presence, which detracts from the plants' appearance. Mealybugs weaken plants as they suck sap and remove nutrients. As a result, the plants often become stunted, distorted, or yellowed. Honeydew covers leaves with a sticky coating that fosters sooty mold. Ants seen foraging on honeydew may be used as an indicator of an infestation of foliage-feeding mealybugs.

Figure 18.2. The long-tailed mealybug, *Pseudococcus longispinus* (Targioni-Tozzetti), is commonly found infesting plants in greenhouses and plant conservatories.
Photo by M. P. Parrella.

Most mealybugs colonize the aerial parts of plants, but some species (*Rhizoecus* spp.) are root feeders. These are rather different from other mealybugs in that infestations are not readily visible. Root-feeding mealybugs can spread in infested soil or plant debris, thus their control centers on detection and sanitation by destruction of infested plants. Prevention of both aerial and soil-inhabiting species involves examination of new plants entering a greenhouse and disinfestation or destruction of all infested plant material.

Of the two mealybugs of concern in greenhouses, most work has been done on citrus mealybug. Previous studies investigated the impact of mixed complexes of predators and parasitoids for control of citrus mealybug in gardenia production (Doutt 1951), greenhouse citrus (Summy, French, and Hart 1986), and mixed ornamentals (Hennekam et al. 1987). Information is lacking on biological control of long-tailed mealybug in greenhouses. The agents that are relatively effective against citrus mealybug may be less so against this species.

The mealybug destroyer, *C. montrouzieri,* is the natural enemy most often used for biological control of mealybugs. Adult beetles, 0.16 in. (4 mm) long, actively fly in search of prey. Their preferred prey is mealybug eggs. Mated females lay up to 500 eggs, primarily among mealybug colonies, in their fifty-day lifetime. Predator eggs hatch in five to six days at 81°F (27°C). The four larval stages have waxy protuberances that cause them to resemble mealybugs. This often leads to misidentifications by the inexperienced user. The larvae of this beetle consume up to 250 early instar mealybugs in a lifetime. Because of their relatively large

size, older larvae are capable of feeding on any developmental stage of the mealybug. *Cryptolaemus montrouzieri* pupate and remain for seven to ten days in sheltered places on stems or greenhouse structures. The life cycle (egg to egg) requires about forty-five days at 70°F (21°C) and thirty-one days at 81°F (27°C).

The two parasitoids that have been studied in most detail as potential biological control agents of mealybugs in protected culture are the encyrtids *Leptomastix dactylopii* Howard and *Leptomastidea abnormis* (Girault) (Tingle and Copland 1988; de Jong and van Alphen 1989; van Baaren and Nenon 1996; Cadee and van Alphen 1997). Most work has been done on *L. dactylopii* as a parasitoid of citrus mealybug. As a result, information about its host stage preferences and reproductive rates are available (de Jong and van Alphen 1989; Tingle and Copland 1989; van Baaren and Nenon 1996). Less information is available on the suitability of long-tailed mealybug as a host of these parasitoid species. Blumberg and Van Driesche (2001) found that 54 to 68% of *L. dactylopii*'s eggs were encapsulated by *P. longispinus* (depending on rearing temperature), making this parasitoid a poor biological control agent for long-tailed mealybug. Two other parasitoids, *Pseudaphycus angelicus* (Howard) and *Anagyrus fusciventris* (Girault) are recognised as potentially better parasitoids of long-tailed mealybug. Only 6% of *A. fusciventris*'s eggs were found to be encapsulated by long-tailed mealybug (Blumberg and Van Driesche 2001).

The parasitoid *L. dactylopii* can be an effective control agent for citrus mealybug. It is most effective at low mealybug densities, used to complement the action of the predator *C. montrouzieri,* which works best at high host densities. The female wasp lays an average of eighty eggs over its lifetime, choosing third-stage nymphs and adult mealybugs as its preferred hosts. This parasitoid is most effective in a sunny, warm (75 to 81°F [24 to 27°C]), and humid environment. Developmental time is twenty-eight days at 75°F (24°C) and eighteen days at 81°F (27°C). Additional information on the biology and life cycle of this parasitoid is reviewed by Clausen (1978).

Control of ants is an important part of a mealybug control program, as ants may attack beneficial species to protect mealybugs and their honeydew. In plantscapes, washing infested plants with water can be of value as it removes the honeydew sought by ants. If mealybugs occur only on one or two high value plants, hand removal or swabbing infested leaves with rubbing alcohol will provide control. If infested plants are not high value specimens, discard heavily infested plants.

Family Psyllidae: Psyllids

The tomato/potato psyllid

The tomato/potato psyllid, *Paratrioza cockerelli* (Šulc.) has been a periodic pest in greenhouse tomato and pepper crops in the United States and Canada (Ferguson and Shipp 2000). As a pest of tomato and potato crops outdoors, the psyllid makes northward migrations from overwinterijng locations in New Mexico and Texas (Wallis 1955). Invasions into greenhouse apparently occur during these migrations, and possibly also from second and third generation adults from crop plants and weeds. Host plants are in the Solanaceae, and tomato and potato are the most important crop hosts. Greenhouse pepper crops in British Columbia have also been heavily attacked by *P. cockerelli.*

Adults resemble aphids somewhat, are strong fliers, and are easily disturbed from foliage. Females lay slightly stalked eggs on the margins of leaves. These eggs hatch into a scale-like nymphs that resemble whitefly nymphs to some degree. There are five nymphal stages and all are capable of limited movement. Development from egg to adult requires 21 days at 68°F (20°C). Adults and nymphs produce distinctive honeydew, which occurs in pellets coated with a waxy membrane. These pellets are white and closely resemble granulated sugar in size and appearance. The presence of this characteristic honeydew is diagnostic for the presence of psyllids.

The primary damage from *P. cockerelli* on tomato is a syndrome called psyllid yellows. The upper quarter of the plant becomes chlorotic, leaves are thin, and fruit set is greatly reduced. The condition is induced by moderate to large numbers of nymphs. Plants outgrow symptoms once nymphs are removed. On pepper, psyllid yellows do not appear to develop and the main injury is from sticky fruit and the accumulation of honeydew in the fruit calyx.

Biological control of psyllids

Green lacewings were tested as biological control agents on potato and, although larvae fed on the eggs and nymphs of *P. cockerelli,* they did not provide control (Al-Jabr 1999). A specialist parasitoid *Tamarixia triozae* (Burks) (Hymenoptera: Eulophidae) was reared in limited number by a biological control agent producer and was released against tomato/potato psyllid populations on tomato in British Columbia. Female parasitoids laid eggs in older nymphs, and developed as ectoparasitoids, underneath the body of psyllid nymphs. Although records of parasitism and numbers of psyllids were not maintained in these trials, anecdotal accounts by growers and IPM advisors involved suggest that this parasitoid established successfully and reduced psyllids below economic injury levels on tomatoes. The sporadic nature of demand for the parasitoid apparently made continued production uneconomical, and it is no longer available.

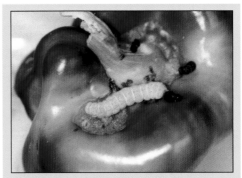

Figure 18.3. Caterpillars of the variegated cutworm, *Peridroma saucia* (Hübner), bore into fruit, where they are protected from natural enemies.
Photo by D. Gillespie.

Pest Caterpillars

Family Noctuidae: Armyworms, loopers, leafworms, fruitworms, and cutworms

The Noctuidae is a large, diverse group of over 5000 moth species worldwide (Hill 1994). Adults are medium sized, grey to brown moths that are strong fliers. Eggs are laid singly or in groups. The mature caterpillars are large and heavy-bodied, and are light green, brown, or black. The various terminology applied to the common names (e.g., loopers and inchworms) is frequently associated with various aspects of larval biology such as the numbers of abdominal prolegs, types of movement, and feeding modes.

It is not feasible to cover all of the noctuid caterpillars that might be found in greenhouses in the world, given the numbers and diversity of species. As a result, only the most common species are discussed. In addition, cutworms (fig. 18.3) and climbing cutworms are not treated because natural enemies are not presently used to control them.

Crop advisors should remember that specialists in moth identification rely on examination of specialized structures under high-powered microscopes to obtain identifications. Many moth species are difficult to distinguish based on external characteristics. Growers should obtain species identification from experts. Correct species identifications form the foundation of any management program, since such identifications provide access to a great deal of information on pest biology and guide the correct choice of natural enemies.

Autographa gamma (L.)

This migratory species is widely distributed in Europe and Asia (Hill 1994). It frequently invades and overwinters in greenhouses in the northern areas of its geographic distribution. Malais and Ravensberg (1992) provide a summary of *A. gamma*'s life cycle. Greyish-white eggs, laid singly or in small clusters on the undersides of leaves, hatch in about six days. Caterpillars are light green loopers with yellowish heads and six longitudinal white lines on the body. The adults have brownish to grey forewings, with a characteristic white spot in the center that resembles the Greek letter γ (gamma). Caterpillars feed on leaves for about thirty days before spinning loose cocoons and pupating in folded leaves on plants. Several other species of loopers that occur in greenhouses have a white or off-white spot on the forewing, and these are frequently misidentified as *A. gamma*. Loopers similar in appearance to *A. gamma* include the golden twin-spot or green garden looper (*Chrysodeixis chalcites* [Esper]), the alfalfa looper (*Autographa californica* [Speyer]), and the cabbage looper (*Trichoplusia ni* [Hübner]). The primary injury caused by these caterpillars is defoliation, although young fruit may be attacked.

Several natural enemies have been used for biological control of loopers. Foliar applications of *Bacillus thuringiensis* Berliner targeted against early instar larvae are the most common and are generally successful. Several predators that feed on immature loopers have received some attention. The predatory bug *Podisus maculiventris* (Say) feeds on caterpillars of all sizes. The mirid bug *Macrolophus caliginosus* (Wagner) and the anthocorid bugs in the genus *Orius* will feed on both eggs and small caterpillars. Among the parasitoids examined are *Cotesia marginiventris* (Cresson), which attacks first-instar larvae, and several species of *Trichogramma*, which parasitize the eggs.

Spodoptera exiguae *(Hübner)*

The beet armyworm is widely distributed in western North America (Arnett 1993), Africa, southern Europe, and Asia (Hill 1994). It infests greenhouses in northern Europe,

where it is known as the Florida moth. This species survives year-round in northern European greenhouses, but is unable to overwinter elsewhere in northern climates.

A female moth lays green eggs, covered with hairs and scales from her abdomen, in masses of approximately 150. The eggs darken with time and hatch after two days at 77 to 81°F (25 to 27°C). The larval stages last approximately thirteen days and are followed by a two-day pupal stage that occurs in the soil (Patana 1985). Larvae feed gregariously during the first two instars and then disperse. By their feeding, they defoliate vegetable, ornamental and floral crops, bore into pepper and tomato fruits, and damage flowers. The caterpillars are yellow-green and darken with age. They have a characteristic pair of yellow dorsolateral stripes. The relatively small-sized adult possesses a kidney-shaped, yellow spot on a grey forewing. Species of similar appearance to *S. exigua* are *Spodoptera frugiperda* (J. E. Smith), which occurs in South America and North America, and the cotton leafworm, *Spodoptera littoralis* (Boisduval), which occurs in Africa and the Mediterranean region (Hill 1994).

Efficacy among control strategies varies greatly. The efficacy of *B. thuringiensis* to control *S. exigua* has been questioned by field workers, but we are unaware of published studies. Some beet armyworm caterpillars feed inside fruits, where they are not exposed to natural enemies or most biopesticides. Egg masses are protected from parasitism by *Trichogramma* spp. parasitoids by the hairs and scales deposited by the female moth. However, good control has been obtained using the parasitoid *Cotesia marginiventris* (Cresson) and predators such as *Podisus maculiventris* (Say) (Rajapahse, Ashely, and van Waddill 1988; Carpenter, Hidrayani, and Sheenan 1996).

Mamestra brassicae *(L.)*

The cabbage armyworm, also called the cabbage moth, is only known to occur in Europe and Asia (Hill 1994). This pest may have many generations per year in greenhouses, where it often infests peppers and chrysanthemums (Malais and Ravensberg 1992). Female moths lay eggs in groups of 20 to 30 on the underside of leaves, and a female lays an average of 500 eggs during her lifetime (Sannina and Espinosa 1998). Newly deposited eggs are transparent, but later turn brownish black (Malais and Ravensberg 1992). Eggs hatch in twelve to eighteen days, and the young caterpillars feed gregariously before dispersing. Caterpillars are initially yellow, later turning green, and then turn, brownish black just before pupation. Feeding lasts for thirty to fifty days. Pupation occurs in the soil and the pupal stage can last for several months. Adults have greyish-brown to black wings with a span of 1.8 in. (45 mm). The wings have a kidney-shaped, white-edged spot in the center.

Biological control is possible using *B. thuringiensis* and the predator *P. maculiventris.* The parasitoids *Trichogramma brassicae* Bezdenko and *Eulophus pennicornis* (Nees) (Eulophidae) provide successful biological control of cabbage armyworm (van de Veire 1993, Hassan and Wuher 1997).

Helicoverpa zea *(Boddie)*

The corn earworm, also called the tomato fruitworm, is a pest of tomato and pepper crops in North America. Moths migrate annually from the southern U.S. and invade greenhouses in Canada and the northern U.S. The moths are large (with a 1.8- to 2.6-in. [45- to 65-mm] wingspan) and yellowish-brown. Females lay pale green eggs singly in a somewhat random distribution on the plant foliage. Larvae grow to 1.6 in. (40 mm) and have yellow heads, black legs, and light and dark longitudinal stripes on a background that varies from light green to brown or black. Damage occurs when larvae bore into tomato and pepper fruits. Pupation occurs in the soil. Species similar in appearance found attacking greenhouse crops include *Helicoverpa assulta* (Guenée) in Asia and *Helicoverpa armigera* (Hübner) in Europe.

Control strategies such as natural enemies or pesticides do not kill larvae in fruits. Hence, efforts have been directed toward disrupting adult mating (and thus reduce egg laying) with sex pheromones, and by mass trapping of adults with and light traps. The success of these methods to control *H. zea* in protected cultures has not been conclusively demonstrated.

Trichoplusia ni *Hübner*

The cabbage looper is an important pest of greenhouse vegetable crops in Canada (Gillespie, Raworth and Shipp, 2002). Canadian populations originate from adult moths migrating from the south (Lafontaine and Poole 1991). There is some evidence that cabbage loopers can overwinter in greenhouses in cold climates. There are several generations per year inside greenhouses, and tomato, pepper, and cucumber are attacked. The caterpillars are foliage feeders, and may also feed directly on cucmber fruits, scarring them. The most important damage is from contamination of fruit by caterpillar frass, which accumulates in the calyx of pepper fruit, and by meconium, which the adult moths void soon after emergence.

Biological control is possible using *B. thuringiensis* in conjunction with *T. brassicae* and integrated IPM techniques. There is evidence that cabbage loopers are becoming resistant to *B. thuringiensis* (Janmaat and Myers 2003). The efficiency of biological control using *Trichogramma* may be lower on tomato than on pepper, due to a slower walking speed for wasps on tomato, perhaps due to the glandular hairs on tomato leaves (McGregor, Prasad and Henderson 2002). *Podisus maculiventris* can be used as a predator on pepper and cucumber, and *C. marginiventris* releases can enhance biological control.

Family Torticidae: Leafrollers and budmoths

Leafrollers feed in protected shelters made of leaves held together by silk strands, whereas budmoths tend to feed inside buds and growing tips. Two leafrollers, *Clepsis spectrana* Treitschke (the straw-colored tortix) and *Cacoecimorpha pronubana* (Hübner), are periodic pests of protected crops. There is little else reported for *C. pronubana* except that it is known to attack carnations (*Dianthus caryophyllus* L.) in greenhouses in Europe (Jarrett 1985, Quaglia 1993).

Clepsis spectrana is found in greenhouses in Europe (Malais and Ravensberg 1992) and is found outdoors, but not in greenhouses in western British Columbia, Canada (Dang, Duncan, and Fitzpatrick 1996). Adults are straw-colored, with two brown spots on each wing that join together when the wings are folded to form a V. Female moths lay eggs

on leaves in groups of ten to seventy eggs. Common host plants include rose (*Rosa* spp. and hybrids), alstroemeria (*Alstroemeria* spp.), gerbera (*Gerbera jamesonii* Bolus ex Adlam), cyclamen, and kalanchoe (*Kalanchoe* spp.) (Malais and Ravensberg 1992). The larvae (up to 1 in. [25 mm] long) are grey to dark brown with a dark green to black head. They feed in silk webs (where pupation occurs) and the larvae vigorously wriggle backwards when disturbed. This distinguishes the species from other caterpillars found in greenhouses (Ibid.). There are eight to twelve generations per year in greenhouses.

Multiple applications of *B. thuringiensis* control these species (Jarrett 1985, Malais and Ravensberg 1992). Repeated applications are needed because the susceptible caterpillar feeds under the protection provided by webbed leaves and it is often not exposed to the biopesticide. *Trichogramma* spp. and predators like *P. maculiventris* and *M. caliginosus* can also be used.

Family Gelechiidae: Tomato pinworm

The tomato pinworm, *Keiferia lycopersicella* (Walshingham), has become an important pest of tomato crops in Ontario, Canada (Wang, Fergusen, and Shipp 1998). Although this species will not overwinter outdoors in northern climates, populations persist in greenhouses for several years. Eggs are laid on both upper and lower surfaces of leaves and hatch in six to eight days (Schuster 1989). First instar larvae mine leaves while older larvae feed either as leafrollers or they bore into fruit, the latter causing severe economic losses (Wang, Ferguson, and Shipp 1998). The time for development from an egg to an adult is twenty-one days at 79 to 81°F (26 to 27°C) (Schuster 1989). Effective control strategies within protected cultures include the use of pheromones for mating disruption (Wang, Ferguson, and Shipp 1998), releases of the egg parasitoid *Trichogramma pretiosum* Riley at host-to-parasitoid ratios of 1:1 to 1:10, and releases of *T. pretiosum* combined with mating disruption (Shipp, Wang, and Ferguson 1998).

Family Pyralidae: European corn borer

The European corn borer, *Ostrina nubilalis* (Hübner), is a pest of greenhouse grown pepper in North America and Europe. One to two generations occur annually, with female moths laying eggs in masses on leaves or on the calyx of the fruit. After hatch, larvae feed on leaves and then bore into fruit. As with the other fruit boring pests, this feeding behaviour results in severe damage and it protects the pest from both natural enemies and insecticides. Mature caterpillars are approximately 1.2 in. (30 mm) long, they are grey to tan with a spotted overlay of brown plates, and they have setae. Pupation occurs inside fruit. Adult moths have a 1-in. (25-mm) wingspan and the wings are light brown with dark cross bands. Releases of *Trichogramma* species may suppress populations by reducing the numbers of eggs producing corn borer larvae. In addition, *B. thuringiensis* applications timed to coincide with egg hatch may effectively suppress corn borer populations.

Natural enemies of Lepidoptera

Egg parasitoids

Trichogramma wasps are primary egg parasitoids of various Lepidoptera. Adults lay one to several eggs inside host eggs. Parasitoid eggs hatch in twenty-four to forty-eight hours and larvae feed on the contents of the host egg, killing it. The feeding activity generally turns pale host eggs dark, but this can be obscured in host species with naturally dark eggs. The adult wasp emerges after ten to twenty days, leaving a round exit hole in the host egg.

Trichogramma species are released by placing parasitized eggs (packaged loose or placed on cards) within the targeted area. Many species are reared commercially in eggs of stored products moths or in artificial eggs; the latter reduces the price of wasps to end users (Greensberg, Nordland, and Wu 1998). While most commercial insectaries produce and sell high quality natural enemies, purchasers ultimately regulate quality control. To insure successful biological control, *Trichogramma* wasps should be periodically assessed for their ability to fly. Examples of wasps improperly maintained within commercial mass-rearing cultures have been reported to either be unable to fly or to locate hosts (Dutton, Cerotti, and Bigler 1996; Xie et al. 1997). Flight ability may be assessed directly by letting wasps emerge from a portion of the parasitized eggs received from the insectary into a clear cage and observing their flight. An indirect assessment of flight may be accomplished by the recovery of wasps released into a greenhouse on sticky traps suspended within or above the crop. By monitoring levels of host parasitism after release of the wasps, practitioners can assess the wasps' ability to locate hosts.

Only a small number of the *Tricho-gramma* species available commercially have been sufficiently studied to assess their ability to control caterpillars in greenhouses. Three releases of *Trichogramma evanescens* Westwood, made fourteen days apart from fifteen locations in a tomato greenhouse and at a rate of 0.7 parasitized eggs per ft.^{2} (8/m^2), resulted in parasitism of 82% of the eggs oviposited by the pest moth, *Chrysodeixis chalcites* (Esper) (Pizzol, Voegele, and Marconi 1997). *Trichogramma brassicae*, released twice weekly at 37 adults per ft.^{2} (400/m^2), reduced damage from European corn borer, *O. nubilalis*, to the fruit of peppers grown in protected culture from 20% in areas without wasps to 5% in areas receiving parasitoid releases (Maini and Burgio 1991). Achieving a ratio of one *T. pretiosum* for every ten *K. lycopersicella* hosts may control pinworm when used as part of an integrated approach for greenhouse grown tomatoes (Shipp, Wang, and Ferguson 1998). In summary, releases of *Trichogramma* alone are unlikely to provide satisfactory biological control of Lepidoptera in greenhouses. For this reason, it is best to use them as part of a larger management program.

Eulophus pennicornis *and* Cotesia marginiventris

Although many parasitoid species in addition to *Trichogramma* spp. attack Lepidoptera, only two species have been investigated for their potential for biological control in greenhouse crops. These are the eulophid *E. pennicornis* and the braconid *C. marginiventris*.

Eulophus pennicornis is a gregarious ectoparasitoid that attacks several noctuid species commonly found in greenhouses (van de Veire 1993). Females attack late-instar larvae

and parasitoid development requires approximately twenty days (Marris and Edwards 1995). Inoculative and inundative releases show promise against tomato moth, *Lacanobia oleracea* (L.) (Lepidoptera: Noctuidae), and other Lepidoptera species in greenhouses (van de Veire 1993, Marris and Edwards 1995).

Cotesia marginiventris is a solitary endoparasitoid of many species of noctuid caterpillars. Females lay eggs inside newly emerged larvae, or more rarely, inside eggs about to hatch (Ruberson and Whitfield 1996). Parasitoid larvae hatch in about two days and require six to eight days to complete development. Mature larvae emerge from the host caterpillar and pupate inside white silk cocoons located on leaves or stems of plants (Boling and Pitre 1970). *Cotesia marginiventris* parasitizes cabbage loopers in greenhouses (Gillespie et al. 1997) and is a key parasitoid of *Spodoptera* and *Helicoverpa* species on a variety of crops (Carpenter, Hidrayani, and Sheehan 1996; Cortesero et al. 1997). It should be tested for its ability to provide biological control of various Lepidoptera pests in greenhouses.

Predators

Many of the generalist predators used in greenhouse biological control attack many species and developmental stages of lepidopteran pests and thus contribute to their biological control. While the level of control achieved by these predators depends on the abundance of alternative and preferred prey, their activity can contribute to the overall level of pest suppression achieved by natural enemy releases. Predation by the bug *M. caliginosus* reduces numbers of *L. oleracea* on greenhouse tomatoes (Sampson and King 1996), and when used in combination with parasitoids may provide acceptable pest control. Minute pirate bugs, *Orius* spp., often immigrate and become abundant in greenhouse crops grown in the subtropical and tropical regions. In many regions of the world they are released for biological control of thrips (Malais and Ravensberg 1992). These predators also feed on moth eggs and small caterpillars and may reduce pest caterpillar numbers (Jacobsen and Kring 1994). Other general predators such as ladybird beetles and green lacewings also feed on the eggs of Lepidoptera.

Spined soldier bugs, particularly *P. maculiventris*, may be useful in controlling many caterpillar pests in greenhouses (van der Linden 1996). Nymphs of these bugs require approximately thirty days to complete development at 73°F (23°C). Female bugs live for over sixty days and lay several hundred eggs (De Clerq and Degheele 1992, 1993). Fourth instar nymphs of *P. maculiventris* released into tomato greenhouses at a rate of 1 predator per 3.3 *C. chalcites* caterpillars resulted in rapid reduction of caterpillar numbers (De Clerq et al. 1998). Again, however, effective biological control that limits crop damage requires the integration of natural enemies with other control practices. Current experience in greenhouses suggests that inoculative releases of *P. maculiventris* should be made early in the cropping season, and these releases should be coupled with releases of *Trichogramma* spp. or *C. marginiventris*. Mating disruption with pheromones, mass trapping with light traps, and biological control with *B. thuringiensis* may also be integrated with the use of this predator.

Diseases

The bacterium *B. thuringiensis* is widely used for biological control of caterpillar pests in many countries. It is applied, together with a carrier and other ingredients, to the foliage where it remains viable for less than forty-eight hours. When a caterpillar ingests a spore, the spore dissolves and releases enzymes that break down the midgut wall of the caterpillar. This allows invasion of bacteria into the body cavity and causes general septicemia and eventual death. *Bacillus thuringiensis* insecticides are not effective against all immature Lepidoptera. Host specificity of this bacterial insecticide is achieved in part by its requirement for an alkaline gut (pH > 9) within its host. Because spores must be consumed for insecticidal activity to occur, caterpillars that feed in protected enclosures such as inside fruits, webs, or leaf mines, are either not exposed or are exposed to low doses; consequently caterpillars are often not controlled by *B. thuringiensis*. There must be sufficient time for the infection cycle to be completed, thus early instar caterpillars are generally more susceptible than are late instar caterpillars (which have a short period of time remaining until they pupate). Species differences can be striking. For example, beet armyworm is less susceptible than other noctuids and is therefore more difficult to manage with this pathogen (Malais and Ravensberg 1992, Yoshida and Parrella 1987).

References Cited

Al-Jabr, A. M. 1999. Integrated pest management of tomato/potato psylli, *Paratrioza cockerelli* (Sulc) (Homoptera: Psyllidae) with emphasis on its importance in greenhouse grown tomatoes. Ph.D. Thesis, Department of Bioagricultural Sciences and Pest Management Colorado State University. 89 pp.

Arnett, R. H., Jr. 1993. *American Insects: A Handbook of the Insects of America North of Mexico*. Gainesville, Fla.: Sandhill Crane Press.

Blumberg, D., and R. G. Van Driesche. 2001. Encapsulation rates of three encyrtid parasitoids by three mealybug species (Homoptera: Pseudococcidae) found commonly as pest in commercial greehouses. *Biological Control* 22: 191–9.

Boling, J. C., and H. N. Pitre. 1970. Life history of *Apanteles marginiventris* with descriptions of immature stages. *Journal of the Kansas Entomological Society* 43:465–70.

Brodeur, J., A. Bouchard, and G. Turcotte. 1997. Potential of four species of predatory mites as biological control agents of the tomato russet mite, *Aculops lycopersici* (Masse) (Eriophyidae). *Canadian Entomologist* 129:1–6.

Cadee, N., and J. J. M. van Alphen. 1997. Host selection and sex allocation in *Leptomastidea abnormis*, a parasitoid of the citrus mealybug, *Planococcus citri. Entomologia Experimentalis et Applicata* 83:277–84.

Carpenter, J. E., Hidrayani, and W. Sheenan. 1996. Compatibility of F_1 sterility and a parasitoid, *Cotesia marginiventris* (Hymenoptera: Braconidae), for managing *Spodoptera exiguae* (Lepidoptera: Noctuidae): acceptability and suitability of hosts. *Florida Entomologist* 79:289–95.

Clausen, C. P., ed. 1978. *Introduced Parasites and Predators of Arthropod Pests and Weeds: A World Review.* USDA-ARS, Agriculture Handbook No. 480.

Cortesero, A. M., C. M. de Moraes, J. O. Stapel, J. H. Tumlinson, and W. J. Lewis. 1997. Comparisons and contrasts in host-foraging strategies of two larval parasitoids with different degrees of host specificity. *Journal of Chemical Ecology* 23(6):1589–606.

Costello, R. A., and D. R. Gillespie. 1993. The pepper weevil, *Anthonomus eugenii,* as a greenhouse pest in Canada. *IOBC/WPRS Bulletin* 16:31–4.

Cranshaw, W. S. 1993. An annotated bibliography of the potato/tomato psyllid, *Paratrioza cockerelli* (Sulc) (Homoptera: Psyllidae*). Technical Bulletin* TB93-5, Department of Entomology, Colorado State University Agriculture Experiment Station.

Dang, P. T., R. W. Duncan, and S. Fitzpatrick. 1996. Occurrence of two palearctic species of *Clepsis Guenée, C. spectrana* Treitschke, and *C. consimilana* (Hübner) (Tortricidae), in British Columbia, Canada. *Journal of the Lepidopterists Society* 50:321–8.

Day, W. H. 1996. Evaluation of biological control of the tarnished plant bug (Hemiptera: Miridae) in alfalfa by the introduced parasite *Peristenus digoneutis* (Hymenoptera: Braconidae). *Environmental Entomology* 25:512–8.

De Clerq, P., and D. Degheele. 1992. Development and survival of *Podisus maculiventris* (Say) and *Podisus sagitta* (Fab.) (Heteroptera: Pentatomidae) at various constant temperatures. *The Canadian Entomologist* 124:125–33.

——. 1993. Quality assessment of the predatory bugs of *Podisus maculiventris* (Say) and *Podisus sagitta* (Fab.) (Heteroptera: Pentatomidae) after prolonged rearing on a meat-based artificial diet. *Biocontrol Science and Technology* 3:133–9.

De Clerq, P., F. Merlevede, I. Mestdagh, K. Vanderdurpel, J. Mohaghegh, and D. Degheele. 1998. Predation on the tomato looper, *Chrysodeixis chalcites* (Esper) (Lep.: Noctuidae), by *Podisus maculiventris* (Say) and *Podisus nigrispinus* (Dallas) (Het.: Pentatomidae). *Journal of Applied Entomology* 122:93–8.

de Jong, P. W., and J. J. M. van Alphen. 1989. Host size selection and sex allocation in *Leptomastix dactylopii*, a parasitoid of *Planococcus citri. Entomologia Experimentalis et Applicata* 50:161–9.

de Moraes, G. J. and H. C. Lima. 1983. Biology of *Euseius concordis* (Chant) (Acarina: Phytoseiidae) a predator of the tomato russet mite. *Acarologia* 24 (3):251–5.

Doutt, R. L. 1951. Biological control of mealybugs infesting commercial greenhouse gardenias. *Journal of Economic Entomology* 44:37–40.

Dutton, A., F. Cerotti, and F. Bigler. 1996. Quality and environmental factors affecting *Trichogramma brassicae* efficiency under field conditions. *Entomologia Experimentalis et Applicata* 81:71–9.

Fan, Y., and F. L. Petitt. 1994. Biological control of broad mite, *Polyphagotarsonemus latus* (Banks), by *Neoseiulus barkeri* Hughes on pepper. *Biological Control* 4 (4):390–5.

Ferguson, G., and L. Shipp. 2002. New pests in Ontario greenhouse vegetables Bulletin OILB/SROP, 2002, Vol. 25, No. 1, pp. 69–72, 12 ref.

Gillespie, D., G. Opit, R. McGregor, M. Johnston, D. Quiring, and M. Foisy. 1997. Use of *Cotesia marginiventris* (Cresson) (Hymenoptera: Braconidae) for biological control of cabbage loopers, *Trichoplusia ni* (Lepidoptera: Noctuidae), in greenhouse vegetable crops in British Columbia. Technical report, Agriculture and Agri-Food Canada, Research Branch, Pacific Agri-food Research Centre Agassiz 14 p.

Gillespie, D. R., D. A. Raworth, and J. L. Shipp. 2002. *Trichoplusia ni* Hübner (Lepidoptera: Noctuidae) Cabbage looper. In *Biological Control Programmes in Canada 1981-2000*, ed. P. Mason and J Hübner, 269–272. New York: CABI Publishing.

Green, J. L. 1978. Special: cyclamen mite alert. Ornamentals Northwest Feb./Mar. '78. pp 6 – 9.

Greenberg, S. M., D. A. Nordland, and Z. X. Wu. 1998. Influence of rearing host on adult size and ovipositional behavior of mass-produced female *Trichogramma minutum* Riley and *Trichogramma pretiosum* Riley (Hymenoptera: Trichogrammatidae). *Biological Control* 11:43–8.

Hassan, S. A., and B. C. Wuhrer. 1997. Present status of research and commercial utilization of egg parasitoids of the genus *Trichogramma* in Germany. *Gesunde Planzen* 49:68–75.

Hennekam, M. M. B., M. Kole, K. van Opzeeland, and J. J. M. van Alphen. 1987. Biological control of citrus mealybug in a commercial crop of ornamental plants in the Netherlands. *Mededelingen Faculteit Landbouwwetenschappen, Rijksuniversiteit Gent*s 52 (2a):329–38.

Hill, D. H. 1994. *Agricultural Entomology*. Portland, Ore.: Timber Press.

Jacobsen, D. A., and T. J. Kring. 1994. Predation of corn earworm (Lepidoptera: Noctuidae) eggs and young larvae by *Orius insidiosus* (Say) (Heteroptera: Anthocoridae) on grain sorghum in greenhouses. *Journal of Entomological Science* 29:10–7.

Janmaat, A. F. and J. Myers. 2003. Rapid evolution and the cost of resistance to *Bacillus thuringiensis* in greenhouse populations of cabbage loopers, *Trichoplusia ni.* Proceedings of the Royal Society of London, Series B, 270 (1530): 2263–2270.

Jarrett, P. 1985. Experience with the selective control of caterpillars using *Bacillus thuringiensis*. In *Biological Pest Control: The Glasshouse Experience*, ed. N. W. Hussey and N. E. A. Scopes, 142–4. Poole, U.K.: Blandford (Ithaca, N.Y.): Cornell University Press.

Jeppson, L. R., H. H. Keifer, and E. W. Baker. 1975. *Mites Injurious to Economic Plants*. Berkeley, Calif.: University of California Press.

Kamau, A. W., J. M. Mueke, and B. M. Khaemba. 1992. Resistance of tomato varieties to the tomato russet mite, *Aculops lycopersici* (Masse) (Acarina: Eriophyidae). *Insect Science and Its Application* 13 (3):351–6.

Keifer, H. H., E. W. Baker, T. Kono, M. Delfinado, and W. E. Styer. 1982. *An Illustrated Guide to Plant Abnormalities Caused by Eriophyid Mites in North America*. United States Department of Agriculture Handbook No. 573.

Kuhlman, U., P. G. Mason, and D. J. Greathead. 1998. Assessment of potential risks for introducing European *Peristenus* species as biological control agents of native *Lygus* species in North America: A cooperative approach. *Biocontrol News and Information* 19:83N–90N.

Lafontaine J. D. and R. W. Poole. 1991. Notuoidea, Noctuidae (part) Plusiinae. In *The Moths of America North of Mexico*, Hodges, R. W., D. R. Davis, T. Dominick, D. G. Ferguson, J. G. Fraclemont, E. G. Munroe and J. A. Powell (Eds). Fasicle 25.1. Washington, D.C.: The Wedge Entomological Research Foundation.

Maini, S., and G. Burgio. 1991. Biological control of the European corn borer in protected pepper by *Trichogramma maidis* Pint. and Voeg. and *Bacillus thuringiensis* Berl. subsp. *kurstaki*. *Colloques de l'INRA* 56:213–5.

Malais, M., and W. J. Ravensberg. 1992. *Knowing and Recognizing: The Biology of Glasshouse Pests and Their Natural Enemies*. Berkel en Rodenrijs, the Netherlands: Koppert Biological Systems.

Marris, G. C., and J. P. Edwards. 1995. The biology of the ectoparasitoid wasp, *Eulophus pennicornis* (Hymenoptera: Eulophidae), on host larvae of the tomato moth, *Lacanobia oleracea* (Lepidoptera: Noctuidae*). *Bulletin of Entomological Research* 85:507–13.

McGregor, R. R., R. P. Prasad, and D. E. Henderson. 2002. Searching behaviour of *Trichogramma* wasps (Hymenoptera: Trichogrammatidae) on tomato and pepper leaves. J. Entomol. Soc. Brit. Col. 99: 93-98

Norton, A. P., and S. C. Welter. 1996. Augmentation of the egg parasitoid *Anaphes iole* (Hymenoptera: Mymaridae) for *Lygus hesperus* (Heteroptera: Miridae) management in strawberries. *Environmental Entomology* 25:1406–14.

Patana, R. 1985. *Spodoptera exiguae*. In *Handbook of Insect Rearing, Vol. II*, ed. R. Singh and R. R. Moore, 465–8. Amsterdam, the Netherlands: Elsevier.

Peña, J. E., and L. Osborne. 1996. Biological control of *Polyphagotarsonemus latus* (Acarina: Tarsonemidae) in greenhouses and field trials using introductions of predacious mites (Acarina: Phytoseiidae). *Entomophaga* 41: 279–85.

Perring, T. M., and C. A. Farrar. 1986. Historical perspective and current world status of the tomato russet mite (Acari: Eriophyidae*). *Miscellaneous Publications of the Entomological Society of America, 1986, No. 63, 19 pp.*

Pizzol, J., J. Voegele, and A. Marconi. 1997. Efficiency of *Trichogramma evanescens* against *Chrysodeixis chalcites* (Lepidoptera: Noctuidae) in greenhouses in tomato crops. *International Conference on Pests in Agriculture, June 6–8, 1997, Corum, Montpellier, France* 3: 751–7.

Quaglia, R. 1993. Population dynamics of tortricids *Cacoecimorpha pronubana* (Hbn.) and *Epichoristodes acerbelle* (Walk.) on ornamentals with special reference to the potential use of sex pheromone for monitoring, mass trapping, and mating disruption. *Frustula Entomologica* 16:1–7.

Rajapahse, P. H. J., T. R. Ashely, and H. van Waddill. 1988. Interspecific competition of fall armyworm parasites. *Brighton Crop Protection Conference—Pests and Diseases 1988* 3: 113–4.

Rice, E. R., and F. E. Strong. 1962. Bionomics of the tomato russet mite, *Vasates lycopersici* (Masse). *Annals of the Entomological Society of America* 55: 431–5.

Riley, D. G. 1992. The pepper weevil and its management. *Fact Sheet Texas A&M University*, Agricultural Extension Service, Publication No. L-5069.

Royalty, R. N., and T. M. Perring. 1989. Reduction in photosynthesis of tomato leaflets caused by tomato russet mite (Acari: Eriophyidae). *Environmental Entomology* 18 (2):256–60.

Ruberson, J. R., and J. B. Whitfield. 1996. Facultative egg-larval parasitism of the beet armyworm, *Spodoptera exiguae* (Lepidoptera: Noctuidae), by *Cotesia marginiventris* (Hymenoptera: Braconidae). *Florida Entomologist* 79:296–302.

Sampson, A. C., and V. J. King. 1996. *Macrolophus caliginosus*: Field establishment and pest control effect in protected tomatoes. *IOBC/WPRS Bulletin* 19 (1):143–6.

Sannina, L., and B. Espinosa. 1998. Biological cycle of *Mamestra brassicae* and damage to horticultural crops in Campania. *Informatore Fitopatologico* 48:56–67.

Schuster, D. J. 1989. Development of the tomato pinworm (Lepidoptera: Gelechiidae) on foliage of selected plant species. *Florida Entomologist* 72:216–9.

Shipp, J. L., K. Wang, and G. Ferguson. 1998. Evaluation of commercially produced *Trichogramma* spp. (Hymenoptera: Trichogrammatidae) for control of pinworm, *Keiferia lycopersicella* (Walshingham) (Lepidoptera: Gelechiidae), on greenhouse tomatoes. *Canadian Entomologist* 130 (5):721–31.

Stauffer, S., and M. Rose. 1997. Biological control of soft scale insects in interior plantscapes in the U.S.A., pp 183 – 205. In *Soft Scale Insects: Their Biology, Natural Enemies, and Control, Vol. 7B*, ed. Y. Ben-Dov and C. J. Hodgson. New York (Amsterdam): Elsevier.

Steiner, M. Y., and D. P. Elliott. 1983. *Biological Pest Management for Interior Plantscapes.* Publication No. 83-E1. Vegreville, Canada: Alberta Environmental Centre.

Summy, K. R., J. V. French, and W. G. Hart. 1986. Citrus mealybug (Homoptera: Pseudococcidae) on greenhouse citrus: Density-dependent regulation by an encyrtid parasite complex. *Journal of Economic Entomology* 79:891–5.

Tingle, C. C. D., and J. W. Copland. 1988. Effects of temperature and host-plant on regulation of glasshouse mealybug (Homoptera: Pseudococcidae) populations by introduced parasitoids (Hymenoptera: Encyrtidae). *Bulletin of Entomological Research* 78:135–42.

———. 1989. Progeny production and adult longevity of the mealybug parasitoids *Anagyrus pseudococci, Leptomastix dactylopii* and *Leptomastidea abnormis* (Hymen.: Encyrtidae) in relation to temperature. *Entomophaga* 34:111–20.

van Baaren, J., and J. P. Nenon. 1996. Host location and discrimination mediated through olfactory stimuli in two species of Encyrtidae. *Entomologia Experimentalis et Applicata* 81:61–9.

van der Linden, A. 1996. Control of caterpillars in integrated pest management. *IOBC/WPRS Bulletin* 19:91–4

van de Veire, M. 1993. First observations in glasshouse sweet peppers in Belgium and laboratory rearing of the parasitic wasp *Eulophus pennicornis* (Hymenoptera: Eulophidae). *Entomophaga* 38:61–2.

Visser, M. E., and J. J. M. van Alphen. 1987. *Metaphycus helvolus* (Hymenoptera: Encyrtidae), a biological control agent of *Coccus hesperidum* (Homoptera: Coccidae). *Mededelingen Faculteit Landbouwwetenschappen, Rijksuniversiteit Gent* 52 (2a):319–28.

Wallis, R. L. 1955. Ecological studies on the on the potato psyllid as a pest of potatoes. Technical Bulletin of the U.S. Department of Agriculture no 1107. 25 pp.

Wang, K., G. Fergusen, and J. L. Shipp. 1998. Incidence of pinworm, *Keiferia lycopersicella* (Walshingham) (Lepidoptera: Gelechiidae), on greenhouse tomatoes in southern Ontario and its control using mating disruption. *Proceedings of the Entomological Society of Ontario* 128:93–8.

Xie, Z. N., W. C. Nettles Jr., G. Saladana, and D. A. Nordland. 1997. Elmer's School Glue and Elmer's Glue All: Arrestants and probing/oviposition enhancers for *Trichogramma* spp. *Entomologia Experimentalis et Applicata* 82:115–8.

Yoshida, H. A., and M. P. Parrella. 1987. The beet armyworm in floriculture crops. *California Agriculture* 41:13–5.

19

BIOLOGICAL CONTROL OF ARTHROPOD PESTS IN THE SOIL

R. D. Oetting

Entomology Department
University of Georgia; College of Agriculture and Environmental Sciences
Griffin, Georgia

and

S. K. Braman

Entomology Department
University of Georgia; College of Agriculture and Environmental Sciences
Griffin, Georgia

Introduction

Most growers are familiar with the management of pests on the foliage of ornamental plants but are not as comfortable dealing with pests in the soil or potting media. Many of the common groups of foliar pests also have counterparts in the growing media. There are mealybugs, mites, thrips, leafminers, aphids, and other major pests that are found in the potting media, either as permanent soil inhabitants or species that spend part of their life cycle in the soil. Pests that spend part of their life cycle in the soil, not discussed in other chapters, will be covered here. Fungus gnats (*Bradysia* spp., Diptera: Sciaridae) and black vine weevils (*Otiorhynchus sulcatus* [Fabricius], Coleoptera: Curculionidae) are two important greenhouse pests that spend their immature stages in the soil, but emerge as adults to move between host plants. Biological agents used against these pests are directed at the larvae in the soil or potting media. Shore flies (*Scatella* spp., Diptera:

Ephydridae), another media-breeding pest, are similar to fungus gnats and the management tactics used against them are similar to those used against fungus gnats.

Fungus Gnats

Fungus gnats were considered only as a nuisance pest for many years. However, the damage caused by larval feeding on ornamental plant roots, reductions in mushroom yields, and their role in disseminating plant pathogens shows them to be a more serious pest (Harris, Oetting, and Gardner 1995; Harris, Oetting, and Moody 1995). Fungus gnats in the genus *Bradysia* (fig. 19.1) are commonly referred to as the darkwinged fungus gnats. They inhabit moist shady areas within woodlands, greenhouses, mushroom cellars, and field crops (Springer and Carlton 1993).

Biology

Adult fungus gnats are small (males are 0.10 in. [2.5 mm] and females are 0.11 in. [3 mm]

Figure 19.1. Adult fungus gnats *Bradysia* spp.) are weak fliers commonly found in the area between the soil and the lower foliage. *Photo: J. L. Shipp.*

in length), weak fliers, but active runners. They are inconspicuous and found most often in the area between the soil and the lower foliage (Harris, Gardner, and Oetting 1996). Adults are short-lived (approximately three days) and males usually live longer than females, which die soon after oviposition (Kennedy 1976). Female fungus gnats are less active and, therefore, less conspicuous than males. Females can be found standing on the underside of leaves, on the soil, and on the vertical surfaces near the soil surface (Harris, Gardner, and Oetting 1996). They lay approximately 150 eggs, which usually hatch within two days. When diseased tissue is present, females will lay their eggs on that tissue but in the absence of diseased plant tissue they will oviposit on healthy tissue. There are four

larval instars and an obtect pupa. The presence of a shiny black head capsule on an otherwise translucent or white vermiform body (fig. 19.2) distinguishes fungus gnat larvae from other immature dipterans commonly found in potting media (Harris, Gardner, and Oetting 1996).

Severity of problems and crops attacked

Direct damage, resulting from larval feeding, was long considered insignificant because such insect-caused damage was considered secondary to effects of plant pathogens on roots. Larval fungus gnats actively feed on the root systems of a variety of plants. Direct damage from fungus gnat larval feeding is hard to detect because the normal symptom is a reduction in plant growth. In the case of young, slow-growing seedlings, feeding damage can result in plant death. Larval feeding predisposes the plant to attack by pathogens (Leath and Newton, 1969). Hamlen and Mead (1979) considered five to ten larvae per potted plant to represent a moderate infestation.

This ability of fungus gnats to spread plant diseases increases the seriousness of this insect as a pest within protected culture. Adults may disseminate the spores of fungal pathogens among plants as the spores adhere to their legs and bodies (Charles and Popenoe 1928; Kalb and Millar 1986; Gillespie and Menzies 1993). Fungal spores can also survive passage through the digestive tract of fungus gnats and be disseminated by fungus gnat excretion (Gardiner, Jarvis, and Shipp 1990; Stanghellini and Rasmussen 1994; Harris, Oetting, and Gardner 1995).

Figure 19.2. Fungus gnat larvae are characterized by having shiny black head capsules on otherwise clear to milky-white worm-like bodies. These characteristics distinguish them from other immature dipteran larvae commonly found in potting media. *Photo: R. Cloyd.*

Natural enemies

Three groups of natural enemies used to manage fungus gnats are pathogens, nematodes, and predators.

Pathogens

Bacillus thuringiensis Berlinger subspecies *israelensis* (serotype H-14) was marketed in the United States as Vectobac in the 1980s. This strain of *B. thuringiensis* is effective against fly larvae, unlike the earlier strains that were primarily used against lepidopteran larvae. This pathogen must be ingested by mouth and is only effective against the larval stage. Adult fungus gnats do not feed on foliage and as a result do not ingest the pathogen. More recently, this bacterium is marketed under the U.S. trade name Gnatrol with a label specially designed for use against fungus gnats in greenhouses. Another pathogen group sometimes used for insect management in greenhouses is the entomo-

pathogenic fungi, but research on the abilities of these fungi to produce biological fungus gnat control are preliminary at this time.

Nematodes

Nematodes are biological control agents that are similar to parasitoids because the immature stages develop at the expense of the host (fig. 19.3) and the host is eventually killed (Ehler 1990). Unlike parasitoids, nematodes have a mutualistic association with a bacterial pathogen that actually kills the host (Ibid.). There are two nematode species in the family Steinernematidae that have been widely used for the management of fungus gnats: *Steinernema carpocapsae* (Weiser) and *Steinernema feltiae* (Filipjev). These nematodes commonly attack fungus gnat larvae in the soil.

Predators

Both naturally occurring parasitoids and predators attack fungus gnats, but only the

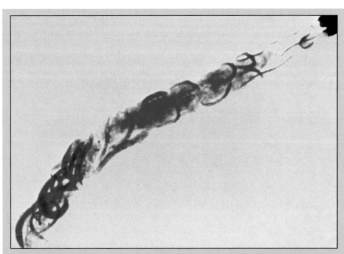

Figure 19.3. In the latter stages of infection, immature nematodes frequently occupy most of the body cavity of their fungus gnat host. *Photo: L. Osborne.*

predators have been developed as commercially available biological control agents. Two species of *Hypoaspis* mites are commercially available for the management of fungus gnats and shore flies: *Hypoaspis aculeifer* (Canestrini) and *Hypoaspis miles* (Berlese) (Hunter 1997). These two predatory mite species are similar in habitat and activity, but *H. miles* has been studied more and is the primary predator discussed here. *Hypoaspis miles* is a soil-dwelling mite that preys on the soil-inhabiting stages of several organisms: fungus gnat and shore fly larvae, collembola, nematodes, mold mites, and other insects; but, they prefer fungus gnat larvae (Gillespie and Quiring 1990; Wright and Chambers 1994; Ydergaard, Enkegaard, and Brödsgarrd 1997). This mite's environmental requirements for development from egg to adult are similar to those of fungus gnats, thus permitting it to coexist with its

preferred prey. The developmental time is influenced by temperature, decreasing with increasing temperature from forty-six days at 59°F (15°C) to ten days at 86°F (30°C) (Ydergaard, Enkegaard, and Brödsgarrd 1997). The highest rate of survival occurs at 77°F (25°C), and females survive for about sixty days at 68°F (20°C) and thirty-nine days at 77°F (25°C) (Ibid.). Male longevity is substantially longer than the values reported for females. Prolonged longevity permits *H. miles* to feed on fungus gnat larvae for extended periods. When the preferred fungus gnat larvae are unavailable, *H. miles* is capable of sustaining itself on other types of prey.

Biological control programs

The primary method used for the control of fungus gnats is the application of pesticides. In recent years, most of the insect growth regulators registered for greenhouse use have added fungus gnats to their labels. These new registrations should help the practical deployment of biological control programs because these materials are compatible with biological agents used in fungus gnat management.

Pathogens

Experimental trials with the bacterium *B. thuringiensis* var. *israelensis* have demonstrated successful control of fungus gnat larvae by causing up to 92% larval mortality (Osborne, Boucias, and Lindquist 1985). The ease of application and familiarity with the use of *B. thuringiensis* for control of lepidopterous larvae facilitate rapid adoption of this form of biological fungus gnat control by growers. *Bacillus thuringiensis israelensis*, formulated in a manner similar to chemical insecticides, is applied as a soil drench using a conventional sprayer or applied through the irrigation system. *Bacillus thuringiensis israelensis* is applied at the rate of approximately 2.2 to 4.4 billion International Toxic Units per 100 gal. of diluted mix for light infestations and at higher rates for heavy infestations. This microbe is only effective against the larvae of fungus gnats and has little effect on shore flies.

Nematodes

Methods have been developed to commercially produce insect-pathogenic nematodes on a large scale, and they have been formulated in different media for delivery to growers for use in biological control programs (Friedman 1990). Although production methods continue to improve, poor storage characteristics remain a problem. Nematodes are living organisms and, even though they are formulated in a resting state, they have a limited shelf life. Refrigeration extends shelf life, as survival is higher in cool compared to hot conditions. Oetting and Latimer (1991) found that *S. carpocapsae* might survive a wide range of environmental conditions associated with various potting media, plant growth regulators, pH levels, fertilizers, and salts.

Application technique is critical for successful use of nematodes. Some nematodes can move through the media searching for hosts, but searching distance is on the order of millimeters, an exceptionally short distance compared to arthropod natural enemies. The presence of an insect host stimulates the movement of nematodes capable of doing so (Moyle and Kaya 1981). Nemotodes may also be dispersed passively through the movements of infected hosts (Timper, Kaya, and Gaugler 1988). Thus, nematodes should be delivered close to the pest insect to facilitate ease in contacting the host. Successful biological control depends on getting the nematodes into the potting media or soil where the target insect is feeding. Nematodes are usually applied at concentrations exceeding 1 billion nematodes per acre to increase the probability of nematode encounters with potential hosts (Georgis 1990).

Nematode products are formulated so they can be applied with the same equipment used for chemical insecticides. However, their sensitivity to insecticides requires that application equipment is free of pesticide residues before application, or that equipment specifically designated for nematode application is used. Nematodes can withstand application pressures of 300 pounds/square in. and can be delivered with all common types of spray nozzles, producing droplets fifty microns or larger (Ibid.). However, sprayers with pumping mechanisms that produce excessive heat (above 90°F [32°C]) can harm nematodes. Other methods of delivery include application through irrigation systems and spreading of granule-like formulations directly on the potting media.

Four species of *Steinernema* are commercially available in the United States:

S. carpocapsae, S. feltiae, Steinernema glaseri (Steiner)*, and Steinernema riobravis* Cabanillis et al. (Hunter 1997). Much of the research on fungus gnat management with nematodes has been with *S. carpocapsae* and *S. feltiae.* Reduction of fungus gnats has been achieved with applications of both species (Nedstam and Burman 1990, Lindquist and Piatkowski 1993). Research has also been conducted on *Heterorhabditis bacteriophora* Poinar for fungus gnat control, but that species is less effective than *S. feltiae* (Harris, Oetting, and Moody 1995). The results of tests on efficacy of *Steinernema* spp. are not consistent, probably because of the variation within species or strains obtained from different commercial suppliers and because of environmental conditions present at different locations.

Predators

Hypoaspis miles is available from many commercial suppliers (Hunter 1997). Adult and immature mites are normally shipped in bottles containing a mixture of sphagnum moss, vermiculite and grain mites; the latter serves as food for the predators. The predators are introduced by sprinkling the contents of each bottle onto the soil or media surface. Treatments are preventative if applied soon after planting and before fungus gnats have infested the media, or curative if applied soon after observing fungus gnats. The most successful method is to start mite introductions soon after planting and continue introductions throughout the cropping period (Chambers, Wright, and Lind 1993). Recommended rates in commercial nurseries are about one-half dozen to several dozen mites per container or ft.^{2} (twenty to dozens/m^2) of media applied before pests become abundant.

Black Vine Weevil

The black vine weevil, *Otiorhynchus sulcatus* (F.), is a highly polyphagous and serious pest of woody ornamental shrubs. This species is of European origin, but it was discovered in North America when collected in Connecticut in 1910 (Smith 1932). It is now found throughout the United States and other countries of North America, Australia, and Asia. Although it feeds on a variety of plants, it is most commonly found on species of *Taxus*, *Rhododendron*, *Tsuga*, and *Conium*.

There is one generation of the black vine weevil a year. Most adults emerge from pupae between mid-May and late July. Adults are about 0.20 in. (5 mm) long, black, flightless, and parthenogenetic (males are unknown) (Burlando, Kaya, and Timper 1993). Adults hide during the day in the soil or litter under the plants, are active only at night, and feign death when disturbed. Females lay as many as 550 eggs in the soil around plants. Eggs hatch in about two weeks and grubs feed on roots.

The larvae have limited mobility and are restricted to the host plant selected by their parents. Even though adults have a large host range, they are selective in choosing plants on which to lay their eggs, seeking out species that are best for larval development (Hanula 1988). Larvae that hatch from eggs laid early in the season may pupate before cold weather. Younger larvae overwinter and pupate in the spring. The few adults found early in the spring may have overwintered as adults. Several easily recognized features help identify larvae of root weevils; all are legless, C-shaped, and white with brown heads. Larvae are sometimes present in soil as deep as 12 in. (30 cm), but most (>90%) are found in the top 6 in. (5 cm) (Hanula 1993). The pupae are found near the surface of the soil and are white with visible appendages.

Severity of problems and crops attacked

Feeding by adult black vine weevils on plant foliage causes a distinctive injury that aids in determining the cause. On broad-leaved evergreens, this injury consists of marginal notching of the leaves. These notches are easy to distinguish from the feeding of other insects, such as caterpillars. However, where several weevil species are present, it is hard to distinguish the damage symptoms caused by particular weevils. Feeding by adult black vine weevil on yew (*Taxus* sp.) is uniquely characteristic as they notch and cut-off needles. If there are many notches on the host plant's foliage, the roots are probably being injured by weevil larvae. Adults feed only at night and the injury they cause is primarily cosmetic. By contrast, heavy infestations of grubs can destroy most of a plant's small feeder roots, and larvae may girdle large roots and the crown. Destruction of the root system reduces the plant's ability to absorb water, and as a result plants may be stunted, show little growth, frequently have yellow foliage, or die if the pest is not controlled.

In nurseries, the close proximity of a large number of host plants is ideal for development of black vine weevil populations. Further, the exchange of infested plant material among nurseries provides a second avenue for rapid spread of an infestation within the industry. Monitoring for signs of black vine weevils or their damage should be most carefully done in spring and summer. Due to the cryptic nature of black vine weevils, an infestation may go undetected for several years and only be noticed when plants start to show dieback. Even though injured plants may survive in the nursery, customer complaints may increase if the plants die soon after they are transplanted into the landscape.

Natural enemies

Only nematodes and pathogenic fungi are commercially available for black vine weevil biological control.

Fungi

The primary microbial agents for management of black vine weevils are entomopathogenic fungi. Under natural conditions, such fungi may reduce or even eliminate black vine weevil populations. However, these fungal epizootics often occur in dense weevil populations and are too late to prevent extensive damage to crops. Spores of such fungal pathogens attach themselves to the insect body wall and normally invade the insect through its cuticle, without having to be ingested to initiate the disease cycle (Lacey and Goettel 1995). Sites of invasion occur where a humid microclimate promotes spore germination and the cuticle is nonsclerotized, including the mouthparts, intersegmental folds, and the spiracles (Charnley 1997). The ability of fungal hyphae to penetrate the insect body wall increases the range of insect hosts that fungi can infect. Once the fungus breaks through the cuticle and epidermis, it may grow profusely in the blood causing death by starvation or biochemical disruption (Ibid.). More commonly, the fungi produce insecticidal secondary metabolites that contribute to the death of the insect (Gillespie and Claydon 1989). Fungi can infect non-feeding stages such as eggs and pupae, but only do so when a spore-contacted host is located in a suitable environment. Some pathogens are more selective and appear to have more specific requirements, such as an ability to tolerate contact with anti-fungal compounds and with short chain fatty acids found in the insect cuticle (Boucias and Pendland 1991).

Two species of fungi have been extensively studied as candidates for management of black vine weevil. *Beauveria bassiana* (Balsamo) Vuillernin was the first species of entomopathogenic fungi made available for use in U.S. greenhouses. Two U.S. manufacturers have registered formulations available for use in protected culture. *Metarhizium anisopliae* (Metchnikoff) Sorokin is one of the most common mycopathogens found infecting soil insects, especially beetles, in the temperate regions. This fungus appears to be an excellent candidate for black vine weevil management, but it is not available commercially in North America.

Nematodes
Nematodes for black vine weevil management include species of both *Steinernema* and *Heterorhabditis*. Descriptions of species are provided earlier in the section on fungus gnat management.

Biological control programs

Fungal pathogens
Both of the species of fungal agents mentioned above have promise for management of weevils, but only *B. bassiana* is currently registered in the United States. *Metarhizium anisopliae* is registered for use on other pests and in other countries. Test results suggest it to be a potentially effective biopesticide for control of black vine weevil (Gillespie, Moorhouse, and Sellers 1989; Easterbrook, Cantwell, and Chandler 1992; Moorhouse, Gillespie, and Charnley 1993; Booth, Tanigoshi, and Shanks 2002). Commercial production methods of these fungal insect pathogens are similar to those used for *B. thuringiensis*, and conventional chemical spray equipment is used to apply them. Unlike chemical insecticides, these fungi are living organisms that are affected by environmental conditions. Fungal pathogens survive and infect hosts best under warm, humid conditions.

Nematodes
Nematode species in the genera *Steinernema* and *Heterorhabditis* can control black vine weevil larvae. However, experiments indicate that *H. bacteriophora* (Poinar 1990) (which may be conspecific with *Heterorhabditis heliothidis* is more effective at controlling black vine weevil larvae than *Steinernema* spp. A drawback, though, is the difficulty associated with rearing and storing *Heterorhabditis* species compared to species of *Steinernema* (Stimmann et al. 1985). Nematode species vary in their effectiveness on different stages of black vine weevils. Georgis and Poinar (1984) found better control of small larvae with *H. bacteriophora,* but *S. carpocapsae, S. glaseri,* and *H. bacteriophora* all controlled third and fourth instar larvae. Several species of both groups have been studied and some have been commercialized.

The application of the T327 strain of *H. bacteriophora (heliothidis)* resulted in 100% parasitism of weevil larvae on yew, raspberries, and grapes in nurseries and there was usually >90% parasitism in one month with other strains of that species (Bedding and Miller 1981). Trials under greenhouse conditions, using 10,000 to 20,000 juvenile nematodes per pot, with *H. bacteriophora* and *Heterorhabditis megidis* (Poinar et al.) caused more than 78% mortality of black vine weevil larvae (Kakouli-Duarte, Labuschagne, and Hague 1997). These authors found that early and later instar larvae, pupae, and adults were all susceptible to both nematodes. These nematodes were most efficacious during the first two weeks of larval development. *Heterorhabditis marelatus* Lui and Berry caused reductions in both numbers of weevils and proportion of infested strawberry plants, whereas *H. bacteriophora* did not (Wilson, Nitzsche, and Shearer 1999).

Species of *Steinernema* and *Heterorhabditis* are commercially available, and they are formulated in a way that allows them to be applied through commercial pesticide spray equipment. *Heterorhabditis bacteriophora* is typically applied at a rate of 1 billion nematodes per acre (400 million/ha) or 25,000 per ft.^{2} (8,000/m^2), and 10,000 per 6-in. pot. Two to ten gal. of the spay slurry are applied per 1,000 ft.^{2} (3 to 13 l/10 m^2). Plants should be watered both before and after the application to aid nematode penetration of the soil.

Heterorhabditis spp. provide excellent control when soil temperatures are between 64 and 86°F (18 and 30°C), but the level of control declines significantly at lower temperatures, i.e., 54 to 58°F (12 to 14°C) (Rutherford, Trotter, and Webster 1987). One reason for this failure to control black vine weevil at low temperatures may be the tendency of nematodes to aggregate rather than disperse and search when temperatures are low (Westerman 1999). When temperatures are optimal, nematodes move through the soil under their own power and also are carried along as water percolates downward in the soil. Hanula (1993) reported finding *S. carpocapsae and S. feltiae* 7 to 8 in. (18 to 20 cm) deep in an 8-in. (20-cm) column of soil, whereas *H. bacteriophora* was not found below 5 in. (13 cm). The potential of a cold-active entomopathogenic nematode, *Steinernema kraussei* Mamiya to control black vine weevil has been reported (Long, Richardson, and Fenlon 2000; Willmott et al. 2002).

Shore Flies

The most common species of shore fly found on ornamental plants in greenhouses is *Scatella stagnalis* (Fallén). The adults are robust with short legs and bristlelike antennae that are somewhat inconspicuous as the antennae are shorter than the head (fig. 19.4). The wings are dark with five light spots. Shore flies are often confused with fungus gnats because they are similar in size and found in the same habitat. However, shore flies are robust in appearance, while fungus gnats are slender and resemble mosquitoes in body shape and leg length. Shore flies are stronger, faster fliers than fungus gnats, but they have less tendency to take flight in comparison with fungus gnats. Shore fly larvae have a plump maggot-like or wedge-shaped body, up to about ⅛ in. (3 mm) long. Larvae have no distinct head capsule, but their dark mouthparts and internal organs are visible through their outer skin. Shore fly larvae have a distinctive forked, dark-tipped breathing tube on the end of the body. In temperate greenhouse conditions, shore flies have several generations each year.

Eggs of shore flies are scattered on algal mats found on the soil, potting mix, cooling pads, or other surfaces in the greenhouse. The eggs hatch in two to three days and the larvae are found feeding on bacteria and other microorganisms within the algal mat. Shore fly larvae mature and pupate in about three to six days. The pupae are usually found near the surface of the potting media or algal mat

and adult flies emerge in about four to five days (Baker 1994).

Shore flies have also been associated with the spread of plant pathogens similar to fungus gnats. Compared to fungus gnats, there is little information regarding biological control. *Bacillus thuringiensis* does not appear to be effective against shore flies, but most other natural enemies have not been evaluated sufficiently to support or refute their use in biological control programs.

Figure 19.4. Although found in similar habitats as fungus gnats, shore flies (adult shown above) are more robust in size, their wings are dark with light-colored spots, and they are strong fliers. *Photo: J. L. Shipp.*

References Cited

Baker, J. R., ed. 1994. Insect and related pests of flowers and foliage plants. AG-136 No. 50. Raleigh, North Carolina: North Carolina Cooperative Extension Service.

Bedding, R. A., and L. A. Miller. 1981. Use of a nematode, *Heterorhabditis heliothidis,* to control black vine weevil, *Otiorhynchus sulcatus*, in potted plants. *Annals of Applied Biology* 99:211–6.

Boucias, D. G., and J. C. Pendland. 1991. Attachment of myco-pathogens to cuticle: The initial event of mycosis in arthropod hosts. In *The Fungal Spore and Disease Initiation in Plants and Animals,* ed. G. T. Cole and H. C. Hoch, 101–28. New York: Plenum Press

Booth, S. R., L. K. Tanigoshi, and C. H. Shanks, Jr. 2002. Evaluation of entomopathogenic nematodes to manage root weevil larvae in Washington State cranberry, strawberry and red raspberry. *Environmental Entomology* 31:895–902.

Burlando, T. M., H. K. Kaya, and P. Timper. 1993. Insect-parasitic nematodes are effective against black vine weevil. *California Agriculture* 47 (3):16–8.

Chambers, R. J., E. M. Wright, and R. J. Lind. 1993. Biological control of glasshouse sciarid larvae (*Bradysia* spp.) with the predatory mite, *Hypoaspis miles,* on cyclamen and poinsettia. *Biocontrol Science and Technology* 3:285–93.

Charles, V. K., and C. H. Popenoe. 1928. Some mushroom diseases and their carriers. Circular 27. Washington, D.C.: U.S. Department of Agriculture.

Charnley, A. K. 1997. Entomopathogenic fungi and their role in pest control. *In The Mycota: A Comprehensive Treatise on Fungi as Experimental Systems for Basic and Applied Research, IV, b, Environmental and Microbial Relationships*, ed. K. Esser and P. A. Lemke, 185–200. Berlin: Springer-Verlag.

Easterbrook, M. A., M. P. Cantwell, and D. Chandler. 1992. Control of the black vine weevil, *Otiorhynchus sulcatus,* with the fungus *Metarhizium anisopliae. Phytoparastica* 20:17–9.

Ehler, L. E. 1990. Some contemporary issues in biological control of insects and their relevance to the use of entomopathogenic nematodes. In *Entomopathogenic Nematodes in Biological Control*, ed. R. Gaugler and H. K. Kaya, 1–16, Boca Raton, Fla.: CRC Press.

Friedman, M. J. 1990. Commercial production and development. In *Entomopathogenic Nematodes in Biological Control*, ed. R. Gaugler and H. K. Kaya, 153–70. Boca Raton, Fla.: CRC Press.

Gardiner, R. B., W. R. Jarvis, and J. L. Shipp. 1990. Ingestion of *Pythium* spp. by larvae of the fungus gnat *Bradysia impatiens* (Diptera: Sciaridae*). Annals of Applied Biology* 116:205–12.

Georgis, R. 1990. Formulation and application technology. In *Entomopathogenic Nematodes in Biological Control*, ed. R. Gaugler and H. K. Kaya, 173–87, Boca Raton, Fla.: CRC Press.

Georgis, R., and G. O. Poinar Jr. 1984. Greenhouse control of the black vine weevil *Otiorhynchus sulcatus* (Coleoptera: Curculionidae) by *Heterorhabditid* and *Steinernematid* nematodes (*Neoaplectana carpocapsae, Neoaplectana glaseri, Heterorhabditis heliothidis*). *Environmental Entomology* 13:1138–40.

Gillespie, A. T., and N. Claydon. 1989. The use of entomogenous fungi for pest control and the role of toxins in pathogenesis. *Pesticide Science* 27:203–15.

Gillespie, A. T., E. R. Moorhouse, and E. K. Sellers. 1989. *Metarhizium anisopliae*: A promising biological control agent for the black vine weevil, *Otiorhynchus sulcatus. Aspects of Applied Biology* 22:389–93.

Gillespie, D. R., and J. G. Menzies. 1993. Fungus gnats vector *Fusarium oxysporum* F. sp. *Radicis-lycopersici. Annals of Applied Biology* 123:539–44.

Gillespie, D. R., and D. M. J. Quiring. 1990. Biological control of fungus gnats, *Bradysia* spp. (Diptera: Sciaridae) and western flower thrips, *Frankliniella occidentalis* (Pergande) (Thysanoptera: Thripidae), in greenhouses using a soil-dwelling predatory mite, *Geolaelaps* sp. nr. *aculeifer* (Canestrini) (Acari: Laelapidae). *The Canadian Entomologist* 122:975–83.

Hamlen, R. A., and F. W. Mead. 1979. Fungus gnat larval control in greenhouse plant production. *Journal of Economic Entomology* 72:269–71.

Hanula, J. L. 1988. Oviposition preference and host recognition by the black vine weevil, *Otiorhynchus sulcatus* (Coleoptera: Curculionidae). *Environmental Entomology* 17:694–8.

———. 1993. Vertical distribution of black vine weevil (Coleoptera: Curculionidae) immatures and infection by entomogenous nematodes in soil columns and field soil. *Journal of Economic Entomology* 86:340–7.

Harris, M. A., W. A. Gardner, and R. D. Oetting. 1996. A review of the scientific literature on fungus gnats (Diptera: Sciaridae) in the genus *Bradysia*. *Journal of Entomological Science* 31:252–76.

Harris, M. A., R. D. Oetting, and W. A. Gardner. 1995. Use of entomopathogenic nematodes and a new monitoring technique for control of fungus gnats, *Bradysia coprophila* (Diptera: Sciaridae), in floriculture. *Biological Control* 5:412–8.

Harris, M. A., R. D. Oetting, and E. H. Moody. 1995. Dissemination of *Thielaviopsis basicola* and *Fusarium proliferatum* by fungus gnats. Proceedings of 40th Southern Nurserymen's Association Research Conference, August 3-4, 1995, Atlanta, Georgia: 63–4.

Hunter, C. D. 1997. *Suppliers of Beneficial Organisms in North America*. Sacramento, Calif.: California Environmental Protection Agency.

Kakouli-Duarte, T., L. Labuschagne, and N. G. M. Hague. 1997. Biological control of the black vine weevil, *Otiorhynchus sulcatus* (Coleoptera: Curculionidae) with entomopathogenic nematodes (Nematoda: Rhabditidae). *Annals of Applied Biology* 131:11–27.

Kalb, D. W., and R. L. Millar. 1986. Dispersal of *Verticillium albo-atrum* by the fungus gnat (*Bradysia impatiens). Plant Disease* 70:752–3.

Kennedy, M. K. 1976. The interaction of *Bradysia impatiens* (Joh.) (Diptera: Sciaridae), a fungal host, and the root systems of vascular plants. Ph.D. dissertation. Ithaca, N.Y.: Cornell University.

Lacey, L. A., and M. S. Goettel. 1995. Current developments in microbial control of insect pests and prospects for the early 21st century. *Entomophaga* 40:3–27.

Leath, K. T., and R. C. Newton. 1969. Interaction of a fungus gnat, *Bradysia* sp. (Sciaridae) with *Fusarium* spp. on alfalfa and red clover. *Phytopathology* 59:257–8.

Lindquist, R. K., and J. Piatkowski. 1993. Evaluation of entomopathogenic nematodes for control of fungus gnat larvae. *IOBC/WPRS Bulletin* 16:97–100.

Long, S. J., P. N. Richardson, and J. S. Fenlon. 2000. Influence of temperature on the infectivity of entomopathogenic nematodes (*Steinernema* and *Heterorhabditis* spp.) to larvae and pupae of the vine weevil *Otiorhynchus sulcatus,* (Coleoptera: Curculionidae). *Nematology.* 2:309-17.

Moorhouse, E. R., A. T. Gillespie, and A. K. Charnley. 1993. Selection of virulent and persistent *Metarhizium anisopliae* isolates to control black vine weevil (*Otiorhynchus sulcatus)* larvae on glasshouse Begonia. *Journal of Invertebrate Pathology* 62:47–52.

Moyle, P. L., and H. K. Kaya. 1981. Dispersal and infectivity of the entomogenous nematode, *Neoaplectana carpocapsae* Weiser (Rhabditida: Steinernematidae). in sand. *Journal of Nematology* 13:295–300.

Nedstam, B., and M. Burman. 1990. The use of nematodes against sciarids in Swedish greenhouses. *IOBC/WPRS Bulletin* 8 (5):147–8.

Oetting, R. D., and J. G. Latimer. 1991. An entomogenous nematode *Steinernema carpocapsae* is compatible with potting media environments created by horticultural practices. *Journal of Entomological Science* 26:390–4.

Osborne, L. S., D. G. Boucias, and R. K. Lindquist. 1985. Activity of *Bacillus thuringiensis* var. *israelensis* on *Bradysia coprophila* (Diptera: Sciaridae). *Journal of Economic Entomology* 78:922–5.

Poinar, G. O. 1990. Taxonomy and biology of Steinernematidae and Heterorhabditidae. In *Entomopathogenic Nematodes in Biological Control*, ed. R. Gaugler and H. K. Kaya, 23–61, Boca Raton, Fla.: CRC Press.

Rutherford, T. A., D. A. Trotter, and J. M. Webster. 1987. The potential of heterorhabditid nematodes as control agents of root weevils. *The Canadian Entomologist* 119:67–73.

Smith, F. F. 1932. Biology and control of the black vine weevil. Technical Bulletin No. 325. Washington, D.C.: U.S. Department of Agriculture.

Springer, T. L., and C. E. Carlton. 1993. Oviposition preference of dark-winged fungus gnats (Diptera: Sciaridae) among *Trifolium* species. *Journal of Economic Entomology* 86:1420–3.

Stanghellini, M. E., and S. L. Rasmussen. 1994. Hydroponics a solution for zoosporic pathogens. *Plant Disease* 78:1129–38.

Stimmann, M. W., H. K. Kaya, T. M. Burlando, and J. P. Studdert. 1985. Black vine weevil management in nursery plants. *California Agriculture* 39 (1):25–6.

Timper, P., H. K. Kaya, and R. Gaugler. 1988. Dispersal of the entomogenous nematode *Steinernema feltiae* (Rhabditidae: Steinernematidae) by infected adult insects. *Environmental Entomology* 17:546–50.

Westerman, P. R. 1999. Aggregation of entomopathogenic nematodes, *Heterorhabditis* spp. and *Steinernema* spp., among host insects at 48 and 68°F (9 and 20°C) and effects on efficacy. *Journal of Invertebrate Pathology* 73:206–13.

Willmott, D. M., A. J. hart, S. J. Long, R. N. Edmonson, and P. N. Richardson. 2002. Use of a cold-active entomopathogenic nematode *Steinernema kraussei* to control overwintering larvae of the black vine weevil *Otiorhynchus sulcatus* (Coleoptera:Curculionidae) in outdoor strawberry plants. *Nematology* 4:925-32.

Wilson, M., P. Nitzsche, and P. W. Shearer. 1999. Entomopathogenic nematodes to control black vine weevil (Coleoptera:Curculionidae) on strawberry. *Journal of Economic Entomology* 92:651-57.

Wright, E. M., and R. J. Chambers. 1994. The biology of the predatory mite *Hypoaspis miles* (Acari: Laelapidae), a potential biological control agent of *Bradysia paupera* (Dipt.: Sciaridae). *Entomophaga* 39:225–35.

Ydergaard, S., A. Enkegaard, and H. F. Brödsgaard. 1997. The predatory mite *Hypoaspis miles*: Temperature dependent life table characteristics on a diet of sciarid larvae, *Bradysia paupera* and *B. tritici*. *Entomologia Experimentalis et Applicata* 85:177–87.

20

BIOLOGICAL CONTROL IN CHRYSANTHEMUM

G. D. Murphy
Ontario Ministry of Agriculture and Food
Ontario, Canada

and

A. B. Broadbent
Agriculture and Agri-Food Canada
Ontario, Canada

Chrysanthemum (*Chrysanthemum mori-folium* Ramat=*Dendranthema grandi-flora* Tevelev.) is a short-day plant and one of the world's most popular floral crops. The crop cycle begins with cuttings, which when rooted are transplanted into beds or pots, given a period of long-day photoperiod to promote stem and leaf development, followed by short days to initiate flowering. A complex of insects and mites is a major limiting factor in producing high-quality chrysanthemum. Natural enemies are available for each key pest; however, combining them into a successful integrated pest management (IPM) program is challenging. IPM programs for chrysanthemum have been developed, especially in the United Kingdom and the United States, but subsequent emergences of new pests, and the increased availability of natural enemies, make a review of the topic necessary (Hussey and Bravenboer 1971, Cross et al. 1983, Wardlow 1985, Parrella and Jones 1987).

Pest Complex

The most important pests attacking chrysanthemum are thrips, especially *Frankliniella occidentalis* (Pergande); aphids, including *Myzus persicae* (Sulz.) and *Aphis gossypii* Glover; leafminers such as *Liriomyza trifolii* (Burgess), *Liriomyza bryoniae* (Kalt) and *Liriomyza huidobrensis* Blanchard; two-spotted spider mite, *Tetranychus urticae* Koch; and lepidopteran pests, especially *Spodoptera exigua* (Hübner). For potted chrysanthemum, fungus gnats (*Bradysia* spp.) are also important.

Biological control of a large pest complex is difficult. Failure to control one pest may require intervention with pesticides, compromising the entire IPM program. The economics of controlling many different pests must also be considered. In chrysanthemum, successful biological control of each of the major pests has been documented, but it is too simplistic to concentrate on control of just one pest. Biological control for one pest in a complex must be compatible with control methods used for other pests (Tauber and Helgesen 1978).

Natural Enemies

Commercially available natural enemies for control of chrysanthemum pests include parasitoids, predators, entomopathogenic fungi, nematodes, a bacterial toxin, and a virus (Fransen 1995). The reader should refer to other chapters for more detailed information on individual natural enemies.

Having a wide selection of natural enemies does not guarantee successful biological control. There are potential interactions between the crop and natural enemy (e.g. for *Phytoseiulus persimilis* Athias-Henriot and *Orius* spp. [Fransen, Boogaard, and Tolsma 1993; Gillespie and Quiring 1994]) or between different species of natural enemies (e.g., between the leafminer parasitoid *Diglyphus begini* Ashmead and various parasitic nematodes; *D. begini* and *Cephalosporium* [= *Verticillium*] *lecanii* Zimmermann; *Orius* and the predatory mite *Neoseiuls cucumeris* [Oudemans] [Sher and Parrella 1996, Bethke and Parrella 1989, Ramakers 1993]); and among predators (such as *Hypoaspis* spp. and soil-dwelling life stages of various predators [Brødsgaard, Sardar, and Enkegaard 1996]). When interactions among natural enemies are accompanied by an increased suppression of the targeted pest populations, such interactions become a scientific curiosity rather than a detriment to biological control. However, when such interactions occur without an additive suppression of the pest populations, as may occur when generalist predators or hyperparasitoids are involved, the interactions may hinder the ability to accomplish biological control.

Monitoring

Monitoring pests in chrysanthemum is similar to that in other greenhouse crops. Sticky cards (for flying insects) and crop inspection (for nonflying pests and immature life stages) are most commonly used and essential for successful IPM.

Differential attractiveness exists between blue and yellow sticky cards to *F. occidentalis*, but the range of flying insects attracted to yellow makes them a better choice for insect monitoring in chrysanthemum (Brødsgaard 1989, Broadbent 1994). If thrips populations must be detected at low levels (e.g., where there is a history of thrips-borne tospoviruses), then blue cards are particularly useful. For monitoring natural enemies, the same principles apply. Yellow sticky cards attract a number of parasitoids including species of *Aphidius*, *Diglyphus*, *Dacnusa*, as well as other beneficial arthropods such as *Orius* spp. Growers may express reservations about removing natural enemies by inadvertently trapping them, but the advantages of tracking natural enemy populations to evaluate ongoing biological control programs outweigh the relatively minuscule loss from trapping. Crop inspection is important for monitoring predatory mites, immature stages of insects such as species of *Orius* or *Aphidoletes*, and for obtaining direct measures of the impact of natural enemies on the pest (e.g., parasitism of leafminer larvae and aphids). Post-release evaluation of beneficials should be an integral component of biological control in chrysanthemum.

Influence of Production Variables on Biological Control

Production systems

Different production systems (e.g., cut vs. potted flowers, weekly vs. holiday crops, and finished crop vs. stock plants) affect the application of biological control. For example, in cut chrysanthemum, the first four to six weeks of vegetative growth is not harvested, allowing a higher threshold of damage early in the crop (Parrella, Jones, and Christie 1987). In potted chrysanthemum, the whole plant is sold, requiring minimal damage from the outset. Additionally, pests such as fungus gnats that work at the soil interface, detract from the value of potted chrysanthemum, but are not a factor in cut chrysanthemum sales.

In a weekly production schedule, all growth stages of the crop are grown concurrently (fig. 20.1) and on a long-term basis, allowing time to establish biological control. However, in chrysanthemum grown specifically for holidays (e.g., Easter and Christmas), biological control presents a different challenge, and success depends on: (i) crops grown prior to and concurrently with the chrysanthemum crop; (ii) pest populations in other crops and when the chrysanthemum crop is started; and (iii) whether biological control is used in other crops. If biological control must be re-established whenever a holiday crop is grown, it increases costs and difficulty, as the grower must repeatedly overcome the initial obstacles of establishment, (e.g., pesticide residues and well-established pest populations).

Figure 20.1. In year-round chrysanthemum grown for fresh cut flowers, plantings of new cuttings are typically placed beside a mature crop ready to harvest. When this production schedule is conducted over a long period, it permits the time necessary to allow biological control to take place. *Photo: G. D. Murphy.*

Flowering crops and stock plants grown to propagate cuttings are also treated differently. In a flowering crop, aesthetic value and low tolerance for pests (van Lenteren and Woets 1988) drives the decision-making process. In stock crops (particularly if grown by growers for their own use), a higher action threshold provides greater opportunity for successful control. If cuttings are sold, however, there may be grower resistance if biological control results in low levels of pests on the cuttings.

The importance of pollen to natural enemies such as *N. cucumeris* and *Orius* spp. may limit use of biological control in stock plants where no naturally occurring pollen is available (van Rijn and Sabelis 1990, Ramakers and van den Meiracker 1991). An alternative food source may help in establishing natural enemies, especially at lower pest densities (Fransen, Boogaard, and

Tolsma 1993). Hessein and Parrella (1990) showed that adding pollen could be useful with chrysanthemum in a biological control program using predatory mites, particularly at lower thrips densities. Murphy and Broadbent (1996) suggested that removal of cuttings from stock plants might also remove predators preying on western flower thrips in the terminals, and as a result have a detrimental effect on the existing biological control.

Market destination

The potential of biological control in chrysanthemum is influenced by its market destination. Crops grown for export have little tolerance for pests and pest damage. Flowers entering the United States from Colombia, one of the largest chrysanthemum producers in the world, require a "zero tolerance" for pests and diseases, severely limiting use of biological control (Nicholls, Parrella, and Altieri 1998). Implying that pesticides ensure "zero-tolerance" is equally fraught with problems. Perfect kill, or 100% mortality of the target pest, is rarely accomplished with insecticides due to the inability to achieve perfect coverage or due to within-population variation in susceptibility to any given insecticide. The solution to this quandary lies in the adoption of IPM strategies with a reliance on biological control as an alternative to prophylactic applications of insecticides. While this solution applies to all crops regardless of market, biological control will likely be adopted more readily in crops marketed domestically.

Cultivar susceptibility

Chrysanthemum cultivars vary in their susceptibility to pests and are used in IPM in different ways (Wyatt 1965; Price et. al. 1980; Oetting 1982; Broadbent and Blom 1983; Broadbent, Matteoni, and Allen 1990; Yoshida and Parrella 1991; Fransen and Tolsma 1992; de Jager and Butôt, 1993). A grower may discontinue growing susceptible cultivars or use them as indicators of pest presence. Parrella and Jones (1987) suggested that growers place susceptible chrysanthemum cultivars together and away from doorways and vents, and that they concentrate their IPM programs on those areas.

Fransen and Tolsma (1992) found enhanced control of western flower thrips in chrysanthemum by using resistant cultivars and noted the potential of resistant cultivars in biological control programs. The importance of host plant resistance is recognised by plant breeders. For example, a company object of one of largest plant propagators (Yoder Brothers Inc., Alva, Florida) is to include the breeding of pest resistance into new chrysanthemum introductions (Begley 1992).

Compatible pesticides

Selective or compatible pesticides have an important role in biological control. These pesticides can be used to control pests and diseases when no other methods are available, or they may redress an imbalance in the desired pest/natural enemy complex. Further, an application of a compatible pesticide may be used as an emergency control measure if biological control fails or used as a method to reduce pest numbers prior to implementing biological control (Oomen 1992).

Many pesticides that are compatible with natural enemies are available to control chrysanthemum pests. However, efficacy and number of products varies, and disparities exist in their availability between countries. This places some growers at a disadvantage in implementing biological control. The use of compatible pesticides is critical to successful biological control in many crops with multiple pests (van Lenteren and Woets 1988, Parrella 1990b, Ramakers and van den Meiracker 1991). Most documented programs in chrysanthemum rely on selective pesticides.

Limitations of Biological Control in Chrysanthemum

Economics

Given the need to purchase many different types of natural enemies to control the potential range of pests, start-up costs of biological control in chrysanthemum are considerable. For ornamental crops in general, Wardlow, Brough, and Need (1992) noted that biological control-based IPM might cost twice as much as conventional insecticide control. For chrysanthemum, Murphy and Broadbent (unpublished data) have developed biological control programs for chrysanthemum growers in Ontario, Canada, costing US $0.37 to 0.47 per ft.^{2} (CD $6 to 7/m^2), with 90% of the cost for control of *F. occidentalis*. High costs of biological control in chrysanthemum are also reported by Ravensberg and Altena (1993) in the Netherlands and Hesselein et al. (1993) in the United States.

However, start-up costs in year-round chrysanthemum are unlikely to represent on-going costs. During the initial experiences with biological control, a grower must endure several obstacles that include (i) inexperience in handling natural enemies,

(ii) excessive pest densities often associated with reductions in the use of broad spectrum insecticides, and (iii) pesticide residues having lethal or sub-lethal effects on natural enemies. With experience and reduced dependence on pesticides, these problems are reduced or eliminated and biological control should become more economically attractive.

Secondary pests

Ending of frequent pesticide use can encourage development of secondary pest problems, and natural enemies necessary for their control may not be commercially available. Of particular importance in chrysanthemum are plant-feeding bugs, especially *Lygus* spp. and other capsids (Hemiptera: Miridae). *Lygus* spp. damage chrysanthemum by feeding on growing points and developing flowers (Price and Poe 1991). Fransen (pers. comm.) noted extensive damage to chrysanthemums from this pest where biological controls for other key pests were being implemented in the Netherlands. Murphy and Broadbent (1993, 1996) reported several cases of biological control in chrysanthemum being abandoned because of an inability to effectively manage *Lygus* damage using compatible measures. The egg parasitoid *Anaphes iole* (Girault) is available for control of *Lygus* species outdoors, but there is no documentation of its use in greenhouses. In the United Kingdom, capsids, symphilids, and millipedes are frequently secondary pests, with capsids in particular often causing programs to be abandoned (Helyer, pers. comm.). The threat of secondary pests is a strong argument for using insect-exclusion screening in biological control programs.

New pests

A number of hypotheses have been formulated in an attempt to explain the causes of new pest outbreaks. The major hypotheses include: (i) dramatic changes in the physical environment; (ii) changes in intrinsic genetic or physiological properties; (iii) trophic interactions between plants and herbivores or prey (or hosts) and predators (or parasitoids); (iv) qualitative or quantitative changes in host plants; (v) occurrence of a particular life history strategy; (vi) escape from the influence of natural enemies; and (vii) overwhelming the defensive systems of their hosts (Berryman 1987). Considering variation among greenhouse environments (and in relation to unprotected environments), pesticide resistance, continuous introductions of new plant species and varieties, and variations in cultural and control practices; numerous examples may be cited to support each of these hypotheses. Regardless of the cause of new pest outbreaks, global shipment of plant material has spread pests around the world at an alarmingly fast rate (Van Lenteren and Woets 1988). Since 1980, new pests such as *L. trifolii, L. huidobrensis, F. occidentalis, A. gossypii* and *Thrips palmi* Karny have emerged to cause significant economic losses for chrysanthemum growers. New pests can limit or preclude the use of biological control. For each additional pest, a new species of natural enemy is often required for its control. A breakdown in the biological control of any single pest within a complex may compromise the implementation or success of the biological control program for the entire pest complex. For example, the emergence of *F. occidentalis* as

a greenhouse pest has had long-term detrimental effects on biological control in many crops including chrysanthemum.

Introduction Rates of Natural Enemies

Van Lenteren and Woets (1988) discuss difficulties in determining release rates for natural enemies in greenhouse crops. For growers of ornamental plants including chrysanthemum, lack of specific release rate recommendations represents a pressing need (Osborne and Oetting 1989, Parrella 1990a, Fransen 1992). Some biological control producers now provide recommendations for major ornamental crops; however, lack of relevant data has resulted in excessive introductions to enhance establishment and success (Mumford 1992; Hesselein et al. 1993; Murphy and Broadbent 1996; Nicholls, Parrella, and Altieri 1998). This approach depends on long-term success offsetting high initial costs.

Another approach to setting release rates is the use of mathematical models based on biological parameters of the pest and natural enemy. Sabelis et al. (1983) describes a model for *T. urticae* and *P. persimilis* on cucumber, but it has not been tested on chrysanthemum. Heinz, Nunney, and Parrella (1990) developed and validated a model to control *L. trifolii* using the parasitoid *D. begini* on chrysanthemum. Some caution should be exercised with using such single pest and crop models since they currently do not include the complexities associated with the inclusion of interactions with other natural enemies, specifics associated with production practices, or the effects of pesticide applications. Despite these concerns, using models can assist in the biological control decision-making process.

Major chrysanthemum pests are discussed below, with a range of producer recommendations on release rates of natural enemies where available. Use of natural enemies may depend on importation requirements, quarantine restrictions, or registration requirements. Therefore, recommendations may not apply in all countries.

Aphids

The two most common aphids attacking chrysanthemum are *M. persicae* and *A. gossypii*, although other species such as *Macrosiphum euphorbiae* (Thom.), *Aulacorthum solani* (Kaltenbach), or *Macrosiphoniella sanborni* (Gill.) also cause damage. Until the early 1990s, *Aphidius matricariae* Haliday was the most commonly used natural enemy against aphids (primarily *M. persicae*) (Scopes 1970; Hussey and Bravenboer 1971; Scopes and Biggerstaff 1973; Hussey and Scopes 1977; Wardlow, Brough, and Need 1992; Buxton and Wardlow 1992). *A. matricariae* has also been used in chrysanthemum in Colombia (Nicholls, Parrella, and Altieri 1998).

Aphis gossypii was described by Hussey and Bravenboer (1971) as an occasional pest of chrysanthemum, but it has reached greater pest status more recently (Price and Poe 1991; Vehrs, Walker, and Parrella 1992). As *A. gossypii* became more problematic, the ineffectiveness of *A. matricariae* against it became evident. Another *Aphidius* species, *Aphidius colemani* Viereck was shown to provide good control (van Steenis 1993) and has been used successfully in commercial

chrysanthemums against both these aphids (Murphy and Broadbent 1996). Success of biological control of *A. gossypii* and *M. persicae* with *A. colemani* can be enhanced by optimising the spacing of parasitoid release points (Heinz 1998). Other aphid species, such as *M. euphorbiae* and *A. solani* are becoming more prevalent in Europe and the United Kingdom, and the parasitoid *Aphidius ervi* Haliday is recommended for their control. Hyperparasitism of *Aphidius* spp. may occur during the summer requiring the use of compatible pesticides or other natural enemies.

Use of the predatory midge *Aphidoletes aphidomyza* (Rondoni) on chrysanthemum has been reported, but without comment on its effectiveness (Buxton and Wardlow 1992, Buxton and Finlay 1993). Generalist predators, such as coccinellid beetles and lacewings, may be useful against aphid species not well controlled by the specialist parasitoids or predators described above. Some, such as *Hippodamia convergens* Guerin-Meneville, *Harmonia axyridis* Pallas, and *Chrysoperla rufilabris* (Burmeister) are commercially available, but there is little documentation of their use in chrysanthemum. Wardlow (1985) recommended the entomopathogenic fungus *V. lecanii* against aphids in chrysanthemum and Helyer et al. (1992) used it successfully. Aphicides showing some compatibility with natural enemies include pirimicarb, kinoprene and pymetrozine.

Recommendations by commercial producers for biological control of aphids range from 0.009 to 0.09 *A. colemani* per ft.^{2} (0.1 to 1.0/m^2) per week for *A. gossypii* and *M. persicae*; *A. ervi* at the same rates for *M.*

euphorbiae and *A. solani*; and *A. aphidomyza* at 0.09 to 0.9 per ft.^{2} (1 to 10/m^2) per week. These rates depend on the size of the aphid infestation. Biological control of aphids is a viable option, limited principally by other pests that are not controlled as easily without pesticides.

Thrips

Western flower thrips, *F. occidentalis*, is the most important insect pest of chrysanthemum (fig. 20.2) and frequently the major limiting factor in developing biological control for this crop. Control is complicated by susceptibility of chrysanthemum to thrips-borne tospoviruses, whose presence greatly reduces tolerance for thrips compared to a system where the pest arthropod does not vector a plant disease.

A number of thrips predators are commercially available and a system using multiple natural enemies, targeting different life stages, will likely be more effective than one using a single control agent. The most commonly used species is the predatory mite *N. cucumeris,* which feeds on first-instar

Figure 20.2. *Frankliniella occidentalis* (Pergande) damage to chrysanthemum flowers. *Photo: M. P. Parrella.*

larvae and was introduced for thrips control in 1985 (van Lenteren 1992). There are many reports of its use in chrysanthemum (Hessein and Parrella 1990, Buxton and Wardlow 1992, Buxton and Finlay 1993, Hesselein et al. 1993, Ravensberg and Altena 1993, Murphy and Broadbent 1996) at different introduction rates, either alone or with various other natural enemies or insecticides. Despite general observations by the above authors that control was inconsistent or uneconomical at the levels used, or that it was difficult to separate its impact from other natural enemies used, *N. cucumeris* remains the most commonly used predator for thrips biological control. Because it feeds on first instar thrips and later instars are immune to attack, it is most effective when used preventatively.

Iphiseius degenerans (Berlese) is an effective predator of western flower thrips and best utilized within a biological control program using a banker plant introduction system (Ramakers and Voet 1995). Due to the mite's requirement for pollen, supplemental addition of apple pollen may be needed to achieve biological control in chrysanthemum where the crop is harvested before significant pollen production. Scientific documentation of the use of *I. degenerans* in chrysanthemum is lacking.

The anthocorids in the genus *Orius* feed on all life stages of thrips and became commercially available in 1991 (Van Lenteren 1992). Fransen and Tolsma (1992) and Fransen, Boogaard, and Tolsma (1993) found that *Orius insidosus* (Say) (one per plant or one per two plants, four applications, two weeks apart [against high thrips populations]; or one per eleven plants, four applications, two weeks apart [for low populations]), could be successful, especially when used in conjunction with thrips-resistant chrysanthemum cultivars. Buxton and Finlay (1993) used *Orius majusculus* (Reuter) on chrysanthemum (3 introductions at 0.09 per ft.^{2} [1/m^2]) and found it reasonably effective at suppressing thrips populations; however, recoveries of *O. majusculus* from the crop were few. Murphy and Broadbent (1996) reported on a grower's use of *O. insidiosus* (5 introductions over 8 weeks, totalling 2.3 per ft.^{2} [25/m^2]) giving excellent control of a large thrips population in commercial chrysanthemums.

Verticillium lecanii is sold in some countries for control of thrips. Buxton and Wardlow (1992) used *V. lecanii* and *N. cucumeris* together to achieve good control of *F. occidentalis*, but noted that infected thrips could not be found. Similarly, Ravensberg and Altena (1993) used *V. lecanii, O. insidiosus* and *N. cucumeris* in combination against western flower thrips in chrysanthemum, but found the individual effect of *V. lecanii* difficult to evaluate. Other entomopathogenic fungi, such as *Beauveria bassiana* (Balsamo) Vuillemin, are sold for thrips control under the U.S. names BotaniGard and Naturalis-O; however, results of spray trials have been inconsistent. *B. bassiana* (BotaniGard) suppressed populations of western flower thrips infesting chrysanthemums grown in California (Murphy et al. 1998), and Georgia (Ludwig and Oetting 2002), but trials conducted in Texas using BotaniGard and Naturalis-O failed to control western flower thrips populations infesting potted chrysanthemums (Thompson, Krauter, and Heinz 1999).

The entomopathogenic nematode *Steinernema feltiae* (Filipjev) used as a foliar application has demonstrated excellent potential for control of *F. occidentalis* in commercial chrysanthemum crops (Wardlow, Piggot and Goldsworthy 2001). Control of female thrips was shown to be particularly effective over two successive years of production. Another nematode species being investigated for thrips control is *Thripinema nicklewoodi* (Siddiqui) (Lim, Van Driesche, and Heinz 2001; Arthurs and Heinz 2002). Laboratory studies resulted in infection and sterilization of female *F. occidentalis*, but the commercial applicability of this natural enemy remains doubtful.

The soil-dwelling pre-pupal and pupal stages of western flower thrips offer an alternative target for biological control. Helyer et al. (1995) found that the fungus *Metarhizium anisopliae* (Metchnikoff) Sorokin and the nematode *Steinernema carpocapsae* Weiser gave best control (>70%) of thrips pupae in the soil. The predatory mite *Hypoaspis* (=*Geolaelaps) miles* Berlese also attacks thrips pupae, and a single release of 9 per ft.^{2} (100/m^2) may control thrips in commercial greenhouses (Gillespie and Quiring 1990; Brødsgaard, Sardar, and Enkegaard 1996; Murphy and Broadbent 1996). Improvement upon control achieved by *H. miles* may be on the horizon as research conducted in the Netherlands (Ravensberg, pers. comm.) suggests that *Hypoaspis aculeifer* (Canestrini) consumes nearly 50% more pupae than *H. miles* in laboratory experiments.

Producer recommendations for biological control of thrips in chrysanthemum focus on *N. cucumeris* and *Orius* species. *Neoseiulus cucumeris* is sold in bulk or in slow-release envelopes that function as breeding chambers to release mites over a prolonged period. Recommended release rates are 9 per ft.^{2} (100/m^2), with frequency depending on the densities of thrips populations and which product is used (bulk or slow-release). *Orius* species (0.09 to 0.9 per ft.^{2} [1 to 10/m^2] repeated after two weeks) are recommended when rapid control of established populations is necessary.

Thrips control is currently the greatest obstacle to biological control in chrysanthemum. Pesticides that are effective and compatible with other natural enemies are currently unavailable for thrips control (Ramakers and van den Meiracker 1991). While successful biological thrips control has been achieved in individual trials, it is far from assured in commercial operations, and the economics of applying large quantities of several different natural enemies must be evaluated.

Leafminer

Historically, leafminers have been important pests of chrysanthemums. Before the 1980s the chrysanthemum leafminer, *Chromatomyia (=Phytomyza) syngenesiae* (Hardy), was the major leafminer pest of chrysanthemum. In the 1980's *L. trifolii* nearly devastated the chrysanthemum industry, with losses in California alone estimated at US $93 million between 1982 and 1986 (Newman and Parrella 1986). In the mid-1980s, the introduction of the insecticide abamectin dramatically reduced damage (fig. 20.3) from this pest. As frequently occurs when control depends on one insecticide, the status of this pest began to rebound during the 1990s (Parrella 1996). In addition, another species

Figure 20.3. *Liriomyza trifolii* **(Burgess) damage to chrysanthemum foliage.** *Photo: A .B. Broadbent.*

of leafminer, *L. huidobrensis,* has become a key pest in Colombia. There, the leafminer limits the use of biological control since cut chrysanthemum flowers are exported to the United States, where the pest has quarantine status (Nicholls, Parrella, and Altieri 1998).

Early biological control programs were directed against *C. syngenesiae* (Hussey and Bravenboer 1971, Scopes and Biggerstaff 1973, Wardlow 1985). Natural enemies used against leafminers include early trials with *Chrysocharis* spp. by Hussey and Bravenboer (1971) and Parrella, Jones, and Christie (1987), but parasitoids such as *Diglyphus isaea* (Walker) and *Dacnusa sibirica* Telenga are now more commonly recommended.

A combination of *D. sibirica* and *D. isaea* (0.09 per ft.^{2} [1/m^2] every three weeks) was successful against leafminer in the United Kingdom (Buxton and Finlay 1993) and in the Netherlands (Ravensberg and Altena 1993). Murphy and Broadbent (unpublished data) used the same combination of parasitoids (0.18 per ft.^{2} [2/m^2], two applications, two weeks apart) to control a high *L. trifolii* population (>800 leafminers per sticky trap per week) in a commercial chrysanthemum stock crop in Canada. Current recommendations from producers of natural enemies include: a combination of *Dacnusa/Diglyphus* (90:10) at 0.02 to 0.18 per ft.^{2} (0.25 to 2/m^2) per week (depending on infestation level) or *Diglyphus* alone (recommended rates use different criteria, e.g., 1 per 10 plants per week or 0.009 to 0.09 per ft.^{2} [0.1 to 1/m^2] for three consecutive weeks). Determining proper release rates has long been a burning issue in augmentation biological control. In an effort to solve this problem, Heinz, Nunney, and Parrella (1990) used a predictive computer model to determine release rates of *D. begini* against *L. trifolii*. Hesselein et al. (1993) also used this model.

Biological control of leafminers can be a viable part of chrysanthemum IPM, if introductions begin before leafminer populations build up. Chances of success may improve in greenhouses where residual leafminer populations are supressed between crops, providing a well-defined starting point to begin natural enemy introductions. Where all stages of crop growth are present, a bed of newly planted cuttings is often found adjacent to a mature crop. This provides obvious complications in treating new crops separately from previous plantings and applications of compatible pesticides may be appropriate. The insect growth regulator cyromazine is compatible with *D. begini* and most other natural enemies, and where registered is a useful adjunct to biological control of leafminer (Parrella 1990a, Koppert 1995).

Another potential option, although not yet proven under commercial situations is the use of entomopathogenic nematodes for leafminer control. Williams and Walters (1994) discussed the important role of humidity and temperature in the efficacy of *S. feltiae* against *L. huidobrensis*. *Steinernema carpocapsae* was demonstrated by Broadbent and Olthof (1995) to control *L. trifolii* in chrysanthemum in research greenhouses. Sher, Parrella and Kaya (1999) further developed this concept by combining the use of *S. carpocapsae* with the parasitoid *D. begini* and Wardlow (pers. comm.) noted the effective control of *S. feltiae* against *C. syngenesiae* in commercial chrysanthemum greenhouses in the United Kingdom.

Spider mites

Biological control of the two-spotted spider mite, *T. urticae*, using the predatory mite *P. persimilis* is well established in greenhouse crops, and *P. persimilis* remains the most important natural enemy for this pest. Recently, predatory midges in the genus *Feltiella* (=*Theridiplosis*) and the predatory mite *Neoseiulus californicus* (McGregor) have also become available for purchase from commercial insectaries, but there is no documentation of their use against *T. urticae* in chrysanthemum.

Biological control of mites in chrysanthemum is usually part of a broader IPM program concentrating on more difficult to control pests such as thrips. Various introduction rates have been recommended by Hussey and Bravenboer (1971), Scopes and Biggerstaff (1973), Wardlow (1985), and Buxton and Wardlow (1992). Ravensberg and Altena (1993) and Buxton and Finlay (1993) achieved excellent control of *T. urticae* by releasing 0.09 *P. persimilis* per ft.^{2} (1/m^2). Commercial producers' recommendations range from using *P. persimilis* in infested areas at 1.8 per ft.^{2} (20/m^2), to using one predator per ten plants every two weeks.

Sciarid flies

Sciarid flies or fungus gnats are capable of causing damage in chrysanthemum, primarily in potted plants (Price and Poe 1991). Biological control studies on fungus gnats in chrysanthemum are limited, probably because it is less serious than other pests.

Two entomopathogenic nematodes, *S. feltiae* and *S. carpocapsae*, are sold for fungus gnat control. Recent work in chrysanthemum and other crops (Buxton 1993; Lindquist, Buxton, and Piatkowski 1994; Gouge and Hague 1994) suggest *S. feltiae* is the more effective species. Predatory mites in the genus *Hypoaspis* will also consume sciarid larvae in the soil (Gillespie and Quiring 1990; Brødsgaard, Sardar, and Enkegaard 1996). Lindquist, Buxton, and Piatkowski (1994) were able to achieve effective biological fungus gnat control using 25 *H. miles* per 4-in. (10.5-cm) pot diameter in chrysanthemum. Current recommendations from natural enemy producers are to apply *S. feltiae* at 46,000 per ft.^{2} (500,000/m^2) (two applications for heavy infestations) and/or 10 to 50 *Hypoaspis* per ft.^{2} (100 to 500/m^2), depending on population size and whether the mites are applied in the crop or beneath benches.

The staphylinid *Atheta coriaria* Kraatz has been shown to be a voracious predator of sciarid larvae, with long-term resident populations of naturally occurring predators being documented in Ontario, Canada (Carney et al. 2002). *Atheta coriaria* is being produced and sold commercially with recommended introduction rates of 2 per m^2.

Lepidopteran pests

Many lepidopterans are sporadic pests on chrysanthemum, although outbreaks of the beet armyworm (*S. exigua*) have been severe at times in the United States and the Netherlands (Yoshida and Parrella 1991). Control of *S. exigua* has focused on two biological insecticides, *Bacillus thuringiensis* Berliner *kurstaki* and *S. exigua* nuclear polyhedrosis virus (SeNPV). *Bacillus thuringiensis* is recommended against *S. exigua* in California by Parrella and Jones (1987), but van der Linden (1996) suggests that *B. thuringiensis* is ineffective against *S. exigua* in Europe. Shinoyama et al. (2002) produced the first Bt transgenic chrysanthemum and demonstrated its potential for controlling lepidopteran pests. *Spodoptera exigua* NPV was identified as a potential control for beet armyworm in 1977 soon after the pest was introduced into Europe, and a commercial product was subsequently registered for use in the Netherlands in 1993 (Smits and Vlak 1994). An insect virus that attacks beet armyworm was also used in chrysanthemum production in the United States (Begley 1989), but a formulation of the virus has not yet been registered in North America. Other forms of control have also been proposed with varying degrees of success. These include the use of pheromone traps, insect exclusion screening, black light traps, and host plant resistance (Parrella and Jones 1987, Begley 1989, Price and Poe 1991, Yoshida and Parrella 1991).

Final Remarks

For many chrysanthemum growers, implementation of biological control represents a dramatic shift by comparison to prophylactic applications of insecticides. Because natural enemy releases rates are based on pest densities, a biological control program in chrysanthemum must include a structured, regular monitoring program. Keeping pest densities to a minimum by implementing good sanitation practices and using insect-exclusion screening will improve chances of success. Because chrysanthemums are suitable hosts for a variety of pests, several different strategies (summarized in Table 20-1) must be used when attempting to control a complex of pests. Breaking chrysanthemum ranges into smaller management units will also increase opportunities for biological control by isolating severe pest outbreaks and minimizing variation associated with planting dates, cultivars, and environment.

The future of biological control in chrysanthemum depends on effectiveness, consistency, and economic feasibility. Availability of new natural enemies, new pesticides, and resistant cultivars will influence its adoption. Environmental constraints on pesticides in many countries will

Table 20-1. Biological Control–Driven IPM Strategies against Major Chrysanthemum Pests.

Pest	Treatment
Thrips	If thrips are present, reduce populations with short residual pesticides. Introduce *N. cucumeris* regularly, and *Hypoaspis* spp. in the soil and *Orius* spp. if needed. Use entomopathogenic fungi such as *V. lecanii* or *B. bassiana* if available. Consider regular applications of the entomopathogenic nematode *S. feltiae*. If thrips are not present, release *N. cucumeris* regularly as a preventive measure.
Aphids	Release *Aphidius* spp. (with compatible pesticides if necessary). Banker plants may be effective preventatively if aphids are not present. If hyperparasitism occurs, release *A. aphidomyza* and/or use a compatible pesticide.
Leafminer	At first sign of mines or adults release *D. isaea/D. sibirica*. If populations still become damaging, use a compatible pesticide.
Spider mites	Introduce *P. persimilis* as required. Consider using *N. californicus* or *Feltiella spp.* preventatively and spot sprays with short residual pesticides if necessary.
Fungus gnats	Use *S. feltiae, B. thuringiensis, Hypoaspis* spp. or *A. coriaria* as necessary and compatible pesticides if required.
Caterpillars	Use *B. thuringiensis* if needed.

provide added impetus to growers to explore biological control opportunities. Inconsistency of thrips control on chrysanthemum is a primary concern, but as new natural enemies become available, better control should ensue. Likewise, the increasing trend towards pesticides that are very specific, or have shorter persistence, offers hope that more pesticides that are effective in controlling isolated pest outbreaks while being compatible with biological control will become available.

Other pest problems not easily controlled biologically fall into the category of secondary, sporadic, or region-specific pests. Many are outdoor pests that seasonally move into the greenhouse, for example, lygus bugs, other Hemiptera or Lepidoptera. The increasing use of natural enemies will underscore the value of insect-exclusion screening. Development of chrysanthemum cultivars resistant to pests will play a significant role in the future of biological control. Traditional breeding programs will be important, but the greatest advances will likely come from genetic manipulation of the plant.

The future for biological control in chrysanthemum is promising. There are many field examples of successful control and new technological developments will result in increased areas of chrysanthemum being grown under biological control–driven IPM programs. Change is inevitable as more growers worldwide demonstrate successful use of biological control in chrysanthemum.

Acknowledgments

We wish to thank Applied Bionomics Ltd., Biobest Ltd., Syngenta BioLine, and Koppert Biological Systems for their advice on introduction rates of natural enemies.

References Cited

Arthurs S. and K. M. Heinz. 2002. In vivo rearing of *Thripinema nicklewoodi* (Tylenchida: Allantonematidae) and prospects as a biological control agent of *Frankliniella occidentalis* (Thysanoptera: Thripidae). *Journal of Economic Entomology.* 95(4):668-74

Begley, J. W. 1989. How integrated pest management reduced pesticide applications at Yoder Brothers. In *Proceedings for the Fifth Conference on Insect and Disease Management on Ornamentals,* ed. M. Daughtrey and J. Begley, 8–18. Alexandria, Virginia, USA: Society of American Florists.

———. 1992. Plant breeding with the goal of pest management, in *Proceedings for the Eighth Conference on Insect and Disease Management on Ornamentals.* February 22–24, 1992, ed. M. Daughtrey, 12–25. Alexandria, Virginia, USA: Society of American Florists.

Berryman, A. 1987. The theory and classification of outbreaks. In *Insect Outbreaks,* ed. P. Barbosa and J. C. Schultz, 3–30. San Diego, Calif.: Academic Press.

Bethke, J. A., and M. P. Parrella. 1989. Compatibility of the aphid fungus *Cephalosporium lecanii* with the leaf miner parasite, *Diglyphus begini* (Hymenoptera: Eulophidae). *Pan-Pacific Entomology* 65 (4):385–90.

Broadbent, A. B. 1994. The integrated pest management of western flower thrips. In *Proceedings for the Tenth Conference on Insect and Disease Management on Ornamentals,* ed. K. Robb, 68–78. Alexandria, Virginia, USA: Society of American Florists.

Broadbent, A. B., and T. J. Blom. 1983. Comparative susceptibility of chrysanthemum cultivars to *Liriomyza trifolii* (Diptera: Agromyzidae). *Proceedings of Entomological Society of Ontario* 114:91–3.

Broadbent, A. B., J. A. Matteoni, and W. R. Allen. 1990. Feeding preferences of the western flower thrips, *Frankliniella occidentalis* (Pergande) (Thysanoptera: Thripidae), and incidence of tomato spotted wilt virus among cultivars of florist's chrysanthemum. *The Canadian Entomologist* 122:1111–7.

Broadbent A. B. and T. H. A. Olthof. 1995. Foliar application of *Steinernema carpocapsae* (Rhabditida: Steinernematidae) to control *Liriomyza trifolii* (Diptera: Agromyzidae) larvae in chrysanthemums. *Environmental Entomology.* 24:431-5.

Brødsgaard, H. F. 1989. Coloured sticky traps for *Frankliniella occidentalis* (Pergande) (Thysanoptera: Thripidae) in glasshouses. *Journal of Applied Entomology* 107:136–40.

Brødsgaard, H. F., M. A. Sardar, and A Enkegaard. 1996. Prey preference of *Hypoaspis miles* (Berlese) (Acarina: Hypoaspididae): Non-interference with other beneficials in glasshouse crops. *IOBC/WPRS Bulletin* 19 (1):23–6.

Buxton, J. H. 1993. Control of sciarid flies with parasitic nematodes. *IOBC/WPRS Bulletin* 16 (2):23–5.

Buxton, J. H., and R. Finlay. 1993. Integrated pest management in AYR chrysanthemums. *IOBC/WPRS Bulletin* 16 (8):33–41.

Buxton, J. H., and L. Wardlow. 1992. Two years of trials with biological control programmes in year-round chrysanthemums. *Bulletin OEPP/EPPO* 22:503–11.

Carney V. A., J. C. Diamond, G.D. Murphy and D. Marshall. 2002. The potential of *Atheta coriaria* (Coleoptera: Staphylinidae), as a biological control agent for use in greenhouse crops. *IOBC/WPRS Bulletin* 25(1):37-40

Cross, J. V., L. Wardlow, R. Hall., M. Saynor, and P. Bassett. 1983. Integrated control of chrysanthemum pests. *IOBC/WPRS Bulletin* 6 (3):181–5.

de Jager, C. M., and R. P. T. Butôt. 1993. Thrips (*Frankliniella occidentalis* [Pergande]) resistance in chrysanthemum; the importance of pollen as nutrition. *IOBC/WPRS Bulletin* 16 (8):113–8.

Fransen, J. J. 1992. Development of integrated crop protection in glasshouse ornamentals. *Pesticide Science* 36:329–33.

Fransen, J. J. 1995. Integrated pest and disease management in floriculture: the experience in the Netherlands. In *Simposio Internacional "El Manejo Integrado de Plagos y Enfermedades en Floricultura,"* February 1995, 3–15, Santafe de Bogota, Colombia.

Fransen, J. J., M. Boogaard, and J. Tolsma. 1993. The minute pirate bug *Orius insidiosus* (Say) (Hemiptera: Anthocoridae), as a predator of the western flower thrips, *Frankliniella occidentalis* (Pergande), in chrysanthemum, rose and Saintpaulia. *IOBC/WPRS Bulletin* 16 (8):73–7.

Fransen, J. J., and J. Tolsma. 1992. Releases of the minute pirate bug, *Orius insidiousus* (Say) (Hemiptera: Anthocoridae), against western flower thrips, *Frankliniella occidentalis* (Pergande), on chrysanthemum. *Mededelingen Faculteit Landbouwwetenschappen Rijksuniversiteit Gent* 57 (2b): 479–84.

Gillespie, D. R, and D. M. J. Quiring. 1990. Biological control of fungus gnats, *Bradysia* spp. (Diptera: Sciaridae), and western flower thrips, *Frankliniella occidentalis* (Pergande) (Thysanoptera: Thripidae), in greenhouses using a soil-dwelling predatory mite, *Geolaelaps* sp. nr. *aculeifer* (Canestrini) (Acari: Laelapidae). *The Canadian Entomologist* 122:975–83.

———. 1994. Reproduction and longevity of the predatory mite, *Phytoseiulus persimilis* (Acari: Phytoseiidae) and its prey, *Tetranychus urticae* (Acari: Tetranychidae) on different host plants. *Journal of the Entomological Society of British Columbia* 91:3–8.

Gouge, D. H., and N. G. M. Hague. 1994. Control of sciarids in glass and propagation houses, with *Steinernema feltiae*. *Brighton Crop Protection Conference–Pests and Diseases–1994*:1073–8. British Crop Protection Council; Farnham, U.K.

Heinz K.M. 1998. Dispersal and dispersion of aphids (Homoptera: Aphididae) and selected natural enemies in spatially subdivided greenhouse environments. *Environmental Entomology.* 27(4):1029-38.

Heinz, K. M., L. Nunney, and M. P. Parrella. 1990. Predictability of biological control of the leaf miner *Liriomyza trifolii*, infesting greenhouse cut chrysanthemums. *IOBC/WPRS Bulletin* 13 (5):76–82.

Helyer, N., G. Gill, A. Bywater, and R. Chambers. 1992. Elevated humidities for control of chrysanthemum pests with *Verticillium lecanii*. *Pesticide Science* 36 (4):373–8.

Helyer, N. L., P. J. Brobyn, P. N. Richardson, and R. N. Edmondson. 1995. Control of western flower thrips (*Frankliniella occidentalis* Pergande) pupae in compost. *Annals of Applied Biology* 127:405–12.

Hessein, N. A., and M. P. Parrella. 1990. Predatory mites help control thrips on floricultural crops. *California Agriculture* 44 (6):19–21.

Hesselein, C., K. Robb, J. Newman, R. Evans, and M. Parrella. 1993. Demonstration/integrated pest management program for potted chrysanthemums in California. *IOBC/WPRS Bulletin* 16 (2):71–6.

Hussey, N. W. and L. Bravenboer. 1971. Control of pests in glasshouse culture by the introduction of natural enemies. In *Biological Control*, ed. C. B. Huffaker, 195–216. New York: Plenum.

Hussey, N. W., and N. E. A. Scopes. 1977. The introduction of natural enemies for pest control in glasshouses: Ecological considerations. In *Biological Control by Augmentation of Natural Enemies,* ed. R. L. Ridgway and S. B. Vinson, 349–77, New York: Plenum.

Koppert Biological Systems. 1995. *Koppert Side Effects List.* Koppert B.V.

Lim, U. T., R. G. Van Driesche, and K. M. Heinz. 2001. Biological attributes of the nematode, *Thripinema nicklewoodi*, a potential biological control agent of western flower thrips. *Biological Control.* 22:300–306.

Lindquist, R. K., J. Buxton, and J. Piatkowski. 1994. Biological control of sciarid flies and shore flies in glasshouses. *Brighton Crop Protection Conference–Pests and Diseases–1994* 3:1067–72.

Ludwig S.W. and R.D. Oetting. 2002. Efficacy of *Beauveria bassiana* plus insect attractants for enhanced control of *Frankliniella occidentalis* (Thysanoptera: Thripidae). *Florida Entomologist* 85(1):270-2

Mumford, J. D. 1992. Economics of integrated pest control in protected crops. *Pesticide Science* 36:379–83.

Murphy, B. C., T. A. Morisawa, J. P. Newman, S. A. Tjosvold, and M. P. Parrella. 1998. Fungal pathogen controls thrips in greenhouse flowers. *California Agriculture* 52 (3):32–6.

Murphy G. D., and A. B. Broadbent. 1993. Development and implementation of IPM in greenhouse floriculture in Ontario, Canada. *IOBC/WPRS Bulletin* 16 (2):113–6.

———. 1996. Case studies of biological control in Canadian floriculture. In *Proceedings of the 12th Conference on Insect and Disease Management on Ornamentals*, ed. M. Daughtrey and J. Hall, 1–16. Alexandria, Virg.: Society of American Florists.

Newman J. P., and M. P. Parrella. 1986. A license to kill. *Greenhouse Manager* 5(3):86–92.

Nicholls, C. I., M. P. Parrella, and M. A. Altieri. 1998. Advances and perspectives in the biological control of greenhouse pests with special reference to Colombia. *Integrated Pest Management Reviews* 3:99–109.

Oetting, R. D. 1982. Susceptibility of selected chrysanthemum cultivars to *Liriomyza trifolii*. *Journal of Georgia Entomological Society* 17 (4):545–52.

Oomen, P. A. 1992. Chemicals in integrated control. *Pesticide Science* 36:349–53.

Osborne, L. S. and R. D. Oetting. 1989. Biological control of pests attacking greenhouse-grown ornamentals. *Florida Entomologist* 72 (3): 408–13.

Parrella, M. P. 1990a. Biological control in ornamentals: Status and objectives. *IOBC/WPRS Bulletin* 13 (5):161–8.

Parrella, M. P. 1990b. The development of IPM strategies in chrysanthemums and gerberas with an emphasis on biological control. In *Proceedings of the Latin American Symposium of Flowering and Ornamental Plants, June 1989,* Asociación Colombiana de Exportadores de Flores ed. V. O. Sing, M. Maldonado, and M. Pizano, 43–59. Bogota, Colombia.

Parrella, M. P. 1996. Leaf miners—Part I: Accurate identification. *Grower Talks*, October, 34–43.

Parrella, M. P., and V. P. Jones. 1987. Development of integrated pest management strategies in floricultural crops. *Bulletin of the Entomological Society of America* 33:28–34.

Parrella M. P., V. P. Jones, and G. D. Christie. 1987. Feasibility of parasites for biological control of *Liriomyza trifolii* (Diptera: Agromyzidae) on commercially grown chrysanthemum. *Environmental Entomology* 16:832–37.

Price J. F., A. J. Overman, A. W. Englehard, M. K. Iverson, and V. W. Yingst. 1980. Integrated pest management in commercial chrysanthemums. *Proceedings of the Florida State Horticultural Society* 93:190–4.

Price, J. F., and S. L. Poe. 1991. Management of insect and mite pests of Florida chrysanthemums. *University of Florida Agricultural Experimental Station Bulletin* No. 881.

Ramakers, P. M. J. 1993. Coexistence of two thrips predators, the anthocorid *Orius insidiosus* and the phytoseiid *Amblyseius cucumeris* on sweet pepper. *IOBC/WPRS Bulletin* 16 (2):133–6.

Ramakers, P. M. J., and R. A. F. van den Meiracker. 1991. Biological control of western flower thrips with predatory mites and pirate bugs: can two do better than one? *Annual Report 1991 of DLO Research Institute for Plant Protection*: 9-21.

Ramakers, P. M. J., and S. J. P. Voet. 1995. Use of castor bean, *Ricinus communis,* for the introduction of the thrips predator *Amblyseius degenerans* on glasshouse grown sweet peppers. *Mededelingen Faculteit Landbouwwetenschappen Rijksuniversiteit Gent.* 60 (3a): 885–91.

Ravensberg, W. J., and K. Altena. 1993. IPM in glasshouse ornamentals: The first steps in practice. *IOBC/WPRS Bulletin* 16 (8):119–22.

Sabelis, M. W., F. van Alebeek, A. Bal, J. van Bilsen, T. van Heijningen, P. Kaizer, G. Kramer, H. Snellen, R. Veenenbos, and J. Vogelezang. 1983. Experimental validation of a simulation model of the interaction between *Phytoseiulus persimilis* and *Tetranychus urticae* on cucumber. *IOBC/WPRS Bulletin* 6 (3):207–29.

Scopes, N. E. A. 1970. Control of *Myzus persicae* on year-round chrysanthemums by introducing aphids parasitized by *Aphidius matricariae* into boxes of rooted cuttings. *Annals of Applied Biology* 66:323–27.

Scopes, N. E. A., and S. M. Biggerstaff. 1973. Progress towards integrated pest control on year-round chrysanthemums. *Proceedings of the 7th British Insecticide and Fungicide Conference, Brighton*: 227–234. British Crop Protection Council

Sher, R. B., and M. P. Parrella. 1996. Integrated biological control of leaf miners, *Liriomyza trifolii,* on greenhouse chrysanthemums. *IOBC/WPRS Bulletin* 19 (1):147–50.

Sher R. B., M. P. Parrella and H. K. Kaya. 1999. Biological control of the leafminer *Liriomyza trifolii* (Burgess): implications for intraguild predation between *Diglyphus begini* Ashmead and *Steinernema carpocapsae* (Weiser). *Biological Control* 17:155-63

Shinoyama H., M. Komano, Y. Nomura and T. Nagai. 2002. Introduction of delta-endotoxin gene of *Bacillus thuringiensis* to chrysanthemum [*Dendranthema* x *grandiflorum* (Ramat.) Kitamura] for insect resistance. *Breeding Science* 52:43-50.

Smits, P. H., and J. M. Vlak. 1994. Registration of the first viral insecticide in the Netherlands: The development of Spod-X, based on *Spodoptera exigua* nuclear polyhedrosis virus. *Mededelingen Faculteit Landbouwwetenschappen Rijksuniversiteit Gent.* 59 (2a): 385–92.

Tauber, M. J., and R. G. Helgesen. 1978. Implementing biological control systems in commercial greenhouse crops. *Bulletin of the Entomological Society of America* 23 (1):424–6.

Thompson, S., P. C. Krauter, and K. M. Heinz. 1999. Battling bugs biologically. *Greenhouse Grower*, February, 26–34.

van der Linden, A. 1996. Control of caterpillars in integrated pest management. *IOBC/WPRS Bulletin* 19 (1):91–4.

van Lenteren, J. C. 1992. Biological control in protected crops: Where do we go? *Pesticide Science* 36:321–7.

van Lenteren, J. C., and J. Woets. 1988. Biological and integrated pest control in greenhouses. *Annual Review of Entomology* 33:239–69.

van Rijn, P. C. J., and M. W. Sabelis. 1990. Pollen as an alternative food source for predatory mites and its effect on the biological control of thrips in greenhouses. *Proceedings of Experimental and Applied Entomology* 1:44–8.

van Steenis, M. J. 1993. Suitability of *Aphis gossypii* Glov., *Macrosiphum euphorbiae* (Thom.), and *Myzus persicae* (Sulz.) (Hom.: Aphidiidae) as host for several aphid parasitoid species (Hym.: Braconidae). *IOBC/WPRS Bulletin* 16 (2): 157–60.

Vehrs, S. L. C., G. P. Walker, and M. P. Parrella. 1992. Comparison of population growth rate and within-plant distribution between *Aphis gossypii* and *Myzus persicae* (Homoptera: Aphidiidae) reared on potted chrysanthemums. *Journal Economic Entomology* 85(3):799–807.

Wardlow, L. R. 1985. Chrysanthemums. In *Biological Pest Control: The Glasshouse Experience.* ed. N. W. Hussey and N. E. A. Scopes, 180–5. Ithaca, N.Y.: Cornell University Press (Poole, U.K.: Blandford Press).

Wardlow, L. R., W. Brough, and C. Need. 1992. Integrated pest management in protected ornamentals in England. *Bulletin OEPP/EPPO* 22:493–8.

Wardlow L. R., S. Piggot and R. Goldsworthy. 2001. Foliar application of *Steinernema feltiae* for the control of flower thrips. *Mededelingen Faculteit Landbouwwetenschappen, Rijksuniversiteit Gent.* 66(2a):285-91.

Williams E. C. and F. F. A. Walters. 1994. Nematode control of leafminers: efficacy, temperature and timing. *Brighton Crop Protection Conference Pests and Diseases–1994*:1079–84. British Crop Protection Council; Farnham, UK.

Wyatt, I. J. 1965. The distribution of *Myzus persicae* (Sulz.) on year-round chrysanthemums. *Annals of Applied Biology* 56:439–59.

Yoshida, H. A. and M. P. Parrella. 1991. Chrysanthemum cultivar preferences exhibited by *Spodoptera exigua* (Lepidoptera: Noctuidae). *Environmental Entomology* 20 (1):160–5.

21

BIOLOGICAL CONTROL IN POINSETTIA

J. P. Sanderson
Department of Entomology
Cornell University, Ithaca, New York

Biological control of pests on poinsettia must be integrated with other control tactics, including cultural, physical, and perhaps chemical methods for it to be successful. The short duration of the crop, the demand for extremely low pest levels, and the effectiveness of currently available natural enemies require the concerted integration of multiple tactics to produce acceptable plants. This chapter will review biologically based pest management tactics for poinsettia pests in relation to biological control.

Crop Background

Poinsettias (*Euphorbia pulcherrima* Willd. ex Koltz.) are the most valuable and popular potted floral crop in the United States, purchased for decoration for the Christmas holidays. In the United States in 2001, 1,749 producers grew 67 million pots worth $255 million in wholesale value (NASS 2003). Poinsettias are grown and sold in a wide variety of forms (Figure 21.1), including potted trees, hanging baskets, tiny personal poinsettias, multiple plants per pots of various sizes, and the standard single pinched plant grown in a 6-in. (15-cm) pot.

Figure 21.1. Poinsettia production ranges frequently contain a variety of cultivars, each with a characteristic bract color that gives the crop grown for Christmas its aesthetic value.
Photo: M. P. Parrella

Poinsettias are vegetatively propagated. In the United States, cuttings are taken in late winter/spring from stock plants grown by several primary propagators and distributed to secondary propagators around the world. Cuttings from the stock plants grown by secondary propagators are then distributed during summer to producers who grow the finished crops, which are sold in November and December. Propagators usually also grow a Christmas crop themselves. Consumers purchase the plants from a variety of outlets, including retail florist shops, garden centers, grocery stores, and growers who sell directly to the public. While plant quality, including pest tolerances, vary depending on market outlet, propagators selling cuttings for export face strict requirements for pest-free plant material.

The poinsettia crop for Christmas holidays is grown from cuttings placed into peat-based growing media in August. The typical crop grown in 6-in. (15-cm) pots is "pinched" to promote branching after roots are well established. The crop is usually grown for fourteen weeks after planting. The colorful bracts of a poinsettia give the plant its aesthetic appeal. These bracts are formed as upper leaves begin to change color in response to shortened daylength, after about two-thirds of the duration of the crop cycle.

Pest Complex

Whiteflies

Three species of whiteflies (Homoptera: Aleyrodidae) infest poinsettias. Before 1986, the greenhouse whitefly, *Trialeurodes vaporariorum* (Westwood), was the most severe pest of poinsettias. Greenhouse whitefly can still be a serious pest if not managed. In 1986, infestations of a new whitefly pest, then

identified as *B. tabaci*, the sweetpotato whitefly, were observed on poinsettia (Price, Schuster, and Short 1987). Subsequently this whitefly was referred to as *B. tabaci* Strain B, the Florida strain, the poinsettia strain, or the B-biotype (Perring et al. 1992). It has subsequently been described as a new species, *B. argentifolii*, the silverleaf whitefly (Bellows et al. 1994). The only *Bemisia* species reported on greenhouse poinsettias is *B. argentifolii* (Brown, Frohlich, and Rosell 1995). Liu, Oetting, and Buntin (1994) reported that *B. argentifolii* could displace *T. vaporariorum* within two generations when they both infest a poinsettia crop.

The third species of whitefly associated with poinsettia is the bandedwinged whitefly, *Trialeurodes abutilonea* (Haldeman). It has occasionally been found on yellow sticky traps over poinsettia crops in the eastern United States in the fall, but rarely reproduces on the crop (Gill 1991; G. Murphy, pers. comm.). Bandedwinged whitefly occurs across the United States, Mexico, and the Caribbean (Mound and Halsey 1978).

Whitefly damage to greenhouse grown poinsettias reduces the attractiveness of the plant, and the presence of even low densities of whiteflies may severely reduce marketability (Heinz and Nelson 1996, Hoddle, Van Driesche, and Sanderson 1998). Whitefly levels of 1.9 to 4.5 nymphs per in.^{2} (0.3 to 0.7/cm^2), reported as acceptable by Helgesen and Tauber (1974), would probably not be accepted today in most markets. For example, Hoddle et al. (1998) examined seventy-two poinsettias from five Massachusetts retail outlets in 1994 and found an average of only 1.5 whitefly nymphs per leaf. Furthermore, high populations of silverleaf whitefly can cause the stems and bracts of red poinsettia cultivars to lose color and become pale yellow (Fig. 21.2), referred to as "stem blanching" or "white stem" (Schuster, Stansly, and Polston 1996; Oetting and Buntin 1996). Severity of these symptoms is related to degree of whitefly control (Schuster, Stansly, and Polston 1996). High populations of silverleaf whitefly can also reduce poinsettia growth and cause a decreased number of bracts (Oetting and Buntin 1996). Though *B. argentifolii* is capable of transmitting numerous viruses, none have yet been reported on poinsettia (Brown, Frohlich, and Rosell 1995). Chapter 8 reviews whitefly identification and life history.

Fungus gnats

Larvae of darkwinged fungus gnats, *Bradysia coprophila* (Lintner) and *Bradysia impatiens* (Johannsen) (in North America) and *Bradysia paupera* Tuomik and *Bradysia tritici* (Coquillett) (in northern Europe) (Diptera: Sciaridae), infest poinsettia growing media feeding on fungi and organic material as well as on poinsettia roots. (Note: *B. paupera* and *B. impatiens* may be a single species). Larval feeding damage to roots can predispose a plant to infection by fungal phytopathogens (Leath and Newton 1969). Based on research results under controlled conditions, fungus gnats have also been implicated in the transmission of several root disease organisms in commercial greenhouses (Harris 1995). Poinsettias are particularly susceptible to fungus gnat direct damage early in the crop during establishment of the root system. At time of sale, the presence of adults, if numerous, can reduce marketability. Further information on life history and damage caused by fungus gnats is covered in chapter 19.

Figure 21.2. The pale coloration of new leaves and bracts, termed "stem blanching" or "white stem," is a phytotoxic response to high populations of silverleaf whitefly. The response is reversible if whiteflies are suppressed to sufficiently low numbers.
Photo: M. P. Parrella

Shore flies

Greenhouse workers and consumers consider adult shore flies, *Scatella stagnalis* Fallen (Diptera: Ephydridae), a nuisance pest. Dense infestations deposit unsightly black fecal specks on foliage. Larvae are considered algae feeders and do not feed on crop plant tissue. Adult shore flies can transmit root pathogens such as *Pythium* species, but whether such transmission commonly occurs in commercial greenhouses is unknown. However, because algal growth and shore flies are common in misted propagation areas, and root rot diseases are particularly severe among young plants during propagation, some growers aggressively manage shore flies in their poinsettia propagation facilities.

Lewis mites

The Lewis mite, *Eotetranychus lewisi* (McGregor) (Acari: Tetranychidae), has recently become an occasional pest of poinsettias. Originally found on poinsettia in California and Washington (Doucette 1962; Jeppson, Keifer, and Baker 1975), more recently this spider mite has been reported across the United States, following the widespread adoption of the insecticide imidacloprid for whitefly control (Gill 1996). Imidacloprid is not effective against spider mites, but its widespread use has precluded the need for applications of other insecticides that were used in the past and were most likely suppressing Lewis mites. Poinsettias damaged by Lewis mites display fine stippling on the leaf surface, caused by the mites' stylet mouthparts, which are used to puncture leaf cells and remove chlorophyll. These mites can produce substantial amounts of webbing.

Western flower thrips

Growers who have had inadequate control of western flower thrips (*Frankliniella occidentalis* [Pergande]) (Thysanoptera: Thripidae) on spring and summer crops may experience thrips damage to the leaves of their fall poinsettia crop. Though thrips do not seem to reproduce well on poinsettia, they can feed on young leaf tissue, causing cells to collapse and resulting in leaf distortion as the young leaves mature.

Scale and mealybugs

Scale and mealybug species, such as brown soft scale, *Coccus hesperidum* L. (Homoptera: Coccidae), and citrus mealybug, *Planococcus citri* Risso (Homoptera: Pseudococcidae), can infest poinsettias, especially poinsettias that may be growing near species of foliage plants that are better hosts for these pests.

Advantages and Challenges for Biological Control

Compared with many floral crops, poinsettias have several advantages that make the use of biological control on the crop more feasible than is the case on many other floral crops. First, the pest complex is simple, consisting of whiteflies as the primary pest, with fungus gnats generally as secondary pests, and shore flies and most of the other arthropod pests as occasional pests. Most commonly, control tactics for whiteflies need only be compatible with those for fungus gnats, and vice versa. Second, the crop is usually grown as a monoculture, reducing the number of pest species and horticultural practices compared to the case in which several crops are grown together within the same greenhouse. Third, at low levels, the primary pests (whiteflies) do not cause visible damage to the plants; so total pest eradication is not necessarily required on the plants at time of sale of the finished crop. Fourth, several species of effective natural enemies are commercially available for the most serious pests (*B. argentifolii* and *T. vaporariorum*).

However, there are challenges to biological control on poinsettias. The short duration of the crop provides little time to correct unexpected pest problems. Poinsettias are generally a fourteen-week crop. Whiteflies complete about four generations during this time (about one per month). Because numbers are very low (0.01 to 1.0 nymph per cutting) when the crop is begun, growers often do not find whiteflies on their plants until late in the crop. However, by week nine or so, the bracts begin to color, and applications of foliar pesticides to reduce a whitefly infestation become too great a risk because phytotoxicity may result, ruining the plants. Thus, timely supplies of adequate numbers of high quality natural enemies must be dependable. There is a very low tolerance for the presence of pests, especially on plant material that is sold for export. Control tactics for some of the minor pests (e.g., thrips and Lewis mites) may be incompatible with biological control for other pests.

Biological control on poinsettias grown in temperate areas may be easier to achieve than on poinsettias grown in subtropical regions. In subtropical areas, the milder climate allows for year-round whitefly infestations on outdoor weeds and crops, leading to continuous whitefly invasions of the greenhouse. In temperate climates, the greenhouse can be closed for much of the crop cycle, and the pest whiteflies of poinsettia usually cannot overwinter outdoors. However, growers who grow stock plants for cutting production will have poinsettias in their greenhouses for a longer period, and whitefly infestations can increase on these stock plants and later spread to other poinsettias. Also, the current supply of effective insecticides for whiteflies greatly reduces grower interest and incentive to use biological control. An important reason why growers should, however, stay up-to-date on poinsettia biological control is that resistance to many of these insecticides has been documented in *Bemisia* populations at certain locations in the world (Horowitz and Ishaaya 1994, Cahill et al. 1996a, b) and may develop in greenhouse whitefly populations.

Origins of the Pests

Natural enemies are rarely able to reduce sizeable pest populations and successful biological control is often confounded by sudden influxes of pests from external sources. Thus, it is important to recognize and eliminate as many of the original sources of pests as possible.

Whiteflies can infest a poinsettia crop from four sources: residual plant materials, concurrent crops, outside sources, and the cuttings themselves. (i) *Residual infestations* may exist on plant material from the previous crop(s) in the greenhouse. This plant material may include weeds under and around the benches, unsold plants, hanging baskets, and stock plants held over between crops for cuttings of favored or non-commercial varieties. All such sources of whiteflies should be eliminated before a new poinsettia crop is introduced. (ii) *Concurrent crops,* such as poinsettia stock plants or other plants are common sources of whiteflies and should be grown in separate greenhouses away from the finished crop, or by screening off the plants using insect screens. (iii) *Outside whiteflies* should be prevented from entering the greenhouse by using insect screening to isolate crops from outside whitefly sources, such as from weeds or crop plants (Ross and Gill 1994, Robb 1995, Anon 1996, Bell and Baker 2000). (iv) Lastly, whiteflies can be present on the *incoming poinsettia cuttings.* Cuttings should be inspected for whiteflies as soon as possible after arrival. On a typical cutting with six leaves, 90% of whitefly nymphs are found on the oldest three leaves (Sanderson and Davis 1996). These leaves are often removed from the plant or eventually senesce; removing them as soon as possible may eliminate a substantial portion of a whitefly population. Before planting, or immediately after, inspect the bottom three leaves for whiteflies to determine if the initial whitefly population exceeds a level that can be controlled by natural enemies (probably anything greater than two whitefly nymphs, pupae, or adults per cutting [Hoddle, unpublished data]). Fixed precision level sampling plans for cuttings for three infestation levels have been developed (Sanderson and Davis 1996).

Fungus gnats are attracted to soil and growing media with active microbial activity (Lindquist 1994; Lindquist and Casey 1994; Harris, Gardner, and Oetting 1996). Careful sanitation in areas beneath the benches, removal of spilled growing media, and relocation of compost piles are important steps to reduce sources of fungus gnats. Fungus gnats have also been found in bales of prepared growing media (R. Cloyd and D. Smitley, pers. comm.) and in growing media mixed on-site. See chapter 19 for further information on the sources of fungus gnat infestations.

Shore flies are associated with algae, and removal of algae between crops can minimize shore fly problems. Normal sources of Lewis mites have not been determined, but these mites may arrive on poinsettia plant material at levels too low to be detected. Scale and mealybug infestations may spread to poinsettias from any nearby plants that are hosts for these pests. Growers who are unable to manage serious infestations of western flower thrips on previous crops may sustain thrips damage to their poinsettia crop.

Monitoring/Sampling

Regular monitoring is important for successful biological control on poinsettias.

Monitoring must provide a sufficiently accurate estimate of the location and trends of pest populations in order to make appropriate pest management decisions. Accuracy in monitoring is important because the duration of the crop is too short and the pest tolerances too low to easily remedy mistakes. Monitoring information can be used, for example, to make decisions as to when to begin natural enemy releases, to confirm that control is being maintained by releases, or to provide growers an early warning that the pest has escaped control and that insecticide applications are needed.

Whiteflies

A complete estimate of the size and life-stage distribution of a whitefly population provides helpful information for control decisions. Monitoring only the levels of adult whiteflies provides no information on the immature stages, which may be a large proportion of the total population. Monitoring the levels of the various nymphal stages can rapidly reveal whether the population is increasing in number and developmental stage or is being controlled by the natural enemies. Monitoring can also provide the information needed to time releases of natural enemies or pesticide applications to when susceptible life stages are most abundant.

Both yellow sticky traps and foliage inspections are needed to assess the total whitefly population. Adult whitefly numbers are best monitored with yellow sticky traps. The optimal number and spacing of traps per unit area has not been determined, so growers currently use traps in an ad hoc manner, using whatever works best for them. Unfortunately, adult whitefly parasitoids such as *Encarsia formosa* Gahan and *Eretmocerus eremicus* Rose and Zolnerowhich are also attracted to yellow sticky traps, and a significant proportion of the wasps may be lost to the traps. A minimal number of the traps should be used when wasps are employed, or the adult whitefly levels should be assessed by leaf inspections alone. Inspect the lower surfaces of leaves to monitor sedentary nymphs. Inspecting ten plants per 1000 pots has been suggested (Ferrentino et al. 1993, Pundt 1997). Leaves from the top, middle, and bottom of the plant should be inspected to estimate the whitefly population age distribution.

Sequential sampling plans have been developed and validated for both greenhouse whitefly and silverleaf whitefly on poinsettias grown in standard 6-in. (15-cm) diameter pots (Sanderson, Davis, and Ferrentino 1994; Sanderson 1995, 1999). This sampling plan can be used to determine whether a whitefly population is above or below one of three different action thresholds. The low and moderate action thresholds are based on actual end-of-season whitefly levels sampled from poinsettias from 107 greenhouse establishments in New York in 1991. In the 1991 survey, growers who participated in the New York State Poinsettia IPM Program had an average of 10% of their plants infested with at least one whitefly of any life stage at time of sale. Growers in New York who were not participating in the program had an average of 25% of their plants infested at time of sale. Extension professionals in two southern U.S. states, where whitefly control can be more difficult, suggested that a higher threshold such as 50% infested plants was also needed. The low (10% infested plants), moderate (25% infested plants), and high (50% infested

plants) thresholds correspond to whitefly levels of an average of 0.017, 0.1, and 1.2 nymphs per leaf, respectively, based on the relationship between whitefly densities per leaf and the proportion of infested plants. Growers can use the sampling plan at any time or at regular intervals during the growth of the crop. It is useful in a biological control program to determine if the natural enemies are maintaining control at any time during the crop. A fixed precision level sampling scheme for whiteflies on poinsettia cuttings (Sanderson and Davis 1996) can be used to determine if initial whitefly levels on the crop exceed levels that can be suppressed by natural enemies.

Fungus gnats

Growers can monitor populations of adult fungus gnats with yellow sticky traps. Traps positioned vertically just above the crop canopy can be used to monitor whiteflies, fungus gnats, thrips, and most other flying insect pests of poinsettias. Adult fungus gnats and shore flies are trapped in greater numbers if the yellow traps are placed horizontally at the level of the soil surface (Lindquist, Faber, and Casey 1985; Lindquist 1998). Fungus gnat larvae can be monitored by placing raw potato disks or wedges on the media surface (L. Osborne, pers. comm.; Harris, Oetting, and Gardner 1995). Larval monitoring with potato disks provides a more direct and rapid evaluation of larval mortality caused by natural enemies or pesticides than does waiting for surviving adults to become captured on sticky traps. Potato disks are currently more useful for determining survival of fungus gnat larvae after treatment than for estimating fungus gnat population levels. Because fungus gnat larvae are most destructive to poinsettias at the beginning of the crop when roots are developing, monitoring should be started before planting to determine if background fungus gnat levels are likely to injure newly potted cuttings.

Shore flies

Yellow sticky traps are useful in monitoring adult shore flies. These traps should be used in the same manner as for fungus gnats: positioned either horizontally just above the soil surface for the greatest trap catch or vertically just above the plant canopy for general pest monitoring. Larvae can sometimes be seen by examining algae-covered areas with a hand lens. Potato disks do not work for monitoring shore fly larvae because shore fly larvae are not attracted to potato disks.

Other pests

Thrips are monitored with yellow or blue sticky traps (see chapters 14 and 15). In addition to monitoring thrips on the crop, monitoring thrips levels in a greenhouse before the crop is planted is important to determine if potentially damaging levels may already be present. During weekly scouting of the foliage for whitefly nymphs, inspect the foliage for infestations of Lewis mites, scales, mealybugs, and other pests or diseases.

Influence of Cultivar and Fertilizer

Population growth rates of both greenhouse whitefly and silverleaf whitefly can be affected by poinsettia cultivars (Fischer and Shanks 1974, Bilderback and Mattson 1977, Sanderson 1992). Nevertheless, no commercial poinsettia cultivar to date has sufficient resistance to whiteflies to provide substantial control. However, the performance of natural enemies can also differ among poinsettia cultivars. The life histories and searching efficiencies of whitefly parasitoids and the predaceous beetle *Delphastus catalinae* (Horn) (previously referred to incorrectly in the whitefly literature as *Delphastus pusillus* [LeConte]) can be adversely affected on cultivars with higher leaf trichome densities (Heinz and Parrella 1994a).

The amount and form of nitrogenous fertilizer used on a plant can affect some whitefly parasitoids. Bentz (1993) found significantly more *E. formosa* Beltsville strain adults on poinsettias fertilized with 500 ppm of either ammonium nitrate or calcium nitrate than on unfertilized control poinsettias. Parasitism of silverleaf whiteflies was higher on plants fertilized with calcium nitrate than on plants fertilized with ammonium nitrate or on control plants. In no-choice tests, host feeding was higher on fertilized plants than on the control plants. Boorse (1993) used choice tests to measure silverleaf whitefly levels after six weeks on poinsettias fertilized with 100, 285, or 640 ppm of nitrate nitrogen. She found small but significant differences in whitefly population levels, but did not examine affects on parasitoids. Poinsettias fertilized with 285 ppm nitrogen had more whitefly nymphs than those fertilized with 640 ppm nitrogen.

Lindquist, Faber, and Casey (1985); Lindquist (1998); and Evans, Smith, and Cloyd (1998) all noted differences in fungus gnat populations among different growing media, but little is known about the possible influence of these media or other aspects of the soil environment on fungus gnats and most of their natural enemies. Notably, Oetting and Latimer (1991) found no effect on the nematode *Steinernema carpocapsae* (Weiser) for a range of soil environmental factors.

Biological Control

Whiteflies

Various natural enemies are available for whitefly biological control on poinsettia. Chapters 6 and 8 review the scientific literature on these species.

Pathogens

Fungal entomopathogens are useful for whitefly management because of their ability to penetrate the insect cuticle and cause infection leading to death. Three species of fungal pathogens are currently under commercial development or available for use against whiteflies on poinsettias. *Verticillium lecanii* (Zimmerman) Viégas is available for use on poinsettias in Europe (Meekes, Fransen, and van Lenteren 1994), with variable reports of levels of effectiveness (Nedstam 1992). *Paecilomyces fumosoroseus* (Wize) Brown and Smith is under development in the United States. Three formulations of *Beauveria bassiana* (Balsamo) Vuillemin are currently available for use in the United States. *Aschersonia aleyrodis* Webber may be commercialized in the future, though interactions with the poinsettia leaf environment may reduce its effectiveness (Meekes et al. 2000). All mycoinsecticides (i.e., formulations of fungal pathogens) are applied to the foliage and coverage of lower leaf surfaces must be thorough for effective control. Also, these products must be applied while whitefly densities are still low. Season-long applications at weekly or biweekly intervals are needed to achieve good coverage with adequate spore densities to contact susceptible life stages (Osborne and Landa 1994). In some subtropical regions, natural invasions of whitefly parasitoids into greenhouses have added to the whitefly population suppression provided by these mycoinsecticides. Humid environments are important for pathogenicity (see chapter 8). A few unpublished efforts have been made to evaluate the efficacy of applications of mycoinsecticides while poinsettia cuttings are under mist propagation. Though not all combinations of species have been evaluated, these mycoinsecticides appear to be compatible with whitefly parasitoids and some predacious coccinellids (Lacey, Fransen, and Carruthers 1996). Fungicides should not be applied closer than two days before or after the use of a mycoinsecticide.

Predators

The most common commercially available predators for control of whiteflies on poinsettia are green lacewings (*Chrysoperla carnea* [Stephens], *Chrysoperla rufilabris* [Burmeister]), and the tiny predaceous ladybeetle *D. catalinae*. Green lacewings, though relatively inexpensive if purchased as eggs, are not very effective for control of whiteflies on poinsettia. Lacewing larvae (also commercially available) are difficult to apply effectively due to their cannibalistic nature and their tendency to fall off the foliage unless plant canopies interlock. Once on the ground, larvae rarely make their way back onto plants on benches (Heinz 1996). Very high numbers (twenty-five to fifty per plant, applied at two week intervals) of green lacewing larvae were needed for adequate silverleaf whitefly control in a study by Breene et al. (1992).

Lastly, whitefly nymphs appear to be an inadequate diet for green lacewings (Nordlund and Legaspi 1996, Senior and McEwen 1998). *Delphastus catalinae* is a relatively expensive predator, but has been used effectively at low release rates in combination with parasitoids for silverleaf whitefly on poinsettia (Heinz and Parrella 1994b) and also at higher release rates directed only at whitefly hot spots. Life history traits are affected and the searching ability of *D. catalinae* is reduced on poinsettia cultivars that have higher leaf hair densities (Heinz and Parrella 1994a).

Parasitoids

The aphelinid whitefly parasitoids *E. formosa* and *Eretmocerus eremicus* Rose and Zolnerowich (formerly known as *Eretmocerus* sp. nr. *californicus*) are commercially available for use against both greenhouse whitefly and silverleaf whitefly. *Encarsia formosa* has long been used against greenhouse whitefly on tomato, but is less effective against silverleaf whitefly. Some studies have reported adequate silverleaf whitefly control on poinsettia with releases of *E. formosa* (Albert and Sautter 1989; Benuzzi, Nicoli, and Manzaroli 1990; Stenseth 1993), but this differs from results from other studies (Parrella et al. 1991; Hoddle and Van Driesche 1996, 1999a, b). Differences in market acceptance of whitefly levels may explain this discrepancy.

Hoddle and Van Driesche (1996, 1999a, b), and Van Driesche et al. (1999) also indicate that *E. eremicus* performs consistently better than *E. formosa* against silverleaf whitefly on poinsettia under commercial conditions, in the northeastern United States. The wasps are introduced to the crop in weekly inundative releases. Given the high number of wasps needed to reduce whiteflies to acceptable, essentially non-detectable levels, host-feeding and superparasitism, rather than parasitism, causes the greatest mortality to the whitefly nymphs. Parasitoid reproduction in the greenhouse is inconsequential (Hoddle et al. 1998; Hoddle, Sanderson, and Van Driesche 1999). Releases of three female *E. eremicus* per plant per week provide commercial whitefly control, but are prohibitively expensive (Van Driesche et al. 1999). A release rate of one female per plant per week is less expensive and adequately suppresses whitefly levels, but generally only for the first two-thirds of the crop (Hoddle et al. 1998). In an effort to reduce costs, Hoddle, Sanderson, and Van Driesche (1999) and Van Driesche et al. (2001) compared fixed release rates with variable release rates. Releasing a high rate (five females/plant/week) of wasps for the first half of the crop, followed by a low release rate (one female/plant/week) for the last half, provided better control than the reverse. But this was not different from the level of control achieved by the constant release rate of three females/plant/week.

Finally, Hoddle, Van Driesche, and Sanderson investigated the integration of insect growth regulator (IGR) insecticides for whiteflies with releases of *E. eremicus*. Buprofezin, fenoxycarb, kinoprene, pymetrozine, and pyriproxyfen were evaluated for effects on parasitoids under laboratory conditions (Hoddle et al. 2001). Only kinoprene harmed adult parasitoids. Subsequent studies (Van Driesche et al. 2001) indicated that when combined with a mid-crop (just before bracts begin to color) double application of an IGR, a low release rate of one female/plant/week provided control equal to or better than a release rate of three females/ plant/week with no IGR applications. Lastly, Van Driesche et al. (2002) found that a release rate of 0.5 female *E. eremicus* per plant per week plus two mid-crop IGR applications provided commercially acceptable control of *B. argentifolii* at a cost comparable to a standard pesticide program. The advantages of this integration of chemical and biological control include reduced cost and a probable delay of insecticide resistance to the IGRs due to their limited use. In poinsettia crops infested with a mixture of both greenhouse whitefly and silverleaf whitefly, *E. eremicus* readily attacks both species. It has been effective on infestations of pure greenhouse whitefly (Van Driesche et al. 1999, 2001). Chapter 8 includes a discussion of the use of parasitoids for whitefly control on poinsettia, and chapter 7 discusses the possible effects of residues of particular pesticides on whitefly parasitoids and predators. Some growers have "integrated" chemical and biological control by relying on natural enemies for most of the crop and using pesticides such as sulfotepp at the end of the crop.

The research described above provides guidelines for the use of parasitoids on poinsettias grown in temperate climatic regions. In such regions, there is little concern over movement of whiteflies onto the crop from outdoor sources for most of the crop cycle. In subtropical regions, however, biological control may be more difficult to achieve due to possible year-round entrance of whiteflies into the greenhouse from outdoor plants. In such situations, whitefly natural enemies often accompany the whiteflies. If compatible management tactics are employed using such as applications of mycoinsecticides, these natural enemies may assist in suppressing whiteflies.

Fungus gnats

Chapter 19 discusses the natural enemies of fungus gnats, which include parasitic nematodes (e.g., *Steinernema feltiae* [Filipjev]), some strains of the bacterial pathogen *Bacillus thuringiensis* Berliner, and some predaceous mites that are active in the soil (e.g., *Hypoaspis* spp.). All these natural enemies can be used on poinsettia and are compatible with the parasitoids and predators used in the crop for whitefly biological control. Conversely, the compatibilities of some mycoinsecticides used against whiteflies, such as *B. bassiana* and *P. fumosoroseus*, with the natural enemies of fungus gnats have not been determined.

If sampling shows fungus gnats to be present before or at the start of the poinsettia crop, growers should release fast-acting natural enemies or establish them in abundant numbers to protect the crop during root formation. Vanninen (2003) found that preventative applications of *S. feltiae* could delay the fungus gnat infestation of poinsettia cuttings during rooting by two weeks and reduce the proportion of infested cuttings. Alternatively, compatible insecticides, such as some of the IGRs, may be applied to protect the crop initially, and natural enemies may be employed once the roots are established.

If insecticides must be used for whitefly management, IGRs such as pyriproxyfen, buprofezin, azadirachtin, and fenoxycarb are likely to be more compatible with natural enemies of fungus gnats than are other kinds of pesticides. Some of these IGR insecticides, such as pyriproxyfen and azadirachtin, are effective against fungus gnat larvae. Imidacloprid, a systemic insecticide widely used for whitefly control on poinsettias, is very harmful to the fungus gnat predator *Hypoaspis miles* (Berlese) (Acari: Laelapidae) for two to four weeks after a drench application, though it does kill fungus gnat larvae.

Fungus gnat biological control is especially useful on poinsettia stock plants, where the roots are well established, the plants can tolerate somewhat higher populations, and consumer aesthetic demands are not an issue. The various possible natural enemies— *H. miles*, *B. thuringiensis* var. *israelensis*, and *S. feltiae*—can be used alone or in combination.

Other minor pests

Though natural enemies such as predaceous mites may be commercially available for Lewis mites, infestations of the mites are sufficiently infrequent that preventative releases of predaceous mites may be wasted. Cosmetic damage might appear and spread quickly before predaceous mites provide control. To counter such problems, acaricides compatible with the natural enemies in use for other pests should be used (Zchori-Fein, Roush, and Sanderson 1994). Likewise, it may be impractical to control damage by western flower thrips on poinsettia with releases of predators. Applications of mycoinsecticides or compatible insecticides may be a better choice.

IPM Guidelines for Poinsettias

The following guidelines for control of pest arthropods are particularly applicable to poinsettia production in regions with a temperate climate. In other climates, substantial differences could occur.

Locate sources of pests prior to planting

Existing infestations within a greenhouse are detected by the use of yellow sticky traps and foliage inspection. Begin locating these infestations well before the start of the poinsettia crop to provide sufficient time to eliminate pest sources. Inspect stock plants, hanging baskets, unsold plants, and weeds. Eliminate these sources of pests, or move infested plant material to separate greenhouses, or use screening within the greenhouse to confine the infestation, or reduce the infestations with compatible control tactics, before the start of the poinsettia crop. Keep stock plants in a separate greenhouse. To reduce existing infestations of fungus gnats and shore flies, clean up spilled potting mix, thoroughly remove algal growth from floors, benches, and walls, keep plant refuse/compost piles well away from the greenhouse, and eliminate perpetually wet or moist areas. In warmer climates, install insect screens over the intake vents, doorways, or other paths of entry to reduce influx of pests from outdoor sources, if ventilation needs permit.

Sample cuttings for pests

Inspect the bottom three leaves of a cutting for whiteflies and other pests. Inspect thirty to sixty-five cuttings per batch of 500 to 2000 cuttings to estimate the initial whitefly population (Sanderson and Davis 1996). Ideally, the initial whitefly infestation should be less than an average of two nymphs, pupae, or adults per cutting inspected. Use alternative control measures to reduce whitefly density if initial levels on cuttings are higher. Control measures that may be used compatibly with parasitoids and predators include soaps, horticultural oils, and insect growth regulators.

Control fungus gnats at the beginning of the crop

Fungus gnats are most destructive to poinsettias at the start of the crop when the root system is young and developing. Apply preventative natural enemies such as *H. miles*, nematodes, and/or *B. thuringiensis* var. *israelensis*, making multiple applications at the beginning of the crop. Most insect growth regulators applied for fungus gnat larvae will not affect whitefly natural enemies. Use potato disks to determine if larval numbers are declining because of control measures.

Weekly releases or applications

For whitefly control, begin weekly releases of *E. eremicus* (particularly for silverleaf whitefly) or *E. formosa* (particularly for greenhouse whitefly) at potting. See "Case Study: Biological Control of *Bemisia tabaci* Strain B on Poinsettias" in chapter 8 for details on the use of *E. eremicus*. There are no published reports that demonstrate consistently successful use of mycoinsecticides in commercial poinsettia production; yet they appear to have potential. Follow the label and the manufacturer's directions for rates and frequency of mycoinsecticide applications. Some growers use natural enemies to keep whiteflies at a low level for most of the crop, and switch to insecticides toward the end of the season for a final cleanup.

Monitor the crop weekly

Use yellow sticky traps to monitor adult whiteflies, fungus gnats, shore flies, and thrips. However, if *E. eremicus* is used for whitefly control, use very few traps or assess adult whitefly numbers via foliage inspection alone. For foliage monitoring, inspect six leaves on each of ten randomly selected plants per 1000 plants weekly to assess nymphal populations or use the sequential sampling plan of Sanderson (1999). Look for infestations of minor pests during weekly plant inspections. Locate a few leaves with live whitefly nymphs several times during the crop and inspect these weekly with a hand lens to see if natural enemies kill them. Monitoring should be particularly thorough in the weeks before the onset of bract coloration to assess if control is adequate or if pesticide applications are needed. This must be determined before the risk of phytotoxicity to the bracts restricts the potential use of insecticides for "rescue" treatments.

Be prepared to control occasional pests

If weekly monitoring reveals an infestation of a minor pest such as Lewis mites or thrips, it will likely be more cost-effective to control these pests with pesticides that are compatible with natural enemies for whiteflies and fungus gnats than to attempt to use natural enemies such as predators against them. Have these pesticides on hand at the beginning of the crop in case they are needed.

Common Situations That Can Lead to Failure

Movement of large numbers of adult whiteflies from weeds, discarded plant material, or outdoor sources, or the introduction into a poinsettia crop of older, heavily infested plants such as stock plants being grown as finished plants, can overwhelm the pest control capability of natural enemies. Overhead watering can wet the wasp pupae that are released weekly and increase their mortality, resulting in inadequate wasp emergence. There may be insecticide residues toxic to parasitoids and predators on poinsettia leaves, benches, or walls, or residues may drift or fume into the crop from a nearby spray application. If several shipments of natural enemies are delayed, missed, or dead on arrival, the biological control program may fail. A reliable, knowledgeable supplier is critical. Mishandling of shipments after their arrival (e.g., not releasing natural enemies immediately, inadvertently exposed them to temperature extremes, or releasing them improperly) can also cause control failure.

Keep Records

Consideration of historical records of a pest management program helps identify cost-effective improvements and opportunities for increased efficiency. Growers should annually review records from previous crops to determine what went wrong and why, what was and was not necessary to do, when various tasks needed to be done, and costs associated with various aspects of the IPM program. This sort of analysis can help improve the process in subsequent crops.

References Cited

Albert, R., and H. Sautter. 1989. Parasitoids protect Christmas stars from whiteflies. *Deutscher Gartenbau* 43:1671–3.

Anon. 1996. Insect screening: Installation considerations for greenhouse operators. Littleton, Colo.: National Greenhouse Manufacturer's Association.

Bell, M. L., and J. R. Baker. 2000. Comparison of greenhouse screening materials for excluding whitefly (Homoptera: Aleyrodidae) and thrips (Thysanoptera: Thripidae). *Journal of Economic Entomology* 93(3): 800-804.

Bellows, T. S., T. M. Perring, R. J. Gill, and D. H. Headrick. 1994. Description of a new species of *Bemisia* (Homoptera: Aleyrodidae). *Annals of the Entomological Society of America* 87:195–206.

Bentz, J. 1993. The influence of nitrogen content of poinsettia, *Euphorbia pulcherrima*, on the sweetpotato whitefly, *Bemisia tabaci*, and its parasitoid *Encarsia formosa*. PhD diss., University of Maryland.

Benuzzi, M., G. Nicoli, and G. Manzaroli. 1990. Biological control of *Bemisia tabaci* (Genn.) and *Trialeurodes vaporariorum* (Westw.) by *Encarsia formosa* Gahan on poinsettia. *IOBC/WPRS Bulletin* 13(5):27–31.

Bilderback, T. E., and R. H. Mattson. 1977. Whitefly host preference associated with selected biochemical and phenotypic characteristics of poinsettias. *Journal of the American Society for Horticultural Science* 102:327–31.

Boorse, D. F. 1993. The effect of fertilizer nitrate level and cultivar on the biology of *Bemisia tabaci* (Gennadius) (Homoptera: Aleyrodidae) and poinsettia (*Euphorbia pulcherrima* Willd.). Master's thesis, Cornell University.

Breene, R. G., R. L. Meagher, D. A. Nordlund, and Y. T. Wang. 1992. Biological control of *Bemisia tabaci* (Homoptera: Aleyrodidae) in a greenhouse using *Chrysoperla rufilabris* (Neuroptera: Chrysopidae). *Biological Control* 2:9–14.

Brown, J. K., D. R. Frohlich, and R. C. Rosell. 1995. The sweetpotato or silverleaf whiteflies: Biotypes of *Bemisia tabaci* or a species complex? *Annual Review of Entomology* 40:511–534.

Cahill, M., I. Denholm, K. Gorman, S. Day, A. Elbert, and R. Nauen. 1996a. Baseline determination and detection of resistance to imidacloprid in *Bemisia tabaci* (Homoptera: Aleyrodidae). *Bulletin of Entomological Research* 86:343–9.

Cahill, M., W. Jarvis, K. Gorman, and I. Denholm. 1996b. Resolution of baseline responses and documentation of resistance to buprofezin in *Bemisia tabaci* (Homoptera: Aleyrodidae). *Bulletin of Entomological Research* 86:117–22.

Doucette, C. F. 1962. The Lewis mite, *Eotetranychus lewisi*, on greenhouse poinsettia. *Journal of Economic Entomology* 55:139–40.

Evans, M. R., J. N. Smith, and R. A. Cloyd. 1998. Fungus gnat population development in coconut coir and *Sphagnum* peat-based substrates. *HortTechnology* 8(3):406–9.

Ferrentino, G., J. Grant, M. Heinmiller, J. Sanderson, and M. Daughtrey. 1993. IPM for poinsettias in New York: A scouting and pest management guide. New York State Integrated Pest Management Program Publication No. 403. Ithaca, N.Y.: Cornell University.

Fischer, S. J., and J. B. Shanks. 1974. Host preference of greenhouse whitefly: Effect of poinsettia cultivars. *Journal of the American Society for Horticultural Science* 99(3): 261–2.

Gill, S. 1991. Bandedwinged whitefly turns up in Maryland. *Greenhouse Manager*, November, 58.

Gill, S. 1996. Mites on poinsettias: A problem again? *GrowerTalks,* August, 48.

Harris, M. A. 1995. Dissemination of the phytopathogen *Thielaviopsis basicola* by the fungus gnat *Bradysia coprophila* and biological control of these pests by *Fusarium proliferatum* and steinernematid nematodes. PhD diss., University of Georgia.

Harris, M. A., W. A. Gardner, and R. D. Oetting. 1996. A review of the scientific literature on fungus gnats (Diptera: Sciaridae) in the genus *Bradysia*. *Journal of Entomological Science* 31:252–76.

Harris, M. A., R. D Oetting, and W. A. Gardner. 1995. Use of entomopathogenic nematodes and a new monitoring technique for control of fungus gnats, *Bradysia coprophila* (Diptera: Sciaridae), in floriculture. *Biological Control* 5:412–8.

Heinz, K. M. 1996. Predators and parasitoids as biological control agents of *Bemisia* in greenhouses. In *Bemisia: 1995 Taxonomy, Biology, Damage, Control, and Management*, ed. D. Gerling and R. T. Mayer, 435-449, Andover, U.K.: Intercept.

Heinz, K. M., and J. M. Nelson. 1996. Interspecific interactions among natural enemies of *Bemisia* in an inundative biological control program. *Biological Control* 6:384–93.

Heinz, K. M. and M. P. Parrella. 1994a. Poinsettia (*Euphorbia pulcherrima* Willd. ex Koltz) cultivar mediated differences in performance of five natural enemies of *Bemisia argentifolii* Bellows and Perring n. sp. (Homoptera: Aleyrodidae). *Biological Control* 4:305–18.

Heinz, K. M., and M. P. Parrella. 1994b. Biological control of *Bemisia argentifolii* (Homoptera: Aleyrodidae) infesting *Euphorbia pulcherrima*: Evaluations of releases of *Encarsia luteola* (Hymenoptera: Aphelinidae) and *Delphastus pusillus* (Coleoptera: Coccinellidae). *Environmental Entomology* 23:1346–53.

Helgesen, R. G., and M. J. Tauber. 1974. Biological control of greenhouse whitefly, *Trialeurodes vaporariorum* (Homoptera: Aleyrodidae), on short-term crops by manipulating biotic and abiotic factors. *The Canadian Entomologist* 106:1175–88.

Hoddle, M. S., J. P. Sanderson, and R. G. Van Driesche. 1999. Biological control of *Bemisia argentifolii* (Hemiptera: Aleyrodidae) on poinsettia with inundative releases of *Eretmocerus eremicus* (Hymenoptera: Aphelinidae): Does varying the weekly release rate affect control? *Bulletin of Entomological Research* 89:41–51.

Hoddle, M. S., and R. G. Van Driesche. 1996. Evaluation of *Encarsia formosa* (Hymenoptera: Aphelinidae) to control *Bemisia argentifolii* (Homoptera: Aleyrodidae) on poinsettia (*Euphorbia pulcherrima*): A lifetable analysis. *Florida Entomologist* 79:1–12.

Hoddle, M. S., and R. G. Van Driesche. 1999a. Evaluation of *Eretmocerus eremicus* and *Encarsia formosa* Beltsville strain in commercial greenhouses for biological control of *Bemisia argentifolii* on colored poinsettia plants. *Florida Entomologist* 82(4):556–70.

Hoddle, M. S., and R. G. Van Driesche. 1999b. Evaluation of inundative releases of *Eretmocerus eremicus* and *Encarsia formosa* Beltsville strain in commercial greenhouses for control of *Bemisia argentifolii* on poinsettia stock plants. *Journal of Economic Entomology* 92:811–24.

Hoddle, M. S., R. G. Van Driesche, and J. P. Sanderson. 1998. Biology and use of the whitefly parasitoid *Encarsia formosa*. *Annual Review of Entomology* 43:645–69.

Hoddle, M. S., R. G. Van Driesche, J. P. Sanderson, and O. P. J. M. Minkenberg. 1998. Biological control of *Bemisia argentifolii* on poinsettia with inundative releases of *Eretmocerus eremicus* (Hymenoptera: Aphelinidae): Do release rates affect parasitism? *Bulletin of Entomological Research* 88: 47-58.

Hoddle, M. S., R. G. Van Driesche, S.M. Lyon, and J. P. Sanderson. 2001. Compatibility of insect growth regulators with *Eretmocerus eremicus* (Hymenoptera: Aphelinidae) for whitefly (Homoptera: Aleyrodidae) control on poinsettias. I. Laboratory Assays. *Biological Control* 20: 122-131.

Horowitz, A. R., and I. Ishaaya. 1994. Managing resistance to insect growth regulators in the sweetpotato whitefly (Homoptera: Aleyrodidae). *Journal of Economic Entomology* 87:866–71.

Jeppson, L. R., H. H. Keifer, and E. W. Baker. 1975. *Mites Injurious to Economic Plants*. Berkeley, Calif.: University of California Press.

Lacey, L. A., J. J. Fransen, and R. Carruthers. 1996. Global distribution of naturally occurring fungi of *Bemisia*, their biologies and use as biological control agents. In *Bemisia: 1995 Taxonomy, Biology, Damage, Control, and Management*, ed. D. Gerling and R. T. Mayer, 401–33. Andover, U.K.: Intercept.

Leath, K. T., and R. C. Newton. 1969. Interaction of a fungus gnat, *Bradysia* sp. (Sciaridae) with *Fusarium* spp. on alfalfa and red clover. *Phytopathology* 59:257–8.

Lindquist, R. K. 1994. Integrated management of fungus gnats and shore flies. In *Proceedings of the Society of American Florists 10th Conference on Insect and Disease Management on Ornamentals*, ed. K. Robb, 58–67. Alexandria, Va.: Society of American Florists.

Lindquist, R. K. 1998. Fungus gnat and shore fly management. In *Proceedings of the Society of American Florists 14th Conference on Insect and Disease Management on Ornamentals*, ed. J. Hall and K. Robb, 45–51. Alexandria, Va.: Society of American Florists.

Lindquist, R. K., and M. A. Casey. 1994. Integrated management of fungus gnats and shore flies. *Ohio Florist's Association Bulletin*, May, 3–5.

Lindquist, R. K., W. R. Faber, and M. L. Casey. 1985. Effect of various soilless root media and insecticides on fungus gnats. *HortScience* 20:358–60.

Liu, T. X., R. D. Oetting, and G. D. Buntin. 1994. Evidence of interspecific competition between *Trialeurodes vaporariorum* (Westwood) and *Bemisia tabaci* (Gennadius) (Homoptera: Aleyrodidae) on some greenhouse-grown plants. *Journal of Entomological Science* 29:55–65.

Meekes, E. T. M., J. J. Fransen, and J. C. van Lenteren. 1994. The use of entomopathogenic fungi for the control of white-flies. *Mededelingen Faculteit Landbouwwetenschappen, Rijksuniversiteit Gent* 59(2a): 371–7.

Meekes, E. T. M., S. vanVoorst, N. N. Joosten, J. J. Fransen, J. C. vanLenteren. 2000. Persistence of the fungal pathogen, *Aschersonia aleyrodis*, on three different plant species. *Mycological Research* 104(10):1234-1240.

Mound, L. A., and S. H. Halsey. 1978. *Whitefly of the World: A Systematic Catalogue of the Aleyrodidae (Homoptera) with Host Plant and Natural Enemy Data.* Chichester, U.K.: British Museum of Natural History and John Wiley and Sons.

National Agricultural Statistics Service (NASS), Agricultural Statistics Board. 2003. *Floriculture Crops 2001 Summary.* Washington, D.C.: U.S. Department of Agriculture.

Nedstam, B. 1992. Biological control of pests in Swedish pot plant production. *Bulletin OEPP/EPPO* 22:417–9.

Nordlund, D. A., and J. C. Legaspi. 1996. Whitefly predators and their potential for use in biological control. In *Bemisia: 1995 Taxonomy, Biology, Damage, Control, and Management*, ed. D. Gerling and R. T. Mayer, 499–513. Andover, U.K.: Intercept.

Oetting, R. D., and G. D. Buntin. 1996. *Bemisia* damage expression in commercial greenhouse production. In *Bemisia: 1995 Taxonomy, Biology, Damage, Control, and Management*, ed. D. Gerling and R. T. Mayer, 201–8, Andover, U.K.: Intercept.

Oetting, R. D., and J. G. Latimer. 1991. An entomogenous nematode *Steinernema carpocapsae* is compatible with potting media environments created by horticultural practices. *Journal of Entomological Science* 26:390–4.

Osborne, L. S., and Z. Landa. 1994. Utilization of the entomogenous fungus *Paecilomyces fumosoroseus* against sweetpotato whitefly, *Bemisia tabaci.* *IOBC/WPRS Bulletin* 17(1):201–6.

Parrella, M. P., T. D. Paine, J. A. Bethke, K. L. Robb, and J. Hall. 1991. Evaluation of *Encarsia formosa* (Hymenoptera: Aphelinidae) for biological control of sweetpotato whitefly (Homoptera: Aleyrodidae) on poinsettia. *Environmental Entomology* 20:713–9.

Perring, T. M., A. D. Cooper, D. Kazmer, C. Shields, and J. Shields. 1992. Identification of the poinsettia strain of *Bemisia tabaci* (Homoptera: Aleyrodidae) on broccoli by electrophoresis. *Journal of Economic Entomology* 85:1278–84.

Price, J. F., D. Schuster, and D. Short. 1987. Managing the sweetpotato whitefly. *Greenhouse Grower.* December, 55–7.

Pundt, L. 1997. New England integrated pest management scouting guide for poinsettias. Office of Communication and Information Technology, Storrs, Conn.: University of Connecticut.

Robb, K. L. 1995. Screening to exclude insects. *Ohio Florist's Association Bulletin*, November, 12–3.

Ross, D. S., and S. A. Gill. 1994. Insect screening for greenhouses. *Maryland Cooperative Extension Service, Agricultural Engineering Facts* No. 186.

Sanderson, J. P. 1992. Planning ahead for sweetpotato and greenhouse whiteflies. In *Proceedings of the Society of American Florists 8th Conference on Insect and Disease Management on Ornamentals*, ed. M. Daughtrey, 26–36. Alexandria, Va.: Society of American Florists.

———. 1995. Total whitefly identification and control. *GrowerTalks*, September, 32–44.

———. 1999. Biology and management of arthropod pests of greenhouse florist crops: Whiteflies. In *Recommendations for the Integrated Management of Greenhouse Florist Crops. Part II. Management of Pests and Crop Growth.* 58–66, Ithaca, N.Y.: Cornell Cooperative Extension Distribution Center.

Sanderson, J. P., and P. M. Davis. 1996. Pest-free poinsettias. *Greenhouse Grower*, July, 39–42.

Sanderson, J. P., P. M. Davis, and G. Ferrentino. 1994. A better, easier way to sample for whiteflies on poinsettias. *Greenhouse Manager*, August, 71–6.

Schuster, D. J., P. A. Stansly, and J. E. Polston. 1996. Expressions of plant damage by *Bemisia*. In *Bemisia: 1995 Taxonomy, Biology, Damage, Control, and Management*, ed. D. Gerling and R. T. Mayer, 153–65. Andover, U.K.: Intercept.

Senior, L. J., and P. K. McEwen. 1998. Laboratory study of *Chrysoperla carnea* (Stephens) (Neuroptera: Chrysopidae) predation on *Trialeurodes vaporariorum* (Westwood) (Homoptera: Aleyrodidae). *Journal of Applied Entomology* 122:99–101.

Stenseth, C. 1993. Biological control of cotton whitefly *Bemisia tabaci* (Genn.) (Homoptera: Aleyrodidae) by *Encarsia formosa* (Hymenoptera: Aphelinidae) on *Euphorbia pulcherrima* and *Hypoestes phyllostachya*. *IOBC/WPRS Bulletin* 16(2):135–40.

Van Driesche, R. G., M. S. Hoddle, S. M. Lyon, and J. P. Sanderson. 2001. Compatibility of insect growth regulators with *Eretmocerus eremicus* (Hymenoptera: Aphelinidae) for whitefly (Homoptera: Aleyrodidae) control on poinsettias. II. Trials in commercial poinsettia crops. *Biological Control* 20:132-146.

Van Driesche, R. G., M.S. Hoddle, S. Roy, S. Lyon, and J. P. Sanderson. 2001. Effect of parasitoid release pattern on whitefly (Homoptera: Aleyrodidae) control in commercial poinsettia. *Florida Entomologist* 84(1):63-69.

Van Driesche, R. G., S. M. Lyon, M. S. Hoddle, S. Roy, and J. P. Sanderson. 1999. Assessment of cost and reliability of *Eretmocerus eremicus* (Hymenoptera: Aphelinidae) for whitefly (Homoptera: Aleyrodidae) control in commercial poinsettia crops. *Florida Entomologist* 82(4):570–94.

Van Driesche, R. G., S. Lyon, K. Jacques, T. Smith, and P. Lopes. 2002. Comparative cost of chemical and biological whitefly control in poinsettia: Is there a gap? *Florida Entomologist* 85(3):488-493.

Vanninen, I. 2003. Control of sciarid flies with *Steinernema feltiae* in poinsettia cutting production. *International Journal of Pest Management* 49(2):95-103.

Zchori-Fein, E., R. T. Roush, and J. P. Sanderson. 1994. Potential for integration of biological and chemical control of greenhouse whitefly (Homoptera: Aleyrodidae) using *Encarsia formosa* (Hymenoptera: Aphelinidae) and abamectin. *Environmental Entomology* 23:1277–82.

22

BIOLOGICAL CONTROL IN CUT FLOWERS

G. Murphy

Ontario Ministry of Agriculture and Food
Ontario, Canada

Several unrelated factors affect the chances for successful biological control in cut flowers. (i) In flowers grown for export, the low legal tolerance for pests on the crop (by the importing country) often precludes the use of biological control (van Lenteren and Woets 1988). (ii) In production areas with warm climates (e.g., Central and South America), greenhouses are often open-sided to facilitate ventilation. These openings allow outside pests to enter the greenhouse year-round and make it difficult to predict the natural enemy release rates needed to drive pest populations to very low levels (Nicholls, Parrella, and Altieri 1998). (iii) Shifts in crop cultural practices may change pest complexes, requiring important changes to existing biological control programs. Some crops, such as roses, traditionally were grown in soil beds using open irrigation systems. Conversion to the use of nutrient recycling systems may alter the severity of root diseases. Replacement of soil beds with soilless media may lead to increased populations of fungus gnats and reductions in root nematodes and black vine weevil (*Otiorhynchus sulcatus* F.). Further, modifications to the training and pruning of rose stems affects the spatial distribution of spider mites and hence requires modifications of predator release strategies.

Agronomic characteristics of some cut flowers greatly facilitate the use of biological control. The long cropping cycles in some species (e.g., roses and orchids) allow sufficient time for biological control systems to become established because the crop exhibits seasonal variability in production of harvestable commodities or because of the inherent stability of the system due to few crop destruction phases. In other crops (e.g., gerbera and gypsophila), small amounts of foliage are harvested or sold, thus reducing a stringent adherence to near-zero damage tolerance levels associated with other aesthetically important plant structures. Many crops may meet one or both of these criteria, but the current use and study of biological control for cut flowers is concentrated on rose and gerbera.

Roses

Roses (*Rosa* × *hybrida*) are one of the most economically important cut flower crops in the world with most production exported. The pest complex is large. Two-spotted spider mite (*Tetranychus urticae* Koch) and western flower thrips (*Frankliniella occidentalis* [Pergande]) are the most widespread and chronic arthropod pests. Whitefly and aphids are also important, but infestations are often sporadic. Powdery mildew, a frequent disease in roses, is most commonly suppressed by vaporizing sulfur. Use of this disease control strategy conflicts with the use of biological control because the sulfur fumes are toxic to natural enemies, especially predacious mites (Simmonds 1972; Wardlow, Brough, and Need 1992; Jackson 1995).

The practice of arching vegetative stems, introduced into rose production in the early 1990s, has changed the rose canopy from being upright and relatively dense to a canopy with dense lower foliage opening up to flowering stems. This canopy structure makes it easier to direct pesticide applications at flowers, but also makes it difficult to achieve good pesticide coverage on the thick foliage at the base of the crop. However, the arching of vegetative stems should create an environment favorable for natural enemies. Pesticide residue levels on the foliage are reduced by the poor coverage, and predator movement among plants is facilitated by the dense foliage and numerous leaves in contact with one another that create a series of interconnecting bridges. The importance of bridging to enhance the movement of *Phytoseiulus persimilis* Athias-Henriot between rose plants has been demonstrated by Casey and Parrella (2002).

Two-spotted spider mite is probably the most chronic pest of roses. Its reproductive capacity and damage are greater on rose than on chrysanthemum or gerbera (van de Vrie 1985). Nevertheless, the potential of *P. persimilis* to control *T. urticae* on roses was demonstrated by Simmonds (1972) and Burgess (1984). This predator was able to increase its numbers twenty-fold in ten days when feeding on *T. urticae* reared on roses (Popov and Khudyakova 1989). In Colombia in research greenhouses, successful control of *T. urticae* in rose crops with *P. persimilis* and *Neoseiulus californicus* (McGregor) was demonstrated by de Vis and Barrera (1999), although pesticide residues were considered an obstacle to success in commercial crops. In systems where miticides must be used, an insecticide-resistant strain of another predatory mite, *Metaseiulus* (=*Typhlodromus*) *occidentalis* (Nesbitt), can be used in combination with certain miticides (Field and Hoy 1984). Integration of predatory mites with chemical control is achieved by differentially treating the upper and lower portions of the crop canopy (Sanderson and Zhang 1995, Nicetic et al. 2001).

Frankliniella occidentalis is not as consistent a problem on roses as are mites, although in Colombia, rose growers routinely accept 2% losses from this pest (Corredor 1999). As in other flower crops, western flower thrips damage occurs primarily in the flower, and control of this pest is difficult. The ability to implement a biological control program on this crop depends upon the capability to manage *F. occidentalis* (Jackson 1995; Martin, Workman, and Marais 1996). Unfortunately, biological thrips control in roses appears to be especially problematic.

Thrips management in roses cannot depend on the use of *Orius* spp., as roses appear to be an unsuitable host plant for this important group of western flower thrips natural enemies (Beekman et al. 1991; Smitley 1993; Fransen, Boogaard, and Tolsma 1993; Nicholls, Parrella, and Altieri 1998). Predatory mites also do not seem to be effective in providing biological thrips control in roses. *Neoseiulus cucumeris* (Oudemans) did not provide satisfactory control, even when combined with releases of the predacious bug *Orius majusculus* (Reuter) (Blümel and Schausberger 1996). Similarly, *Neoseiulus barkeri* Hughes, released at 13 per ft.^{2} (140/m^2) was also unsuccessful (Del Bene and Landi 1991). In addition, parasitoids of thrips seem unable to provide control on roses or any other crop. While both *Ceranisus menes* (Walker) and *Ceranisus americensis* (Girault) established when released against western flower thrips in roses, parasitism rates were low and the crops suffered extensive damage (Loomans et al. 1995).

Although the presence of *F. occidentalis* on roses greatly complicates creating biological control programs for this crop, recent studies suggest that thrips control with minimal insecticide input is possible. Robb (1989) noted that thrips adults lay eggs in rose buds after sepal split (less than a week before harvest), leaving insufficient time for thrips to complete development before the flower is harvested. This means that apart from movement of thrips into greenhouses from outside, increases in thrips numbers in roses depend on unharvested flowers being left in the greenhouse. Teerling and Murphy (1998) confirmed this finding and observed that 95% of *F. occidentalis* eggs were laid in rose buds that were within seven to eight days of harvest. This makes it impossible for the eggs to hatch and the larvae to develop and leave the plant before the flower is ready to be cut and sold. Leaves, stems, and smaller buds were largely ignored as oviposition sites. Results from trials in a commercial rose crop lend support to the theory that rigorous removal of all nonharvested flowers before they open plays an important role in reducing thrips populations, even without additional control measures (Teerling and Murphy, unpublished data). Further studies to quantify the impact of this management practice on thrips populations in roses are needed.

Other rose pests are less severe than mites and thrips, yet they may still be common. *Aphelinus abdominalis* Dalman provides successful biological control of the potato aphid *Macrosiphum euphorbiae* (Thomas) (Blümel and Schausberger 1996). Rose aphid, *Macrosiphum rosae* (L.), has been controlled with the predacious midge *Aphidoletes aphidomyza* (Rondani) (Smitley 1993). The parasitoid *Aphidius colemani* Viereck controls green peach aphid *Myzus persicae* (Sulzer) (Murphy unpubl. data).

Beck (1992) reported control of black vine weevil (*O. sulcatus*) in soil beds using the entomopathogenic fungus *Metarhizium anisopliae* (Metchnikoff) Sorokin. However, with the greater use of soilless growth media, pests such as root nematodes and *O. sulcatus* have become less important.

Gerbera

There is great potential for successful use of biological control in gerbera (*Gerbera jamesonii* Bolus ex Adlam.) (Parrella 1990a, b; Ravensberg and Altena 1993; Sütterlin and van Lenteren 1996). Flower stems are detached directly from the crown of the plant and sold without foliage (Fig. 22.1), permitting growers to tolerate a higher density of pests on the foliage in this crop. The arthropod pest complex of gerbera includes thrips, leafminers, spider mites, whitefly, aphids, and beet armyworm, *Spodoptera exigua* (Hübner) (Nucifora and Calabretta 1986; Wardlow, Brough, and Need 1992; Ravensberg and Altena 1993); whereas the major disease is powdery mildew.

While crop phenology lends itself well to implementation of biological control, several factors may also hinder its use. Powdery mildew is most often suppressed by vaporizing sulphur. This practice impedes the use of some biological control agents (especially predacious mites) as discussed earlier.

Additionally, the leaf hairs on gerbera can disrupt natural enemy behavior and reduce their effectiveness. Both *Encarsia formosa* Gahan and *P. persimilis* show reduced walking speed and searching ability on gerbera (Sütterlin and van Lenteren 1996, Kleijn et al. 1997) as compared to other plants.

Whitefly, particularly greenhouse whitefly, *Trialeurodes vaporariorum* (Westwood), is very damaging on gerbera. Gerbera is difficult to treat due to the dense canopy and the inability to reach the undersides of leaves with pesticides. Most studies of biological control in gerbera have concentrated on using *E. formosa* to suppress greenhouse whitefly. Reported introduction rates vary greatly and

Figure 22.1. Gerbera flowers being detached from the plant. Note the single stem and the absence of foliage, a major factor in the potential of biological control in this crop.
Photo: by G. D. Murphy.

may depend on pest infestation level. For example, rates have included: 0.3 to 0.8 wasps per ft.^{2} (3 to 9/m^2) each week; 0.6 wasps per ft.^{2} (6/m^2) every two weeks; and 1.9 wasps per ft.^{2} (20/m^2) each week (Parrella 1990b; Del Bene and Landi 1991; Ravensberg and Altena 1993). Sütterlin and Lamour (1994) obtained effective control of this pest with one release of three *E. formosa* per plant. Despite disagreement on introduction rates many of these trials were successful, although applications of compatible pesticides were sometimes necessary (Parrella 1990a; Del Bene and Landi 1991; Blümel 1992; Ravensberg and Altena 1993).

Western flower thrips is the only major pest of gerbera whose damage is concentrated on the flowers. Effective thrips control using *N. cucumeris* and *Orius insidiosus* (Say) was achieved by Ravensberg and Altena (1993), who reported that these predators reproduce on the pollen of gerbera. Parrella (1990a) reported preliminary successes against thrips, mites, aphids and leafminers. Ravensberg and Altena (1993) likewise achieved good control of the leafminer *Liriomyza trifolii* (Burgess), with *Diglyphus isaea* (Walker) and *Dacnusa sibirica* Telenga; of spider mites with *P. persimilis*; of aphids with *Aphidius* species and *A. aphidomyza*; and of Lepidoptera with *Bacillus thuringiensis* Berliner *kurstaki*. Stolz (1996) reported good control of the leafminer *Liriomyza huidobrensis* (Blanchard) with *D. isaea, D. sibirica,* and the compatible pesticide cyromazine.

Other Cut Flower Crops

Like gerbera, carnation (*Dianthus caryophyllus* L.) is a crop in which the prospects for use of biological control appear good (Parrella 1990a), even though current use is minimal (Bolckmans, Koppert B.V., pers. comm.). Two-spotted spider mite (*T. urticae*) is a major pest of carnation, but biological control of this pest on carnation using the predator *P. persimilis* is not reliable. In the environmental conditions commonly encountered during a crop production cycle, the rate of increase of *P. persimilis* on *T. urticae* reared on carnation is greatly reduced compared to use of hosts fed on plants such as rose and soybean (Popov and Khudyakova 1989). In addition, this predator is easily dislodged from carnation leaves (Martin, Workman, and Marais 1996).

Other important cut flower crops include alstroemeria (*Alstroemeria × hybrida)* and bulb crops such as lily (*Lilium* spp.) and freesia (*Freesia × hybrida*). These crops are grown at cooler temperatures that may reduce the efficacy of natural enemies (Fransen 1995). However, several commercial growers of alstroemeria in Ontario, Canada, have been using biological control successfully against western flower thrips and other pests for several years (Murphy, unpublished data). Reports from the Netherlands suggest that increasing numbers of alstroemeria growers are using biological control (Bolckmans, pers. comm.).

Of the other cut flowers, orchids have the most potential for successful use of biological control because, like gerbera, the foliage is not harvested. Successful biological control programs have been reported for cymbidium orchids in New Zealand, with an estimated 9% of growers in 1993 using *P. persimilis* for control of *T. urticae* (see chapter 10) (Beck, Workman, and Martin 1993).

Conclusions

The degree of use of biological control in cut flowers depends on many variables, perhaps most importantly the crop. Gerbera is probably the most favorable crop for such use because of the greater tolerance for pests where no foliage is harvested. While the diversity of pests in this crop is a concern, the success demonstrated in many studies offers good evidence of the potential of biological control.

Roses should also be an excellent crop for the use of natural enemies, but important obstacles have slowed progress. Western flower thrips control has been difficult; however, strict adherence to sanitation and removal of unharvested flowers may help reduce the importance of this pest. The other major hindrance is the use of vaporized sulfur, which is toxic to the natural enemies, to control powdery mildew. Without the use of sulfur, successful biological control of other pests should be possible.

Questions still exist over the use of biological control in other crops. In carnations, there appears to be inherent difficulties in use of *P. persimilis* and control of western flower thrips remains problematic. For alstroemeria and bulb crops there is little documented research on using biological control, although anecdotal information suggests some potential.

While the crop itself is obviously important, in cut flowers as in any other cropping situation, other components of the IPM program may determine the success of biological control releases. The importance of a regular monitoring program, good record keeping, sanitation, weed control, and the use of screening to exclude pests cannot be overestimated.

References Cited

Beck, D. F. 1992. Effects of *Metarhizium anisopliae* applications in greenhouse roses to biologically control the black vine weevil, *Otiorhynchus sulcatus. Mededelingen Faculteit Landbouwwetenschappen, Rijksuniversiteit Gent* 57 (2b):523–31.

Beck, N. G., P. Workman, and N. Martin. 1993. IPM for cymbidium orchids in New Zealand: Grower acceptance. *IOBC/WPRS Bulletin* 16 (8):12–5.

Beekman, M., J. J. Fransen, R. D. Oetting, and M. W. Sabelis. 1991. Differential arrestment of the minute pirate bug, *Orius insidiosus* (Say) (Hemiptera: Anthocoridae), on two plant species. *Mededelingen Faculteit Landbouwwetenschappen, Rijksuniversiteit Gent* 56 (2a):273–6.

Blümel, S. 1992. Glashausversuche zur bekampfungvon *Trialeurodes vaporariorum* (Westwood) auf gerbera mit der parasitischen erzwespe *Encarsia formosa* Gahan. (Abstract only). *Journal of Applied Entomology* 113:1–7.

Blümel, S., and P. Schausberger. 1996. Current status of IPM in greenhouses in Austria. *IOBC/WPRS Bulletin* 19 (1):19–22.

Burgess, E. P. 1984. Integrated control of two-spotted mite on glasshouse roses. In *Proceedings of the Thirty-seventh New Zealand Weed and Pest Control Conference, Russley Hotel, Christchurch, August 14–16, 1984*, 257–61. Wellington, New Zealand: New Zealand Weed and Pest Control Society.

Casey C. and M. Parrella. 2002. Distribution, thresholds and biological control of the twospotted spider mite (Acari: Tetranychidae) on bent cane cut roses in California. *IOBC/WPRS Bulletin* 25(1):41-44.

Corredor D. 1999. Integrated pest management in cut flower crops grown in plastic houses at the Bogota Plateau. *Proceedings of the International Symposium On Cut Flowers in the Tropics*. International Society of Horticultural Science. *Acta Horticulturae.* 482:241-6.

Del Bene, G., and S. Landi. 1991. Biological control in glasshouse ornamental crops in Tuscany. *IOBC/WPRS Bulletin* 14 (5):13–21.

de Vis R. and A.J.Barrera. 1999. Use of two predators *Phytoseiulus persimilis* Athias-Henriot (Acari: Phytoseiidae) and *Neoseiulus californicus* (McGregor) (Acari: Phytoseiidae) for the biological control of *Tetranychus urticae* Koch (Acari: Tetranychidae) in roses in the Bogota plateau. *Proceedings of the Int. Symp. On Cut Flowers in the Tropics.* International Society of Horticultural Science. *Acta Horticulturae.* 482:259-67.

Field, R. P., and M. A. Hoy. 1984. Biological control of spider mites on greenhouse roses. *California Agriculture* 38 (3/4):29–32.

Fransen, J. J. 1995. Integrated pest and disease management in floriculture: The experience in the Netherlands. In *Simposio Internacional "El Manejo Integrado de Plagos y Enfermedades en Floricultura,"* Asociación Colombiana de Exportadores de Flores. February 1995, 3–15, Santafe de Bogota, Colombia.

Fransen, J. J., M. Boogaard, and J. Tolsma. 1993. The minute pirate bug *Orius insidiosus* (Say) (Hemiptera: Anthocoridae), as a predator of the western flower thrips, *Frankliniella occidentalis* (Pergande), in chrysanthemum, rose, and Saintpaulia. *IOBC/WPRS Bulletin* 16 (8):73–7.

Jackson, A. 1995. Biological control in ornamentals. *The Horticulturist* 4 (2):25–9.

Kleijn, P. W., O. E. Krips, P. E. L.Willems, and M. Dicke. 1997. The influence of leaf hairs of *Gerbera jamesonii* on the searching behavior of the predatory mite *Phytoseiulus persimilis*. *Proceedings of the Section Experimental and Applied Entomology of the Netherlands Entomological Society* 8:171–6.

Loomans, A. J. M., J. Tolsma, J. P. N. F. Van Heest, and J. J. Fransen. 1995. Releases of parasitoids (*Ceranisus* spp.) as biological control agents of western flower thrips (*Frankliniella occidentalis*) in experimental greenhouses. *Mededelingen Faculteit Landbouwwetenschappen, Rijksuniversiteit Gent* 60 (3a):869–77.

Martin, N. A., P. J. Workman, and T. Marais. 1996. IPM for greenhouse crops in New Zealand: Progress, problems and prospects. IOBC/WPRS *Bulletin* 19 (1):99–102.

Nicetic O., D. M. Watson, G. A. C. Beattie, A. Meats, and J. Zheng. 2001. Integrated pest management of two-spotted mite *Tetranychus urticae* on greenhouse roses using petroleum spray oil and the predatory mite *Phytoseiulus persimilis*. *Experimental and Applied Acarology* 25: 37-53.

Nicholls, C. I., M. P. Parrella, and M. A. Altieri. 1998. Advances and perspectives in the biological control of greenhouse pests with special reference to Colombia. *Integrated Pest Management Reviews* 3:99–109.

Nucifora, A., and C. Calabretta. 1986. Advances in integrated control of gerbera protected crops (Abstract only). *Acta Horticulturae* 176: 191–7.

Parrella, M. P. 1990a. Biological control in ornamentals: Status and objectives. *IOBC/WPRS Bulletin* 13 (5):161–8.

Parrella, M. P. 1990b. The development of IPM strategies in chrysanthemums and gerberas with an emphasis on biological control. In *Proceedings of the Latin American Symposium of Flowering and Ornamental Plants, June 1989*, Asociación Colombiana de Exportadores de Flores. ed. V. O. Sing, M. Maldonado, and M. Pizano, 43–59, Bogota, Colombia.

Popov, N. A., and O. A. Khudyakova. 1989. Development of *Phytoseiulus persimilis* (Acarina: Phytoseiidae) fed on *Tetranychus urticae* (Acarina: Tetranychidae) on various food plants. *Acta Entomologica Fennica* 53:43–6.

Ravensberg, W. J., and K. Altena. 1993. IPM in glasshouse ornamentals: The first steps in practice. *IOBC/WPRS Bulletin* 16 (8):119–22.

Robb, K. L. 1989. Analysis of *Frankliniella occidentalis* (Pergande) as a pest of floricultural crops in California greenhouses. PhD diss., University of California, Riverside.

Sanderson, J. P., and Z. Q. Zhang. 1995. Dispersion, sampling, and potential for integrated control of two-spotted spider mite (Acari: Tetranychidae) on greenhouse roses. *Journal of Economic Entomology* 88 (2):343–51.

Simmonds, S. P. 1972. Observations on the control of *Tetranychus urticae* on roses by *Phytoseiulus persimilis*. *Plant Pathology* 21:163–5.

Smitley, D. R. 1993. Biocontrol of thrips and mites on roses. *Roses Incorporated Bulletin*, November, 53–6.

Stolz, M. 1996. Investigations on the occurrence of agromyzid leafminers and their natural enemies in greenhouse cut gerbera in Austria. *IOBC/WPRS Bulletin* 19 (1):167–70.

Sütterlin, S., and A. Lamour. 1994. Movements among plants and population development of the greenhouse whitefly (*Trialeurodes vaporariorum*) in gerbera with and without parasitoids (*Encarsia formosa*). *Proceedings of the Section Experimental and Applied Entomology of the Netherlands Entomological Society* 5:159–64.

Sütterlin, S., and J. C. van Lenteren. 1996. Hairiness of *Gerbera jamesonii* leaves and the walking speed of the parasitoid *Encarsia formosa*. *IOBC/WPRS Bulletin* 19 (1): 171–4.

Teerling, C., and G. Murphy. 1998. Potential of flower removal for thrips control on roses. *Greenhouse Canada* 18 (11):37–8.

van de Vrie, M. 1985. Greenhouse ornamentals. In *Spider Mites: Their Biology, Natural Enemies, and Control*. Vol. 1B, ed. W. Helle and M. W. Sabelis, 239–83. New York (Amsterdam): Elsevier.

van Lenteren, J. C., and J. Woets. 1988. Biological and integrated pest control in greenhouses. *Annual Review of Entomology* 33:239–69.

Wardlow, L. R., W. Brough, and C. Need. 1992. Integrated pest management in protected ornamentals in England. *Bulletin OEPP/EPPO* 22:493–8.

23

BIOLOGICAL CONTROL IN FOLIAGE PLANTS

L. S. Osborne
University of Florida, IFAS
Mid-Florida Research and Education Center, Apopka, Florida

N. C. Leppla
Department of Entomology and Nematology
University of Florida, Gainesville, Florida

and

R. S. Osborne
Department of Entomology and Nematology
University of Florida, Gainesville, Florida

Insecticides and acaricides have traditionally controlled the primary pests of foliage
plants—aphids, thrips, mealybugs, whiteflies,
scales, and spider mites. However, it is
increasingly clear that the strategy of unilat-
eral reliance on chemical control is not an
ideal solution to pest problems. There are
four major problems associated with chemical control: (i) development of resistance to
pesticides by pest species; (ii) increasing
governmental regulation; (iii) the damaging
(or detrimental) effect of these chemicals on
non-target species resulting in resurgence of
pests and secondary pest outbreaks; and (iv)
phytotoxic reactions of treated plants.
However, for foliage plants, strict reliance on
biological control is frequently not a viable
alternative either.

Biological control programs are
currently available for the management of
two-spotted spider mite, *Tetranychus urticae*

Koch, in ornamental foliage production.
Many of the remaining pest species, particularly thrips, aphids, mealybugs, and scales,
still require considerable research before
biological control programs can be implemented. Although many of these pests have
effective natural enemy complexes outside
the greenhouse, the effectiveness of a given
natural enemy under greenhouse conditions
may be limited or, if effective, the species
may not be commercially available. The
prospects for integrated programs are much
more promising. There is considerable
progress on chemical techniques that are
compatible with natural enemies especially
with the use of predatory mites for the
management of two-spotted spider mite.

Two-Spotted Spider Mite

Any program designed to change pesticide
use patterns in the ornamental foliage plant

industry should focus first on mite control as one of its major target areas (Hudson et al. 1996). Among possible spider mite natural enemies, predatory mites have excellent potential for biological control of pest mites. Biological control of two-spotted spider mite has been practiced in vegetable crop greenhouses throughout Europe for decades. Because of the many problems and economic consequences associated with chemical mite control, research on the implementation of mite control programs on ornamentals has been underway for many years. Potentially useful predatory mites for controlling *T. urticae* on ornamental plants are *Neoseiulus californicus* (McGregor)*, Neoseiulus fallacis* (Garman), and *Phytoseiulus persimilis* Athias-Henriot. These predators are commercially available from a number of different commercial sources in many countries for the control of this pest and other mite pest species (Hunter 1997).

The ability of predatory mites to control *T. urticae* on various ornamental plants has been demonstrated (Osborne et al.1998), but commercially viable programs with explicit directions for use on ornamental crops are rare. Difficulties arise when protocols are not applicable to all situations. For example, *Phytoseiulus macropilis* (Banks) can significantly reduce *T. urticae* on greenhouse grown *Dieffenbachia maculata* (Lodd.) Bunting (fig. 23.1) when introduced twice, three weeks apart, at the rate of ten predators per infested plant with an initial *T. urticae* density of about thirty-eight mites per leaf

Figure 23.1. *Dieffenbachia maculata* **(Lodd.) Bunting is a major foliage crop grown in protected structures located primarily in tropical and subtropical regions. Spider mites are a frequent pest of this crop, but they may be brought under biological control with releases of** *Phytoseiulus macropilis* **(Banks).** *Photo: P. Krauter.*

(Hamlen 1978, 1980). Similar studies with *Chamaedorea elegans* Martius (parlor palms) as the host plant have not yielded such promising results. Thus, certain ornamental plants may be better candidates for biological control programs than other plants because of varying abilities of natural enemies to suppress an identical pest among host plants.

There are release methods that increase the probability of successfully controlling *T. urticae* with predatory mites on vegetables. Most guidelines call for the release of predators once natural infestations of spider mites are found (French et al. 1976). Further, sufficient predators must be released to create a predator: prey ratio of 1:10 in cucumbers (Markkula and Tiittanen 1976) or 1:6 to 1:25 in ornamentals (Hamlen and Lindquist 1981). Once the mite population has reached a high density, the cost of releasing adequate numbers of predatory mites can be prohibitive, especially in vegetables. However, predators are frequently released prophylactically in greenhouses producing ornamentals due to the high value and high aesthetic value of these crops. Releases of approximately 0.2 predators per ft.^{2} (2/m^2) are made once each month even if no mites are present in the crop, on the assumption that the crop is likely to become infested.

Because foliage plants offered for sale must be nearly free of insects and mites, the use of predatory mites will have its greatest acceptance on stock plantings where more damage can be tolerated. These plants are usually grown for relatively long periods—one to two years for smaller plant types such as ivy and dieffenbachia. These stock plantings are grown very close together and produce very dense canopies. Dense canopies

preclude thorough spray coverage with acaricides. Because most acaricides are not systemic, mites that are not directly contacted by the spray escape control. As a result, chronic mite problems occur in these areas and are often spread to other parts of the greenhouse when cuttings are taken for propagation. Inadvertent spread of these mite infestations may be greatly reduced by dipping them in the pyrethroid fluvalinate (Osborne 1986) that causes little or no phytotoxicity to cuttings of many plant species. Although dipping of cuttings may reduce *T. urticae* densities by 90%, propagators desire cuttings free of insect pests when shipping to their customers.

Production of cleaner cuttings is possible if predatory mites were released in "stock" plantings to seek out and suppress high-density patches of *T. urticae* and followed by a dip of an effective pesticide. Palms are good candidates for biological control programs because the pests other than mites that attack them do not quickly develop damaging populations. Palms are commonly infested with long-tailed mealybug (*Pseudococcus longispinus* [Targioni Tozzetti]), Florida red scale (*Chrysomphalus aonidum* L.), false oleander scale (*Pseudaulacaspis cockerelli* [Cooley]), banana moth (*Opogona sacchari* [Bojer] Tineidae), and various snails. These pests are very slow to develop damaging populations; they are attacked by indigenous natural enemies or controlled with selective pesticides.

Broad Mite

Gerson's 1992 review of the biology and control of the broad mite, *Polyphagotarsonemus latus* (Banks), indicates that pesticide applications tend to provide the most effective control. However, situations exist in which control measures must have minimal adverse effects on the environment. To guarantee the safety of their visitors and to highlight biological control–based IPM systems, "The Land/Epcot Center," an agricultural exposition located within a Florida tourist attraction, relies heavily on the use of biological control. During the summer and spring production of peppers at "The Land," ten to thirty *Neoseiulis barkeri* Hughes per plant per week were released to provide adequate control of broad mite on peppers (Petitt 1993). In laboratory studies, adult females of *N. barkeri* consume a mean of fifteen adult female broad mites in twenty-four hours. However, during the fall of each year, the commercially reared *N. barkeri* released at "The Land" enter reproductive diapause so sulfur applications must replace the use of predatory mites during late fall through early spring. To solve this problem, colonies of *N. barkeri* that did not exhibit this diapause behavior were reared at the Epcot Center. Weekly releases of mites from this source were used to control broad mites on pepper throughout the year. In recent years, "The Land" has used *Neoseiulus cucumeris* (Oudemans) instead of *N. barkeri*.

A similar strategy is effective at controlling broad mite infestations on foliage plants. *N. barkeri* is no longer commercially available in the United States, so foliage growers must choose from either *N. cucumeris* or *N. californicus*. *N. californicus* is an excellent predator of *P. latus* and *T. urticae* (Peña and Osborne 1996). Because thrips are considered a minor pest in most crops and *N. cucumeris* will not control *T. urticae*, growers rely on *N. californicus* for managing both *T. urticae* and *P. latus*.

Fungus Gnats and Shore Flies

Foliage plant producers have used both the nematode *Steinernema feltiae* (= *bibionis*) (Filipjev) (when available) (Lindquist, Buxton, and Piatkoski 1994) and the predatory mite *Hypoaspis miles* Berlese (Gillespie and Quiring 1990) for the management of *Bradysia* spp. (fungus gnats). The problem faced by most growers is that control options for shore flies, *Scatella stagnalis* Fallen, are inadequate and populations of this pest often reach economically damaging levels. Natural enemies of this pest do exist (e.g., a species of eucoilid wasp in the genus *Hexacola*), but none are commercially available. Populations of *Atheta coriaria* Kraatz occur naturally in commercial Florida greenhouses where foliage plants are grown, but their effectiveness has not been determined.

Aphids

The green peach aphid, *Myzus persicae* (Sulzer), and the cotton or melon aphid, *Aphis gossypii* Glover, are the primary pest aphids on foliage plants and are the targets of both chemical and biological control programs. In much of the southeastern United States, *M. persicae* within greenhouses are commonly parasitized by the braconid wasp *Diaeretiella rapae* (McIntosh) and *A. gossypii* is parasitized by the braconid *Lysiphlebus testaceipes* Cresson. The encyrtid hyperparasitoid *Aphidencyrtus aphidivorus* (Mayr) develops on both of the braconid aphid parasitoids and frequently disrupts the natural control exerted by the aphid parasitoids.

Few scientific studies have been conducted to assess the abilities of commercially reared parasitoids to provide successful biological aphid control. Despite this lack of data of practical importance, studies conducted with the wasp *Aphidius colemani* Viereck have identified several parameters that will influence the outcome of a biological control program. The method of release can significantly affect the success of a biological control program (Hofsvang and Hågvar 1978, Heinz 1998b). Work on the dispersal behavior of *A. colemani* in chrysanthemum suggests that biological control may be enhanced by releasing sufficient numbers of these wasps from points approximately 10.5 ft. (325 cm) apart (Heinz, 1998b). Wasps with no previous encounters with aphids show no preferential attraction to uninfested plants or to plants heavily infested with green peach aphid (Grasswitz 1998). Releases of *A. colemani* are likely to generate a delayed biological control response until they gain experience through random encounters with aphids. In addition, populations of *A. colemani* exhibit different genetically based predispositions as to the host aphid species they will parasitize (Messing and Rabasse 1995). Thus, insectaries and end users should be careful in matching the parasitoid rearing practices with the pest species.

Several predators have also been proposed for use against aphids in greenhouses, including various species of Coccinellidae (Hallborg 2003), Syrphidae, and Chrysopidae. The green lacewing *Chrysoperla* (=*Chrysopa*) *rufilabris* (Burmeister) is used to suppress *M. persicae* on eggplant, tomatoes,

and peppers. *Chrysoperla rufilabris* larvae are also released to control *A. gossypii* on cucumbers (Pettit 1993). However, the cost of lacewing larvae is quite high, and there is very little reproduction of this species in the greenhouse. In addition, larvae must be released onto each aphid infested plant or plant foliage must be interlocking for biological control from lacewing larval releases to be successful (Heinz 1998b). The predatory gall midge *Aphidoletes aphidomyza* (Rondani) has given good control of aphids in many northern greenhouses (Markkula et al. 1979, Gilkeson and Hill 1987), but results of evaluation studies conducted in more southern regions are lacking (LeFevre and Adams 1982). The native coccinellid, *Diomus terminatus* (Say) as been suggested for the biological control of greenhouse aphids (Osborne, 2003). This predator occurs in Florida greenhouses and is reported by growers to be very effective. Hallborg (2003) studied its biology and developed rearing systems for this predator. He considered it a potential candidate for use in Florida greenhouses.

Various fungi have been proposed as candidates for managing pest aphids. One species, *Verticillium lecanii* (Zimmerman) Viégas, was commercially formulated and used for *M. persicae* control in England (Hall 1985). Critical environmental factors affecting *V. lecanii's* efficacy are the need for high humidity and cooler temperatures. Maximum infection occurs only if free water is present. In the United States, commercial formulations of the fungus *Beauveria bassiana* (Balsamo) Vuillernin has been used successfully to control aphid in research trials, yet widespread use of this fungus for control of aphid outbreaks in foliage plants has not been documented (Heinz 1998a; Murphy, Von Damm-Kattari, and Parrella 1999).

Mealybugs

Mealybugs are important pests of foliage plants grown in protected culture or in interior landscapes such as hotel lobbies, malls, or restaurants. Since the importation of new species and the loss of the systemic pesticides aldicarb and oxamyl in the United States, mealybugs and scales have become more difficult for U.S. growers to control. As a result, growers have an increased interest in biological control as an alternative. Fortunately, many parasitoids, predators, and fungal diseases attack mealybugs (Copland et al. 1985, Goolsby 1994). In addition, greenhouse temperatures may be manipulated to favor population growth of predators and parasitoids to the detriment of the mealybug pest population (Copland and Varley 1987).

Suppression of the citrus mealybug, *Planococcus citri* (Risso), for four months after establishment of several encyrtid parasitoid species in greenhouse citrus (Summy, French, and Hart 1986) represents the best-documented case of biological control of a mealybug in protected culture. Most attempts to control mealybugs in commercial settings have resulted in less than acceptable control, primarily due to improper identification of the pest mealybugs. There are several mealybugs that cause significant problems and matching the pest with the appropriate natural enemy is key to the success of biological control. One pest, the long-tailed mealybug (*P. longispinus*), is a poor host for the para-

sitoids that are commonly purchased for control of mealybugs, i.e., *Leptomastix dactylopii* Howard, *Leptomastidea abnormis* Girault and *Anagyrus pseudococci* (Girault) (Goolsby 1994, Copland et al. 1985). In contrast, longtailed mealybugs infesting pothos (*Epipremnum aureum* [Linden and Andréy] Bunt) planted in hotel atria can be permanently suppressed by establishment of the encyrtid wasp *Pseudaphycus angelicus* (Howard) (Goolsby 1994), a species that is not sold commercially.

Predators, which are frequently less host-specific than are parasitoids, have also been examined for biological control of mealybugs. The mealybug destroyer, *Cryptolaemus montrouzieri* Mulsant (Coccinellidae), is useful against most mealybugs if densities are high. However, the densities needed for establishment and oviposition of this predator are probably too high to be acceptable on most ornamental plants. Also, the large size of the adults and the resemblance of the larvae to mealybugs are objectionable to some producers or end users, especially if plants are in hotels or restaurants. Other predators such as the green lacewings *Chrysoperla carnea* (Stephens) and *C. rufilabris* against mealybugs have also been unable to provide consistent successful mealybug control.

Other Arthropod Pests

Many species of soft scales (Coccidae) attack foliage plants (Hamon and Williams 1984), but there have been few attempts to use natural enemies to control them. Hamlen (1975) demonstrated the effective integration of pesticides with the parasitoid *Encyrtus infelix* Embleton to control hemispherical scale (*Saissetia coffeae* [Walker]), yet the parasitoid remains unavailable from commercial insectaries and the program has not been implemented in commercial nurseries. False oleander scale (*P. cockerelli*) is considered the most important diaspidid scale pest of ornamentals in Florida (Dekle 1976). There are few known natural enemies of this scale and management of this pest relies on culling of infested plants and aggressive use of pesticides. For example, in some situations, the brown soft scale (*Coccus hesperidum* L.) can be permanently controlled in indoor plantscapes after establishing a population of the encyrtid wasp *Metaphycus alberti* (Howard) (Stauffer and Rose 1997).

Whiteflies are an occasional problem on foliage plants. On some plants (e.g., *Aphelandra squarrosa* Nees or *Hedera helix* L.) The damage threshold is exceedingly low because as few as five nymphs on a leaf can result in significant chlorosis and damage to newly developed leaves (Osborne et al. 1990). Other plants having much higher damage thresholds are candidates for biological control either through releases of the commercially available parasitoid *Eretmocerus eremicus* Rose and Zolnerowhich or through natural controls by natural enemies indigenous to the area.

Banana moth (*O. sacchari*) can devastate potted ornamental plants in both nurseries and interior landscapes (Peña, Schroeder, and Osborne 1990). Applications of the entomogenous nematodes *S. feltiae* or *Heterorhabditis bacteriophora* (=*heliothidis*) Poinar directed to the sites of infestation can result in 58 to100% reduction of larval numbers (Ibid.). Nematode applications are frequently used by growers releasing predatory mites against *T. urticae* on palms as a way of saving their highly effective biological control programs. The most common method for control of foliage feeding Lepidoptera is to make preventative applications of *Bacillus thuringiensis* Berliner subsp. *kurstaki*.

Effective methods for biological control of thrips on foliage crops are not available. There are a number of pest thrips that attack foliage plants, but all of them are being controlled chemically at this time.

Other Pests

Damage from snails and slugs results from the feeding on plant tissues, but more important they are quarantine pests of most states and the presence of certain species prohibits international or interstate movement of infested plants. As a result, growers rely on the use of molluscicides to provide complete control of snails and slugs. Foliar applications of molluscicides can disrupt the use of predatory mites for biological control of *T. urticae*. Bait formulations of molluscicides are less damaging, but some baits deteriorate very quickly and acceptable control is difficult to achieve. Recently available formulations that last longer appear to be gaining grower acceptance and may allow slug and mite control to be integrated.

IPM on Foliage Crops

The prospects for developing integrated control programs for foliage plants improved during the 1990s. Selective compounds that are less likely to disrupt the actions of beneficial insects and mites are common and provide effective control of the target pest.

For example, use of imidacloprid in ivy (*H. helix*) crops offers long-term control of most Homoptera such as aphids and whiteflies, together with acceptable suppression of *Echinothrips americanus* Morgan, a foliar feeding thrips. In combination with imidacloprid, biweekly releases of the predatory mite *N. californicus* can suppress both *T. urticae* and broad mites on the crop. This program has been used successfully in demonstration plots.

Several problems remain that limit implementation of biological control programs in foliage plants (Osborne et al. 1994). One important limiting factor is the lack of scouts and good scouting programs. With very few exceptions (see Parrella et al. 1989), statistically valid yet economically feasible sampling and/or monitoring for pests and their natural enemies are not available to growers or their scouts. A second problem delaying the adoption of biological control methods is the perceived competitive superiority of chemical control to provide cheap and effective control solutions. For example, in the 1980s, Florida foliage growers were achieving less than acceptable levels of mite control using the pesticides available to them. Sensing a crisis, many growers were ready to adopt the use of *P. persimilis* to control *T. urticae*. Adoption of any new control strategy requires that individual growers make specific adjustments. During this adjustment period, growers are susceptible to casting aside long-term solutions in favor of returning to the comfortable short-term strategies. During the mite biological control adjustment period the highly effective miticide, abamectin, was registered for use on foliage crops. As a result, most growers lost

interest in learning the new biological control tactic. Recently, mite control has again become increasingly more difficult in Florida. Some chemicals have been removed from the market and many growers feel that *T. urticae* and *P. latus* are now resistant to abamectin. As growers begin to show renewed interest in biological mite control, it will likely be subjected to competition to another suite of new chemical control products. Whether the above cycle will repeat itself is yet to be seen.

While basing all pest management solutions in ornamental foliage plants on biological control is not possible, there is a critical need to integrate biological control with existing cultural and chemical controls. Important to the entire industry is the collective need to preserve the current pesticides that are safe, effective, and registered. These materials have to be considered a valuable common resource and be managed appropriately. Development of resistance to these pesticides would be of great concern, since in many cases there are no effective and feasible alternative control strategies. The use of biological controls during specific phases in the production of ornamental plants will slow the development of resistance in some target pests.

Current Trends

Two of the largest growers in Florida are rigorously pursuing natural enemy mass production programs. One grower in South Florida began the production of *B. bassiana, P. fumosoroseus,* and *P. persimilis* five years ago. This has proven so effective he has begun to develop rearing systems for mealybug and scale natural enemies. He also has plans to begin production of fungi that can be used to control plant pathogens. The other company is located in central Florida and has a rearing system for *N. californicus*. This facility continues to purchase *N. californicus* but doesn't release them directly into their crops. Their program utilizes a banker plant system with corn plants infested with the Banks grass mite, *Oligonychus pratensis* (Banks). This mite does not feed on ivy or croton, which are the crops being protected from *T. urticae* and *P. latus*. The Banks grass mite serves as an excellent alternate host for *N. californicus* and other mite predators. When the predatory mites arrive from the producer they are distributed on the Banks grass mite-infested corn plants, which are then dispersed throughout the crop to be protected. The predatory mites increase in numbers on the corn plants and then move into the crop. The grower feels this makes the use of predatory mites economical and, during this past year, has tripled the acreage on which the system is used. Banker plants also serve as a method to check the quality of commercially obtained predatory mites. Because of the success this grower has had with biological control of mites he is developing other mass rearing systems for other natural enemies.

References Cited

Copland, M. J. W., C. C. D. Tingle, M. Saynor, and A. Panis. 1985. Biology of glasshouse mealybugs and their predators and parasitoids. In *Biological Pest Control: The Glasshouse Experience*, ed. N. W. Hussey and N. E. A. Scopes, 82–6. Ithaca, N.Y.: Cornell University Press (Poole, U.K.: Blandford).

Copland, M. J. W., and M. J. Varley. 1987. Progress in developing a controlled glasshouse environment to promote biological pest control. *IOBC/WPRS Bulletin* 2 (10):41–5.

Dekle, G. W. 1976. *Florida Armored Scale Insects: Arthropods of Florida and Neighboring Land Areas*, Vol. 3., 2d print (rev.). Gainesville, Fla.: Florida Dept. of Agriculture and Consumer Services, Div. of Plant Industry.

French, N., W. J. Parr, H. J. Gould, J. J. Williams, and S. P. Simmonds. 1976. Development of biological methods for the control of *Tetranychus urticae* on tomatoes using *Phytoseiulus persimilis*. *Annals of Applied Biology* 83:177–89.

Gerson, V. 1992. Biology and control of the broad mite, *Polyphagotarsonemus latus* (Banks) (Acari: Tarsonemidae). *Experimental and Applied Acarology* 13:163–78.

Gilkeson, L. A., and S. B. Hill. 1987. Release rates for control of green peach aphid (Homoptera: Aphidiidae) by the predatory midge *Aphidoletes aphidomyza* (Diptera: Cecidomyiidae) under winter greenhouse conditions. *Journal of Economic Entomology* 80 (1):147–50.

Gillespie D. R., and D. M. J. Quiring. 1990. Biological control of fungus gnats, *Bradysia* spp. (Diptera: Sciaridae), and western flower thrips, *Frankliniella occidentalis* (Pergande) (Thysanoptera: Thripidae), in greenhouses using a soil-dwelling predatory mite, *Geolaelaps* sp. nr. *aculeifer* (Canestrini) (Acari: Laelapidae). *Canadian Entomologist* 122:975–83.

Grasswitz, T. R. 1998. Effect of adult experience on the host-location behavior of the aphid parasitoid *Aphidius colemani* Viereck (Hymenoptera: Aphidiidae). *Biological Control* 12 (3):177–81.

Goolsby, J. A., III. 1994. Biological control of longtailed mealybug, *Pseudococcus longispinus* (Targioni-Tozzetti) (Homoptera: Pseudococcidae) in the interior plantscape. Ph.D. diss., Department of Entomology, Texas A&M University, College Station.

Hall, R. A. 1985. Aphid control by fungi. In *Biological Pest Control: The Glasshouse Experience*, ed. N. W. Hussey and N. E. A. Scopes, 138–41. N.Y.: Cornell University Press (Poole, U.K.: Blandford).

Hallborg, K. M. 2003. Biology and rearing of *Diomus terminatus* (Coleoptera: Coccinellidae) on *Rhopalosiphum maidis* (Homoptera: Aphididae) and artificial diet. Master's thesis, Department of Entomology and Nematology, University of Florida, Gainesville, FL.

Hamlen, R. A. 1975. Survival of hemispherical scale and an *Encyrtus* parasitoid after treatment with insect growth regulators and insecticides. *Environmental Entomology* 4:972–4.

———. 1978. Biological control of spider mites on greenhouse ornamentals using predaceous mites. *Proceedings of the Florida State Horticultural Society* 91: 247–9.

———. 1980. Report of *Phytoseiulus persimilis* management of *Tetranychus urticae* on greenhouse-grown dieffenbachia. *IOBC/WPRS Bulletin* 3:65–74.

Hamlen, R. A., and R. K. Lindquist. 1981. Comparison of two *Phytoseiulus* species as predators of two-spotted spider mites on greenhouse ornamentals. *Environmental Entomology* 10:524–7.

Hamon, A. B., and M. L. Williams. 1984. *The Soft Scale Insects of Florida (Homoptera: Coccoidea): Arthropods of Florida and Neighboring Land Areas,* Vol. 11. Gainesville, Fla: Florida Department of Agriculture and Consumer Services, Div. of Plant Industry.

Heinz, K. M. 1998a. Biological control approaches for southern nursery and greenhouse growers. *Proceedings of the Southern Nursery Association Research Conference.* 43:154–7.

Heinz, K. M. 1998b. Dispersal and dispersion of aphids (Homoptera: Aphidiidae) and selected natural enemies in spatially subdivided greenhouse environments. *Environmental Entomology* 27 (4):1029–38.

Hofsvang, T. and E. B. Hågvar. 1978. Biological control of the green peach aphid (*Myzus persicae*) (Sulzer) on greenhouse paprika. Two methods of parasite introduction (*Ephedrus cerasicola* Stary) biological control. *Kontoret for informasjon og rettleiing i landbruk* 26 (6):565–72.

Hudson, W. G., M. P. Garber, R. D. Oetting, R. F. Mizell, A. R. Chase, and K. Bondari. 1996. Pest management in the United States greehouse and nursery industry: V. Insect and mite control. *HortTech* 6(3):216–21.

Hunter, C. D. 1997. *Suppliers of Beneficial Organisms in North America* (PM 97-01). Sacramento, Calif.: California Environmental Protection Agency.

LeFevre, V. F., and R. G. Adams. 1982. Bibliography of the aphid predator, *Aphidoletes aphidomyza* (Diptera: Cecidomyiidae) biological control of phytophagous pests. *Bulletin of the Entomological Society of America* 28 (2):129–33.

Lindquist, R. K., J. Buxton, and J. Piatkowski. 1994. Biological control of sciarid flies and shore flies in glasshouses. In *Brighton Crop Protection Conference on Pests and Diseases 1994: Proceedings of an International Conference*, Vol. 3, 1067–72. Farnham, U.K.: British Crop Protection Council.

Markkula, M. and K. Tiittanen. 1976. "Pest in first" and "natural infestation" methods in the control of *Tetranychus urticae* Koch with *Phytoseiulus persimilis* Athias-Henriot on glasshouse cucumbers. *Annales Agriculture Fenniae* 15:81–5.

Markkula, M., K. Tiittanen, M. Hämäläinen, and A. Forsberg. 1979. The aphid midge *Aphidoletes aphidomyza* (Diptera: Cecidomyiidae) and its use in biological control of aphids. *Annales Entomologici Fennici* 45:89–98

Messing, R. H., and J. M. Rabasse. 1995. Oviposition behavior of the polyphagous aphid parasitoid *Aphidius colemani* Viereck (Hymenoptera: Aphidiidae). *Agriculture, Ecosystem and Environment* 52 (1):13–7.

Murphy, B., D. Von Damm-Kattari, and M. P. Parrella. 1999. Interaction between fungal pathogens and natural enemies: Implication for combined biocontrol of greenhouse pests. *IOBC/WPRS Bulletin* 22 (1):181–4.

Osborne, L. S. 1986. Dip treatment of tropical ornamental foliage cuttings in fluvalinate to prevent spread of insect and mite infestations. *Journal of Economic Entomology* 79:465–70.

Osborne, L. S. 2003. Biological cntrol of foliage pests. *Society of American Florists' 19th Annual Conference on Insect and Disease Management on Ornamentals* 19:36–48.

Osborne, L. S., K. A. Hoelmer, and R. K. Yokomi. 1990. Foliage disorders in Florida associated with feeding by the sweetpotato whitefly, *Bemisia tabaci*. In *Sweetpotato Whitefly Mediated Vegetable Disorders in Florida*, ed. R. K. Yokomi, K. R. Narayanan, and D. J. Schuster, 49–52. Miami, Fla.: University of Florida and Lumoprint.

Osborne, L. S., J. E. Peña, R. L. Ridgway, and W. Klausen. 1998. Predaceous mites for mite management on ornamentals in protected cultures. In *Mass Reared Natural Enemies: Application, Regulation, and Needs*, ed. R. L. Ridgway, M. P. Hoffman, M. N. Inscoe, and C. Glenister, 116–38. Lanham, Md.: Entomological Society of America.

Osborne L. S., F. L. Petitt, Z. Landa, and K. A. Hoelmer. 1994. Biological control of pests attacking crops grown in protected cultivation: The Florida experience. In *Pest Management in the Subtropics: Biological Control—A Florida Perspective*, ed. D. Rosen, F. D. Bennett, and J.L. Capinera, 327–42, Andover, U.K.: Intercept.

Parrella, M. L., V. P. Jones, M. S. Malais, and K. M. Heinz. 1989. Advances in sampling in ornamentals. *Florida Entomologist* 72:394–403.

Peña, J. E., and L. Osborne. 1996. Biological control of *Polyphagotarsonemus latus* (Acarina: Tarsonemidae) in greenhouses and field trials using introductions of predacious mites (Acarina: Phytoseiidae). *Entomophaga* 41:279–85.

Peña, J. E., W. J. Schroeder, and L. S. Osborne. 1990. Use of entomogenous nematodes of the families Heterorhabditidae and Steinernematidae to control banana moth (*Opogona sacchari*). *Nematropica* 20 (1):51–5.

Petitt, F. L. 1993. Biological control in the integrated pest management program at The Land, EPCOT. Center. *IOBC/WPRS Bulletin* 16 (2):129–32.

Stauffer, S., and M. Rose. 1997. Biological control of soft scale insects in interior plantscapes in the USA. In *Soft Scale Insects: Their Biology, Natural Enemies and Control*, vol. 7b, ed. Y. Ben-Dov and C. J. Hodgson, 183–205. Amsterdam: Elsevier.

Summy, K. R., J. V. French, and W. G. Hart. 1986. Citrus mealybug (Homoptera: Pseudococcidae) on greenhouse citrus: Density-dependent regulation by an encyrtid parasite complex. *Journal of Economic Entomology* 79:891–5.

24

BIOLOGICAL CONTROL IN WOODY ORNAMENTALS

P. M. Shrewsbury
Department of Entomology
University of Maryland, College Park, Maryland

and

M. J. Raupp
Department of Entomology
University of Maryland, College Park, Maryland

Woody ornamental plants are a major growing component of the wholesale and retail nursery industry in the United States. Nursery plants grown under protected culture have an annual value of several billion dollars nationwide (Decker 1997). This estimate includes not only woody plants grown in containers and liners under glass but also those grown in hoop houses, on gravel pads, and in fields. The pest complex and opportunities for biological control vary with the type of production system, type of plant material, geographic location, duration of the production cycle, and the market for the plants.

For biological control programs to be effective, they must be tailored to the pest's host-plant range and environmental conditions within which the system operates. Two-spotted spider mite (*Tetranychus urticae* Koch) is often not an important pest on many woody plants when grown outdoors. However, Smith, Orr, and Hart (1993) found *T. urticae* to be a severe pest of poplars (*Populus* spp.) grown under glass. Hence, one biological control strategy will not fit all growing situations. Some pests such as two-spotted and spruce spider mites (*Oligonychus ununguis* [Jacobi]), black vine weevil (*Otiorhynchus sulcatus* [Fabricius]) (fig. 24.1), and many aphid species attack many different plant species. Others such as the azalea lace bug (*Stephanitis pyrioides* [Scott]), gypsy moth (*Lymantria dispar* [Linnaeus]), and ash whitefly (*Siphoninus phillyreae* [Haliday]) attack relatively few plant species. In most cases, biological control is easier to obtain in plant systems harboring few rather than numerous plant pests.

The market for the crop will also have a significant effect on the feasibility of implementing specific types of biological control. Extremely low levels of insect and mite injury often render woody plants in retail nurseries unmarketable (Sadof and Raupp 1987). This clearly reduces the potential for biological

Figure 24.1. Adult black vine weevil (*Otiorhynchus sulcatus* [Fabricius]) attacks many different species of woody plants grown in commercial greenhouses and nurseries. *Photo: S. Gill.*

control where the natural enemies used require multiple seasons to reduce pest populations or are unable to reduce pest populations below economic thresholds. However, this extreme intolerance to insect and mite injury is frequently less severe during the years of production prior to the time of sale. Quarantine regulations, which when enforced prohibit the movement of infested plant material across geographic boundaries, prevent sole reliance on biological control but not its utilization in an integrated management program.

Despite the numerous challenges associated with full implementation in woody ornamental plant production systems, opportunities for use of biological control of insect and mite pests of woody plants in protected culture have increased significantly during the past two decades. While there have been relatively few attempts to implement comprehensive IPM programs based on biological control in woody ornamental crops, many examples exist of programs that have

enhanced levels of biological control on woody plants in protected culture.

Classical Biological Control

Classical biological control has not been widely explored as a direct approach for managing insect and mite pests of woody plants in protected culture. The most significant effects of classical biological control in nurseries have come as ancillary benefits of importation efforts directed at forest and landscape pests. Many of these programs have reduced forest and landscape pest populations on an area wide basis, thereby reducing pest abundance in nurseries. These efforts date back to some of the earliest successes with classical biological control such as the area-wide reduction of the cottony cushion scale (*Icérya púrchasi* Maskell) by the Vedalia beetle (*Rodòlia cardinàlis* [Mulsant]). Cottony cushion scale has a broad host range and is a pest of many nursery crops. While this premier example of classical biological control is credited with saving the citrus industry in California, the impacts of this program clearly extend to many types of ornamental plants grown in protected culture. Other recent cases further demonstrate the importance of classical biological control in protected culture.

The ash whitefly, *S. phillyreae*, invaded southern California in 1988 and caused in excess of $200 million dollars worth of damage to woody landscape plants annually (Pickett et al. 1996). Soon after invading the region, ash whitefly (fig. 24.2) became established in nurseries throughout the state and hampered normal operations such as the interstate shipment of woody landscape

Figure 24.2. The ash whitefly (*Siphoninus phillyreae* [Haliday]), an exotic pest to the United States, became established in California nurseries, hampering normal operations such as the interstate shipment of woody landscape plants. The pest was eventually controlled by the introduction of a parasitoid that parasitized the nymphal stage of the whitefly (the stage shown above) as part of a classical biological control program. *Photo: M. P. Parrella.*

plants. After the introduction of the parasitoid *Encarsia inaron* (Walker) from Europe, populations of the whitefly declined dramatically on a regional basis and significant levels of biological control occurred in nurseries as well as in landscapes (T. Paine, pers. comm.).

In the eastern United States, the gypsy moth has been a key pest of natural and urban forests for more than a century (Doane and McManus 1981). This pest has become a significant pest in nurseries and tree plantations, especially in the northeast and mid-Atlantic area (Davidson et al. 1988). In these areas, nurseries and greenhouses are often interspersed with forest stands that serve as reservoirs for the gypsy moth. During the last decade, the fungal pathogen *Entomophaga maimaiga* Humber, Shimazu and Soper has spread rapidly throughout the northeast region, decimating gypsy moth populations (Reardon and Hajek 1997). This pathogen has made gypsy moth a far less serious problem in protected culture than was the case a decade ago.

Introductions of the sevenspotted lady beetle, *Coccinella septempunctata* L., helped reduce aphids in agricultural crops (Angalet, Tropp, and Eggert 1979; Horn 1996). However, this beetle now occurs in a number of crop production systems and is regularly found in nurseries (Staines, Rothschild, and Trumbule 1990). The lady beetle *Harmonia axyridis* (Pallas) was originally imported to control aphids in pecan plantations in the southern United States. It is now widely dispersed throughout the country and feeds on a variety of aphids in arboreal habitats and nurseries. The predatory beetles *Chilocorus kuwanae* (Silvestri) and *Cybocephalus* sp. nr. *nipponicus* Endrody-Younga were imported for control of the euonymus scale, *Unaspis euonymi* (Comstock), in landscapes (Drea and Carlson 1990). Release of these beetles is providing significant control of euonymus scale in eastern nurseries (R. Chianese, pers. comm.).

Augmentative Releases of Natural Enemies

In this section, the groups of natural enemies most commonly used in augmentative releases on woody ornamentals, such as predatory beetles and mites, lacewings, and pathogens, are discussed. Other groups of natural enemies such as true bugs and parasitoids have been used mainly in experimental settings or only anecdotal information is available. Therefore, they will not be discussed here.

Predacious beetles

There have been many attempts to reduce insect and mite pests in protected culture through the augmentation of natural enemies. Most studies have examined the releases of predatory insects and mites, nematodes, and pathogens under laboratory or experimental greenhouse conditions. Few have been conducted in commercial operations. With respect to predator releases, one of the most widely promoted predators with potential use in nurseries is the convergent lady beetle, *Hippodamia convergens* Guérin-Méneville. Dreistadt and Flint (1996) noted that despite long-standing beliefs that releases of *H. convergens* were ineffective, relatively few rigorous studies have been conducted to evaluate efficacy of this predator. Raupp et al. (1994) found releases of *H. convergens* and *C. septempunctata* to effectively reduce spirea aphid, *Aphis spiraecola* Patch, on potted firethorn (*Pyracantha coccinea* Roem 'Lalandei') in the greenhouse only when placing firethorns in cages restricted dispersal of beetles. Beetles released on uncaged firethorns rapidly dispersed from plants and left the greenhouse via the vents. In the same study, Raupp et al. (1954) found a woolly aphid, *Erisoma* sp., attacked by neither species of lady beetle even when plants were enclosed in cages. In a similar study, Flint et al. (1995) reported significant reductions in numbers of rose aphids feeding on roses following releases of *H. convergens* on potted plants outdoors. Unlike the study by Raupp et al. (1994), Flint et al. (1995) found that *H. convergens* remained on potted roses several days after the release.

Lacewings

At least two studies have examined the ability of lacewings (Chrysopidae) to reduce populations of pest aphids and true bugs in nursery settings. White fir, *Abies concolor* (Gord. and Glend.), is regularly attacked by the aphid *Mindaris kinseyi* Voegtlin in nursery plantations in the western United States. Ehler and Kinsey (1995) described a comprehensive approach to managing this pest that involved regular monitoring, the use of decision-making guidelines, and a variety of intervention strategies. During the first year of their field demonstration, regular releases of *Chrysoperla rufilabris* (Burmeister) larvae alone and in conjunction with applications of insecticidal soaps reduced the number of seedlings damaged. In the second year of the study, releases of *C. rufilabris* in aphid-infested patches reduced aphid populations to undetectable levels for more than three weeks in 69% of the study plots. This experiment was repeated using *Chrysoperla carnea* (Stephens) larvae with similar results. Aphid populations were significantly reduced for a period of three weeks following the release of *C. carnea* and a 65% reduction in plants injured by aphids was reported.

Recently Shrewsbury and Smith-Fiola (2000) evaluated the ability of *C. carnea* larvae to reduce populations of azalea lace bugs, *S. pyrioides*, infesting azaleas in commercial nurseries. A series of greenhouse studies using containerized azaleas determined that inundative releases of *C. carnea* could reduce lace bug populations by as much as 96% on individual plants. A release rate of one green lacewing to eight or sixteen azalea lace bug nymphs resulted in 86% and 68%

lace bug mortality, respectively. Studies conducted on containerized azaleas in a commercial nursery revealed that *C. carnea* provided levels of control comparable to those obtained by conventional insecticides. A second field release also conducted in a wholesale nursery under normal production conditions confirmed the results of the previous smaller scale studies. The second field release revealed that single releases at an average rate of one green lacewing to three lace bugs reduced lace bug populations by more than 95%. Both Ehler and Kinsey (1995) and Shrewsbury and Smith-Fiola (2000) found that lacewings readily dispersed from release sites and were rarely recovered even a few days following release.

Predatory mites

Predatory mites have been investigated for use in augmentative releases to control pests of roses. One of the first attempts to use predatory mites to manage spider mites was conducted by Boys and Burbutis (1972) who made sequential releases of *Phytoseiulus persimilis* Athias-Henriot on potted roses infested with two-spotted spider mites, *T. urticae*, in a greenhouse. Several weeks after the release, predators virtually eliminated spider mites from the roses. Simmonds (1972) also examined releases of *P. persimilis* at three densities to reduce two-spotted spider mite populations on roses. Spider mite populations collapsed at all three predator densities within two months of the release. Zhang and Sanderson (1995) successfully managed two-spotted spider mite populations on potted roses in greenhouses with multiple releases of *P. persimilis*. *Phytoseiulus persimilis* nearly eliminated populations of *T. urticae* after one

month. Gough (1991) achieved long-term cycling of *T. urticae* and *P. persimilis* populations on hedge roses grown under normal production conditions in plastic covered tunnels. Multiple releases of predators provided excellent control of spider mites with no economic losses for the thirty-month period of the study (Ibid.). Hamlen and Lindquist (1981) released *Phytoseiulus macropilis* (Banks) on roses (*Rosa* sp.) in mixed plantings with schefflera (*Schefflera actinophylla* [Endl.]) and dracaena (*Dracaena sandeirana* Hort.). Within a month, predators released at two different densities reduced two-spotted spider mite populations by more than 80%. However, see chapter 22 for complications in spider mite biological control in roses due to the practice of sulfur vaporization for control of powdery mildew.

Augmentative releases of predatory mites have also been used to control pests of other woody plants. Multiple releases of the predatory mites *P. persimilis* and *Neoseiulus californicus* (McGregor) proved equally efficacious and more cost effective than applications of conventional miticides for controlling populations of *T. urticae* attacking poplars in a research greenhouse (Smith, Orr, and Hart 1993). Cashion, Bixler, and Price (1994) used multiple releases of *P. persimilis* to effectively manage *T. urticae* populations on 2,500 areca palms, *Chrysalidocarpus lutescens* H. Wendl., grown in one-gallon containers in open greenhouses. Augmentative releases of this predatory mite provided better control than miticides applied at ten to fourteen day intervals. In a similar study conducted under laboratory conditions, Boyne and Hain (1983) were able to dramatically reduce populations of spruce spider mite, *O. ununguis*, on small Fraser fir, *Abies fraseri* (Pursh) Poir., seedlings by releasing single gravid females of the predatory mite *Neoseiulus fallacis* (Garman). Populations of spider mites were reduced by more than 70% on seedlings receiving predatory mites after three weeks.

Pratt and Croft (1998) achieved high levels of control of citrus red mite, *Panonychus citri* (McGregor), on *Skimmia japonica* Thunberg growing in containers in a nursery by releasing three adult females of *N. fallacis* per plant. In a later study Pratt and Croft (2000b) investigated the use of *N. fallacis, N. californicus* and *Galendromus occidentalis* (Nesbitt) to control populations of *T. urticae* on rootstock of apples and on small field-grown maples and spiraea. Levels of control by *N. fallacis* ranged from 0 to about 90% and control improved as the season progressed. The same pattern was found for *N. californicus* released on maple and spiraea. *Galendromus occidentalis* also produced good control of mites on apple and maple by the end of the season. Pratt and Croft (2000b) also released *N. fallacis and N. californicus* to control *Oligonychus illicis* (McGregor) on *Rhododendron* and found that *N. fallacis* provided relatively good levels of control, up to 90%, while *N. californicus* provided no detectable reduction in mite populations.

Pratt, Rosetta, and Croft (2002) evaluated *N. fallacis* releases in outdoor beds of several kinds of herbaceous and woody landscape plants infested with *T. urticae, O. ununguis, O. illicis*, and *Panonychus citri* (McGregor). Plant morphology and foliage density affected the success of the predator release with unacceptable and moderate levels of control on tall, vertical plants with sparse canopies. Low-growing and some dense-canopied tall plants also experienced acceptable levels of control. Control was equally effective on field grown and containerized plants and the species of spider mite targeted for release did not affect the level of control. Skirvin and De Courcy Williams (1999) also examined the effects of prey abundance and plant species on the movement of the predatory mite *P. persimilis*. While plant species did not affect the movement of the predator, the density of prey, *T. urticae*, and structure of the host plant did. Predators were more active at low prey densities.

Shrewsbury and Hardin (2003) evaluated sequential releases of *N. fallacis* and *G. occidentalis* singly and in combination to control *O. ununguis* on containerized junipers. Releases were based on the grower's estimation of mite abundance and perception of damage. The efficacy and cost effectiveness of releases based on grower recommendations and release rates recommended by the supplier of the predator were compared to applications of conventional miticides. Predators reduced spider mites by 10-20%, compared to about 50% with miticides. Predators did not prevent plant injury. The cost of predatory mite releases was 2 to 7 times greater than the application of miticides. Shrewsbury and Hardin (2003) recommend the development of better methods for estimating target mite abundance and basing predator release rates on ratios of predator and prey densities rather than by production units such as plants or beds.

Entomopathogenic nematodes

Van Tol and Raupp (in press) reviewed more than fifty studies involving the use of entomopathogenic nematodes to control several pests of woody plants growing in containers and open nursery fields. Augmentative releases of *Heterorhabditis* and *Steinernema* species have been evaluated in nursery settings for control of larvae of root feeding Coleoptera such as the black vine weevil (fig. 24.3) and Japanese beetle (*Popillia japonica* Newman). Levels of control of both pests can be quite high, often exceeding 90% in both containers and the field. In general *Heterorhabditis* species provide better control of these pests than *Steinernema*. While control generally increases with the application rate, Van Tol and Raupp (in press) recommended rates of 0.5 x 10^6 / 1 liter for containers and 1.0 x 10^6 / m^2 for field applications. Soil temperatures should exceed 12° C at the time of the release in containers and for field applications soil temperatures should exceed 12° C for at least one week following the application. Control of wood boring beetles, including Scolytidae and Cerambycidae, with nematodes has been poor to moderate (15-60%). Control of leaf beetles was moderate (50-70%). Root and wood boring caterpillars showed variable levels of control, but in several cases such as the iris borer, carpenter worm, and clearwing borers, control using *Steinernema* species exceeded 90%. Variable levels of control (0-98%) have been observed for defoliating caterpillars and sawflies (Van Tol and Raupp in press). In addition to the variables enumerated above, host plant and the levels of injury may also affect efficacy of nematodes. In general conifers such as *Thuja* and *Taxus* are more attractive to *Heterorhabditis* than angiosperms and plants wounded by root weevils are more attractive than undamaged plants (Van Tol and Raupp in press).

Entomopathogenic fungi

Recently, there has been increased interest in the use of fungi as augmentative control agents. Moorhouse et al. (1993) evaluated the use of *Metarhizium anisopliae* (Metchnikoff) as a control agent for black vine weevil feeding on twenty-two genera of woody plants growing in containers. Larval control was highly variable, ranging from 0 to 96%, and dependent on the type of plant material evaluated and strain of fungus applied. Van Tol (1993a,b) found that *M. anisopliae* provided moderate (50%) to excellent (90%) control of black vine weevil when used alone or in combination with nematodes in containers and the field.

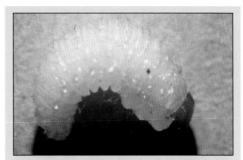

Figure 24.3. The larva of the black vine weevil (*Otiorhynchus sulcatus* [Fabricius]) controlled in nursery pots by applications of entomopathogenic nematodes.
Photo: S. Gill.

Table 24.1. Releases of Predators to Manage Arthropod Pests of Woody Ornamentals in Protected Culture

Natural Enemy	Pest	Crop	Rate	Control	Reference
Beetles					
Hippodamia convergens	*Macrosiphum rosae*	*Rosa*	14–20 adults/ plant	~90%	Flint et al. 1995
Hippodamia convergens	*Aphis spiraecola*	*Pyracantha*	10/plant	~0–90%	Raupp et al. 1994
Hippodamia convergens	*Erisoma sp.*	*Pyracantha*	10/plant	0%	Raupp et al. 1994
Coccinella septempunctata	*Aphis spiraecola*	*Pyracantha*	10/plant	~0–80%	Raupp et al. 1994
Coccinella septempunctata	*Erisoma sp.*	*Pyracantha*	10/plant	0%	Raupp et al. 1994
Lacewings					
Chrysoperla rufilabris	*Mindarus kinseyi*	*Abies*	2 larvae/ seedling	~90%	Ehler and Kinsey 1995
Chrysoperla carnea	*Mindarus kinseyi*	*Abies*	100 larvae/ plot	~75%	Ehler and Kinsey 1995
Chrysoperla carnea	*Stephanitis pyrioides*	*Rhododendron*	5/plant	~79%	Shrewsbury and Smith-Fiola 2000
Chrysoperla carnea	*Stephanitis pyrioides*	*Rhododendron*	10/plant	~88%	Shrewsbury and Smith-Fiola 2000
Mites					
Phytoseiulus persimilis	*Tetranychus turkestani*	*Rosa*	20–40/plant	100%	Boys and Burbutis 1972
Phytoseiulus persimilis	*Tetranychus urticae*	*Rosa*	2–10/plant	100%	Simmonds 1972
Phytoseiulus persimilis	*Tetranychus urticae*	*Rosa*	N/A	~100%	Zhang and Sanderson 1995
Phytoseiulus persimilis	*Tetranychus urticae*	*Rosa*	21,000– 80,000/house	Excellent	Gough 1991

(continued)

Table 24.1. *(continued)*

Natural Enemy	Pest	Crop	Rate	Control	Reference
Phytoseiulus persimilis + Neoseiulus californicus	*Tetranychus urticae*	*Populus*	13/plant	Good	Smith et al. 1993
Phytoseiulus persimilis	*Tetranychus urticae*	*Chrysalido-carpus*	1–3/plant	~75%	Cashion et al. 1994
Phytoseiulus macropilis	*Tetranychus urticae*	*Rosa*	2–5/plant	80–>90%	Hamlen and Lindquist 1981
Neoseiulus fallacis	*Oligonychus ununguis*	*Abies*	1–3/plant	~75–80%	Boyne and Hain 1983
Neoseiulus fallacis	*Panonychus citri*	*Skimmia*	3/plant	~60-95%	Pratt and Croft 1998
Neoseiulus fallacis	*Tetranychus urticae*	*Malus*	2100/ha	~60-90%	Pratt and Croft 2000b
Neoseiulus fallacis	*Tetranychus urticae*	*Acer*	2/plant	~0-60%	Pratt and Croft 2000b
Neoseiulus fallacis	*Tetranychus urticae*	*Spirea*	5/35 m	~0-80%	Pratt and Croft 2000b
Neoseiulus fallacis	*Oligonychus illicis*	*Ilex*	N/A	~20-90%	Pratt and Croft 2000b
Neoseiulus californicus	*Tetranychus urticae*	*Acer*	2/plant	~0-70%	Pratt and Croft 2000b
Neoseiulus californicus	*Tetranychus urticae*	*Spirea*	5/35 m	~0-70%	Pratt and Croft 2000b
Neoseiulus californicus	*Oligonychus illicis*	*Ilex*	N/A	0%	Pratt and Croft 2000b
Galendromus occidentalis	*Tetranychus urticae*	*Malus*	2100/ha	~70-95%	Pratt and Croft 2000b
Galendromus occidentalis	*Tetranychus urticae*	*Acer*	2/plant	~0-50%	Pratt and Croft 2000b

(continued)

Table 24.1. *(continued)*

Natural Enemy	Pest	Crop	Rate	Control	Reference
Neoseiulus fallacis	*Tetranychus urticae*	*Acer*	3/plant	Unacceptable	Pratt et al. 2002
Neoseiulus fallacis	*Tetranychus urticae*	*Azalea*	0.25/plant	Acceptable	Pratt et al. 2002
Neoseiulus fallacis	*Tetranychus urticae*	*Buddleia*	2/plant	Acceptable	Pratt et al. 2002
Neoseiulus fallacis	*Tetranychus urticae*	*Euonymus*	2/plant	Acceptable	Pratt et al. 2002
Neoseiulus fallacis	*Tetranychus urticae*	*Ilex*	5/plant	Acceptable	Pratt et al. 2002
Neoseiulus fallacis	*Tetranychus urticae*	*Magnolia*	1/plant	Unacceptable	Pratt et al. 2002
Neoseiulus fallacis	*Tetranychus urticae*	*Malus*	4000/ha	Acceptable	Pratt et al. 2002
Neoseiulus fallacis	*Tetranychus urticae*	*Potentilla*	2/plant	Acceptable	Pratt et al. 2002
Neoseiulus fallacis	*Tetranychus urticae*	*Skimmia*	5/plant	Acceptable	Pratt et al. 2002
Neoseiulus fallacis	*Tetranychus urticae*	*Spirea* spp.	2-5/plant	Acceptable	Pratt et al. 2002
Neoseiulus fallacis	*Tetranychus urticae*	*Tilia*	2/plant	Unacceptable	Pratt et al. 2002
Neoseiulus fallacis	*Tetranychus urticae*	*Viburnum* spp.	2-3/plant	Acceptable	Pratt et al. 2002
Neoseiulus fallacis	*Tetranychus urticae*	*Viburnum*	7500/ha	Acceptable	Pratt et al. 2002
Neoseiulus fallacis	*Tetranychus urticae*	*Weigela*	2-5/plant	Acceptable	Pratt et al. 2002
Neoseiulus fallacis	*Oligonychus ununguis*	*Abies*	10/plant	Unacceptable	Pratt et al. 2002

(continued)

Table 24.1. *(continued)*

Natural Enemy	Pest	Crop	Rate	Control	Reference
Neoseiulus fallacis	*Oligonychus ununguis*	*Abies*	16,000/ha	Acceptable	Pratt et al. 2002
Neoseiulus fallacis	*Oligonychus ununguis*	*Picea*	5/plant	Acceptable	Pratt et al. 2002
Neoseiulus fallacis	*Oligonychus ununguis*	*Thuja*	3/plant (April)	Unacceptable	Pratt et al. 2002
Neoseiulus fallacis	*Oligonychus ununguis*	*Thuja*	3/plant (June)	Acceptable	Pratt et al. 2002
Neoseiulus fallacis	*Oligonychus ununguis*	*Thuja*	6/plant	Acceptable	Pratt et al. 2002
Neoseiulus fallacis	*Oligonychus illicis*	*Rhododendron*	2/plant	Acceptable	Pratt et al. 2002
Neoseiulus fallacis	*Panonychus citri*	*Skimmia*	10/plant	Acceptable	Pratt et al. 2002
Neoseiulus fallacis	*Oligonychus ununguis*	*Juniperus*	114/plant x 3 releases	~10%	Shrewsbury and Hardin 2003
Galendromus occidentalis	*Oligonychus ununguis*	*Juniperus*	114/plant x 3 releases	~15%	Shrewsbury and Hardin 2003
Neoseiulus fallacis + *Galendromus occidentalis*	*Oligonychus ununguis*	*Juniperus*	114/plant x 3 releases	~20%	Shrewsbury and Hardin 2003

Conservation of Natural Enemies

Perhaps the single most significant development that has facilitated the conservation of natural enemies of pests of woody plants in protected culture is the development, implementation, and widespread adoption of IPM programs. Prior to demonstration IPM programs in the 1980s, a survey of commercial nurseries in Pennsylvania revealed that on average 2.2 lbs. (1 kg) of active ingredient of insecticides and miticides were applied per acre each year to control pests (Shetlar and Hellar 1984). This rate has been greatly reduced by IPM programs that incorporate regular monitoring, decision-making guidelines, and the use of non-chemical and least toxic methods of intervention in place of traditional pesticide applications (Davidson and Cornell 1988, Studebaker 1992, Flint et al. 1993, Ehler and Kinsey 1995, Cowles and Abbey 1997). With the adoption of IPM, large reductions in pesticides have occurred. Davidson et al. (1988) reduced pesticide use by 98% in a commercial nursery in Maryland with the adoption of IPM. A commercial grower in Ohio was able to cut pesticide use in half with IPM (Studebaker 1992). Flint et al. (1993) reduced insecticide use in an institutional nursery by 40% by implementing IPM. Undoubtedly, pesticide reductions of this order do much to conserve natural enemy communities.

Relatively few studies have examined specific methods designed to conserve natural enemies in production nurseries. A notable exception is the work of Cowles and Abbey (1997). By eliminating or reducing the use of pyrethroids and carbamates, increasing the use of horticultural oil and selective miticides, and intervening only when dictated by results of careful pest monitoring, populations of predatory mites were conserved and further intervention was often unnecessary to control spider mites in commercial nurseries. This saved growers money and reduced their pesticide use by 77 to 99%. Similarly, Ehler and Kinsey (1995) combined careful monitoring with non-chemical tactics such as the use of reflective tape that reduced pest colonization of the crop, low impact insecticides (insecticidal soap), and predator releases to successfully manage aphids on seedlings in an institutional nursery.

Banker plants have been used as a technique for increasing the abundance and dispersal of predatory mites in greenhouses (Ramakers and Voet 1996). Pratt and Croft (2000a) discussed the potential use of banker plants to increase the abundance and dispersal of predatory mites in landscape nurseries.

Future Needs

Despite the progress made in implementing biological control for woody plants in protected culture, significant challenges remain. A recent survey conducted by the nursery industry revealed that only 18% of 114 wholesale nursery growers use IPM fully (Higginbotham 1993). Remarkably, 30% of the growers surveyed used pesticides on a fixed basis. The same study found that the majority of growers used IPM strategies that would clearly help to conserve natural enemies in nurseries such as monitoring (88%), careful pesticide selection and timing (79%), and using horticultural oils, soaps, or other alternatives (59%). However, relatively few growers used biological control (21%) or other cultural pest control methods (17%). When asked what could be done to increase adoption of IPM, growers suggested increased education of both the industry and the consumer and demonstration of the competitiveness and effectiveness of IPM. Other assessments of grower needs ranked the development of new biological tactics for several key pests including mites, weevils, scales, borers, lace bugs, and grubs and strategies for conserving biological control agents in nurseries as high priorities (Raupp and Hoitink 1996). Clearly, much work lies ahead before biological control becomes a reality for insect and mite pests of woody plants in protected culture.

References Cited

Angalet, G. W., J. M. Tropp, and A. N. Eggert. 1979. *Coccinella septempunctata* in the United States: Recolonization and notes on its ecology. *Environmental Entomology* 8:896–901.

Boyne, J. V., and F. P. Hain. 1983. Responses of *Neoseiulus fallacis* (Acarina: Phytoseiidae) to different prey densities of *Oligonychus unungis* (Acarina: Tetranychidae) and to different relative humidity regimes. *The Canadian Entomologist* 115:1607–14.

Boys, F. E., and P. P. Burbutis. 1972. Influence of *Phytoseiulus persimilis* on populations of *Tetranychus turkestani* at the economic threshold on roses. *Journal of Economic Entomology* 65:114–7.

Cashion, G. J., H. Bixler, and J. F. Price. 1994. Nursery IPM trials using predatory mites. *Proceedings of the Florida State Horticulture Society* 107: 220–2.

Cowles, R. S., and T. Abbey. 1997. Integration of biological and chemical controls is used to manage the two-spotted spider mite in container-grown nurseries. *Yankee Nursery Quarterly,* Spring, 18–9.

Davidson, J. A. and C. F. Cornell. 1988. IPM: Parts and parcel. What makes an effective pest control program? *American Nurseryman*, April, 80–91.

Davidson, J. A., C. F. Cornell, M. E. Zastrow, and D. C. Alban. 1988. Making the pilot fly. *American Nurseryman,* May, 51–60.

Decker, D. 1997. *Floriculture and Environmental Horticulture: Situation and Outlook Report, FLO-1997.* Washington, D.C.: U.S. Department of Agriculture, Economic Research Service.

Doane, C. C., and M. L. McManus, eds. 1981. *The Gypsy Moth: Research Toward Integrated Pest Management.* USDA Forest Service Technical Bulletin No. 1584. Washington, D.C.: U.S. Department of Agriculture.

Drea, J. J., and R. W. Carlson. 1990. Establishment of *Cybocephalus* sp. (Coleoptera: Nitidulidae) from Korea on *Unaspis euonymi* (Homoptera: Diaspididae) in the eastern United States. *Proceedings of the Entomological Society of Washington* 90:307–9.

Dreistadt, S. H., and M. L. Flint. 1996. Melon aphid (Homoptera: Aphididae) control by inundative convergent lady beetle (Coleoptera: Coccinellidae) release on chrysanthemum. *Environmental Entomology* 25:688–97.

Ehler, L. E., and M. G. Kinsey. 1995. Ecology and management of *Mindarus kinseyi* Voegtlin (Aphidoidea: Mindaridae) on white fir seedlings at a California forest nursery. *Hilgardia* 62 (1):1–62.

Flint, M. L., S. Dreistadt, E. M. Zagory, and R. Rosetta. 1993. IPM reduces pesticide use in the nursery. *California Agriculture* 47 (4):4–7.

Flint, M. L., S. H. Dreistadt, J. Rentner, and M. P. Parrella. 1995. Lady beetle release controls aphids on potted plants. *California Agriculture* 49 (2):5–8.

Gough, N. 1991. Long-term stability in the interaction between *Tetranychus urticae* and *Phytoseiulus persimilis* producing successful integrated control on roses in southeast Queensland (Australia). *Experimental and Applied Acarology* 12:83–102.

Hamlen, R. A., and R. K. Lindquist. 1981. Comparison of two *Phytoseiulus* species as predators of two-spotted spider mites on greenhouse ornamentals. *Environmental Entomology* 10:524–7.

Higginbotham, J. S. 1993. Pest control. *American Nurseryman,* June, 70–7.

Horn, D. J. 1996. Impacts of nonindigenous arthropods in biological control. *Midwest Biological Control News* 3 (12):1–6.

Moorhouse, E. R., M. A. Easterbrook, A. T. Gillespie, and A. K. Charnley. 1993. Control of *Otiorhynchus sulcatus* (Fabricius) (Coleoptera: Curculionidae) larvae on a range of hardy ornamental nursery stock species using the entomogenous fungus *Metarhizium anisopliae. Biocontrol Science and Technology* 3 (1):63–72.

Pickett, C. H., J. C. Ball, K. C. Casanave, K. M. Klonsky, K. M. Jetter, L. G. Bezark, and S. E. Schoenig. 1996. Establishment of the ash whitefly parasitoid *Encarsia inaron* (Walker) and its economic benefit to ornamental street trees in California. *Biological Control* 6(2):260–72.

Pratt, P. D. and B. A. Croft. 1998. *Panonychus citri* (Acari: Tetranychidae) on ornamental *Skimmia* in Oregon, with assessment of predation by native phytoseiid mites. *Pan-Pacific Entomologist* 74(3): 163–168.

Pratt, P. D. and B. A. Croft. 2000a. Banker plants: Evaluation of release strategies for predatory mites. *Journal Environmental Horticulture* 18:(4): 211-217.

Pratt, P. D. and B. A. Croft. 2000b. Screening of predatory mites as potential control agents of pest mites in landscape plant nurseries of the Pacific Northwest. *Journal of Environmental Horticulture* 18:(4): 218-223.

Pratt, P. D., R. Rosetta, and B. A. Croft. 2002. Plant-related factors influence the effectiveness of *Neoseiulus fallacis* (Acari: Phytoseiidae), a biological control agent of spider mites on landscape ornamental plants. *Journal of Economic Entomology* 95(6): 1135-1141.

Ramakers, P. M. J. and S. J. P. Voet. 1996. Introduction of *Amblyseius degenerans* for thrips control in sweet peppers with potted beans as banker plants. *IOBC Bulletin* 19:127-30.

Raupp, M. J., M. R. Hardin, S. M. Braxton, and B. B. Bull. 1994. Augmentative releases for aphid control on landscape plants. *Journal of Arboriculture* 20(5):241–9.

Raupp, M. J. and H. Hoitink. 1996. *Proceedings of the Third National IPM Symposium/Workshop: Broadening Support for 21st Century IPM,* No. 1542, ed. S. Lynch, C. Greene, and C. Kramer-LeBlanc, pp. 205-10 . Washington, D.C.: U.S. Department of Agriculture, Economic Research Service.

Reardon, R., and A. E. Hajek. 1997. *The gypsy moth fungus* Entomophaga maimaiga *in North America.* FHTET 97–11. Fort Collins, Colo.: Forest Health Technology Enterprise Team.

Sadof, C. S., and M. J. Raupp. 1987. Consumer attitudes toward the defoliation of American arborvitae, *Thuja occidentalis*, by bagworm, *Thyridopteryx ephemeraeformis*. *Journal of Environmental Horticulture* 5 (4):164–6.

Shetlar, D. J., and P. R. Hellar. 1984. Survey of insecticide and miticide usage by 158 nurseries in Pennsylvania. *Journal of Environmental Horticulture* 2 (1):16–20.

Shrewsbury, P. M. and M. R. Hardin. 2003. Evaluation of predatory mite (Acari: Phyotseiidae) releases to suppress spruce spider mites, *Oligonychus ununguis* (Acari: Tetranychidae), on juniper. *Journal of Economic Entomology.* 96: 1675-1684.

Shrewsbury, P. M. and D. C. Smith-Fiola. 2000. Evaluation of green lacewings for suppressing azalea lace bug populations in nursuries. *Journal of Environmental Horticulture* 18(4):207-11.

Simmonds, S. P. 1972. Observations on the control of *Tetranychus urticae* on roses by *Phytoseiulus persimilis*. *Plant Pathology* 21:163–5.

Skirvin, D. J. and M. De Courcy Williams. 1999. Differential effects of plant species on a mite pest (*Tetranychus urticae*) and its predator (*Phytoseiulus persimilis*): implications for biological control. *Experimental and Applied Acarology* 23: 497-512.

Smith, V. A., D. B. Orr, and E. R. Hart. 1993. Economic analysis of two-spotted spider mite management on greenhouse grown poplars. *Tree Planters' Notes* 44 (4):154–6.

Staines, C. L., M. J. Rothschild, and R. B. Trumbule. 1990. A survey of the Coccinellidae (Coleoptera) associated with nursery stock in Maryland. *Proceedings of the Entomological Society of Washington* 92 (2):310–3.

Studebaker, D. W. 1992. Practical IPM. *American Nurseryman,* October, 41–54.

Van Tol, R.W.H.M. 1993a. Control of the black vine weevil (*Otiorhynchus sulcatus*) with different isolates of *Heterorhabditis sp.* and *Metarhizium anisopliae* in nursery stock. *Proceedings Experimental and Applied Entomology, N.E.V. Amsterdam* 4:181-186.

Van Tol, R.W.H.M. 1993b. Efficacy of control of the black vine weevil (*Otiorhynchus sulcatus*) with strains of *Heterorhabditis sp.*, *Steinernema sp.* and the fungus *Metarhizium anisopliae* in nursery stock. *Mededelingen Faculteit Landbouwwetenschappen Universiteit Gent* 58/2a: 461-467.

Van Tol, R. and Raupp, M. J. in press. Nursery and tree application. In: *Nematodes as Biocontrol Agents* (P. S. Grewal, R. U. Ehlers and D. Shapiro-Ilan, Eds.), *CABI Publishing,* Wallingford, United Kingdom.

Zhang, Z-Q. and J. P. Sanderson. 1995. Two-spotted spider mite (Acari: Tetranychidae) and *Phytoseiulus persimilis* (Acari: Phytoseiidae) on greenhouse roses: Spatial distribution and predator efficacy. *Journal of Economic Entomology* 88:352–7.

25

BIOLOGICAL CONTROL IN BEDDING PLANTS

S. A. Gill

Central Maryland Research and Education Center
University of Maryland Cooperative Extension, Ellicott City, Maryland

and

R. A. Cloyd

Department of Natural Resources and Environmental Sciences
University of Illinois, Urbana, Illinois

Bedding plants are annual flowering herbaceous plants that complete their life cycle in one year and do not persist. The majority of commercially available bedding plants are grown from plugs, although they may also be grown from seeds or cuttings. Bedding plants have a high crop value ($10 to 12 per ft.^{2} [$108 to 129/m^2]) and short crop times of two to eight weeks. Plants are typically sold for use in the landscape, with common examples of such plants including garden impatiens (*Impatiens walleriana* Hook. f.), ageratum (*Ageratum houstonianum* Mill.), salvia (*Salvia splendens* F. Sellow ex Roem. & Schult.), and zinnia (*Zinnia elegans* Jacq.). Bedding plant production is a rapidly expanding sector of the floriculture and nursery industry within the United States. The USDA National Agricultural Statistics Service Floriculture Crops 1997 Summary showed that bedding plants, in the United States, had a wholesale value of $1.57 billion dollars, a 10% increase from 1996 (NASS 1998).

Production Practices Influencing Biological Control

Automated watering systems, including watering booms, subirrigation, and automated drip irrigation, are widely used to keep cost of producing bedding plants low. However, growers may have little direct contact with crops because of such automation. This reduces the grower's chance of detecting pest problems early. In addition, plug production facilities generally produce plugs year around, thus providing a continuous source of plants for pests to infest. Plugs are often kept moist to prevent drying out and death of the roots. This moist environment is favorable for development of fungus gnats, shore flies, and drain moth populations. Plugs are often grown on the ground where penetration and contact with pesticide sprays is difficult.

Pests that infest plants in the plug stage may inadvertently be shipped to customers. Growers purchasing plugs seldom closely inspect plugs that have been shipped from another location to their greenhouse operation. Pests can be present on plugs as eggs or other sessile stages, which are frequently difficult to detect and hence go unnoticed by those growing the plants to a finished stage. In the two to eight weeks of production time, populations of pest aphids, whiteflies, thrips, or mites can virtually exploded on a crop. Suppliers of plugs must be especially vigilant in keeping pests at extremely low populations by spraying pesticides to prevent passing on pest problems to the finished product grower.

Challenges associated with short cropping cycle

Because bedding plants mature rapidly, little time is available for predators or parasitoids to establish and reproduce and thus produce future generations of natural enemies that may effectively control pest populations. As a result, inundative releases of natural enemies are required to rapidly control developing pest populations. This approach to biological control requires the release of large numbers of natural enemies that virtually eradicate the pest population within the natural enemy's life span. Because bedding plants grown from plugs flower in as few as fourteen days (in the case of impatiens) or in fifteen to twenty days (in the case of petunias and others), sole reliance on inundative biological control may not be cost effective in many cases.

Challenges associated with a rotation of multiple cropping systems

Greenhouses are dynamic growing areas that contain within a single greenhouse many different species of bedding plants, each with its own growing requirements and maturation times. For example, marigold may reach market size in four weeks whereas salvia may stay in the greenhouse for eight weeks. When the marigolds are sold, the empty growing area is refilled with a new set of plants at the beginning of their growth cycle. While new plants may sustain some minor damage, soon-to-be harvested plants must be relatively damage-free to be marketable. As a result, the spatial patchwork of fast growing plant material is often managed as a single unit with all plants receiving the same pest control measures. Due to the expense associated with inundative releases of predators and parasitoids, growers frequently apply insecticides to the entire range to achieve the aesthetic quality demanded by consumers.

An additional complication occurs when hanging baskets are placed above bedding plants growing on greenhouse benches. Annual flowering plants grown in baskets are frequently hung in bedding plant greenhouses from the rafters supporting the greenhouse roof. Because these plants are grown to a larger size and in larger pots than are bedding plants, they may take four to six weeks longer to reach market size than do the bedding plants below. At times, these baskets can serve as sources of pest populations that infest the bedding plants (Gill and Sanderson 1998). However, because plants in hanging baskets are maintained for eight to twelve weeks, they are well suited to inoculative releases of beneficial predators or parasitoids.

Components to the Management of Major Pests

The primary pests of bedding plants are thrips, aphids, whiteflies, fungus gnats, caterpillars, shoreflies, drain flies, mealybugs, and mites (Lindquist and Powell 1997, Gill and Sanderson 1998). Thrips, such as the western flower thrips (*Frankliniella occidentalis* [Pergande], are a serious insect pest because of their ability to spread the tospoviruses impatiens necrotic spot virus (INSV) and tomato spotted wilt virus (TSWV). In addition, thrips can develop resistance to many pesticides, especially pesticides with similar modes of action (Daughtrey et al. 1998, Broadbent and Pree 1997).

Scouting and monitoring systems

Scouting of bedding plants pests, particularly for nonflying pests such as immature aphids, thrips, mites, whitefly nymphs, mealybugs, and caterpillars requires examining whole plants. A qualified IPM scout or a grower, trained in pest identification, should inspect plants on a weekly basis. It is necessary to examine the undersides of leaves since many of the immature nonflying pests occur there. Flying insects such as adult thrips, whiteflies, fungus gnats, shore flies, drain flies, and winged aphids can be monitored with colored sticky card traps. These traps are best used for early detection and for monitoring of insect population trends, provided the numbers of insects caught are counted and recorded weekly. Examination of recorded data is useful in assessing the success of biological control or any other pest management practice.

Screening to exclude pests

Greenhouses are easily invaded by insect and mite pests via open inlet and exhaust ventilation openings. Covering of openings with fine-mesh screens effectively reduces the numbers of pests entering from the outside.

Use of such screens has resulted in 50 to 90% reduction in pesticide use in some areas of North America, Europe, and Israel (Baker, Bethke, and Shearin 1995; Gill and Sanderson 1998). In addition, screens can facilitate biological control by eliminating the unpredictable events associated with insect movements—either pests immigrating into a greenhouse or natural enemies emigrating outward. Once a biological control program is established in a screened greenhouse, extreme caution should be practiced to avoid the introduction of infested plugs or cuttings from outside sources.

One caveat to the use of fine-mesh screening is the need for maintaining adequate ventilation while trying to exclude small insects and mites. While fine mesh screens are needed for exclusion of small-sized insects (e.g., thrips larvae), such screens are also more resistant to airflow. To maintain adequate ventilation, customize screen construction in individual greenhouses based upon greenhouse size, shape, and type of ventilation system in place (see chapter 3). A structural or agricultural engineer with experience in greenhouse ventilation systems should be consulted before installing a screening system over intake and exhaust vents.

Natural Enemies of Bedding Plant Pests

Table 25.1 lists commercially available natural enemies of the major bedding plant pests. Biological control agents are best suited to use in a proactive IPM program and should be applied early in a pest infestation rather than used to attempt to control a serious pest problem. Growers should seek information on which biological control agents are appropriate for use on particular crops and pests before implementing a biological control program. Some specific guidelines associated with the application of arthropod pathogens are provided here. Emphasis is placed on pathogens because they are more cost-effective relative to predators and parasitoids when used as part of an inundative release program. Due to the demand for high aesthetic quality and the short crop cycle common to bedding plants, inundative natural enemy releases must control pest populations continuously.

Bacillus thuringiensis

Bacillus thuringiensis is one of the most widely used pathogens for control of young caterpillars. Discovered in the early twentieth century, it was not until the 1960s that widespread commercial development of this bacterium occurred. Present formulations stored under cool dry conditions have a storage shelf life of two years. *Bacillus thuringiensis kurstaki* and *B. thuringiensis aizawai* are effective in controlling a number of caterpillar pest species that include cabbage looper (*Trichoplusia ni* [Hübner]), corn earworm (*Helicoverpa zea* [Boddie]), European corn borer (*Ostrina nubilalis* [Hübner]), Florida fern caterpillar (*Callopistria floridensis* [Guenée]), saltmarsh caterpillar (*Estigmene acrea* [Drury]), and the caterpillar *Euptoieta claudia* Cramer. Caterpillars may become pests of bedding plants during warmer months of the year and if not detected early they can cause large losses. Applications of *B. thuringiensis kurstaki* can be used to control most caterpillars, provided it is applied while the larvae are

first or second instars, and they are actively feeding. Correct identification of the caterpillar pest is important as some strains of *B. thuringiensis* are more efficacious against some species than are other strains of the pathogen.

Bacillus thuringiensis israelensis applied to the soil kills fungus gnat larvae. To control fungus gnats, repeated applications are often necessary since fungus gnats often have overlapping generations and because the bacteria is only effective against early instar larvae. Propagation areas kept under mist maintain soil conditions well suited to the use of *B. thuringiensis israelensis*. Periodic drying of the soil media, a common occurrence in normal production conditions, is not conducive to the use of this bacterium for fungus gnat control.

Entomopathogenic nematodes

Entomopathogenic nematodes are insect-parasitic microscopic roundworms that thrive in moist conditions (Kaya and Gaugler 1993). They can cause high rates of mortality to insects inhabiting these conditions such as fungus gnats (*Bradysia* spp.; Sciaridae), pupating thrips, and black vine weevil larvae (*Otiorhynchus sulcatus* [Fabricus]) (Gaugler, Campbell, and McGuire 1989; Gaugler and Campbell 1991; Kakouli 1993; Gill and Dutky 1997; Gill, Shrewsbury, and Reeser 2003). Two taxonomic families of entomopathogenic nematodes, Heterorhabditidae and Steinernematidae, and their associated bacteria have shown the greatest potential among nematodes as biological agents for control of insects (Smith, Miller, and Simser 1992).

Commercial producers rear entomopathogenic nematodes either in vitro on an

Table 25.1. Commercially Available Natural Enemies for the Major Pests of
Bedding Plants.

Pest	Natural Enemies	Release Rate	Source	Comments
Thrips	*Neoseiulus cucumeris* (Oudemans)	90–270/yd.^{2} (8–226 m^2)	Orr and Baker 1997	Release early before pest populations build up. Only attacks young thrips.
	N. cucumeris (predatory mite)	0.02 sachets/ft.^{2} (0.2/m^2)	Gill 1997	
	Orius spp. (minute pirate bug)	2–6/yd.^{2} (2–5/m^2)	Orr and Baker 1997, Stack and Drummond 1997	Enters diapause under short days. Supplemental lighting may prevent this.
Aphids	*Chrysoperla* spp. (green lacewing)	2–12/yd.^{2} (2–10/m^2)	Orr and Baker 1997	Larvae are cannibalistic and should be well dispersed.
	Aphidoletes aphidomyza (Rondani) (aphid midge)	2–9/yd.^{2} (2–8/m^2)	Orr and Baker 1997	Pupates in substrates. Enters diapause under short day conditions.
	Aphidius spp. (aphid parasitoid)	2–8/yd.^{2} (2–7/m^2)	Orr and Baker 1997	Release immediately upon arrival.
Whiteflies	*Beauveria bassiana* (Balsamo) (beneficial fungus)	See label instructions.	N/A	Apply as a fine mist. May require repeat applications.

(continued)

Table 25.1. *(continued)*

Pest	Natural Enemies	Release Rate	Source	Comments
	Encarsia formosa Gahan whitefly parasitoid)	2–8/yd.^{2} (2–7/m^2)	Orr and Baker 1997	Good for green-house whitefly (*Trialeurodes vaporariorum* Westwood).
	Eretmocerus eremicus Rose and Zolnerowich (whitefly parasitoid)	6–18/yd.^{2} (5–15/m^2)	Orr and Baker 1997	Good for silver-leaf whitefly (Bemisia argentifoli).
	Beauveria bassiana (benefi-cial fungus)	See label instructions.	N/A	Apply as a fine mist. May require repeat applications.
Fungus gnats	*Steinernema feltiae* (Filipjev) (beneficial nematode)	See label instructions.	N/A	Only kills larvae.
	Hypoaspis miles (Berlese) (preda-tory mite)	45–100/yd.^{2} (38–84/m^2)	Orr and Baker 1997	Feeds on larvae and thrips pupae. Will reproduce in greenhouses.
Mealybugs	*Cryptolaemus montrouzieri* Mulsant (mealybug destroyer)	2–8/yd.^{2} (2–7/m^2)	Orr and Baker 1997	Works best on large populations of mealybugs.

(continued)

Table 25.1. *(continued)*

Pest	Natural Enemies	Release Rate	Source	Comments
	Leptomastix dactylopii Howard (mealybug parasitoid)	2/yd.^{2} (m^2)	Orr and Baker 1997	Only attacks citrus mealybug (*Planococcus citri* [Risso]), not long-tailed mealybug (*Pseudococcus longispinus* [Targioni-Tozzetti]).
	Chrysoperla carnea (Stephens) (green lacewing)	2–12/yd.^{2} (2–10/m^2)	Orr and Baker 1997	Larvae are cannibalistic and should be well dispersed.
Caterpillars	*Bacillus thuringiensis* Berliner *kurstaki* (beneficial bacterium)	See label instructions.		Only kills larvae.
Mites	*Phytoseiulus persimilis* Athias-Henriot (predatory mite)	1/ft.^{2} (11/m^2)	Orr and Baker 1997	Apply early in crop cycle. May have to repeat release.
Broad mites	*Neoseiulus barkeri* Hughes (predatory mite)	10–30/plant	Orr and Baker 1997	Apply early in crop cycle.

Figure 25.1. This dying Lepidoptera larva has been infected with *B. thuringiensis*.
Photo: M. P. Parrella.

artificial diet or in vivo in living hosts. Nematodes produced *in vitro*, such as *S. carpocapsae* and *S. feltiae*, are usually formulated in a manner enabling them to be stored for up to six months. Nematodes, such as *Heterorhabditis bacteriophora* Poinar, produced in vivo, may be stored for up to three months. Thus, it is important to request information from the supplier on the method of production and suggested storage recommendations to maintain efficacy.

Growers may receive nematodes formulated as slurries, in granules within inert clay carriers, in gels, and on the surface of sponges. With all formulations, water must be added to the nematodes before application. Nematodes are applied as a soil drench to distribute them evenly throughout the substrate and to maximize their contact with soil-dwelling insects. To promote nematode survival, the soil should be kept moist and soil temperatures should remain above 60°F (16°C) and below 90°F (32°C) (Hanula 1993).

When a susceptible host is located, the infective nematodes enter the insect's body through natural openings such as the mouth, spiracles, or anus. Nematodes pierce the gut wall and enter the insect body cavity, where they release bacteria. The bacteria rapidly kills the insect, and the nematodes mature and reproduce in the insect cadaver. Once the food is exhausted, thousands of infective stages leave the insect's body and return to the soil or substrate in search of additional hosts.

Entomopathogenic fungi

Entomopathogenic fungi are pathogens that infect and kill insects. These fungi need not be ingested by insects since the fungi can directly penetrate the insect body. Because entomopathogenic fungi have some ability to suppress populations of several key pests such as thrips, aphids, and whiteflies (Murphy et al. 1998), they may be useful for pest control on bedding plants. For example, *Beauveria bassiana* (Balsamo) Vuillemin is an entomopathogenic fungus that may control infestations of whiteflies, some thrips, and certain aphids species. The fungus has been formulated as suspensions or wettable powders of conidia (spores), which can be sprayed directly onto plants. Spores must contact the host directly to be effective and good spray coverage is critical. Hyphae, small tubes that grow from the conidia, use a combination of mechanical pressure and enzymes to break through the exoskeleton of the insect, enter the body cavity, and then attack the internal organs. The infected insect stops feeding and dies within a few days.

References Cited

Baker, J. R., J. A. Bethke, and E. A. Shearin. 1995. Insect screening. In *New Guinea Impatiens: A Ball Guide*, ed. W. Banner and M. Klopmeyer, 155–70. Batavia, Ill.: Ball Publishing.

Broadbent, A. B., and D. J. Pree. 1997. Resistance to insecticides in populations of *Frankliniella occidentalis* (Pergande) (Thysanoptera: Thripidae) from greenhouses in the Niagara region of Ontario. *The Canadian Entomologist* 129:907–13.

Daughtrey, M. L., R. Jones, J. Moyer, M. Daub, and J. Baker. 1998. Tospoviruses strike the greenhouse industry—INSV has become a major pathogen on flower crops. *Plant Disease* 81 (11):1220–30.

Gaugler, R., and J. Campbell. 1991. Selection for enhanced host finding of scarab larvae (Coleoptera: Scarabaeidae) in an entomopathogenic nematode. *Environmental Entomology* 20:700–6.

Gaugler, R., J. Campbell, and T. McGuire. 1989. Selection for host finding in *Steinernema feltiae*. *Journal of Invertebrate Pathology* 54:363–72.

Gill, S.A., Shrewsbury, P., and Reeser, R. 2003. Controlling a major nursery pest: Black vine weevil, *Otiorhynchus sulcatus* (Fabricius), University of Maryland Fact Sheet 805

Gill, S. 1997. You can control thrips biologically. *GrowerTalks*, July, 114–7.

Gill, S., and E. Dutky. 1997. Identification and control of fungus gnats and substrate-borne diseases. *FloraCulture International*, March, 26–9.

Gill, S., and J. Sanderson. 1998. *Ball Identification Guide to Greenhouse Pests and Beneficials*. Batavia, Ill.: Ball Publishing.

Hanula, J. L. 1993. Vertical distribution of black vine weevil (Coleoptera: Curculionidae) immatures and infection by entomogenous nematodes in soil columns and field soil. *Journal of Economic Entomology* 86 (2):340–7.

Kakouli, T. 1993. Evaluation of the entomopathogenic nematodes, *Steinernema carpocapsae*, against black vine weevil, *Otiorhynchus sulcatus*: Test of agrochemicals and cultivars. *Supplement to Annals of Applied Biology* 27 (14):190–1.

Kaya, H. K., and R. Gaugler. 1993. Entompathogenic nematodes. *Annual Review of Entomology* 38:181–206.

Lindquist, R., and R. Powell. 1997. *Ball Pest and Disease Manual*, 2nd ed. Batavia, Ill.: Ball Publishing.

Murphy, B. C., T. A. Morisawa, J. P. Newman, S. A. Tjosvold, and M. P. Parrella. 1998. Fungal pathogen controls thrips in greenhouse flowers. *California Agriculture* 52 (3):32–6.

National Agricultural Statistics Service (NASS), Agricultural Statistics Board. 1998. *Floriculture Crops 1997 Summary*. Washington, D.C.: U.S. Department of Agriculture.

Orr, D. B., and J. R. Baker. 1997. Biocontrol in greenhouses. *North Carolina Flower Growers' Bulletin*, August, 5–14.

Smith, K. A., R. Miller, and D. Simser. 1992. Entomopathogenic nematode bibliography: Heterorhabditid and Steinernematid nematodes. *Southern Cooperative Series, Arkansas Agricultural Experiment Station Bulletin* 370.

Stack. P. A., and F. A. Drummond. 1997. Reproduction and development of *Orius insidiosus* in a blue light-supplemented short photoperiod. *Biological Control* 9:59–65.

26

IPM Program for Cucumber

J. L. Shipp

Agriculture and Agri-Food Canada
Greenhouse and Processing Crops Research Centre, Harrow, Ontario, Canada

English cucumber (*Cucumis sativus* L.) (Fig. 26.1) is a major greenhouse vegetable crop throughout the world. Many different cultivars of cucumbers are grown in the greenhouse with cultivar selection depending on the geographic region, time of year, disease resistance or tolerance, overall productivity, fruit quality, fruit shelf life, and plant growth habit and vigor. Greenhouse cucumbers are unique in that the plants are gynoecious and thus, only produce female flowers. Fruit development is parthenocarpic (i.e., pollination is not necessary for fruit development). Cucumber plants are very sensitive to unfavorable conditions such as lack of water, nutrient imbalance, or pest pressure. They will quickly display reduced productivity or vigor (Papadopoulos 1994).

Production Systems

The number of crops per year varies from two to three. In northern climates, more growers are switching to three crops (late winter, spring and fall crop) to increase fruit quality and due to the lack of adequate control measures for diseases. When three crops per season are grown in Finland and Norway, artificial lights are used for the winter crop.

Figure 26.1 English cucumber (*Cucumis sativus* L.) is a major greenhouse-grown vegetable in many regions of the world that produces fruit (inset) without the need for pollination. *Photos: A. Papadopoulos and L. Shipp (inset).*

The growing medium for cucumber varies from soil in less developed countries to soilless media in developed countries. Rockwool is the predominant soilless medium with peat bags also being very popular in certain areas such as Canada, Finland, and Russia. Other soilless media used are clay pellets, vermiculite, perlite, coconut fiber, polyurethane foam and polystyrene beads (Papadopoulos 1994). Cucumber plants are pruned using the umbrella system or modified versions of it. Fruit is thinned to improve fruit size and overall yield. Harvested fruits are usually individually wrapped in a thin plastic film to conserve moisture and stored at 50 to 55°F (10 to 13°C) and 90 to 95% relative humidity (RH) (Ibid.).

Overall Pest Problems

Greenhouse cucumber has the largest pest complex of any greenhouse vegetable crop (Table 26.1). Many of these pests, such as greenhouse whitefly (*Trialeurodes vaporariorum* [Westwood]), spider mites and western flower thrips (*Frankliniella occidentalis* [Pergande]), are major problems throughout the world. Others, especially sweet potato whitefly (*Bemisia tabaci* [Grennadius]), leafminers and onion thrips (*Thrips tabaci* [Lindeman]), are important pests in some regions and minor problems in other areas. Table 26.1 also lists the more common minor pests. These minor pests usually cause sporadic problems; however, damage can be severe if densities become high or the pests are disease vectors.

Pests of cucumbers can directly damage the fruit (e.g., *F. occidentalis* and cucumber beetles) and indirectly affect yield and fruit

quality by reducing plant vigor. Black sooty molds (*Cladosporium* spp.) grow on the honeydew deposits of whiteflies and aphids, thus interfering with photosynthesis and transpiration on the leaves. Other pests (mites, leafminers and thrips) feed on the sap and chlorophyll in the leaves. Plant bugs and aphids stunt and distort new growth by feeding on growing points. The larvae of fungus gnats feed on the fine root hairs, weakening the plant and providing sites for pathogen entry (fig. 26.2).

Some pest species can vector disease agents as well as cause feeding damage. Transmission of beet pseudo-yellows virus by *T. vaporariorum* can be a major concern where the virus occurs outdoors. Other viral

Figure 26.2. The larvae of fungus gnats (upper photo) feed on the fine root hairs, weakening the plant and providing sites for pathogen entry, such as *Pythium* (*Pythium* damage symptoms shown in lower inset).
Photos: L. Shipp and W. Jarvis [inset].

Table 26.1. Pests of Greenhouse Cucumber

Major Pests	Minor Pests
Greenhouse whitefly (*Trialeurodes vaporariorum* [Westwood])	Fungus gnats (*Bradysia spp., Corynoptera spp.*)
Sweet potato whitefly (*Bemisia tabaci* [Gennadius])	Cabbage looper (*Trichoplusia ni* [Hübner])
Silverleaf whitefly (*Bemisia argentifolii* Bellows &Perrring)	Cutworms (Noctuidae)
Two-spotted spider mite (*Tetranychus urticae* Koch)	Spotted cucumber beetle (*Diabrotica undecimpunctata howardi* Barber)
Western flower thrips (*Frankliniella occidentalis* [Pergande])	Striped cucumber beetle (*Acalymma vittata* [Fabricius])
Onion thrips (*Thrips tabaci* [Lindeman])	*Thrips fuscipennis* Haliday
Melon thrips (*Thrips palmi* Karny)	Green peach aphid (*Myzus persicae* [Sulzer])
Melon (cotton) aphid (*Aphis gossypii* Glover)	Potato aphid (*Macrosiphum euphorbia* [Thomas])
Tomato leafminer (*Liriomyza bryoniae* [Kaltenbach])	Plant bugs (*Lygus lineolaris* [Palisot de Beauvois]) (*Lygus rugulipennis* Poppius)
Serpentine leafminer (*Liriomyza trifolii* [Burgess])	Silver "y" moth (*Autographa gamma* L.)
	Green leafhopper (*Empoasca decipiens* Paoli)

diseases, such as cucumber and watermelon mosaic viruses (fig. 26.3), are transmitted by aphids. The cucumber beetle is an effective carrier of bacterial wilt. Also, studies have shown that even root pathogens (*Pythium sp.*) can be transmitted by larvae of fungus gnats (Jarvis, Shipp, and Gardiner 1993).

Economic Impact

The effect of greenhouse pests on cucumber can vary from little or none to complete

Figure 26.3. Fruit exhibiting symptoms of cucumber mosaic virus. The virus overwinters in perennial weeds and is transmitted to healthy plants by aphid vectors or by mechanical means. The cucumber mosaic virus cannot withstand drying or persist in the soil. *Photo: W. Jarvis.*

destruction of the crop. Unless the pest is vectoring a disease agent, high densities are necessary to reduce fruit quality or yield. In countries closer to the equator, pest problems are generally more numerous and severe. The result is that in warmer climates economic losses as a percentage of crop yields are much greater and pest control is usually based on pesticides, not biological control (van Lenteren et al. 1992). In northern Europe, pest control expenses are 2 to 6% of greenhouse production costs (Ibid., Jacobson 1997), whereas, pest control in Spain averages 16.5% of production costs (Cabello and Cañero 1994).

In the Mediterranean area, whiteflies (*T. vaporariorum* and *B. tabaci*) are the most economically important pests. In this area, diseases associated with whiteflies are an important problem and cause significant crop losses. In Japan, consumer demand for very

high quality product has resulted in little damage by *B. tabaci* being tolerated in the marketplace. Sooty mold deposits on honeydew, excreted by both the adult and immature whiteflies, coats the leaves and fruit. Thus, high consumer demand has resulted in frequent applications of pesticides for pest control in Japan (Matsui and Nakashima 1992).

In Europe and North America, *F. occidentalis* and *Tetranychus urticae* Koch (two-spotted spider mite) are the most economically important pests. Both pests cause damage by sucking the contents out of plant cells. The result is a speckling of the leaves with spots that eventually coalesce thus causing the leaves to turn yellow or brown and die. Thrips also causes longitudinal feeding striations on the fruit. Extensive feeding damage results in unmarketable fruit. Early feeding damage on young developing fruit can result in fruit curling. Extensive damage by *F. occidentalis* can result in complete crop loss, requiring replanting (Jacobson 1997).

Aphids can also cause significant damage to cucumber because of their rapid population increase over a short period. Populations can increase ten to twelve fold on cucumber within a week (Wyatt and Brown 1977). Infestations of 2,000 aphids per leaf will cause leaves to wilt and collapse. Aphids excrete honeydew with the same associated problems as with whiteflies. Once aphids reach a damaging level, even if controlled with pesticides, five to seven weeks will be needed before normal yields return (Gilkeson 1994). Aphids are the most important vectors of viral plant diseases (Ponsen 1987) and without adequate control will destroy a complete crop.

Monitoring Systems

It is important to monitor the population densities of pests to effectively time control measures and determine the efficacy of implemented measures. All growers should implement a basic monitoring program to detect pests present in their crops. Materials required are a hand lens (10×), a map of the crop layout in the greenhouse, sticky traps, brightly colored plastic tags or tape, and a clipboard and notebook for recording observations and keeping records. An enthusiastic and responsible integrated pest management (IPM) manager to coordinate the program is essential. People involved in the program must know how to identify the pests, understand their life cycles and recognize the various damage symptoms on the crop.

Sticky traps should be checked at least weekly and replaced frequently. All pests on the traps should be identified and recorded. The crop should also be directly inspected for pests and damage symptoms. When a pest or pest damage is found on a plant, the plant should be marked with brightcolored tape or a tag. Different colors should be used for different pest species. Color pins coded for the different pests can be used to mark the locations of the infested plants on the map of the greenhouse. This map will show the infested areas and how the infestation spreads throughout the greenhouse. Early control of small areas of high pest infestation is critical for the prevention of large-scale pest outbreaks.

The most commonly used method to monitor pests is colored sticky traps (various hues of yellow or blue). Blue is generally recommended as the color that collects the most *F. occidentalis* (Brødsgaard 1993, Shipp 1995) and *Thrips palmi* Karny (Kawai and Kitamura 1987). Whiteflies, aphids, leafminers and fungus gnats, however, are highly attracted to yellow traps (Powell and Lindquist 1992). The result is that yellow is the standard color of sticky traps used with cucumber crops because yellow traps can monitor more pest species than blue traps. For most pests, traps are hung vertically with the base of the trap at or just above the canopy. Sweet potato whiteflies, fungus gnats, and leafminers, can also be monitored by placing traps horizontally just above the growing medium surface (Ibid.).

Direct counts of pests on leaves or flowers are an alternative to sticky traps to monitor pest densities in cucumbers. Counts can be pest numbers in flowers or on leaves or numbers dislodged by plant tappings. These methods can monitor both adult and immature stages of some pests. However, these methods are more time consuming and are usually not done by growers. Pest management consultants will use these sampling methods to get a more accurate estimate of pest trends in the greenhouse.

Direct observation of the crop and the surrounding greenhouse area is perhaps the most important sampling method. Growers and their workers should routinely inspect the plants when they are working in the crop. Once a pest or signs of pest damage are detected, control strategies should be implemented. It is especially important to inspect plants near doors, vents, and alongside outside walls (Ibid.).

For *F. occidentalis*, several fixed precision-level sampling programs have been developed and are recommended for monitoring this species (Steiner 1990; Cho, Kang, and Lee 1998; Taylor, Lindquist, and Shipp 1998; Wang and Shipp 2001). The recommended numbers of yellow sticky traps needed to estimate different population densities of adult thrips at precision levels of 10 to 20% accuracy are presented in Table 26.2 (Taylor, Lindquist, and Shipp 1998). The number of samples recommended in this sampling program is given on a per day basis. Steiner (1990) developed a fixed precision-level sampling program based on presence-absence sampling (rather than actual counts) of thrips on the middle strata leaves of cucumber plants. This program recommends sampling 50 leaves per 21,525 ft.^{2} (2,000 m^2) at low thrips density and 25 per 21,525 ft.^{2} (2,000 m^2) leaves for high densities. The fixed precision-level sampling program suggested by Cho, Kang, and Lee (1998) uses leaf samples too, but is based on actual counts of thrips. A fixed precision-level sequential sampling program has also been recommended based on counts of adult thrips in the flowers. In addition, Wang and Shipp (2001) developed a population classification sequential sampling program based on economic thresholds of 3 and 5 adult thrips per flower.

Generally, fixed precision-level sampling programs are designed to estimate population densities for situations where actual counts of thrips densities are required. For example, accurate estimates are necessary to determine when to initiate control measures. A sequential sampling plan for classifying thrips populations is primarily used in decision-making for whether or not to apply a pesticide application. This plan has the advantage of a smaller sample size requirement for decision-making when pest population densities differ greatly from the critical density (i.e., economic thresholds). When the population density is close to the critical density, using a combination of both sampling plans should be considered.

Economic injury levels have been determined for *T. urticae* and *F. occidentalis* on cucumber. Hussey and Parr (1963) related leaf damage caused by *T. urticae* to yield loss with a damage index scale that ranged from

Table 26.2. Number of Recommended Sticky Trap Samples, Using the Precision Levels (10–20%), to Estimate Densities of *Frankliniella occidentalis* (Pergande) on Greenhouse Crops (Taylor et al. 1998)

Precision level (%)	Number of thrips/sticky card/day					
	0.14	0.43	1.43	4.29	14.29	42.86
10	66*	55	46	38	32	26
15	29	25	20	17	14	12
20	16	14	11	10	9	7

*If 0.14 thrips/sticky card/day is collected, then sixty-six sticky card samples are needed in a 10,764 ft.^{2} (1,000 m^2) greenhouse for estimating a thrips population density with a 0.10 level of precision.

0 to 4. The economic injury level at which crop loss occurred was at an index value of 1.9 (30% reduction in photosynthetic area of the leaf). A higher index value of 2.5 will result in 40% crop loss five weeks later. Economic injury levels for *F. occidentalis* range from 20 to 50 adults per sticky card per day or 3 to 7.5 per flower as determined under greenhouse production conditions in Ontario, Canada (Shipp, Wang, and Binns 2000). Steiner (1990) was able to correlate thrips density with leaf damage, but not with fruit damage. It was felt, however, since thrips and mite damage to the leaf are similar, a density of 9.5 larvae or 1.7 adults per middle leaf (equivalent to 30% leaf damage) may cause economic damage to cucumber.

Growers typically modify sampling programs mentioned above to suit their particular needs. The number of sticky traps currently recommended to growers ranges from one trap per 1,076 to 1,615 ft.^{2} (100–150 m^2). This number needs to be validated against the number recommended by Taylor et al. (1998). In reality, many growers just use sticky traps to detect the initial presence of a pest or to monitor general population trends. Traps are often not changed weekly or even counted on a regular basis. However, the trend is moving towards monitoring pest densities more on a regular basis, especially as individual greenhouse operations get larger. To implement control measures in a timely fashion in larger operations, it is very important to be organized and to know when pest outbreaks occur.

Effective Natural Enemies

Growers of greenhouse cucumber are fortunate to have commercially available biolog-ical control agents for all its major pests plus some of the minor pests (Table 26.3). These agents may not be available in all countries depending upon the policies set by each nation for importing and registering biological control agents. The rates and schedules for introduction of the different natural enemies are presented in Table 26.3. These rates are guidelines as growers usually modify the rates to suit their own situation. When initially starting to use biological control, growers often use the high rate or even above the recommended rates to insure success. Even then, success may not last all season.

Whitefly natural enemies

Encarsia formosa (Gahan) is a very effective biological control agent for *T. vaporariorum* and can be effective against *B. tabaci* and *B. argentifolii* Bellows and Perring on cucumber when the rate is doubled. However, success against the latter pest species is much more variable than for *T. vaporariorum*. In contrast, *Eretmocerus eremicus* Rose and Zolnerowhich is more effective against *B. tabaci/B. argentifolii* than against *T. vaporariorum*. *Encarsia formosa* is less effective under conditions of low light intensity and short-day lengths, and as a result higher release rates are needed to achieve biological whitefly control (Stenseth 1985). Additional control measures, such as vacuuming or mass-trapping adult whiteflies, may also be necessary when low light and short day conditions occur.

Generalist predators, such as *Dicyphus tamaninii* Wagner, have achieved successful control of whiteflies on cucumbers in caged experiments (Gabarra, Castañé, and Albajes

1995). Functional response trials on cucumber leaf disks showed that *D. tamaninii* exhibited good potential as a biological control agent for *T. vaporariorum* (Montserrat, Albajes, and Castañé 2000). Recently, the phytoseiid mites, *Euseius scutalis* (Athias-Henriot) and *Typhlodromips swiskii* (Athias-Henriot) were found to decrease population densities of *B. tabaci* by 16 to 21 fold on cucumber when provided weekly with an alternative food source, *Typha* sp. pollen (Nomikou et al. 2002).

Spider mite natural enemies

Phytoseiulus persimilis Athias-Henriot is an effective biological control agent for spider mites in greenhouse cucumber and has been used commercially since the late 1960s (van Lenteren et al. 1992). The main restraints in using this predatory mite are temperature and humidity. At temperatures >86°F (30°C), the reproductive capacity of *P. persimilis* becomes less than that of *T. urticae* and *P. persimilis* no longer provides control (Scopes 1985). Also, oviposition and survival rates of *P. persimilis* decrease dramatically at humidities <60% RH (Pralavorio and Rojas 1980).

The predatory midge (*Feltiella acarisuga* [Vallot]) is another biological control agent that is commercially available for control of spider mites. The midge is most effective at higher humidities and it should be introduced in combination with *P. persimilis*. The predatory coccinellid beetle *Stethorus punctillum* Weise is effective for reducing isolated patches of high populations of *T. urticae*. *Stethorus punctillum* works best in combination with *P. persimilis*.

Thrips natural enemies

For control of thrips, several predatory mite species (*Neoseiulus cucumeris* [Oudemans], *Hypoaspis aculeifer* (Canestrini) and *Hypoaspis miles* Berlese) and predatory Hemiptera (*Orius* spp.) are commonly used. Slow-release "sachets" that contain a colony of the predator and prey mites (harmless grain mites) have become the preferred method for introducing *N. cucumeris*. The sachets come in sizes of 250 and 1000 mites/sachet. The larger sizes are recommended for use in areas with high thrips infestations. Correct timing for introduction of the sachets is critical to prevent establishment of *F. occidentalis*. In England, the sachets are introduced at a rate of one per plant immediately after transplanting (Jacobson 1995a). *Neoseiulus cucumeris* can also be released in loose bran. This method of introduction is best suited for releasing high numbers of mites in small areas where a rapid reduction of thrips densities is required. *Orius* spp. ("minute pirate bugs") can also be used to control thrips in small areas with high pest densities. In Canada, *Orius insidiosus* (Say) is recommended at a rate of two to four bugs per plant when thrips counts reach five to twenty adult thrips per flower and five to ten bugs per plant when thrips exceed twenty thrips per flower. In Finland, a rate of five to ten *Orius* sp. is also recommended for small areas of high thrips infestation (I. Väninnen, pers. comm.). The soil-dwelling predatory mites *H. aculeifer* and *H. miles* provide partial control (40 to 78%) of the prepupal and pupal stages of *F. occidentalis* when applied at the same rate as recommended for control of fungus gnats *Bradysia* spp. (Borgemeister et al.

2002, Gillespie and Quiring 1990). In the Mediterranean area, the predatory bug, *D. tamaninii,* at a ratio of 3:10 (predator:prey) was also found to maintain *F. occidentalis* population densities under the economic injury level (Castañé, Alomar and Riudavets 1996).

Aphid natural enemies

Aphis gossypii Glover is usually the predominate aphid on greenhouse cucumber. Its biological control agent, *Aphidius colemani* Viereck, can be introduced as loose parasitized aphid mummies mixed with sawdust or via an open-rearing system (in which the parasitoids develop on cereal aphids maintained on cereal plants). The open-rearing system, frequently termed as banker plants, is the more effective method for aphid control over the whole crop season. Ladybird beetles, *Harmonia axyridis* (Pallas) and *Hippodamia variegate* Goeze, show promise as future biological control agents for *A. gossypii* (El Habi et al. 2000, Kuroda and Miura 2003). In Japan, the introduction of egg mass sheets and flightless adults of *H. axyridis* reduced the population levels of aphids by 86 to 98% depending on the introduction rate (Kuroda and Miura 2003). The green peach aphid (*Myzus persicae* [Sulzer]) may also be a pest of greenhouse cucumber. Releases of *Aphidoletes aphidimyza* (Rondani) or *A. matricariae* Haliday are often used for this pest.

Fungus gnat natural enemies

For control of *Bradysia* spp. and *Corynoptera* spp. (Sciaridae), nematodes provide more rapid control than the predatory mites *H. aculeifer* or *H. miles*, and nematodes can be applied through the irrigation system. If the population densities of *Bradysia* spp. or *Corynoptera* spp. are high (>75 flies/card/week), nematodes are the preferred control measure. However, *H. aculeifer* and *H. miles* can be applied as a prophylactic treatment, as the soil-dwelling mites will survive on other organisms in the soil or growing media. Nematodes cannot be applied as a preventive treatment. In addition, a soil-dwelling predatory staphylinid, *Atheta coriaria* Kraatz, is also commercially available for control of the immature stages of fungus gnats (Carney et al. 2002).

Caterpillar natural enemies

Bacillus thuringiensis Berliner provides effective control of some lepidopteran pests (e.g., *Trichoplusia ni* [Hübner]), but is not effective against the spotted (*Amathes c-nigrum* [L.]) and variegated (*Peridroma saucia* [Hübner]) cutworms.

Fungal pathogens

Fungal entomopathogens have recently gained popularity for use in controlling some greenhouse pests (Butt, Jackson, and Magan 2001; Shipp et al. 2003). Improvements in formulation and in maintaining proper environmental conditions within greenhouses have increased the effectiveness of these fungi. Entomopathogens are most effective when integrated with other biological control agents. They can be used to control isolated outbreaks and to supplement other biological control agents (such as *E. formosa* for whiteflies) when such agents are not effective (when there are conditions of low light intensity and short-day lengths) (Jacobson et al. 2001). One of the major obstacles to the use

of entomopathogens is in obtaining registration for use in a given country. *Beauveria
bassiana* (Balsamo) Vuillernin is registered
widely for use on greenhouse ornamentals
and vegetables. To a lesser degree,
Verticillium lecanii (Zimmerman) Viégas is
registered for use in several European countries, but not in many other countries. Even
more restricted in its registration (geographi-
cally) is the fungal pathogen, *Paecilomyces
fumosoroseus* (Wize) Brown and Smith.

Adoption of IPM by Industry

The large number of pest species, the various
types of damage caused by these pests, and
the different biologies among the pest species
present numerous challenges to the implementation of IPM in greenhouse grown
cucumbers. Although biological control is
often the main control measure in cucumber
IPM programs, other components include
physical exclusion (screening), sanitation,
plant resistance, and other cultural control
methods. Pesticides are used selectively when
populations increase too fast for the biological
control agents or for cleaning up greenhouses
between cropping seasons. In many regions of
the world, sole reliance on biological control
is very difficult (due to growing conditions)
and too costly for growers. In areas where
biological control-based IPM is implemented
most successfully, growers are supported by
specialized advisors who are employed by the
producers of beneficial organisms, agricultural supply companies, and government and
private consultants (Ramakers and Rabasse
1995). It is important for insectaries not just to
provide a product, but also to ensure proper
handling, application, and monitoring.

In Canada, the percentage of cucumber
acreage using biological control (outlined in
Table 26.4) varies from 38% (Ontario) to
100% (British Columbia). Ontario has the
greatest acreage of cucumbers (329 acres
[133 ha], 68% of the total acreage for
Canada), but it also has the largest problem
with diseases that are vectored by insects
(beet pseudo-yellows, bacterial wilt, and
cucumber and watermelon mosaic viruses).
In Ontario, there is considerable pest pressure
on greenhouse crops from field pests during
the summer months, especially with whiteflies and aphids. This type of pest influx into
the greenhouses is not as severe in the other
greenhouse-production regions in Canada. In
Canada, the area with the greatest adoption of
biological control (British Columbia) has the
greatest number of suppliers of biological
control agents. In addition, British Columbia
had a greater number of advisors (compared
to other areas of Canada) from a variety of
sources that assist the growers. The number
of advisors has increased considerably in
recent years in Ontario with a corresponding
increase in biological control adoption in
cucumber. This vast and diverse supply of
continuing grower education is critical for
large-scale adoption of IPM.

In northern Europe (the Netherlands, the
United Kingdom, Denmark, France, Finland,
Norway, and Sweden), biological control is
practiced on 80 to 100% of the greenhouse
acreage as the main method for pest control
(van Lenteren 1992; Jacobson 1995b;
Maisonneuve 2002; H. F. Brødsgaard, pers.
comm.; I. Vänninen, pers. comm.). In the
Mediterranean region of southern Europe, the
adoption rate for IPM is very low and, in
many cases, nonexistent (van Lenteren et al.

Table 26.3. Biological Control Agents and Their Application Rates for Pests of Greenhouse Cucumber

Natural Enemies	Pest	Rate	Frequency
Encarsia formosa Gahan (parasitic wasp)	*Trialeurodes vaporariorum* (Westwood)	Preventive: 0.07–0.1/ft.^{2} (0.7–1.5/m^2) Curative: 0.3–0.8/ft.^{2} (3–9/m^2)	Biweekly; weekly when whiteflies are present outdoors Weekly until 80% parasitism
Eretmocerus eremicus (Rose and Zolnerowich) (parasitic wasp)	*Trialeurodes vaporariorum*	Preventive: 0.13/ft.^{2} (1.5/m^2) Curative: 0.3–0.8/ft.^{2} (3–9/m^2)	Every 1–2 weeks Minimum of 3 introductions
Phytoseiulus persimilis Athias-Henriot (predatory mite)	*Tetranychus urticae* Koch	Curative: 0.4–0.5/ft.^{2} (4–6/m^2) throughout the greenhouse and 1.8–4.5/ft.^{2} (20–50/m^2) on infested plants	Weekly until predatory mites are present on infested leaves
Feltiella acarisuga (Vallot) (predatory midge)	*Tetranychus urticae*	Curative: 0.9–22.5/ft.^{2} (10–250/m^2)	Minimum of 3 weekly introductions in infested areas
Stethorus punctillum Weise (predatory coccinellid)	*Tetranychus urticae*	Curative; 100-200 per hot spot 0.09-0.4ft^2 (1–4/ m^2)	3-4 weekly introductions or until established
Neoseiulus cucumeris (Oudemans) (predatory mite)	*Frankliniella occidentalis* (Pergande)	Preventive: 2.5 cc per transplant Curative: 9/ft.^{2} (100/m^2) 1–2 slow-release bags/plant	1 introduction, every 1–2 weeks Variable; see local pest management advisor
Orius spp. (predatory bug)	*Frankliniella occidentalis*	Curative: 0.1–0.9/ ft.^{2} (1–10/m^2)	1–2 weekly introductions

(continued)

Table 26.3. *(continued)*

Natural Enemies	Pest	Rate	Frequency
Aphidoletes aphidimyza (Rondani) (predatory midge)	*Aphis gossypii* (Glover) *Myzus persicae* (Sulzer)	Curative: 0.1–0.9/ft.^{2} (1–10/m^2)	Weekly until numerous midge larvae are present
Aphidius colemani Viereck (parasitic wasp)	*Aphis gossypii*	Preventive: 0.009/ft.^{2} (0.1/m^2) Aphidbanks 1/186–372 ft.^{2} (1/2,000–4,000 m^2) Curative: 0.05–0.09/ft.^{2} (0.5–1/m^2)	Weekly, see local pest management Weekly until >80% parasitism
Harmonia axyridis (Pallas) predatory beetle)	*Aphis gossypii*	Curative: 0.9–4.5/ ft.^{2} (10-50/m^2)	1 introduction for hot spots
Hippodamia convergens (Guérin-Ménéville) (predatory beetle)	*Aphis gossypii*	Curative: 2.3–9.0/ft.^{2} (25–100/m^2)	1 introduction for hot spots
Diglyphus isaea (Walker) (parasitic wasp)	*Liriomyza bryoniae* (Kaltenbach) *Liriomyza trifolii* (Burgess) *Liriomyza huidobrensis* (Blanchard)	Curative: 0.01–0.02/ft.^{2} (0.1–0.25/m^2)	Weekly for at least 3 introductions
Dacnusa sibirica (Telenga) *Diglyphus isaea* (parasitic wasps)	Same as above	Curative: 0.02/ft.^{2} (0.25/m^2)	Weekly for at least 3 introductions

(continued)

Table 26.3. *(continued)*

Natural Enemies	Pest	Rate	Frequency
Hypoaspis miles Berlese *Hypoaspis aculeifer* (Canestrini) (predatory mite)	*Bradysia* spp. *Corynoptera* spp.	Preventive: 100/m^2 Curative: 200–500/m^2	1 introduction
Atheta coriaria Kraatz (predatory beetle)	*Bradysia* spp. *Corynoptera* spp.	Preventive; 0.2/ft^2 (2/m^2)	1 introduction
Steinernema carpocapsae (Weiser) *Steinernema feltiae* (Filipjev) (parasitic nematodes)	Same as above	Curative: 40,000–90,000/ft.^{2} (0.5–1 million/m^2), see label	Weekly for 1–2 introductions
Verticillium lecanii (Zimmerman) Viégas *Beauveria bassiana* (Balsam) Vuillemin (fungal pathogen)	*Trialeurodes vaporariorum* *Aphis* spp. *Frankliniella occidentalis*	Curative: See label	See label
Bacillus thuringiensis (Berliner) (bacterium)	*Trichoplusia ni* (Hübner) *Autographa gamma* L.	Curative: Depends upon formulation, see label	See label
Trichogramma evanescens (Westwood) *Trichogramma brassicae* Bezdenko *Trichogramma pretiosum* Riley (parasitic wasps)	Same as above	Curative: 0.9–2/ft.^{2} (10–22/m^2)	Weekly until >80% parasitism

1992; C. Castañé, pers. comm.). In Austria, Germany, Hungary, and other countries from middle Europe, the adoption rate is intermediate (Albert 1990; Hatala-Zsellér et al. 1993; Blümel and Schausberger 1996).

In the Mediterranean area, pests and natural enemies move freely into greenhouses through open sides or ventilation vents. Greenhouses in this region (see chapter 3) are open to maintain adequate ventilation in the relatively warm climate. A concerted effort is being conducted by some countries such as Italy and Spain to survey the natural enemies in their area for possible use in greenhouses (Riudavets, Castañé, and Gabarra 1995; Albajes et al. 1996). Four species that show potential are *Dicyphus tamaninii* Wagner, *Macrolophus caliginosus* Wagner, *Orius laevigatus* (Fieber), and *Orius majusculus* (Reuter) (Riudavets, Castañé, and Gabarra 1995; Montserrat, Albajes, and Castañé 2000). It is hoped with reduced pesticide application, these natural predators will move into the greenhouse and provide control, especially with additional augmentative releases (Albajes et al. 1996).

Limitations to IPM in Cucumber Production

Limitations to the use of biological control in cucumber production vary according to the region and previous success rate with this control measure. Grower education concerning the advantages of IPM, the different strategies involved, how biological control programs may be implemented, the biology of the natural enemies involved, and what conditions are important for success are critical for successful implementation of IPM. In areas where biological control is generally successful, the main limitations are the lack of pesticides compatible with key natural enemies, the development of regulations for the use of new indigenous and non-indigenous biological control agents, and the attitude of growers towards the use of biological control agents. There are over twenty species of biological control agents (parasitoids, predators, and pathogens) introduced against arthropod pests of cucumber. However, many situations still occur where the balance between the biological control agent and the pest is upset in favor of the pest or there are no suitable biological control agents for a particular pest, as in the case for biological control of noctuid caterpillars. In these cases, selective pesticides, especially insect growth regulators, need to be used to reduce pest densities to non-economic levels or levels at which the biological control agents can again exert control. Information regarding the compatibility and the effects of pesticides on biological control agents is available from several sources (see chapter 7 and Koppert 1999). It is important to remember that even some fungicides used to control plant diseases are also harmful to biological control agents.

A potential limitation to the use of biological control worldwide is the trend for government regulations on the use of parasitoids and predators for arthropod pest management. Many countries throughout the world are developing regulations to control the use of indigenous and the importation of non-indigenous arthropods for biological control (van Lenteren 2003). The purpose of such regulations is to protect local natural ecosystems and to ensure that new agents meet minimum quality standards.

Table 26.4. IPM Program for Greenhouse Cucumber Pests in Ontario, Canada

Pest	Strategy	Control Actions/Agents
All pests	Cultural	1. Thorough clean up between crops using high temperatures or short-residual fumigants. 2. Control weeds inside and around greenhouse.
	Monitoring	1. Monitor pest populations using yellow sticky cards. 2. Inspect crop regularly for development of pest hot spots and for location of non-flying pests.
Western flower thrips (*Frankliniella occidentalis* [Pergande])	Biological	1. *Neoseiulus cucumeris* (Oudemans): After transplanting in the greenhouse, place small piles of the mite/bran mixture at the base of plants but away from the stem. When plants are at the wire, slow-release sachets are used. 2. *Orius insidiosus* (Say): Apply in hot spots. 3. *Hypoaspis miles* Berlese/*H. aculeifer* (Canestrini): Apply these predators to seedlings and immediately after transplanting in the greenhouse to assist in suppressing thrips pupae.
Greenhouse whitefly (*Trialeurodes vaporariorum* [Westwood])	Biological	1. *Encarsia formosa* (Gahan): Release preventively and in response to detection of whiteflies. 2. *Eretmocerus eremicus* (Rose and Zolnerowhich): Release during late winter, spring and summer.
Two-spotted spider mite (*Tetranychus urticae* Koch)	Biological	1. *Phytoseiulus persimilis* Athias-Henriot: Once spider mites have been detected for several weeks, release predator on infested and surrounding plants. 2. *Feltiella acarisuga* (Vallot): Will provide additional control when combined with *P. persimilis*. 3. *Stethorus punctillum* Weise: Use only for hot spots.

(continued)

Table 26.4. *(continued)*

Pest	Strategy	Control Actions/Agents
	Chemical	Fenbutatin oxide may be applied as soon as spider mites are detected, and before release of predators, particularly if diapausing stages are observed.
Fungus gnats (*Bradysia impatiens* [Johannsen])	Cultural	Provide good drainage throughout greenhouse to minimize water puddles and algal growth.
	Biological	1. *Hypoaspis miles*/*H. aculeifer* (Canestrini)/*Atheta coriaria* Kraatz: Apply during seedling stage and after planting in the greenhouse. 2. *Steinernema feltiae* (Filipjev): Apply to reduce larval populations. 3. *Bacillus thuringiensis* (VectoBac) : Apply to reduce larval populations.
Aphids (*Aphis gossypii* [Glover], *Myzus persicae* [Sulzer])	Biological	*Aphidius colemani* (Viereck): Use banker plants to release this parasitoid preventively and at first sign of aphids.
	Chemical	1. Use insecticidal soap on hot spots. 2. Apply nicotine smokes for general reduction in population.
Cabbage loopers (*Trichoplusia ni* [Hübner])	Monitoring/ Trapping	1. Use UV light traps to detect adults and reduce adult populations during winter months. 2. Inspect plants to detect feeding damage.
	Biological	*Bacillus thuringiensis* (Berliner): Apply formulations (Dipel, Foray, Thuricide) to suppress larval populations.

Grower attitudes toward pest management can also limit successful implementation and long-term adoption of biological control. Many growers use biological control agents as if they were pesticides. In part, this is due to recommendations for the release of biological control agents as number of organisms per ft.^{2} or m^2. This terminology for release rates is virtually identical to the unit of application (active ingredient [AI] per unit of area) associated with pesticide recommendations. Parasitoids, predators, and pathogens used in biological control, however, are living organisms, and differ in important ways from pesticides. The organisms used in biological control are as perishable as the crops that they are used to protect. Most natural enemies cannot be stored, even for short periods. Because living organisms respond to the environment around them, release rates should be based upon temperature and humidity conditions, the size of the plant canopy, and the densities of pest species. As a result, biological control programs must typically be tailored to the greenhouse production conditions used by individual growers.

In areas where implementation of biological control is low, various issues such as the climatic conditions of the area, incidence of diseases that are vectored by greenhouse pests, management practices, differences in greenhouse structures, and lack of selective pesticides often act as limiting factors. Climatic conditions that favor pest development on a year-round basis make it difficult to control pest species within greenhouses because of frequent opportunities for movement into greenhouses from the field (van Lenteren et al. 1992, Cabello and Cañero 1994). In northern Italy, *T. urticae* undergoes five to eight generation per year, whereas in southern Italy, spider mites can have more than thirty generations per year (van Lenteren et al. 1992). On the other hand, even in temperate climates such as Alberta and Ontario, Canada, extremes between the cold dry winters and hot humid summers make it challenging to maintain a greenhouse climate that is beneficial to biological control (Shipp, Boland, and Shaw 1991).

Similarly, the occurrence of plant diseases vectored by arthropods is a much greater problem in warm climates. In the Mediterranean area, beet pseudo yellow and cucumber mosaic viruses are important problems both outdoors and in the greenhouses (Ramakers and Rabasse 1995). In Ontario, bacterial wilt, which is vectored by cucumber beetles, is a major obstacle to biological control in the spring.

Production practices can also have a major influence on the implementation of IPM. In the Mediterranean area, growers often have several crops, at various stages within their production cycle, all growing at once in their greenhouses. Complete sanitation of a greenhouse is not possible when there are continuous overlapping crop production cycles. In this geographic region and with this production cycle, growers prefer the intensive use of broad-spectrum pesticides to control their pests and diseases (van Lenteren et al. 1992, Cabello and Cañero 1994).

Greenhouse structures in warmer climates often are frame structures covered with plastic and with open sides (see chapter 3). If there are vents in these structures, they are normally controlled manually, as there is little automation of climate control systems. Ventilation is so important that screening is seldom used or even considered. Greenhouses located in these climates are seldom heated: only 10% of Italian greenhouses are heated. Thus, the poorly controlled temperature fluctuations and the absence of barriers to prevent or reduce the incidence of pest movement often make the greenhouses unsuitable for biological control (van Lenteren et al. 1992).

Finally, the lack of selective pesticides that can be integrated with biological control agents is an important limitation. Such pesticides should have short residual times so natural enemies can be re-introduced as soon as possible after a pesticide application (Shipp, Wang and Ferguson 2000; Jones et al. 2002). Also, these pesticides should be selective to specific groups of pests or have a mode of action (systemic or growth regulator) that will only be harmful to a certain group of pests. Still needed are chemicals and other strategies that control plant diseases and are not harmful to the natural enemies eliciting biological control of arthropod pests.

References Cited

Albajes, R., O. Alomar, J. Riudavets, C. Castañé, J. Arnó, and R. Gabarra. 1996. The mirid bug *Dicyphus tamaninii*: An effective predator for vegetable crops. *IOBC/WPRC Bulletin* 19 (1):1–4.

Albert, R. 1990. Experiences with biological control measures in glasshouses in southwest Germany. *IOBC/WPRS Bulletin* 13 (5):1–5.

Borgemeister, C., L. Ebssa, D. Premachandra, O. Berndt, R. Ehlers, and H. Pochling. 2002. Biological control of soil-dwelling life stages of western flower thrips *Frankliniella occidentalis* (Pergande) (Thysanoptera: Thripidae) by entompathogenic nematodes and *Hypoaspis* spp. (Acari: Laelapidae). *IOBC/WPRC Bulletin* 25(1):29-32.

Blümel, S., and P. Schausberger. 1996. Current status of IPM in greenhouses in Austria. *IOBC/WPRS Bulletin* 19 (1):19–22.

Brødsgaard, H. F. 1993. Coloured sticky traps for thrips (Thysanoptera: Thripidae) monitoring on glasshouse cucumbers. *IOBC/WPRS Bulletin* 16 (2):19–22.

Butt, T. M., C. W. Jackson, and N. Magan. 2001. *Fungi as Biocontrol Agents – Progress, Problems and Potential.* New York, NY: CAB International.

Cabello, T., and R. Cañero. 1994. Technical efficiency of plant protection in Spanish greenhouses. *Crop Protection* 13:153–9.

Carney, V. A., J. C. Diamond, G. D. Murphy, and D. Marshall. 2002. The potential of *Atheta coriaria* Kraatz (Coleoptera: Staphylinidae), as a biological control agent for use in greenhouse crops. *IOBC/WPRC Bulletin* 25 (1):37-40.

Castañé, C., O. Alomar, and J. Riudavets. 1996. Management of western flower thrips on cucumber with *Dicyphus tamaninii* (Heteroptera: Miridae). *Biological Control* 7:114-120.

Cho, K., S. H. Kang, and J. O. Lee. 1998. Spatial distribution of thrips in greenhouse cucumber and development of a fixed-precision sampling plan for estimating population density. *Journal of Asia-Pacific Entomology* 1:163-170.

El Habi, M., A. Sekkat, L. El Jadd, and A. Boumezzough. 2000. Biologie d'*Hippodamia variegate* Goeze (Col., Coccinellidae) et possibilité de son utilisation contre *Aphis gossypii* Glov (Hom., Aphididae) sous serres de concombre. *Journal of Applied Entomology* 124:365-74.

Gabarra, R., C. Castañé, and R. Albajes. 1995. The mired bug *Dicyphus tamaninii* as a greenhouse whitefly and western flower thrips predator on cucumber. *Biocontrol Science and Technology* 5:475-488.

Gilkeson, L. A. 1994. Greenhouse cucumber: Melon (cotton) aphid. In *Diseases and Pests of Vegetable Crops in Canada*, ed. R. J. Howard, J. A. Garland, and W. L. Seaman, 321–2, Ottawa, Canada: Canadian Phytopathology Society and Entomological Society of Canada.

Gillespie, D. R., and D. M. J. Quiring. 1990. Biological control of fungus gnats, *Bradysia* spp. (Diptera: Sciaridae), and western flower thrips, *Frankliniella occidentalis* (Pergande) (Thysanoptera: Thripidae), in greenhouses using a soil-dwelling predatory mite, *Geolaelaps* sp. nr. *aculeifer* (Canestrini) (Acari: Laelapidae). *The Canadian Entomologist* 122:975–83.

Hatala-Zsellér, I., E. Simon, P. Szabó, and E. Ceglarska-Hódi. 1993. Integrated pest and disease management in Hungarian greenhouses. *IOBC/WPRS Bulletin* 16 (2):55–8.

Hussey, N. W., and W. J. Parr. 1963. The effect of glasshouse red spider mite (*Tetranychus urticae* Koch) on the yield of cucumbers. *Journal of Horticultural Science* 38:255–63.

Jacobson, R. 1995a. Integrated pest management in cucumbers: Prevention of establishment of *Frankliniella occidentalis* (Pergande). *Mededelingen Faculteit Landbouwwetenschappen, Rijksuniversiteit Gent* 60:857–63.

Jacobson, R. J. 1995b. Resources to implement biological control in greenhouses. In *Thrips Biology and Management*. eds. Parker, B. L., Skinner, M., and T. Lewis, 211-219, New York: Plenum Press.

Jacobson, R. J. 1997. Integrated pest management (IPM) in glasshouses. In *Thrips as Crop Pests*, ed. T. Lewis, 639–66. Wallingford, U.K.: CAB International.

Jacobson, R. J., D. Chandler, J. Fenlon, and K. M. Russell. 2001. Compatibility of *Beauveria bassiana* (Balsamo) Vuillemin with *Amblyseius cucumeris* Oudemans (Acarina: Phytoseiidae) to control *Frankliniella occidentalis* Pergande (Thysanoptera: Thripidae) on cucumber plants. *Biocontrol, Science and Technology* 11:391-400.

Jarvis, W. R., J. L. Shipp, and R. B. Gardiner. 1993. Transmission of *Pythium aphanidermatum* to greenhouse cucumber by the fungus gnat *Bradysia impatiens* (Diptera: Sciaridae). *Annals of Applied Biology* 122:23–9.

Jones, T., C. Scott-Dupree, R. Harris, L. Shipp, and B. Harris. 2002. Spinosad: An effective biocide for inclusion in integrated pest management programs for *Frankliniella occidentalis* Pergande (Thysanoptera: Thripidae) on greenhouse cucumber. *IOBC/WPRC Bulletin* 25 (1):119–122.

Kawai, A., and C. Kitamura. 1987. Studies on population ecology of *Thrips palmi* Karny. XV. Evaluation of effectiveness of control methods using a simulation model. *Applied Entomology and Zoology* 22:292–302.

Koppert Biological Systems. 1999. *Side Effects Guide*. Berkel en Rodenrijs, the Netherlands: Koppert B.V.

Kuroda, T., and K. Miura. 2003. Comparison of the effectiveness of two methods for releasing *Harmonia axyridis* (Pallas) (Coleoptera: Coccinellidae) against *Aphis gossypii* Glover (Homoptera: Aphididae) on cucumbers in a greenhouse. *Applied Entomology and Zoology* 38:271-274.

Maisonneuve, J. C. 2002. Biological control in France in greenhouse vegetables and ornamentals. *IOBC/WPRS Bulletin* 25 (1):151-154.

Matsui, M., and T. Nakashima. 1992. Damage to vegetables and ornamental plants by the sweet potato whitefly and its control in Japan. *Japanese Pesticide Information* 60:15–8.

Montserrat, M., R. Albajes, and C. Castañé. 2000. Functional response of four heteropteran predators preying on greenhouse whitefly (Homoptera: Aleyrodidae) and western flower thrips (Thysanoptera: Thripidae). *Biological Control* 29:1075-1082.

Nomikou, M., A. Janssen, R. Schraag, and M. W. Sabelis. Phytoseiid predators suppress populations of *Bemisia tabaci* on cucumber plants with alternative food. *Experimental and Applied Acarology* 27:57-68.

Papadopoulos, A. P. 1994. Growing greenhouse seedless cucumbers in soil and in soilless media. Agriculture and AgriFood Canada Publication 1902/E.

Ponsen, M. B. 1987. Alimentary track. In *Aphids: Their Biology, Natural Enemie,s and Control*, Vol. 2A, ed. A. K. Minks and P. Harrewijn, 79–97, New York (Amsterdam): Elsevier.

Powell, C. C., and R. K. Lindquist. 1992. *Ball Pest and Disease Manual*. Geneva, Ill.: Ball Publishing.

Pralavorio, M., and A. Rojas. 1980. Influence de température et de l'humidité relative sur le développement et la reproduction de *Phytoseiulus persimilis*. *IOBC/WPRS Bulletin* 3 (3):157–62.

Ramakers, P. M. J. and J. M. Rabasse. 1995. Integrated pest management in protected cultivation. In *Novel Approaches to Integrated Pest Management*, ed. R. Reuveni, 198–229. Boca Raton, Fla: Lewis Publishers.

Riudavets, J., C. Castañé, and R. Gabarra. 1995. Native predators of western flower thrips in horticultural crops. In *Thrips Biology and Management*, ed. B. L. Parker, M. Skinner, and T. Lewis, 255–8. New York: Plenum Press.

Scopes, N. E. A. 1985. Red spider mite and the predator *Phytoseiulus persimilis*. In *Biological Pest Control: The Glasshouse Experience*, ed. N. W. Hussey and N. E. A. Scopes, 43–52. Poole, U.K.: Blandford (Ithaca, N.Y.: Cornell University Press).

Shipp, J. L. 1995. Monitoring of western flower thrips on glasshouse and vegetable crops. In *Thrips Biology and Management*, ed. B. L. Parker, M. Skinner, and T. Lewis, 547–55. New York: Plenum Press.

Shipp, J. L., Boland, G. J., and L. A. Shaw. 1991. Integrated pest management of disease and arthropod pests of greenhouse vegetable crops in Ontario: Current status and future possibilities. *Canadian Journal of Plant Science* 71:887–914.

Shipp, J. L., Y. Zhang, D. W. A. Hunt, and G. Ferguson. 2003. Influence of humidity and greenhouse microclimate on the efficacy of *Beauveria bassiana* (Balsamo) for control of greenhouse arthropod pests. *Biological Control* 32:1154-1163.

Shipp, J. L., K. Wang, and M. R. Binns. 2000. Economic injury levels for western flower thrips (Thysanoptera: Thripidae) on greenhouse cucumber. *Journal of Economic Entomology* 93:1732-1740.

Shipp, J. L., K. Wang, and G. Ferguson. 2000. Residual toxicity of avermectin b1 and pyridaben to eight commercially produced beneficial arthropod species used for control of greenhouse pests. *Biological Control* 17:125–31.

Steiner, M. Y. 1990. Determining population characteristics and sampling procedures for the western flower thrips (Thysanoptera: Thripidae) and the predatory mite *Amblyseius cucumeris* (Acari: Phytoseiidae) on greenhouse cucumber. *Environmental Entomology* 19:1605–13.

Stenseth, C. 1985. Whitefly and its parasite *Encarsia formosa*. In *Biological Pest Control: The Glasshouse Experience*, ed. N. W. Hussey and N. E. A. Scopes, 30–3. Poole, U.K.: Blandford (Ithaca, N.Y.: Cornell University Press).

Taylor, R. A. J., R. K. Lindquist, and J. L. Shipp. 1998. Variation and consistency in spatial distribution: Significance for pest management. *Environmental Entomology* 27:191–201.

van Lenteren, J. C. 1992. Biological control in protected crops: Where do we go? *Pesticide Science* 36:321–7.

van Lenteren, J. C. 2003. *Quality Control and Production of Biological Control Agents – Theory and Testing Procedures*. Cambridge, MA: CABI Publishing.

van Lenteren, J. C., M. Benuzzi, G. Nicoli, and S. Maini. 1992. Biological control in protected crops in Europe. In *Biological Control and Integrated Crop Protection: Towards Environmentally Safer Agriculture*, ed. J. C. van Lenteren, A. K. Minks, and O. M. B. De Ponti, 77–89. Wageningen, the Netherlands: Pudoc Scientific Publishers.

Wang, K., and J. L. Shipp. 2001. Sequential sampling plans for western flower thrips (Thysanoptera: Thripidae) on greenhouse cucumbers. *Journal of Economic Entomology* 94:579-585.

Wyatt, I. J., and S. J. Brown. 1977. The influence of light intensity, day length and temperature on increase rates of four glasshouse aphids. *Journal of Applied Ecology* 14:391–9.

27

IPM Program for Sweet Pepper

P. M. J. Ramakers

Applied Plant Research Division, Glasshouse Horticulture
Naaldwijk, The Netherlands

Peppers are grown worldwide on 1.5 million hectares, mainly as an outdoor crop (FAO 2002). Fruit development and ripening require considerable periods with high temperatures. Commercial production in temperate climates is therefore only possible in greenhouses. In areas warm enough for outdoor production, the acreage of peppers produced under some kind of protection is also increasing as the practice extends the production season, generates higher quality fruit, and provides some insurance against crop damage from weather. Production within technologically advanced greenhouses generates yields up to 300 tons/ha (van Woerden 2003) compared to 12 tons or even less for outdoor crops (FAO 2002). Peppers are grown as protected crops in spring/summer in continental climates (e.g., Hungary), in winter/spring or autumn in subtropical areas (e.g., Spain, Italy), and year-round (planted in winter) in heated greenhouses in temperate climates (e.g., northern Europe, Canada).

History of Use of Biological Control in Sweet Peppers

Protected cultivation of sweet peppers was still in an experimental phase when the first growers tried to emulate the biological control of spider mites practiced by cucumber growers. Biological control in greenhouses was itself in its infancy, and few natural enemy species were available from commercial suppliers. In addition there were no assurances that sufficient numbers of natural enemies would be available as needed, a prerequisite for successful biological control, even if the desired species were mass produced by a commercial insectary.

During the 1970s, the number of growers adopting biological control increased steadily (Woets, Ramakers, and van Lenteren 1980). However, the type of IPM being applied was still dominated heavily by insecticides. After planting in December, growers typically applied broad-spectrum pesticides in a preventative manner. Fumigation treatments were preferred, and frequencies like once every 10 days were common. Spider mites characteristically first appeared in March at which time growers had to choose between either (1) chemical control, including incorporation of specific acaricides rather than general insecticides, foliar rather than fumigation treatments, and stepping up the application frequency to weekly, or (2) an integrated approach, including predatory mites and selective chemicals as far as available. Beginning in June and continuing until replanting, most IPM growers reverted back to sole reliance on chemical control due to arrival of immigrating secondary pests. While there was an increase in the numbers of growers implementing biological control during the 1970s, the practice was actually used for only a short portion of the cropping cycle.

Use of biological control in greenhouse peppers accelerated in the mid-1980s, not only in terms of acreage (Fig. 27.1), but also in terms of the biological input per hectare. The gross volume of natural enemies purchased by pepper growers in the Netherlands increased ninety-fold in that decade (Ramakers 1996b). In the same period, sweet pepper evolved from a minor greenhouse vegetable crop to one of major importance. Sweet pepper is now considered the best example of successful IPM in protected cultivation with respect to both complexity (number of biological control agents involved) and duration (period during which natural enemies are operational). Factors that triggered and supported this development included:

(i)   An initiative by the Dutch Central Bureau for Fruit and Vegetable Auctions to promote the export of pesticide-residue-free fresh peppers to the United States (de Klerk and Ramakers 1986, Ravensberg and Altena 1987).

(ii) An increase in the availability of natural enemies produced by commercial insectaries (Ravensberg 1992).

(iii) The adoption by many developed countries of a policy to reduce dependence on pesticides used in agriculture (van Lenteren, Minks, and de Ponti 1992). An agreement in the Netherlands between the Ministries of Agriculture, Economics, and Environment and growers' representatives to set environmental targets for the greenhouse industry as a whole (van Aartsen et al., 1997).

(iv) Incorporation of IPM into marketing approaches to consumers (Gerritsen 1991, Ramakers 1996a).

(v)   Occurrence of pesticide resistance in aphids (van der Staay and van Steenis 1994).

(vi) Agreements between international (often British) supermarkets and individual growers or growers associations about standards for good agricultural practice, including guidelines for plant protection.

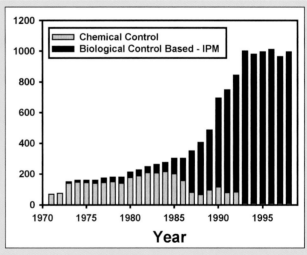

Figure 27.1. Adoption (No. of hectares) of biological control-based IPM in glasshouse-grown sweet pepper in the Netherlands.

If and to what extent an individual grower will choose an IPM approach, depends on his or her knowledge of biological control, the local availability of both natural enemies and compatible pesticides (especially insecticides), demands of supermarkets and consumers, local climatic conditions, and most importantly the local pest and disease pressure. In particular, the expectation of problems with virus diseases transmitted by aphids or thrips is a major impediment for biological control in peppers. Biological control–based IPM is therefore more likely to succeed in areas or seasons where there is little chance of pest populations immigrating into greenhouses, which is the case in the relatively closed type of greenhouse located in the northern parts of Europe and Canada. For similar reasons, winter planted crops are more suitable than crops planted in full summer. Peppers in subtropical

areas are often grown in half open structures, and growers of such crops frequently choose chemical control over biological control (Table 27.1).

Local differences in crop production practices, weather, attitude of individual growers and pest pressure yield a variety of IPM programs practised in sweet pepper. One may distinguish three levels of IPM, according to the scope of the biological component (Table 27.2).

The "basic program" includes integrated control of spider mites and thrips, with chemical control being used for all other pests. Systems of "expanded use of biological control" integrate chemical and biological control for spider mites, aphids, noctuid moths, thrips, and leafminers. In "maximum use of biological control" programs, all available biological control agents are used and chemical control is highly restricted.

Table 27.1 Acreage of Sweet Pepper Production under IPM for Selected Countries in Europe and North America.*

Country	Total area (ha)	Protected area (ha)	Yield protected (ton/ha)	IPM area (ha)
Spain	22,800	—	43	1,100
Italy	13,700	2,600	24	130
Holland	1,200	1,200	260-300	1,200
Hungary	—	—	20–30	25–30
France	760	760	36	—
Canada	—	200	—	200
Belgium	80	80	—	80

*Sources: FAO, Eurostat

Table 27.2 IPM Programs Using Different Levels of Biological Control for Sweet Peppers Grown in Protected Culture in The Netherlands

Pest	Biological Control Agents	Chemicals
Basic Program		
Spider mites*	*Phytoseiulus persimilis*	Abamectin (at propagation, before flowering, later only spots) Fenbutatinoxide Hexythiazox
Thrips	*Neoseiulus cucumeris* *Orius laevigatus*	Pending: Spinosad
Aphids	None	Pirimicarb Imidacloprid (systemic) Thiacloprid (systemic or spots) Pymetrozine
Leafminers	None	Abamectin (at propagation) Cyromazine
Caterpillars	None	Teflubenzuron
Other insects	None	Pyrethroids (spots, end of season) Pyridaben (fumigation, foliar applications)
Expanded Use of Biological Control		
Spider mites	*Phytoseiulus persimilis* *Feltiella acarisuga*	Abamectin (at propagation, before flowering, later only spots) Fenbutatinoxide Hexythiazox
Aphids	*Aphidius colemani* on banker plants with *Rhopalosiphum* sp. *Aphidius ervi* on bankers with *Sitobion* sp. *Aphidoletes aphidimyza* *Adalia bipunctata* (at hot spots only)	Pirimicarb (fumigation) Imidacloprid (systemic) Thiacloprid (systemic or spots) Pymetrozine

(continued)

Table 27.2 *(continued)*

Pest	Biological Control Agents	Chemicals
Thrips*	*Neoseiulus cucumeris* *Orius laevigatus* *Iphiseius degenerans*	Abamectin (at propagation, before flowering, for *Echinothrips*) Pending: Spinosad (start and end of season)
Noctuids, Tortricids	*Bacillus thuringiensis* Baculovirus (for *Spodoptera* sp.) Light traps	Teflubenzuron
Leafminers	*Diglyphus isaea* (after March) *Dacnusa sibirica* (natural control) *Opius pallipes* (natural control)	Abamectin (at propagation) Cyromazine
Mirid bugs	None	Imidacloprid (systemic)
Whiteflies	*Eretmocerus eremicus* *Eretmocerus mundus* (from May)	Pyriproxyfen Buprofezin Thiacloprid Imidacloprid (systemic, high rate) Pyridaben (aerial appl., spraying only end of season)
Maximum Use of Biological Control		
Spider mites	*Phytoseiulus persimilis* (pest in first) *Feltiella acarisuga* *Neoseiulus californicus*	Fenbutatinoxide Hexythiazox
Aphids*	*Aphidius colemani* on bankers with *Rhopalosiphum* sp. *Aphidius ervi* on banker plants with *Sitobion* sp. *Aphidoletes aphidimyza* *Aphelinus abdominalis* *Adalia bipunctata* (at hot spots only)	Pirimicarb (fumigation) Thiacloprid (systemic or at hot spots) Pymetrozine

(continued)

Table 27.2 *(continued)*

Pest	Biological Control Agents	Chemicals
	Chrysoperla carnea (at hot spots only) *Episyrphus balteatus* (near banker plants or hot spots)	
Thrips	*Neoseiulus cucumeris* *Orius laevigatus* *Orius majusculus* (for *Echinothrips* sp.) *Iphiseius degenerans* (on castor beans as banker plants)	None
Noctuids, Tortricids	Light traps Pheromone traps for monitoring *Spodoptera* sp. and *Clepsis* sp. *Bacillus thuringiensis* *Trichogramma brassicae* Baculovirus (for *Spodoptera* sp.)	Teflubenzuron
Leaf miners	Sample larvae to assess percent parasitism *Dacnusa sibirica* *Diglyphus isaea* (after March) *Opius pallipes* (natural control)	Cyromazine
Mirid bugs	None	Imidacloprid (systemic)
Whiteflies	*Encarsia formosa* *Eretmocerus eremicus* *Eretmocerus mundus* (from May) *Macrolophus caliginosus* Eggplants for monitoring whiteflies and as banker plants for natural enemies	Pyriproxyfen Buprofezin Thiacloprid

*Crucial pest in the particular control program

Table 27.3. Recommended Release Rates for Natural Enemies in Sweet Pepper.

Target Pest	Control Agent	Application Methods/Comments	Rate (# / ha)	GRID (release points / ha)
Spider mites	*Phytoseiulus persimilis*	1) Pest-in-first 2) Inoculative 3) Inundative	10,000 60,000 10–25 per plant	2,000 4,000 Spot treatment
	Neoseiulus californicus	Inoculative	12,000	along green-house walls and central path
Thrips	*Neoseiulus cucumeris*	1) Predator-in-first (early introduction on rockwool)	2,500,000	30,000
		2) Predator-in-first (in paper bags on plants)	4,000,000	4,000
	Orius spp.	1) Predator-in-first, on flowering crop	2 x 5,000– 10,000	200
		2) Inundative	25 per m^2	Spot treatment
	Iphiseius degenerans	1) Inoculative, on flowering crop	2,000	25
		2) Banker plants (*Ricinus communis*)	15 bankers with >1,000 predators each	Move bankers weekly
Aphids	*Aphidius* spp.	1) Preventive weekly	1,000–1,500	25
		2) Banker plants (barley seedlings with cereal aphids)	5 pots, each with four tussocks	Add weekly, replace when necessary
	Aphidoletes aphidimyza	1) Curative	10,000	25
		2) Inundative hot spot	1,000 per	Spot treatment
	Coccinellids	Inundative	2.5 per m^2	Spot treatment
	Chrysopids	Inundative	10 per m^2	Spot treatment
	Syrphids	Inundative	5 per m^2	Spot treatment

(continued)

Table 27.3. *(continued)*

Target Pest	Control Agent	Application Methods/Comments	Rate (# / ha)	GRID (release points / ha)
Leafminers	*Dacnusa sibirica*	If insufficient natural parasitization	2 × 5,000	20
	Diglyphus isaea	From March onwards, in case of high levels of pest attack	2,500	release adults while walking through affected area
Whiteflies	Aphelinid parasitoids	1) Preventive, from mid February onwards	10,000 weekly	300
		2) Curative	30,000 weekly until 90% parasitization	600
		3) Inundative	100 per m²	Spot treatment
	Macrolophus caliginosus	1) Inoculative, from March onwards	2 × 5,000	400
		2) Inundative	250 per hot spot	Spot treatment

Recommended release rates for each of the natural enemies used in biological control in sweet pepper crops are listed in Table 27.3.

Spider Mites

The basic program indicated in Table 27.2 is meant to prevent or overcome problems with resistance in spider mites. Acaricides are still used, but with a reduced frequency. A cropping season can usually be completed with only one or two full-scale pesticide treatments. Because spider mites can complete up to fifteen generations per year, there is relatively weak selection for the development of resistance from this level of acaricide use. If the organophosphate (OP)–resistant strain of *Phytoseiulus persimilis* Athias-Henriot (Schulten, van de Klashorst, and Russel 1976) is applied, this basic program can be used even with non-selective insecticides. An IPM scheme that was popular for several years in The Netherlands included predatory mites and fenbutatinoxide against spider mites, pirimicarb against aphids, and tetrachlorvinphos against thrips (Ramakers 1980). For an OP-compound, tetrachlorvinphos is a relatively persistent chemical, and an occasional light application to only the tops of the plants (rather than a thorough spray of the foliage) was sufficient to prevent fruit damage by thrips. Since pirimicarb could also be applied in rather simple ways (fumigation or low volume misting rather than spraying), this program was considered both effective and convenient.

Thrips

The basis program (Table 27.2) is applicable only if the local thrips population is sufficiently susceptible to insecticides compatible with the use of *P. persimilis*. This approach to control of spider mites was jeopardized by the introduction of highly resistant strains of western flower thrips, *Frankliniella occidentalis* (Pergande), into European greenhouses in the mid-1980s (zur Strassen 1986). The invasion of this resistant strain of western flower thrips complicated the IPM program since the few insecticides effective against western flower thrips were incompatible with the use of predator mites. As a result, it became necessary to use biological control against both spider mites and thrips (see the "expanded use" scheme in Table 27.2). Biological control of western flower thrips was accomplished by the combined use of a predatory mite, *Neoseiulus cucumeris* (Oudemans), and minute pirate bugs (*Orius insidiosus* [Say]). These predators complement each other by preying on different instars of western flower thrips (*N. cucumeris* feeding on young larvae and *O. insidiosus* feeding on old larvae and adults) and by occupying different plant microhabitats (*N. cucumeris* occurring on fruit, *O. insidiosus* in flowers, and both occurring together on the foliage). (Anticipating new faunal protection legislation by the E.U., European suppliers of beneficials have replaced the Nearctic species

O. insidiosus with the Palearctic species *Orius laevigatus* [Fiefer], which has a wide European distribution.) Peppers are particularly suitable for biological thrips control, since the pollen that is continuously produced by this crop acts as a food source for both the phytoseiids and the anthocorids. Hence, colonization of the crop by predators is completed even before the pest is present (predator-in-first), resulting in considerable improvement of the reliability of the control program (Ramakers and Rabasse 1995).

Later, another phytoseiid, *Iphiseius degenerans* (Berlese), was found to be a more suitable predator of thrips in peppers than *N. cucumeris* (van Houten and van Stratum 1995). As the mass rearing of this species is far more expensive, growers are advised to make an inoculative introduction (several thousand per hectare) of this species after an inundative introduction (several million per hectare) of *N. cucumeris*. Some growers accelerate *I. degenerans* colonization using a castor bean (*Ricinus communis* L.) banker plant system (Fig. 27.2) (Ramakers and Voet

Figure 27.2. **Castor bean (*Ricinus communis* L.) is used by some growers as a banker plant to facilitate prolonged releases of *Iphiseius degenerans*, to help control western flower thrips.** *Photo: P. M. J. Ramakers.*

1995). In most greenhouses, *N. cucumeris* is the dominant predator in winter and spring, while *I. degenerans* replaces it in mid-summer. After being introduced at the end of winter, *Orius* spp. bugs become common in spring and coexist with the phytoseiids until the late autumn when they cease reproduction with the declining day length. Because of the complexity of this system and the lack of a selective insecticide for emergency control of thrips, growers are encouraged to respond rapidly to changing conditions and intensively monitor pest and predator densities. A decision support model, emphasising the interactions between thrips and thrips predators, is available to assist in making effective pest management decisions (Ramakers and van der Maas 1996).

This model requires the examination of various plant structures for both thrips and predators. Growers should examine the undersides of thirty pepper leaves with a hand lens to assess the abundance of phytoseiid mites, paying special attention to the trichomes within the pits along the veins of leaves, where the predator's eggs are often attached. Anthocorids and thrips should be counted on 100 fully opened flowers. To achieve a more accurate determination, insects are counted with the aid of a microscope after flowers have been placed in alcohol. Sticky traps detect initial thrips infestations and show the trends in the abundance of adults thrips and anthocorids. If a grower appears to have sufficient predators, but the numbers of adult thrips in flowers and on sticky traps remain high, then growers should dissect some second quality fruits to detect the possible presence of thrips larvae in the narrow space between the pericarp and the calyx. If such a sample reveals few thrips larvae but a high number of phytoseiids, further fruit damage is unlikely and the grower may confidently continue with the pest management program without resorting to chemical applications.

Once established, thrips predators will remain present in detectable numbers in the crop throughout the season. It has been suggested to use them as "biological indicators" of environmentally friendly production practices for growers or growers' organizations that want to specially label their products in the marketplace. For pepper growers the presence of phytoseiids on three out of four leaves, or the occurrence of fifty *Orius* bugs in a sample of one hundred flowers was suggested as a minimum standard for earning the IPM label (Ramakers 1996a).

Suppression of thrips with predators is sufficient to minimize feeding damage. However, if thrips are transmitting tospoviruses, growers are likely to switch to an intensive chemical campaign and abandon biological control for the rest of the season. Studies are underway to determine whether a zero tolerance for thrips is justified under such circumstances.

Aphids

If spider mites and thrips are controlled with predators, aphids tend to become the dominant pest. Aphids are more destructive to peppers than thrips, but have received less attention because of the availability (in Europe) of pirimicarb, a selective aphicide. Aphids have the widest spectrum of natural enemies, many of which occur spontaneously in greenhouses. In the past, most pepper growers made an inoculative introduction of braconid wasps or relied on their spontaneous occurrence. Local aphid outbreaks were subsequently controlled by spot applications of pirimicarb. Aphid parasitoids, such as *Aphidius matricariae* Haliday or *Praon volucre* (Haliday), have often been observed in sweet pepper greenhouses in mid-winter, suggesting these species are not affected by short-day conditions (Ramakers 1989). Today, most commercial companies offer *Aphidius colemani* Viereck since this species is effective against both *Myzus persicae* (Sulzer) and *Aphis gossypii* Glover (van Steenis 1993).

A significant but temporary increase in the use biological aphid control occurred in the early 1990s, as pepper growers were facing very serious problems with carbamate resistance in a "red strain" of *Myzus persicae* (Sulzer) (also called *Myzus nicotianae* Blackman) (Field et al. 1997). However, sole reliance on biological aphid control (using releases and naturally occurring braconid parasitoids, cecidomyiid predators, and field collected coccinellid beetles for spot treatments) was soon abandoned because it provided unsatisfactory control and because of the development of new effective systemic pesticides (nitromethylene derivatives). Although these insecticides are considered to be broad spectrum in their activity, they act against phloem feeders in a rather selective way when applied through the irrigation system. Imidacloprid was the first compound in this group to be registered for use on greenhouse vegetables. It is compatible with most natural enemies, including aphid parasitoids and phytoseiid predators, but it does adversely affect *Orius* spp., aphid predators

and pollinators. For this reason, and to slow the development of pesticide resistance, it is recommended that full-scale applications be made as infrequently as possible. In hydroponic systems, imidacloprid is rather persistent and effective at extremely low rates. Growers who scout their crops for aphids and treat localized infestations before they become serious may obtain adequate control with only very low inputs of chemicals and biological control agents. The registration of imidacloprid is therefore perceived as an important component to an aphid IPM program. However, growers are attracted to the ease of use associated with this highly efficacious insecticide thus placing it in strong competition with the sale of aphid natural enemies. Greenhouse growers still use pirimicarb, usually by fumigation, against minor aphid pests (*Aulacorthum solani* [Kaltenbach] and *Macrosiphum euphorbiae* [Thomas]) as they occur. Newer aphicides with apparently even better IPM profiles are thiacloprid (another nitromethylene derivative), pymetrozine, and triazamate.

Caterpillars

Tactics for the management of noctuid moths and other Lepidoptera known to attack sweet peppers have focused on reducing the chance of an infestation occurring, as well as attempting to control an infestation once it occurs. Mating success (necessary to initiate egg laying) can be disrupted using pheromones in ways that make it difficult for male moths to locate females. Registrations of several mating disruption pheromones for use in protected culture are pending in some

European countries. To suppress caterpillars, pepper growers use *Bacillus thuringiensis* Berliner and the insect molt inhibitor teflubenzuron. Traps baited with a pheromone lure are used for early detection of infestations and to properly time the *B. thuringiensis* or teflubenzuron applications. Because teflubenzuron may damage or even eliminate *Orius* populations, the control strategy is to start with *B. thuringiensis* to kill small caterpillars and to delay the application of teflubenzuron as long as possible. For species that lay their eggs in clusters (species of *Spodoptera* or *Lacanobia*), local applications of broad-spectrum chemicals soon after egg hatch before the larvae disperse are useful in controlling outbreaks. However, for species in the genera *Chrysodeixis* and *Autographa*, which deposit eggs singly and scatter them over many plants, spot treatments are not effective and effective control usually requires treatment of the entire crop.

Simultaneous with the attempt to control aphids with biological means only, pepper growers have tried to control noctuids without pesticides by frequent introductions of extremely high numbers of egg parasitoids (*Trichogramma* spp.), by introducing *Podisus maculiventris* (Say) as a predator of larvae, and by repeated spraying or dusting with *B. thuringiensis*. Some control has been achieved using these natural enemies but not without considerable damage to the crop. Until methods yielding better control can be developed, this approach is not recommended.

Some natural control by native parasitoids may occur (van der Linden 1996), but none are considered suitable species for mass rearing given existing technologies, market conditions, and rates of parasitization observed in the field. Because even small larvae may cause considerable damage to the crop, natural enemies acting on the egg stage are preferable to those attacking larvae. *Orius* spp. feed on noctuid eggs and they often occur at high densities in pepper crops. Dutch pepper growers have frequently reported that native birds that have inadvertently entered the greenhouse feed on caterpillars. In response, some growers actively encourage bird visits by scattering bird food or placing cage birds in their greenhouses. A systematic study has been started to select a bird species well adapted to the crop, the growing conditions, and the target pest. A Timaliid species was found highly effective (van der Linden 1999), but does not breed easily in captivity. However, making biological control depend on harvesting relatively rare birds from nature does not fit very well in the concept of sustainable agriculture.

Other Pests and Diseases

As growers apply fewer broad-spectrum insecticides, minor pests tend to occur more frequently. *Liriomyza* leafminers were once thought to be a serious pest limiting the implementation of biological control-based IPM in peppers until it was realized that the problem was induced by existing pest management practices. Occasional use of pyrethroids can produce leafminer outbreaks by eliminating their associated parasitoids. If pyrethroids are not applied, natural control by larval parasitoids becomes commonplace, even in winter plantings. To assess the level of leafminer parasitization, leaf samples are collected during the first generation of the outbreak and the mines and/or larvae dissected to detect parasitism (van der Linden 1986, van der Linden and van Achterberg 1989). Most biological control companies in Holland offer this service, which is cheaper than a potentially unneeded introduction of parasitoids. If the level of natural control is considered unable to provide satisfactory control, one or two introductions of parasitoids are then made against the young larvae of the second generation. The occurrence of punctures made in foliage by adult leafminers is a helpful sign for marking the onset of a new generation and thus for correctly timing the release of larval parasitoids. In addition to controlling feeding damage caused by leafminer larvae, growers also fear the occurrence of pupae that may drop onto fruit and thus may be in violation of quarantine regulations associated with intercontinental export. To combat this potential problem, growers frequently increase the rate of leafminer parasitoid releases in an effort to virtually eliminate the pest from their greenhouses. Natural occurrence of leafminer parasitoids, as well as the recent registration of the IGR cyromazine, have reduced the interest for artificial introductions of parasitoids.

Broad mites, *Polyphagotarsonemus latus* (Banks), are controlled by maintaining good sanitation standards in the nurseries, by treating young plants preventively with a relatively persistent acaricide like abamectin, and by applying sulphur dust or specific acaricides when necessary in the production house. It is believed that the use of vaporized sulphur as a preventive measurement to control mildew may reduce the probability of broad mite outbreaks.

Whiteflies are not considered serious pests, since peppers are poor hosts for *Trialeurodes vaporariorum* (Westwood) and only a moderately good host for *Bemisia tabaci* (Gennadius). Hence, full rate introductions of *Encarsia formosa* Gahan are seldom applied. Problems with *B. tabaci* seem to increase from year to year; growers having suffered from it in the previous season may introduce *Eretmocerus* spp. in the next season. Some growers place a few eggplants (a far more attractive host plant than peppers) in their greenhouses as indicator plants for whiteflies. Initially these plants are useful to detect the first occurrence of whiteflies in the greenhouse and later to serve as banker plants for production of parasitoids (Ramakers and Rabasse 1995).

The other phloem feeders (mirid bugs, leafhoppers, aphids) that may emigrate from surrounding vegetation may often be controlled with systemic insecticides. Systematic monitoring with yellow sticky traps, identification of the species trapped, and knowledge of the damage to be expected from each of them, may help reduce the need for applications of insecticides for control of these species. Apart from crop pests, miscellaneous arthropods may became a nuisance for the people working in the greenhouse (skin irritation by alate males from ant colonies, curtains of cobwebs produced by high numbers of spiders, etc.). These problems have created a growing interest in predators such as lizards, toads and snakes. Such biological control is not practical and there is no experimental evidence supporting the benefits of using such vertebrate predators.

Chemical control of fungal diseases is in general not an obstruction for biological pest control in this crop. There is some concern, however, about the growing trend to operate sulphur vaporizers for the prevention of mildew outbreaks. Frequent use of these vaporizers (several times per week or even daily) may amplify minor adverse effects on natural enemies. High rates of sulphur vapor have been reported to reduce the dispersal capabilities of *I. degenerans*, and IPM advisors report that *P. persimilis* has difficulties in controlling spider mites in the immediate vicinity of the vaporizers. Since sulfur is vaporized during the night when the greenhouse is closed, it may also affect the ability of *A. aphidimyza* to locate its prey, as the adult midges are active at night.

IPM During Propagation

It is a matter of dispute whether IPM is more likely to succeed if the young plants have been propagated without insecticides. Natural enemies introduced later in the production greenhouses will initially suffer less from pesticide residues. In addition, releases of some natural enemies can begin while plants are still in the propagation room. Opponents, however, argue that crops managed with IPM should start with the lowest possible numbers of pests, and that from an environmental viewpoint chemicals were better used in the relatively small propagation areas rather than later in the much larger areas of the crop production greenhouses.

A study conducted by the Dutch Plant Protection Service from 1994 to1997 (Visser and Roosjen 1997) resulted in the following recommendations. First, it is important to reduce insect movement into propagation facilities by screening ventilators with a mesh (600 µ) appropriate to exclude insects the size of whiteflies and larger. Second, inundative releases of natural enemies are necessary to protect plants from thrips (using releases of *N. cucumeris*) and aphids (*A. colemani* released from banker plants). Third, "blind" application of insecticides should be replaced by supervised control based on frequent monitoring of insect pests using yellow sticky traps and visual inspections by trained personnel, conducted in the propagation greenhouse and to be continued in the production houses. Fourth, target specific rather than broad spectrum insecticides should be applied only if necessary; suggested were the uses of imidacloprid against aphids and cyromazine against leafminers. Fifth, leafminer-infested leaves should be removed and destroyed to avoid quarantine problems associated with international commerce.

The project had an immediate effect on plant protection as practiced by propagators, changing from making prophylactic applications of insecticides to making pest control decisions based upon monitoring data. Further, monitoring data demonstrated that most of the pest problems occurring in production greenhouses did not originate in propagation facilities. Propagation facilities with their concrete floors, compartmentalization, and screened ventilators can more easily maintain high sanitary standards than production greenhouses In production facilities, year-round cultivation, with less than a week's gap between crop destruction and subsequent replanting, is common practice. Soil is usually covered but seldom disinfected. It was found that with the current replanting practices some pests, especially leafminers, aphids and thrips, survive in much higher numbers in the production house than could possibly come from propagation. Transfer of beneficials from propagation and subsequent survival in production areas have been observed only for the thrips predator, *N. cucumeris*. On the other hand, the movement of aphids from propagation to production, even if part of the population is parasitized, is considered unacceptable by pepper growers.

The response from the production growers was less positive. Propagators found it difficult to sell young plants originating from an IPM nursery. Most growers insist on a final insecticide treatment before the delivery of the plants to ensure the lowest possible number of pests, or treat young plants themselves, using chemicals like abamectin and imidacloprid. Those growers who wish to start biological control early request that propagators avoid chemicals during the second half of the propagation period. Hardly any pepper grower was prepared to pay a higher price for such "IPM" plants. While propagators considered IPM during propagation an additional cost factor, the growers perception was that such practices were an additional risk rather than an advantage.

Prospects

In the early 1990s, some pepper growers in both Holland and Canada attempted to rely solely on biological pest control. Pepper was thought to be one of the most suitable crops (second only to tomato) for this approach, especially when starting with plants from propagation houses using biological control. Excessive numbers of natural enemies were being released, but the costs of the releases were found to be disproportional to the savings on chemicals. Above all, the suppression of aphids and caterpillars was insufficient. Eventually some growers ended up using higher rates of insecticides than colleagues using regular IPM schemes.

These attempts were abandoned, and most Dutch growers currently use a variant of IPM close to what is called "expanded use" in Table 27.2. In Canada, growers are seeking registration of some modern pesticides that are more compatible with natural enemies.

Rewarding growers by an IPM label for releasing a minimum amount of natural enemies (Gerritsen 1991) is no longer practiced. A proposal to link an IPM label to the actual presence of natural enemies in the crop (Ramakers 1996a) was not adopted. The reason is that plant protection policy has shifted from "prescription of means" to "prescription of aims". In this philosophy, biological control is merely a tool, while reducing negative effects on the environment is considered the ultimate goal. In the future, growers will not be judged for the number of beneficial agents released, but for the amount of pesticides used. "Kilogram-reduction" as was imposed during the 1990s will be replaced by a more adequate parameter: the amount of pesticides used multiplied by an environmental risk factor calculated for each chemical (Leendertse *et al.* 1997, see http://library.wur.nl/milieumeetlat/glas.html).

It is increasingly understood that the market and thus finally the consumers should pay for the efforts, risks, and additional costs associated with the further development and implementation of biological control programs. In northern Europe, the production costs of organically grown (including organic fertilization) greenhouse vegetables is estimated to be 40 to 45% higher than vegetables grown using conventional techniques (Boonekamp 1999). Organic production of peppers in greenhouses is thought to cover a small market niche that is not expected to grow in the foreseeable future. More important are the initiatives being taken by mainstream supermarkets to promote IPM-grown vegetables. Migros in Switzerland was a pioneer in promoting integrated, not necessarily organic, production (Tschabold and Wertheim 1993). A system called EUREPGAP was developed in 2000 and became operational in 2002. Certification of individual growers, minimizing of pesticide use, registration of all plant protection measurements, and "tracing & tracking" throughout the trade channels are important features of this system (see http://www. eurep.org).

It is anticipated that the acreage of IPM peppers in protected cultivation will remain steady or may slightly grow worldwide, but that growers will introduce fewer species and numbers of natural enemies. Products and antagonists with insufficient or unproven efficacy will be eliminated, both by growers and by manufacturers. New regulations concerning protection of local fauna discourage introduction of exotic natural enemies. Most of all, some biocontrol components in the IPM programs are competing with new insecticides with low environmental risk profiles (low toxicity to non-target organisms and/or low emission rates).

References Cited

Boonekamp, G. 1999. Greenery gaat voor topsegment ecologische producten. *Groenten en Fruit* 9 (8):18–20.

de Klerk, M. L. and P. M. J. Ramakers. 1986. Monitoring population densities of the phytoseiid predator *Amblyseius cucumeris* and its prey after large-scale introduction to control *Thrips tabaci* on sweet pepper. *Mededelingen Faculteit Landbouwwetenschappen Rijksuniversiteit Gent* 51 (3a):1045–48.

FAO. 2002. *FAO Yearbook 2001 Production*, Vol. 55-2001, FAO Statistics Series, No. 170. Rome, Italy FAO.

Field, L. M., A. P. Anderson, I. Denholm, S. P. Foster, Z. K. Harling, N. Javed, D. Martinez-Torres, G. D. Moores, M. S. Williamson and A. L. Devonshire. 1997. Use of biochemical and DNA diagnostics for characterising multiple mechanisms of insecticide resistance in the peach-potato aphid, Myzus persicae (Sulzer). *Pesticide Science* 51:283–9.

Gerritsen, M. 1991. Milieubewust telen heeft de toekomst. *Groenten en Fruit* 1 (50):6–7.

Leendertse, P. C., J. A. W. A. Reus, P. J. A. de Vreede and J. K. Nienhuis. 1997. Meetlat voor middelengebruik in de glastuinbouw. Centrum voor Landbouw en Milieu, Utrecht, The Netherlands. *CLM publication nr. 298-1997.*

Ramakers, P. M. J. 1980. Biological control of *Thrips tabaci* (Thysanoptera: Thripidae) with *Amblyseius* spp. (Acari: Phytoseiidae). *IOBC/WPRS Bulletin* 3(3):203–7.

———. 1989. Biological control in greenhouses. In *Aphids: Their Biology, Natural Enemies, and Control,* Vol. 2C, ed. A. K. Minks and P. Harrewijn, 199–208. New York (Amsterdam): Elsevier.

———. 1996a. Use of natural enemies as 'indicators' for obtaining an IPM label. *IOBC/WPRS Bulletin* 19 (1):119–22.

———. 1996b. Using natural enemies as environmental indicators for marketing purposes in integrated production. *International Workshop on Biological and Integrated Pest Management in Greenhouse Pepper,* June 10–14, 1996, Hódmezővásárhely, Hungary.

Ramakers, P. M. J., and J. M. Rabasse. 1995. Integrated pest management in protected cultivator. In *Novel Approaches to Integrated Pest Management*, ed. R. Reuveni, 198–229. Boca Raton, Fla.: Lewis Publishers.

Ramakers, P. M. J., and A. A. van der Maas. 1996. Decision support system 'CAPPA' for IPM in sweet pepper. *IOBC/WPRS Bulletin* 19 (1):123–6.

Ramakers, P. M. J., and S. J. P. Voet. 1995. Use of castor bean, *Ricinus communis,* for the introduction of the thrips predator *Amblyseius degenerans* on glasshouse-grown sweet peppers. *Mededelingen Faculteit Landbouwwetenschappen Rijkuniversiteit Gent* 60 (3a):885–91.

Ravensberg, W. J. 1992. The use of beneficial organisms for pest control under practical conditions. *Pflanzenschutz Nachrichten Bayer* 45 (1):49–72.

Ravensberg, W. J., and K. Altena. 1987. Recent developments in the control of thrips in sweet pepper and cucumber. *IOBC/WPRS Bulletin* 10 (2):160–4.

Schulten, G. G. M., G. van de Klashorst, and V. M. Russell. 1976. Resistance of *Phytoseiulus persimilis* A. H. (Acarina: Phytoseiidae) to some insecticides. *Zeitschrift für Angewandte Entomologie* 80:337–41.

Tschabold, J. L., and S. J. Wertheim. 1993. Marketing experiences within the Migros-Sano programme. *Acta Horticulturae* 347:285–90.

van Aartsen, J. J., M. de Boer, A. Jorritsma-Lebbink, G. J. Weijers, P. A. C. Beelaerts van Blokland, H. A. van de Meer, J. Boeve, and G. J. Doornbos. 1997. Convenant Glastuinbouw en Milieu 1995 – 2010 met integrale milieu taakstelling.

van Houten, Y. M., and P. van Stratum. 1995. Control of western flower thrips on sweet pepper in winter with *Amblyseius cucumeris* (Oudemans) and *A. degenerans* Berlèse. In *Thrips Biology and Management*, ed. B.L. Parker, M. Skinner, and T. Lewis, 245–8. New York: Plenum Press.

van Lenteren, J. C., A. K. Minks, and O. M. B. de Ponti, eds. 1992. Biological control and integrated crop protection: Towards environmentally safer agriculture. *Proceedings of an International Conference Organized by the IOBC/WPRS*, Veldhoven, the Netherlands, September 8–13, 1991. Wageningen, the Netherlands: Centre for Agricultural Publishing and Documentation.

van der Linden, A. 1986. Mineervliegbestrijding eindigt nooit. *Tuinderij* 66 (26):34–5.

———. 1996. Control of caterpillars in integrated pest management. *IOBC/WPRS Bulletin* 19 (1):91–4.

———. 1999. Insectivorous birds for biological control of pests in glasshouses. *IOBC/WPRS Bulletin* 22 (1):149–52.

van der Linden, A., and C. van Achterberg. 1989. Recognition of eggs and larvae of the parasitoids of *Liriomyza* spp. (Diptera: Agromyzidae; Hymenoptera: Braconidae and Eulophidae). *Entomologische Berichten, Amsterdam* 49 (9):138–40.

van der Staay, M., and M. van Steenis. 1994. Rode luis is te bestrijden. *Groenten en Fruit* 4 (26):9.

van Steenis, M. J. 1993. Suitability of *Aphis gossypii* Glov., *Macrosiphum euphorbiae* (Thom.), and *Myzus persicae* Sulz. (Hom.: Aphidiidae) as host for several aphid parasitoid species (Hym.: Braconidae). *IOBC/WPRS Bulletin* 16 (2):157–60.

van Woerden, S. 2003. Kwantitatieve informatie voor de glastuinbouw 2003-2004. Wageningen, The Netherlands: Applied Plant Research, Division Glasshouse Horticulture.

Visser, A., and M. Roosjen. 1997. Eindverslag demonstratieproject geïntegreerde bestrijding in uitgangsmateriaal van vruchtgroenten 1994–1997. *Verslagen en Mededelinge* nr. 189, Wageningen, the Netherlands: Plantenziektenkundige Dienst.

Woets, J., P. M. J. Ramakers, and J. C. van Lenteren. 1980. Progress report on development and application of integrated pest control in glasshouses in the Netherlands with an indication about limiting factors. *IOBC/WPRS Bulletin* 3 (3):247–57.

zur Strassen, R. 1986. *Frankliniella occidentalis* (Pergande 1895), ein nordamerikanischer Fransenflügler (Thysanoptera) als neuer Bewohner europäischer Gewächshäuser. *Nachrichtenblatt des Deutschen Pflanzenschutzdienstes* 38 (6):86–8.

28

IPM Program for Tomato

R. J. Jacobson
Stockbridge Technology Centre Ltd.
Cawood, North Yorkshire, United Kingdom

In northern Europe and Canada, integrated pest management (IPM) is probably further advanced in protected tomato crops than for any other agricultural or horticultural crop in the world. The IPM programs are based largely on biological control, but also draw on physical and cultural control measures, supported by the occasional use of target specific chemicals. Tomato crops may be attacked by over ten arthropod species, and there are often two or more control measures used against each pest. With so many species present simultaneously, the overall programs can become complex and difficult to manage. If just one of the control measures fails and it becomes necessary to apply a nonspecific pesticide, the whole program is disrupted. IPM practitioners must therefore have a good understanding of the biology of the pests and beneficial species, and of the complex interactions that occur between them.

This chapter focuses on the IPM program that is now used effectively in conventional greenhouse tomato crops in the United Kingdom, with notes to show how approaches differ in other parts of northern Europe and Canada. The additional difficulties faced by growers in warmer climates are also discussed.

One of the original driving forces in the development of IPM in protected tomatoes in the U.K. was the difficulty in controlling greenhouse whiteflies (*Trialeurodes vaporariorum* [Westwood]) and two-spotted spider mites (*Tetranychus urticae* Koch) with the pesticides that were available during the 1970s. The natural enemies *Encarsia formosa* Gahan and *Phytoseiulus persimilis* Athias-Henriot were effective against these pests. However, both natural enemy species were vulnerable to chemicals used against other pests, so compatible control options were sought for those pests too. More recently, the forces driving the adoption of IPM in the crop have changed. Consumers are becoming increasingly sensitive to the potential risks of pesticide residues in food and there are strong indications that many people seek produce that has received no or only a few applications of chemicals. Several leading European food retailers require growers to adopt crop production standards that include minimal use of pesticides (Hilborn 1998). If growers wish to gain access to these important market outlets they must abide with the retailers' Codes of Practice, which are guidelines established by retailers sometimes without consulting suppliers. Another important driving force is the adoption of biological pollination using bumblebees (*Bombus terrestris* L.). Compared to the manual techniques previously used to pollinate tomato crops, biological pollination offers huge labor savings and improved fruit set. The latter results in greater income from higher yields of better quality produce. However, to maximize these benefits, growers must avoid the use of broad-spectrum insecticides and maintain their IPM programs throughout the growing season.

Tomato Production in the U.K.

The cultivated tomato, *Lycopersicon esculentum* Miller, is a native of South America, where it grows as a rambling, small-fruited plant. The genus *Lycopersicon* includes six other species, some that have been used in the extensive breeding programs that produced the range of tomato cultivars now available to growers (Luckwill 1943). There are six basic groups of tomato cultivars grown in the U.K.: medium sized (approximately 2 in. [5 cm]) "classic round"; smaller and sweeter "cherry" and "cocktail"; larger "beef"; oval-shaped "plum"; and "vine," which are allowed to ripen on the plant. The cherry and cocktail varieties are generally the most susceptible to pests. Vine-ripened tomatoes are often marketed as whole trusses. This increases the importance of any damage that results in an incomplete truss.

In most cases, the plants are propagated during October and November and planted in the production house in November or December. Bumblebees that are systematically introduced to the greenhouse throughout the season pollinate the flowers.

Fruit picking begins in late February or early March and is then continuous until the crop is terminated in October. It is common practice to remove leaves below the fully swollen fruit to facilitate air movement and to reduce the establishment of disease.

Crops in the United Kingdom are grown in high quality greenhouses (13 to 16 ft. [4 to 5 m.] in height) with computerized environments enriched with carbon dioxide to improve growth and yield (fig. 28.1). The temperature is typically maintained at a minimum of 61°F (16°C) at night and 64°F (18°C) in the day, with automatic ventilation at 70°F (21°C). The ground is covered with white plastic to reflect light and minimise the risk of attack by soilborne pests and pathogens. The plants are either grown in artificial substrates such as rock wool or perlite or growers use a substrate-less Nutrient Film Technique (NFT) system. A single strong stem is trained up a vertical string to a horizontal support wire positioned 6 to 10 ft. (2–3 m) above ground. When the plant reaches the wire, it is layered so that only the most recent 6 to 10 ft. (2–3 m) growth is ever vertical. By the end of the growing season, the stem of each plant may be over 40 ft. (14 m) long.

The principal diseases of tomato are controlled with chemical fungicides that are compatible with the natural enemies used in the IPM program. Occasionally, conflicts arise between the use of entomopathogenic fungi and the control of important diseases.

Between 1976 and 1996, the adoption of new technologies enabled U.K. tomato growers to double their yield to approximately 11 lbs. per ft.^{2} (52 kg/m^2), while reducing fuel usage by 41% and labor costs by 64% per 2 lbs. (1 kg) of fruit produced

Figure 28.1. A typical glasshouse tomato crop in the United Kingdom. Note the height of the crop and the difficulty this presents when monitoring pests and releasing natural enemies such as *Phytoseiulus persimilis* Athias-Henriot on the upper leaves.
Photo: R. Jacobson.

(G. Hayman, pers. comm.). These improvements were due to a combination of factors including new cultivars, better equipment (i.e., greenhouse structures, irrigation, environmental control), carbon dioxide enrichment, biological pollination, and more effective pest and disease control.

Biological Pollination

The use of bumblebees to pollinate tomato crops was the most rapidly adopted innovation in the recent history of horticulture in northern Europe. Trials with bumblebees began in U.K. tomato crops in 1989. By 1992, bumblebees were being used by virtually all long-season tomato growers.

In the wild, fertilized female bumblebees (queens) hibernate in isolation through the winter and emerge in spring to begin a colony in a small hole in the ground (Alford 1975). Each queen lays a batch of eight to sixteen eggs and forages for pollen and nectar to feed the developing young. This brood is composed of sterile females (workers). When mature, these workers take over the task of gathering food, allowing the queen to devote herself to egg production. By midsummer, the colony may contain over one hundred individuals. Towards autumn, the production of workers stops and consecutive swarms of males and functional females are produced. The workers then die, as do the males after mating, and the fertilized females disperse for hibernation. There is only one such cycle per year.

The commercialization of bumblebees became possible with the development of reliable systems of mass rearing that could provide a continuous supply of bees throughout the entire tomato-growing season. As pollination was required in late winter and early spring when the bees were normally inactive, the rearing system had to include a means of breaking diapause. Colonies are established in the rearing units using individual queens and colonies are supplied to growers in disposable hives when they have built up to about eighty workers. The workers visit the tomato flowers (fig. 28.2) to collect pollen to feed to young in the hive and in doing so effect pollination. As there is no nectar in tomato flowers, a concentrated sugar solution is supplied within the hive. Each colony can pollinate approximately 11,000 ft.^{2} (1000 m^2) of classic round tomatoes for about two months, and colonies are replaced systematically throughout the growing season.

Potential Role of the Tomato Plant in IPM

Both the morphological features and the chemical components of tomato plants can influence the establishment and survival of herbivorous insects (Farrar and Kennedy 1991). The most important features are the hair-like trichomes that clothe the leaves and stems of the plants, but there are other factors associated with secondary metabolites in the leaf lamella.

Luckwill (1943) and Reeves (1977) described seven types of trichomes, including four with apical glands, and showed that the

Figure 28.2. Bumblebees (*Bombus terrestris* L.) are systematically introduced into the greenhouse throughout the season to pollinate the flowers of tomato plants.
Photo: R. Jacobson.

combination and numbers of the various types differed on different species of tomatoes. Both glandular (fig. 28.3) and non-glandular trichomes impede the movement of arthropods, but those with glands have the greatest effect because they produce exudates that are sticky and repellant (Gentile, Webb, and Stoner 1969; Cantelo, Boswell, and Argauer 1974). Two of the major components in the exudates from type VI trichomes are the methyl ketones 2-tridecanone and 2-undecanone (Luckwill 1943, Williams et al. 1980, Farrar and Kennedy 1988). The former has been shown to be toxic to tomato fruitworm (*Heliothis zea* [Boddie]), tobacco hornworm (*Manduca sexta* L.), melon cotton aphid (*Aphis gossypii* Glover), Colorado potato beetle (*Leptinotarsa decemlineata* [Say]), and two-spotted spider mites (*T. urticae*); and the latter to *H. zea* (Williams et al. 1980; Dimock and Kennedy 1983; Kennedy and Farrar 1987; Chatzivasileiadis and Sabelis 1997). Other chemicals in type VI trichomes that have been associated with resistance to insects include two catecholic phenolic compounds, rutin and chlorogenic acid, and several sesquiterpenes.

The resistance of the host plant to herbivorous arthropods is loosely correlated to the type and density of trichomes. For example, the wild tomato *Lycopersicon hirsutum* Humboldt and Bonpland is densely clothed with type VI trichomes and is very resistant to two-spotted spider mites, while *Lycopersicon peruvianum* Miller has few of these trichomes and is very susceptible to the pest. The numbers of type VI trichomes on the cultivated varieties of *L. esculentum* are intermediate, and these cultivars show variable susceptibility to the pest (P. Croft, pers. comm.). However,

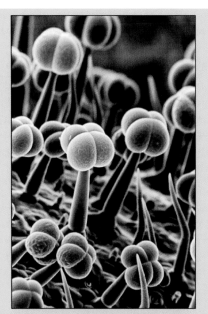

Figure 28.3. Glandular trichomes produce exudates that are sticky and repellant to both beneficial and pest arthropods. Two major compounds in type VI glandular trichomes on the surface of a tomato leaf (scanning electron micrograph) affording this type of protection are the methyl ketones 2-tridecanone and 2-undecanone.
Micrograph: John Pegler, Horticulture Research International, Littlehampton, U.K.

the link between tomato cultivar and spider mite resistance is complicated because the density of trichomes on each cultivar varies with leaf age, light intensity, temperature, and photoperiod (Nihoul 1993).

Several secondary metabolites in the tomato leaf lamella have been linked to resistance to pests. Alpha-tomatine occurs in vari-

able quantities in *L. esculentum* and has been shown to be toxic to several pest species, including potato leafhopper (*Empoasca fabae* Harris) (Dahlman and Hibbs 1967). The proteinase inhibitors I and II are synthesized in response to mechanical wounding and have been associated with toxicity to several arthropod species, for example, reduced growth rate of beet armyworm (*Spodoptera exigua* [Hübner]) (Broadway and Duffey 1986). However, the primary significance of these compounds may be in relation to insects that do not normally feed on tomato plants.

The features of the plant that provide resistance to herbivorous arthropods may also impede the performance of natural enemies. For example, van Haren et al. (1987) demonstrated that while glandular trichomes act as a defense mechanism against spider mites, the overall effect of these structures in the IPM program was detrimental because they also affected the dispersal and searching efficiency of the predator *P. persimilis*.

There are numerous potentially valuable sources of insect- or mite-resistant germ plasma in tomato and the long-term prospect for development of arthropod-resistant cultivars would appear to be promising. However, it is important that the role of the host plant in IPM is always evaluated in the broader context of the tritrophic interaction with the pests and their natural enemies.

Typical Tomato IPM Program in the U.K.

The most successful pest control systems within IPM programs usually do not rely on single control measures. Ideally, there should be one or more sustainable control measures to suppress each pest species throughout the growing season, supported by other compatible control measures that can be used as a second line of defence at critical times. The sustainable control measures are typically cultural, physical, and biological control agents, while the remedial treatments are target specific chemicals or entomopathogens. Full details of the biology and behavior of the pests and natural enemies are provided elsewhere in this volume. The intention here is show how the control measures have been brought together in U.K. tomato crops to form a truly integrated package.

One unfortunate side effect of the introduction of IPM programs in tomato crops has been the creation of opportunities for some arthropod species to change their pest status. Insects such as leafminers and leafhoppers, which were of only minor importance in chemical-based regimes because they were killed by pesticides applied against the primary pests, now survive and also require compatible control measures. In some cases these "secondary" pests have become the most difficult to control.

Greenhouse whitefly

The control of greenhouse whitefly (*T. vaporariorum*) in U.K. tomato crops has improved significantly since Woets (1985) described it as the key pest in integrated control in tomatoes. There is now a better understanding of the interaction of greenhouse whitefly with its principal natural enemy *E. formosa* (van Roermund and van Lenteren 1992), and there are additional products that can be used to control the pest. Consequently, control of greenhouse whitefly is routine in almost all

situations. The parasitic wasp *E. formosa* suppresses the pest throughout the season. The wasp is inexpensive (about US $5 per 1000 wasps) and can be released weekly in relatively large numbers from planting until August. The actual application rates vary between greenhouses, but a typical program would include weekly releases of about 3,000 parasitized whitefly nymphs per acre (7,500/ha) at planting, increasing to 5,000 per acre (12,500/ha) either when whiteflies are first seen or when the plants reach a height of about 8 ft. (2.5 m). This program has been so successful that it is rare for any other action to be required unless *E. formosa* are killed by pesticides applied against other pests, or if parasitized nymphs are removed by over enthusiastic trimming of lower leaves before adult wasps have emerged. If the primary biological control system does break down, then both the insect growth regulator buprofezin and the entomopathogenic fungi *Verticillium lecanii* (Zimmerman) Viégas are available for remedial use (Kanno et al. 1981, Hall 1982). The nonspecific predator *Macrolophus caliginosus* Wagner, available in the United Kingdom for whitefly control in the mid-1990s, is described separately.

Leafhoppers

The greenhouse leafhopper, *Hauptidia maroccana* (Melichar), is a sporadic but important pest of tomato crops in parts of the United Kingdom. Outbreaks are controlled with a combination of the leafhopper egg parasitoid *Anagrus atomus* L. and the insect growth regulator buprofezin (Wardlow and Tobin 1990; Cooper 1993; Maisonneuve, Blum, and Wardlow 1995; Jacobson and Chambers 1996). A single application of buprofezin in late January provides acceptable control until mid April, thus reducing the dependence on the parasitoid until later in the season when it is most effective. When buprofezin is applied against leafhoppers, the secondary benefit of control of whitefly must be taken into account in the overall IPM program. Following treatment, introductions of *E. formosa* may be delayed for several weeks and the financial saving equates to the cost of the buprofezin (Jacobson and Chambers 1996).

Leafminers

Tomato leafminer (*Liriomyza bryoniae* [Kaltenbach]) is currently one of the most important pests of tomato crops in the United Kingdom. The larvae tunnel in leaf mesophyll tissue, reducing photosynthetic output, and eventually kill the plants if left untreated. The parasitic wasps *Dacnusa sibirica* Telenga and *Diglyphus isaea* (Walker) are included in most IPM programs. *Dacnusa sibirica* is most effective in the early season, while *D. isaea* provides control during the summer (Minkenberg and van Lenteren 1986). Despite their use, many growers have experienced difficulties controlling tomato leafminers during May and June, and this has led to unacceptable crop damage and application of organophosphate insecticides. The latter disrupted biological pollination and other components of the IPM program. As the parasitoids are relatively expensive (e.g., *D. isaea* costs about US $110 per 1000 parasitoids), they cannot be used as freely as *E. formosa,* and this limits the options for control strategies. Many growers physically remove mined leaves in the early stages of infestation to delay the start of the biological program.

Recent experimentation suggests that it may be more effective to use these leafminers to establish parasitoids as early as possible (Sampson and Walker 1998). The complex interactions between the leafminers and the parasitoids are being further investigated and it is hoped that a better understanding will lead to improved control at an acceptable cost. Other biological control agents, including the parasitic wasp *Opius pallipes* Wesmael and the predatory bug *M. caliginosus,* are also being evaluated. Foliar applications of parasitic nematodes (*Steinernema feltiae* Filipjev) have been shown to be effective alternatives to organophosphate insecticides for remedial action (Williams and Macdonald 1995, Jacobson 2000).

Aphids

Three species of aphids are commonly found in U.K. tomatoes: green peach aphid (*Myzus persicae* [Sulzer]), greenhouse potato aphid (*Aulacorthum solani* [Kaltenbach]), and potato aphid (*Macrosiphum euphorbiae* [Thomas]). They are usually controlled with localized applications of the selective aphicide pirimicarb, or the anti-feedant chemical pymetrozine, but biological control options exist. The parasitic wasps *Aphidius colemani* Viereck, *Aphidius ervi* Haliday, and *Aphelinus abdominalis* Dalman are effective against *M. persicae, M. euphorbiae,* and *A. solani,* respectively (Feng, Johnson, and Halbert 1992; van Steenis 1993; van Lenteren et al. 1997). All are now available from commercial insectaries. It is quite common for natural enemies of aphids to enter greenhouses during the summer, and in the absence of insecticidal residues these species often become established and control the pests without any specific action from the grower. This contribution from nature is yet another benefit of the minimal pesticide regimes employed in IPM.

Spider mites

Control of two-spotted spider mites (*T. urticae*) in U.K. tomato crops has been based on the combined use of the predatory mite *P. persimilis* and the target specific acaricide fenbutatin oxide. The predators are used to suppress the pest population throughout the season, while the acaricide is used as a second line of defense when spider mite populations become unacceptably dense. Although this control system has been used for many years, tomato growers still find it difficult to manage. This was illustrated by the results of a survey commissioned by the British Tomato Growers' Association in 1998 that proclaimed spider mites to be the most difficult pest to control within the IPM program (G. Hayman, pers. comm.). The problems arise because establishment of *P. persimilis* on tomatoes is slow, which often results in unacceptable damage in the early season. Furthermore, spider mites breed more successfully than the predators in the tops of the plants during hot weather and this some-times results in control failures in the middle of the summer. These difficulties are exacer-bated in crops that suffer the hyper-necrotic response to spider mites (Zhang and Jacobson 2000). In these situations, severe damage occurs at quite low population densities, and fenbutatin oxide must be applied as soon as the pests are seen. As a consequence, there is too much dependence on remedial treatments of fenbutatin oxide and there are indications that some spider mite populations are

becoming resistant to the chemical (Jacobson and Croft 1999).

In 1998, the pesticide abamectin was registered for use in U.K. tomato crops. This acaricide is extremely effective against spider mites and reduced the dependence on fenbu-tatin oxide. However, abamectin has a broad spectrum of activity and has to be integrated with care because it is not compatible with all the natural enemies used in the IPM program (Jacobson, Croft and Sampson 2000). The starch-based polymer Eradicoat has also been used as an alternative second line of defense against spider mites. This product is reputed to suffocate the mites by blocking spiracles and is therefore dependent on very good spray coverage.

Recent studies have shown that the ento-mopathogenic fungus *Beauveria bassiana* (Balsamo) is at least as effective as fenbu-tatin oxide as a second line of defense against spider mites (Chandler, Davidson and Jacobson, 2004). This entomopathogen is not yet approved in U.K. but should become available to tomato growers in the near future.

Both scientists and growers are actively seeking means of improving this important component of the IPM program. There are strong indications that the initial establish-ment of *P. persimilis* may be improved by preconditioning the predators to tomato plants (Drukker 1997, Croft et al. 1999). Additional natural enemies are being sought that would complement the role of *P. persim-ilis*. For example, the predatory midge *Feltiella acarisuga* (Vallot) is being used experimentally and makes a positive contri-bution to the overall control of the pest in some circumstances (Opit, Roitberg, and

Gillespie 1997). The adult midge can fly and thus has an advantage in locating the spider mites. However, its biology and behavior are poorly understood, and it is not yet known how this midge can best be used. The predatory bug *M. caliginosus* can help eliminate residual populations of spider mites at the end of the growing season, and this can significantly reduce pest problems at the start of the following crop. However, there are specific problems associated with the use of this insect (see the section on *Macrolophus* bugs).

In the longer term, it is envisaged that the IPM program for spider mites will be based on plant cultivars that provide an advantage to the natural enemies, and that biopesticides such as entomopathogenic fungi will replace chemical acaricides as the second line of defense.

Russet mites

The tomato russet mite, *Aculus lycopersici* (Massee), is an eriophyid mite that causes tanning of tomato stems and bronzing of leaves (Rice and Strong 1962). The damage is usually most evident on the lower parts of the plant and rarely becomes serious until late in the season. It is not a widespread pest in the United Kingdom, but it can be difficult to control and causes complications in the IPM program. It has been controlled by physical removal of lower leaves and applications of horticultural petroleum oil to the remaining stems and petioles.

Caterpillars

The tomato hawk moth, *Lacanobia oleracea* L., is the most important lepidopteran pest in U.K. tomato crops. The females lay clusters of 50 to 300 eggs on the undersides of leaves.

Newly hatched caterpillars feed gregariously on the undersides of leaves for about two days before dispersing to feed more generally on the plant. The large caterpillar (1.8 in. [45 mm] long when fully grown) may feed on the fruit before pupating in crevices in the greenhouse structure or under debris. There are two generations per year; the first adults appear in April or May, and the second brood is present in late summer. The pupae of the second generation survive between crops (Lloyd 1920, Speyer and Parr 1948). The microbial insecticide *Bacillus thuringiensis* Berliner applied as a high-volume spray effectively controls the caterpillars (Jarrett and Burgess 1982). It is critical to time control measures to coincide with the peak of activity of first generation larvae so that more serious damage can be avoided later in the season. Several other species of moths may stray into U.K. tomato crops during the summer and early autumn, but the damage is usually localized and the use of specific control measures is rarely necessary.

Mealybugs

The greenhouse mealy bug, *Pseudococcus viburni* (Signoret), is becoming more common in U.K. tomato crops, although the reasons for this are not clear. It survives between crops on the structure of the greenhouse and on equipment and fittings, such as irrigation pipes. The development time from egg to egg at the temperatures maintained in tomato crops is relatively long (forty to sixty days), and mealybug populations do not usually reach damaging levels until the late summer or early autumn. The insects are most commonly found on the lower parts of the plant, particularly on the stripped stems.

Although several predators and parasitoids are produced commercially for use against mealybugs (Steiner and Elliot 1983), they are not very effective in the tomato-growing environment and are rarely used in this crop.

The insect growth regulator buprofezin is effective against the citrus mealybug, *Planococcus citri* (Risso) (Bedford et al. 1996). Buprofezin is commonly used to control mealybugs in tomatoes because it is compatible with other components of the IPM program. Because it acts by preventing larval development by disrupting chitin production, it may be several weeks before there is a visual effect on the mealybug population density.

Recent studies have shown that the efficacy of the entomopathogen *V. lecanii* can be considerably enhanced against mealybugs if it is applied after an insecticidal soap (Jacobson 2003). It has been hypothesized that the soap breaks down the waxy deposits and allows more spores to come into contact with the insect's body. The results of this sequence of treatments have been variable but complete mortality has been achieved in some circumstances.

Macrolophus bugs

The predatory mirid bug *M. caliginosus* was originally offered commercially for the control of whiteflies in southern Europe (Malausa, Drescher, and Fraco 1987). Under Mediterranean conditions, it was also found to suppress populations of spider mites, aphids, and caterpillars (Fauvel, Malausa and Kasper 1987; Trottin-Caudal and Millot 1994). Sampson and King (1996) subsequently demonstrated that the predator could make a useful contribution to biological control programs in northern Europe.

Macrolophus caliginosus is not indigenous to the U.K. and was first released in tomato crops in 1995 with promising results, particularly against leafminers and spider mites. However, in the latter half of the 1996 growing season, there was concern because the predators were causing direct damage to tomato plants (Hayman and Jacobson 1996). The main damage symptoms were leaf distortion that was not thought to be important, and premature flower and fruit drop that significantly reduced yield, particularly in cherry tomato crops (Sampson and Jacobson 1999). Premature fruit drop was most serious in cultivars that were vine ripened and harvested as complete trusses, as the loss of just one fruit from the middle of a truss could render the whole truss unmarketable. Although most of the growers who suffered damage in 1996 decided not to release *M. caliginosus* in their crops again, the bugs survived between seasons to colonize the new plants in both 1997 and 1998. Additional infestations of *M. caliginosus* were recorded at sites where the predators had never been released. As a consequence, many of the most vulnerable crops were sprayed with broad-spectrum insecticides. There is now some debate among U.K. tomato growers concerning the status of *M. caliginosus*; some believe that it is a useful predator, while others consider it to be a pest. There is little doubt that this predator could make a useful contribution to IPM in tomatoes if the populations were manipulated to avoid injury to plants and subsequent financial loss to the grower.

Pest Monitoring

Pests must be detected as early as possible and the correct control action must be taken promptly. Any delay will allow the pests to multiply, requiring use of larger numbers of natural enemies, which ultimately can become uneconomic. Therefore, accurate information about pest abundance and the establishment of beneficial organisms is gathered regularly as part of IPM programs. There are some shortcuts, such as the use of yellow sticky traps for the early detection of whiteflies and leafminers, but the best results are generally obtained from regular examination of plants. After assessing the size of the arthropod populations, crop managers must make personal judgements on the best course of action, taking into account any side effects these actions may have on other components in the IPM program. There are few fixed rules for growers to follow, and they must learn when it is appropriate to release additional natural enemies and when to use remedial pesticide sprays. These decisions are complex, and mistakes can be costly due to the high-value of the crops. To simplify the procedures, computer-based decision support systems have been developed in Europe and Canada and are likely to become widely used in the United Kingdom (Squires 1998, Shipp and Clarke 1999). Though time consuming, an efficient pest monitoring system will pay for itself in terms of reduced crop damage, reduced expenditures on crop protection materials, and reduced labor for pest control.

IPM on Greenhouse Tomatoes in Other Parts of the World

Temperate regions

The methods used for tomato production in northern mainland Europe and Canada are essentially the same as those described for the United Kingdom. However, there are variations in the IPM programs due to differences in the pest complexes and the availability of both biological control products and target specific chemicals.

In the Netherlands, the green garden looper (*Chrysodeixis chalcites* [Esper]) has become a year-round pest in tomato crops. The microbial pesticide most commonly used to control this pest is *B. thuringiensis*, but it is only partially effective and several applications are usually required during the season. An interesting project has recently evaluated the efficacy of brown-capped fulvetta (*Alcippe brunnea* Gould) birds as predators of these caterpillars in pepper crops (van der Linden 1999), and there may be potential for their use in tomato crops too. Another lepidopteran pest, tomato pinworm (*Keiferia lycopersicella* [Walshingham]), causes serious damage in Ontario (Wang, Ferguson, and Shipp 1998). These caterpillars penetrate the fruit, leaving inconspicuous entry holes that can easily be overlooked during packing. Such infested fruit results in serious marketing difficulties. Several control measures are being used against this pest, including improved crop hygiene, use of light traps, pheromone traps, disruption of mating by slow release of a sex pheromone, and the release of various species of egg parasitoids (*Trichogramma* spp.) (Ibid.; Shipp, Wang, and Ferguson 1998; G. Ferguson, pers. comm.). Another caterpillar, the cabbage looper (*Trichoplusia ni* [Hübner]), causes substantial losses of tomato production in British Columbia (D. Gillespie, pers. comm.). It is primarily a foliage feeder but contaminates fruit with frass, which collects around the calyx and provides a site for bacterial infection. Cabbage loopers are commonly controlled within IPM programs with *B. thuringiensis* and releases of *Trichogramma* spp. Populations of cabbage loopers in B.C. are displaying resistance to *B. thuringiensis* (Milks and Myers 2003). In addition, the predatory bug *Podisus maculiventris* (Say) and the larval parasitoid *Cotesia marginiventris* (Cresson) have been evaluated experimentally, but without great success in tomato crops.

Warmer climates

In warmer climates, chemical pesticides still form the basis of pest control in the majority of commercial greenhouse tomato crops. The main factors limiting the adoption of IPM in these countries are the difficulties in combating sudden large pest invasions, the speed of development of pests in the crops, and the fear of plant virus infections spread by insects, particularly *Frankliniella occidentalis* (Pergande) and *Bemisia tabaci* (Gennadius).

One option is to reduce pest invasion by screening greenhouse doors and ventilators, and there are examples of this being successfully done in a range of crops in southern Europe, Israel, and the southern United States. The use of screens against larger insects, such as whiteflies, is well advanced (Berlinger, Mordech, and Leeper 1991), but it is more difficult to exclude thrips because they can penetrate through smaller apertures. Screens that can exclude thrips purely by mesh size also impede airflow, the primary purpose of ventilators. However, the color of a screen enhances its effect (Berlinger et al. 1993). A loose shading net, through which

whiteflies and thrips passed freely in the laboratory, reduced penetration of thrips if it were "aluminum colored." These results were reinforced in field trials in which an aluminum-colored screen performed much better than an otherwise identical white one. Screens and covers will probably make a substantial contribution to future IPM programs, particularly in warmer climates.

The Future

The British Tomato Growers' Association is dedicated to the development of production systems that are completely free from synthetic chemical toxins, but they also recognize that this will be one of their greatest challenges in the coming years (G. Hayman, pers. comm.). The elimination of target specific chemical pesticides from IPM will clearly place more emphasis on the primary biological control methods. Pesticides will probably be replaced with a wider range of beneficial organisms and plant cultivars that provide advantages to the arthropod natural enemies. It is anticipated that a greater range of entomopathogens, particularly host-specific strains of parasitic fungi and baculoviruses will support the primary biological control systems.

IPM will ultimately become the norm in the warmer climates, but this will present a much greater challenge than in temperate regions. Screens and covers will probably make a substantial contribution, reducing pest invasion to levels that can be managed with cultural and biological control methods.

It is envisaged that the type of chemicals used in IPM throughout the world will change. Arthropod poisons will be phased out gradually and replaced by synthetic analogues of pheromones, allomones, and kairomones used to manipulate the behavior of pests or incorporated as attractants in traps. The use of such semiochemicals will, of course, require a much more detailed knowledge of the interactions between plants, herbivorous arthropods, and beneficial organisms. There is no doubt that the future development of IPM must be built on a sound scientific foundation.

References Cited

Alford, D. V. 1975. *Bumblebees*. London: Davis-Poynter.

Foster, G. N., and Barker, E. 1978. A new biotype of red spider mite causing atypical damage on tomatoes. *Plant Pathology* 27: 47-48.

Bedford, I. D., A. Kelly, P. G. Markham, and R. P. Tucker. 1996. The effects of buprofezin against the citrus mealybug, *Planococcus citri*. In *Proceedings Brighton Crop Protection Conference—Pests and Diseases*, 3: 1065–70, Brighton, U.K.: British Crop Protection Council.

Berlinger, M. J., S. L. Mordechi, D. Fridja, and N. Mor. 1993. The effect of types of greenhouse screens on the presence of western flower thrips: A preliminary study. *IOBC/WPRS Bulletin* 16 (2):13–6.

Berlinger, M. J., S. Mordechi, and A. Leeper. 1991. Application of screens to prevent whitefly penetration into greenhouses in the Mediterranean Basin. *IOBC/WPRS Bulletin* 14 (5):105–10.

Broadway, R. M., and S. S. Duffey. 1986. Plant proteinase inhibitors: Mechanism of action and effect on the growth and digestive physiology of larval *Heliothis zea* and *Spodoptera exiguae*. *Journal of Insect Physiology* 32:827–33.

Cantelo, W. W., A. L. Boswell, and R. J. Argauer. 1974. *Tetranychus* mite repellent in tomato. *Environmental Entomology* 3:128–30.

Chandler, D., G. Davidson, and R. J. Jacobson 2004. Laboratory and glasshouse evaluation of entomopathogenic fungi against the two-spotted spider mite, *Tetranychus urticae*, on tomato, *Lycopersicon esculentum*. *Biocontrol Science and Technology,* In press.

Chatzivasileiadis, E. A., and M. W. Sabelis. 1997. Toxicity of methyl ketone from tomato trichomes to *Tetranychus urticae* Koch. *Experimental and Applied Acarology* 21:473–84.

Cooper, S. 1993. The biology and application of *Anagrus atomus* (L.) Haliday. *IOBC/WPRS Bulletin* 16 (8):42–3.

Croft, P., J. Fenlon, R. J. Jacobson, and J. Dubas. 1999. Effect of tomato conditioning on *Phytoseiulus persimilis* Athias-Henriot (Acari: Phytoseiidae) population growth**. *IOBC/WPRS Bulletin* 22 (1):45–8.

Dahlman, D. L., and E. T. Hibbs. 1967. Responses of *Empoasca fabae* (Homoptera: Cicadellidae) to tomatine, solanine, leptine I, tomatadine, solanidine, and demissidine. *Annals of the Entomological Society of America* 60:732–40.

Dimock, M. B., and G. G. Kennedy. 1983. The role of glandular trichomes in the resistance of *Lycopersicon hirsutum f. glabratum* to *Heliothis zea*. *Entomologia Experimentalis et Applicata* 33:263–8.

Drukker, B. 1997. Improved control capacity of the mite predator *Phytoseiulus persimilis* (Acari: Phytoseiidae) on tomato. *Experimental and Applied Acarology* 21:507–18.

Farrar, R. R., Jr. and G. G. Kennedy. 1988. 2-Undecanone, a pupal mortality factor in *Heliothis zea*: Sensitive larval stage and *in planta* activity in *Lycopersicon hirsutum f. glabratum*. *Entomologia Experimentalis et Applicata* 47:205–10.

Farrar, R. R., Jr. and G. G. Kennedy. 1991. Insect and mite resistance in tomato. In *Monographs on Theoretical and Applied Genetics*, ed. G. Kalloo, 121–42, Berlin: Springer-Verlag.

Fauvel, G., J. C. Malausa, and B. Kaspar. 1987. Etude en laboratoire des principles caracteristiques biologiques de *Macrolophus caliginosus* (Heteroptera: Miridae). *Entomophaga* 32:529–43.

Feng, M. G., J. B. Johnson, and S. E. Halbert. 1992. Parasitoids (Hymenoptera: Aphidiidae and Aphelinidae) and their effect on aphid (Homoptera: Aphidiidae) populations in irrigated grain in southwestern Idaho. *Environmental Entomology* 21:1433–40.

Gentile, A. G., R. E. Webb, and A. K. Stoner. 1969. *Lycopersicon* and *Solanum* spp. resistant to the carmine and the two-spotted spider mite. *Journal of Economic Entomology* 62:834–6.

Hall, R. A. 1982. Control of whitefly, *Trialeurodes vaporariorum,* and the cotton aphid, *Aphis gossypii*, in glasshouses by *Verticillium lecanii*. *Annals of Applied Biology* 101:1–11.

Hayman, G., and R. Jacobson. 1996. Not so beneficial insects? *Grower* 126 (29):13.

Hilborn, R. G. 1998. Food safety and pesticides: A retailer's view. In *Proceedings Brighton Crop Protection Conference—Pests and Disease,* 2: 471–4, Brighton, U.K.: British Crop Protection Council.

Jacobson, R. J. 2000. Early season control of tomato leaf miner. *HDC Fact Sheet.* 08/00. 4.pp. Horticultural Development Council, East Malling, U.K.

Jacobson, R. J. 2003. Mealybugs on the increase. *HDC News*, 94, 24-26.

Jacobson, R. J., and R. J. Chambers. 1996. Control of greenhouse leafhopper (*Hauptidia maroccana*: Homoptera, Cicadellidae) within an IPM programme in protected tomatoes. *IOBC/WPRS Bulletin* 19(1):67–70.

Jacobson, R. J., and P. Croft. 1999. Response to fenbutatin oxide in populations of *Tetranychus urticae* Koch (Acari: Tetranychidae) in U.K. protected crops. *Crop Protection* 18 (1):47–52.

Jacobson, R. J., P. Croft, and C. Sampson. 2000. Optimising the use of abamectin in cucumber and tomato IPM programmes. *HDC Fact Sheet*, 18/00. 4pp. Horticultural Development Council, East Malling, U.K.

Jarrett, P., and H. D. Burgess. 1982. Control of tomato moth, *Lacanobia oleracea*, by *Bacillus thuringiensis* on greenhouse tomato crops and the influence of larval behavior. *Entomologia Experimentalis et Applicata* 31 (3): 239-244.

Kanno, H., K. Ikada, T. Asai, and S. Maekawa. 1981. 2-tert-butylimino-3-isopropyl-5-phenylperhydro-1,3,5-thiadi-azin-4-one (NNI-750): A new insecticide. In *Proceedings Brighton Crop Protection Conference–Pests and Diseases,* 1: 59-66. Brighton, U.K.: British Crop Protection Council.

Kennedy, G. G., and R. R. Farrar Jr. 1987. Response of insecticide-resistant and susceptible Colorado beetle, *Leptinotarsa decemlineata*, to 2-tridecanone and resistant tomato foliage : The absence of cross-resistance. *Entomologia Experimentalis et Applicata* 44:213–9.

Lloyd, L. L. 1920. The habits of the greenhouse tomato moth, *Hadena (Polia) oleracea* and its control. *Annals of Applied Biology* 7:66–102.

Luckwill, L. C. 1943. *The Genus Lycopersicon: Historical, Biological, and Taxonomic Survey of the Wild and Cultivated Tomatoes*. Aberdeen, Scotland: The University Press.

Maisonneuve, J. C., J. Blum, and L. R. Wardlow. 1995. Contre la cicadelle de la tomate en serre. *Un nouvel auxiliaire: Anagrus atomus. Phytoma–La Defense des vegetaux* 471, April 1995: 24–7.

Malausa, J. C., J. Drescher, and E. Fraco. 1987. Perspectives for the use of predacious bug *Macrolophus caliginosus* Wagner (Heteroptera: Miridae) on glasshouse crops. *IOBC/WPRS Bulletin* 10 (2):106–7.

Milks, M. L. and J. H. Myers. 2003. Cabbage looper resistance to a nucleopolyhedrovirus confers cross-resistance to two granuloviruses. *Environmental Entomology* 32 (2): 286-289.

Minkenberg, O. P. J. M. and J. C. van Lenteren. 1986. The leaf miners: *Liriomyza bryoniae and L. trifolii* (Diptera: Agromyzidae), their parasites and host plants: A review. *University of Wageningen papers* 86 (2):50.

Nihoul, P. 1993. Do light intensity, temperature and photoperiod affect the entrapment of mites on glandular hairs of cultivated tomatoes? *Experimental and Applied Acarology* 17:709–18.

Opit, G., B. Roitberg, and D. R. Gillespie. 1997. The functional response and prey preference of *Feltiella acarigusa* (Vallot) (Diptera: Cecidomyiidae) for two of its prey: Male and female two-spotted spider mites, *Tetranychus urticae* (Koch) (Acari: Tetranychidae). *The Canadian Entomologist* 129:221–7.

Reeves, A. F. 1977. Tomato trichomes and mutations affecting their development. *American Journal of Botany* 64(2):186–9.

Rice, R. E., and F. E. Strong. 1962. Bionomics of the tomato russet mite, *Vasates lycopersici* (Massee). *Annals of the Entomological Society of America* 55:431–5.

Sampson, A. C., and V. J. King. 1996. *Macrolophus caliginosus*: Field establishment and pest control effect in protected tomatoes. *IOBC/WPRS Bulletin* 19 (1):143–6.

Sampson A. C., and P. Walker. 1998. Improved control of *Liriomyza bryoniae* using an action threshold for the release of *Diglyphus isaea* in protected tomato crops. *Mededelingen Faculteit Landbouwwetenschappen, Rijksuniversiteit Gent* 63 (2b):415–22.

Sampson, C., and R. J. Jacobson. 1999. *Macrolophus caliginosus* Wagner (Heteroptera: Miridae): A predator causing damage to U.K. tomatoes. *IOBC/WPRS Bulletin* 22 (1):213–6.

Shipp, J. L., and N. D. Clarke. 1999. Decision tools for integrated pest management in greenhouses. In *Integrated Pest and Disease Management in Greenhouse Crops*, ed. R. Albajes, M. L. Gullino, J. C. van Lenteren, and Y. Elad, 168–82. Dordrecht, the Netherlands: Kluwer Academic Publisher.

Shipp J. L., K. Wang, and G. Ferguson. 1998. Evaluation of commercially produced *Trichogramma* spp. (Hymenoptera: Trichogrammatidae) for control of pinworm, *Keiferia lycopersicella* (Walshingham) (Lepidoptera: Gelechiidae), on greenhouse tomatoes. *The Canadian Entomologist* 130 (5):721–31.

Speyer, E. R., and W. J. Parr. 1948. The tomato moth. In *1947 Report of the Experimental Research Station*, 41–62, Cheshunt. Ministry of Agriculture, Fisheries and Food, London, U.K.

Squires, P. 1998. Watch it with Crop-It. *Grower* 129 (9):22.

Steiner, M. Y., and D. P. Elliot. 1983. *Biological Pest Management for Interior Plantscapes*. Publication No. 83-E1.Vegreville, Canada: Alberta Environmental Centre.

Trottin-Caudal, Y., and P. Millot. 1994. Lutte integrée contre les ravageurs sur tomate sus abri. Situation et perspectives en France. *IOBC/WPRS Bulletin* 17 (5):5–13.

van der Linden, A. 1999. Insectivorous birds for biological control of pests in glasshouses. *IOBC/WPRS Bulletin* 22 (1):149–52.

van Haren, R. J. F., M. M. Steenhuis, M. W. Sabelis, and O. M. B. de Ponti. 1987. Tomato stem trichomes and dispersal success of *Phytoseiulus persimilis* relative to its prey Tetranychus urticae. Experimental and Applied Acarology 3:115–21.

van Lenteren, J. C., Y. C. Drost, H. J. W. van Roermund, and C. J. A. M. Posthuma-Doodeman. 1997. Aphelinid parasitoids as sustainable biological control agents in greenhouses. *Journal of Applied Entomology* 121:473–85.

van Roermund, H. J. W., and J. C. van Lenteren. 1992. Life-history parameters of the greenhouse whitefly *Trialeurodes vaporariorum* and the parasitoid *Encarsia formosa*. *Wageningen University papers*, 92–3.

van Steenis, M. J. 1993. Suitability of *Aphis gossypii* Glov., *Macrosiphum euphorbiae* (Thom.), and *Myzus persicae* (Sulz.) (Hom.: Aphidiidae) as hosts for several aphid parasitoid species (Hym.: Braconidae). *IOBC/WPRS Bulletin* 16 (2):157–60.

Wang, K., G. Ferguson, and J. L. Shipp. 1998. Incidence of tomato pinworm, *Keiferia lycopersicella* (Walshingham) (Lep.: Gelechiidae), on greenhouse tomato in southern Ontario and its control using mating disruption. *Proceedings of the Entomological Society of Ontario* 128:93–8.

Wardlow, L. R., and A. Tobin. 1990. Potential new additions to the armory of natural enemies for protected tomatoes. *IOBC/WPRS Bulletin* 13 (5):225–7.

Williams, E. C., and O. C. Macdonald. 1995. Critical factors required by the nematode *Steinernema feltiae* for the control of the leaf miners *Liriomyza huidobrensis, Liriomyza bryoniae* and *Chromatomyia syngenesiae. Annals of Applied Biology* 127:329–41.

Williams, W. G., G. G. Kennedy, R. T. Yamamoto, J. D. Thacker, and J. Bordner. 1980. 2-Tridecanone, a naturally occurring insecticide from the wild tomato *Lycopersicon hirsutum f. glabratum. Science* 207, 22 February 1980: 888–9.

Woets, J. 1985. Tomatoes. In *Biological Pest Control: The Glasshouse Experience*, ed. N. W. Hussey and N. E. A. Scopes, 166–74, Poole, U.K.: Blandford Press (Ithaca, N.Y.: Cornell University Press).

Zhang, Z-Q., and R. J. Jacobson. 2000. Using adult female morphological characters for differentiating *Tetranychus urticae* complex (Acari: Tetranychidae) from greenhouse tomato crops in the UK. *Systematic and Applied Acarology.* 5: 69-76.

29

BIOLOGICAL CONTROL FOR MUSHROOM

C. B. Keil
Department of Entomology and Wildlife Ecology
University of Delaware

and

P. F. White
Plant Pathology and Microbiology Department
Horticulture Research International

Overview of *Agaricus* Mushroom Production

White and brown mushrooms commonly grown for consumption, *Agaricus bisporus* (Lange) Imbach, are produced using several variations upon a central theme. Production facilities may be: houses with fixed beds or shelves containing compost; farms with a series of growing rooms with different environmental conditions into which trays of compost are moved for each stage of production; or simple sheds with compost in large, 25-gal. [100-l] plastic bags. Whichever production system is used, growers must carefully regulate temperature, humidity, airflow, and moisture in the compost to produce high yields of fresh, market quality mushrooms.

Mushroom production begins with a two-phase process for the preparation of growing substrate or compost. The ingredients of mushroom compost are straw or straw-bedded horse manure that has been mixed with a carbohydrate source (typically corncobs, cocoa hulls, or cottonseed hulls), a nitrogen source such as chicken manure, a buffer such as gypsum or lime, and water. In Phase I, these ingredients are placed outdoors on a concrete wharf and mixed thoroughly with specialized machinery or they are placed in specially constructed bunkers or tunnels through which fresh air is forced. Temperatures in the interior of a pile typically reach 140°F (60°C), which together with the mixing or aeration encourages aerobic fermentation.

Phase II is characterized by a peak heating followed by a cool down period, and thus requires controlled conditions either in growing rooms or rooms specially constructed to regulate the temperature of the fermenting compost. During Phase II, the high temperatures derived from aerobic fermentation pasteurize the compost. This pasteurization drives off ammonia, it converts nitrogen in the compost to microbial protein, and it facilitates the succession of a series of thermophilic microbial communities. The result is a nutrient rich substrate for the growth of *A. bisporus*.

When the compost has cooled to approximately 72°F (22°C), *A. bisporus* mycelia in the form of spawn is mixed into the substrate. Spawn consists of pure cultures of various strains of *Agaricus* grown on sterile rye or millet grains. White button mushrooms are from hybrids derived from white and off-white strains that combine good yields, high quality for fresh market sales, and favorable characteristics for processing. Portobello and crimini mushrooms are from older brown strains that are not as high yielding but have good shelf life and stronger flavor. Growth supplements are usually added to the compost at the time of spawning. These supplements typically consist of denatured corn, soy, or feather meal combinations to provide delayed release of protein and lipids for mushroom nutrition later in the crop. The proliferation of the *A. bisporus* mycelia through the compost is referred to as *spawn run*. Moderate temperatures, generally 70 to 81°F (21 to 27°C) but 77 to 82°F (25 to 28°C) in the United Kingdom, and high carbon dioxide concentrations are necessary for maintaining mycelia in a vegetative state and for generating a vigorous spawn run. This is essential to combating pest and disease infestation.

A 1.5-in. (4-cm) thick layer of peat mixed with gypsum or lime, termed *casing*, is applied when the mycelium has fully colonized the compost. The casing is often steam-pasteurized before application to make the media contaminant free. When the mycelia have fully colonized the casing, the fruiting process is initiated by lowering the temperature of the growing room by introducing outside air. During this period, it is important to water the growing beds frequently to provide free water to the developing fruit bodies.

This environmental shock results in simultaneous appearance of fruiting bodies throughout the growing room. Typically there are three or four synchronized fruiting events in each eleven-week crop, which yield up to 8.2 lb. per ft.² (40 kg/m²) of white button mushrooms per crop. The cropping cycle is continuous, and ranges of growing rooms are typically filled with all stages of crop production present on a farm at all times. At the end of each crop, the growing room is sterilized with live steam before being emptied of spent compost.

Pests Affecting Mushroom Production

Sciaridae

Three sciarid flies infest commercially grown mushrooms. *Lycoriella solani* Winnertz was the most destructive fly pest until the widespread introduction of organophosphorous pesticides into mushroom production in the 1970s. The development of resistance to the organophosphates by *Lycoriella auripila* (Winnertz) allowed this species to supplant *L. solani*, and *L. auripila* is now the dominant sciarid pest in Britain and Ireland (Fletcher, White, and Gaze 1989). The sciarid infesting mushrooms grown in the United States and most of the world is *Lycoriella mali* (Fitch), and it is now found in the United Kingdom. There is speculation that *L. mali* may have displaced other sciarid flies in the United States with the introduction and widespread application of organophosphorous, carba-mate, and pyrethroid pesticides.

All three sciarid species infest compost as it is cooling from peak heating (Phase II of compost preparation) and during spawn run. Females enter mushroom growing rooms and lay up to 150 eggs per female in the compost. The larvae hatch in three to five days and begin to feed on the compost and developing mycelia. Moderate numbers of larvae are tolerated in the compost at this early stage of crop development. However, high larval populations can inhibit proliferation of the *A. bisporus* mycelia and break down the physical and chemical structure of the compost rendering it unable to support the crop. Because the temperature of the compost is uniform during spawn run and infestation of the crop tends to occur on the day of spawning, the development of the first gener-ation of sciarid larvae is remarkably synchro-nous. In the United States, adult flies emerge from the substrate twenty-six to twenty-eight days after infestation, just as the primordia of the fruiting bodies form. In the United Kingdom, spawn run temperatures are higher and sciarid emergence takes place just after casing, eighteen to twenty-two days after spawning. Larval feeding during this stage of crop development can result in significant yield losses as feeding often severs the mycelial attachments and destroys the primordia.

Most control efforts directed at sciarids prevent the emergence of the first-generation adults. Insect growth regulators (IGR) can be very effective against first generation sciarid larvae because synchronous development allows for precise timing of IGR applications. Growers monitor the infestation of growing rooms with blacklight traps to better time IGR applications. Although there are no empirically derived economic thresholds for sciarids, most growers begin control efforts when they detect five to ten sciarid adults per day on the black light traps.

First-generation adults that emerge in the mushroom house mate and lay eggs in the casing. Larval feeding of the second and subsequent generations can be very destruc-tive as it occurs during fruit body formation. Moderate populations of larvae in the casing may significantly affect subsequent fruiting events and reduce yields of marketable mush-rooms. When larval populations are high, they may tunnel into the stipes (stem) of developing mushrooms. This tunneling results in the formation of an infection court, stipe discoloration, and occasional malforma-tion of the cap itself.

Adult sciarids are also mechanical vectors of fungal and bacterial diseases of mushrooms caused by *Trichoderma harzianum* Rifai, *Verticillium fungicola* (Preuss) Hassebrauk, and *Pseudomonas tolaasii* Paine (White 1981). Damage from sciarid-vectored diseases often causes greater economic loss of marketable mushrooms than damage from larval feeding. In addition, large numbers of adult flies can be very irritating and can result in loss of efficiency and complaints from workers. An estimated 20% of crop losses are attributed to sciarids even with regular pesticide application (Cantwell and Cantelo 1984).

Pesticide resistance is a serious problem in sciarid control. *Lycoriella auripila* has become resistant to diazinon over a wide geographic range throughout the United Kingdom (White and Gribben 1989). In the

United States, *L. mali* has become resistant to organophosphates, DDT, diazinon, dichlorvos, permethrin, pyrethrin, and diflubenzuron (Brewer and Keil 1989, Bartlett and Keil 1997). Currently, the most effective pesticides for sciarid control include methoprene, azadirachtin, and cyromazine. The widespread development of pesticide resistance has stimulated the development of biological control methods (primarily microbial controls) for these important pests of cultivated mushrooms.

Phoridae

A number of phorid flies in the genus *Megaselia* affect commercial mushroom production worldwide (White 1985). The most economically important species, *Megaselia halterata* (Wood), affects mushroom cropping both by direct larval feeding and by the transmission of fungal pathogens (White 1981; Rinker and Snetsinger 1984). Gravid female flies are attracted to volatiles from the growing mycelium after it has been spawned (Burrage 1981, Grove and Blight 1983). Specifically, females prefer to lay eggs in compost that has been spawn run for seven to twelve days (Richardson and Hesling 1978). Once the crop has been cased, fresh mycelial growth will again attract phorid females. After the final surge of mycelial growth, the attractiveness of the crop diminishes as harvest progresses. Fly emergence can occur at any time from casing onwards.

Presently, *M. halterata* does not appear to be resistant to organophosphate insecticides. Even when using an effective OP such as diazinon, larval control is complicated by difficulties in mixing the insecticide into the compost at spawning and by fungitoxicity to

A. bisporus mycelia (Wyatt and Gurney 1974; Cantelo, Henderson, and Argauer 1982). Although efficacy may vary among farms, control of adults can be achieved with a range of products including pirimiphosmethyl, dichlorvos, and synthetic and natural pyrethrins (Keil 1986).

Cecidomyiidae

Two cecidomyiid species commonly affect mushroom production: *Mycophila speyeri* (Barnes) and *Heteropeza pygmaea* Winnertz. A third species, *Mycophila barnesi* Edwards, is a less frequent pest. *Mycophila* spp. larvae are orange-colored, while *H. pygmaea* larvae are white. All three species can cause substantial losses in yield both due to mycelial browsing by larvae and due to spoilage of harvested mushrooms (Wyatt 1960, White 1990). Adult flies of these pests are attracted to the crop in ways similar to phorids, since cecidomyiid larvae are found readily in decaying wood and rotten vegetation. Interestingly, reproduction in these species occurs during the larval stage (a process known as paedogenesis). As a result, growing material with very small infestations of larvae can soon generate crop-damaging pest populations. Larval infestations can arise from inadequate sterilization of trays or bed timbers, or by transport on the workers' hands and tools. Due to the lack of accurate easy-to-use larval monitoring techniques, infestations are often only detectable when moderate or severe. When larval densities are sufficiently high, adult flies develop and only then may the minute flies be seen and the infestation detected. Chemical control of these pests is extremely difficult due to difficulty in achieving insecticide-to-pest contact.

Additionally, many countries have few to no compounds registered for use against these pests.

Nematodes

Nematodes associated with mushroom production have two different feeding habits. They may be mycophagous (feeding on fungus) or saprophagous (feeding on dead organic material). Two nematodes that may destroy mushroom mycelia are *Ditylenchus myceliophagus* Goodey and *Aphelenchoides composticola* Franklin (Hussey, Read, and Hesling 1969). An early infestation by either species can result in dead, sodden patches of compost, which can increase in size from the second flush onwards. However, pest nematodes seldom cause serious problems provided standard short cropping periods are utilized and normal hygienic conditions are followed.

Most nematodes found in mushroom beds belong to the family Rhabditidae, with individuals characteristically having a saprophagous feeding habit. Although these species are typically not primary pests of mushrooms, if *Caenorhabditis elegans* (Maupas) Dougherty survives through Phase II pasteurization or if it is inadvertently introduced during casing, this species may have a deleterious effect on the crop (Grewal and Richardson 1991).

Typically, an infestation of either form of nematode is an indication that compost preparation was inadequate or that pasteurization was not complete. Thus, nematode control is generally achieved by cultural methods and sanitation. Flies can spread both types of nematodes once an infestation occurs, and as a result, good fly control is also required to prevent the spread of a nematode infestation.

Biological Control Agents and Methods

Insect parasitoids

Populations of the key mushroom pests are seldom affected by insect parasitoids. Hussey, Read, and Hesling (1969) reported that *Synaldis concolor* Nees parasitizes larvae of the mushroom phorid *Megaselia nigra* (Meigen). Because parasitized *M. nigra* larvae continue to feed and develop normally until pupation, damage to the immediate mushroom crop may be severe even if parasitism rates are high. The benefits of this type of natural enemy activity may only be observed in crops planted sequentially, as parasitism of a current crop may provide an overall reduction of the population infesting future crops.

Muscidifurax raptor Girault and Sanders, *Muscidifurax zaraptor* Kogan and Legner, and *Muscidifurax raptorellus* Kogan and Legner are used extensively by most producers of mushroom compost to control manure-breeding flies, such as *Musca domestica* L., *Fannia canicularis* (L.), and *Stomoxys calcitrans* (L.) on the compost wharf. These flies characteristically breed on the margins of the compost production areas and in decomposing piles of raw ingredients. Parasitoids are commonly shipped as pupae by commercial insectaries, and wharf managers release them weekly during the warm months of the year to control manure-breeding flies.

Entomopathogenic nematodes

Several entomopathogenic nematodes affect mushroom pests. *Howardula husseyi* Richardson is an obligate parasite of the mushroom phorid *M. halterata*. Extensive research was carried out to determine its potential as a biological control agent (Richardson and Chanter 1979). However, due to a number of factors peculiar to the life cycle and development of the parasite, its initial promise as a biological control agent was not realized (Richardson and Chanter 1981).

The most extensively used biological agent for control of *L. mali* and *L. auripila* is *Steinernema feltiae* (Filipjev) (Steiner-nematidae). Richardson (1987) established that *S. feltiae* and a species of *Heterorhabditis* were able to use *L. auripila* larvae as hosts, and they established a provisional concentration range for field applications. Nickle and Cantelo (1991) obtained a 72 to 81% reduction in adult emergence of *L. mali* using a concentration of 4,000 infective juveniles per in.^{2} (620/cm^2) of spawned compost. This was about one third of the concentration used by Richardson (1987) to obtain similar reductions in emergence of *L. auripila*. Nickle and Cantelo (1991) also found that the third instar larvae of *L. mali* were most susceptible to nematode infection and that mortality decreased if insects were exposed to the nematodes as fourth instar larvae or pupae. They speculated that the fourth instar larvae avoided searching nematodes by burrowing deep into the spawned compost. The lack of free water in this stratum may restrict movement of the nematodes.

Grewal and Richardson (1993) conducted trials under commercial production conditions to determine the best concentration of *S. feltiae* to apply for control of *L. auripila*. In their experiment, four concentrations of nematodes were compared to an untreated control and a grower standard of diazinon-diflubenzuron tank mixed together. Nematodes and insecticide treatments were applied to the casing, as it was placed on the growing trays, approximately two weeks after spawning and infestation by *L. auripila* females. At the third week after casing and continuing to the eighth week, the two highest nematode concentrations (13,948 and 6,974 nematodes per in.^{2} [2,162 and 1,081/cm^2]) provided control equivalent to the insecticide standard. No differences in pest suppression were observed between the two highest nematode concentrations. After the fifth week, all nematode concentrations, including the two lowest concentrations (3,483 and 1,741 nematodes per in.^{2} [540 and 270/cm^2]), were as effective as the diazinon-diflubenzuron combination. During the trials, nematode numbers declined during the first two weeks after application, remained constant until the eighth week, then they rose slightly. Grewal and Richardson (1993) attributed this pattern to recycling of the nematodes in the larger host larvae. Nematodes invade suitable hosts immediately following application, and they develop within their infected hosts during weeks three through eight. The next generation infective juveniles emerge from host cadavers during week eight and beyond.

Rinker et al. (1995) conducted nine commercial scale trials to test the abilities of *S. feltiae* to control *L. mali*. Nematode concentrations ranged from 71 to 7,225 infective juveniles per in.^{2} (11 to 1,120/cm^2) applied the day of casing, about two weeks after the spawned compost was exposed to gravid L. *mali* females. At all concentrations above 903 nematodes per in.^{2} (140/cm^2), the reduction in emergence of L. *mali* was 95% or greater compared to an untreated control. Concentrations in the range of 361 to 903 nematodes per in.^{2} (56 to 140/cm^2) reduced emergence by 80 to 85%. Not reported previously by other researchers, these investigators also described harmful effects to the crop from nematode application densities. For example, the amount of visible mycelia on the casing surface at pin set (which is indicative of the total amount of mycelia) was reduced even at a very low application rate of 71 to 181 nematodes per in.^{2} (11 to 28/cm^2). While these low nematode application rates (up to 181 nematodes per in.^{2} [28/cm^2]) did not translate into yield reductions, significant reductions in the mushroom yields during the first break were observed for application rates of 7,225 nematodes per in.^{2} (1,120/cm^2). Crop yields in the high nematode application treatments returned to normal in later breaks.

A number of strategies have been proposed to improve effectiveness of S. *feltiae* in commercial settings. Grewal et al. (1993) attempted to select a strain of S. *feltiae* with an improved ability to detect L. *mali* larvae. The selected strain and a standard strain of S. *feltiae* were applied at 323 and 645 infective juveniles per in.^{2} (50 and 100/cm^2) of growing surface on a commercial mushroom farm. In addition, there was an untreated control and a chemical standard (diflubenzuron applied at the recommended concentration listed on the label). At the 645 infective juveniles per in.^{2} (100/cm^2) concentrations, both the selected and standard nematode strains reduced emergence of L. *mali* adults similar to the emergence rate observed in the diflubenzuron treatment. No adverse effects of nematode applications on crop production were observed during the study. Current recommendations call for application of S. *feltiae* at 781 infective juveniles per in.^{2} (121/cm^2) of growing surface at casing or several days later.

Predators

Al-Amidi and Downes (1990) reported the predatory mite *Parasitus bituberosus* Karg (Parasitidae) to be an effective predator of the cecidomyiid, H. *pygmaea* in laboratory trials. Deutonymphs preferred as prey the first and second instars of H. *pygmaea* and first instars of L. *solani* when presented with a range of prey sizes (instars) on plates of corn meal agar. In laboratory tests conducted in small pots of spawned compost, P. *bituberosus* densities increased in the presence of H. *pygmaea* larvae, and when fly larvae were absent they persisted by foraging on soilborne nematodes. By contrast, cecidomyiid larvae increased dramatically in pots where P. *bituberosus* was not present. In field trials conducted in commercial growing bags in Ireland, Al-Amidi, Dunne, and Downes (1991) demonstrated that P. *bituberosus* was able to reduce the emergence of adult L. *solani* by about 66% when larval population densities were low.

Fungal pathogens

Pandora gloeospora (Vuillemin) Humber (Entomophthorales: Zygomycetes), an entomopathogenic fungus, has been described from field-collected *L. mali* adults in Delaware and Pennsylvania (Miller and Keil 1990). This pathogen was originally described from an unidentified midge in France and is likely to have a widespread geographical distribution. As with most entomopathogens, infectivity and pathogenicity are related to density and duration of spore contact with the hosts. Conidiospores of this fungus can infect large larvae, pupae and adults of *L. mali* (Table 29.1). When conidia were topically applied to fourth-instar larvae, the insects pupated normally and emerged as adults at about the same proportion as water-treated controls. However, the adults derived from the treated larvae were killed by *P. gloeospora* and developed an extensive spore-producing layer (hymenium) within a day of emergence. Topical application of one hundred conidia to less than one day old *L. mali* pupae resulted in about 78% of the resulting adults developing a fatal mycosis. Application of conidia to four-day old pupae produced a fatal mycosis in only 25% of the adults (Table 29.1). When adult *L. mali* were exposed to showers of *P. gloeospora* conidia in a flight cage for twenty-four hours, external mycosis developed in 22 to 97% of the flies exposed. Natural epizootics can occur in mushroom growing rooms when sciarid populations are very high, thus maximizing the probability of contact of infected insects with healthy hosts. These epizootics can result in dramatic declines in population density.

Table 29.1. Ability of *Pandora gloeospora* to Infect Various Life Stages of *Lycoriella mali*

L. mali Life Stage	Individuals	Treatment[1]	% Emergence[2]	% Infection[2]
Fourth Instar	60	Conidia	90.0 ± 12.7	100
	50	Water	94.0 ± 8.9	0
Late Pupa	40	Conidia	98.0 ± 4.5	25.6 ± 12.7
Early Pupa	50	Conidia	100	78.0 ± 4.5
Early Pupa	10	Water	90	0
Adult	100	Conidial Shower	N/A	22
Adult	100	Conidial Shower	N/A	43
Adult	100	Conidial Shower	N/A	97

[1]Treatments consisted of one hundred conidia applied topically. Controls were treated with water. Insects were grouped in replicates of ten individuals.
[2]Values within columns represent means ± 1 standard error of the mean (when available).

Bacteria

The *israelensis* strain of *Bacillus thuringiensis* (*Bti*) is a dipteran-active, highly effective bacterium for control of mosquito larvae (Goldberg and Margalit 1977). Osborne, Boucias, and Lindquist (1985) showed that *Bti* could control a greenhouse sciarid, *Bradysia coprophila* (Lintner), while it infests mushrooms. Cantwell and Cantelo (1984) showed that *Bti* had promise as a control agent for *L. mali*, although at application rates that were uneconomical. Keil (1991), using an experimental formulation of *Bti*, demonstrated control of *L. mali* and *M. halterata* in commercial trials equal to the control provided by grower applications of diflubenzuron and methoprene. The application of *Bti* to compost and casing may also result in increased yields of *Agaricus* mushrooms. Keil (1991) and Keil and Miller (1995) reported yield increases ranging from 4.7 to 10.7 % by weight in field applications on commercial farms and 8.1 to 19.3% by weight in the laboratory. By contrast, Cantwell and Cantelo (1984) failed to detect an increase in yield associated with *Bti* applications. White et al. (1995) showed that a number of *Bt* isolates provided better control of *L. auripila* larvae than did *Bti*. Control from these isolates was comparable to that from diflubenzuron. Results of this work have produced patents for two new strains, GC315 and GC327, for use against mushroom pests (Jarrett, White, and Pethybridge 1996).

In addition to producing a protein crystal and a vegetative spore, *B. thuringiensis* can produce a number of exotoxins. In contrast to the crystal and spore, the exotoxins are general toxins and, in consequence, have a wide range of activity, including mammalian toxicity. Although these toxins in general are active against a range of insects and plant mite pests, the beta-exotoxin in *Bti* is only active against the mushroom sciarid *L. auripila* at very high doses.

Bacterial blotch is a serious disease of *A. bisporus* caused by *Pseudomonas tolaasii* Paine. Diseased mushrooms exhibit slightly sunken brown lesions with smooth margins on the cap and stipe. This disease is a significant factor in reducing mushroom quality and shelf life of the harvested fruiting bodies. Most growers in the United States add sodium or calcium hypochlorite to irrigation water as a prophylactic treatment for *P. tolaasii* (Wong and Preece 1985). These sodium or calcium hypochlorite applications can interfere with the effectiveness of *Bti* and *S. feltiae* (Keil 1991; Grewal, Weber, and Betterley 1998).

Other Considerations for Pest Management

Physical exclusion of insects

Physical exclusion of invading populations of sciarids and phorids is an essential part of successful biological control programs in mushrooms. Most growers try to exclude flying insects from the critical phases of commercial mushroom production, such as the cool-down from Phase II pasteurization, spawn run, and pre-cropping. The use of sixteen mesh screening to cover entry ways is fine enough to stop the progress of flies but not too fine to prevent the flow of air. Many growers use the placement of foam gaskets treated with insect adhesives (i.e., Tanglefoot) on doors, door jams, and other openings. Cracks and joints in walls and ceilings are sealed with spray-on polyurethane foam. This practice not only excludes invading flies but also reduces heating and cooling costs as the foam has significant insulation value. The use of water or J-traps on drain lines of air conditioning units has effectively eliminated those pipes as a point of fly invasion.

Monitoring fly populations

Growers commonly base insect control decisions on data collected from trap counts. Trap data are useful in both timing pest control activities and selecting techniques appropriate to the size of an invading population. Most growers in the United States regularly use blacklight traps equipped with removable panels constructed of freezer paper coated with an insect adhesive. These traps are placed in growing rooms during cool down after peak heating in Phase II of compost preparation and monitored daily for invading female flies. The efficiency of these trapping systems might be improved if used in conjunction with a pheromone cocktail capable of attracting both phorid and sciarid adults (Kostelc, Girard, and Hendry 1980; Burrage 1981; Baker et al. 1982). Trapping techniques are unlikely to be effective as stand-alone pest control measures. Suction and sticky traps provide little control of flying pest populations (Lelley 1984, Wardlow and O'Brien 1988).

Pest Management in Mushroom Crops

Several issues limit development of biological control based pest management strategies for cultivated mushrooms. Mushrooms are a minor crop in most states and countries where they are grown. Consequently, there are few new reduced risk pesticides registered for use in mushrooms simply because the potential market is too small. Complicating the use of chemical controls are the highly restricted pesticide registrations in many countries for use on mushrooms. Currently, chemical pest control in the United States relies primarily on a single compound, cyromazine. Sciarids have rapidly developed resistance to a diversity of insecticides, including IGRs, organophosphates, and pyrethroids. Development of sciarid resistance to cyromazine could be disastrous to United States growers. Similar situations also apply to fungicides used to control mushroom disease organisms.

Compounding the pest management problem is the unavailability of biological control options, with the exception of several microbial biological control organisms. Optimal deployment of entomopathogenic nematodes and *Bti*, however, are viewed more as resistance management techniques for preserving currently registered pesticides rather than as a reliable pest control tactic. However, the current trend toward organic mushroom production should stimulate the use of existing biological control agents and development of new ones. Furthermore, products based on azadirachtin provide the possibility of integrating rescue applications of a relatively benign botanical pesticide with the use of natural enemies, thus possibly giving growers the confidence needed to begin learning how to best use biological control agents. Natural controls such as the entomopathogen *P. gloeospora* are additional tools that could be integrated into a biological control-based pest management strategy.

Equally important to taking the proper steps in preventing pest problems or implementing the appropriate management strategy once a pest problem occurs is to anticipate pest problems and to plan accordingly. Nematodes effectively control low to moderate sciarid populations. However, high populations of flies may require multiple control techniques that include larvicides and adulticides, especially if the flies may be vectoring a plant pathogen.

Pest management in mushrooms is based on five factors: sanitation, exclusion, monitoring, biological control, and the use of a variety of pesticides only when pest pressure demands their use. The foundation for pest management in mushroom production is a healthy spawn run. Dense mycelial growth is inhibitory to the development of insect larvae and pathogens. Only recently have scientists and growers begun to understand the interactions between *A. bisporus*, normal compost microorganisms, arthropod pests, and diseases. This is underscored by the development of a variety of microorganisms for biological control, many of which are naturally occurring in the compost and casing. The optimization and effective implementation of these techniques will require an understanding of the complex microbial ecology of the mushroom growing substrate. It is likely that this understanding will suggest additional organisms and techniques for microbial control and optimization of the substrate for *A. bisporus* production.

References Cited

Al-Amidi, A. H. K., and M. J. Downes. 1990. *Parasitus bituberosus* (Acari: Parasitidae): A possible agent for biological control of *Heteropeza pygmaea* (Diptera: Cecidomyiidae) in mushroom compost. *Experimental and Applied Acarology* 8:13–25.

Al-Amidi, A. H. K., R. Dunne, and M. J. Downes. 1991. *Parasitus bituberosus* (Acari: Parasitidae): An agent for control of *Lycoriella solani* (Diptera: Sciaridae) in mushroom crops. *Experimental and Applied Acarology* 11:159–66.

Baker, R., A. H. Parton, V. B. Rao, and V. J. Rao. 1982. The isolation, identification and synthesis of 3,6-dimethylheptan-2,4-dione, a pheromone of the mushroom fly, *Megaselia halterata* (Diptera: Phoridae). *Tetrahedron Letters* 23:3103–4.

Bartlett, G. R., and C. B. Keil. 1997. Identification and characterization of a permethrin resistance mechanism in populations of the fungus gnat, *Lycoriella mali* (Fitch) (Diptera: Sciaridae). *Pesticide Biochemistry and Physiology* 58:173–81.

Brewer, K. K., and C. B. Keil. 1989. Permethrin resistance in *Lycoriella mali* (Diptera: Sciaridae). *Journal of Economic Entomology* 82:17–21.

Burrage, K. J. 1981. Ecological biochemistry of the mushroom phorid, *Megaselia halterata* (Wood) (Dipt.). Bach. thesis, University of Southampton.

Cantelo, W. W., D. Henderson, and R. J. Argauer. 1982. Variation in sensitivity of mushroom strains to diazinon compost treatment. *Journal of Economic Entomology* 75:123–5.

Cantwell, G. E., and W. W. Cantelo. 1984. Effectiveness of *Bacillus thuringiensis* var. *israelensis* in controlling a sciarid fly, *Lycoriella mali*, in mushroom compost. *Journal of Economic Entomology* 77:473–5.

Fletcher, J. T., P. F. White, and R. H. Gaze. 1989. *Mushrooms: Pest and Disease Control*, 2nd ed. Andover, U.K.: Intercept.

Goldberg, L. J., and J. Margalit. 1977. A bacterial spore demonstrating rapid larvicidal activity against *Anopheles sergentii, Uranotaenia unguiculata, Culex univitattus, Aedes aegypti* and *Culex pipiens. Mosquito News* 37:355–8.

Grewal, P. S., and P. N. Richardson. 1991. Effects of *Caenorhabditis elegans* (Nematoda: Rhabditidae) on yield and quality of the cultivated mushroom *Agaricus bisporus. Annals of Applied Biology* 118:381–94.

———. 1993. Effects of application rates of *Steinernema feltiae* (Nematoda: Steinernematidae) on biological control of the mushroom fly, *Lycoriella auripila* (Diptera: Sciaridae). *Biocontrol Science and Technology* 3:29–40.

Grewal, P. S., M. Tomalak, C. B. Keil, and R. Gaugler. 1993. Evaluation of a genetically selected strain of *Steinernema feltiae* against the mushroom sciarid, *Lycoriella mali. Annals of Applied Biology* 123:695–702.

Grewal, P. S., T. Weber, and D. A. Betterley. 1998. Compatibility of the insect-parasitic nematode, *Steinernema feltiae*, with chemicals used in mushroom production. *Mushroom News* 46 (4):6–10.

Grove, J. F., and M. M. Blight. 1983. The oviposition attractant for the mushroom phorid, *Megaselia halterata*: The identification of volatiles present in mushroom house air. *Journal of Science: Food and Agriculture* 34:181–5.

Hussey, N. W., W. H. Read, and J. J. Hesling. 1969. *The Pests of Protected Cultivation: The Biology and Control of Glasshouse and Mushroom Pests*. New York: American Elsevier Publishing Co. (London: Edward Arnold).

Jarrett, P., P. F. White, and N. J. Pethybridge. 1996. Biological control of dipteran pests of the genus *Lycoriella* using Bacillus *thuringiensis*. U.S. Patent Office, No. 5,512,279.

Keil, C.B. 1986. Control of adult *Lycoriella mali* and *Megaselia halterata*. In *Cultivating Edible Fungi,* ed. P. J. Wuest, D. J. Royse, and R. B. Beelman, 587–97. New York: Elsevier.

———. 1991. Field and laboratory evaluation of a *Bacillus thuringiensis* var. *israelensis* formulation for control of fly pests of mushrooms. *Journal of Economic Entomology* 84:1180–8.

Keil, C. B., and M. W. Miller. 1995. Interaction of *Agaricus bisporus* with *Bacillus thuringiensis* var. *israelensis* applied for control of *Lycoriella mali*. In *Science and Cultivation of Edible Fungi*, ed. T. J. Elliot, 525–32. Rotterdam, the Netherlands: A.A. Balkema.

Kostelc, J. G., J. E. Girard, and L. B. Hendry. 1980. Isolation and identification of a sex attractant of a mushroom-infesting sciarid fly. *Journal of Chemical Ecology* 6:1–11.

Lelley, J. 1984. New methods for insect control in mushroom culture. Results of testing an air suction insect-catching apparatus. *Champignon* 270 (1):16–7.

Miller, M. W., and C. B. Keil. 1990. Redescription of *Pandora gloeospora* (Zygomycetes: Entomophthorales) from *Lycoriella mali* (Diptera: Sciaridae). *Mycotaxon* 38:227–31.

Nickle, W. R., and W. W. Cantelo. 1991. Control of a mushroom-infesting fly, *Lycoriella mali* with *Steinernema feltiae*. *Journal of Nematology* 23:145-7.

Osborne, L. S., D. G. Boucias, and R. K. Lindquist. 1985. Activity of *Bacillus thuringiensis* var. *israelensis* on *Bradysia coprophila* (Diptera: Sciaridae). *Journal of Economic Entomology* 78:922–5.

Richardson, P. N. 1987. Susceptibility of mushroom pests to the insect-parasitic nematodes, *Steinernema feltiae* and *Heterorhabditis heliothidis*. *Annals of Applied Biology* 111:433–8.

Richardson, P. N., and D. O. Chanter. 1979. Phorid fly (Phoridae: *Megaselia halterata*) longevity and the dissemination of nematodes *Howardula husseyi* (Allantonematidae) by parasitized females. *Annals of Applied Biology* 93:1–11.

———. 1981. Aspects of the laboratory production of mushroom flies (*Megaselia halterata*) parasitized by the nematode *Howardula husseyi*. *Annals of Applied Biology* 99:1–9.

Richardson, P. N., and J. J. Hesling. 1978. Laboratory rearing of the mushroom phorid, *Megaselia halterata* (Diptera: Phoridae). *Annals of Applied Biology* 88:211–7.

Rinker, D. L., T. H. A. Olthof, J. Dano, and G. Alm. 1995. Effects of entomopathogenic nematodes on control of a mushroom-infesting sciarid fly and on mushroom production. *Biocontrol Science and Technology* 5:109–19.

Rinker, D. L., and R. J. Snetsinger. 1984. Damage threshold to a commercial mushroom by a mushroom-infesting phorid (Diptera: Phoridae). *Journal of Economic Entomology* 77:449–53.

Wardlow, L. R., and A. O'Brien. 1988. Reducing the fly nuisance in mushroom houses. *International Symposium on Crop Protection— Ghent* 53:789–92.

White, P. F. 1981. Spread of the mushroom disease, *Verticillium fungicola* by *Megaselia halterata* (Diptera: Phoridae). *Protection Ecology* 3:17–24.

———. 1985. Pests and pesticides. In *The Biology and Technology of the Cultivated Mushroom*, ed. P. B. Flegg, D. M. Spencer, and D. A. Wood, 279–93. Chichester, U.K.: John Wiley and Sons.

———. 1990. Effects of the paedogenetic mushroom cecid, *Heteropeza pygmaea* (Diptera: Cecidomyiidae) on cropping of the cultivated mushroom (*Agaricus bisporus*). *Annals of Applied Biology* 117:63–72.

White, P. F., P. Butt, N. J. Pethybridge, and P. Jarrett. 1995. The story of a strain: Development of GC327, a dipteran-active strain of *Bacillus thuringiensis* effective against the mushroom sciarid, *Lycoriella auripila*. In *Science and Cultivation of Edible Fungi*, ed. T. J. Elliot, 499–506. Rotterdam, the Netherlands: A.A. Balkema.

White, P. F., and D. A. Gribben. 1989. Variation in resistance to diazinon by the mushroom sciarid, *Lycoriella auripila*. *Mushroom Science* XII:851–9.

Wong, W. C., and T. F. Preece. 1985. *Pseudomonas tolaasii* in cultivated mushrooms (*Agaricus bisporus*) crops: Effects of sodium hypochlorite on the bacterium and on blotch disease severity. *Journal of Applied Bacteriology* 58:259–67.

Wyatt, I. J. 1960. Cecidomyiidae as pests of cultivated mushrooms. *Annals of Applied Biology* 48:430–2.

Wyatt, I. J., and B. Gurney. 1974. The efficiency of spawning machines for mixing insecticides into mushroom compost. *Annals of Applied Biology* 78:125–38.

30

EXTENSION/ADVISORY ROLE IN DEVELOPING AND DELIVERING BIOLOGICAL CONTROL STRATEGIES TO GROWERS

J. Bennison

ADAS, Boxworth, Cambridge
United Kingdom

Biological control of pests in greenhouses became a commercial reality in the early 1970s. A few innovative growers began to use the first commercially available biological control agents on cucumber and tomato, supported by researchers and advisors who helped them develop the new techniques. Today, biological control of most pests on several greenhouse vegetable and ornamental crops is a routine part of integrated pest management (IPM) in many countries. In northern Europe, the United States and Canada, successful commercial use of biological control has inspired grower confidence, enthusiasm, and commitment. Today's crop protection advisors only encounter the problems faced by early advisors (i.e., convincing growers to try novel pest control methods) in countries where IPM is not yet widely adopted, or on crops where biological control is still a relatively new technique. Whatever the level of grower experience, the role of the advisor is still critical in promoting and supporting the use of biological control and other successful IPM strategies.

Definitions of Biological Control and IPM

The terms *biological control* and *IPM* are often used synonymously, but IPM practices do not necessarily include biological control methods in all countries. The commercial use of biological control could be defined as the manipulation of natural enemies to maintain pest densities below the level at which economic plant damage would occur. The pest density at which economic damage occurs varies with the crop. On vegetable crops such as cucumber or tomato, the grower aims to maintain damage below the level at which either yield or quality of fruit might be reduced. However, for crops in which the whole plant is marketed (e.g., ornamentals or edible herbs) there is a near complete intolerance of pests or the damage they cause. As a result, inundative 'overkill' biological control methods have been developed for use in these highly sensitive crops. These methods aim to produce finished plants completely free from pests and their damage.

IPM embraces various complementary methods of maintaining pest populations below the appropriate threshold. In most northern European countries, IPM in protected crops is generally understood to mean the integration of biological control methods with cultural and physical techniques, and minimal use of those pesticides that are least harmful to natural enemies. In the United Kingdom, comprehensive IPM programs are used on the majority of protected cucumbers, tomatoes, and peppers and on an increasing area of protected fruit and ornamental plants (Garthwaite and Thomas 2001).

In the United States and Canada, although biological control is the fundamental approach to IPM on protected vegetable crops (Gillespie 2002), the term IPM does not always imply a biological control component on ornamental crops. Advisors of IPM on ornamentals in Ontario, a major area for floriculture in Canada, defined IPM as "a philosophy/strategy of pest control integrating all available tactics to reduce pest populations to an acceptable level in a cost-effective, environmentally rational manner" (Murphy and Broadbent 1996). The first phase of IPM is what is known in northern Europe and Israel as supervised control (i.e., the use of a sound monitoring and record-keeping system to rationalize pesticide use). This basic IPM strategy, together with cultural control techniques such as good nursery hygiene and weed control, is now increasingly being extended to include the use of biological control agents on ornamentals in North America (Murphy et al. 2002, Murphy 2002). As this chapter concerns the adoption of biological control methods, the term IPM will be used to encompass a range of control strategies including the use of natural enemies.

Reasons for Adopting IPM Systems Based on Biological Control

Historically, growers of greenhouse crops first became interested in biological control methods to overcome severe problems with pesticide resistance. Despite advances in pesticide technology, resistance remains the main reason that growers adopt biological control techniques today, along with increasing pressures from retailers, the public, and governments to use environmentally- friendly production methods. Many of today's growers utilize sophisticated technology to produce high-quality crops and accept that IPM with a biological control component is an essential part of production. The attitude of the grower is arguably the most important factor affecting the successful use of available biological control methods. In considering changing attitudes, it is necessary to understand what motivates growers to adopt biological control strategies, and what needs have to be met in order to put these methods into practice within an effective IPM program.

Resistance

Biological control techniques were first developed for commercial use in the United Kingdom in the 1970s in response to resistance to organophosphorus pesticides by the two-spotted spider mite, *Tetranychus urticae* Koch. Soon after, resistance to various groups of broad-spectrum pesticides was also detected in the greenhouse whitefly, *Trialeurodes vaporariorum* (Westwood), and in the green peach aphid, *Myzus persicae* (Sulzer) (Gould 1985). A similar situation occurred in other countries during the 1970s, e.g., in Canada, 'biological controls were adopted in greenhouse crops out of desperation' (Gillespie 2002). Today's growers are faced with similar problems despite the development of new and more specific pesticides. Examples of how the development of pesticide resistance has affected grower attitudes towards control strategies and the adoption of biological methods are given below.

Whiteflies

Whiteflies infesting protected crops have largely evaded the attempts of the pesticide industry to develop effective insecticides for their control. In the early 1980s, many British growers relied on the newly developed synthetic pyrethroids for greenhouse whitefly control. As a result, the parasitoid *Encarsia formosa* Gahan was used on only 30% of the area of tomatoes and on 46% of the area of cucumbers (Gould 1985). The first cases of pyrethroid resistance were confirmed in 1982, and by 1985 resistance was widespread (Wardlow 1985). Growers of cucumbers and tomatoes had no other choice but to adopt the routine use of *E. formosa*. The role of the national advisory service (ADAS) was instrumental in this increased adoption, both in testing for whitefly resistance and in helping growers to develop effective parasitoid management strategies.

The tobacco whitefly, *Bemisia tabaci* (B biotype, also known as *B. argentifolii* Bellows and Perring), proved to be equally adept at developing resistance to pesticides (Cahill et al. 1995). This occurrence is even more serious due to the importance of this pest as a vector of plant viruses (e.g., tomato yellow leaf curl virus, TYLCV). In Israel, a crisis with pesticide resistance accompanied by severe problems with TYLCV led to the implementation of IPM programs on tomatoes by the extension service in 1992 (Ausher 1997). As biological control agents are not yet fully effective under the environmental conditions in plastic greenhouses in Israel, the IPM program relies heavily on physical methods such as the use of insect-proof screens and UV-absorbing plastic sheets, as well as on sticky traps for mass trapping of *B. tabaci*. Screening to prevent entry of viruliferous whiteflies is also used in the Mediterranean countries, especially Spain. Here, severe problems with pesticide resistance have led to the adoption of biological control methods for whiteflies, but only on virus-resistant tomatoes or on other less susceptible crops, or in areas where virus pressure is lower (Castañé 2002).

The wider availability of pesticides approved for control of whiteflies on ornamentals delayed the adoption of biological control methods. But the development of resistance (e.g., to buprofezin in both greenhouse whitefly and tobacco whitefly [Gorman, Cahill, and Denholm 1998]) has led to the increased use of biological control methods on ornamentals. *Encarsia formosa* is now routinely used on the majority of poinsettias and on an increasing number of other whitefly-susceptible ornamental plant species grown in northern Europe. The parasitoid *Eretmocerus eremicus* Rose and Zolnerowich has recently become available in northern Europe and this is now being used in addition to *E. formosa* on crops such as poinsettias that are also susceptible to the tobacco whitefly, against which *E. formosa* is less effective.

In the United States, the continued use of the neonicotinoid pesticide imidacloprid has inhibited the use of biological control agents for whiteflies on pot plants, particularly poinsettias, on which the pesticide offers persistent control of the only two significant pests, whiteflies and fungus gnats. Growers of these crops may only turn to biological control methods when resistance to imidacloprid develops, as is occurring in *B. tabaci* populations elsewhere (Cahill et al. 1996, El Kady and Devine 2003). However, recent research and commercial availability of *E. eremicus* in the United States now offers a cost-effective biological alternative to imidacloprid for the control of tobacco whitefly, which should encourage the adoption of biological control on poinsettias (Van Driesche and Lyon 2003.). In northern Europe, growers of ornamentals who are using IPM have not abandoned biological control methods in favor of imidacloprid. These growers, having gained confidence with biological control methods and mindful of previous resistance problems with other pesticides, are currently reserving the use of imidacloprid for plants particularly susceptible to whiteflies, or on those crops grown at temperatures too low for effective use of parasitoids.

Western flower thrips

The most important pest influencing the development and adoption of biological control methods since the late 1980s has been the western flower thrips, *Frankliniella occidentalis* (Pergande). In the United Kingdom, western flower thrips was first detected on imported chrysanthemums (*Dendranthema grandiflora* Tzvelev) in 1986, and it then rapidly spread to most greenhouses growing susceptible crops. Control with pesticides proved extremely difficult due to problems with resistance, phytotoxicity of the more effective pesticides, and adverse effects on biological control agents being used against other pests in established IPM programs.

Before the arrival of western flower thrips, the main thrips species in protected crops was the onion thrips, *Thrips tabaci* Lindeman. This pest had been controlled with applications of diazinon on chrysanthemums, and in cucumber crops within IPM programs with applications of Thripstick (sticky polybutenes, combined with the insecticide deltamethrin) to the floor (Pickford 1984). Neither of these control measures proved effective against western flower thrips. Cucumber and sweet pepper growers sought biological control methods for the pest, as there was no other practical choice. Grower pressures to find a biological solution led to the commercial release of a predatory mite (*Neoseiulus cucumeris* [Oudemans]) and later predatory bugs (*Orius* spp.), before sufficient research and development had been carried out. However, within a few years, biological control of western flower thrips with *N. cucumeris* was reliable on peppers (Altena and Ravensberg 1990, Buxton et al. 1990, Ramakers 1990), and this stimulated the widespread adoption of full IPM programs on this crop. Cucumbers proved a more difficult crop on which to achieve effective biological control of western flower thrips. However, a period of intensive research and development led to more reliable techniques by the mid-1990s

(Jacobson 1995), and these are now used within IPM programs on the majority of cucumber crops in northern Europe and Canada.

Adoption of biological control methods for western flower thrips on ornamentals has been slower due to the lower tolerance of thrips damage on the marketable plants. In the late 1980s, attempts to control the pest within established IPM programs on chrysanthemums failed due to the inability of the biological control agents to maintain control during flowering, leading to unacceptable damage and problems with tomato spotted wilt virus transmission. Growers were forced to abandon biological control methods and return to the intensive use of pesticides. However, a group of innovative British growers of pot and bedding plants, disillusioned with frequent applications of increasingly ineffective pesticides, sought advice on developing biological control methods for western flower thrips. With the guidance of the advisory service (ADAS), tentative comprehensive IPM programs were set up on a range of crops. These initial programs were successful and stimulated further interest and development of IPM on many pot and bedding plant species (Wardlow 1990; Wardlow, Davies, and Brough 1993). Western flower thrips has been a major catalyst for the development and adoption of IPM programs on ornamental crops in northern Europe and Canada. There are now effective IPM programs even for 'difficult' host crops such as chrysanthemums, on which the entomopathogenic nematodes *Steinernema feltiae* (Filipjev) is now being used successfully against western flower thrips (Wardlow 2002, Piggott and Wardlow 2002).

Aphids

Until the mid-1980s, most greenhouse vegetable IPM programs in northern Europe used the selective aphicide pirimicarb for aphid control, even though international research on biological control methods had been carried out and natural enemies were commercially available. But increasing resistance to pirimicarb, particularly in the green peach aphid and in the melon and cotton aphid, *Aphis gossypii* Glover (Furk and Hines 1993), stimulated more research and adoption of biological control strategies. Other factors encouraging biological control of aphids were the demand for residue-free sweet peppers exported from The Netherlands and Canada to the United States (Gilkeson 1990) and evidence that pirimicarb could have adverse effects on *N. cucumeris* used for thrips control (van der Staay 1991).

Biological control of *M. persicae* was shown to be possible in sweet peppers, using the braconid parasitoid *Aphidius matricariae* Haliday and the predatory cecidomyiid midge *Aphidoletes aphidimyza* (Rondani) (Gilkeson 1990). Following research demonstrating that *Aphidius colemani* Viereck was the most effective parasitoid against both *A. gossypii* and *M. persicae* (van Steenis 1994, van Tol and van Steenis 1994), *A. colemani* has become widely used against these aphid species on both peppers and ornamentals. *Aphidius colemani* also provides effective control of *A. gossypii* on cucumbers and can be made more cost-effective by using open rearing units or banker plants (Bennison and Corless 1993, Mulder et al. 1999). Banker plants for aphid parasitoids are now used on both edible and ornamental crops, and the technique is also being developed for natural enemies of various other pests (Maisonneuve 2002).

More recently, new strains of *M. persicae* with total resistance to the dimethyl carbamates, such as pirimicarb and triazamate (Wege *et al*. 1998), have further encouraged the adoption of biological control methods. In the United Kingdom, although the incidence of resistant strains is still low, cases have been confirmed in various protected crops. The antifeedant pymetrozine is now available and effective against resistant aphids, and can be integrated safely with biological control agents within IPM programs.

Reduced availability of effective pesticides

Commercial withdrawal or government banning of pesticides is another factor encouraging the adoption of biological control methods. The organochlorine pesticide aldrin was withdrawn in the United Kingdom in 1989 due to its environmental hazard. This led to the use of entomopathogenic nematodes for the control of the black vine weevil, *Otiorhynchus sulcatus* (F.), on susceptible pot plants, such as cyclamen and hardy ornamental species. Although the availability of compost-incorporated formulations of both chlorpyrifos and imidacloprid in the United Kingdom during the mid-1990s led to a reduction in the use of nematodes particularly on outdoor ornamentals, the recent availability of *Steinernema kraussei* (Steiner), which is tolerant of low temperatures, is leading to a return to the use of nematodes for control of this pest.

The withdrawal of cyhexatin in the United Kingdom in 1988, due to applicator health risks, stimulated further use of biological control methods for spider mites. Cyhexatin was widely used in IPM programs in both tomatoes and cucumbers, and its withdrawal left fenbutatin oxide as the main acaricide that could be safely integrated with natural enemies. However, limitations in the effectiveness of fenbutatin oxide encouraged research on natural enemies to supplement control by *P. persimilis*. The predatory midge *Feltiella acarisuga* (Vallot), formerly *Therodiplosis persicae* Keiffer, was shown to have potential for use on tomatoes (Wardlow and Tobin 1990) and has now been adopted successfully by growers of both tomatoes and ornamentals. Although newer acaricides such as abamectin and tebufenpyrad are now available, they do not always give reliable control and they are not fully compatible with IPM. Thus research on improving biological control of spider mites is continuing, and additional natural enemies such as *Neoseiulus californicus* (McGregor) are now being used on ornamental crops.

There are now very few pesticides registered for use on certain 'minor' edible protected crops such as lettuce, other leafy salads and herbs. Effective biological control methods are now used on protected herbs in the United Kingdom, despite the zero tolerance of pest damage. Potted herbs can be treated like ornamental pot plants as subjects for biological control; both products need to be free from pests or damage and require an 'overkill' approach justified by the high value of the crops. Similar restraints on fresh herbs exported from Israel have led to IPM strategies being implemented, with a drastic reduction in the use of pesticides (Ausher 1997).

On demonstration plots and farms managed by the Israeli Extension Service, IPM methods have achieved the zero tolerance goals for both pests and pesticide residues and these methods have now been adopted by the whole fresh herbs industry in Israel. Lettuce and other leafy salad greens are more challenging crops for biological control, as they are lower in value and grown at cooler temperatures during the winter. However, the shortage of approved pesticides for use on these crops and increasing problems with pesticide-resistant aphid and leafminer populations are stimulating research on biological control methods (Bennison et al. 1999, Jacobson et al. 1999, Head et al. 2002). The current EU Pesticide Review will shortly lead to the revocation of further pesticides and this will encourage further development and adoption of novel IPM methods on various crops.

Increasing pressures to reduce pesticide usage

Public pressure to reduce pesticide usage is increasing in many countries. Concerns about residues in food, health risks to growers and consumers, contamination of ground and surface water, and other potential adverse effects on the environment are strongly influencing market demand for both edible and ornamental crops grown with minimal risks to the environment. "Crop protection has become a political item" (van Alphen 1997), and government policies are responding accordingly. In the United Kingdom, government objectives include minimizing the use of pesticides and promoting sustainable and environmentally responsible crop production methods, and a national pesticides strategy is being developed (Williams 2002). The

European and Mediterranean Plant Protection Organization (EPPO) promotes good plant protection practices, which include guidelines on rational use of pesticides and use of biological or integrated approaches where appropriate (Smith 1997). Some governments have set targets for the reduction in pesticide usage. In The Netherlands, the 'GLAMI Convenant' for growers of glasshouse crops has set various environmental targets, including a 60% reduction in the use of pesticides by 2010.

Consumer concerns have encouraged various market initiatives to introduce Quality Assurance schemes, codes of practice for growers, and IPM labelling systems in various European countries. British growers are now unavoidably tied to their retail outlets, whose demands for quality assurance exert a powerful influence on suppliers. The major British supermarkets now require both British and overseas suppliers to adhere to the various Integrated Crop Management Systems (ICMS) protocols within supermarket Assured Produce and other accreditation schemes, and this is stimulating further use of biological control methods on both edible and ornamental crops.

Specific accreditation schemes for ornamentals include the BOPP (British Ornamental Plant Producers) scheme and the Dutch Milieu Project Sierteelt (MPS) scheme, which is also open to growers from other countries. The 'Dansk I.P.' (Danish Integrated Production) scheme for fruit and vegetables is similar to the British and Dutch accreditation systems, but is controlled by the Plant Health authorities. The label gives growers a market advantage and a price premium due to consumer demand for "green" produce. EUREPGAP is a recently established European quality assurance scheme that sets 'benchmark' standards for good agricultural practice and for the safety of food and the environment. It is likely that there will soon be mutual recognition among these various accreditation schemes.

Health and safety considerations for greenhouse staff

In most countries where IPM is used, growers and their staff are now more aware of potential health risks in using pesticides, and this is stimulating further use of biological control methods. U.K. legislation now requires operators to be trained in competent pesticide use and to make safety assessments before each application, selecting the product with least risk to humans, animals and the environment. This approach has led to safer, more rational use of pesticides. Applying pesticides in greenhouses is an unpopular task and staff members prefer not to handle treated plants. Once nursery staff start to use biological control methods and appreciate the benefits to their working practices and environment, they often become even more reluctant to use pesticides and this encourages the use of more comprehensive IPM programs.

Protection of bumble bees and other beneficial species

Since the late 1980s, the widespread use of bumble bees for pollination of tomatoes and peppers has been an important stimulus to increase the use of biological control methods. Likewise, the lack of a native biological pollinator in Australia and restrictive legislation on importing bees is impeding adoption of biological control. Due to the adverse effects of pesticides on bees and biological control agents, even so-called "minor" pests on tomatoes such as the glasshouse leafhopper, *Hauptidia maroccana* (Melichar), have become the target of biological control in IPM programs. This leafhopper, which until the 1990s was controlled with heptenophos, can now be controlled by the egg parasitoid *Anagrus atomus* Haliday. The U.K. advisory service was instrumental in developing techniques for using this parasitoid and together with commercial producers, facilitated its adoption (Wardlow and Tobin 1990).

As growers invest in more comprehensive biological control programs, the potential financial risks of using an incompatible pesticide increase. In addition, the status of pests can change once broad-spectrum pesticides are no longer used; species that were once considered only minor nuisances such as mirid bugs can cause considerable damage as, for example, is now the case in hardy ornamental plants and cucumbers grown under IPM. Other 'new' pests that can disrupt IPM programs include those that have spread with the increasing plant traffic around the world, such as *Echinothrips americanus* Morgan (van Schelt *et al.* 2002). Such new pests require the development of even more complex biological control programs. During the mid-1980s, the main biological control agents used in the United Kingdom were *P. persimilis* for control of spider mites, *E. formosa* for whiteflies, and parasitoids for leafminers. There are now over thirty species of natural enemies available, and on some ornamentals susceptible to a wide range of pests, at least a dozen of these may be used in an IPM program. This increased complexity in IPM programs creates new challenges for researchers in understanding the interactions between all the pests and beneficial agents, and for advisors in recommending successful management strategies to growers.

Growers' Needs for Successful Use of Biological Control

The success of today's IPM programs has been made possible by research and development, well-informed advice, and improved availability and quality of an increasing range of natural enemies. The factors affecting successful implementation of IPM are considered below.

Information and advice

"Successful integrated control is largely a matter of confidence" (Hussey 1985). When switching from reliance on pesticides to IPM, the grower needs access to a large amount of information and the means to assimilate it before it can be put into practice. The grower may feel daunted by the need to be an expert on the biology of all the pests and biological control agents and how to use and manage them in an IPM program.

There are now many sources of such information, but this does not always help the inexperienced grower who sometimes receives conflicting advice. The grower new to biological control needs reliable information and guidance from a specialist advisor. Experienced growers need continued support and advice, particularly as more complex IPM programs are developed. The availability of effective specialist advisors in biological

control is a key factor in the successful use of IPM in greenhouses around the world.

Government-funded extension services now exist in very few countries, and even where they do, they do not necessarily provide enough specialist advisors in IPM. Growers in some Canadian provinces, the United States, and Israel still have access to free, well-coordinated advice from extension workers specializing in IPM, whereas a shortage of such advisors is limiting the adoption of biological control in countries such as Australia, New Zealand, Greece, and Japan. In many European countries, the national extension services have suffered cutbacks or been wholly or partially privatized, which has led to the establishment of private or grower funded services. In the United Kingdom, the privatization of the national advisory service, together with associated staff reductions and advisory fees, has led to increased grower reliance on the biological control suppliers for advice. However, growers still value the impartial and comprehensive advice given by the advisory service and are prepared to pay for it, particularly for crops such as hardy nursery stock for which biological control is less developed. The biological control companies are increasingly important sources of information and guidance, particularly in those countries where independent extension workers or advisors are not available or are in short supply. The inability of some growers to put the available advice on biological control into practice can limit adoption. For example, in some areas of Australia, many growers of protected crops are from a non-English speaking background, and literacy and language can lead to communication problems between growers and advisors. In New South Wales, the Department of

Agriculture has provided IPM training courses and manuals for growers, and employs bilingual staff to help IPM specialists deliver the training to non-English speaking growers.

The continued availability of information and advice on biological control and IPM can only be sustained if sufficient research is conducted to fill the gaps in existing knowledge in order to supply solutions to new or persistent problems. Funding for research on biological control is inadequate in many countries. The IOBC working group "IPM in Greenhouses" helps to alleviate this problem by offering opportunities for international collaboration and for sharing research results and practical experience.

Availability of effective and affordable natural enemies

In northern Europe, Canada, and the United States, a wide range of natural enemies are available, but in other countries availability or cost-effectiveness is limited either by exten-

Figure 30.1. Advice and information are critical to the success of biological control. Jude Bennison, ADAS adviser, with Alistair Hazel, technical manager at Darby Nursery Stock, Norfolk, United Kingdom
(Photograph courtesy of H. Maher)

sive reliance on imported beneficials, as in Greece and Japan, or by dependence on those produced locally, such as in Australia and New Zealand. This limitation can restrict access to the range of natural enemies needed for comprehensive IPM programs. However, progress has been made in commercialization of native natural enemies in Japan (Yano 1999) and Australia (Goodwin and Steiner 2002, Steiner and Goodwin 2002), and developments in Australia have allowed further commercial adoption of IPM on a range of crops. Native natural enemies often perform better than exotic imported ones as they are adapted to local conditions (Yano 1999, Castañé 2002) and they are viewed by regulators as being less risky to native non-target invertebrates. The importation of non-indigenous organisms is subject to legislation in most countries and a European working group is currently developing guidelines for risk assessment procedures before exotic natural enemies can be imported or released (van Lenteren et al. 2002). The IOBC global working group "Quality Control of Mass-Reared Arthropods" has helped to improve the quality and reliability of natural enemies in recent years by developing standardized quality control tests. Quality control issues are discussed in detail in Chapter 31. Advisors still encourage growers to carry out simple quality checks on arrival because even if biological control agents leave the producer in good condition, packaging and transportation systems can affect viability.

Suitable growing environment and greenhouse structures

In temperate climates, growing conditions for the greenhouse crops on which IPM is most commonly applied are suitable for the successful use of most of the available biological control agents, although some can only be used for part of the year or part of the production cycle. Biological control programs used in northern countries are not always applicable to countries with warmer climates. Biological control can be particularly difficult in countries where greenhouse structures are open-sided to increase ventilation, creating the need for screening to minimize pest immigration. High technology greenhouses help growers cope with temperature extremes and these are beginning to be used in places such as Australia, where they are allowing increased use of biological control.

Availability of compatible pesticides

Although it is sometimes possible to grow certain crops (e.g., cyclamen, poinsettia, and sweet pepper) solely with biological pest control methods, in many crops some intervention with pesticides may be needed, either for pests not controlled adequately by natural enemies, or more often, for diseases. Research into plant breeding for resistance to pests and diseases and into improved methods for biological and cultural control will continue to reduce the need for pesticides within IPM programs, but in the meantime, compatible pesticides are still required. Limited availability of such pesticides can inhibit the adoption and success of IPM, particularly in those countries where the range of available natural enemies is not extensive, and increasing pest resistance to available safe pesticides is a serious threat. There has been a recent increase in the avail-

ability of plant-derived pesticides able to be integrated with biological control agents, and these are helping to fill some gaps in IPM programs. Knowing when such natural enemy–compatible pesticides are needed is a key skill in IPM management, and one where the advisor often plays an important role in supporting the grower.

Market acceptance of crops grown under biological control

For widespread adoption of biological control measures, growers have to be confident of the market acceptance of their produce. Retail demands can be contradictory; although pressures to reduce the use of pesticides encourage IPM, zero tolerance of pests, their damage, or natural enemies on the finished product can limit the use of biological control methods on some crops, especially ornamentals and herbs. However, improved IPM programs are now allowing growers to meet these quality standards. Zero tolerance of quarantine pests on propagation material or plants grown for export can also inhibit the use of IPM, although resistance to pesticides in pests such as *B. tabaci* and *Liriomyza huidobrensis* (Blanchard) is forcing the adoption of biological control methods and research into integrated eradication or containment techniques (Cheek 1997).

Methods for Helping and Encouraging Growers to Adopt Biological Control Methods

Growers seeking information and advice on adopting biological control methods are usually strongly motivated, as they are often experiencing difficulties controlling resistant pests with pesticides, or market demand for produce grown with reduced pesticides is forcing them to use IPM. In order to make the necessary commitment to biological control, growers must be confident of success. However, they should also be prepared to accept some risks. Innovative growers are more ready to take these risks and more cautious growers will follow later.

The role of the advisor and skills needed

The role of the advisor in providing information, reassurance, and support is critical in inspiring grower confidence and in helping even those skeptical of biological control to begin using this method. The advisor needs to have a thorough knowledge of the biology of both pests and natural enemies, be up to date with recent information and research results, and be able to translate these into practical and cost effective strategies for growers. There will always be problems for which there are no current solutions, and while continuing research aims to fill these gaps in knowledge, growers ask the advisor to provide answers. The advisor often needs to make judgments based on both established facts and personal experience and, together with growers, to develop workable solutions through trial and error. Thus, most advisors have an individual but important role in the development of new techniques under commercial conditions. This role is more effective if the advisor is involved in a coordinated strategy for research and development. In many countries, extension workers do not have a research role, in which case it is essential that there is close liaison with researchers and producers to ensure the necessary technology transfer.

Good communication and listening skills are essential so that the advisor establishes a relationship of trust and understanding with the grower. Enthusiasm for biological control should be balanced by practicality and realism, e.g., consideration of plant quality and of the grower's budget. The advisor should support the adoption of new ideas and technology but also prescribe caution with new or unreliable natural enemies, or with crops for which a robust biological control program has not yet been developed. The advisor's job is to help growers make informed decisions and to take the calculated risks needed to successfully manage their IPM programs.

Methods of giving information and advice

There are many ways to make new information available to growers and the effectiveness of these methods largely depends on the resources available to the advisor. Ideally, there should be a coordinated extension approach including a range of activities. However, in most countries, advisors have to use limited human and financial resources to best effect.

Workshops, demonstrations and grower groups

True understanding of IPM can only be achieved by personal experience. Workshops are used successfully by advisors in many countries to introduce groups of growers to the concepts and practical aspects of IPM, and to update more experienced growers on new techniques. Combining a workshop with a visit to a grower using IPM works well, as the knowledge and expertise gained in the workshop is reinforced by seeing the theory put into commercial practice. Such experiences give growers the confidence and enthusiasm to start using IPM, particularly on crops or in countries where IPM is not widely adopted. In the United Kingdom, ADAS-led workshops on IPM on ornamentals, funded by both industry and the government, have contributed to a significant increase in the successful uptake of IPM on protected hardy ornamental nursery stock (Bennison et al. 2002). An industry-funded extension initiative with state government support in Australia is helping to expand the adoption of IPM by providing groups of growers with accredited training courses, IPM demonstrations and subsequent technical support. In many countries, the transfer of new technology is a key component of research projects and most research institutes hold demonstrations for growers to view practical trial results, in either experimental or commercial greenhouses. Other demonstrations of biological control agents and methods are given by producers and researchers at trade shows, which play a valuable role in increasing awareness of IPM in both the horticultural industry and the general public.

Grower groups in many countries visit each other's greenhouses, together with their advisors, to compare production techniques including IPM. In Canada, monthly focus groups have been successful in promoting biological control and addressing common problems (Murphy 2002). Such exchanges provide vital peer support and encourage-

ment, help maintain confidence, and standardize commercial practices.

Planning the individual IPM program and on-site training

It is vital that adequate technical support and advice is available to help individual growers implement the new techniques discussed in workshops or seen at demonstrations. For a grower new to biological control, an individual visit by the advisor is essential to discuss the crops grown, the history of the grower's pest problems, particular environmental conditions, and budget for pest control. The advisor can then plan a detailed IPM program for each crop, tailored to conditions at that particular location. For growers of ornamentals, it is wise to try IPM first on a relatively easy crop such as cyclamen or poinsettia, using biological control agents for only one or two pests. As confidence is gained, the grower becomes interested in expanding the range of beneficial species employed and using IPM on additional crops. An annual review of the IPM program with the advisor is useful at the beginning of each season in order to consider experiences from the previous season, discuss new developments, and plan a new IPM program as needed.

Cost is an inevitable factor when designing comprehensive IPM programs. Costs of the natural enemies can sometimes be higher than for pesticides, particularly on ornamentals that are attacked by a wide range of pests and require many beneficial species. But a cost-effective IPM program can be designed for most crops, and even the most skeptical growers often become enthusiasts after only one season when the benefits of improved plant quality and reduced labor costs are clearly demonstrated. As the grower gains expertise with biological control, costs can be further reduced by fine-tuning introduction rates and monitoring techniques. Once an IPM program has been designed, grower commitment to training of greenhouse employees is then vital for successful implementation. It is useful if all workers can recognize pests, damage, and biological control agents. Employees responsible for pest control need a more detailed understanding of the biology of pests and their natural enemies, the use of biological control agents, and how to monitor and manage a successful IPM program. The advisor can provide this training and should develop a good working relationship with these employees, as their knowledge and experience is critical to successful IPM.

Decision making and support in IPM

Successful use of IPM depends on regular and efficient monitoring of both pests and biological control agents. Monitoring is necessary to detect potential or actual problems quickly, so that timely and appropriate action can be taken before the crop is put at risk. Pest populations can develop rapidly in greenhouse crops, which are usually of high value. Diagnosing the problem and deciding on the best course of action within IPM requires a great deal of knowledge, information, and experience. An advisor will usually be needed to help identify and evaluate problems, review the options, and assist in making informed decisions. Growers new to biological control need more technical back up than those who are more experienced, but all growers benefit from regular visits, supplemented as neces-

sary by diagnostic services and advice by telephone, fax or email. Even if no major problems are found during the advisor's visit, the value of reassurance and maintaining confidence cannot be overestimated.

Monitoring is discussed in detail in chapter 5. The monitoring system needs to be adequate to supply the required information, but should also be manageable in the time available. The advisor can show the grower how to monitor efficiently. In some countries, such as Israel and the United States, commercial scouts are used, with technical backup from the extension service.

Growers in the United Kingdom who are registered in any of the quality assurance accreditation schemes must use an efficient monitoring system and keep records for auditing purposes. Although computer-aided monitoring systems linked to decision support systems are likely to be used more widely in the future, personal contact with an advisor will still be needed.

Publications and electronic communication methods

Articles in the horticultural press effectively bring new information to the attention of a wide international audience and these, together with presentations at grower meetings and conferences, stimulate further interest in biological control and in new developments. Fact sheets, pest and natural enemy recognition booklets, posters, and IPM manuals all play a valuable role, particularly if they are combined with practical workshops or training courses. However, printed publications can quickly become out of date if techniques are changing rapidly, thus electronic communication methods are now increasingly being used as extension tools as they can be easily updated However, even the most advanced growers tend to prefer 'hard copy' information which can be more widely available at the business site and is quicker to access. In the United Kingdom, a Best Practice Guide for Integrated Pest and Disease Management on protected herbs that is currently being developed by ADAS will be produced both as a booklet and as a website at the growers' request. Regular newsletters are a cost-effective method for updating grower knowledge and are widely distributed by most advisory services and biological control companies, either as paper copies or by email. A wealth of information on biological control and IPM is available on the Internet, but growers are advised to treat this with caution if the source is not known to be reliable. *The Harrow Greenhouse Manager* is a computer-based decision-support system developed in Canada for IPM on cucumbers and tomatoes (Clarke et al. 1999), which has been commercially available since 1998 and is being used by growers, advisors and greenhouse suppliers in various countries.

The Advisor, the Researcher, and Commercial Producers of Natural Enemies

The extent and sophistication of biological control methods currently used within IPM on greenhouse crops has been made possible by the joint efforts and close collaboration between growers, advisors, researchers, and natural enemy producers. Continued development and adoption of biological control will depend on the maintenance and growth of this essential teamwork. Growers and their advi-

sors need to keep researchers and producers informed of new problems. Researchers and producers can then look for the answers and the natural enemies, and the advisors can then work with the growers to develop these into practical commercial solutions and improved IPM programs.

This ideal situation cannot always be realized in all countries. Researchers, advisors, and producers are not always available and they do not always work together in a coordinated approach. Inevitably there is an element of competition between producers, and this sometimes leads to duplication of research effort or the premature release of new natural enemies in order to gain a commercial advantage. However, the formation of the IBMA (International Biological Manufacturers Association), with a code of conduct, has enhanced cooperation among producers. IPM researchers and advisors are sometimes in short supply or poorly coordinated and there can be problems with competition among those who are privately funded.

In most countries the relationships between researchers, advisors, and commercial producers are still good. But in the United Kingdom, competition for research funding and the subsequent role of technology transfer has led to reluctance by researchers to share ideas, which is eroding the earlier cooperation and impeding progress. Fortunately, the recent emphasis on collaborative research and extension projects funded by both government and industry is now restoring vital links between the laboratory and the greenhouse. Hopefully this will improve coordination and use of the available expertise and resources.

International collaboration between researchers, advisors, and producers has always played an essential role in the worldwide development of IPM, and the IOBC working group "Integrated Control in Greenhouses" has been instrumental in providing a unique forum for the open exchange of ideas, results, and experience. Attendance and contribution to IOBC working group meetings is growing rapidly and leading to further international collaboration and the generation of an increasing flow of valuable information. If this can be channeled efficiently to growers, this combined international effort will accelerate the continued successful development of biological control within sustainable IPM systems around the world.

Acknowledgements

Thanks are due to the following advisors and researchers who provided international information for this chapter: R. Albajes, Spain; R. Ausher, Israel; S. Blumel, Austria; A. Enkegaard and H. Brodsgaard, Denmark; G. Ferguson, G. Murphy and L.Shipp, Canada; J. Fransen and P. Ramakers, The Netherlands; S. Goodwin, Australia; F. Hashimoto, Japan; M. Hommes, Germany; R. Lindquist, D. Mahr, and J. Newman, United States; the late G. Nicoli, Italy; N. Roditakis, Greece; N. Treanor, Jersey; P. Workman, New Zealand, I. Bedford and C. Sampson, United Kingdom.

References Cited

Altena, K., and W. J. Ravensberg. 1990. Integrated pest management in the Netherlands in sweet peppers from 1985 to 1989. *IOBC/WPRS Bulletin* 13 (5):10–13.

Ausher, R. 1997. Implementation of integrated pest management in Israel. *Phytoparasitica* 25 (2):119–41.

Bennison, J. A., and S. P. Corless. 1993. Biological control of aphids on cucumbers: Further development of open rearing units or "banker plants" to aid establishment of aphid natural enemies. *IOBC/WPRS Bulletin* 16 (2):5–8.

Bennison, J., K. Maulden, and G. Wardell. 1999. Integrated control of the South American leaf miner *Liriomyza huidobrensis* on UK glasshouse lettuce and Chinese leafy salad crops. *IOBC/WPRS Bulletin* 22 (1):9–12.

Bennison, J., R. Umpelby, and J. Buxton. 2002. IPM on protected hardy nursery stock in the UK. *IOBC/WPRS Bulletin* 25 (1):13–16.

Buxton, J. H., R. Jacobson, M. Saynor, R. Storer, and L. Wardlow. 1990. An integrated pest management programme for peppers: Three years trials experience. *IOBC/WPRS Bulletin* 13 (5):45–50.

Cahill, M., F. J. Byrne, K. Gorman, I. Denholm, and A. L. Devonshire. 1995. Pyrethroid and organophosphate resistance in the tobacco whitefly, *Bemisia tabaci* (Homoptera: Aleyrodidae). *Bulletin of Entomological Research* 85:181–7.

Cahill, M., K. Gorman, S. Day, and I. Denholm. 1996. Baseline determination and detection of resistance to imidacloprid in *Bemisia tabaci* (Homoptera: Aleyrodidae). *Bulletin of Entomological Research* 86 (4):343–9.

Castañé, C. 2002. Status of biological and integrated control in greenhouse vegetables in Spain: Successes and challenges. *IOBC/WPRS Bulletin* 25 (1): 49–52.

Cheek, S. 1997. Biological control and plant health in the United Kingdom. *Bulletin OEPP/EPPO* 27 (1):37–43.

Clarke, N. D., J. L. Shipp, A. P. Papadopoulos, W. R. Jarvis, S. Khosla, T. J. Jewett, and G. Ferguson. 1999. Development of the Harrow Greenhouse Manager: a decision-support system for greenhouse cucumber and tomato. *Computers and Electronics in Agriculture* 24:195–204.

El Kady, H., and G. J. Devine. 2003. Insecticide resistance in Egyptian populations of the cotton whitefly, *Bemisia tabaci* (Hemiptera : Aleyrodidae). *Pest Management Science* 59 (8):865–71.

Furk, C., and C. M. Hines. 1993. Aspects of pirimicarb resistance in the cotton and melon aphid, *Aphis gossypii* Glover (Homoptera: Aphidiidae). *Annals of Applied Biology* 123:9–17.

Gallagher, E. 2002. *The BCPC International Congress – Crop Science & Technology* 2003 (1):171–6.

Garthwaite, D. G. and M. R. Thomas. 2001. *Pesticide Usage Survey Report 164: Protected crops (edible and ornamental) in Great Britain 1999.* London: DEFRA, (PB 6166) 65p.

Gilkeson, L. A. 1990. Biological control of aphids in greenhouse sweet peppers and tomatoes. *IOBC/WPRS Bulletin* 13 (5):64–70.

Gillespie, D. R. 2002. Biological and integrated control in vegetables in British Columbia: The challenge of success. *IOBC/WPRS Bulletin* 25 (1):73–76.

Goodwin, S., and M. Steiner. 2002. Developments for IPM for protected cropping in Australia. *IOBC/WPRS Bulletin* 25 (1): 81–4.

Gorman, K., M. Cahill, and I. Denholm. 1998. Response of European populations of the glasshouse whitefly, *T. vaporariorum*, to conventional and novel insecticides. *Brighton Crop Protection Conference–Pests and Diseases–1998* 2:491–6.

Gould, H. J. 1985. The advisory problem. In *Biological Pest Control: The Glasshouse Experience*, ed. N. W. Hussey and N. E. A. Scopes, 219–23. Poole, U.K. Blandford Press (Ithaca, N.Y.: Cornell University Press).

Head, J., L.F. Palmer, and K.F.A. Walters. 2002. Development of an integrated control strategy for leaf miners in leafy salads with potential for extrapolation to other cropping systems. *IOBC/WPRS Bulletin* 25 (1):97–100.

Hussey, N. W. 1985. The economic equation. In *Biological Pest Control: The Glasshouse Experience*, ed. N. W. Hussey and N. E. A. Scopes, 224–8. Poole, U.K.: Blandford Press (Ithaca, N.Y.: Cornell University Press).

Jacobson, R. J. 1995. Integrated pest management in cucumbers: Prevention of establishment of *Frankliniella occidentalis* (Pergande). *Mededelingen Faculteit Landbouwwetenschappen, Riksuniversiteit Gent* 60 (3a):857–63.

Jacobson, R. J., P. Croft, and J. Fenlon. 1999. *Scatella stagnalis* Fallen (Diptera: Ephydridae): Towards IPM in protected lettuce crops. *IOBC/WPRS Bulletin* 22 (1):117–20.

Maisonneuve, J. C. 2002. Biological control in France in greenhouse vegetables and ornamentals. *IOBC/WPRS Bulletin* 25 (1):151–4.

Mulder, S., H. Hoogerbrugge, K. Altena, and K. Bolkmans. 1999. Biological pest control in cucumbers in the Netherlands. *IOBC/WPRS Bulletin* 22 (1):177–80.

Murphy, G. D., and A. B. Broadbent. 1996. Adoption of IPM by the greenhouse floriculture industry on Ontario, Canada. *IOBC/WPRS Bulletin* 19 (1):107–10.

Murphy, G. D., G. Ferguson, K. Fry, L. Lambert, M. Mann, and J. Matteoni. 2002. The use of biological control in Canadian greenhouse crops. *IOBC/WPRS Bulletin* 25 (1):193–6.

Murphy, G. D. 2002. Biological and integrated control in ornamentals in North America: successes and challenges. *IOBC/WPRS Bulletin* 25 (1):197–200.

Pickford, R. J. J. 1984. Evaluation of soil treatment for control of *Thrips tabaci* on cucumbers [*Phytoseiulus persimilis*, *Encarsia formosa*]. *Annals of Applied Biology* 104 (suppl.):18–9.

Piggott, S. and Wardlow, L. 2002. A fresh solution for the control of western flower thrips, dramatic results in trials. *The Commercial Greenhouse Grower* February 2002.

Ramakers, P. M. J. 1990. Manipulation of phytoseiid thrips predators in the absence of thrips. *IOBC/WPRS Bulletin* 13 (5):169–72.

Smith, I. M. 1997. EPPO Council colloquium on strategies for reducing use of plant protection products. *Bulletin OEPP/EPPO* 27:205–6.

Steiner, M., and S. Goodwin. 2002. Development of a new thrips predator, *Typhlodromips montdorensis* (Schica) (Acari: Phytoseiidae) indigenous to Australia. *IOBC/WPRS Bulletin* 25 (1):245–7.

van Alphen, C. A. M. 1997. A strategy for reduced use of plant protection products in the Netherlands. *Bulletin OEPP/EPPO* 27:209–11.

van der Staay, M. 1991. Side effects of pesticides on predatory mites. *Mededelingen Faculteit Landbouwwetenschappen, Riksuniversiteit Gent* 56 (2a):355–8.

Van Driesche, R. G. and S. Lyon. 2003. Commercial adoption of biological-based IPM for whiteflies in poinsettia. *Florida Entomologist* 86 (4):481–3.

Van Lenteren, J. C., F. Bigler, G. Burgio, H. M. T. Hokkanen, and M.B. Thomas. 2002. Risks of importation and release of exotic biological control agents: how to determine host specificity. *IOBC/WPRS Bulletin* 25 (1):281–4.

Van Schelt, J., H. Hoogerbrugge, Y. van Houten, and K. Bolkmans. 2002. Biological control and survival of *Echinothrips americanus* in pepper. *IOBC/WPRS Bulletin* 25 (1):285–8.

van Steenis, M. J. 1994. Evaluation of four aphidiine parasitoids (Hym.: Braconidae) for biological control of *Aphis gossypii* Glov. (Hom.: Aphidiidae). *Mededelingen Faculteit Landbouwwetenschappen, Riksuniversiteit Gent* 59 (2a):267–71.

van Tol, S., and M. J. van Steenis. 1994. Host preference and host suitability for *Aphidius matricariae* Hal. and *A. colemani* Vier. (Hym.: Braconidae), parasitizing *Aphis gossypii* Glov., and *Myzus persicae* Sulz. (Hom.: Aphidiidae). *Mededelingen Faculteit Landbouwwetenschappen, Riksuniversiteit Gent* 59 (2a):273–9.

Wardlow, L. R. 1985. Pyrethroid resistance in glasshouse whitefly. *Mededelingen Faculteit Landbouwwetenschappen Riksuniversiteit Gent* 50 (2b): 555–7.

Wardlow, L. R. 1990. Integrated pest management in protected ornamental crops. *IOBC/WPRS Bulletin* 13 (5):222–4.

Wardlow, L. R., P. J. Davies, and W. Brough. 1993. Integrated pest management techniques in protected ornamental plants. *IOBC/WPRS Bulletin* 16 (8):149–57.

Wardlow, L. R., and A. Tobin. 1990. Potential new additions to the armoury of natural enemies for protected tomatoes. *IOBC/WPRS Bulletin* 13 (5):225–7.

Wardlow, L. 2002. EPNs do it again. *Grower* 31 January: 16-17.

Wege, P. J., W. Parker, I. Denholm, S. P. Foster, Z. K. Harling, G. D. Moores, and A. L. Devonshire. 1998. Resistance in *Myzus persicae*: Current status in Europe and future prospects. *Brighton Crop Protection Conference-Pests and Diseases-1998* 2:497–502.

Williams, D. P. E. 2002. Developing a national pesticides strategy. *The BCPC International Congress – Crop Science and Technology* 2003 (1):163–70.

Yano, E. 1999. Recent advances in the study of biocontrol with indigenous natural enemies in Japan. *IOBC/WPRS Bulletin* 22 (1):291–4.

31

Quality Control of Mass-Produced Beneficial Insects

J. C. van Lenteren
Laboratory of Entomology, Wageningen University
Wageningen, The Netherlands

and

G. Nicoli
Istituto di Entomologia "G. Grandi"
University of Bologna, Bologna, Italy

Why Quality Control?

IOBC initiative on quality control

Although biological control of arthropod pests in protected cultures has been applied since 1926, large-scale production of natural enemies only began in the 1970s (van Lenteren and Woets 1988; van Lenteren 1995, 2003). Initial mass rearing efforts involved the production of not more than several thousand individuals per week of two beneficial species. None of the early publications on commercial aspects of biological control in greenhouses mention the topic of quality control of natural enemies. Quality control in mass rearing of beneficial insects was first mentioned in relation to greenhouse biological control in the mid-1980s, and shortly after that the topic became popular (van Lenteren 1986a, b). The fifth workshop of the International Organization for Biological Control (IOBC) global working group "Quality Control of Mass-Reared Arthropods" in Wageningen, the Netherlands, formed the starting point for a heated discussion among producers of natural enemies and scientists on how to approach quality control in the commercial setting at that time (Bigler 1991).

A series of workshops followed in Horsholm, Denmark, in 1992; Rimini, Italy, in 1993; Evora, Portugal, in 1994; Antibes, France, in 1996; and in Barcelona, Spain, in 1997 (Nicoli, Benuzzi, and Leppla 1994; van Lenteren, Bigler, and Waddington 1993; van Lenteren 1994, 1996, 1998). As a result of these meetings, quality control guidelines were written for about twenty species of natural enemies, and these have been tested and adapted by commercial producers of biological control agents in Europe (van Lenteren 1998, van Lenteren and Tommasini 1999). Also, fact sheets about natural enemies and pests were composed for training purposes. These guidelines cover features that are relatively easy to determine in the laboratory (e.g., emergence, sex ratio, life span, fecundity, adult size, and predation/parasitism rate). Recently the 20 old and 10 new guidelines have been published together with chapters providing the scientific background for the development of quality-control methods (van Lenteren 2003). Work is now focused on development of flight tests and of a test relating these laboratory characteristics to field efficiency.

Trends in commercial mass production of natural enemies

The appearance and disappearance of natural enemy producers have characterized commercialization of natural enemies over the past thirty years. Only a few producers active in the 1970s are still in business today. In addition to many small insectaries producing at the "cottage industry" level, four large facilities (i.e., having more than fifty persons employed) exist, which provide material of good quality. At these four production sites, more than five to ten million agents per agent/per week are produced (van Lenteren and Woets 1988, van Lenteren and Tommasini 1999, van Lenteren 2000, van Lenteren 2003). These facilities provide the full spectrum of natural enemies needed for an entire IPM program in a specific commodity (Albajes et al. 1999, van Lenteren 2000). As the sale of biological control agents is still an emerging market that is composed of small competing companies, product quality and prices are continuously affected by competitive pressure. While such pressure may be profitable in the short-term by lowering costs of natural enemies, in the long run such price competition could lead to biological control failures. Natural enemies were properly evaluated before commercial use some twenty years ago, but nowadays some species of natural enemies are sold without tests under practical cropping situations that determine if the natural enemies are effective against the target pest (van Lenteren and Manzaroli 1999). Lack of stability or inadequate guidance at the producer level has resulted in the sale and use of natural enemies of poor quality. These problems have in some cases resulted in failure of biological control.

Natural enemy producers are a rather diverse group. Rearing of natural enemies can be a full-time business or a part-time activity of greenhouse growers. But natural enemies may also be reared by companies in associated industries like seed companies or producers of fertilizers. In some cases, production of natural enemies has been started by a research group with governmental support and later continued as a private endeavor. The number of individuals produced per natural enemy species and the number of biological control agents that are commercially available has increased dramatically over the past twenty-five years (fig. 31.1). Now, about one hundred natural enemy species are on the market for greenhouse biological control, and thirty of these are produced in commercial insectaries in very large quantities (Table 31.1). These natural enemies are reared by some fifty companies, of which twenty-six can be found in Europe. For prices of natural enemies in Europe and the United States, see van Lenteren, Roskam, and Timmer (1997) and Cranshaw, Sclar, and Cooper (1996), respectively.

Commercial natural enemy producers mainly rear predators and parasitoids (Table 31.1). Only some companies produce nematodes, entomopathogenic fungi, bacteria, or viruses. Chemical companies are the main producers of microbial agents and it is expected that all activities in this area will in the future be exclusively the domain of the pesticide industry. Mass-rearing methods for parasitoids and predators are usually developed on an *ad hoc* basis, an approach that may result in natural enemies of poor quality. The technology to rear natural enemies on artificial diets is not well developed yet and seems to be hampered not only by physiological problems but also by ethological and ecological ones (requirements for associative learning of host-habitat and host finding cues; see chapters in van Lenteren, 2003). Conflicts between attributes favored in mass-rearing programs and those needed for greenhouse performance form another obstacle for cost-effective production of natural enemies. Artificial selection that occurs during mass-rearings may lead to reduced performance in greenhouses. The suggested cures for this problem are often expensive and time consuming and are, therefore, very seldom applied.

Professional natural enemy producers may have research facilities, procedures for monitoring product quality, an international distribution network, promotional activities, and an advisory service. The market for high-quality, effective natural enemies will certainly increase with the growing demand for unsprayed food and a cleaner environment. The growing pesticide resistance problem, which is particularly serious in crop protection in greenhouses, will also move growers to adopt biological control methods.

Developments in the area of mass production, quality control, storage, shipment, and release of natural enemies (van Lenteren 2000, 2003) have decreased production costs and led to better product quality, but much more can be done. Innovations in long-term storage (e.g., through induction of diapause), shipment, and release methods may lead to a further increase in natural enemy quality with a concurrent reduction in costs, thereby making biological control easier and more economically attractive to apply. Even if the natural enemies leave the insectary in good condition, shipment and handling by the producers, distributors, and growers may result in deterioration of the biological control agents before they are released in the greenhouse.

Quality control programs that address not only natural enemy numbers but also natural enemy quality (greenhouse performance) are a necessity. Simple and reliable

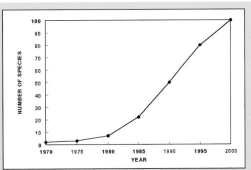

Figure 31.1. Number of species of natural enemies commercially available for biological control in greenhouses in Europe.

Table 31.1. Major Species of Biological Control Agents Commercially Available for Pest Control in Greenhouses in Europe

Biological control agent	Pest species	In use since
Iphiseius degenerans (Berlese)	*Frankliniella occidentalis* (Pergande)	1993
	Thrips tabaci Lindeman	1993
Neoseiulus californicus (McGregor)	*Tetranychus urticae* Koch	1995
Neoseiulus cucumeris (Oudemans)	*Frankliniella occidentalis* (Pergande)	1986
	Thrips tabaci Lindeman	1985
Aphelinus abdominalis (Dalman)	*Macrosiphum euphorbiae* (Thomas)	1992
	Aulacorthum solani Kaltenbach	1992
Aphidius colemani Viereck	*Aphis gossypii* Glover	1992
	Myzus persicae (Sulzer)	1992
Aphidius ervi Haliday	*Macrosiphum euphorbiae*	1996
Aphidoletes aphidimyza (Rondani)	Aphids	1989
Chrysoperla carnea (Stephens)	Aphids	1987
Cryptolaemus montrouzieri Mulsant	Pseudococcidae, Coccidae	1992
Dacnusa sibirica Telenga	*Liriomyza bryoniae* (Kaltenbach)	1981
	Liriomyza trifolii (Burgess)	1981
	Liriomyza huidobrensis (Blanchard)	1990
Delphastus catalinae (Horn)	Whiteflies	1993
Diglyphus isaea (Walker)	*Liriomyza bryoniae*	1984
	Liriomyza trifolii	1984
	Liriomyza huidobrensis	1990
Encarsia formosa Gahan	*Trialeurodes vaporariorum* (Westwood)	1970 (1926)
	Bemisia spp.	1988
Eretmocerus eremicus Rose and Zolnerowich (formerly *E. californicus*)	*Bemisia spp.*	1995
Eretmocerus mundus Mercet	*Bemisia spp.*	1995

(continued)

Table 31.1. *(continued)*

Biological control agent	Pest species	In use since
Harmonia axyridis (Pallas)	Aphids	1995
Heterorhabditis megidis Poinar	*Otiorhynchus sulcatus* (F.)	1984
Hippodamia convergens Guerin-Meneville	Aphids	1993
Hypoaspis aculeifer (Canestrini)	*Rhizoglyphus echinopus* Fumouzze and Robin, Sciaridae	1996
Hypoaspis miles Berlese	*Rhizoglyphus echinopus*, Sciaridae	1994
Leptomastidea abnormis Girault	Pseudococcidae	1984
Leptomastix dactylopii (Howard)	*Planococcus citri* (Risso)	1984
Leptomastix epona Walker	Pseudococcidae	1992
Lysiphlebus testaceipes Cresson	*Aphis gossypii*	1990
Macrolophus caliginosus Wagner	Whiteflies	1994
Opius pallipes Wesmael	*Liriomyza bryoniae*	1980
Orius insidiosus (Say)	Thrips	1991
Orius laevigatus (Fieber)	Thrips	1996
Orius majusculus (Reuter)	Thrips	1994
Phytoseiulus persimilis Athias-Henriot	*Tetranychus urticae*	1968
Steinernema feltiae (Filipjev)	Sciaridae and two other species	1984
Trichogramma evanescens Westwood	Lepidoptera	1992
Verticillium lecanii (Zimmerman) Viégas	Whiteflies, aphids	1990

quality control programs for natural enemies are now emerging as a result of intensive cooperation between researchers and the biological control practitioners. These developments will result in a quick improvement of the biological control industry.

What Is Quality Control?

Quality control programs are applied to mass-reared organisms to maintain the quality of the population. The overall quality of an organism is defined as the ability to function as intended after release into the greenhouse. The aim of quality control programs is to check whether the overall quality of a species is maintained, but that is too general a statement to be useful. Characteristics that affect overall quality have to be identified. These characteristics must be quantifiable and relevant for the greenhouse performance of the parasitoid or predator. This is a straightforward statement, but very difficult to actually carry out (Bigler 1989).

Rather than discussing the development of quality control in strictly scientific terms (see for this approach chapters in van Lenteren 2003), this discussion will outline a more pragmatic approach. The aim of releases of mass-produced natural enemies is to control a pest. In this context the aim of quality control should be to determine whether a natural enemy is still in a condition to properly control the pest. Formulated in this way we do not need to consider terms like maximal or optimal quality, but rather acceptable quality. Some researchers believe the aim of quality control should be to keep the quality of the mass-reared population identical to that of the original field population. This is not only an illusion, it is an unnecessary and expensive goal to pursue. Another important consideration is that quality control programs are not applied for the sake of the scientist, but as a mere necessity. Leppla and Fisher (1989) formulated this dilemma as "Information is expensive, so it is important to separate need to know from *nice to know*." Only if characteristics to be measured are very limited in number, but directly linked to greenhouse performance, will companies producing natural enemies ever be able to apply quality control programs on a regular basis.

Basic Considerations for Quality Control

The problem of quality control of beneficial insects can be approached from either of two directions: (i) measure how well the biological control agent functions in its intended role. If it does not function well enough, trace the cause and improve the rearing method; or (ii) list what changes we can expect when a mass-rearing is started. Measure these and if the changes are undesirable, improve the rearing method.

The disadvantage of the first method is that changes may have occurred that cannot be corrected because the material has already changed so much that the original causes of the observed effects cannot be identified. The disadvantage of the second method is that too many measurements may be needed. The second approach has the advantage that potential problems are forecast, and if seen, it may be possible to make changes in time to correct the problem. Bartlett (1984a), for example, approached the problem from the second viewpoint. He stated that many authors have suggested remedial measures for assumed genetic deterioration, but that causes for deterioration are not easily identified. Identification demands detailed genetic studies, and it is often difficult to define and measure detrimental genetic traits. He concluded, "I believe an unappreciated element of this problem is that the genetic changes taking place when an insect colony is started are natural ones that occur whenever any biological organism goes from one environment to another. These processes have been very well studied as evolutionary events and involve such concepts as colonization, selection, genetic drift, effective population numbers, migration, genetic revolutions, and domestication theory."

In two other articles Bartlett (1984b, 1985) discussed what happens to genetic variability in the process of domestication, what factors might change variability, and which ones might be expected to have little or no effect. In laboratory domestication insects are selected that have suitable genotypes to survive in this new environment, a process called *winnowing* by Spurway (1955) or, the less appropriate but widely used "forcing insects through a bottleneck." The changes that a field population may undergo when introduced into the laboratory are given in Table 31.2.

Variability in performance traits is usually abundantly present in natural populations and can remain large even in inbred populations (Yamazaki 1972, Prakash 1973, and chapters in van Lenteren 2003). But

Table 31.2 Factors Influencing Changes in Field Populations after Introduction into the Laboratory

1. Laboratory populations are kept at constant environments with stable abiotic factors (light, temperature, wind, humidity) and constant biotic factors (food, no predation or parasitism). There is no selection to overcome unexpected stresses. The result is a change in the criteria that determine fitness and a modification of the whole genetic system (Lerner 1958).

2. There is no interspecific competition in laboratory populations, resulting in a possible change in genetic variability (Ibid.).

3. Laboratory conditions are made suitable for the average, sometimes even for the poorest genotype. No choice of environment is possible as all individuals are confined to the same environment. The result is a possible decrease in genetic variability (Ibid.).

4. Density-dependent behaviors (e.g., searching efficiency) may be affected in laboratory situations (Bartlett 1984b).

5. Mate-selection processes may be changed because unmated or previously mated females will have restricted means of escape (Ibid.).

6.. Dispersal characteristics, specifically adult flight behavior and larval dispersal, may be severely restricted by laboratory conditions (Bush, Neck, and Kitto 1976).

differences between field and laboratory environments will result in differences in variability. When natural enemy cultures are started, part of the "open population" from the field, where gene migration can occur and environmental diversity is large, is brought into the laboratory and becomes a "closed population." Thereafter, all future genetic changes act on the limited genetic variation present in the original founders (Bartlett 1984b, 1985). The size of the founder population will directly affect how much variation will be retained from the native gene pool. Although there is no agreement on the size of founder populations needed for starting a mass production, a minimum number of a thousand individuals is suggested (Bartlett 1985). Founder populations for commercial cultures of a number of natural enemies were, however, much smaller, sometimes fewer than twenty individuals. Fitness characteristics appropriate for the greenhouse environment will be different than those for the laboratory. These environments will place different values on the ability to diapause or to locate hosts/prey or mates. Such laboratory selection may produce a genetic revolution, and new balanced gene systems will be selected (Mayr 1970, Lopez-Fanjul and Hill 1973).

One of the methods often suggested to correct for genetic revolutions is the regular introduction of wild individuals from the field or greenhouse. But if the rearing conditions remain the same in the laboratory, the introduced wild individuals will be subjected to the same process of genetic selection. Furthermore, if a genetic differentiation has developed between laboratory and field populations this may lead to genetic isolation (Oliver 1972). Also, positive correlation has been found between the incompatibility of such races and the differences between the environments (laboratory, field) where the races occur, and for the length of time two populations have been isolated. Given these processes, introduction of native individuals to mass-rearing colonies is likely to be useless if incompatibility between field and laboratory populations is complete. If one wants to introduce wild genes, it should be done regularly and from the start of a laboratory rearing onwards. It should not be delayed until problems occur. Introducing field-collected insects into mass rearing also poses risks of introduction of parasitoids, predators or pathogens into the colony (Bartlett 1984b).

Another effect of laboratory colonization is inbreeding—mating of relatives and production of progeny that are more genetically homozygous than when random mating occurs in large populations. Genetically homozygous individuals often express harmful traits. The degree of inbreeding is directly related to the size of the founder population. Because artificial selection in the laboratory often results in an initial decrease in population size, the rate of inbreeding increases. The result is often a definite and rapid effect on the genetic composition of the laboratory population (Bartlett 1984b). Inbreeding can be prevented by various methods that maintain genetic variability (Joslyn 1984), including:

(i)   *Precolonization methods*: selection and pooling of founder insects from throughout the range of the species to provide a wide representation of the gene pool, resulting in a greater fitness of the laboratory material.

(ii)   *Postcolonization methods:*

(iia)   *Variable laboratory environments* (variation over time and space). Although the concept of varying laboratory conditions is simple, putting it into practice is difficult. Consider for example the investments for rearing facilities with varying temperatures, humidities, and light regimes, or the creation of possibilities to choose from various diets or hosts, or the provision of space for dispersal, etc.

(iib)   *Gene infusion*: the regular rejuvenation of the gene pool with wild insects.

A fundamental question concerning inbreeding is: How large must the population size be to keep genetic variation sufficiently large? Joslyn (1984) said that to maintain sufficient heterogeneity, a colony should not decline below the number of founder insects. The larger the colony, the better. Very few data are available about effective population size; Joslyn mentioned a minimum number of five-hundred individuals.

The above discussion suggests several criteria that should be considered before a mass-rearing colony is started (Table 31.3, Bartlett 1984b).

A Broader Approach to Quality Control

Chambers and Ashley (1984) and Leppla and Fisher (1989) put quality control in a much wider perspective. These articles are food for thought for all in mass production of beneficial arthropods. They present some refreshing, and for most entomologists, new ideas.

Table 31.3 Criteria to Be Considered Before Starting a Mass-Rearing Program

1.   The effective number of parents at the start of a mass-rearing is much lower than the number of founder individuals, so start with a large population.

2.   Compensate for density-dependant phenomena.

3.   Create a proper balance of competition, but avoid overcrowding.

4.   Set environmental conditions for the best, not the worst or average genotype; use fluctuating abiotic conditions.

5.   Maintain separate laboratory strains and cross them systematically to increase F_1 variability.

6.   Measure frequencies of biochemical and morphological markers in founder populations and monitor changes.

7.   Develop morphological and biochemical genetic markers for population studies.

8.   Determine the standards that apply to the intended use of the insects, and then adapt rearing procedures to maximize those values in the domesticated strain.

These authors approach quality control from the industrial side and consider three elements as essential: product control, process control, and production control. Product control rejects faulty products, and production control maintains consistency of production output. Process control tells how the manufacturing processes are performing. These elements of quality control are seldom applied to arthropod massrearing programs.

Mass-rearing, usually done by small private companies, is developed by trial-and-error. Knowledge about mass-rearing techniques is often limited in such organizations and the time or money for extensive experimentation is lacking. If success is to be obtained, quality control of the end product is essential, but producers are generally more than happy if they can meet deadlines for providing certain numbers of natural enemies. Although most experts on quality control have adopted tools and procedures needed to regulate the processes of arthropod production so that product quality can be assured (Chambers and Ashley 1984), such tools and procedures are not yet widely used by the many small companies that compose 95% of all producers. The main reason most of the small companies do not develop and use such product, process, and production controls is that they lack the extra financial resources that are required. This limitation can be a serious constraint for new producers.

Quality control seems to be developed best when mass rearing is done in large governmentally supported units. Chambers and Ashley stated that entomologists often concentrate too much on production control, while they are at best only partially controlling production processes and products.

Quality control is frequently, but wrongly, seen as an alarm and inspection system that oversees and intimidates production personnel.

What Makes Quality Control So Difficult?

Obstacles in Mass Rearing of Arthropods

Artificial selection forces in mass-rearing may lead to problems related to performance of natural enemies in the greenhouse if rearing conditions differ strongly from the situation in which natural enemies are to be released (Table 31.4). For example, if temperature in the mass-rearing facility differs considerably from the greenhouse situation, synchronization problems can be expected. Also, rearing on non-target hosts or host plants can create problems with natural enemy quality or recognition by natural enemies of essential semiochemicals.

Any of the preceding obstacles (Table 31.4) may be encountered in mass production programs. One of the main obstacles to economic success seems to be the difficulty to produce qualitatively good natural enemies at a low price. But with a sharply decreasing number of available pesticides, increasing costs per unit of volume for chemical pesticides, and taxation of pesticides (as is presently taking place in several European countries), the price disadvantage of natural enemies will decrease.

Also, effective techniques to mass-produce natural enemies on artificial diets are often not available. Fewer than ten species of natural enemies can be produced on artificial diets, but generally their field performance is

Table 31.4 Obstacles in Mass Rearing of Natural Enemies

1. Production of good quality natural enemies at low costs may be difficult (Beirne 1974).

2. Artificial diets are often not available for some natural enemies (Ibid.).

3. Techniques that prevent selection pressures leading to genetic deterioration are usually lacking (Mackauer 1972, 1976).

4. Cannibalism by predators or superparasitism by parasitoids generally occurs.

5. Rearing on unnatural hosts/prey or under unnatural conditions may cause behavioral changes in pre-imaginal and imaginal conditioning (Morrison and King 1977, Vet et al. 1990).

6. Reduced vigor can occur when natural enemies are reared on unnatural hosts (Morrison and King 1977).

7. Reduced vigor can also be the result when natural enemies are reared on hosts that are reared on an unnatural host diet (Ibid.).

8. Contamination by pathogens may occur (Bartlett 1984b).

poorer than natural enemies reared on a host insect. Although mass production on artificial diets may lead to reduction of costs, the risks of changing natural enemy effectiveness should not be underrated.

Another obstacle for mass production is the lack of techniques to prevent selection pressures leading to genetic deterioration of the mass-produced organisms. Through such a deterioration, the natural enemy could loose its effectiveness (Boller 1972, Boller and Chambers 1977, and chapters in van Lenteren 2003).

Cannibalism among predators may make individual rearing (e.g., for *Chrysopa* spp.) or rearing at relatively high prey densities (e.g., many phytoseiid mites) necessary and will lead to high costs. Superparasitism with parasitoids has the same effect.

Rearing of parasitoids and predators under "unnatural" conditions on "unnatural" hosts or prey, or on artificial media may change their reactions to natural host or host plant cues as a result of missing or improper pre-imaginal or imaginal conditioning. Rearing parasitoids on unnatural hosts may lead to reduced vigor as the result of an inadequate supply of nutrition (quantity or quality) from the unnatural host. The same effect can occur when the host is reared on an unnatural diet, even if the host itself remains apparently unaffected.

Finally, the rearing colonies can become infected by pathogens. One of the problems often encountered in insect rearing is the occurrence of pathogens and microbial contaminants leading to high mortality, reduced fecundity, prolonged development, small adults, wide fluctuations in the quality of insects, or direct pathological effects. Goodwin (1984), Shapiro (1984), Sikorowski (1984), Singh and Moore (1985), and chapters in van Lenteren (2003) give information on the effects of microorganisms on insect cultures and the measures available to minimize or eliminate the pathogens or contaminants. Further, they discuss the recognition of diseases and microorganisms in insect rearing and the common sources of such microbial contaminants. The most common microbial contaminants encountered in insect rearing are fungi, followed by bacteria, viruses, protozoa, and nematodes. Field collected insects used to start a laboratory colony can be a major source of microbial contaminants. Another source is the various dietary ingredients. Disinfection of insects and dietary ingredients are recommended to prevent such contamination. Microbial contamination is usually rapidly recognized, but elimination of the pathogens from insect colonies is difficult (Bartlett 1984a).

Behavioral variation in natural enemies

The variation and changes in behavior of natural enemies caused by rearing conditions need a more detailed discussion as exciting new information has emerged in recent years. The lead question is: Can erratic behavior of natural enemies be prevented or cured? Recently, several papers have appeared on how to interpret and deal with variability in natural enemy behavior (Lewis et al. 1990, Vet et al. 1990, Vet and Dicke 1992, and chapters in van Lenteren 2003). Most ecologists are aware that variability in natural enemy behavior occurs frequently. It is important to

know how natural enemies function in agroecosystems. Such understanding may help in designing systems where natural enemies play an even more important role in inundative and seasonal inoculative releases made in greenhouses. Basic natural enemy behaviors for host-habitat and host location show great variability that often leads to inconsistent results in biological control. Most studies aimed at understanding such variability have focused on extrinsic factors as causes for any inconsistencies seen in foraging behavior. Typically, however, foraging behavior remained irregular even when using precisely the same set of external stimuli. These irregularities are caused by intraspecific individual variation in behavior. In order to understand erratic behavior and to be able to manipulate such variation, biological control researchers need to know the origins and width of variation.

Two types of adaptive variation have been recognized in the foraging behavior of natural enemies (Lewis et al. 1990): genetically fixed differences and phenotypic plasticity.

Genetically fixed differences

Differences exist among individuals (so called fixed-behaviors or innate responses). For example, natural enemy strains have different capabilities for searching in different habitats or have different host acceptance patterns. Such variation is now used in commercial selection of natural enemies. Genetically different strains of the same natural enemy species may react in very different ways to the same set of chemical stimuli from hosts and their host plants. To choose the best strain of a natural enemy for a particular task, it is important to have knowledge of these inherited preferences for particular environments and to match such inherited preferences with the stimuli present in the environment where natural enemy strains will be released. For a population of natural enemies to provide consistent biological control, the strain must have a proper blend of genetic traits appropriate to the target environment, and these traits must occur with sufficient uniformity in the population. This statement has been broadly recognized as true, but has been used only at a very gross level in applied programs (e.g., climate, habitat, and host matching).

Phenotypic plasticity

Unfixed, learned, or plastic behaviors arise as a result of experience accumulated by natural enemies as individuals. These learned behaviors allow the natural enemies to forage more effectively in any one of a variety of circumstances that might be encountered. Preferences develop for habitats in which suitable hosts have been encountered. The response of a foraging natural enemy can be quite plastic and can be modified within the bounds of its genetic potential and its experience as an individual. Modifications can be initiated during pre-imaginal ("larval") stages and at eclosion.

The response of a *naive* adult (one which has not yet encountered a host) will already be affected by its rearing conditions. Such alterations have seldom been quantified, but changes in preference have been observed as a result of different rearing hosts or host diets. Particularly for inundative and seasonal inoculative programs of biological control, quantification of this variability is essential. An individual can often change its inherited response range, so it can develop an increased response for particular foraging environments as a result of experience with stimuli of these environments. Absence of reinforcement (i.e., absence of contact with host-related stimuli) will result in a waning of the level of that response and a reversion to the naive preference. Natural enemies are plastic in their behavior, but operate within genetically defined boundaries.

Only recently have we begun to appreciate the extent to which natural enemies can learn. Many parasitoid species are able to acquire by experience an increased preference for and ability to forage in a particular environmental situation (Vet et al. 1990, Vet and Dicke 1992). There is some evidence for learning by immature stages and abundant evidence for learning by adults of various natural enemies. Learning is mostly by a matter of association of two and more stimuli, such as the odors of a host-plant and a host encounter, resulting later in orientation towards the odors of that specific host-plant species. Foraging behavior can continuously be modified according to the foraging circumstances encountered (Vet and Dicke 1992).

Physiological state of the natural enemy

Foraging behavior can also be strongly influenced by the physiological condition of the natural enemy. Natural enemies face varying situations in meeting their food, mating, reproductive, and safety requirements. Presence of strong chemical, visual, or auditory cues; cues related to presence of enemies of the natural enemy; and temporary egg depletion can all reduce or disrupt the response to cues used to find hosts. For example, hunger may result in increased foraging for food and decreased attention to hosts. In that case, the reaction to food and host cues will be different than when the natural enemy is well fed.

The sources of intrinsic variation in foraging behavior (genetic, phenotypic, and those related to the physiological state) are not mutually exclusive but overlap extensively, even within a single individual. The eventual foraging success of a natural enemy is determined by how well the natural enemy's net intrinsic condition is matched with the foraging environment in which it operates (Lewis et al. 1990 and chapters in van Lenteren 2003).

How to manage variability in behavior of natural enemies

In order to be "efficient" as biological control agents, natural enemies must be able to (i) effectively locate and attack a host and (ii) stay in a host-infested area until most hosts are attacked. "Efficient" is used here in the anthropocentric sense (i.e., an agent able to provide pest control) that does not necessarily mean efficiency in a natural selection sense.

Management of natural enemy variation is particularly important when species are mass-produced in the laboratory, especially if rearing is done in factitious hosts (species different from the target pest). Such laboratory rearings remove natural enemies from the context of natural selection and expose them to artificial selection for traits that are useless in the greenhouse or field (van Lenteren 1986a). In addition to the genetic component, associative learning may lead to many more changes in behavioral reactions.

Managing genetic qualities

Successful predation or parasitism of a target host in a confined situation does not guarantee that released individuals will attack that host under greenhouse conditions (see chapters in van Lenteren 2003). When selecting among strains of natural enemies, we need to ensure that the traits of the natural enemies are appropriately matched with the targeted use situations in the greenhouse. Natural enemy populations chosen for mass rearing should perform well on the target crop and under the specific greenhouse climate conditions.

Managing phenotypic qualities

Without care, insectary environments lead to agents with weak or distorted responses. If we understand the mechanism of natural enemy learning and the stimuli that affect it we can, in theory, provide the appropriate level of experience before releasing a natural enemy to correct defects from mass rearing. Prerelease exposure to important stimuli can help improve the responses of natural enemies through appropriate associative learning, leading to reduction in the escape response and an increase in natural enemy arrestment in target areas. An example of this approach is the exposure of species of *Trichogramma* wasps to cues associated with the intended target greenhouse pest after they have been mass reared on an alternate laboratory host species.

Managing physical and physiological qualities

Natural enemies should be released in a physiological state in which they are most responsive to herbivore or plant stimuli and will not be hindered by deprivations that might interfere with host searching. Thus, adult parasitoids should be well fed (honey or sugar source available in mass rearing), have had opportunities to mate, and have had time for the pre-oviposition period before releases are made.

Laboratory rearing and greenhouse performance of natural enemies

In view of all these obstacles, it clearly is best to rear natural enemies under conditions that are as natural as possible—a conclusion that is supported by a number of researchers with experience in mass production (van Lenteren 2003). Another important conclusion based on the new information about rearing is that the host habitat and the host should provide the same cues in mass rearing as in the greenhouse. If this is not possible, the natural enemies should be exposed to these cues after rearing, but before being released in the field. The problems that remain, even when rearing is done as naturally as possible, are related to obstacles 3, 4, 5, and 8 (Table 31.4). Anyone starting a mass-rearing facility should be prepared to not only overcome these obstacles, but should also recognize the conflicting requirements placed on natural enemies in mass production and during greenhouse performance (Table 31.5).

How to Develop and Implement Quality Control

Natural enemies for greenhouse biological control are often mass-produced under greenhouse conditions that are similar to those found in commercial crops, with the exception that pest densities are much higher. Because of this difference, most of the points listed in Table 31.5 are applicable and must be considered in quality control programs. The development of quality control programs for greenhouse natural enemy production has been rather pragmatic. Guidelines have been

Table 31.5 Conflicting Requirements Concerning Performance of Natural Enemies in a Mass-Rearing Colony and under Greenhouse Conditions

Features Valued in Mass Rearing	Features Important for Performance in Greenhouses
1. polyphagy (makes rearing on unnatural host/prey easier)	monophagy or oligophagy (more specific agent often have a greater pest reduction capacity)
2. high parasitism or predation rates at high pest densities	high parasitism or predation rates at low pest densities
3. no strong migration as a result of direct or indirect interference	strong migration as a result of direct or indirect interference
4. dispersal behavior unnecessary and unwanted, ability to disperse minimal	dispersal behavior essential
5. associative learning not appreciated	associative learning appreciated

developed for thirty species of natural enemies (Table 31.6). Descriptions of the various quality control tests included in these guidelines can be found in van Lenteren (1996, 1998, 2003) and van Lenteren and Tommasini (1999). The standard elements of quality control are given in Table 31.7. In Table 31.8 an example of a quality control test for *E. formosa* is presented. Flight tests are discussed later.

The guidelines developed until now refer to product control procedures, not to production or process control. They were designed to be as uniform as possible so they can be used in a standardized manner by many producers, distributors, pest management advisory personnel, and farmers. These tests should preferably be carried out by the producer after all handling procedures and just before shipment. It is expected that the user (farmer or grower) only needs to perform a few quality tests, e.g., checking the percent emergence or number of live adults in the package. Some tests are to be carried out frequently by the producer, i.e., on a daily, weekly or per-batch basis. Others will be done less frequently, i.e., on an annual or seasonal basis, or when rearing procedures are changed. In the near future, flight tests and field performance tests will be added to these guidelines. Such tests are needed to show the relevance of the laboratory measurements. Laboratory tests are only adequate when a good correlation has been established between the laboratory measurements, flight tests, and field performance.

In addition to the quality control tests it was decided by the European Quality Control Group of the IOBC that fact sheets on the biologies of key natural enemies and pests

were needed for new quality control personnel and plant protection services.

Proposed Flight Tests for *Encarsia formosa*

Two flight tests have been developed for *E. formosa*, i.e., tests in which the parasitoid has to fly a distance of ca. 1.6 in. (4 cm) and ca. 20 in. (50 cm) to reach the trap, respectively. Distances of ca. 1.6 in. (4 cm) are similar to distances between leaves in a plant, and distances of 20 in. (50 cm) correspond to distances between plants in the greenhouse. Some methods of producing or storing *E. formosa* can lead to defective individuals that are unable to fly.

The short-range flight test is run in a glass cylinder that has a glass cover with sticky material on the underside. A barrier of repellent material (Blistex lip pomade), 1.6 in. (4 cm) in height, is applied to the vertical wall of the cylinder to prevent wasps from walking to the sticky material on the glass cover plate at the top (fig. 31.2). Parasitoids are put (on leaves or on cards) on the bottom of the cylinder. The whole setup consists of standardized parts, is easy to assemble and reusable, and uses a small amount of space (6 in.^{2} [40 cm^2]) per glass cylinder. Counting of the trapped wasps can be done rapidly (two minutes per cylinder) and without manipulation of the cylinder. The effects of parasitoid rearing, handling, and storage conditions can be evaluated with this test. This test can be used also for concurrent measurement of immature mortality and the parasitoid emergence pattern, elements that are included in the present quality control criteria.

The long-range flight test is run in a flight cage of 3.5 ft.^{3} (1 m^3) with glass walls,

Table 31.6 Natural Enemies for Which Quality Control Guidelines Have Been Developed

Iphiseius degenerans (Berlese) (Acarina: Phytoseiidae)

*Anthocoris nemoralis (*Fabricius*)* (Hemiptera: Anthocoridae)

Aphelinus abdominalis (Dalman) (Hymenoptera: Aphelinidae)

Aphidius colemani Viereck (Hymenoptera: Braconidae)

Aphidius ervi (Haliday) (Hymenoptera: Braconidae)

Aphidoletes aphidimyza (Rondani) (Diptera: Cecidomyiidae)

Aphytis lingnanensis Compere & *A. melinus* DeBach (Hymenoptera: Aphelinidae)

Chrysoperla carnea Steph. (Neuroptera: Chrysopidae)

Cryptolaemus montrouzieri Mulsant (Coleoptera: Coccinellidae)

Dacnusa sibirica Telenga (Hymenoptera: Braconidae)

Dicyphus hesperus Wagner (Hemiptera: Miridae)

Diglyphus isaea (Walker) (Hymenoptera: Eulophidae)

Encarsia formosa Gahan (Hymenoptera: Aphelinidae)

Eretmocerus eremicus (Rose and Zolnerowich) (Hymenoptera: Aphelinidae)

Eretmocerus mundus Mercet (Hymenoptera: Aphelinidae)

Hypoaspis miles Berlese (Acari: Laelapidae)

Leptomastix dactylopii Howard (Hymenoptera: Encyrtidae)

Macrolophus caliginosus Wagner (Hemiptera: Miridae)

Neoseiulus californicus (McGregor) (Acarina: Phytoseiidae)

Neoseiulus cucumeris (Oudemans) (Acarina: Phytoseiidae)

Orius laevigatus, O. insidiosus, O. majusculus, O. aldibipennis (Hem.: Anthocoridae)

Phytoseiulus persimilis Athias-Henriot (Acarina: Phytoseidae)

Podisus maculiventris Say (Hemiptera: Pentatomidae)

Trichogramma brassicae Bezd. (=*T. maidis*) (Hymenoptera: Trichogrammatidae)

Trichogramma cacoeciae Marchal (Hymenoptera: Trichogrammatidae)

Trichogramma dendrolimi Matsumura (Hymenoptera: Trichogrammatidae)

Table 31.7 General Quality Control Criteria for Rearing Arthropod Parasitoids or Predators in Mass Culture

Quantity:	predators:	number of live predators in container
	parasitoids:	if delivered as adults: number of live parasitoids
		if immatures: number of emerging adults in a certain period
Sex ratio:	minimum percentage females; male biased ratio may indicate poor rearing conditions	
Fecundity:	number of offspring produced during a certain period; for parasitoids, fecundity is an indication of the potential maximum host kill rate	
Longevity:	minimum longevity in days	
Predation:	number of prey eaten during a certain period	
Adult size:	hind tibia length, sometimes pupal size (size is often a good indication for longevity, fecundity, and predation capacity if natural enemy is not manipulated during harvest, packaging, shipment, and release)	
Flight:	short-range flight (natural enemy can still fly) long-range flight + predation/parasitization capacity (can fly and perform)	
Field performance:	capacity to locate and consume prey or parasitize hosts in crop under field conditions	

- Fecundity, longevity, and predation capacity tests can often be combined.
- Expiration date for each shipment is given on packaging material.
- All numbers, ratios, and sizes are mentioned on the container or packaging material.
- Quality control is done under standardized test conditions of temperature, relative humidity, and light regime that are specified for each test

in which a yellow sticky trap is hung. Wasps are introduced as black pupae on cards on the bottom of the cage and have to fly 16 in. (40 cm) or more to reach the yellow sticky trap.

The short-range flight test is suitable for evaluating the effect of storage periods, temperature, and handling procedures on the flight capability of *E. formosa* and will, therefore, be included in the standard testing procedure. The test provides important additional information to the quality control measurements discussed previously. Storage

Table 31.8 Quality Control Test for *Encarsia formosa*[1]

Encarsia formosa **Gahan (Hymenoptera: Aphelinidae)**

Test conditions	Temperature:	71.6°F (22°C) ± 2°
	RH:	60–90%
	Light regime:	16L:8D

Quality control criteria

Emergence rate	Given as the number of adults that will emerge over a two-week period from 1000 pupae; test needs to be repeated weekly
Sex ratio	≥ 98% will be females; test 500 pupae, once every four weeks
Adult size	Tibia length of hind leg ≥ 0.9 in. (0.23 mm); n=30 females; an annual test
Fecundity	≥ 7 eggs/female/day for days 2, 3, and 4 after emergence of the adult; n=30 females; an annual test

Description of testing methods

Emergence	Specify the number of adults that should emerge before conducting the test. Take 3 sub samples, which make up 1000 or more full-black pupae in total. Put the samples in a closed container for two weeks and then count the number of adults that emerged. This can be done by counting the number of emerged adult parasitoids or by comparing the number of empty pupal exuviae at the start and at the end of the test. A combination of both counting methods will give the most reliable results. The number of emerged adults should equal the number specified on the label.
Sex ratio	Take a sample of 500 of the adults from the emergence test and count the number of male wasps. These are completely black and easily distinguished from the females that have a yellow abdomen. The percentage of females should be ≥ 98%.
Adult size	To measure the size of the tibia of the hind leg of adults, freshly emerged female parasitoids, no more than 24 hours old, are collected from a container and killed (by freezing them at a temperature of 5°F [-15°C], or with ether). Measure the tibia length using a light microscope at a magnification of 400x. Convert the ocular micrometer units into millimeters. Measure 30 females. All measured females should have a minimum hind tibia length of 0.9 in. (0.23 mm). This test should be performed in the period from August to October.

(continued)

Table 31.8 *(continued)*

Fecundity

Day 1	Put an ample number of black pupae that are close to emergence in a container. Remove all adult parasitoids the night before the test animals will be collected from the container.
Day 2	Collect 30 freshly emerged females at about 10 o'clock; put each into a small container with a droplet of honey until the following day. This is to feed them and to get them through the pre-oviposition period.
Day 3	The test is conducted on individual females in small, round plastic Petri-dish-type trays (diameter 1.3 in. [32 mm] and height 0.6 in. [15 mm] that can be closed very tightly. A nylon mesh is incorporated into the lid to facilitate air exchange. Trays are filled with agar solution (1%) to a depth of 0.2 in. (5 mm). Just before the agar solidifies a leaf disc is placed with its upper surface in contact with the agar. The fecundity test can be performed using tobacco leaf discs with whitefly nymphs. Care should be taken to ensure that the leaf bears enough whitefly nymphs. Provide each female with at least 25 whitefly nymphs (*Trialeurodes vaporariorum* [Westwood]) in the third- and fourth-instar. Use 30 females in total.
Day 4	Provide the female with a new supply of whitefly nymphs by placing her in a new tray. Do this around 10 o'clock in the morning, again.
Day 5	Repeat Day 4.
Day 6	Remove the parasitoids from the whitefly nymphs. Keep all white flies that were exposed to *E. formosa* in closed containers to prevent unwanted parasitism after the test. Count all black pupae after 10 and 14 days. The average number of black pupae per female per day should be ≥ 7.

[1]van Lenteren 1996, 1998

of parasitoids at a low temperature (46°F [8°C]) for two and sixteen days, respectively, gives similar percentages of emergence, but the capability to fly is much lower for the parasitoids that were stored for sixteen days (fig. 31.4). The test also clearly demonstrates the effect of temperature on ability to fly: while many parasitoids reach the top of the cylinder at 77°F (25°C), very few do so at 64 and 59°F (18 and 15°C).

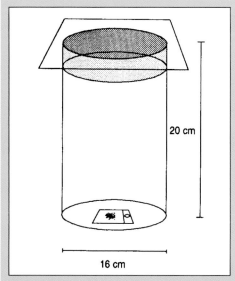

Figure 31.2. Setup of short-range flight test for _Encarsia formosa_. The cylinder (6 in. [16 cm] diameter and 8 in. [20 cm] high) is covered with a glass plate that has a circle of glue at the underside. On the inside wall at the upper part of the cylinder, a 1.5-in. (4-cm) strip of repellent material is applied so that the parasitoids cannot walk into the glue, but have to fly. Pupae on leaves or paper are put at the bottom of the cylinder.

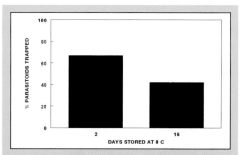

Figure 31.3. Percentage _Encarsia formosa_ females capable of flying (=reaching trap in short-range flight test) when stored for two and sixteen days at 46.4°F (8°C).

2003). The quality control criteria now employed relate to product control and are based on laboratory measurements that are easy to carry out. These criteria will be complemented with flight tests and field performance tests.

Quality control programs should be designed to obtain acceptable quality, not necessarily the best possible quality. The number of necessary tests will be smallest if the natural enemies are reared under the same

The long-range flight test gave similar results as the short-range test, but because it is very cumbersome to manage, this long-range flight test is not recommended for inclusion in quality control procedures (fig. 31.3).

Conclusions

Quality control procedures for natural enemies are presently being developed for additional natural enemy species used commercially in greenhouses (van Lenteren

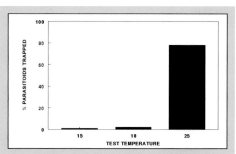

Figure 31.4. Percentage _Encarsia formosa_ females capable of flying (=reaching trap in short-range flight test) at 59°, 64.4°, and 77°F (15°, 18°, and 25°C).

conditions as those under which they also have to function in the greenhouse in terms of same climate, host, and host plant. The more artificial the rearing conditions become and the more the natural enemies are "handled" before use (removed from the plant or host, counted, put in contains, glued to a substrate, manipulated to induce diapause, shipped, released, etc.), the larger the number of tests that will have to be performed. Also, under these circumstances, pre-release training of the natural enemies may be needed so that they can perceive relevant cues from the pest insect or infested plant.

Companies just beginning the production of a natural enemy are often rather ignorant about the obstacles and complications entailed in mass rearing programs. New producers are even more ignorant about the need to develop and apply quality control testing criteria to their products. A special point of concern is the lack of knowledge about the sources of variability of natural enemy behavior and methods to prevent genetic deterioration of natural enemies (van Lenteren 2003). If the biological control industry is to survive and flourish, the production of reliable natural enemies that meet basic quality standards is essential.

Acknowledgements

My good friend and colleague Dr. Giorgio Nicoli died in a car accident in 1999, a few days after we discussed the final version of this chapter. European producers of natural enemies are thanked for cooperation in development of quality control guidelines and for providing unpublished data on quality control. Development of quality control guidelines was financially supported by the Commission of the European Communities, Directorate General for Agriculture, DG VI, Concerted Action "Designing and Implementing Quality Control of Beneficial Insects: Towards more reliable biological pest control."

References Cited

Albajes, R., M. L. Gullino, J. C. van Lenteren, and Y. Elad, eds. 1999. *Integrated Pest and Disease Management in Greenhouse Crops.* Dordrecht, the Netherlands: Kluwer Publishers.

Bartlett, A. C. 1984a. Establishment and maintenance of insect colonies through genetic control. In *Advances and Challenges in Insect Rearing,* ed. E.G. King, and N.C. Leppla, 1. New Orleans, La.: Agricultural Research Service, Southern Region, U.S. Department of Agriculture.

———. 1984b. Genetic changes during insect-domestication. In *Advances and Challenges in Insect Rearing,* ed. E.G. King and N.C. Leppla, 2–8. New Orleans, La.: Agricultural Research Service, Southern Region, U.S. Department of Agriculture.

———. 1985. Guidelines for genetic diversity in laboratory colony establishment and maintenance. In *Handbook of Insect Rearing,* Vol. 1, ed. P. Sing and R. F. Moore, 7–17. Amsterdam: Elsevier.

Beirne, B. P. 1974. Status of biological control procedures that involve parasites and predators. In *Proceedings of the Summer Institute on Biological Control of Plant Insects and Diseases,* ed. F. G. Maxwell and F. A. Harris, 69-76. Jackson, Miss.: University Press of Mississippi.

Bigler, F. 1989. Quality assessment and control in entomophagous insects used for biological control. *Journal of Applied Entomology* 108:390–400.

Bigler, F., ed. 1991. *Fifth Workshop of the IOBC Global Working Group,* Quality control of mass reared arthropods, Wageningen, the Netherlands, 25–28 March.

Boller, E. F. 1972. Behavioral aspects of mass-rearing of insects. *Entomophaga* 17:9–25.

Boller, E. F., and D. L. Chambers. 1977. Quality aspects of mass-reared insects. In *Biological Control by Augmentation of Natural Enemies,* ed. R. L. Ridgway and S. B. Vinson, 219–236, New York: Plenum.

Bush, G. L., R. W. Neck, and G. B. Kitto. 1976. Screwworm eradication: Inadvertent selection for noncompetitive ecotypes during mass rearing. *Science* 193:491–3.

Chambers, D. L. and T. R. Ashley. 1984. Putting the control in quality control in insect rearing. In *Advances and Challenges in Insect Rearing,* ed. E. G. King and N. C. Leppla, 256–60. New Orleans, La.: U.S. Department of Agriculture, Agricultural Research Service, Southern Region.

Cranshaw, W., D. C. Sclar, and D. Cooper. 1996. A review of 1994 pricing and marketing by suppliers of organisms for biological control of arthropods in the United States. *Biological Control* 6:291–6.

Goodwin, R. H. 1984. Recognition and diagnosis of diseases in insectaries and the effects of disease agents on insect biology. In *Advances and Challenges in Insect Rearing*, ed. E. G. King and N. C. Leppla, 96–129. New Orleans, La.: U.S. Department of Agriculture, Agricultural Research Service, Southern Region.

Joslyn, D. J. 1984. Maintenance of genetic variability in reared insects. In *Advances and Challenges in Insect Rearing*, ed. E. G. King and N. C. Leppla, 20–9. New Orleans, La.: U.S. Department of Agriculture, Agricultural Research Service, Southern Region.

Leppla, N. C., and W. R. Fisher.1989. Total quality control in insect mass production for insect pest management. *Journal of Applied Entomology* 108:452–61.

Lerner, I. 1958. *Genetic Basis of Selection*. New York: John Wiley.

Lewis, W. J., L. E. M. Vet, J. H. Tumlinson, J. C. van Lenteren, and D. R. Papaj. 1990. Variations in parasitoid foraging behavior: Essential element of a sound biological control theory. *Environmental Entomology* 19:1183–93.

Lopez-Fanjul, C., and W. G. Hill. 1973. Genetic differences between populations of *Drosophila melanogaster* for quantitative trait. II. Wild and laboratory populations. *Genetical Research* 22:60–78.

Mackauer, M. 1972. Genetic aspects of insect control. *Entomophaga* 17:27–48.

———. 1976. Genetic problems in the production of biological control agents. *Annual Review of Entomology* 21:369–85.

Mayr, E. 1970. *Populations, Species, and Evolution*. Cambridge, Massachusetts: Harvard University Press.

Morrison, R. K., and E. G. King. 1977. Mass production of natural enemies. In *Advances and Challenges in Insect Rearing*, ed. E. G. King and N. C. Leppla, 183–217. New Orleans, La.: U.S. Department of Agriculture, Agricultural Research Service, Southern Region.

Nicoli, G., M. Benuzzi, and N. C. Leppla, eds. 1994. *Proceedings of the Seventh Workshop of the IOBC Global Working Group*, Quality control of mass-reared arthropods. Rimini, Italy, September 13–16, 1993.

Oliver, C. G. 1972. Genetic and phenotypic differentiation and geographic distance in four species of Lepidoptera. *Evolution* 26:221–41.

Prakash, S. 1973. Patterns of gene variation in central and marginal populations of *Drosophila robusta*. *Genetics* 75:347–69.

Shapiro, M. 1984. Microorganisms as contaminants and pathogens in insect rearing. In *Advances and Challenges in Insect Rearing*, ed. E. G. King and N. C. Leppla, 130–42. New Orleans, La.: U.S. Department of Agriculture, Agricultural Research Service, Southern Region.

Sikorowski, P. P. 1984. Microbial contamination in insectaries. In *Advances and Challenges in Insect Rearing*, ed. E. G. King and N. C. Leppla, 143–53. New Orleans, La.: U.S. Department of Agriculture, Agricultural Research Service, Southern Region.

Singh, P. and R. F. Moore, eds. 1985. *Handbook of Insect Rearing*, Vol. 1 and 2. Amsterdam: Elsevier.

Spurway, H. 1955. The causes of domestication: An attempt to integrate some ideas of Konrad Lorenz with evolution theory. *Journal of Genetics* 53:325–62.

van Lenteren, J. C. 1986a. Evaluation, mass production, quality control, and release of entomophagous insects. In *Biological Plant and Health Protection*, ed. J. M. Franz, 31–56. Stuttgart, Germany: Fischer.

———. 1986b. Parasitoids in the greenhouse: Successes with seasonal inoculative release systems. In *Insect Parasitoids*, ed. J. K. Waage and D. J. Greathead, 341–74. London: Academic Press.

———. 1994. Designing and implementing quality control of beneficial insects: Towards more reliable biological pest control. EC concerted action PL 921076. Summary of the Evora/Portugal Workshop (17–20 September 1994). *Sting: Newsletter on Biological Control in Greenhouses* 14:3–24.

———. 1995. Integrated pest management in protected crops. In *Integrated Pest Management: Principles and Systems Development*, ed. D. R. Dent, 311–43. London: Chapman and Hall.

———. 1996. Designing and implementing quality control of beneficial insects: Towards more reliable biological pest control. *Proceedings for Quality Control Meeting IOBC/EU*, February13–18, 1996, Antibes, France:

———. 1998. Quality control guidelines. *Sting, Newsletter on Biological Control in Greenhouses*, 18: 1-32:.

———. 2000. Measures of success in biological control of arthropods by augmentation of natural enemies. In: *Measures of Success in Biological Control*, ed. G. Gurr and S. Wratten, 77-103. Dordrecht, Kluwer Academic Publishers.

———. 2003. *Quality Control and Production of Biological Control Agents. Theory and Testing Procedures*. Wallingford, CABI Publishing.

van Lenteren, J. C., F. Bigler, and C. Waddington. 1993. Quality control guidelines for natural enemies. In *Proceedings of the Seventh Workshop of the IOBC Global Working Group*, Quality control of mass-reared arthropods. Rimini, Italy, September 13–16, 1993, ed. G. Nicoli, M. Benuzzi, and N. C. Leppla, 222–30.

van Lenteren, J. C., and G. Manzaroli. 1999. Evaluation and use of predators and parasitoids for biological control of pests in greenhouses. In *Integrated Pest and Disease Management in Greenhouse Crops*, ed. R. Albajes, M. L. Gullino, J. C. van Lenteren, and Y. Elad, 183–201. Dordecht, the Netherlands: Kluwer Academic Publishers.

van Lenteren, J. C., M. M. Roskam, and R. Timmer. 1997. Commercial mass production and pricing of organisms for biological control of pests in Europe. *Biological Control* 10:143–9.

van Lenteren, J. C., and M. G. Tommasini. 1999. Mass production, storage, shipment and quality control of natural enemies. In *Integrated Pest and Disease Management in Greenhouse Crops*, ed. R. Albajes, M. L. Gullino, J. C. van Lenteren, and Y. Elad, 276–94. Dordecht, the Netherlands: Kluwer Academic Publishers.

van Lenteren, J. C., and J. Woets. 1988. Biological and integrated pest control in greenhouses. *Annual Review of Entomology* 33:239–69.

Vet, L. E. M., and M. Dicke. 1992. Ecology of infochemical use by natural enemies in a tritrophic context. *Annual Review of Entomology* 37:141–72.

Vet, L. E. M., W. J. Lewis, D. R. Papaj, and J. C. van Lenteren. 1990. A variable-response model for parasitoid foraging behavior. *Journal of Insect Behavior* 3:471–90.

Yamazaki, T. 1972. Detection of single gene effect by inbreeding. *Nature* 240:53–4.

32

The Future of Biological Control in Greenhouse Crops

M. P. Parrella
Department of Entomology
University of California, Davis, California

R. G. Van Driesche
Department of Entomology
University of Massachusetts, Amherst, Massachusetts

and

K. M. Heinz
Department of Entomology
Texas A & M University, College Station, Texas

As we enter the new century, biological control will play a greater role in pest management programs in greenhouse vegetable and flower production than at any previous time. Several factors will likely affect the degree of this future use, especially applied IPM research, extension programs, interactions with private industry, regulatory policy, and national and international politics.

Science-Based Biological Control

In greenhouse vegetable crops, use of biological control is already well established and most growers around the world recognize the value of this form of pest control. In vegetable crops, future research needs will be to refine existing systems and to develop controls for new pests as they appear. In contrast, in floriculture crops, many growers do not see the benefit of biological control and feel that it cannot provide the level of pest control flower crops demand. Also, many extension personnel remain unconvinced as to the practical value of biological control in flower crops. These misgivings of growers and extension agents must be reversed if biological control is to become widely used in ornamental production.

The most widely used biological control agents in ornamental greenhouse crops are the predatory mites *Phytoseiulus persimilis* Athias-Henriot for control of spider mites and *Neoseiulus cucumeris* (Oude.) for the control of western flower thrips (*Frankliniella occidentalis* [Pergande]) (Hussey and Scopes 1985a, b). These species are being used by growers and provide clear examples that biological control in flower crops works, is cost effective, and provides a quality product that growers can be proud of. While some

527

successful biological control programs have been based on research, many have been developed by the commercial insectaries themselves. Because of this, while some argue that biological control needs more research to expand, others believe demonstration and implementation programs alone would be sufficient. We feel both are needed and must work together. Without the involvement of researchers and extension personnel in the development and implementation of biological control programs, recommendations for the use of natural enemies are unlikely to be included in formal university recommendations that list pest management options for greenhouse crops. In addition, many of the programs advanced by commercial insectaries could be improved by research. While predatory mites are used successfully in some floriculture crops, questions remain that research could address that would enhance these programs. With respect to predatory mites, we need:

- better sampling plans for both the mites and their prey.
- a better understanding of the optimal release number, frequency and distribution pattern for predatory mites.
- greater assessment of the compatibility of natural enemies with pesticides.
- methods to incorporate new species of predatory mites into crop systems.
- biological controls to address other pests that may occur on the crop.

Information on these topics would help develop more coherent and comprehensive biological control programs. Such programs would be more applicable to additional crops and would demonstrate the general feasibility of biological control. The fact that many growers are already using predatory mites successfully is a powerful incentive to continue research in this area.

Complexity, Efficiency, and Cost of Biological Control

In much of the world, researchers at agricultural universities strongly influence decision making regarding pest control, be it the use of pesticides or natural enemies. Pest control advisors and representatives of commercial insectaries who work in outdoor field, row or orchard crops generally rely on such university-based research in making their recommendations. However, this is not the case in greenhouse crops. For these crops, research at agricultural universities has played only a minor role in formulating the recommendations made by commercial insectaries. This needs to change.

For biological control programs to be adopted by growers, they need to be simple, cost effective, reliable, and predictable. Simplicity of use of biological control agents is very appealing to growers—natural enemies are released into the crop and they seek out and destroy the target pests. Commercial insectaries try to keep programs as simple as possible because ease of use is a powerful marketing tool. The need for efficacy or predictability, however, may require more complex activities than a simple program consisting of a single inoculative release of one species of natural enemy into the crop. Many biological control programs consist of a series of releases of one or several natural enemies, whose efficacy must be assessed to guide further releases. Objective standards for monitoring outcomes of releases are often unavailable and crop advisors or growers often use their personal experience, the past history of the crop, and other insights or intuitions about the crop, pest, or natural enemy to make these decisions. In contrast, science-based IPM programs use sampling methods to estimate the population level and distribution the target pest and the natural enemy. This information is then used to decide whether additional natural enemies should be released, and if so, at what numbers and locations in the greenhouse.

IPM programs that base decision-making on sampling plans that incorporate estimates of pest densities in relation to the economic threshold for the pest on the crop can also include similar information for key natural enemies. The labor costs (i.e., time to take necessary samples) of these programs, however, is a major liability and every effort must be made to speed up the process through the use of sequential or presence-absence sampling schemes. Monitoring schemes, however, make control programs more complicated and there is a risk that such programs will become too expensive for growers to use.

University-based research on the use of biological control in greenhouse crops, conducted in close connection with the insectaries, must increase if future growers are to produce crops with a minimum of pesticide use and a greater reliance on biological control. Stronger relationships must be developed among commercial insectaries and research and extension agencies at both local and international levels.

Fundamental or Applied Research?

A recent review by the National Research Council concluded, "Biological control researchers can boast of many successes, but the factors that lead to success or failure are rarely understood" (NRC 2000). Augmentative biological control, the form practiced in greenhouse crops, is sometimes viewed as a strategy in which natural enemies are used as replacements for pesticides with little understanding of the ecology of how natural enemies actually find pests and suppress their populations (Parrella, Heinz, and Nunney 1992). Research in such systems is often considered low level *ad hoc* applied research of no general interest to ecologists or biological control scientists working in outdoor systems. To correct this problem, scientists working in greenhouse biological controls must fit their applied goals into a broader framework of fundamental concepts about how biological controls function, run well designed tests, and publish the results. Recent examples exist of how applied biological control research in the greenhouse might be framed to also advance basic knowledge of wider interest to ecological and biological control theories (Hoddle et al. 1997, Heinz 1998, Hoddle 2000). With such an approach, greenhouse researchers could become the leaders in advancing biological control theory and practice in all of agriculture, not just in the greenhouse.

The Links Between Extension and Research

Even well-studied and widely used biological control systems, such as the control of spider mites by *P. persimilis,* are based on limited research. Few data exist on such aspects as sampling plans for the pest mite or the natural enemy, their distributions in particular crops, numbers of predatory mites required for control, details of effective release plans, or the influence of the greenhouse environment on the predator-prey interaction. The absence of such research data makes it more difficult for extension agents to provide growers with clear directions on how to use biological control in their crops. Publications on biological control written by cooperative extension specialists usually contain descriptions of natural enemies and their biology, but often lack specific recommendations for use of biological control agents in particular crops. Robust detailed recommendations for the use of biological control agents will only become possible if cooperative extension personnel work with researchers running applied trials. Programs of applied research typically include a research scientist, extension agents, and representatives of commercial insectaries, planning and executing the trials together. To promote the adoption of the results, growers are informed of trial outcomes at demonstration events.

A Systems Approach

A criticism of many entomological research programs is that they are developed independently, and without knowledge of how the arthropod control recommendations resulting from the research might fit with the control of other pests in the crop. The same criticism has been levied at entomologists working in field agriculture (Ehler and Bottrell 2000). There is no longer any room for this fragmented approach. We are rapidly moving towards a systems approach to managing all the inputs going into a greenhouse and biological control needs to be a key compo-

nent. Modern greenhouses of the not so distant future will have complete control over the environment to maximize crop productivity, hydroponic production, optimal use of fertilizers for crop growth, and complete recycling of all components of production. Each component of the system will be tightly connected and dependent on the other components. We assume biological control will be one of these components, but major research obstacles will have to be overcome before this is a reality.

Crop models are being developed in such a way that the greenhouse environment can be modified in an interactive way to affect crop growth, as desired by the grower. One means of manipulating crop growth is to adjust the difference between day and night temperatures. Models of this effect currently exist for Easter lilies and poinsettias. What influence do such manipulations have on the pests of these crops or their natural enemies? These questions must be answered if biological control is to be part of a systems approach. In a similar manner, it may prove possible to manipulate greenhouse environments to improve the performance of a key natural enemy without affecting the quality or timing of the crop (Shipp, Zhang, and Wang 2000).

A final point regarding the need for integration is that the control practices for all pests in the crop must be implemented simultaneously. Recommendations need to be developed for the arthropod, pathogen, and nematode pests that affect the crop. Considerations must be given to recommendations for control of one group of pests that may affect options for the biological control of other groups. This assumes we have biological control options for all members of the pest complex, but often this is not the case. There are few options for biological control of nematodes of plant pathogens, for which chemical control is often the only option. While this is not ideal, it underscores the need to understand the impacts of pesticides on the natural enemies used for biological control of arthropod pests. At the same time, simultaneous recommendations need to be made for control of all pests in the greenhouse—not just the insects and mites. This implies that there are comprehensive sampling plans and thresholds for these other pests and in most cases these do not exist. Entomologists must join with plant pathologists and nematologists to develop comprehensive and inclusive decision making formulae for pest control in the greenhouse.

Pesticides and Integration

Over the last decade, many new rules and regulations governing the use and registration of pesticides have been enacted in the United States. Many growers accustomed to regular use of older pesticides have lost the use of products that they had come to depend on for the majority of their pest control. At the same time, new pesticides being developed have been fewer, more host specific, and not as effective as the products they have replaced. One of the alternatives advocated as a replacement for pesticides was biological control, and many research programs in the United States have focused on developing biological control solutions. While ornamental crops, with their inherent high aesthetic quality and very low tolerance for pests and visible natural enemies, may never completely rely on biological control, the more recently developed pesticides appear to have higher compatibility with natural enemies. Use of these materials is expected to increase by more than twenty percent over the next five years (NRC 2000). Consequently, compatibility of these products with biological control agents is an especially important area of research and it is appropriate that extension specialists and farm advisors provide that research. Both agricultural chemical companies and commodity groups are eager to support this work.

On the other hand, the agrochemical industry is quite creative, and a number of newly developed products have the ability to control pests as well, or even better than products that growers have lost access to. This is a problem for biological control, which is usually at a distinct price disadvantage when competing with such materials. For example, the loss of aldicarb (Temik) coupled with the advent of a new whitefly species, *Bemisia argentifolii* Bellows and Perring, on poinsettia caused growers to struggle to control this pest. This fostered the successful development of programs using biological control (Heinz and Parrella 1994; Van Driesche et al. 2001, 2002). However, the registration of a new, highly effective replacement chemical, imidacloprid (Marathon), relegated these biological control programs to secondary status. In an effort to delay the development of resistance to imidacloprid, use of other control strategies in rotation with imidacloprid is often recommended, but the short-term nature of the poinsettia crop does not really lend itself to such a rotational strategy. It may not be possible to establish biological control as a stand-alone option, but rather it may remain part of an overall pest management scheme that includes chemicals.

Commercial Insectaries

Biological control as practiced in greenhouses is utterly dependent on the commercial insectary industry, and yet very little research is directed at helping insectaries produce higher quality natural enemies. Rather, we are quick to criticize when quality declines (Parrella, Heinz, and Nunney 1992), but little research has been done to support these production facilities. Research could be done in departments of biological and agricultural engineering to optimize mass rearing systems. Also, programs could be developed to answer fundamental questions bearing on insect production, such as those concerning colony size, renewal frequency, and fitness from a genetic perspective (van Lenteren 2003). The development of novel application equipment for mechanical delivery of natural enemies is an area where entomologists and engineers can collaborate. Obtaining funding for this work is difficult—the commercial insectary industry does not have sufficient resources for a large extramural grants program and research at the federal level has been difficult to obtain because of the bias against augmentative biological control. However, this may be changing due to the lobbying of both commercial insectaries and universities and such a change offers the hope of better funding of these important areas of research.

Regulatory Issues and Politics

Laws and treaties governing the movement of plant material and other species around the world directly affect biological control in several ways. First, there is a reluctance to allow the movement of some natural enemies among countries. This is especially true for polyphagous species able to consume plant materials, such as mirid bugs like *Macrolophus caliginosus* Wagner. In other locations, such as Hawaii, increasing concern over the need to protect local endemic species has led to stricter standards for importation of exotic species, including strictly carnivorous biological control agents (Follet et al. 2000). Although there is a clear ecological justification to strengthen policies regulating natural enemy importation, biological control remains an important tool for correcting ecological and economic damage from invasive species of many kinds (Strong and Pemberton 2000; Van Driesche and Van Driesche 2000). In some countries, officials of regulatory agencies are now reluctant to approve the importation of exotic natural enemies not already found in their countries. As a consequence, biological control solutions to pest problems that are based on use of specific natural enemy may not be able to be shared among countries. Rather, a new natural enemy may have to be found in each separate country with the pest problem. However, a minor benefit of this policy is that it promotes the search for new 'endemic' natural enemies in countries with restrictive importation laws. This may lead to the discovery of new natural enemies with the potential to be exported to at least some other parts of the world. This has recently been the case in Australia, where a search for native phytoseiids acting as predators of western flower thrips has led to the rearing of an Australian species for international use. This is a positive development at least in part because there is a pressing need for new natural enemies to use in existing programs. In many cases, we are struggling to obtain effective biological control with what may be inferior natural enemies. Enhanced prospecting in new locations might correct this problem.

Conclusion

The advances made in the use of biological control in vegetable and ornamental greenhouses over the past twenty years are very encouraging and seem likely to continue. More basic research on natural enemies and their use will be needed to advance the reliability and predictability of biological control, but this must be tempered with a view towards simplicity and low cost. A more effective partnership between University research and extension and commercial insectaries is essential to promote grower acceptance and expansion of the use of biological control. Researchers and practitioners must take a more holistic, systems approach to pest management in the greenhouse and understand how biological control fits with all aspects of crop production. Finally, research into more thorough and effective integration of biological control with pesticides may be essential if biological control is continue to expand, especially in ornamental production.

References Cited

Ehler, L. E., and D. G. Bottrell. 2000. The illusion of integrated pest management. *Issues in Science and Technology* 16:61–4.

Follet, P. A., J. Duan, R. H. Messing, and V. P. Jones. 2000. Parasitoid drift after biological control introductions: Re-examining Pandora's box. *American Entomologist* 46:82–94.

Heinz, K. M. 1998. Dispersal and dispersion of aphids (Homoptera: Aphididae) and selected natural enemies in spatially subdivided greenhouse environments. *Environmental Entomology* 27:1029–1038.

Heinz, K. M., and Parrella, M. P. 1994. Biological control of *Bemisia argentifolii* (Homoptera: Aleyrodidae) infesting *Euphorbia pulcherrima*: Evaluations of releases of *Encarsia luteola* (Hymenoptera: Aphelinidae) and *Delphastus pusillus* (Coleoptera: Coccinellidae). *Environmental Entomology* 23:1346–53.

Hoddle, M. S. 2000. Are parasitism rates of whiteflies affected by parasitoid release rates? *California Conference on Biological Control*, July 11–12, 2000, Riverside, California. 22–8.

Hoddle, M. S., R. G. Van Driesche, J. S. Elkinton, and J. P. Sanderson. 1997. Discovery and utilization of *Bemisia argentifolii* (Homoptera: Aleyrodidae) patches by *Eretmocerus eremicus* and *Encarsia formosa* (Beltsville strain) (Hymenoptera: Aphelinidae) in greenhouses. *Entomologia Experimentalis et Applicata* 87:15–28.

Hussey, N. W., and N. E. A. Scopes, eds. 1985a. *Biological Pest Control: The Glasshouse Experience*. Poole, U.K.: Blandford Press (Ithaca, N.Y.: Cornell University Press).

———. 1985b. Greenhouse vegetables (Britain). In *Spider Mites: Their Biology, Natural Enemies, and Control*, eds. W. Helle and M. W. Sabelis, 285–97. New York (Amsterdam): Elsevier.

National Research Council (NRC). 2000. *The Future Role of Pesticides in U.S. Agriculture*. Washington, D.C.: National Academy Press. 163.

Parrella, M. P., K. M. Heinz, and L. Nunney. 1992. Biological control through inundative releases of natural enemies: A strategy whose time has come. *American Entomologist* 38:172–9.

Shipp, J. L., Y. Zhang, and K. Wang. 2000. Using greenhouse environment to augment biological control. *Proceedings of the XXI International Congress of Entomology*, p. 369, Iguacu, Brazil.

Strong, D. R., and R. W. Pemberton. 2000. Ecology: Biological control of invading species—Risk and reform. *Science* 223:1969.

Van Driesche, R. G., M. S. Hoddle, S. Lyon, and J. P. Sanderson. 2001. Compatibility of insect growth regulators with *Eretmocerus eremicus* (Hymenoptera: Aphelinidae) for whitefly control (Homoptera: Alyerodidae) control on poinsettia: II. Trials in commercial poinsettia crops. *Biological Control*. 20:132–146.

Van Driesche, R. G., S. Lyon, K. Jacques, T. Smith, and P. Lopes. 2002. Comparative cost of chemical and biological whitefly control in poinsettia: is there a gap? *Florida Entomologist* 85:488–493.

Van Driesche, R. G., and J. S. Van Driesche. 2000. *Nature Out of Place: Biological Invasions in a Global Age*. Washington, D.C.: Island Press.

van Lenteren, J. C. 2003. Quality *Control and Production of Biological Control Agents: Theory and Testing Procedures*. Wallingford, U.K.: CABI Pub.

INDEX

Bold numbers indicate photographs; italic numbers indicate tables.